Rebels, Believers, Survivors

Rebels, Believers, Survivors

Studies in the History of the Albanians

NOEL MALCOLM

OXFORD
UNIVERSITY PRESS

OXFORD

UNIVERSITY PRESS

Great Clarendon Street, Oxford, OX2 6DP,
United Kingdom

Oxford University Press is a department of the University of Oxford.
It furthers the University's objective of excellence in research, scholarship,
and education by publishing worldwide. Oxford is a registered trade mark of
Oxford University Press in the UK and in certain other countries

First Edition published in 2020

Impression: 1

Published in the United States of America by Oxford University Press
198 Madison Avenue, New York, NY 10016, United States of America

British Library Cataloguing in Publication Data
Data available

Library of Congress Control Number: 2020933229

ISBN 978-0-19-885729-7

DOI: 10.1093/oso/9780198857297.001.0001

Printed and bound in Great Britain by
Clays Ltd, Elcograf S.p.A.

This book is dedicated to the memory of Robert Elsie

Contents

Preface

That the history of the Albanian lands is poorly known and little studied, outside those territories themselves, is a disappointing fact but not a very surprising one. For half a century, Albania itself was under a Communist regime of an unusually inward-looking and autarkic kind; there was very little cultural contact between it and the outside world. Kosovo fared somewhat better in Titoist Yugoslavia, but the academic establishment in that country was much more interested in the historical development of the South Slavs than in the history and culture of what it regarded as a very backwaterish province.

Previously, for roughly half a millennium, the Albanian lands—a phrase used here simply as a historical term, to mean the territories of present-day Albania and Kosovo, plus some other nearby areas that have had significant Albanian-speaking populations—had formed part of the Ottoman Empire. Despite the initial resistance of the Albanians under Skanderbeg, and various subsequent rebellions, the Ottoman sultans tended to take their Albanian subjects for granted. This was partly because the Albanians supplied so many soldiers and administrators to defend and run the Ottoman state, and partly because the conversion of a majority of the Albanian population to Islam meant that the sultans saw these subjects as belonging to a different category from the other peoples of the Balkans, whose 'national' rights were gradually recognized. As a consequence, even in the late Ottoman period there was no general provision for Albanian-language education within the Albanian lands. Belgrade had an institution of higher education—which later became the University of Belgrade—from 1808; Athens had a university from 1837. In both Serbia and Greece, therefore, major works of history were being written and printed at a time when few Albanians were even being taught to write in their own language. In the field of Balkan studies, the relatively greater influence of those other schools of national historiography has continued to this day.[1]

'National' historiography can be, of course, problematic in itself. For all the former subject peoples in the Balkans, the task of establishing a positive narrative of nationhood was felt to be a high priority; everything was to be fitted, if at all possible, into a simplistic long-term story of national resistance and national liberation. When Albanian writers began producing serious works of history, from the mid-twentieth century onwards, they were certainly not immune to this tendency. Indeed, the crude nature of Communist ideology in Albania, with—after the break with the Soviet Union in 1961—its incorporation of a peculiarly strident nationalism, made the products of Albanian historians doubly suspect in the eyes of Western readers, even when those writings did include the fruits of genuine historical research. And such readers were, in any case, very few indeed, not only because these publications were poorly distributed, but also because so few Westerners had any knowledge of the Albanian language. Even in the post-Communist period, when valuable work has been published by historians in Albania and Kosovo, that last problem remains a major one.

For all these contingent reasons, the history of the Albanians may seem, to the casual observer, a rather self-enclosed and inward-looking affair. But the truth is the opposite: this is a history that radiates outwards in all kinds of directions. The Albanian lands have long been a meeting-ground of religions, and Catholicism, Orthodoxy and Islam all connected Albanians with larger currents of culture and thought outside their own region. For much of their history, the Albanian lands were a crossroads of cultures and interests—a channel through which Venetian and other Italian powers interacted with the Ottoman Balkans from an early stage, a place of interest to the Habsburgs over several centuries as they tried to extend their own Balkan influence, and a focus for Greek and Slav ambitions both during the later period of Ottoman rule and, crucially, at the time of that empire's disintegration. In addition, the Albanians have been a very active and mobile people; there were large-scale, long-term settlements of Albanian populations in Greece and southern Italy, and—as I have illustrated in a previous book, *Agents of Empire*—many individuals pursued careers, as soldiers, merchants, administrators and intellectuals, much further afield in Western Europe and the Ottoman Empire.

A single volume of essays cannot possibly do justice to the full extent of these contacts and connections. While this book covers quite a broad range of subject-matters, and extends chronologically from the fifteenth century to the twentieth, it makes no attempt to be systematic; this is a collection of writings on a variety of topics that have caught my interest, for a variety of reasons, over the years. But since each essay is based on the study of primary sources, manuscript as well as printed, a glance at the list of archives in different countries provided in the 'List of Manuscripts' will give at least some sense of the wide range of European resources on which students of Albanian history can draw. (I should state at the outset that I have not studied Ottoman manuscript materials; but readers should not imagine that I have thereby missed the Ottoman equivalent of the sort of qualitatively rich documentation that is available in Vienna, Venice, Rome or the Vatican. Up until the nineteenth century, the relevant Ottoman archival materials consist primarily of tax registers and records of executive decrees; more personal and discursive documentation is not preserved in the Ottoman state archives to anything like the extent that it is in their West European counterparts. Much important work has in any case been done on those Ottoman documents that relate to the Albanian lands, by scholars such as Selami Pulaha, Skënder Rizaj, Petrika Thëngjilli and Ferit Duka, and I have benefited greatly from their researches.)

While the topics discussed in this book connect in many ways with specific developments and interests outside the Albanian lands, the essays also try to shed some light on larger thematic issues, the significance of which goes far beyond their immediate Albanian context. These include religious conversion, the phenomenon of 'crypto-Christianity' among Muslims, methods of enslavement in the Ottoman Empire, the development of nationalist historiography, and the nature of modern myth-making about national identity. Even for readers who have no specialist concern with the history of the Albanians, therefore, my hope is that this book will contain many things of interest.

One essay, on Ali Pasha and his relations with Great Britain during the Napoleonic Wars, is so much longer than the others that it deserves some comment here. After Skanderbeg, Ali Pasha of Tepelenë (or of Ioannina) is the best-known of all the figures in pre-twentieth-century Albanian history. Lord Byron's visit to Tepelenë as his guest in 1809 was commemorated in *Childe Harold's Pilgrimage*; the novelist Alexandre Dumas published a biography of Ali Pasha; the composer Albert Lortzing even wrote an operetta about him. There have been many literary works featuring Ali, and several bellelettristic biographies; yet serious academic study of his life and actions has been surprisingly rare. Only one monograph has been written about him in English within the last eighty years, and its central arguments are, as I explain in my essay, quite unconvincing. Yet Ali remains a very significant figure, not because of his romantic allure, but because he played a crucial role in the geopolitics of south-eastern Europe throughout the period of the Napoleonic Wars. The territories he controlled were of huge potential importance where any plans for a French invasion of the Ottoman Empire were concerned. Napoleon knew that, and so too did the British, who maintained diplomatic agents at Ali's court over many years. My essay here uses, for the first time, all of the extensive materials in British archives that were generated by that relationship; it supplies much new information, thereby helping, I hope, to fill a gap in the political, diplomatic and military history of the Napoleonic period. I believe that the intrinsic interest of this material, and of the whole story that I tell here, justifies the length of the essay. At the same time, I must emphasize that it does not claim to offer a general biography of Ali, even for the years it covers; and to attempt to biographize him fully would of course be out of the question here, as that would be a much larger task, involving the use of many other bodies of evidence.

While the essays in this volume vary greatly in size, I hope I can truthfully say that each has the length appropriate to its subject-matter. They are arranged here in a general chronological sequence. Since each was written quite separately, however, there is no reason why readers should feel obliged to read the book sequentially. (One individual, Pjetër Bogdani, who is the primary subject of chapter 6, also features more briefly in two other chapters, nos. 2 and 7; the degree of overlap is very slight, and those chapters do not need to be read in any particular order.) In a few cases cross-references have been given. Also in a few cases, I have added either an introductory note, to offer a little background information to the non-specialist reader, or an additional note, to supply some further details.

Four of the essays appear here for the first time: chapters 1, 5, 8 and 10. Since these include by far the longest two items in the volume (as well as the fourth-longest), they represent roughly 60 per cent of the total. In addition: when chapter 3 was previously published, the main text it presents was given only in the original Italian; it appears here in English for the first time. And the same is true of the entire text of chapter 9, which was previously published only in Albanian. Two other items, chapters 6 and 11, were published by the Kosovan Academy of Sciences and Arts and by the Albanian Institute in Zurich, respectively; both are hard-to-find publications, absent from most research libraries in the UK, Western Europe and North America. And so far as I know, only one item, chapter 2, has hitherto been available online in academic libraries. So, although eight out of the twelve essays have been published before, I am encouraged to think that bringing them together in this volume may perform a useful service.

In each essay, all quotations from foreign-language sources are given in English (my own translation, unless otherwise stated) in the text, with the original given in the notes. In a few cases, where the previous printing lacked the original word-ings, they have been supplied here. Ottoman terms are given in their modern Turkish forms, unless there is a standard English version (e.g. 'pasha', 'Janissary'). Similarly, where a particular form of a place-name has become standard usage in English, that form is used: I therefore have 'Tirana' and 'Prishtina', but other Albanian place-names are given in their indefinite form in Albanian. Generally, I use the place-names that belong to the official or primary language of the country where the place is now situated.

For permission to reprint the previously published items, I am very grateful to the following publishers and institutions. (I list the items by chapter-number here; full details of the original publications can be found in the Bibliography.) 2: *Südost-Forschungen* (De Gruyter, Berlin); 3: *Revue des études sud-est européennes* (the Institute of South-East European Studies of the Romanian Academy, Bucharest; with special thanks also to Professor Andrei Pippidi); 4: the School of Slavonic and East European Studies, London; 6: *Studime* (the Academy of Sciences and Arts of Kosovo); 7: De Gruyter, Berlin; 9: the Institute of History, Prishtina (publishers of the Albanian translation); 11: the Albanian Institute, Zurich (with special thanks to Dr Albert Ramaj); 12: C. Hurst & Co.

During my many years of study of Albanian history, I have accumulated very many debts of gratitude. Some individuals are thanked in particular essays; here I would like to add the names of Oliver Schmitt, who invited me to the conference at which the first version of chapter 7 was given as a paper, and Peter Bartl, the doyen of historians of Albania in Western Europe, in whose honour that confer-ence was held. I am also deeply grateful to the staff of all the libraries and archives where I have carried out these researches. Thirty-eight are mentioned in the List of Manuscripts, and to those I would add the following libraries: All Souls College, Oxford; the Bodleian Library, Oxford; Cambridge University Library, Cambridge; the Österreichische Staatsbibliothek, Vienna; the School of Oriental and African Studies, London; the School of Slavonic and East European Studies, London; the Skilliter Centre for Ottoman Studies, Cambridge; the Taylor Institution, Oxford; the Warburg Institute, London; the Widener Library, Harvard. I particularly wish to thank my editor at the Oxford University Press, Luciana O'Flaherty, for her encouragement and support. And, as always, I am extremely grateful to the Warden and Fellows of All Souls College, Oxford, for enabling me to carry out much of this research, and for providing such an ideal scholarly environment in which to work.

But my greatest and most long-standing debts in this case are to two individuals. Robert Elsie, to whose memory this book is dedicated, was not only an exceptionally gifted and extraordinarily productive—and generous—scholar, but also a much-valued friend; his loss is deeply felt by all who knew him, and by everyone in the field of Albanian studies. Bejtullah Destani has also been a generous friend, and an encouraging one: the idea of collecting these essays came from him first of all. Over many years, his energy and expertise in seeking out the records of Albanian history have been matched only by his persistence and resourcefulness as an editor and a publisher. Between them, these two individuals have done more during the last three decades than any others I can think of in the world, both to extend our knowledge of the culture and history of the Albanian lands and to propagate it to a wider readership.

Finally, for non-Albanian speakers, some approximate guidance on the pronunciation of words and names:

c	'ts'
ç	'tch' (as in 'match')
dh	'th' (always voiced, as in 'this'; Albanian writes 'th' for the unvoiced 'th', as in 'thin')
ë	a light 'uh' (like the 'u' in 'radium'; virtually silent at the end of a word)
gj	'dj' (as in 'adjure')
j	'y' (as in 'you')
ll	like 'l', but a slightly heavier, longer sound
q	like 'tch', but a slightly thinner sound
rr	like 'r', but a slightly heavier, more rolled sound
x	'dz' (as in 'adze')
xh	'j' (as in 'jam')
y	acute 'u' (as in French 'tu' or German 'über')
zh	'zh' (as in 'Zhivago')

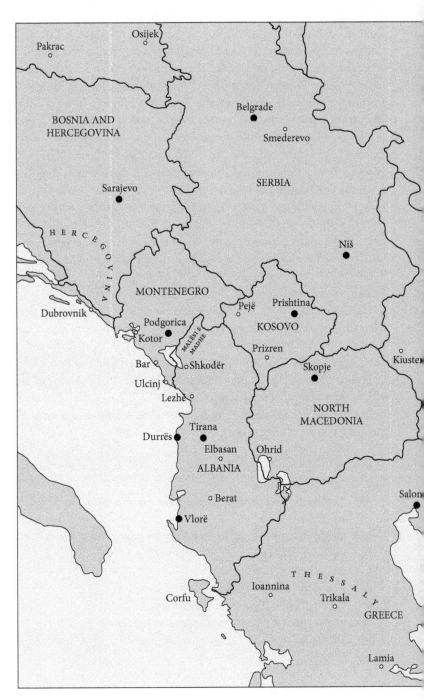

I: The Albanian lands and the Balkans (with modern borders)

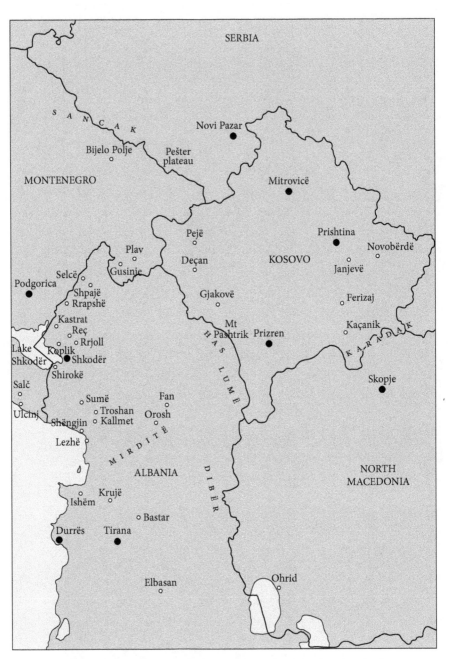

II: The northern Albanian lands and adjoining areas (with modern borders)

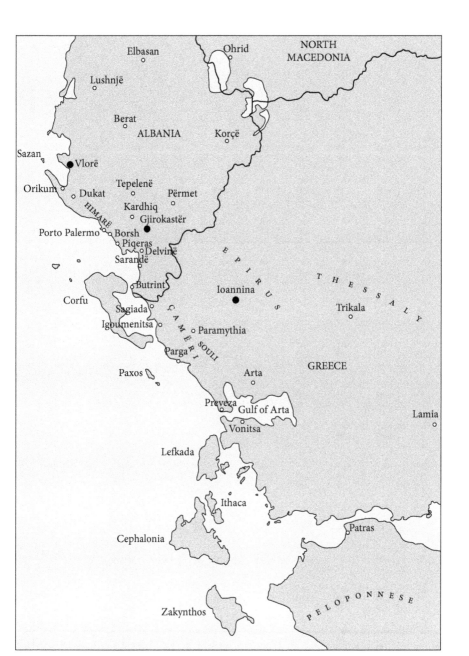

III: The southern Albanian lands and adjoining areas (with modern borders)

1

Glimpses of Fifteenth-Century Albania

The Pilgrim Narratives

The fifteenth century has a special importance in the history of Albania: this was the period of the Ottoman conquest, and of the long-drawn-out war of resistance led by Gjergj Kastrioti 'Skanderbeg'. The interest of outsiders in Albanian affairs was quickened by these events; Skanderbeg had frequent contact with two major powers on the other side of the Adriatic, the republic of Venice and the Kingdom of Naples, and his anti-Ottoman struggle would eventually capture the imagination of a broad European public. Yet Albania remained a little-known and largely unvisited place. Historians have been able to draw on Venetian sources concerning the administration and commerce of those northern cities that were under Venetian control for most or all of the century (especially Shkodër, Durrës and Lezhë); external sources make it possible to document to some extent the commercial life of the southern city of Vlorë, which fell under Ottoman rule in 1417; and, of course, there are a variety of Ottoman administrative records, which give valuable information about demographic and other changes in much of the country. One source, however, has been curiously neglected: the narratives of Western pilgrims, who sailed along the eastern Adriatic coast on their way to and from Jerusalem.[1] The only such narrative from this period to have received any attention from scholars of Albanian history is that of Arnold von Harff, who earned a special place in the history of 'Albanology' by jotting down—with a fair degree of accuracy—a list of Albanian words and phrases during his visit to Durrës in 1496. But there were many other pilgrims who found something to say about the Albanian lands. And whilst their accounts may lack the hard-edged historicity of administrative records or commercial documents, they do have some things that are normally missing from those other categories of documentation: personal narrative and general description. These are texts suffused with human subjectivity—even though some of their apparent first-hand testimony was not (as we shall see) quite as subjective as it might seem.

II

Of the three great sites of Christian pilgrimage, Jerusalem, Rome and Santiago de Compostela, the most important was Jerusalem.[2] A typical visit might last two

Rebels, Believers, Survivors: Studies in the History of the Albanians. Noel Malcolm,
Oxford University Press (2020). © Noel Malcolm. DOI: 10.1093/oso/9780198857297.001.0001

weeks, taking in other holy places such as Nazareth and Bethlehem; more adventurous pilgrims could add a trip to the monasteries of Mt Sinai. Many hundreds of Western Christians made the voyage to the Holy Land each year. Those who came from Spain, the south of France or southern Italy would find passage on trading ships which went from those areas to the Greek islands, and then on to the ports of Syria or Egypt. But for those who lived in northern Italy and most parts of northern Europe, the standard sea-route started from Venice. A rich nobleman who travelled with a large entourage would hire his own galley: examples included Count Wilhelm of Thüringen, who had with him 43 nobles and knights, seven ecclesiastics and 41 others, or Duke Albrecht of Saxony, who brought a total of 140 people.[3] For individual travellers who could afford to pay for a tailor-made service, passage could be bought on one of the pilgrim galleys, which left Venice at two fixed times of year (soon after Easter, and soon after Ascension Day), and were regulated by the state. On payment of a price that varied between 30 and 60 ducats, the pilgrim would have a guaranteed place on the boat, two meals a day, an escorted tour of the Holy Land (also with meals included), and an equally guaranteed return journey.[4] Poorer pilgrims found places on ordinary sailing ships—whether large bulk carriers or smaller 'cog' boats—that traded with the Levant. There were some advantages to this form of travel: as one English writer advised, 'in a shipe is grete space and ese, yef he be newe, large and a good sailler', whereas in the cramped space of a galley 'the eyre therynne waxeth sone contrariouse and groweth alle-wey fro evill into wers'. Nevertheless, he advised, travel by galley was 'the more sure'.[5] Another English pilgrim, the pious Fellow of Eton College William Wey, also recommended going by galley, and gave detailed advice on the contents of the contract with the galley captain; he particularly recommended securing a berth in the uppermost part of the ship, 'for in the lawyst vnder hyt ys ryght smolderyng hote and stynkynge'.[6] With their banks of oars, galleys could make steady progress in conditions of complete calm; and, as another author observed, they had the advantage that they could be brought to land quite easily (unlike sailing ships, which, above a certain size, required proper harbours), and could thus take on fresh water and food whenever those were needed.[7] The great majority of the pilgrims who wrote accounts of their journeys did travel by galley.

As some of these details have already suggested, people from quite a wide social range—excluding the poorest, but rising to the very highest in society—went on these travels. In the second half of the fifteenth century, pilgrimage to the Holy Land seems to have become a status-enhancing fashion among the upper classes in the German lands; prosperous burghers from German and Swiss cities also took part, in some cases developing the practice as a family tradition.[8] Motives for the journey may thus have been mixed. While religious motivation was obviously primary, status-seeking and familial piety were not the only supplementary reasons for pilgrimage; for some people, curiosity about the world (stimulated by works such as the immensely popular *Travels* of the author known as Sir John Mandeville) may have played a part, and for others there are clear signs that humanist interests in the classical past supplied special reasons for wanting to visit the eastern Mediterranean.[9]

Some of these motives can be seen at work in the written narratives that have come down to us. Of course, only a very small minority of pilgrims composed accounts of their travels; and, given that doing so tended to involve not only a certain level of literacy but also some other habits of mind with regard to record-taking, a further narrowing of the field is involved when we turn from pilgrims in general to pilgrim-authors. Typically, these writers would be ecclesiastics, or people with a merchant background, or personal secretaries and assistants to noble pilgrims (who were mostly too grand to write accounts themselves), or else members of princely courts and administrations more generally, with a level of education appropriate to the performance of legal and bureaucratic duties. Within this literate and literarily inclined stratum of society there was thus quite a wide range of variation; so although some standardizing of genres did take place, there was no such thing as the archetypal pilgrim narrative.

At the heart of almost all accounts, naturally, was the description of the Holy Places themselves. Here it is possible that the Franciscans, who acted as 'guardians' of those sites, encouraged a method of performing the pilgrimage, and therefore also a style of writing about it, as a kind of exercise in meditation on the events of Christ's life.[10] But there were many ways of being a pilgrim, and many ways of describing it. Some authors confined themselves to a bare skeleton of dates and facts, perhaps just to provide a personal *aide-mémoire* (or a record to be treasured by their family and descendants); some clearly aimed at setting down practical advice and information for those who would follow; and some incorporated a wider range of details, sometimes drawing on secondary sources, in order to create an account that could be read with interest by those who would never venture in their footsteps. These three types have been distinguished as the 'log', the 'guide' and the 'narration' by one modern scholar; but there were many possible combinations of them or gradations between them.[11] Besides, what might be 'logged' by a merchant could differ greatly, in its choice of focus and degree of detail, from what a more purely religious writer might wish to record. (Not surprisingly, merchants' narratives tend to give more circumstantial detail about such matters as trade, transport, local products and travel costs. Arnold von Harff's interest in compiling useful vocabulary lists may have been another expression of this mentality.)[12] There was nothing monolithic about the religious approach, either; one influential writer, the German Dominican Felix Fabri, produced a total of four different texts (three in German, one in Latin) to serve a variety of purposes, from the devotional to the geographical, with a range of audiences that radiated outwards from the monastic houses of Ulm to broader circles of lay readers.[13] As the new industry of book-printing began to absorb this sort of material from the 1480s onwards, the different physical formats it used demonstrated a difference in intended purposes and readerships. One classic account, by Bernhard von Breydenbach, went through twelve different editions, all in folio, between 1486 and 1522; with its many woodblocks, this was very much a book for armchair reading, for reference and, in view of the lavish amount of illustration and the higher price which that must have generated, for display.[14] Other works, by writers such as Tücher, Capodilista and Brasca, were produced in small quarto, a size more suited to the needs of pilgrims who wished to take such a book with them as a guide to their travels.[15] In short: the concerns of both writers and readers were multiple and various, and could easily include an interest in the details of those parts of the journey—for example, along the Albanian coast—that had no direct relevance to the religious goal of the pilgrimage as such.

To talk of logs and narrations is to raise some assumptions, in the modern reader's mind, about the status of these texts as eye-witness accounts. At a basic level, that is what they all were; there is no equivalent here of Mandeville's *Travels*, where the very nature of the work as an experiential narrative is seriously in doubt. In some cases the writers do refer to their own activity of note-taking. The Burgundian Bertrandon de la Broquière, travelling in 1432–3 (as a pilgrim, but also with a view to supplying his ruler with information that might be useful in planning a new crusade) jotted down his experiences 'in a little booklet'; later in the century an anonymous French pilgrim stated that he summarized in writing every evening what he had seen during the day.[16] Generally, though, we know very little about the circumstances in which the final composition of the texts took place. It is reasonable to assume that this normally happened after the pilgrim's return home; by that stage, well-kept notes would have been important, as memories would already have been fading. In one case—that of the Flemish knight Joos van Ghistele, whose extensive travels in 1481–5 took him as far as Persia, well beyond the usual pilgrim's itinerary—we know that the long narrative account was penned by someone else (not a participant in the pilgrimage) on the basis of van Ghistele's notes.[17] In another case we have two very similar narratives written by two men who travelled together in 1458, the Church functionary Gabriele Capodilista and the nobleman Roberto da Sanseverino; there are many differences between the two texts, but the overlap in material is so large that it seems likely that one of them (probably Capodilista, who had a more literary background) wrote his version first, and then let the other make use of it for his own purposes.[18] Similarly, Sebald Rieter, who travelled with Hans Tücher in 1479, left an account of his travels which overlaps significantly with Tücher's and probably borrows from his.[19]

More problematic, from the modern point of view, are the cases where one account took over textual material from an earlier one. Writers in this period had neither our notion of the nature (and heinousness) of plagiarism, nor our assumptions about travel writing, which privilege first-hand experience. To them, information was information, and its value might actually be enhanced by the fact that it had been drawn, with or without attribution, from a respected work. There are many cases of writers borrowing heavily from earlier texts. The Capodilista/da Sanseverino account was quarried 22 years later by Santo Brasca; Felix Fabri borrowed explicitly from the fourteenth-century writer Ludolf von Sudheim, from Hans Tücher, and also from Bernhard von Breydenbach, who travelled with Fabri and himself drew material from other writers, including Tücher. Von Breydenbach's book, which enjoyed such a publishing success, became a source for many authors: for example, the account of Albania given by the Flemish traveller Jan Aerts (who went first to the Holy Land and then, on a Portuguese commercial mission, to Persia and India) is a simple repetition of von Breydenbach's comments.[20]

Recourse to earlier texts was not the only way in which pilgrims could acquire information at second hand. When Bishop Louis de Rochechouart wrote, in an account of his 1461 pilgrimage, that 'Having asked those who were more knowledgeable, I learned that we had been travelling all night between Albania and Sicily', he evidently meant that he had asked a crew-member or a more experienced passenger.[21] The anonymous author of the *Voyage de la Saincte Cyté de Hierusalem*, describing a pilgrimage of 1480, observed of Vlorë: 'The sailors told us that there was a large garrison of soldiers of the Sultan in that town.'[22] Similarly, Nicole Le Huen, who travelled in 1487, described Vlorë as 'a city belonging to the Sultan which used to be great and powerful and abounding in goods, as they told us'.[23] No doubt much of the information which these pilgrims acquired about Albania as they sailed past it came from the Venetian captains, officers and mariners. Yet even here appearances can be deceptive. The account of Konrad Grunemberg, who travelled in 1486, includes the statement, 'not far from the sea itself, as the sailors told us, lies Durrës, a great destroyed city'; the reference to sailors here gives an air of *actualité* to the account, but this sentence forms part of a passage lifted almost verbatim (with the exception of that phrase) from Hans Tücher's book.[24]

Overall, then, it would be anachronistic to search through these pilgrim narratives solely for eye-witness testimony. Vivid first-hand descriptions do exist, but they are often interwoven with information acquired in other ways. And this should enhance, not diminish, the interest of this whole corpus of writings. For what the study of these texts gives us is not only an entrée into units of individual experience, but also some access to two larger fields of shared knowledge and thinking: the standard views of mariners and others who were familiar with the Albanian coast and had their received opinions about it; and the gradually emerging body of Western European geographical knowledge about Albania, formed by an expanding stock of widely circulated and published texts. And those are two bodies of social knowledge (with the first, thanks to these pilgrim narratives, contributing to the second) of real interest in their own rights.

III

That nearly 30 fifteenth-century pilgrim narratives do contain some comments on Albania, while many others do not, is partly a matter of sheer chance, depending on the vagaries of wind and weather. It was in the interests of the galley captains (who had contracted to feed their pilgrim passengers for however many days they were on board ship) to make the journey quickly, so they would pass down the Adriatic coast as swiftly as conditions allowed. One anonymous account of 1434 stated that with a good wind they had sailed from Zadar to Corfu in two days and a night; in this case, it is likely that the entire coast of Albania was traversed during the hours of darkness.[25] For the benefit of the pilgrims, who did not want the captains' or ship-owners' mercantile business to interfere with their journey, the standard contract stipulated also that there would be no unnecessary stops, and no stops at foreign ports.[26] So only a small minority of these narratives describe a visit to the one significant Albanian port that was in Venetian hands, Durrës. Even though most of these 30-odd pilgrims did not set foot on Albanian soil, however, they did spend long enough travelling along the coast to gain some impression, or pick up some information, that they thought worthy of record.

For some of them, the dominant impression was of mountain fastnesses, and little else. The priest Pierre Barbatre, making the voyage down the coast in June 1480, observed that from the sea off Durrës 'you see the high mountains of Albania, where there are great amounts of snow, for you can see them easily at a distance of 30 or 40 leagues.'[27] Mountains loomed large in the brief characterization of the country given two years later by the south German Franciscan Paul Walther: 'we came to the land and mountains of Albania, a land which, with its neighbouring areas and its mountains, was completely conquered by the Sultan, with the exception of one city, called Durrës, which belongs to the Venetians.'[28] And in 1485, as his galley approached Corfu, the Mayor of Mons, Georges Lengherand, noted that 'on the coast on the left we saw great rocks and mountains, and we were told that beyond those lay the country of Albania, which is ruled by the Sultan.'[29] Ambrosius Zeebout, who wrote up the travel notes of Joos van Ghistele, was untypical in giving a general description of Albania which was both more positive in tone and more detailed in content. 'Now, the aforementioned country of Albania is a very rugged landscape of mountains, with narrow passes, strong cities and castles, and good rivers; many sturdy people live there; it has many woods, and is a good, fertile country.'[30]

The country or territory of 'Albania' which these writers described was not quite co-terminous with the modern state. For most of them, as they travelled southwards, Albania began in what is now Montenegro, at or near the Venetian-ruled city of Kotor (or, at least, the entrance to the Gulf of Kotor, past which they travelled). For Hans Lochner, the physician who attended the Margraves Johann and Albrecht of Brandenburg on their pilgrimage in 1435, 'the country called

Albania' began there; for Gabriele Capodilista, travelling in 1458, that was where 'the mountains of Dalmatia' gave way to 'the mountains of Albania'; in 1493 the Bohemian nobleman Jan Hasišteinský z Lobkovic listed Kotor as the first town in 'the country which is called Albania'.[31] This was in keeping with Venetian practice, which included Kotor and the other Venetian-controlled coastal towns to the south of it (Budva, Bar, Ulcinj) in a territory known as 'Venetian Albania', together with Shkodër, Lezhë and Durrës while those places were ruled by Venice.[32] For some pilgrims the first Albanian town was Budva (Hans Tücher wrote that 'there the country of Sclavonia ends, and Albania begins'), perhaps for the simple reason that Budva was, unlike Kotor, a place they could actually see from their ship.[33] In 1470 Friderich Steigerwalder, a member of the entourage of Count Gaudenz von Kirchberg, noted that ten miles from Kotor there was 'a castle called Budva; and in that place there begin the country, the mountain-range and the language of Albania'.[34]

This reference to the language, although not quite accurate (Budva was Slav-speaking, and the language frontier with Albanian began roughly 20 miles to the south-east of it, just below Bar), is of some interest; it shows that Albania was understood not only as a geographical entity but also as a linguistic one, or at least as the home of a linguistically distinct population. For some pilgrims the fact that the Albanians had their own language was a noteworthy fact, albeit one that strengthened the feeling that they were an alien people. The Genoese-Flemish writer Anselme Adorno penned just two sentences on the subject of Albania, presented as a tiny digression in his description of Corfu: 'From there we looked at the mountains of Albania, a province which is fairly small in its location and boundaries; its people are not rich, and are extremely wicked, having a language of their own. Almost all of Albania, apart from some towns which are Venetian possessions, belongs to the Sultan.'[35] Arnold von Harff, more neutrally, wrote of Durrës: 'this town lies in Albania, where they also have their own language, which cannot properly be written, since they have no alphabet of their own in that country.'[36] Felix Fabri, while making no comment on the Albanian language, did put forward a historical claim which reinforced the notion that the Albanians were an alien people, both savage and essentially non-European. He wrote that there were two Albanias; the other one was close to the Caspian Sea (he was referring to the Caucasian territory known as Albania, which was located to the north-east of Armenia), and it produced 'extremely fierce men' who could see better by night than by day. 'From those people there once came an army to the Peloponnese, and when they had spread up the coast they called that region Albania too.'[37] In geographical works of the sixteenth century, the idea that the Albanians were Asiatics who had migrated to the Balkans became a standard view; this coincidental linkage with the Caucasian place-name was evidently one of the main reasons for it.[38]

IV

As they sailed down the coast of 'Venetian Albania', the pilgrims acquired some fragments of information about the towns which were currently, or had been until recently, under Venetian rule; these, after all, were the places with which their Venetian informants were most familiar. There is no description of Budva or Ulcinj by anyone who actually stopped there, though in one case the galley may have called at the former, and in another it was just about to do so (to give some relief to the passengers after they had been tossed at sea by fierce storms for three days) when a favourable wind sprang up that took it to Corfu.[39] The most detailed account of Ulcinj occurs in Zeebout's version of van Ghistele's travels:

> They sailed past a fine-looking little city, located on the left-hand side, in Albania, called Ulcinj; it is situated on a cliff with an inlet on the seaward side which is very steep, to a large extent cut out with chisels and much labour, and the city itself is built on the very tip, almost surrounded by the sea. The land-ward side is so strongly fortified, and has such deep and wide ditches carved out of the rock, that it would be impossible to conquer. It has a very good port and harbour for ships and galleys.[40]

Capodilista's account makes a brief mention of the castle of Ulcinj, before proceeding to what he calls the castle of 'Ludrino'—that is, lo Drino, at the mouth of the river Drin. (The castle he refers to at this point was presumably that of Lezhë, the town—described by another pilgrim as an 'oppidulum' or little town—which was set back a little from the final stretch or stretches of the river.)[41] 'They found themselves at a castle called Ulcinj, and at another called Ludrino, in the land of Albania, where there is a very bad bay called the Bay of Ludrino, where they would willingly have found a haven, if there had been a berth for the galley, but since there was none, they had to stay out at sea, at the mercy of God, thus spending the whole day off the shore of that castle.'[42] Zeebout's account, once again, is the fullest here:

> Not far from the aforementioned town [of Ulcinj] there is a fine port and harbour, also on the left-hand side, at which place a fine river debouches into the sea; it is called Labajona [the river Bunë; Ital.: la Boiana], around which there are very many hills and remarkably many woods. Now, near there is another good town in Albania, held by the Ottomans, called Allijssio [Lezhë; Ital.: Alessio], which also has many woods around it. Not far from there another fine river, called Loudrijn, debouches into the sea, but its water is not especially good, according to what people say.[43]

Having sheltered in the mouth of the Drin from a violent storm, 'they came to anchor in a port and harbour belonging to a great town, which also lay on the left-hand side, in Albania, called Durassen [Durrës]; it is held by Christians.'[44] This city, which stayed under Venetian rule until 1501, was the one major Albanian port at which pilgrim galleys did sometimes call. The accounts by Capodilista and Sanseverino give a vivid description of what led up to their visit to the city. Having passed Ulcinj and reached Lezhë on 29 May 1458, they were struck on the following day by a strong contrary wind, accompanied by heavy rain; 'several times they tried to come to land, but the force of the wind held the galley as if it were fixed.' The waves were smashing into the boat, causing the pilgrims, and some of the crew, to lie motionless with fear on the deck. Eventually the wind subsided, and on the 31st they were able to row southwards until they came in sight of Durrës; but now another storm sprang up, which sent them back to where they had been the previous night. On 1 June, still with poor conditions and contrary winds, 'the captain decided that at all events they should go to Durrës, and stop in that port, so that the pilgrims, who were all tired and distressed, could take some rest.' Once again the wind drove them back. But in the evening

> there came out the galley of the squadron of the most illustrious government of Venice, which keeps fifteen armed galleys there at all times to guard that Gulf. The captain of that galley was Messer Alessandro Contarini. As they approached us, and saw that ours was a pilgrim galley, at a distance of one mile they began to lower their sail and mast, to pay respect to us, as is their custom. Then, when the galleys came close, and the captains recognized each other, our comito [i.e., approximately, first lieutenant] began to ask them for their news.

After the exchange of news, and the gift (at the request of the captain of the pilgrim galley) of some barrels of water and some wood, they parted; it was only on the following day that, with a favourable wind, the pilgrims were able to approach Durrës. For the last two miles they were helped by Contarini, who came out to meet them and towed them into port; they arrived three hours before sunset.[45]

The English pilgrim William Wey was almost certainly on the same galley, though he gives 31 May as the date of arrival at Durrës, and makes no mention of the storm. His account includes at this point almost the same information about the Venetian armed galleys (putting their number at sixteen). He adds one other item of information which he heard—or mis-heard—at Durrës, about a huge Ottoman defeat near Belgrade and the subsequent movement of Ottoman forces to north-eastern Greece, to besiege the Venetian-held island of Euboea; but unfortunately he does not describe the city of Durrës at all.[46]

Luckily, Capodilista and Sanseverino more than make up for that. They note that on their arrival they were met by Nicolò Barbo, the governor of the city. As Sanseverino recorded:

he gave them a thousand courtesies and offers of help, and accompanied signor Roberto [da Sanseverino] and his companions, together with the said don Alessandro [Contarini], to the church of San Francesco, where they had decided to stay the night. But not having found a place that could be made available for them, they left that church and went to stay at San Domenico, where they found better lodging for the entire company, which was received and lodged with great charity by those friars.[47]

Then, in Capodilista's words,

having had dinner, they decided to look at this very ancient city, which was once great, but nowadays is very much ruined and undone. It is built on hills next to the coast, and surrounded on three sides by very large walls. When they had climbed up onto those walls they found a bronze statue, of a horse with an emperor on it, which is said to have been the Emperor Constantine; that statue stands with one hand raised, looking towards Thessaly. From there one could see the walls which Caesar had made when he was pursuing Pompey, within which he contained him in order to besiege him, and they are very large. One could also see Emathia, which is a part of Albania; that is where Pompey's army was destroyed by Caesar, after which he fled to Egypt and was decapitated by Ptolemy. In those fields, which are within roughly twelve miles of Durrës, it is said that when they plough they find pieces of weaponry, so great was the massacre of the men who stayed in those fields. Nearby there was a city called Thessaly, which nowadays is ruined and destroyed and almost disinhabited—as is Durrës, where very few people live, and which was called Epirus in ancient times.[48]

The description of Durrës as 'very much ruined' is matched by other accounts, even by pilgrims who did not set foot there: the Franciscan Alessandro Ariosto, who travelled in 1476, described it as 'formerly a huge and very spacious city, now fallen into ruin'; Hans Tücher, who passed by three years later, called it 'a great destroyed city', and his phrase was repeated by Bernhard von Breydenbach and Konrad Grunemberg.[49] Clearly the effects of the massive earthquake of 1267 remained permanently visible.[50] Tücher's phrase also resurfaces in the very brief description by von Harff, who visited the place in 1496: 'a great city destroyed by the Turks, and now subject to the Venetians'.[51] (It seems that, not knowing the true explanation of its dilapidated state, he had turned to the usual suspects.)

The presumed connection of this city with the Emperor Constantine was another recurrent theme, part of the historical lore that was handed down to—and by—many pilgrims. According to Hans Lochner, who sailed past Durrës in 1435, 'this city of Durrës, together with Constantinople and Rana, was built and converted [to Christianity] by Constantine'; Bishop Louis de Rochechouart, who travelled in 1461, called it 'formerly the city of Constantine the Great'.[52] Hans Tücher wrote that 'The Emperor Constantine began to build this city with the intention of setting up Constantinople and his palace there. But as he reconsidered the matter, he did not like the nature of the country there. So he moved on to the place where Constantinople now stands, having it built as an imperial residence for himself'.[53] Fabri repeated essentially the same story, and von Breydenbach, embroidering a little on Tücher, said that the Emperor changed his mind 'because of the infertility and unsuitability of the soil'; Zeebout, probably borrowing from one or more of those writers, explained that 'It was first founded by the emperor Constantine, and was intended to be Constantinople, but the air and soil of the area around it did not please him, so that he did not stay longer there, and founded Constantinople in the place where it now stands.'[54]

The origins of this myth are mysterious; there seems to be no basis for it in Byzantine historical writings.[55] Perhaps the popular identification of the bronze equestrian statue with Constantine was the essential generator of the story. Little is known about this statue, which does not survive today. It was mentioned in the twelfth century by Anna Comnena, who said that it stood on 'the gate that opens to the East'; the humanist traveller Ciriaco of Ancona, who visited Durrës in 1436, described it as mounted on the northern gate.[56] Domenico Malipiero, a Venetian official who was stationed in Shkodër in 1474, wrote of Durrës: 'Now it is almost disinhabited, because of the bad quality of the air; it has many remains of ancient statues, among them an Emperor on horseback. Some said it was Theodosius, others Constantine.'[57] The narrative of the pilgrimage of Alexander, Count Palatine of the Rhine, in 1495–6 adds one further detail: 'as they tell me, Durrës is a fine city; Constantine, the son of Helen, had it built, and there in front of the cathedral chapter-house stands an image or representation of Constantine on a great bronze horse, covered in gilt, with a piece of paper in his hand which says "This is the way", etc.'[58] Such an inscription, if present, might well have encouraged an identification with the first Emperor to favour Christianity (it is from Isaiah 30: 21, 'This is the way, walk ye in it...'); however, the other inaccuracies here, and the fact that the inscription goes unmentioned in the accounts of those who actually visited Durrës (including Ciriaco, who made a point of noting down such things), must cast some doubt on this detail.

Zeebout's description of Joos van Ghistele's pilgrimage also gives quite a full account of a visit to Durrës.

It was founded a very long time ago, and is ringed by walls made of brick, of the kind they use in this country. In it is also a very fine strong castle, guarding the landward side, and situated on a hill; round about this aforementioned city it was now mostly swampy ground, so that one can scarcely approach with horses and carts, or even on foot, when it has rained. It is said that Pierus, the son of Achilles, was king of this city, and that the country of Epirus was subject to it.

Now, at the gate of the city on the landward side there are two square columns, which sufficiently support the archway of the gate itself; they are roughly one and a half feet wide on each side, and may be roughly four fathoms high, which is a really remarkable thing to see. They are very shiny with many colours; in them, you can see pieces of human bones, such as fragments of hands and feet, pieces of skulls, jawbones and teeth, and pieces of arm-bone and leg-bone, so that one can see in detail inside the bones, in the way that you see flowers in those glass apples. From this it is believed that in ancient times, these columns—of which one sees many, of various colours, in the lands beyond the sea—were made by craft, and not all cut out of rock-faces. Also, on the gate there is a horse with a man sitting on it, of marvellous size, both made of metal, placed there presumably as memorials. This city was in earlier times founded on an island, and the land was dug so deep that the water flowed from one side to the other, but now it is all filled in and you can ride over it anywhere.[59]

This is the most detailed description of the gate itself; the shiny multi-coloured stone, which so fascinated van Ghistele, was probably a variety of breccia, or possibly a fossiliferous limestone, both of which can be packed with differently coloured pieces including white ones resembling (to an imaginative viewer) fragments of bone.[60] The description of the walls as 'made of brick' is very accurate; in the words of one recent study of these fortifications, 'The circuit at Durres stands, uniquely in late antiquity, as an entirely brick-built defensive wall, without any rubble core.'[61] (These walls, which supervened in places on much earlier structures, post-dated the devastating earthquake of 345 AD. They were probably built in the reign of the Emperor Anastasius (r. 491–518), who was himself a native of the city—which surely makes him a strong candidate for identification with the bronze emperor on horseback.)[62] Because of the demographic contraction of Durrës during the medieval period, at some stage a transverse wall was built, cutting across the area enclosed by the old walls, after which the population was concentrated within the new, smaller space; archaeologists and historians have debated whether this had already happened by 1436 (when Ciriaco of Ancona described the statue on the 'northern gate') or whether it took place after the Ottoman conquest of 1501. The evidence of the pilgrim narratives, while not conclusive, does suggest that in 1458 and 1481 that gate was still located in what could be naturally described as the wall of the city—which tends to support the post-Ottoman theory.[63]

The other physical detail mentioned by Zeebout also corresponds to known facts: the surrounding land, especially on the northern side, was indeed very marshy. Malipiero's comment in 1474 on the 'the bad quality of the air' was doubtless a reference to malaria ('mal'aria', bad air), which remained a problem until the district was properly drained in the twentieth century. And the notion, picked up by van Ghistele, that 'This city was in earlier times founded on an island, and the land was dug so deep that the water flowed from one side to the other' may have been based at least in part on the plans, seriously entertained by the Venetian authorities in the 1390s and the 1450s, to dig a channel around the city in order to turn it into an island—a measure that was expected to have health benefits as well as strategic ones.[64]

One other aspect of these descriptions of Durrës by Capodilista/Sanseverino and van Ghistele/Zeebout deserves comment: their apparent interest in classical history and in what we would now call classical archaeology. In the earlier case, it is fairly clear that it was the local informants who prompted the references to ancient history, pointing out the more distant walls which they believed to be the ones constructed by Caesar during his siege of Dyrrachium in 48 BC. (More probably, the walls in question were part of the outermost circuit, six kilometres from the centre of Durrës, of the concentric fortifications built by Anastasius.)[65] That siege, together with the battle that ended it, was the one moment in Roman history when this city took centre-stage; as the conflict was described at length by Plutarch, it is not surprising that fifteenth-century residents were able to refer to it. The other details given by Capodilista may be his own garblings of other things his informants said: he confuses 'Epirus' with 'Epidamnus' (the earlier name, according to writers such as Pliny, of Dyrrachium); 'Emathia' was a classical term for Macedonia, which could be extended (by writers such as Lucan) to areas further to the south; and the 'Thessaly' ('Thesalia') he mentioned was not a city twelve miles away but the province of north-central Greece containing the town or village of Pharsalos, where Pompey's final defeat took place. (There was probably some aural confusion between 'Farsala', its later Greek name, and 'Thesalia', a more familiar geographical term.) Zeebout's statement 'It is said that Pierus, the son of Achilles, was king of this city, and that the country of Epirus was subject to it' also sounds like a report of a local historical claim; 'Pierus' should have been 'Pyrrhus' (the alternative name of Neoptolemus), and although one must suspect a confusion here with the famous Illyrian ruler and war-leader Pyrrhus (of the late fourth and early third centuries BC), classical writers had also made some association between the son of Achilles and the territory of Epirus. One has to wonder, though, at the historical insouciance of someone who can both locate the son of Achilles in a city and, a few sentences later, assert that that city was founded by the Emperor Constantine.

Some of the other pilgrims managed better than that. A few did have serious interests in classical history and literature, and in some cases such concerns clearly stimulated the attention they paid to these south-east Adriatic territories as they passed them. Thus Louis de Rochechouart noted that Butrint was mentioned by Vergil, identified Corfu with Vergil's Phaeacus, cited a line from the *Aeneid*, and called Ithaca the island of Ulysses.[66] Alessandro Ariosto, who wrote in quite elegant Latin and adopted a humanist genre (the educational dialogue) for his account, referred correctly to the siege of Dyrrachium and the subsequent battle of Pharsalos, and identified Vlorë with the ancient site of Apollonia.[67] The most striking example of this approach is the narrative of Antonio da Crema, a humanist-educated judge and administrator from Mantua, who made his pilgrimage in 1486. While he undoubtedly had some religious motivation, his main reason for travelling seems to have been his desire to see the classical world; at his first main stop, for example (Zadar) he sought out Roman inscriptions, and he went to some trouble to buy classical medallions on Corfu. His pilgrim narrative is stuffed with classical learning: he refers to the geographer Ptolemy on Ulcinj, to Pomponius Mela and Pliny on Durrës, to Pliny again on the southern Albanian coast, to Ptolemy on Vlorë, and to Plutarch on King Pyrrhus of Epirus.[68] This degree of classical-related interest in the Albanian lands was quite exceptional; while it is comparable to that of the non-pilgrim Ciriaco of Ancona, it far exceeds that of any of the other pilgrims.

V

One might expect that interest in recent and contemporary history, on the other hand, would be much more common. Yet here too the record is patchy. Above all, it is surprising that the exploits of Skanderbeg receive very little comment or celebration in these texts. This may reflect the fact that the majority of the pilgrim-narratives that mention Albania are from the period after his death (in 1468); at the same time, it tends to suggest that widespread popular interest in Skanderbeg in Western Europe—even among those whose religious motives should have made them keen to celebrate him as a champion of Christendom—took time to develop, and may have benefited particularly from the later appearance of printed works such as the writings of Marin Barleti. The only pilgrim-narratives from Skanderbeg's lifetime that refer to his activities are those by Capodilista and Sanseverino, whose visit to Durrës took place at the beginning of June 1458. When their 'comito' asked his counterpart on Alessandro Contarini's galley for the latest news, he was told first of all that King Alfonso V of Aragon had died. (This notice was a few weeks premature; Alfonso, who had been the great supporter of Skanderbeg, was on his deathbed, and expired at the end of June.) Then, when asked about the Sultan, the other comito replied that 'it was said that he would go to the Peloponnese, which is a Greek province, partly under the Venetian government and partly under a lord of Greece, but it was not said that he had gone there yet; it was also said that he was making great military preparations to come to Krujë, which is a city in Albania or a castle belonging to the lord Skanderbeg, or perhaps to go to Euboea.'[69] The only narrative to give a general account of Skanderbeg, and indeed of the Ottoman conquest of Albania, was Zeebout's, written more than seventeen years after Skanderbeg's death:

The Sultan has possession of most of the towns and castles situated inland, such as Petrella, Croeya, Scouterij, Drijvasto [Petrela, Krujë, Shkodër, Drisht], and many more, too numerous to name. The Sultan would never have conquered them if the country had been in harmony within itself; but there were various lords who ruled the country of Albania, who were constantly quarrelling, and making war on one another, so that, among these quarrels, the Sultan was sooner and better able to impose his will on the aforementioned country. But there was one lord, called Scanderbec, who was a very stalwart Christian, and strongly resisted the Sultan all the time, so that the Sultan was never able to achieve anything against Scanderbec, but in his time, so people say, he killed almost as many Turks as are now living, and after his death the country was lost, with the exception of some strong cities which are still Christian [possessions], as we have seen.[70]

One other testimony of Albanian anti-Ottoman rebellion survives in the anonymous account by a member of the retinue of Alexander, Count Palatine of the Rhine, who passed down the Albanian coast from 19 to 21 July 1495. After they had passed Ulcinj,

a high mountain was pointed out to my gracious lord on the left-hand side; a short time before this, 10,000 or 12,000 Albanians had gathered there, waiting for the arrival of the King of France in order to make war on the Ottomans. After the aforementioned King of France had obtained the Kingdom of Naples, the Sultan, when he had heard about how the King of France had withdrawn again from the Kingdom of Naples, prepared his forces and killed all or most of those Albanians.[71]

This refers to the dramatic situation that had arisen after the French King, Charles VIII, invaded Italy in September 1494. As his army marched almost unopposed down the peninsula, reaching Naples in February 1495, he let it be known that his plan was to use southern Italy as a springboard for the invasion of the Ottoman Empire and the eventual recovery of the Holy Land. Western sources record that he was in communication with the Catholic Archbishop of Durrës, who promised to raise local forces in support of a French invasion; and there is also some evidence that the Ottoman authorities were seriously alarmed by this prospect. Charles was crowned King of Naples on 10 May, but, knowing that a league of northern Italian states had been formed to fight against him, he began the long march back to France just ten days later.[72] The evidence of this pilgrim narrative is of some importance; although the location is only vaguely referred to (perhaps the informant had gestured rather generally in the direction of the Dukagjin mountain territory), and although the numbers given here, like all such figures in accounts of rebel forces, may have been exaggerated, this testimony does suggest that a major pro-French rising had been organized, whether by the Archbishop or by other local leaders.

Otherwise, the only recent politico-military event on Albanian soil that attracted comment in the pilgrim narratives was the surrender of Shkodër to the Ottomans, which took place, after a siege lasting more than six months, in accordance with a diplomatic agreement made in January 1479.[73] Felix Fabri, whose galley was becalmed off the Albanian coast on 24 December 1483 (during his return journey), commented: 'The city which is the capital of Albania is called Scodra; it belonged to the Venetians, but in 1478 they gave that city by treaty to the Sultan. In common speech we call it Scultur [Ital.: Scutari].' Mournfully, he continued: 'We would willingly have gone there to celebrate the festivities [of Christmas eve], but now there is no worship there, and there are no festivities...'[74] Bernhard von Breydenbach, whose pilgrimage likewise took place in 1483, also commented on the handover of Shkodër, noting with evident regret that the Venetians had yielded it 'together with a certain extremely well armed castle called Tornesius'—a statement which is hard to explicate, as no such name was used for the castle of Rozafat at Shkodër, or for any of the other places ceded by Venice to the Sultan.[75] The fullest account of the fall of Shkodër comes in the narrative of Jan Hasišteinský, who sailed past the mouth of the river Bunë ten years later. Shkodër was, he wrote, 'a very fine and strong fortress and town, which lies on an island. The old Sultan, the father of the present one, spent a long time, so I am informed, attacking it. He stormed it several times, but was never able to conquer it.' The reason for his failure was simply that 'there were brave people in it, and many thousands of Turks were lost in the assaults, when they stormed it, so that the Sultan from shame of them had to break off the attack.' But eventually Venice decided to make a peace agreement, in order to secure its trading rights in the Ottoman Empire. Under the terms of the treaty, 'all the inhabitants of that town of Scutari were able to stay with their possessions, and the Sultan also gave them permission to leave. But no-one wanted to stay, but all of them withdrew to Venice without all their possessions except what they were able to carry with them, taking themselves away for the sake of the Christian faith.' The Venetian authorities, eager to reward 'such constancy towards the faith, and the courage with which they so bravely defended themselves against the Sultan during the siege', gave them all privileged positions as traders or artisans in Venice.[76] One thing at least is clear from Hasišteinský's account: he had been briefed by loyal Venetians, keen to put as positive a gloss as possible on the actions of their government. To see the other side of the coin one has only to turn to the narrative by the Franciscan friar (and non-Venetian) Alessandro Ariosto. His journey had taken place two years before the start of the siege, but when writing his account in 1482 he inserted a passionate declamation against what he regarded as a Venetian act of betrayal:

by the peace agreement made recently (that is, in 1479) by the Venetians with the Sultan, that most savage enemy of the Christians, by which they handed over the castle of Shkodër, the island of Lemnos and the peninsula of Mani in the Peloponnese, which is crammed full of towns and people, and also, amidst such great dangers that threaten Christendom, agreed to assist the Sultan, if he requested it, with 50 galleys fully manned with soldiers, we are given copious reasons to lament, and great suffering is inflicted on the Christian religion, since, indeed, we should very much fear that by means of such a terrible treaty they have thoroughly armed the enemy against us for our final ruin, and that the Turks will destroy us with their raids, devastations, burnings and expulsions.[77]

VI

After Durrës, as the pilgrims continued down the coast, the next significant port they encountered was Vlorë. This town had not been harmed by the Ottoman conquest, having been handed over peacefully in 1417. For its new masters it was an important outlet to the sea, and, before long, it became used at least intermittently as an Ottoman naval base.[78] In the summer of 1480 the local governor, Gedik Ahmed Pasha, assembled there a force of at least 16,000 soldiers, with more than 100 ships on which to transport them, for a major invasion of southern Italy. They landed close to Otranto on 28 July, and conquered that city together with much of the surrounding region. (Although Gedik Ahmed withdrew most of his army in October, he left in Otranto a large garrison which would not abandon its position until September of the following year.) In the third week of June 1480, just a month before that Ottoman fleet set sail for Italy, a pilgrim galley passed by with no fewer than four narrative-writers on board: the German friar Felix Fabri, the French priest Pierre Barbatre, the Milanese civic official Santo Brasca and the anonymous author of the *Voyage de la Saincte Cyté de Hierusalem*.[79] In the words of the last of these: 'we saw all the mountains of Albania, and several towns belonging to the Sultan, among which there is one large stronghold called Vallone [Vlorë; Ital.: Valona] which used to belong to the Venetians. And the sailors told us that there was a large garrison of the Sultan's men in that town, and that there was a great quantity of his ships and galleys at that port.'[80] Barbatre recorded that 'they said that the Sultan had a large part of his army in that town of Waronne [Vlorë], and that near there he had more than 100 sailing vessels', and Brasca gave the same number—which seems a realistic figure, at least as a minimum, for the transportation of 16,000 men.[81] By the time Bernhard von Breydenbach passed by, three years later, popular repute seems to have multiplied the number of ships at Vlorë: he described it as 'a very strong city, next to which the Sultan normally keeps, in a certain river, a huge fleet which commonly consists of 400 vessels'. He immediately added some impassioned sentences about the conquest of Otranto, including the fact that the bishop of that city had been cut down at the altar of his cathedral; clearly the psychological wound inflicted on pious Christians by the Otranto campaign was still quite raw.[82]

A few pilgrim narratives gave more general descriptions of Vlorë and its immediate surroundings—descriptions based, evidently, on what could be seen from a distance, and on such information as the Venetian sailors could supply. Friderich Steigerwalder, who travelled in 1470, noted that between the island of Sazan and the tip of the Karaburun peninsula (which he mistakenly described as another island) you could see 'a castle called Tanina [Kaninë], which was situated on a high mountain. The Sultan built it within the last three or four years; three miles from the castle there lies a town called Velana [Vlorë; Ital.: Valona], which is occupied by Turks and Albanians and belongs to the Sultan.'[83] (In fact the fortress of Kaninë had a continuous history from the late Roman period; but the Ottomans did engage in significant work to strengthen it in the fifteenth century, which this testimony may perhaps help to date.)[84] Zeebout's account of von Ghistele's 1481 voyage recorded that 'they came to a large gulf or bay, all on the left-hand side, on which was a fine, large city, held by the Sultan, called Lavalona. It is not walled, but is surrounded by ditches, earthworks and palisades, of wood and earth. There also stands there a very fine, strong castle, such that, if the city were conquered, but the castle itself were well defended, the city would be impossible to hold without it.'[85] Jan Hasišteinský, who travelled twelve years later, penned a brief description of Vlorë: 'On the coast there is situated a castle on a hill, with quite a large town below it. And the name of that town is Valona. And that castle belongs to the Sultan. And close to that castle the Sultan has many ships, which are called "galee sottili" and "fuste".'[86] A little more detail was supplied by Arnold von Harff, who passed by in 1496: 'To the left side of the harbour, on the mainland there is a very fine, large village called Velona, with a good 2,000 households. This village is able to supply the Sultan with 700 horsemen for war, not counting foot soldiers. Above this village there is a fine castle called Kano [Kaninë], where the Sultan has an official in residence.'[87] In his authoritative study of Ottoman architecture in Albania, Machiel Kiel has used von Harff's testimony to help settle the long-debated question of when the great Ottoman castle of Vlorë (described in the late seventeenth century by Evliya Çelebi, but no longer extant) was constructed: dating in fact from the reign of Süleyman the Magnificent, it was not to be seen in the fifteenth century.[88] While Zeebout fails to give a specific location for the castle he mentions, the accounts of both Steigerwalder and Hasišteinský provide further confirmation of Kiel's argument: the only visible castle was the one 'on a high mountain' or 'on a hill' (the remains of Kaninë castle are at a height of nearly 400 m above sea level), above and beyond the town.

Steigerwalder described the island of Sazan (Ital.: Saseno), and the nearby promontory, as belonging to the Venetians; this was not correct.[89] According to

Zeebout, Sazan (which he called 'Tsasyno') was 'a small island with three stubby promontories, on which there normally lives a caloger, that is, a Greek monk'.[90] Hasišteinský (who called it 'Sazemo') noted that the island belonged to the Sultan, and his galley passed close enough for him to record that 'It did not seem to be inhabited, so far as I could see.'[91] And for von Harff, 'this Saseno is a small island, belonging to the Sultan. On it there are two small Greek chapels, one dedicated to Our Blessed Lady, the other to Saint Nicholas. At this time the Sultan has some very fine stallions grazing on this island.'[92] Such a degree of detailed knowledge does suggest that Venetian ships (or at least local fishing-boats from the Venetian territory of Corfu) did call at the island from time to time.

The most puzzling feature of the entire Albanian coastline was encountered by those pilgrims whose ships took them past the bay of Vlorë and along the Karaburun peninsula in the evening or at night. The fullest description was given by the Swiss-German knight Hans Bernard von Eptingen, who travelled in the retinue of Duke Otto II of Pfalz-Mosbach in 1460:

there we looked between an island and a high mountain, which we approached and below which we passed. The mountain consisted almost entirely of rock, and was covered with snow; it was so bare, that we did not and could not see any trees on it—only, here and there, rosemary, sage and herbs of that kind. We also saw a waterfall which ran and flowed from the mountain into the sea, which was very pleasant to see. After that, in the area on the barren and steep mountain-side we saw many large, tall fires, which all visibly grew larger. When I asked what sort of fire that could be, some said that it was signalling by the Turks; some said that it was iron ore being smelted; and some said that they were fires lit by shepherds. But it was altogether unlikely that people or their livestock could subsist on such a bare mountain; there were higher and more visible mountains from which to signal, and for that purpose the fires would have been even larger and taller, and would also have burnt on and off; and iron ore could hardly be smelted or worked there. Also, from the mountain's appearance it seemed that nobody could get onto it or off it, and besides there was absolutely no wood there. But some were of the opinion that it was the sort of mountain that burns by itself; and I thought that was the most reliable explanation.[93]

Twenty years later, Pierre Barbatre saw something similar, and was satisfied with the first of those explanations: 'towards evening, two or three hours before sunset, we were at sea and the wind was so contrary that we had to stay motionless at sea in front of an island and a castle in Turkey called Waronne [Vlorë]; and there in the evening we saw three fires on the mountains, for it is the custom of the peas-ants to light fires on the mountains in the evening when they see boats, sailing ships or galleys on the sea, so that the people in the towns and cities can be on their guard.'[94] The anonymous French account by another pilgrim on the same galley makes it sound like a much more fraught occasion: 'After sunset, on a high mountain above that town [Vlorë] there were several large fires which were lit by those Turks. Because of them, we were quite amazed, and spent the whole night in great fear and danger; the pilgrims maintained a watch with the sailors all through the night, fearing that those Turks would come and attack our galley.'[95] Paul Walther, a German Franciscan friar who travelled in 1482, saw 'many fires on various mountains, especially around the city of Velona [Vlorë]'. The explanation he received was a different one: 'the commanding officers of the ship said that the peasants made those fires in honour of St John the Baptist (that day, Sunday, being the vigil of his saint's day).'[96] Lighting fires on St John's eve was indeed a custom in some parts of Albania; but from other accounts it is clear that this particular phenomenon was not limited to the dates of Christian festivals.[97] Returning from the Holy Land in 1493, the Silesian knight Heinrich von Zedlitz was on a galley which was driven northwards from Corfu on the evening of 16 September by a strong wind; he noted that 'on the right-hand side, as we passed by during the night, the Turks lit many great fires during the night on their mountains.'[98] Two years later the travelling companion of Alexander, Count Palatine of the Rhine, passing southern Albania on the outward journey, saw something similar on the night of 20 July: 'as the Albanians who live on the high mountains saw our galley going past, they lit many fires; we were told that they lit them to celebrate the coming of our galley, and the fact that we were going to visit the Holy Land, as these Albanians are good Christians.'[99] Yet of all the various explanations offered, the one supported by Hans Bernard von Eptingen was surely the most likely: this probably was 'the sort of mountain that burns by itself'. The region of Vlorë was famous for its production of mineral pitch (bitumen), which was of high quality and also quite easily obtained, as it lay close to the surface. Most likely there were some places on the mountain-sides where, once the pitch— or, at least, a gas derived from it—had caught light for whatever reason, it would burn by itself for a long time. When Henry Holland visited Selenicë, eleven miles inland from Vlorë, in 1813, he observed that 'In two or three different places, in the vicinity of the pitch-mines, I found an inflammable gas issuing from the ground, which easily took fire and spread a flame to some extent over the surface', where it burned 'with considerable vividness'; the miners told him that such fires often happened, 'especially after heavy rains; the gas, once inflamed, frequently continuing to burn for several weeks in succession.'[100]

Those mystery fires were not the only points of interest on the southern Albanian coast. Travelling southwards beyond Vlorë, Louis de Rochechouart observed 'a land rich in grass, wine, oil, olives and sweet oranges', to his surprise, although it was only the first week of June, 'all the hay had already been mown'.[101] Santo Brasca noted that the region of Himarë produced 'a great quantity of grain'.[102] And off its coast, according to Zeebout, 'people often fish up many beautiful pieces of coral, which are very good and fine, though not as big or as strong as the branches of coral which are fished up on the coast of North Africa.'[103] But these were not the main things for which Himarë was famous—or infamous. In Zeebout's words, 'Lasimara' was 'a very large mountain massif' on which 'there lives a type of people, who are Christians, and are the fiercest and most wicked people that you will ever find thereabouts. They have no lords, and obey no one. And although the Sultan has often come with all his force to this massif, among the difficult passes and wildernesses that surround it, he could achieve little or nothing against them, but marched away from there unsatisfied, leaving them as they were, and as they are still.'[104] A similar account was given, rather briefly, by Heinrich von Zedlitz, who travelled in 1493: 'we passed a great mountain massif, where they are their own lords, and the Sultan has not been able to conquer them, as they possess a mountain stronghold and yield to no one.'[105] But the fullest description was given by another pilgrim of that year, Jan Hasišteinský. 'On our left-hand side', he wrote, 'ten Italian miles away, there were some high mountains, which are called Czimera [Himarë]. And those mountains of Czimera are not an island, but very mountainous and rocky headlands, so far as we could see. And they belong to the land of the Sultan. And that region of Czimera is 100 Italian miles in circumference and 60 miles across. And the people of that region are their own masters, and have never been the subjects of anyone.' The area was, he had been informed, productive: 'they have in that region much salt, and a great deal of cattle, grain and wine.' Inland, however, it was almost impenetrable, with 'very high paths because of great cliffs'. When danger threatens, 'they occupy the paths and mountain passes and defend them, so that no-one can get near them. These people and the inhabitants of that region, so far as I can establish, take from all indiscriminately: they inflict harm on Christians, pagans and Muslims, and the great Sultan and his subjects, taking whatever they can.' One year before, 'because of such thieving and raiding the Sultan gathered a great force to conquer them.' But they occupied their high paths and blocked every advance, 'so that he could do nothing, and some thousands of good-quality men were lost, and simply because of the great harm and shame he had to withdraw from them.' As a pious Catholic from a territory where the heresy of the Hussites had found many fol-lowers, Hasišteinský was struck by one other aspect of the situation as it had been described to him: 'in that region of Czimera the inhabitants maintain the custom and way of behaving which exists also, unfortunately, in the Czech lands, that everyone holds the religion he wants to hold, and those Albanians have many different religions among themselves.' Just to add the finishing touches, he wrote: 'Also they have full freedom in all the neighbouring districts to seize, pillage, rob and murder. And no-one dares oppose them. They also make false gold, and from it they make new coins of various kinds, and they are the highest masters of that craft, above all others.'[106]

To the modern traveller, passing down the coast beyond Himarë, the next major place of interest is Sarandë. But this city goes almost unmentioned by the fifteenth-century pilgrims; just two of them refer to it, and their comments serve to explain why it was so neglected. In the words of an anonymous pilgrim from the Rhineland who passed by in July 1472, this was 'a large town, called Cente Quaranta [from "Santi Quaranta", the Italian for the Greek name "Agioi Saranda", meaning the 40 saints—but this writer has turned it into a version of the French for "140"], because that was the number of churches that stood there, which are now destroyed to their foundations, and it is now nothing more than a harbour'.[107] Zeebout painted a very similar picture: 'one passes a certain bay, also lying on the left-hand side, on which there is a fine city, as big as Acre in the Holy Land, called Ayjos Seranda, but it is so ruined and destroyed that one can see nothing more than the foundations and heaps of stones'.[108]

A little further to the south, there was one more place of special interest, then as now: Butrint. The pilgrim who was in the retinue of Count Wilhelm of Thüringen in 1461 described it as 'a fine castle, Bottrinta, which belongs to the Venetians. The Ottomans have twice come there in order to conquer it'.[109] Eleven years later the anonymous pilgrim from the Rhineland, on his return trip to Venice at the end of October, described it as 'a very strong little town'. Such was the lush fertility of the place that it seemed to him 'like the May-time in our country, and thus it was very delightful to be there on the land, or in the field, when the grass there was beginning to grow as it does in our country in the summer. Our galley stayed here for the whole of Sunday, all day long'.[110] But the fullest account, once again, was given by Zeebout, on the basis of Joos van Ghistele's admirably thorough notes. Before reaching Corfu, he wrote,

one passes a small bay, lying on the left-hand side, towards Greece, which is now Turkey, which twists and turns as it runs inland, at the end of which there stands a strong castle on a round, steep cliff, almost surrounded by the sea, and around it it is all marshy, so that one can scarcely reach it by horse, only some of the time with boats, and with difficulty on foot. It is held by the Christians; the Sultan has often attacked it, but has always left with many casualties, and it is a quite unconquerable place. They catch many good fish in that area, especially of two sorts, those called 'cyvale' [kephalos] and those called 'mauvrachi' [mavraki], from the roe of which they make the best botargo in the world, which is a special food and provision much used in that country; the people who live there are almost all fishermen, and very sturdy people. Around it there are very good woods, mostly of laurel trees, extending around it in plains, but nearby, behind it, there is a very high mountain. This castle is called Buventroo.[111]

VII

Finally, some reflections on the general dangers that faced these pilgrims on their journey along the Albanian coast. The threat that most obviously concerned them was that posed by the Ottoman presence. When Santo Brasca's galley was passing the island of Sazan, a scirocco (south-easterly wind) sprang up, which made further progress impossible; and at that moment

> there appeared two Turkish ships, which had come out of Valona [Vlorë]. At this, we were all struck by a degree of fear, and not without reason, above all because in the peace treaty made by the Venetians with the Sultan I believe that no one can think himself safe if he is not from their country. And thereafter the Venetians agreed that whenever their ships are asked to lower their sails on behalf of the Pasha or admiral of the Ottoman fleet, they are obliged to lower them—which is a bad thing for those foreigners who go on their ships.

So, with the scirocco strengthening, they turned aside and tacked westwards, towards the Italian coast.[112] The same episode is described somewhat differently by the anonymous Frenchman: 'At about supper time, we saw a galley coming out from the town [of Vlorë] and were afraid that it was coming towards us; and at that time the wind failed, and our galley could go neither forward nor back.' It was during the night that followed that they observed the mysterious fires on the mountainside near Vlorë, mounting guard in the belief that those were signals for a nocturnal attack; only on the following two days, which were a Friday and a Saturday, were they driven far out towards Apulia. When, on the Saturday evening, they finally made their way to the harbour of Corfu, the men they met from the Venetian naval galleys in that port 'were utterly amazed by our arrival, and said that if it were not for the great and evident miracle which God performed for us when he sent us a contrary wind on the Friday and Saturday that had just passed, we would all have been lost and seized by the Ottomans, who took the course by which we had come; roughly 80 of their ships had passed in front of the port of Corfu, on their way to besiege Ragusa [Dubrovnik], from where we had set off on the previous Wednesday.'[113] Fear of the Ottomans was a constant factor. Felix Fabri recorded that on his way back from the Holy Land in 1483, as night fell on Christmas Day, the wind strengthened, and 'we could not go on at night because of the reefs that were in that sea, nor did we want to enter a safe port in Albania, because of the Turks who lived there.' In the end they managed to find a place on the shore which was 'harbour-like, but deserted, with no people or animals staying near it', where they spent an uneasy night.[114] Fifteen years later, when the Swiss burgher (from Lucerne) Johannes Schürpf reached Corfu on his homeward journey, he was advised that it would be too risky to take the direct route up the Albanian coast, 'as the sea was full of Turks, and unsafe'; so he obtained passage on a trading ship that was going to Apulia instead.[115] And yet, despite this clear evidence of contemporary attitudes, and notwithstanding the legalistic point made by Santo Brasca, it must be said that there is no record of any pilgrim galley being molested by Ottoman naval vessels during this period.

A more valid fear, probably, concerned attacks by corsairs or pirates. These might be Muslim or Christian. The advice to prospective pilgrims by an anonymous English writer included the admonition: 'Be neuere to bolde to shippe you in litell vessels in no costes of the hethene, for drede of such Courssaries as bene aforesaid, as well of the Cristene as well of theyme nought of oure beleve, in euery partie of the see.'[116] On Easter Day (23 April) 1413, somewhere off the southern Albanian coast, the marchese Nicolò da Este and his fellow pilgrims had just finished their lunch when they saw a ship approaching; 'wondering whether it was a corsair ship', he discussed with the captain whether they should confront it—until it unfurled the Genoese flag. (The vessels then came alongside each other and exchanged news: the Genoese ship was returning from Greece, to Venice, with the goods of Venetian merchants on board.)[117] When Hans Bernard von Eptingen's galley was sailing down the northern coast of Albania, one large ship with three sails appeared closer to land, and a smaller, two-sailed vessel seemed to head towards the pilgrims; 'therefore we armed ourselves, with firearms and other things', until they had outrun the suspect ships.[118] Piracy and corsairing were very real problems in this part of the Mediterranean, as in many others. In 1479 Sultan Mehmed II issued orders to Gedik Ahmed to restrain the corsairs of Vlorë, who had been attacking Venetian shipping; it must seem very likely that these corsairs were Greek Orthodox Christians, as the town of Vlorë had no Muslim population at that stage.[119]

But the greatest danger came, in the end, from the elements—or, as the pilgrims might have put it, from God himself. While galleys had the advantage of manoeuvrability, they had the considerable disadvantage that, being oared vessels, they did not ride high in the sea. At its lowest point, the side of a galley was just over a metre above the water. Galleys could be swamped by rough seas; and, as they were relatively light vessels (in comparison with the big, deep-hulled bulk-trading ships), they could also be blown onto reefs or rocky shores by strong winds. Some of the worst conditions, naturally, were experienced by those who left their return journeys until the autumn or winter. Heinrich von Zedlitz's galley, which sailed northwards from Corfu on the evening of 16 September, was struck by a great storm which destroyed one of its sails.[120] The anonymous pilgrim of 1494 (probably Ludwig von Greifenstein), leaving Corfu on 15 October, found that two hours after sunset 'there came an extraordinarily fierce storm, with thunder and lightning, which was almost terrifying, and made the greatest thunderclap I have ever heard in my life'; the pilgrims lit the candles they had bought at the Holy Sepulchre in Jerusalem, after which the storm subsided.[121] And in an account of what may have been one of the latest return journeys of all (written by Johannes of Frankfurt, an adviser to Ludwig III, Count Palatine of the Rhine), we read that on 28 December 1426, one day after leaving Corfu, 'such great tribulation came upon us that the captain and all the sailors despaired of their lives, praying for God's mercy and the intercession of the saints, as the sea was flooding the galley, and it was already close to being entirely swamped.'[122] Even in the summer months, conditions could sometimes be equally bad. When Friderich Steigerwalder's galley was struck by a great storm off Himarë in mid-June 1470, he observed water-spouts in the distance which, he was told, could draw up ships and fill them with water, rapidly sinking them.[123] But perhaps the most humanly touching description is the one given by Capodilista and Sanseverino of the storm which struck them off Lezhë on 29 May 1458, when, as we have seen, not only the pilgrims but also some of the sailors lay prostrate with fear on the deck:

> The captain was greatly amazed to see such a storm, which, he said, would have been bad enough for January. Not seeing any other remedy, he had many saints' names written on pieces of paper and put into a hat, and he told the pilgrims each to pick one of the pieces of paper and make a vow, to the saint whose name he found written on it, that when he reached dry land he would have a Mass said in his honour and reverence; they threw the pieces of paper in the sea, and that is how it was done. And as it pleased God, that evening the rain, the wind, and the sea began to grow calm.[124]

This story, at least, had a happy ending. The stories that ended in the worst possible way have not come down to us, of course. Yet even from those that have, we can gain quite a vivid sense of the sheer difficulty and danger of the conditions in which so many people—not only pilgrims, but traders and other voyagers too—travelled, during the course of the fifteenth century, along the coastline of this understandably little-known territory.

2

The Kelmendi

Notes on the Early History of a Catholic Albanian Clan

Among the clans of the northern Albanian highlands, the 'Malësi e Madhe', one enjoys an extraordinary historical pre-eminence: the Kelmendi (also known as Këlmendi, Klmeni, Klimenti or Clementi). When Franz Baron Nopcsa wrote his survey of the Albanian clans in the 1920s he placed the Kelmendi first in his entire classification, stating that this clan was the most frequently mentioned of all.[1] Edith Durham reserved special praise for the Kelmendi: 'they are', she wrote, 'some of the finest and most intelligent of the tribesmen.'[2] Their political and military importance was noted by the Austro-Hungarian consul in Shkodër, Ritter von Lippich, in November 1878: he described them as the strongest of all the Catholic clans of the Shkodran highlands.[3] Western Europeans had long been aware of the military prowess of the Kelmendi, ever since the Austrian campaign of 1737 in the Balkans, which ended with a large group of Kelmendi highlanders fighting their way northwards in support of the retreating Austrians; the survivors from this Kelmendi force were then incorporated, as a small but distinct Albanian-speaking population, in the Austrian Military Frontier to the west of Belgrade. Long before that episode, the dominance of the Kelmendi over the other clans of the region had been so well established that it was common, in the seventeenth century, to refer to the entire mountain range west of Pejë (Peć) as the 'Kelmendi mountains'; and when the Imperial army came to Kosovo in 1689, its officers used the phrase 'Patriarch of the Kelmendi' to refer to the Catholic Archbishop—thus sowing the seeds of confusion among modem historians, who have puzzled over both the identity of that so-called 'Patriarch' and the meaning of the term 'Kelmendi' itself.[4]

Recent scholarship has shed new light on the history of the Kelmendi, both before and after the epic events of 1737. Two works stand out in particular: Peter Bartl's valuable article 'Die Kelmendi: zur Geschichte eines nordalbanischen Bergstammes', which concentrates especially on the first half of the seventeenth century, and the recent book by Frrok Zefiq, *Shqiptarët Kelmendas ne Hrtkovc e Nikinc (1737–1997)*, which contains a mass of fascinating detail on the history of the Kelmendi population transplanted to the Austrian Military Frontier.[5] The purpose of this essay is not to duplicate the work of either of those two scholars, but merely to contribute some further notes on the pre-1737 history of the

Rebels, Believers, Survivors: Studies in the History of the Albanians. Noel Malcolm,
Oxford University Press (2020). © Noel Malcolm. DOI: 10.1093/oso/9780198857297.001.0001

Kelmendi, offering a few suggestions about the origins of the clan and the reasons for the special position it enjoyed.

Several different explanations of the origins of the Kelmendi (and/or of their name) have been recorded. Some can be discounted, such as the charming piece of local folk-etymology which derived the name from 'Kol mendi', or 'Kolë i men-duar', meaning 'thoughtful Nicholas'.[6] Also implausible is the suggestion, by Milan von Šufflay, that the name came from the Byzantine fortress of Clementiana, on the road from Shkodër to Prizren: so far as is known, the Kelmendi have never lived in the vicinity of that fortress.[7] When von Šufflay was writing, it was still common to suppose that many of the Albanian clans had a continuous history stretching back to the Byzantine or even Illyrian periods. Modern research, in particular by Selami Pulaha and Karl Kaser, has shown that the clans were in most cases formed in the early Ottoman period, especially during the time of instability which followed the break-up of the old Albanian feudal system in the fifteenth century. Groups of families came together for mutual defence; in some cases a single family became the dominant element in such a grouping, giving its name to the whole clan.[8] The evidence that has come down to us about the early history of the Kelmendi suggests that this particular clan offers a classic example of that fifteenth-century process.

The evidence comes in two forms: oral history (recorded at various times, from the seventeenth century to the early twentieth) and Ottoman documents. Some aspects of oral history are, of course, unreliable; details may be altered, with surprising ease, in order to serve economic, social or political purposes. For example, the claim (recorded by Hyacinthe Hecquard in the mid-nineteenth century) that the Kelmendi fought for Sultan Murad at the Battle of Kosovo in 1389 was almost certainly a later invention, designed to perpetuate tax privileges on the grounds that they had been granted as a reward for such military service[9]. Similarly, it is striking that when Edith Durham visited the Kelmendi in 1908, she was told that the four *bajraks* [clan subdivisions] of the Kelmendi derived from the four sons of the original Kelmend, the founder of the clan: one of these four *bajraks*, Boga, had in fact been incorporated into the Kelmendi clan only in the nineteenth century (perhaps as recently as 1897), and the foundation-story of the clan must simply have been adjusted in order to accommodate this new member.[10]

However, the one thing that is least likely to have been falsified in the oral clan-histories of the northern Albanians is the genealogy of the main blood-line of the clan: preserving this knowledge as accurately as possible was of vital importance in a society which operated a strong taboo against marriage to cousins related through the male line. A detailed account of the Kelmendi compiled by a Venetian official or a Catholic priest in or soon after 1707 noted that they counted twelve generations from the founder of the clan; at 25 years per generation, this would date Kelmend himself to the first decade of the fifteenth century.[11] More importantly, a version of the clan genealogy was recorded by Archbishop Pjetër Bogdani in 1685, giving the names of the direct descendants of Kelmend down to the 1630s in a total of eight generations: this version would date the original Kelmend to the 1430s.[12] Combining the two accounts, which would mean reducing the length of a generation to roughly 20 years (to fit four generations between the 1630s and 1707), would place the original Kelmend in the 1470s; that may be the most reliable conclusion to be drawn from this evidence.

The first appearance of any sort of collective entity named 'Kelmendi' in a written document comes from 1497, when the Ottoman administration recorded the tax yields of a 'nahiye Kelmenta' (nahiye being an Ottoman administrative unit) of five katunds or shepherding settlements, one at the village of Selcë, the other four at the village of Shpajë—two places which have remained Kelmendi villages to the present day.[13] This document, drawn up in 1497, covered the territory of four highland clans or groupings (Hoti, Kuçi/Kuči, Piperi and Kelmendi), and was appended to a defter (tax register) of the sancak of Shkodër compiled in 1485. In that earlier defter, only the nahiye of Piperi was mentioned; it seems likely, therefore, that the Kelmendi received their first recognition as a distinct collective unit sometime between 1485 and 1497.[14] The five small Kelmendi settlements contained a total of 152 households; as a group, the Kelmendi area was smaller and poorer than the Hoti (who had six settlements), the Kuçi (who had eleven) or the Piperi (who had 23)—all of which suggests, again, that the Kelmendi in 1497 may have been quite close to the moment of their original coming-together as a collective entity.[15]

So it may be significant that the heads of household in those Kelmendi katunds included six men described as 'son of Kelmend': three in Selcë, at the katund of Liqen, two in Shpajë's katund of Muriq, and one in Shpajë's katund of Gjonoviq.[16] Every version of the foundation-story of the clan emphasizes that the original Kelmend had a large number of sons: four in the modified version noted by Edith Durham, seven in the account given by Pjetër Bogdani, and nine in the oral history recorded by von Hahn.[17] It is surely quite possible that these six sons of Kelmend listed in the Ottoman document were indeed the original group of brothers who gave their patronym first to the nahiye—as a group of settlements in which they formed the most powerful blood-related element—and then, over time, to a clan. Within that clan their own blood-line would have been the predominant one, as the genealogy preserved by Bogdani indicates; but in the original process of formation of that clan, it is likely that non-related people who also lived in the katunds of Selcë and Shpajë would have taken the name 'Kelmendi', not least because that was how their area was now described by the Ottoman administrators.

Since the Ottoman documentary evidence so closely matches the chronology suggested by the oral histories, it may perhaps be worth taking seriously some of the other details given in Bogdani's account. According to Bogdani, the original Kelmend was the son of a Serbian father and an Albanian mother (from the Kuçi clan); his sons wrested control of their area of settlement from 'the Slavs'.[18] There is nothing inherently improbable about this; for a long time, the northern-most part of the Malësi was an area of ethnic interchange and osmosis. The foundation-stories of some of the Montenegrin Slavophone clans declared that they had common ancestors with Albanian clans, and the case of the Kuçi, who were transformed over a long period from Albanian-speakers to Slavophones, is well known.[19] In the case of the Kelmendi, the Ottoman register of 1497 does include a significant number of Slav names, such as Radenko, Radko and Vlad, suggesting at least that this population had long been in contact with Slavs; but the overall pattern of personal names here indicates that these people were definitely Albanian-speaking and Catholic.[20] Albanian-speaking Catholics is what the Kelmendi have remained throughout the more than 500 years of their subsequent history (the only exceptions being the small minority who converted to Islam, and the descendants of the emigrants to Srijem, who eventually became Croat-speakers). The attempt by the early-twentieth-century Serbian historian Jovan Tomić to argue that all Kelmendi were 'really' Serbs, simply on the basis of Bogdani's remark about the father of the original Kelmend, was just a peculiarly gross example of ethnic pseudo-classification for political purposes.[21]

After their first appearance in 1497, the Kelmendi left very little trace in the historical record for more than a century. There is something of a puzzle here. The Ottoman *defters* show that, by the end of the sixteenth century, the Kelmendi villages had actually shrunk, their population falling from 152 households to a mere 70; this would suggest that their importance or influence was falling proportionately.[22] And yet the second half of the sixteenth century is precisely the period in which the Kelmendi displayed the first signs of what might be called their rise to power. An Ottoman document of 1565 noted that the Kelmendi *nahiye* was in revolt, together with the Kuçi and Piperi.[23] Another revolt, in the 1590s, involved the Kelmendi, Kuçi, Piperi and Bjelopavlić (Palabardhe); a Venetian writer, Lazaro Soranzo, commented on these rebel clans as follows: 'among them there are many Albanians, who live by the Roman faith. And these are the ones who, possessing strongholds and being by nature extremely fierce, have still not allowed themselves to be properly subjugated in battle by the Turks.'[24] In 1614 a document compiled at a meeting of Balkan chiefs in the territory of the Kuçi, and sent to political leaders in France and Italy, declared that the Kelmendi, Kuçi, Piperi and Bjelopavlići clans 'have lived in freedom for the last 30 years, and do not pay tribute to the Sultan'; and a similar document, sent to Madrid by the Orthodox Bishop of Ohrid in the same year, referred to 'the Kelmendi, whom the Turk has never been able to subdue'.[25] If the first of these two documents was correct, the turning-point in the history of the Kelmendi had come in the mid-1580s, when they ceased to pay any taxes to the Ottoman state.

Given the clearly hostile relationship which developed in this period between the Kelmendi and the Ottomans, it is perhaps not surprising that the late-sixteenth-century *defter* cited by Selami Pulaha showed such a shrunken population in the Kelmendi villages. For the Ottoman administrators to have carried out such a survey at all, they must have been there during one of the brief periods when Ottoman forces had retaken control of the area—at which time many of the Kelmendi would presumably have retreated to some other, more inaccessible part of the mountains. The sheer mobility of the Kelmendi is one of the striking things that emerges about them in the early seventeenth-century reports, such as the one by the Venetian Mariano Bolizza in 1614, which said that they went raiding as far afield as Plovdiv, in Bulgaria.[26]

Why had this clan, which in 1497 had been such a small and obscure group of people, developed these special characteristics during the next hundred years or so? Two explanations may be deduced from the contents of the 1497 register itself. The first is economic. From the tax data supplied by that register, it is clear that the remote mountain territory of the Kelmendi *nahiye* was particularly unproductive. Settled agriculture was practised (as it was in all the mountain villages), but in this *nahiye* it yielded only a meagre crop of wheat and barley; the Kelmendi were relatively more dependent on stock-raising than any of the other mountain clans.[27] This in itself may have implications for greater mobility; it also suggests that a growing population in that *nahiye* could not have been sustained merely by local agriculture, which must have made raiding a more attractive option. But probably the most significant fact in the 1497 register is the statement added by the Ottoman scribe at the end of the entry on the Kelmendi *nahiye*, which says:

> It is ordained that the Christians of these villages pay the *sancakbeyi* in the form of a lump sum 1,000 *akçes* of *haraç* or *cizye* [poll-tax], and in the form of a lump sum 1,000 *akçes* of *ispence* [land-tax]. They should not pay any other dues or taxes. They are exempted from all *avariz-i divaniye* [extraordinary state taxes] on condition that they are *derbendcis* [mountain pass-keepers] and guard and protect the road which runs from the fortress of Shkodër through the territory of Petrishpan to Altun-ili [near Gjakovë (Djakovica)], and also the road which runs from the fortress of Medun into the mountain of Kuçi, coming down to Plav.[28]

This granting of *derbend* status may have been the single most important factor in determining the subsequent history of the Kelmendi clan. As this document shows, there were three important aspects to the institution of *derbend*. It involved a quasi-military function (guarding roads and passes); it carried with it tax-privileges; and it also meant the treatment of a whole group of people as a collective entity for tax purposes.[29] The strengthening of collective identity which this involved may have played an important part in the development of the Kelmendi as a cohesive clan. And the acquisition of a special collective status (with privileges relating to taxation, and/or other matters) introduces a theme which will run all the way through the history of the northern Albanian territories until the final period of Ottoman rule. What we see in this document of 1497 is one of the first steps in the development of what Selami Pulaha described as 'regions of self-government' in the northern Albanian highlands. A line of historical filiation thus connects this late-fifteenth-century grant of *derbend* status with the late-nineteenth-century autonomist programme of the League of Prizren; indeed, the tradition thus established can be traced as far as the summer of 1911, when the Ottoman government granted a confirmation of privileges not to Albanians in general but specifically to the clans of the Malësi.

Among the privileges which the Albanian movements of the final Ottoman period particularly stressed was the right to carry arms. In the late fifteenth and sixteenth centuries, the quasi-military nature of *derbend* status was probably of particular importance to the development of the Kelmendi; although we know that the Ottoman authorities eventually gave up trying to enforce the general prohibition on the carrying of arms by non-Muslim *raya* (tax-paying subjects), having a formal right to bear arms may have been a valuable privilege in this earliest period of Ottoman rule, and may thus have contributed to the development of the peculiarly warlike tradition of the Kelmendi—whence their description by Soranzo in the late sixteenth century as 'ferocissimi', extremely fierce.

Another feature of the grant of *derbend* status in 1497 is also noteworthy: it gave the Kelmendi responsibility for guarding not only the road which ran to Plav, part of which did pass through the Kelmendis' own territory, but also the main road from Shkodër to Gjakovë, which came nowhere near the valleys of the Kelmendi *nahiye*. Commenting on the oddity of this, Kolë Luka has suggested that perhaps the Kelmendi were employed as general *derbendci*s, placed in various villages along the whole length of that road.[30] If this is correct, it may help to explain how it was that an initially small clan acquired such a leading role across such a large area of the Malësi. It is true that the group of clans among whom the Kelmendi came to enjoy such predominance were not the ones on the Shkodër–Gjakovë road, such as the Mërturi, but the ones to the south-west, west and north-west of the Kelmendi territory—notably the Hoti, Gruda, Piperi, Kuçi and Bjelopavlići. Nevertheless, the experience of maintaining a quasi-military network of Kelmendi clansmen over a wide area of the Malësi may have been what gave the Kelmendi the organizational and leadership qualities that made them the natural leaders of that whole group of neighbouring clans.

Thus it was that Archbishop Marin Bizzi, writing in 1610, used 'Climenti' as a general term covering ten clans: Kelmendi, Gruda, Hoti, Kastrati, Shkreli, Tuzi, Bjelopavlići, Piperi, Bratonožići and Kuçi.[31] The archbishop must have been including all of these clans, and perhaps some others too, when he wrote in another report in 1618 that the Kelmendi could raise a fighting force of 40,000 men.[32] Pjetër Budi gave a much more modest figure in his report of 1621: he wrote that the Kelmendi could raise 6,000 fighters.[33] But this too was a figure that included the members of other clans as well; according to the records of the Franciscans who visited the area in 1641, the Kelmendi themselves had only 700 fighting men.[34]

The prominent role which, as leaders of this grouping of mountain clans, the Kelmendi played in the various rebellions of the seventeenth century has been well described by Peter Bartl, and need not be rehearsed here. Suffice it to say that the Kelmendi were active in the revolts of 1612–13; helped to prepare plans for general Balkan rebellions in 1614, 1616 and 1620; fought the Ottomans in 1624 and 1638, and planned joint actions with the Venetians during 1648–9.[35] They appear to have engaged in fewer major confrontations with Ottoman forces during the second half of the century, but their prominence as leaders of the other mountain clans remained undimmed: when Pjetër Bogdani wrote his account of the Kelmendi in 1685, he declared that they were so full of martial valour that 'the other highlanders depend on them as the heavens depend on the *primo mobile*.'[36]

However, although it is an undoubted fact that the Kelmendi participated in the meetings which planned general uprisings against the Ottomans in the early seventeenth century, it would be anachronistic to suppose that the actions of the Kelmendi throughout that century were aimed consistently and solely at some sort of 'national liberation'. As many contemporary reports make clear, the main aims of the Kelmendi could often be more accurately described as securing their own power and privileges, paying as few taxes as possible, and enriching themselves through raiding in the plains of Kosovo and Novi Pazar, where they extracted a kind of local 'tribute' of their own devising.[37] As the anonymous writer of *c*.1707 put it, when summarizing the history of the Kelmendi during the seventeenth century, they had begun with the area round Pejë (Peć): 'With raiding, arson and destruction they reduced first the territory, then the city itself, to paying annual contributions.' Then they applied the same system to other areas, including much of the territory of the old kingdom of Serbia. 'Every household of the Kelmendi had, in that huge and fertile kingdom, one or more villages which paid it every year whatever was necessary for the dignified subsistence of a noble family.' This writer, who may have been a Catholic priest, put a very positive gloss on these arrangements: he said that they were feared by the Turks but welcomed by the Christians, who regarded them as protectors.[38] Sometimes, indeed, they may have offered protection; at other times, we may suspect that the way in which they demanded those 'contributions' could better be described as a protection racket. Certainly they were not always regarded as national liberators: in 1638 the local inhabitants of Novi Pazar and northern Kosovo sent a petition to the Sultan, pleading for action to be taken to defend them from the raids of the Kelmendi and their associated mountain clans.[39]

It is against this somewhat mixed background that we must assess the role of the Kelmendi in the events surrounding the invasion of the Kosovo region in 1689 by the Imperial troops. In an elaborate piece of speculative historical reconstruction, the Serbian historian Rajko Veselinović has advanced three claims: first, that the 'Patriarch of the Kelmendi' described in Austrian documents as having met the Habsburg General Piccolomini and as having raised local volunteer forces for him was the Serbian Orthodox Patriarch; secondly, that the local forces so raised came exclusively from Orthodox Slavs, including the Orthodox Montenegrin clans in the wider grouping of clans associated with the Kelmendi; and thirdly, that the Kelmendi themselves played no part whatsoever in the anti-Ottoman fighting at that time.[40] The first of these claims is demonstrably false: there is documentary evidence that the Serbian Patriarch was not and could not have been in Prizren at the time of the meeting with Piccolomini.[41] The second claim depends partly on the first, assuming as it does that the Patriarch would have recruited people only from his own religious community. It also depends on setting up a false alternative between the Catholic Albanian Kelmendi on the one hand and Orthodox Slavs on the other, implying that if the local fighters were not the former, they must have been the latter; this is to ignore the mass of local people in the Prizren area, Muslim and Catholic Albanians, whose role as the main component of those volunteer forces is clearly indicated by many of the surviving documents.[42]

As for the actual role played by the Kelmendi at the time of the Habsburg-led invasion, it is true that they did not play a major part in support of the Habsburg army, but it is not true that they played no anti-Ottoman role whatsoever. In 1688 the Venetian general in the coastal area of Montenegro asked the Franciscans in Kotor and Perast to persuade the mountain clans to rise in a pro-Venetian revolt. One friar, Fra Bartolommeo, arranged for the leaders of several Catholic clans, including the Kelmendi, to meet the Venetian general; but news of this came to the ears of Suleiman Bushatli, the pasha of Shkodër, who, in the words of one Franciscan history, 'swore that he would pursue without mercy the inhabitants of Gruda, and the Kelmendi, whom he had discovered to be involved in sedition and in making agreements with the Venetians'. Until that moment, according to the same account, some Kelmendi had been serving in Suleiman Pasha's army; these now turned against the Muslims who served alongside them.[43] This account is confirmed by documents in the Venetian archives, which show that although Suleiman Pasha was boasting about the fact that 'Christians from the mountains' were on his side in May 1688, his army was repelled by an active revolt of the Kelmendi, Kuçi and Gruda in the following month.[44]

Having faced down Suleiman Pasha in this way in the early summer of 1688, however, the Kelmendi seem to have bided their time. In February 1689 they and the Kuçi put out some diplomatic feelers to Austria, sending two priests to see the Austrian envoy in Dubrovnik; nothing further seems to have come of this, though the danger of their siding with Austria rather than Venice worried the Venetian *provveditore* (governor-commander) in Dalmatia so much that he advocated making large payments to the leaders of the Kelmendi, Kuçi and other clans.[45] By the summer of that year, however, some of the Kelmendi were again serving in Suleiman Pasha's army, and it was only thanks to the further efforts of the Venetians that they were persuaded to withdraw from it in early September, on the grounds that it was wrong for Catholics to fight on behalf of an infidel.[46]

It was in the following month (October 1689) that the Imperial army entered north-eastern Kosovo; in early November the Catholic Archbishop, Pjetër Bogdani, encouraged the recruitment of a volunteer force in western Kosovo—made up not of highland clansmen such as the Kelmendi, but predominantly of local Muslim and Catholic Albanians from the Prizren region. While this was happening, the Serbian Orthodox Patriarch was in Montenegro, trying to persuade his flock there to support Venice rather than Vienna. One of his monks, Nikon, told the Venetians that the Patriarch had put together a great 'confederation' of the highland clans, including the Kelmendi.[47] But this sounds like an exaggerated claim, designed to boost the standing of the Patriarch in Venetian eyes; no signs of any confederated or coordinated action on the part of those clans emerges from the subsequent historical evidence.

By the beginning of December rumours had reached Istanbul that the 'Arnauti di Climenti' had risen up in a general revolt; but ten days later the Venetian envoy in Vienna noted that reports that the Kelmendi and their associated clans had sent their chiefs to submit to the Imperial army were not true.[48] A later Venetian report from Montenegro said that four Kelmendi chiefs did go to negotiate with the Austrians at Pejë, but came back discontented because they had not been given suitable presents.[49] Some sporadic actions in support of the Imperial army apparently did take place, such as the sending of a joint Kelmendi-Kuçi force to assist them near Bijelo Polje in mid-November.[50] But the general pattern, it seems, was the one described by the Venetian provveditore in March 1690: 'The peoples of these mountains are still standing at the ready... Some of them, who are in the vicinity of the Austrian troops, join in their raiding parties against the Ottomans; others make raids for their own benefit.'[51]

By that time, the Imperial army had lost its position in Kosovo (with its headlong retreat in early January 1690), and its troops were able to make only occasional incursions into Kosovan territory. For the Ottomans, pushing the Imperial army back to Belgrade (and beyond) was the main strategic aim, and the activities of local Albanian clansmen were very much of secondary significance. Thus the Papal nuncio in Venice reported in April 1690 that the Pasha of Shkodër had been preparing a large campaign against the mountain clans, but that he had been ordered to take his force to join the main Ottoman army in its campaign against the imperial army.[52] The Kelmendi and their allies thus seem to have escaped any major punitive actions, and by July of that year it was reported that they were once again coming down to the plains of Pejë to demand their usual 'contributions' from the inhabitants.[53]

These predations against the territory of Pejë must have been one of the reasons why, in 1700, the pasha of Pejë, Hudaverdi Mahmutbegolli, resolved to take decisive action against the Kelmendi. Having gained allies among the other mountain clans, he used them to block the Kelmendi heartland (the upper Cem valley) on three sides, and then advanced with his own army from Gusinje. Once he had worn down the Kelmendi by starvation, he forced the majority of them to move to the Pešter plateau (north of Pejë, in the Sancak of Novi Pazar), where they could be kept under supervision and control. Only the Kelmendi of Selcë were allowed to stay in their homes; their chief had converted to Islam, and promised to convert his people too.[54]

By 1702 a total of 251 Kelmendi households (1,987 people) were settled in the Pešter area. The Catholic authorities feared that, without any priests to minister to them, they would convert either to Orthodoxy or to Islam; so permission was obtained to send one of the priests from Selcë, and another who came from Italy, to look after their spiritual needs. In a canny political move, these priests were also placed under the formal protection of the leader of the Ragusan merchant community in Novi Pazar.[55] In 1707 more than half of the exiled Kelmendi fought their way back to their mountain homes, and four years later they sent out a large raiding force to bring back some of the others. Fifty families returned this time, to the delight of the Archbishop of Bar, who thought that the residue had been on the point of converting to Islam.[56] But those who still remained in the Pešter region seem never to have wavered in their devotion to Catholicism: according to a report by the Archbishop of Skopje in 1713, these exiled Kelmendi numbered 1,000 souls, and were ministered to by four priests. Two of those were Germans or Austrians, and in 1716 (when Austria entered another anti-Ottoman war) they fled northwards, even though the Kelmendi offered them a large extra payment to stay.[57] The position of these Kelmendi cannot have been helped by the fact that the Kelmendi in the mountains, together with the Gashi and the Mirdita, rose up against the Ottomans during this war.[58] And yet the next report by the Archbishop of Skopje, in 1719, suggests that the Pešter Kelmendi, who still had their two priests, were flourishing: their population was now put at 'more than 2,000', and the Archbishop noted that on his visit to them that year he had confirmed 800 people.[59]

And so the stage was set for the next great conflict, the Austrian campaign of 1737, during which the Kelmendi of the Pešter plateau joined with their brothers in the mountains (and with many of the other clansmen, including Orthodox Slav ones), rising up in support of the Austrians: they were then obliged to retreat northwards in the wake of the Austrian army, suffering huge losses before finally reaching their safe haven in Austrian-controlled territory near Belgrade. The story of those events has been well told by Mita Kostić and Frrok Zefiq, and need not be repeated here.[60] With the uprising and exodus of 1737, more than just a chapter in the history of the Kelmendi seems to have been closed; it would take a long time for the remaining Kelmendi in the Malësi (and in Pešter, where some remained) to recover their strength. Although their pre-eminence among the clans of the Malësi e Madhe was noted, as mentioned at the beginning of this paper, by some nineteenth-century observers, the extraordinary status they had enjoyed as the leaders of a group of marauding clans that could strike terror deep into the territories of Bosnia, Serbia and Kosovo would never be regained.

Looking back at the whole history of the Kelmendi up to 1737, it is possible to make some observations, finally, on the significance of their devotion to Catholic Christianity. This is in fact a recurrent theme in the contemporary descriptions of them. Admittedly, until the Franciscan mission reached the Kelmendi in 1641, their Catholicism must have been of a rough-hewn and approximate kind, since they had by then been without the regular ministrations of the clergy for a very long time. As Pjetër Bogdani later recorded, 'They used to be rather barbarous people, but thanks to the work of the Franciscans they have been transformed into the best Christians of those mountains'.[61] Within ten years of the arrival of the Franciscans, the Kelmendi had built themselves a new church, at Shpajë, in order to serve the nine villages of the surrounding area.[62] And, as we have seen, the exiled Kelmendi in the Pešter region were so keen to retain their priests in time of war that they were willing to pay large sums of their own money for their services. It is also noteworthy that, despite the deliberate policy of Hudaverdi Pasha of encouraging conversion to Islam, and despite all the general advantages that Muslim status could bring, the proportion of the Kelmendi that did convert was extremely small. When Edith Durham visited the Kelmendi villages in 1907, she found that only one *bajrak* (Nikshi) had a partly Muslim population, with just ten Muslim families out of a total of 94.[63]

It might be tempting to say that Catholic Christianity was the one absolute factor in determining the sense of identity of the Kelmendi throughout their history—tempting, but not correct. As we have seen, during the seventeenth century they willingly cooperated with other neighbouring clans, some of whom were Serbian Orthodox, and in 1737 they fought their way northwards accompanied not only by members of those clans, but also by the Orthodox Patriarch himself. On a few occasions the Kelmendi had also served in the army of the Ottoman pasha of Shkodër. An appeal to their loyalty to the Catholic faith was one of the methods used by the Venetians to persuade them to leave that army; we may conclude that a sense of Catholic identity was one powerful element in their self-understanding, but not an exclusive or an absolute one. Nor should we forget that, when a small minority of Kelmendi clansmen did convert to Islam, as in the cases of other mixed Catholic-Muslim clans, the feeling of mutual loyalty as members of the same clan remained essentially unchanged. After all, Kelmendi identity was defined in the first place by blood—that is, descent from the patrilineal family lines of the Kelmendi clan—not by religion.

It makes more sense, surely, to say that the Kelmendi identity, like almost any human identity, was something with different aspects to it, and that these aspects could have different relative significances in different contexts or at different historical moments. One aspect was that they were Catholics; Catholic Christianity supplied many of the social practices and ceremonies, relating to birth, marriage, prayer, thanksgiving, sickness and death, that gave their life its meaning. Another aspect was that they were malësors or highlanders, connected with a particular group of other clans (both Albanian and Slav), with whom they could cooperate for the purposes of raiding or war. And a third aspect was that they were Albanians—though this would acquire its real importance as the principle of their self-identification only in a much later period of their history.

3

An Unknown Account of Ottoman Albania

Antonio Bruni's Treatise on the *Beylerbeylik* of Rumeli (1596)

Of the many treatises about the Ottoman Empire published in Western Europe during the sixteenth century, few are as wide-ranging and well-informed as the one published by Lazaro Soranzo in 1598 under the title *L'Ottomanno*. Soranzo had clearly spent time in Ottoman territory himself, but he had also read widely. Unfortunately he gives, as a rule, very little information about his sources. One important exception to that rule is a manuscript treatise by Antonio Bruni. Soranzo makes explicit reference to it twice in his book: on the first occasion he refers to 'Antonio Bruni, in his treatise on the *beylerbeylik* of Greece [*sc.* the Ottoman administrative province of Rumeli]', agreeing with a point made by Bruni about the danger of stirring up forlorn attempts at rebellion among the Christian subjects of the Sultan, and on the second occasion he introduces a long passage about Albania with the words, 'Of the Catholic Albanians, that same Bruni, who is their compatriot, writes in the aforementioned treatise...'.[1] The text of Antonio Bruni's treatise was never published, and no subsequent author seems ever to have cited it directly.

This entirely forgotten work is, however, still extant; it survives in two scribal copies, in the Vatican Library and the library of the Museo Correr, Venice.[2] The significance of this text is not confined to the fact that it was (as we shall see) a major influence on Soranzo's book, informing many other passages in his writing. It is an unusually interesting work in its own right, quite different in kind from the usual 'relazioni' written about the Ottoman Empire by Western diplomats or travellers. For Antonio Bruni had something a little more like an insider's view of the empire: his work had taken him to such places as Vlorë, on the southern coast of Albania, and Constanța, on the Black Sea coast, and he had also resided for some time in Moldavia, a tributary state within the empire itself. Although he was living outside Ottoman territory when he wrote this treatise, he clearly retained good sources of information within the Ottoman Albanian lands. For Antonio Bruni was—as Soranzo pointed out—an Albanian, and this fact gives his writing a special significance: the description of the Albanian lands given in his treatise is the earliest surviving general account of Albania to have been written by an identifiable Albanian author.

Rebels, Believers, Survivors: Studies in the History of the Albanians. Noel Malcolm,
Oxford University Press (2020). © Noel Malcolm. DOI: 10.1093/oso/9780198857297.001.0001

Antonio Bruni was a member of a remarkable Venetian-Albanian family, from the city of Ulcinj (in present-day Montenegro), which was a Venetian possession at the time of his birth and later fell under Ottoman dominion. The Bruni family had previously been nobles of Shkodër, fleeing from that city when it was conquered by the Ottomans in 1479. Antonio's father, Gasparo, became a Knight of Malta in 1567; thereafter he acted as an intelligence agent for the Knights in Dubrovnik, was captain of the papal flagship in three naval campaigns against the Ottomans—1570, 1571 (the Lepanto campaign) and 1572—and served for thirteen years as an infantry officer in the papal territory of Avignon. Gasparo's brother Giovanni became Archbishop of Bar in 1551, played a prominent role in the final sessions of the Council of Trent, was captured by the Ottomans at the fall of Bar in 1571 and met a tragic end as a galley-slave in the aftermath of the Battle of Lepanto. Their sister Maria (Antonio Bruni's aunt) married Antonio Bruti, a member of a noble family of Durrës which had also found refuge, like the Brunis, in Ulcinj; he was a very active servant of Venice in the southern Adriatic region, as an intelligence-supplier, local diplomat and grain merchant, and was rewarded with the title of 'Cavaliere di San Marco' by the Doge in 1559. He too died in 1571, just after the conquest of Ulcinj. But among his many sons (the first cousins of Antonio Bruni), several also had distinctive careers; the most prominent of them was Bartolomeo Bruti, who became chief minister of Moldavia in the 1580s, before meeting his own tragic end in 1592.[3]

Antonio Bruni's precise year of birth is not known; from the date at which he began his secondary education it can be estimated as 1557 or 1558. Nor is there any information about his mother; all that can be said with reasonable certainty is that, given that Gasparo Bruni later became a Knight of Malta (a position strictly barred to anyone who was or had been married), Antonio must have been an illegitimate son. The earliest documentary evidence of Antonio's existence consists of the record of his entry into the Seminario Romano, the élite Jesuit school and college in Rome, in May 1572.[4] He spent five years at that institution, acquiring classical learning and rhetorical skills; thereafter he studied briefly at the University of Perugia, and possibly also at the University of Padua, before moving to Avignon, where his father, Gasparo, was stationed.[5] Antonio enrolled at the University of Avignon and proceeded rapidly to the degree of Doctor of Law, which was awarded to him in October 1585.[6]

The next few years in Antonio Bruni's life are not well documented. He probably went from Avignon to Koper (Capodistria), the Venetian town on the northern side of Istria, where most of his Bruti cousins had settled after the fall of Ulcinj. He was there by 1587 at the latest, when he took part in a debate at the 'Accademia Palladia', Koper's literary club.[7] But at some point in the next two or three years he moved to Moldavia, where his cousin Bartolomeo Bruti, the chief minister and right-hand man of the Voivod Petru Şchiopul, had evidently found work for him. The nature of that work is not known, though it may be significant that Lazaro Soranzo (who, as we shall see, got to know Antonio personally) wrote at one point in *L'Ottomanno* that 'such is the information which I have obtained from people who have seen the accounts of Moldavia and Wallachia.'[8] By August 1591, however, Antonio Bruni was back in Koper: in that month he was elected one of the overseers of the municipal grain store there.[9]

Antonio's departure from Moldavia had thus preceded—but perhaps not by very long—the decision of Petru Şchiopul to abandon his throne and seek a new life in exile. Wearying of the ever-increasing financial burdens imposed on him by Istanbul, and fearing for the future of his young son Ştefan, the Voivod left Moldavia in mid-August 1591 and moved to Habsburg territory. Early in the following year, he seems to have contacted Antonio Bruni in Koper; for in April 1592 Antonio presented a letter from Petru to the recently elected Pope, Clement VIII, in Rome. The Pope's reply began: 'From your letter, and from a conversation with my beloved son Antonio Bruni, to whom you gave your letter for me and your instructions, I learned how eager you are to visit me...'.[10] (From this it also seems very likely that Antonio Bruni was the person Petru referred to five months later in a letter to Archduke Ferdinand, when he wrote that 'I used to have good friendly relations with the Holy Pope; I had a certain man, called Bruti, whom I sent quite often from my court to the Pope.')[11] Petru did not travel to Rome, however; he eventually settled, with his retinue, in the small town of Bolzano, in the South Tyrol. But his exile was not an untroubled one. Shortly before his departure, he had received a large advance payment from a Ragusan merchant in Moldavia, Giovanni ('Dživa') de Marini Poli, for the right to collect the taxes on cattle and sheep for the coming year; Petru's successor, the Voivod Aron, did not honour the agreement, so de Marini Poli pursued Petru for the return of the money, launching a legal process against him in the Tyrol. In May 1593 Antonio Bruni travelled to Bolzano, where Petru signed a legal document empowering Antonio to speak and act on his behalf.[12] Antonio's duties also included acting as an interpreter for Petru, which shows that he had spent long enough in Moldavia to become fluent in Romanian. For seven months Antonio stayed in the Tyrol, overseeing the successful defence of the ex-Voivod in the law courts.[13] Towards the end of 1593 he helped to transmit to Clement VIII another request by Petru for permission to visit him in Rome; this time, instead of taking the message himself, he made use of a contact in Rome, the Venetian Lazaro Soranzo, who served there as a 'cameriere d'onore' to the Pope. Soranzo would later write (in a passage contained in a manuscript version of *L'Ottomanno*, but omitted from the printed text) that he made arrangements for this visit 'at his [*sc.* Petru's] request, and through the efforts of Antonio Bruni, an Albanian gentleman.'[14]

The ex-Voivod Petru Şchiopul did not, in the end, travel to Rome. He died in the South Tyrol in June 1594. In the aftermath of his death, members of his family and household stripped his house of valuables and took them to Venice; Antonio Bruni (who was once more based in Koper, one or two days' travel from Venice) found out and alerted the Tyrolean authorities. He also gave advice on how to obtain reliable translations of Petru's will, and associated documents.[15] Antonio appears to have felt a special concern for the future of Petru's son, Ştefan; in 1596 he submitted a memorandum to the Austrian authorities suggesting some sort of anti-Ottoman geopolitical stratagem in which, 'merely using his [sc. Ştefan's] name, and with the secrecy that is necessary in such affairs, His Imperial Majesty might make use of him in the most exceptional way, both in Moldavia and else-where'.[16] Perhaps with such aims in mind, he kept up a connection with the Austrian official who acted as one of Ştefan's guardians; and it seems to have been during one of his trips between Koper and Bolzano that Antonio Bruni met own his death—perhaps from the plague—in Trieste in late July 1598.[17]

The reason why political stratagems involving 'Moldavia and elsewhere' had become so important was that since the late summer of 1593 the Holy Roman Empire had been at war with the Ottoman Empire. The strongest political sup-port for the Imperial war effort came from Pope Clement VIII, who was, like several of his sixteenth-century predecessors, a passionate supporter of anti-Ottoman initiatives of various kinds, including warfare (in 1595 he sent a papal force of 12,000 troops to support the Imperial army in Hungary), diplomacy and the fomenting of rebellion in Ottoman territory. His nephew, Cardinal Cinzio, also took a keen interest in these projects, and encouraged intellectuals in his cir-cle to promote such ideas. To give just one example: in 1595 the philosopher Francesco Patrizi, a protégé of the Cardinal, published the second part of his trea-tise on military affairs, *Paralleli militari*, in which he recommended an invasion of the Balkans by an Italian force of 30,000 men. He put forward three options, Dalmatia, Albania and Greece, saying that in each case the local people would immediately rebel against the Ottomans. 'If we landed in Albania', he declared, 'all the Albanians would come to our side; they are a courageous people, so much feared by the Ottomans, both because of the ancient memory of their glory under Skanderbeg, and because of the very fierce hatred they feel at present.'[18]

Between 1592 and 1595 Cardinal Cinzio employed a young Venetian, Angelo Ingegneri, as his secretary and literary assistant. In late September or early October 1596 Ingegneri travelled to Venice; although he was no longer the Cardinal's employee, it seems that he was still carrying out some tasks on his behalf. Towards the end of his stay there he sent a message to Antonio Bruni, who was also in Venice. Antonio's reply, written on 17 October 1596, apologized for the fact that he had just missed him, and stated: 'Now, since you write that you have been notified from Rome that information written up in that way would not be unwelcome to your most distinguished patron, I begin to think that it has been represented by you as something much greater than it really is.' Nevertheless, Bruni concluded, 'I am resolved to embrace your most prudent and kind advice, so that the lord Cardinal may know that the text will be sent by me to him, by means of you, my most especial patron.'[19] It seems very likely that this letter reveals the precise origin of Antonio Bruni's treatise on the *beylerbeylik* of Rumeli (which, in any case, can be dated on internal evidence to some time after August 1596, as it refers to a revolt in Himarë of that month). Cardinal Cinzio and his circle were interested in the possibility of raising an anti-Ottoman revolt in the Balkans, and the Albanian lands were of special interest for that purpose; Angelo Ingegneri had no doubt heard that Bruni was particularly well-informed about conditions in the Balkan provinces of the Ottoman Empire, especially in the Albanian lands. And the text which Antonio Bruni duly wrote conforms in every way to what one might expect to arise from such a commission: it discusses the military weakness of the Ottomans and the willingness of various Balkan peoples to rebel (but with some cautious remarks about the danger of encouraging inef-fective rebellion and starving it of outside help); it also adds some comments on the parlous state of the Roman Catholic Church in the Albanian lands; and it strikes, at the end, a note of due deference towards the Pope—who, if the text found favour, was likely to be one of its readers. 'As it is permitted to anyone to narrate what he has seen and heard', Bruni wrote, 'so it is not permitted to every-one to try to persuade rulers of that which they should or can do'.

Clearly, Antonio Bruni was someone well worth seeking out for his expertise on these matters. Another person who sought him out, at roughly the same time, was Lazaro Soranzo. (As we have seen, Soranzo and Bruni were already acquainted; the origin of their friendship is not known, but it could have been formed in the period 1585–6, when Lazaro may have visited Koper to see his uncle Giacomo, a distinguished Venetian diplomat, who was undergoing a period of exile there.) According to the account he later gave, Lazaro Soranzo began to draft his book on the island of Ischia in 1596. He then moved to Venice, where he was able to make use of many sources of information about the Ottoman Empire. One possible scenario is that after some conversations with his friend Antonio Bruni, he asked Antonio to set down some of the things he had said, and that it was Soranzo who told Angelo Ingegneri (whom he probably knew from Rome) about Bruni's writings, whether actual or in prospect. The form which Antonio's text finally took, however, seems very much tailored to Cardinal Cinzio's require-ments; and it was, in the end, that version of the text that was used by Soranzo when writing his book. The first draft of his *L'Ottomanno* was written in the final months of 1596. By the end of January 1597 a manuscript version of it was sent by Soranzo to Vincenzo Gonzaga, the Duke of Mantua, who was planning a military expedition in support of the Imperial forces in Hungary. One manuscript copy, in the Ambrosian Library in Milan, is dated June 1597. Finally, in May 1598, Soranzo decided to have the book printed; it was published two months later in the city of Ferrara, which had recently been incorporated in the Papal States.[20]

As has already been mentioned, Soranzo referred explicitly to Antonio Bruni's treatise in two passages in his book. In the first of these he echoed Bruni's warn-ings about the danger of encouraging ineffective rebellion; in the second, he reproduced a substantial section of his account of the Albanian lands.[21] But these were not his only borrowings. Elsewhere in his text there were passages drawn directly from Bruni on a variety of topics: the poor state of Ottoman forces; the *devşirme* (the 'collection' of Christian boys for Janissary (and other) service); Ottoman military auxiliaries; the reluctance of spahis (holders of military-feudal estates) to undergo the discomforts of war; the Tatars; Petru Şchiopul's advice to Ferdinand; the clans of the Albanian-Montenegrin highlands; and the revolt in the Himarë. (Details of these are given in the Appendix to this essay.) And there are other items of information in Soranzo's book which, whilst they are not contained in the treatise written by Antonio Bruni, may well have been derived from conversation or correspondence with him. Soranzo's statement that he had spoken to people who had seen the governmental accounts of Moldavia and Wallachia has already been cited; he had also acquired information about the taxes on cattle, the tribute paid by the Moldavian voivods to the Tatars, their relations with Poland, and the different geographical terms used for Moldavia and Wallachia.[22] In addition, he noted many other details about Albania and the Albanians, some or all of which may have been derived from Bruni: about the timber of the Dukagjin highlands which was floated down the river Drin to Lezhë; the manufacture of ship's biscuit in Vlorë; the ports of the Albanian coast from Durrës to Sarandë; the presence of Albanians among the soldiers of the rebel Wallachian Voivod Mihai cel Viteaz; and the feasibility of seizing Ulcinj, Shkodër or Durrës. And it was surely from Antonio that he learned both about the precise origins of the Grand Vizier Sinan Pasha (who was a cousin of the Bruti family), and about the summoning of Gasparo Bruni to papal service before the Lepanto campaign.[23]

The manuscript of Bruni's text that was used by Soranzo does not apparently survive. Nor does the one sent to Angelo Ingegneri for Cardinal Cinzio. Of the two known manuscripts of Bruni's treatise, both are later scribal copies. The one in the Museo Correr is dated February 1598 (i.e. 1599 in the Venetian style of dating), and the other, which is undated, must have been copied in 1598 or later; both of them reproduce a scribal error describing the death of Petru Şchiopul as having happened in 1597 instead of 1594. There are other errors in both of them, from which it becomes clear that they were copied from differing versions, neither of which was the original. (Since neither has any clear textual superiority, and each can be used to correct the other on some particular points, the choice of copy-text is necessarily arbitrary; the transcription given below takes the Vatican manuscript as the copy-text, and records variants in the Museo Correr manuscript, promoting them to the text where necessary.) The scribal publication of such texts—including, most famously, the 'relazioni' of Venetian diplomats—was a flourishing business in Venice and elsewhere, so it is reasonable to expect that many copies were in fact generated, some of which may still survive, as yet unnoticed, in libraries and archives.[24] One example of the transmission of such a copy can be identified. In the late 1590s the soldier, traveller and political writer Filippo Pigafetta was living in Venetian territory and sending a steady stream of 'relazioni' to a friend at the Medici court who passed them on to the Grand Duke. Writing from Padua in mid-January 1599, he said that he was commissioning a copy of 'a discourse about the *beylerbeylik* of Rumeli and the people who live under it'; and at the end of the month he wrote: 'I am sending a relazione of the state of the Ottoman Empire in Europe, written by an experienced man who, being of the Albanian nation, lived for a long time in those parts.'[25]

When Lazaro Soranzo referred in his book to Bruni's treatise, he may well have assumed that it would be possible for an interested reader to track down a copy of that text. Sadly, whatever interest he stimulated was not sufficient to lead to the publication of the treatise in print. Soranzo's own book, on the other hand, was a tremendous publishing success; despite—or even, perhaps, because of—an attempt by the Venetian authorities to suppress it, the work was quickly reprinted in both Ferrara and Milan in 1599, in Naples in 1600, and again in Ferrara in 1607.[26] In 1600 much of it appeared in French translation, incorporated in a history of the Ottoman Empire by Jacques Esprinchard; this work was reprinted in 1609.[27] A German translation, by Christian Cresse, was printed in both Eisleben and Magdeburg in 1601.[28] In 1603 an English version of Soranzo's book appeared, translated by the secretary of the Archbishop of Canterbury.[29] And a Europe-wide readership of the work was assured by the publication of a Latin translation, by Jakob Geuder von Heroltzberg, in 1600; this was re-issued in 1601 and 1664, and a 48-page extract from it was included in the volume on the Ottoman Empire (of 1630, reprinted in 1634) in the best-selling series of politico-geographical books issued by the Elzevier publishing house in Leiden (the so-called 'Elzevier Republics').[30] Several generations of Italian, French, German, English and other European readers thus learned about the Ottoman Empire from Lazaro Soranzo's remarkably well-informed book. And, as they did so, they also learned—though without knowing it—from the treatise on the *beylerbeylik* of Rumeli by Antonio Bruni.[31]

On the Beylerbeylik of Rumeli, by Antonio Bruni of Ulcinj

Many people have written—some according to what they have seen, some according to what they have heard—about the greatness and the government of the Ottoman Empire, telling the story of the advances made, and the power obtained, by that dynasty. I shall briefly discuss the religion, language and condition of life of both the Christians and the Muslims only in that part of this realm that lies in Europe, under the *beylerbeyi* of Rumeli (whom we call the *beylerbeyi* of Greece). He is higher in rank, and in ordinary authority, than the other governors of provinces; he exercises his jurisdiction particularly in Bulgaria, Serbia and Albania, and in Greece—but not in all of it, as some of the coastal *sancak*s, and the island ones (of which the *sancak* of Euboea rules quite an area on the mainland) obey the *kapudan paşa*.[32] Bosnia and Hungary have their own *beylerbeyi*s, who are called—for greater clarity, and as it is a more honourable title—'pashas'. Hungary has two pashas, one of Buda, the other of Temesvár; Bosnia has one, who lives in Banja Luka. Caffa [Feodosiya] too has its own pasha, who governs the coast of that peninsula, together with the seaway through Lake Maeotis [the Sea of Azov] to the river Don, and the shore of the Black Sea as far as the river Dniester.[33] Between the Dniester and the Danube lies Moldavia; the voivod of that principality, just like his neighbour the voivod of Wallachia, used to recognize the superior authority of the *beylerbeyi*.

Now, within the responsibility of that person, between the Danube, the mouth of the river Sava, the Gulf of Kotor and the Black Sea, just as there are different religions, so too you find different languages, which cause a certain disunity among the peoples, and that increases the disagreement that normally obtains as a result of religious difference. The Christian faith is superior in numbers to the Muslim and Jewish ones; but because it is poor, and subordinate, and divided between Orthodox and Roman Catholic, it is declining every day—thanks, in the past, to the competition between those two Churches, and, at present, to the advantage that one finds in being a Muslim. And that is besides the fact that, because of ignorance and the scarcity of prelates, many people are Christians only in name, believing, furthermore, that they are just as pleasing to God if they become Muslims as they are if they remain Christians—for they imagine that a good person can be saved in any religion whatsoever.

All these Christians who speak the Greek language are of the Orthodox rite, with the exception of a few families in Pera, and some islands in the Archipelago which are Roman Catholic (though not entirely). The Bulgarians and the Serbs, who all speak the Slav language (some more elegantly, some more roughly), are Orthodox, except that in Serbia some villages near Skopje,[34] and some families scattered through the territory of that province up to the Danube, still retain the Roman Catholic faith, under the cure of souls of the Archbishops of Bar, the Primates of that kingdom.[35] The Slav language, which was previously used in the Sultan's court itself, is actually disappearing in some places, and the Turkish language is beginning to be the most generally used language: the Christians make an effort to learn it, because the most low-born renegades disdain to speak their native tongue, even though many of them have nothing Muslim about them other than their circumcision.

As I said at the start, Bosnia (including the duchy of Hercegovina), Croatia, Dalmatia and Hungary (which has its own language) are not included in the territories governed by the *beylerbeyi*. In those regions, except in Hercegovina, they mostly keep the Roman Catholic rite and Christian worship; but in Hungary it was almost eliminated by modern heresies[36]—just as, among the superstitions of the Orthodox, there are some remnants of the ancient irreligion of the Arians, the Donatists and the Manichaeans, who call themselves Paulicians. There are some villages of Paulicians in Bulgaria,[37] in Moesia;[38] for that nation took possession not only of Moesia Inferior, but also of a good part of Thrace and Macedonia— the ancient names of those provinces having now completely disappeared.

The Albanians live in part of Epirus, Dardania, Macedonia, and a corner of Illyria; those who are on the Dalmatian side are Roman Catholics, while the others, from Durrës southwards, are all Orthodox. The language of these people is very different from Slav and Greek. It may be Alan, or Gothic, brought there by Alaric, who stayed a long time in Epirus when he was attacking the Roman Empire; or indeed it may be the ancient language of the Macedonians—which seems more likely, as it does not resemble the Slav language, which was perhaps the Goths' own language.[39] The Albanian nation extends quite a lot further than its territory: Albania begins in the west at Ulcinj and the lake of Shkodër, ending in the east at Bastia[40] opposite Corfu, but the Albanians live beyond that in many places in the Peloponnese and Greece,[41] having taken refuge there from wars, or having been transported there by the Byzantine emperors, who dealt in that way with their rebellions. I shall speak at greater length about the Albanian nation, after I have set out the conditions of life of the Muslims.

The Vlachs, who are also Orthodox, are shepherds more than farmers, living in many of the mountain areas of Serbia and Bulgaria, and in almost all the Pindus mountains as far as Larissa. In my opinion they are the remnants of those people who, driven out of the Dacian colonies by the Emperor Aurelian,[42] were placed on this side of the Danube, from Moesia to Macedonia and Dardania, and were later almost entirely exterminated by the Greeks. Now these Vlachs speak the same language as the Moldavians and the Wallachians, as do the Čiči,[43] who are scattered through Croatia and Istria.

Of the other Christians, the Greeks are the most comfortably off, given that most of them live in towns and make their living from trade. But in some places, because of the constant oppressions and insults of the Muslims, they are forced to abandon their lands, rather than sell them. The peasants cannot perform any work except on the land, either because of their indigence, or because of the violence of their masters. And so they have undergone degradation—the upper classes have been degraded by sordid manual labour, and the common people by never being able to attain rest or satisfaction. The Greeks retain the pride of their ancestors, and their hatred of Catholics. They give signs of wishing to rebel, and they would do so; but the peasants of the plains are almost completely deprived of weapons, and the landowners, however warrior-like their dress may make them seem, have no followers, and are fearful, both by nature and because of the risk of losing their property and their families. The ones in the Peloponnese and Thessaly, among whom we may also number the Vlachs, are the best, both in terms of their courage and in terms of their weapons. But those in Thessaly are not so conveniently placed for being roused to rebel, or for being given help; those of the Peloponnese are both more inclined to rebel, if an opportunity arises, and better-placed for being helped by sea. In these two provinces there is an infinite number of Albanians, but rather more in the Peloponnese: their leaders have disturbed the whole of Greece with their uprisings and revolts.

The Bulgarians of Thrace and Moesia, between Mount Haemus (which the Slavs call 'Stara Planina', and the Turks mostly call 'Zalicanac')[44] and the Danube, are not badly equipped with weapons; they are a warlike people, both in their physical make-up and in their enthusiasm for robbery. The Serbians from Skopje to the Danube are more like the Bulgarians of Macedonia than those of Moesia; they too have the same desire to free themselves from the Turkish tyranny, a desire which every slave has.

Westwards from Skopje, those who live in the other part of Dardania and in the mountains bordering Albania, who, thanks to their physical situation and their fierceness, have not yet been tamed by the Turks, should be held in high esteem. These are the Piperi, Kuçi, Kelmendi, Bjelopavlići and others in the Plav region, who are partly Albanian and partly Slav.[45] Of these, the Slavs, who live in accordance with Orthodoxy, are more schismatic than the others of their nation; they abhor the Roman Catholic denomination, which is usually persecuted by the Archbishop of Pejë, who oppresses the Catholic prelates in order to get the recognition of his authority that he demands from them. Not long ago that archbishop, having gained jurisdiction over a very wide area, was enabled by the pasha Mehmed Sokolović (who governed under Süleyman, Selim and Murad) to usurp the title of 'Patriarch'.[46] Pejë is a territory near the White Drin river in the *sancak* of Dukagjin, though it is mostly inhabited by spahis of the *sancak* of Shkodër.[47]

But the Turks are all of one faith, and one language, except for the Yürüks, manufacturers of very fine felt, who were once nomadic shepherds but have now been settled;[48] they are descended from those people from Asia who followed the party and sect of 'Zecchelle' the Persian, whoever he was, and it may be that in their hearts believed more in Ali than in Muhammad.[49] And they live, under their own leader, more in Dobrudža than in the rest of Bulgaria.[50]

Once upon a time, the Turks lived only by their weapons, and those few who engaged in trade did so by making use of Christians. But after they ceased to have the opportunity to commit robbery and arson, when the country they had conquered had been repopulated, they devoted themselves to agriculture and trade, so that they now think of nothing else. And they think most highly of a mercantile life, in view of the benefit and leisure it brings; for the trading activities of the great ones consist of usury, which is also a vice of these Christians. In most of the territories of Greece the Turks [Muslims] do not outnumber the Christians with whom they live, and many territories are inhabited entirely by Greeks. In the territories of Bulgaria, Serbia and Albania almost all the Turks [Muslims] are for the most part foreigners, of various nations, and slavish people (in Albania, however, they are natives), whether merchants or artisans, who are afraid of any revolt; they are armed in the old-fashioned way, with bows and scimitars, though the ones on the coast have some arquebuses. The [Muslim] peasants, who are outnumbered by the Christians, have very few weapons. Those who do not live intermingled with Christians are all Turks, and these are found only in the Thracian and Macedonian parts of Bulgaria, rather than in Moesia. But the ones who live together with Christians, and who have converted to Islam either from fear of some punishment, or to avoid extraordinary taxes other than the tribute, now that they realize that they receive worse treatment, make an effort to demonstrate that they are Muslims. For the Ottoman government ministers do not want all the Christians to abandon their faith, as they do not want to lose the advantage of robbing and enslaving them, and the benefit which they draw from the tithes for the militia.[51]

As for the soldiers who are called timariot spahis [holders of 'timar' military-feudal estates], who serve as cavalry under their own *sancakbeyis*, nowadays their shout is in reality greater than their strength, both qualitative and quantitative. They have given up their arquebuses. They are unwilling to accept discomfort, whether because they are unused to it, or because they vie with one another [in ostentation]; for although most of them have been newly recruited either from tilling the fields and shepherding or from servitude, they nevertheless want to take to the camp all the conveniences of bedding, and cooking facilities—which is why there are so many horses in their armies. And because most of them have bought these timars (which are seldom awarded on merit), they do not wish to risk their lives in the wars, so many either sell their timars again, or send their servants in their place, with the intention of resigning [from their timars]. That is the reason why there is so much disorder in their military discipline, where the cavalry are disobedient and disorderly.[52] Those who want to be regarded as courageous go in front, and all hope of winning the battles depends on them. They march badly, and set up camp far apart. It was with this in view that Petru, the Voivod of Moldavia (the one who, having abandoned his principality, was then detained in Germany by a lawsuit, and died in Bolzano in 1594), said, among other things, in reply to the Archduke Ferdinand, that a large number of Turks had been defeated by a small number of Christians, first by means of God's help, and secondly by means of their superiority in weapons and discipline.[53]

In the interior [of the *beylerbeylik* of Rumeli] there is very little infantry, because there are few fortresses. Many men are enlisted in various places to serve in the navy, but most of them are useless for that purpose, either because of their age, or because of their occupations, which are very remote from military life. In this year's selection of Janissaries they took notice only of physical condition, and advanced age, so that they could send them at length to the war and get them taken for veterans, even though very few of them knew how to put on a sword or handle an arquebus. In the past almost all the soldiers were rich; now very few have money, as they have spent it in this Hungarian war, where they were not able to rob, and victuals were extremely expensive. And because many of them have borrowed money at interest in order to buy their timars, and many have lent out money at interest to other soldiers who have gone bankrupt (apart from the Asian ones, and the cavalry of the Porte, who have wintered in Serbia and Bulgaria in recent years,[54] and who are all called *sipahioğlans*, although they are divided into four regiments and six troops, under six different banners),[55] they have more or less ruined their estates, since in many places the peasants have had no grain to sow. To make themselves seem grander than they are on their campaigns, many of them have dressed as Tatars, making no distinction between Muslims and Christians. But I come back to the infantry, which is stationed in garrisons, and goes under the name of *azabs* and *beşlüs*.[56] Normally they receive no more than four or five *akçes* a day, which comes to two thalers a month:[57] they are badly [*sc.* irregularly] paid, just as the *sipahioğlans* have been kept waiting for their salary-payments.

The *sancaks* governed by the *beylerbeyi* are as follows. In Bulgaria, on the banks of the Danube: Silistra, Nikopol, Vidin. Inland from there: Kırkkilise, Sofia (the residence of the *beylerbeyi*), Vize, in Thrace, and Çirmen [Černomen], in Macedonia. (I have chosen to describe these using the ancient names of those provinces, so that the reader may know where they are.) In Serbia: on the Danube, Smederevo or Belgrade (those two cities forming one *sancak*), and in the interior, Vushtrri [Vučitrn], Alacahisar (which the Serbs call Kruševac), Kiustendil, Skopje, and Prizren, which possesses many places in Albania. In Greece: Ioannina, Angelokastro,[58] Salonica, and Trikala, a *sancak* which belongs to the Turhanlı family.[59] In the Peloponnese there is only one, which the Greeks call Gastuni;[60] for the *sancak* of Mystras, and the others, are under the *kapudan paşa*. In Albania: Shkodër, Dukagjin, Elbasan, Vlorë, Delvinë, all of which reach the coast, and Ohrid, which contains Krujë, of Skanderbeg fame, and has a great mixture of Greeks, Bulgars and Albanians. The *beylerbeyi* also has two tiny *sancaks* (which were previously one *sancak*) beyond the Danube: Bender and Akkerman,[61] both of which have fewer than 100 spahis. The *sancak* of Kiustendil has 1,300 spahis; not one of the others has more than 800, and the normal figure is between 200 and 300. A total of 600 is rare, and some have fewer than 80, such as Skopje, Prizren and Dukagjin. Shkodër has a slightly larger number, and Çirmen has 50–60.[62] (In no case do I include members of the *sancakbeyis*' families in the number of spahis.)

From these extremely accurate figures one can clearly see that the total number of Turks is smaller than it is reputed to be. Realizing this themselves, they have introduced a new militia made up of agricultural labourers and peasants, whom they have enticed to join by offering them various privileges—but above all, by qualifying them to receive honours, and to be called 'brother of a slave', which is the most honoured title among them, so they call themselves *kul kardaşı*.[63] Apart from the spahis, there are the *akıncı*,[64] most of whom are peasants. They are cavalry militia; their service is neither simply voluntary nor simply paid, in view of the fact that they have a certain exemption [from taxes], and permission to plunder everything, in the manner of the Tatars, whom they resemble in many ways. In the old days they were more numerous, and held in higher esteem, before the Sultan made use of the Tatars. Some people wrongly describe them as soldiers of fortune; the Turks call those *gönüllü*.[65] The *akıncı* live mostly in Dobrudža, a province of Bulgaria near the Danube, under their own chief, who is from the Mihaloğlu family.[66]

In Dobrudža, between the Danube and the ruins of that long wall which was extended by the Byzantine emperors from Karasu near Silistra as far as Constanţa on the coast of the Black Sea,[67] there reside the *cebelü*[68] Tatars, by which I mean armed men, of whom there may be 2,000; they are armed with scimitars, arrows, doublets and helmets. The Turks often make use of the name of these Tatars, to give the impression that they have been reinforced by the arrival of the Tatars of the Crimea (a place known by Herodotus, together with its trench, after which those Tatars are called 'people of Perekop' by the Poles and the Russians).[69] And to make people believe that more easily, they bring across the Danube those Tatars who normally live in that corner of Moldavia which, lying between the Dniester and Danube, makes up the *sancak*s of Bender and Akkerman. Bender is the place that the Moldavians and Poles call Tighina, and Akkerman is called 'Bialograd' [Białogród] by the Poles and 'Cittat Alba' [Cetatea Albă] by the Moldavians.[70]

Now some of these Tatars live with their families around Kiliya, a trading area,[71] and some are robbers, who come from the Crimea to raid these territories. Together, they come to no fewer than 6,000 and no more than 8,000. And indeed raising the Tatars costs the Sultan a great deal, for the members of that greedy nation usually will not leave home unless they are first given provisions for the family which they leave behind, as well as weapons for themselves, and clothing—even down to their boots. And as they understand the need for their help, or the danger into which they will be sent, they cause ructions in order to get the payment increased—or else they return home whenever they encounter the slightest difficulty. There is another stratagem of the Turks which I do not want to omit: in order to keep up the number of men whom they are thought to present on campaign, the *sancakbeyi*s very often lend people to one another; or indeed they gather their men so far away that they cannot be seen by their comrades, and then, coming all together towards the rest of the army, they give the appearance of being an innumerable multitude. In this way they even deceive themselves, when they receive the Tatar reinforcements. For those reasons, and because of the way in which the army marches and makes camp, it seems innumerable even to the Turks themselves.

It remains for me to add something about Albania. In this province, as I have said, people follow Orthodoxy from Bastia to Durrës, in the *sancak*s of Delvinë, Vlorë and Elbasan. In the *sancak* of Delvinë almost all of them know the Greek language; in that of Vlorë, the majority do. There are also many villages of Bulgarians there, who extract pitch.[72] Vlorë is the only place in all the territories of Albania to be inhabited by foreign Turks of Asian origin, coming from those who followed Zecchelle.[73] Near Vlorë, a little less than one day's journey away, are the Himariot highlanders; they are indeed fierce people, but not very reliable, and armed mostly with spears and slings. They have now risen up, persuaded by some people, and especially by the efforts of Archbishop Athanasios of Ohrid, who, on the pretext of a visitation (Ohrid being roughly four days' journey from Himarë), has made them think that he had an agreement with the Emperor, and that men would very soon come from the King of Spain—with whom they would be able to reach etc. in order to unite etc.[74] These rebels have eighteen villages; the largest of them can supply 500 fighting men, while the others cannot supply more than 200 [each].[75] But if this revolt of theirs is not supported by outside help, it cannot last long, in which case they will be forced (as on previous occasions) to make peace with the Turks on very disadvantageous terms. That happened recently to their neighbours the people of Dukat (to say nothing of others), who, having been badly treated by Piri Pasha, the then *sancakbeyi* of Delvinë, and reduced to little more than 200 households, were forcibly moved to 'Herico' (which in ancient times was called 'Oricum').[76]

The Albanian Roman Catholics, being the best armed, are also the most faithful Christians of the Ottoman Empire; they are regarded as the most capable ones, and are feared on account of their constant revolts. They rise up for the slightest reason, those of the plains no less than those of the mountains; but then they submit, in spite of themselves, since on their own they are not able to hold out, not so much against the Turks, as against the neighbouring Christians, who harass them more for the sake of seizing their goods than to give an appearance of loyalty to the Sultan. Very often the *sancakbeyi*s provoke them to rebel, either in order to pillage them, or to take revenge on them, or to have an excuse for not going to a distant war; for that reason the *sancakbeyi* of Dukagjin never leaves, just like the one of Angelokastro who, on the pretext of defending his territory against armed Christians, always stays at home. The people of Dukagjin live on mount Scardus[77] on the edge of Prizren, and those who live far from the road do not pay tax, being protected by the roughness of the terrain. The mountain [-range] is called 'the black mountain', and there are many mountains with that name in Turkish territory.[78]

On the side facing the Adriatic, Albania is ringed by very high mountains; as a plain it is watered by frequent and large rivers, which prevent those moving on foot from gathering together. And the Christians have no cavalry, nor do they have the means to make bridges. The strongholds are held by the Ottomans, even if not all of them are garrisoned or guarded. The main ones, at least, are secure enough, so that they cannot be surreptitiously seized by the Christians. I wished to point this out because of the opinion which some have about these people, that they can achieve a lot by themselves, without foreigners, and that the mere rumour of help from Italy and Spain, with the raising of a flag, will be enough to make them rise up. I hope to God that these unfortunate people do not fall into danger, and that these dealings with them, which are so public, do not completely destroy the opportunity to achieve something in the future. I know that rulers cannot be deceived when they do not want to be deceived, even if sometimes they may appear to put their faith in foolish or impossible proposals that they happen to receive—which, if they succeed, bring them glory, and, even if they fail, bring them praise for having proved to the world their great-heartedness and their eagerness to promote the public good. Doubtless, however, it would not be a bad idea to try to maintain these people in the Christian religion, until such time as His Divine Majesty favours these pious intentions with better ways of carrying them out. Perhaps the destruction of the Ottoman Empire is drawing near. Nevertheless, one should procure the safety of so many souls which, because of ignorance and the scarcity of prelates, are at risk of perishing—I mean, the Roman Catholics of Albania and Serbia.

In Albania there are at present only two bishops, both of them called Nicolò: the Bishop of Sapë[79] and the Bishop of Stefani.[80] (For the Bishop of Lezhë, a former Franciscan, lives in his homeland, the territory of Dubrovnik, for reasons of ill-health;[81] and because of his absence, and because he does not speak the language [sc. Albanian], he can achieve little.) As for the Bishop of Stefani, who was also a Franciscan: because he entered into a plan to take Krujë by surprise, by the means of a Muslim highway robber called Nidar Manasi (which may or may not succeed), he has gone into hiding, as the Ottomans have already found out about the plan, and I think they are treating it with ridicule.[82] Thus, because of his lack of security, he can hardly carry out his pastoral function. The Bishop of Sapë cannot be everywhere; besides, this winter he visited the Catholics of Serbia, since he is closest to the see of Bar, which is vacant. Bar, a Slav city conquered by the Ottomans 25 years ago, has begun to use the Albanian language, as it is governed by Muslims from the Albanian, not the Slav, nation. It is certainly necessary that bishops should be native-born, and that they should have servants, and incomes; for if they are foreigners they will be constantly slandered, and it may happen that one of them will gladly make use of such hostility to enjoy the episcopal title, and some little pension, without residing in his see. And if they do not have servants, they will be subjected to abuse not only by the Turks, but also by irreverent Christians; nor will they be able to travel through their dioceses unless they enjoy personal security, and if they are poor they will not be able to keep retainers. Thus episcopal dignity is degraded, and the churches go to ruin, not so much because of the tyranny of the Ottomans, as because of the poverty of the clergy.

As for which are the suitable places and mountain passes through which to enter the provinces of this *beylerbeylik*, and the best way to seize and keep hold of the most advantageous places: it is more difficult for me to give an account of these, not having seen all of them, than it is for others to discuss them on the basis of reading the history-books which show all the routes by which the Roman armies, and those of other nations, penetrated as far as the Danube, or passed from the Danube to the sea.[83] So I shall leave that aspect of things to those better suited to deal with it. I am content to have set out simply and in real terms the present state of the Muslims and Christians. As it is permitted to anyone to narrate what he has seen and heard, so it is not permitted to everyone to try to persuade rulers of that which they should or can do.

Appendix: Soranzo's Borrowings from Bruni's Treatise

The following details in Soranzo's *L'Ottomanno* (listed here by page-number of the first edition) consist of material borrowed from Bruni's treatise on the *beylerbeylik* of Rumeli.

14: *akıncı* are mostly peasants; not simply voluntary, in view of tax exemption; rob country like Tatars; live mostly in Dobrudža; *gönüllü* ('Gionli') are soldiers of fortune

19: recent recruitment of Janissaries took notice only of physical condition and advanced age, so they could be sent to war as if they were veterans

20: garrison infantry are *azabs* ('Asappi') and *beşlüs* ('Besli'); new militia recently introduced of agricultural labourers and peasants, with honorific name *kul kardaşı* ('Culcardasì')

21: spahis have bought timar estates on money borrowed at interest, or have lent at interest to others who have gone bankrupt; have become soft, taking bedding and cooking facilities on campaign, hence also many horses

23: many spahis send servants in their place

25: Crimean Tatars called 'people of Perekop' ('Precopiti') by Poles and Russians because of trench, which is mentioned in Herodotus

28: Akkerman called 'Bialogrod' by Poles, 'Cittat Alba' by Moldavians; Bender called 'Tegina' by both; *cebelü* ('Giebeli', explained as 'armed men') Tatars are up to 2,000, armed with scimitars, arrows, doublets and helmets, in Dobrudža between Danube and ruins of wall from 'Corasuì' to Constanța; Ottomans use them to make people think Crimean Tatars have come

98: conversation between Archduke Ferdinand and Petru Șchiopul, who died in Bolzano, 1594

112: Greeks willing to rebel in Peloponnese and Thessaly, especially those near coast who can receive foreign help; Serbians also willing, especially in

Dardania: Piperi, Kuçi, Kelmendi, Bjelopavlići and others in Plav region, with many Albanians among them

113: as Bruni says, we should not encourage revolt unless we can give enough help for it to succeed; Athanasios raised revolt among Himariots, claiming promised Spanish help; they were forced to make peace on disadvantageous terms

114: same happened to Dukat, badly treated by Piri ('Pirri') Pasha, reduced to 200 households, transported to Orikum

117: Albanians both Catholic and Orthodox; Albania from Ulcinj to Bastia; Albanians also in Greece, whether fled there or transported by Emperors of the East; as Bruni says, Catholic Albanians are the best armed and most faithful Christians, constantly rebelling, but harassed by neighbouring Christians

118: *sancakbeyi*s provoke them, for pillage, or revenge, or excuse not to go to distant war (e.g. *sancakbeyi*s of Dukagjin, Angelokastro); those on Mount Scardus, far from road, do not pay tax; range called 'black mountain', like others in Ottoman territory; Albania ringed by mountains, with rivers, preventing those on foot from gathering; Christians there have no cavalry and cannot make bridges; strongholds held by Ottomans, cannot be taken surreptitiously; we should not think they can achieve all by themselves with mere rumour of help from Italy or Spain, and raising of a flag

4

Crypto-Christianity and Religious Amphibianism in the Ottoman Balkans

The Case of Kosovo

Crypto-Christianity was a widespread phenomenon in the Ottoman Empire, but not a common one. A map of the Empire, with the crypto-Christian communities coloured in, would show specks and patches here and there, scattered over a very wide area; but the communities in each case were fairly small ones, leading, of necessity, somewhat limited and introverted lives. The best-known ones were in the Trebizond region of north-eastern Turkey; in Crete; in Cyprus; and in parts of Albania and Kosovo.[1] What the members of all these communities had in common was that they adhered outwardly to Islam—they made the profession of faith, they went to mosques, their menfolk were (in most cases) circumcised, they bore Muslim names, and so on—while, in the privacy of their own communities, they preserved the rudiments of a Christian faith, saying Christian prayers, having their children baptized if possible, observing Christian feasts and fasts, and performing other Christian rituals. The term 'communities' is emphasized here, because crypto-Christianity is very much a phenomenon of social religious life: individuals may have hidden their faith at all sorts of times and places, but the sort of crypto-Christianity I am concerned with here is a form of life, a tradition, something that can be sustained and transmitted only by a community.

The crypto-Christians of Kosovo form the most distinctive group out of all the Ottoman crypto-Christians, because their form of Christianity was Roman Catholic. But of course the first thing that strikes one about the whole phenomenon of crypto-Christianity is that so many of these communities sprang up, probably without any knowledge of the existence of other such communities in other parts of the Empire, and underwent quite similar patterns of development. Before considering the distinctive history of the Kosovo crypto-Christians, therefore, it is worth looking at some of the general conditions of religious life in the Ottoman-ruled Christian or former Christian territories. For much of this century—and certainly since the publication of F. W. Hasluck's marvellous *Christianity and Islam under the Sultans* in 1929—studies of religious life in the Ottoman Empire, especially in the Ottoman Balkans, have paid great attention to the ways in which Islam and Christianity interacted and became elaborately intertwined. A much fuller and richer picture has emerged, which makes the

Rebels, Believers, Survivors: Studies in the History of the Albanians. Noel Malcolm,
Oxford University Press (2020). © Noel Malcolm. DOI: 10.1093/oso/9780198857297.001.0001

Manichaean vision of the old religious-nationalist historiography (oppressed national churches versus oppressive Islam) seem crude and quite outmoded. Nevertheless, there is a danger that some key distinctions may get lost or blurred in this new, complex, mixed-up, parti-coloured world of Ottoman religion, in which everything seems to have been merging into everything else in a sort of warm syncretist soup. The phenomenon of crypto-Christianity may also get rather blurred when looked at in this way, becoming mixed up with other types of what might in general be called religious amphibianism; so I should like to begin by making some distinctions, and isolating a number of factors or conditions which I think are essentially different from crypto-Christianity, even though they may have helped to provide an environment of amphibianism in which crypto-Christianity could survive or flourish. The examples I shall give here are drawn mainly from the religious history of Kosovo, but they apply much more generally to conditions throughout the Ottoman Balkans. I want to distinguish three factors: the first is social coexistence; the second is religious syncretism; and the third is theological equivalentism.

The social coexistence of Christians and Muslims that matters here is not the general co-presence of the two faiths in towns or country areas, but the close coexistence of people living in such social intimacy that they could not avoid experiencing, and even in some ways sharing, the ritual acts or religious observances of each other's faith. The strongest form this took was the coexistence of religions within a single family. This was something that happened, typically, in either of two ways: a member of a Christian family converted to Islam (usually, a young man, who could then become the head of a Muslim sub-branch of the family); or there was intermarriage. Many examples of this sort of intimate coexistence could be given from all over the Balkans; let me give a few from the Kosovo region.

The modern Franciscan mission to northern Albania started in the 1630s, and in 1637 one of its members, Fra Cherubino, went into Kosovo. At one house in a village outside Gjakovë (Djakovica) he and his companion were welcomed with the words: 'Come in, Fathers: in our house we have Catholicism, Islam and Orthodoxy'. In shocked tones Fra Cherubino reported to his superiors: 'They seemed to glory in this diversity of religions, as if they were wiser than the other people of this world.'[2] In the clan system of the northern Albanians, loyalties to the family, the vëllazëri (bratstvo, group of families) or the clan were always stronger than the claims of religion: some clans, such as the Krasniqi and the Berisha, divided into Catholic and Muslim branches, without any diminution of fellow feeling.[3] In the Thaçi clan of north-eastern Albania there were three branches: one fully Catholic, one fully Muslim, and one Catholic but non-pork-eating. The clan tradition was that there had been three brothers in the late seventeenth or early eighteenth century: the eldest had converted to Islam, the second had remained Catholic, and the third, while remaining Catholic, had stopped

eating pork out of deference to the eldest.[4] Whether this oral tradition was anything more than a fanciful rationalization can only be guessed at; but the example
does suggest that close social coexistence could lead to the blurring of some religious distinctions. In the 1930s and 1940s Mirko Barjaktarović studied a number
of Albanian *zadruga*s (extended family farms) in Kosovo which contained mix-
tures of Catholics and Muslims; not surprisingly, he found a degree of syncretism
in their religious practices. The Muslim members of the family would assist the
Catholics in cutting the *badnjak* (Yule-log), and would also attend prayers on
saints' days; and the Catholics would take part in the Bajram celebrations. When
they had feast-days together the Catholics would not eat pork or drink wine, but
all of them, Catholic and Muslim, would drink *raki* (brandy).[5]

Obviously, the coexistence, however close, of two distinct religious identities is
not the same as crypto-Christianity. Each person in one of these mixed families
was either one thing or the other. The only direct way in which this form of life
may sometimes have created a small-scale simulacrum of crypto-Christianity was
in the opportunity it may have given to some of the Christian members of the
family to pass themselves off as Muslims when they travelled elsewhere, given
that they had an unusually intimate knowledge of Muslim customs and religious
observances. It was also quite common in these mixed *zadruga*s for the Catholic
members to be given, in addition, Muslim names, which they used within the
family and could use in the outside world if it were to their advantage to do so.[6]
More generally, the use of Muslim names by Catholic Albanians in the Malësi
(highlands of northern Albania) was in fact widespread until well into the twentieth century; it may originally have been just a form of camouflage for their dealings with the outside world, but it became a cherished tradition, and continued
long after the need for such protection had passed.[7] Of course the principle
of camouflage is the essential principle of crypto-Christianity; but crypto-
Christianity involves a much more far-reaching form of mimicry than the mere
use of a name for limited social purposes.

Religious syncretism provides my second form of amphibianism. The general
phenomenon here is very well-known: at the level of folk-religion, many practices
were shared between Muslims and Christians, for a range of purposes including
the divinatory, medical and apotropaic. Some forms of folk-religion did not
require the assistance of priests or imams: examples would include the private
celebration of saints' days (Muslims in northern Albania would light a candle on
St Nicholas's day), the celebration in Muslim homes of a *slava* or family patron
saint's day, and the ritual of the *badnjak* at Christmas-time. And some of these
observances would be carried out by Muslims and Christians together: mixed
Muslim-Christian villages in northern Albania, for example, would have joint
celebrations of St Nicholas's day.[8] (There is, incidentally, a tradition of argument
by Serbian ethnographers which claims that all these practices demonstrate that
the Albanians of Kosovo and northern Albania were originally Serbs, as if only

people who had started with pure Serbian blood in their veins could do any of these things. Such an argument misunderstands the whole nature of syncretism; it also misrepresents the origins of many of these practices, all of which can be found in a much wider catchment area and some of which have obviously pre-Christian and pre-Slav origins.)

Other forms of syncretism involved recourse to the priests and clergy, or the shrines and religious buildings, of the other faith. Thus Christians might go to the *türbe* (tomb) of a holy dervish sheikh, or ask a dervish to read the Koran over them when they were sick; and Muslims might visit churches, and ask priests for blessings, holy water or the administration of sacraments. Nineteenth-century travellers noted Albanian Muslims going to visit the monastery of Deçan (Dečani); a Bosnian Franciscan who travelled through northern Albania in 1907 observed in one village that 'On Sunday, five or six Muslims came to church, and a *bula* knelt below the altar during Mass.'[9] For the more or less magical purposes of folk-religion, holy oil (chrism) and holy water were especially prized. Christian baptism was held in high esteem by many Muslims, for a variety of magical purposes: they thought it would give them a longer life, that it would guard them against mental illness, that it would protect them from being eaten by wolves, and—a strange idea, but a very widespread one—that it would prevent them from smelling like dogs.[10]

The reports sent back to Rome by the senior Catholic clergy in Kosovo often show signs of irritation at this magical use of Christian practices. The eighteenth-century Archbishop of Skopje Matija Mazarek reported wearily on one occasion that he had been summoned by the governor of Novobërdë (Novo Brdo), whose wife was suffering from 'a certain curious female malady', and that he had had to bless oil and water for her; more generally, he complained that in order to placate the local Muslims he had to 'visit their sick, and even exorcize and bless their animals'.[11]

And yet these misgivings about folk-religion did not stop the Catholic arch-bishops of Skopje (i.e. in effect, the archdiocese of Kosovo) from presiding over one of the most dramatic examples of syncretism in the whole of the Ottoman Balkans. This was the great two-day festival on the summit of Mt Pashtrik (Paštrik), a few hours' walk to the west of Prizren, to celebrate the Assumption of the Virgin Mary. The mountain had three peaks: more than 1,000 people would gather there, and say vespers on the two lower ones. Then, in the words of the visitation report of Archbishop Pjetër Bogdani in 1681: 'they spend all night there, with drums, whistles, dancing and singing. After midnight they begin a mixed procession—Muslims, Serbians and Greeks with lighted wax candles, their length proportionate to each person's age. They walk round the peak of the highest mountain for three hours in bare feet (with some of the leading Muslims on horseback).' In the morning, the Archbishop held a service on the mountain-top, preaching in Albanian to 'a numberless crowd of all sorts of people'; he was taken to lunch afterwards by the Orthodox Bishop of Prizren.[12] This cult of a mountain-top was evidently a pagan survival; what makes it a peculiarly fascinating example of syncretism is the fact that in later periods it was subsumed under two different interpretations, Muslim and Orthodox. One of the many tombs of the legendary Muslim holy man Sarı Saltık was located there, with celebrations on the day of Ali, the son-in-law of the Prophet, 2 August; and the Orthodox in Prizren in the late nineteenth century had their own version of this story, in which the grave of St Pantaleimon was on the summit—also with appropriate celebrations taking place over a whole night in the summer.[13]

Syncretism, once again, is clearly a different phenomenon from crypto-Christianity. A Christian who visited the *türbe* of a Muslim holy man to cure an illness was not pretending to be a Muslim; more importantly, a Muslim who had his children baptized may not have had any idea in his head of creating a secret Christian identity for them. All we can say is that in indirect ways the common or borrowed practices of syncretism may have helped to sustain an environment in which it was easier for crypto-Christianity to exist—in such an environment, crypto-Christians did not always need to engage in elaborate subterfuges in order to enter churches, have contacts with priests, or engage in some at least of the festivals and other practices of their Christian faith.

The third form of amphibianism I wish to look at very briefly is what I call 'theological equivalentism'. The term 'theological' is used here deliberately, as opposed to 'religious'. Most modern studies of religious life in the Ottoman Balkans, and particularly of its Islamicization, deal almost exclusively with religion as a social phenomenon, and attribute conversion purely to social or economic factors. I should like to put in a small plea for the role of theological arguments, which have been almost pushed out of the picture. Of course most peasants had only the haziest ideas of Christian or Islamic doctrine; of course social and economic factors were important, and probably predominant in most cases. But when reading accounts by seventeenth-century Catholic clerics of their activities in Albania and Kosovo, one frequently finds that they appealed to theological arguments, either to stop people from converting to Islam, or to reconvert them if they had already done so. It does not seem unreasonable to suppose that *hoxha*s (Islamic religious teachers) and dervishes might also have used theological arguments for their own purposes.

The argument which I describe as 'theological equivalentism' stated that both Islam and Christianity were equally valid ways to salvation. I use the clumsy word 'equivalentism' rather than more familiar terms such as 'ecumenism' or 'latitudinarianism', because those terms have too specifically Christian or intra-Christian meanings; another term used in seventeenth-century Christian discourse, 'indifferentism', also has too narrow a focus, as well as suggesting overtones of coldness or even disbelief, which need not apply in this case. It was Muslim proselytizers, not cold or irreligious people, who had recourse to the tactic of theological equivalentism, arguing that Christianity and Islam were hardly opposed to each other at all. In the words of one Franciscan report from the mid-seventeenth century:

> Those impious people also said that the difference between them and the Christians was small; 'After all', they said, 'we all have only one God, we venerate your Christ as a prophet and holy man, we celebrate many of the festivals of your saints with you, and you celebrate Friday, our festive day; Muhammad and Christ are brothers...' And this error was so widespread, that in the same family one person would be Catholic, one Muslim and one Orthodox.[14]

Similarly, a report of 1650 noted that 'the Muslims preach to them that everyone can achieve salvation in his own religion.'[15] This argument, which seems at first sight to strengthen the case against changing one's faith, was in fact a subtle first step towards converting Christians to Islam: the important move was to get them to accept the idea that Muslims too would achieve eternal life. And on a slightly different tack, Archbishop Mazarek reported in 1760 on what he called the 'fine arts and stratagems' of the Muslims in trying to persuade Catholics to convert: they argued, he said, that the Gospels did in fact teach the doctrines of Islam.[16] This may be theologically a different position from strict equivalentism; but it has the same effect of downplaying the importance, or even the possibility, of doctrinal conflict between two religions.

This attitude is clearly conducive to a kind of religious amphibianism; it can be combined—as the quotation from the Franciscan report illustrated—with both syncretism and intimate social coexistence. But once again, although this may have contributed to forming an environment in which it was easier for crypto-Christianity to exist, there is an essential difference in principle between this sort of easy-going religious amphibianism and crypto-Christianity itself. Crypto-Christianity must surely have been based on the idea that the two faiths were not really equivalent at all, but radically opposed, and that one of them (the secretly held Christian faith) gave salvation, while the other did not.

Having made these distinctions, let us now turn to the history of crypto-Christianity in Kosovo. Some previous writers on this subject have offered as evidence of crypto-Christianity things for which—if my distinctions are correctly drawn—there may be quite separate explanations: the baptism of the children of Muslim parents, the celebration of Christian festivals in Muslim homes, the use of Muslim names by Christians, and so on. Nevertheless, there is quite strong evidence of genuine crypto-Christianity, which emerges in the seventeenth century and continues into the twentieth.

The origins of this phenomenon may go back earlier than that, but the evidence simply does not allow us to say with certainty that crypto-Christianity was present before the seventeenth century. The earliest potential evidence comes from an Ottoman report of 1568, which noted disapprovingly that Muslim villa-gers in the Debar (Dibër) area were taking their new-born children first to the priest, who gave them Christian names, and only afterwards to the Muslim clergy.[17] Without further details, we cannot tell whether this was proper crypto-Christianity or merely a quasi-magical syncretist practice. Some of the earliest visitation reports from northern Albania do allude to what might be called a crypto-Christian attitude: a report of 1603 mentions people who think they can profess Islam and at the same time 'retain the Christian faith in their hearts'.[18] People who had converted to Islam for mainly prudential reasons might well have thought that they remained Christians at heart. This is a phenomenon of first-generation converts, an attitude which may either have survived or have died with them; only when the attitude has become transmitted down the family, and established as a tradition, can we speak confidently of the practice of crypto-Christianity.

The Archbishop of Bar (Tivar, Antivari), Marin Bizzi, described in a visitation report of 1618 what does seem like an initial phase of crypto-Christianity: some of the Catholics of northern Albania, he said, 'profess outwardly the Muslim religion...while retaining the Christian faith only in their hearts; and on that assumption, they demanded in vain from the Archbishop on his visitations that he should issue a decree, telling the parish priests to administer secretly to them the sacraments of penitence and the eucharist.'[19] But if this was an early sign of crypto-Christianity, then it cannot have been a common or an established phenomenon at this stage: when Bizzi issued a detailed set of instructions to his priests, including, for example, special requirements to stop the misuse of the sacraments for folk-religious purposes, he made no mention of crypto-Catholicism.[20]

Another report, made by the parish priest of Prizren, Gregor Mazrreku, in 1651, described a very similar request: 'Some of the men (and there are very many of these) say: "We are Christians in our hearts, we have only changed our reli-gious affiliation to get out of paying taxes which the Muslims imposed on us" and for that reason they say... "dear Reverend, come and give us confession and Holy Communion secretly." But I have not done this up till now, nor does it seem right to me.'[21]

Clearly the phenomenon was growing by now. The first use by a Catholic priest in this area of a phrase meaning crypto-Christians, 'christiani occulti' or hidden Christians (in fact he meant 'hidden Catholics': only Catholics were called 'Christians' by the Catholic clergy, while the Orthodox were called 'schismatics') comes in a report of 1672 by Shtjefën Gaspari, describing the Pulat region of northern Albania. He says that the men of this area publicly converted to Islam 20 years ago: 'They are called by Muslim names in the presence of the Muslims, they eat meat and foods forbidden by our holy faith [i.e. during Catholic fasts], but when they are not observed by the Muslims they go to church to hear the Mass, to confess and to receive communion from a certain priest, Martin Politi, who goes sometimes to that region, with the bishop's permission, in order that the holy sacraments may be administered to these people, whom he calls hidden Christians.'[22]

Just two years after that report was written, the first formal decree against crypto-Catholicism was issued, by Andrija Zmajević, the Archbishop of Bar. He ordained that Holy Communion should no longer be given to any Catholics who made a public profession of 'infidelity' and sought to hold their Christian faith 'occulte', in a hidden way, and he damned with anathemas any priest who disobeyed this order.[23] Clearly, crypto-Catholicism was by now an established phenomenon.

Going back to those two reports, by Gaspari in 1672 and Mazrreku in 1651, we can get some further clues about how and why it was established. Note, first of all, that both reports specifically say that it was the men who had converted to Islam. Men-only conversion was a common expedient, reflecting the fact that the main motive for conversion in these cases was to escape the additional taxes on Christians, which were levied only on the male members of the family. The main tax was the *cizye* or *haraç*, which was paid, in normal circumstances, only by non-Muslims; some other taxes had differential rates, such as the *ispence* or *resm-i çift*; and there is evidence that at some times in the seventeenth century when the Ottoman Empire was at war with Catholic powers, special extra taxes or charges were levied on the Catholic community. (There were probably other pressures specifically against Catholics, especially after the two abortive attempts by Catholic bishops to assist the conquest of Shkodër (Scutari) by Venetian forces in the 1640s.[24] These, like the later Austrian invasion of 1689, provoked a fiercely anti-Catholic policy on the part of the Ottoman authorities in the northern Albanian region: this may help to explain why it was that crypto-Christianity developed among the Catholics of Kosovo, but not, so far as we know, among either the Orthodox of Kosovo or the Catholics of other regions such as Bosnia.) Visitation reports frequently describe cases of whole Catholic communities engaging in men-only conversion. In 1637, for example, Gjergj Bardhi noted that the inhabitants of a village near Gjakovë had divided in this way; in 1651 Gregor Mazrreku wrote that all the men in Suharekë (Suva Reka), where there had previously been 160 Catholic households, had gone over to Islam, but that 36 or 37 of their wives remained Catholic; and 21 years later Shtjefën Gaspari found 300 Christian women but no Christian men at all in the Has district west of Gjakovë.[25] Gregor Mazrreku reported that the men who had converted to Islam 'do not want to take Muslim women as their wives, but Christian ones instead, saying, "it's so that in this way the name of Christian will not die out completely in my house."'[26]

For Muslims to take Christian wives was quite a common practice in the Ottoman Empire, so it would not have aroused any suspicions on the part of the authorities or the Muslim clergy. Under Islamic law it is permissible for a Muslim man to marry a Christian or Jewish woman, though not for a Muslim woman to marry a non-Muslim. An anonymous Venetian account of the Ottoman Empire in 1579 described the practice as follows: 'The Turks [i.e. Muslims] take Christian wives without demur, since their law permits it. The male child, at the father's request, is made a Muslim, and the female ones, at the mother's request, become Christians; however, the girls will be brought up as Muslims if the father desires it.'[27] Apparently, therefore, this system of religious differentiation by sex could be continued down the generations. It may thus have been an important mechanism in making crypto-Catholicism possible. With women in the family who were officially Christian, it became possible for priests to enter their homes in order to minister in secret to the menfolk as well. These home visits were an important part of the job of a parish priest: as one priest reported in a deposition to the Vatican in 1728, 'there are 237 Catholic households with 4,695 Catholic souls, scattered among the houses of the Muslims, who are given the sacraments by us.'[28]

If sexual differentiation was one key mechanism in the development of crypto-Catholicism, then the other most important mechanism was priestly complicity. It is no coincidence that Gaspari's report of 1672, the first definite description of fully functioning crypto-Christianity, was also the first to confirm that these 'hidden Christians' were being given the sacraments: quite simply, without the cooperation of the priests, crypto-Christianity could not function properly at all. The prohibition issued by Andrija Zmajević in 1674 seems to have had little effect; the administration of the sacraments continued. In terms of official doctrine, Zmajević was of course quite correct: making a public denial of Christ, such as was implied by conversion to Islam, was a mortal sin, and the sacraments could not be administered to anyone who did not repent of it and return to the Church. A specific decree against crypto-Christianity had been issued by the Congregatio de Propaganda Fide (in response to an enquiry from a missionary in North Africa) as early as 1630.[29] It was precisely in that period, the early seventeenth century, that the Catholic Church developed a sophisticated theory of 'mental reservations' to protect Catholic priests who were questioned about their religious identity in Protestant countries; but although the theory covered various sorts of misleading answers to questions, it could not stretch far enough to include an explicit profession of faith in another religion.[30]

Twenty-nine years after Andrija Zmajević issued his decree, his nephew and successor-but-one as Archbishop, Vicko Zmajević, held a provincial synod (in 1703) which repeated and in some ways strengthened the provisions against crypto-Catholicism. Not only did the decrees of this synod say that those who professed Islam must be denied the sacraments; they also said that even without making an official profession of faith in Islam, if someone lived 'Turcica more', in the Muslim way, using a Muslim name, and eating on Catholic fast-days, that person too should be denied them. Other decisions of this synod were that a Christian girl who married a Muslim must be forbidden the sacraments (though she could continue to receive them if the man had been a Christian when she married him), and that although it was permitted to avoid declaring one's Christian faith when asked by a private person, if asked by public authority one was obliged to profess, even at the risk of death.[31] Further prohibitions, along similar lines, were issued by the Holy Office (the Inquisition) in 1724 and 1730.[32]

Despite all these dire prohibitions, however, the crypto-Catholics continued to receive the sacraments from their local priests. That they did so is hardly surprising: the two Austrian invasions of Kosovo, in 1689 and 1737, unleashed waves of Ottoman anti-Catholic hostility in the region, and must have prompted many prudential conversions to Islam. The fullest description of how crypto-Catholicism worked comes from just after that second Austrian fiasco: it derives from a report to Rome by the Archbishop of Skopje, Gjon Nikollë (Ivan Nikolović) in 1743. (Unfortunately the section of his report describing the crypto-Catholics has not survived; but a long summary of it has.) Nikollë clearly stated that the bishops and priests did administer all the sacraments to these people, in open violation of the decrees of the provincial synod.[33]

He wrote that the Catholics in the cities, and in some villages, professed their faith openly, paid the tribute and suffered persecution; the others, scattered in the villages, 'maintain the Christian faith in a hidden way' ('occultamente'). These, he said, 'profess the Christian faith in an internal way, but so secretly, that sometimes the father does not reveal himself as a Christian to his sons, or the sons to the father, and on their deathbeds they behave as and give themselves out to be Muslims.' He observed that some went to the mosques; in some cases they had themselves circumcised, in order not to be recognized as Christians, and they were buried as Muslims, but on the other hand they professed Christianity at home, baptized their sons, confessed, communicated, observed vigils and Lent, and said masses for the dead. Interestingly, he noted that 'their wives are for the most part publicly Christian, unless they are themselves the daughters of Muslims converted subsequently in the homes of their Christian husbands.'[34] Nikollë's remark about sons not revealing their Christianity to their fathers is puzzling: either it indicates some covert induction of sons into Christianity by Christian mothers, or it may perhaps be attributable to a pattern of rhetorical phrase-making taking over from the sense of Nikollë's argument. But the reference to fathers not telling their sons is interesting, in view of the comparison it prompts with what we know of crypto-Judaism in the seventeenth century: in the case of the 'Marranos' in Spain and Portugal, apparently, it was common for fathers to wait until their sons were aged 20 before beginning their induction into Judaism.[35]

When Archbishop Nikollë sent his report to Rome in 1743, he asked for further guidance on this whole problematic issue. All he got in response, from Pope Benedict XIV, was an even more severe restatement of the official line in an encyclical of 1744. (Another encyclical, ten years later, also tightened up the official position on the use of Muslim names.)[36] The next-but-one Archbishop,

Matija Mazarek, who held the post for most of his adult life (from 1758 to 1807), did make at least a partial attempt to enforce these decrees. In a report of 1760 he wrote that the crypto-Catholics used to receive the sacraments until Benedict XIV's encyclical; now they were rapidly turning to Islam. The saddest cases among them, he wrote, were those of women who had been converted secretly to Christianity after marrying crypto-Christian men, but who were now also refused the sacraments.[37] He also told the story of an eighteen-year-old Albanian who had come to a christening service conducted by Mazarek in Pejë (Peć), had said he was a crypto-Christian, and had asked to be baptized. Mazarek told him to profess his faith openly, and he refused; so Mazarek denied him baptism. But Mazarek wrote that his own conscience was troubled, and that this policy was not only losing souls, but creating enemies: 'because they have been abandoned by us missionaries, they completely embrace Islam, and these people bear an incredible hatred, aversion and contempt towards us, and we suffer worse persecution from them than from the true and original Muslims.'[38] Relenting somewhat, when he visited a mainly crypto-Catholic village near Prizren during the same visitation, he did allow them the sacraments, on condition that they promised him four things: not to eat forbidden foods, not to circumcise, not to enter mosques and not to allow Muslim burial for their dead.[39]

Some such compromises, it seems, must have continued to be applied in practice; otherwise it is very hard to see how the phenomenon of crypto-Catholicism could have continued, as it did, for several more generations. A report by Archbishop Bogdanović in 1846, for example, gave quite detailed statistics, not only for Catholic families in the archdiocese, but also for crypto-Catholic ones: 128 of them in the parish of Prizren, for example, 150 in the Karadak (Skopska Crna Gora), 57 in the parish of Janjevë (Janjevo), 165 in the parish of Pejë, and so on, up to a total of 500 families.[40] Twenty years later a French consular official in Salonica was able to report that the archdiocese of Skopje contained precisely 5,847 open Catholics and 4,735 crypto-Catholics, the latter in 665 families.[41] Such statistics must reflect continual contacts between the crypto-Catholics and the parish clergy.

It was in the 1840s that the first attempts were made by crypto-Catholics to make a public profession of faith on a legal basis. The great reform decree of 1839, the Hatt-i Şerif of Gülhane, had included general promises of equal rights for all subjects, regardless of religion; five years later, after much pressure from the British Ambassador in Istanbul, a declaration was made that Muslim converts from Christianity who wanted to revert to the Christian faith would no longer be subject to the death penalty.[42] In the following two years attempts were made to introduce the new conscription system, and new taxation, to Kosovo: both forms of innovation were resisted, and a large military force was sent to crush the rebellion. When the Ottoman army commander imposed order in Gjakovë in the summer of 1845 and began conscripting the local men, the call-up was applied only to Muslims. (This was the traditional Ottoman policy, although the new army law of 1843 did in principle make Christians liable for military service too.)[43] A group of crypto-Catholics from nearby villages went to the Catholic church in Gjakovë and declared themselves as Christians; and the same happened soon afterwards in Pejë. Seventy of these men then made a public declaration of Christianity in the army camp. This was an act of some bravery: everyone in this part of Kosovo would have remembered the fate of a group of Catholics in Rugovë (Rugovo), a village near Pejë, who had Muslim names but professed Catholicism openly, and were executed by the local pasha in 1817.[44]

The crypto-Catholics who declared themselves in 1845 were also put into prison, but the army commander did at least order an inquiry, at which the Catholic priests were allowed to make their case. When they argued that these people had only simulated Muslim beliefs in order to avoid oppression, the local Ottoman officials raised the counter-example of the Fandi or Fan, a warlike Catholic clan (and sub-branch of the Mirdita) who had moved into the area west of Gjakovë in recent decades. 'Why is it that the Fandi have never been disturbed in their religious affairs?' they asked, rhetorically. The parish priest of Gjakovë replied that they were a powerful clan who could defend themselves, whereas his crypto-Catholics were 'scattered among completely Muslim villages'. After six weeks in gaol (during which two died of dysentery), the Catholics were released, on payment of a fine. Fifty more heads of family promptly came out as Christians, bringing the total to more than 150.[45]

Later that year, and in the spring of 1846, more crypto-Catholics declared themselves in the villages of the Karadak. The treatment they received was harsher: both they and their priest were thrown into prison, and when they failed to pay the allotted fine (despite, or perhaps because of, the confiscation of all their property), they were sent into exile in Anatolia. Roughly 150 people (25 families) underwent this punishment, with their priest; 20 of them perished on the way to Anatolia, and at least 70 more died in exile before they were finally permitted to come home two years later.[46] Similar problems involving the conscription of crypto-Catholics arose again in 1849 and 1850.[47] But the position of the Catholic Church did generally improve, and the leverage exerted by Western diplomats in Istanbul was enormously increased during the period of the Crimean War, when the Ottoman state was allied with European powers against Russia. In 1856 another important reform decree was issued, declaring full equality of rights among Muslim and non-Muslim subjects and full freedom of religion; this decree, which included a remarkable clause against hate-speech (forbidding officials to use words or expressions 'tending to make one class of my subjects inferior to another class on account of religion, language or race'), also confirmed that apostasy from Islam was no longer punishable by death.[48] After this, the general persecution of the Kosovo crypto-Catholics seems to have ceased. Some declared themselves publicly as Catholics soon after 1856; but the Catholic archbishop noted that many remained in their crypto-Catholic state in his report of 1872.[49]

The most persistent community was the small group of crypto-Christian villages in the Karadak. There is some evidence to suggest that the most famous historical figure from this region, the military chief Idriz Seferi (who took part in every Albanian revolt from the League of Prizren in 1878 to the 'kaçak' rebellion of the 1920s) was in fact a crypto-Christian.[50] During the period immediately after the First Balkan War, when Serbian and Montenegrin rule was forcefully imposed on Kosovo, there were reports of pressure being put on crypto-Catholics to convert to Orthodoxy; and in the 1920s it was reported that some of them declared themselves as Muslims in order to emigrate to Turkey.[51] Quite a number did come out as public Catholics in the 1920s and 1930s, but the ethnographer Atanasije Urošević wrote as late as 1935 that the crypto-Catholics were still very 'secretive'.[52] Recent research by Ger Duijzings suggests that it was the active policy of the Bishop of Skopje, Ivan Franjo Gnidovec (who was bishop between 1924 and 1939), to put pressure on the crypto-Christians to become full Catholics.[53] After all, the old decrees anathematizing the adoption of Muslim practices were still valid, and however oppressive the policies of the Yugoslav state may have been during that period, they certainly did not involve pressure to conform to Islam. And yet it is reported that the traditions of crypto-Christianity had become so ingrained that the practice has continued, partly because of close ties with other Muslim families, until this day. Perhaps some element of genuine bi-confessionality has evolved. If so, the paradoxical conclusion must be that crypto-Christianity has been saved from extinction only because it has changed, during the final period of its history, into something else, ceasing to be merely a type of camouflage—a sincerely practised faith conducted in secret behind a simulated one—and becoming, after all, amphibious in the fullest sense: an equal and parallel commitment to two distinct forms of religious life.

5

Early Modern Albanians in the Hands of the Inquisition

When we study any past society, one of the things we most naturally want to do is to hear the voices of ordinary people. While the great institutions of government, religion and learning may have generated (if we are lucky) a mass of information about the social elite, we have to look elsewhere to find ordinary men and women speaking about their lives. Fortunately, in the case of many Western societies, suitable sources exist from the later Middle Ages onwards: personal correspondence, petitions, autobiographical narratives of various kinds, and, above all, the depositions and transcripts of interrogations that can be found—sometimes in large quantities—among some types of judicial records.

Where the history of the Albanians is concerned, on the other hand, such sources are extremely sparse, at least until the nineteenth century. In the few cases where we can learn about individuals from their personal correspondence and other such papers, it is because they led their lives outside Ottoman Albania.[1] Within the Ottoman lands, the judicial system kept records of judgments, but these contained only brief summaries of accusations and defences, not the detailed answers given by the accused, or by witnesses, during the trial.[2] Beyond the basic tax registers compiled by Ottoman officials, the richest body of documentation recording at least some aspects of ordinary life in the Ottoman Albanian lands consists of the reports sent to the 'Propaganda Fide' in Rome by Catholic priests, from the early seventeenth century onwards. For all their wealth of detail, however, these are quite narrowly focused on the practice of Catholic Christianity. We can learn from these documents about various aspects of social behaviour that were of concern to the clergy (such as bigamy, trial marriages, folk-medicine, divination and blood-feuds); but they leave us with very little sense of the specificity of any individual Albanian's life.[3]

Luckily there is one type of source-material from which we can gain a few glimpses of ordinary Albanians' lives during the early modern period: the records of the Inquisition in Western Christendom. Although the quantity of relevant material here is very small, it has—for the reasons just stated—a special value; and, what is more, it even gives us a few precious details about the lives of ordinary women, who are otherwise almost invisible as individuals in the known historical sources. The Inquisition did not operate in the Albanian lands, of course: all these cases involved people who had left their country, whether voluntarily or

Rebels, Believers, Survivors: Studies in the History of the Albanians. Noel Malcolm,
Oxford University Press (2020). © Noel Malcolm. DOI: 10.1093/oso/9780198857297.001.0001

involuntarily. Some of the cases were concerned only with actions committed after they had left. But in the majority of cases we do learn something, however minimal, about these people's background and earlier life in Albanian territory; and in a few cases the glimpse we gain is more than momentary. Above all, we hear early modern Albanians speaking—more or less—in their own words. And that is something that can hardly be supplied, it seems, by any other category of document from this period.[4]

II

In the great majority of the cases that will be discussed here, the Inquisition was the Roman Inquisition, founded in 1542 and known as the 'Sant'Uffizio' (or 'Sant'Ufficio', or 'Sant'Officio'), the 'Holy Office'. Various ad hoc inquisitions had existed during the Middle Ages; Spain had set up its own Inquisition, under royal control, in 1478 (with the primary task, initially, of examining Jews whose conversion to Christianity was suspected of insincerity); and the Portuguese Crown had created its Inquisition, in imitation of the Spanish, in 1536. The Roman Inquisition was a new and distinct formation, governed by its own committee of cardinals in Rome, under the direct supervision of the Pope. Although its initial *raison d'être* was combating the spread of Protestant heresy, it had jurisdiction, like the other two Inquisitions, over offences with serious theological implications, such as diabolic magic or witchcraft, the abuse of the sacraments, blasphemy and apostasy. From the 1560s or 1570s onwards, these other categories—especially the first—predominated in its workload.[5]

Apostasy was a rather special case, typically taking either of two forms: conversion to Judaism (often by baptized Jews who were returning to the faith of their forefathers), and conversion to Islam. Christians who converted to Islam were in almost every case people who had spent time in the Ottoman Empire or North Africa. Some were born within the Ottoman Empire, and converted there; this category included the great majority of the Albanians who appeared before the Inquisition. Others had been born in Christendom; in rare cases they had travelled voluntarily to Muslim lands in order to embrace Islam, but by far the largest category of converts appearing before the Inquisition consisted of Christians (mostly from Western Europe) who had been captured and taken to Muslim territory to be slaves. Their eventual return to Christendom could come about through ransoming, or escape, or recapture at sea. When they did reappear, and when it was known that they had converted to Islam, such people automatically came under the jurisdiction of the Inquisition, which now had the job of examining how they had committed the mortal sin of apostasy and whether they persisted in it. (Note, however, that a 'native' Muslim, born and brought up in that faith, was outside the Inquisitors' jurisdiction, and would come within it only if he or she expressed a wish to convert to Christianity.) It was very common for those Western Christians who had converted to Islam—so-called 'renegades'—to appear voluntarily before the Inquisition on their return to Christian territory. In many cases they were eager to undergo the process of being re-admitted into the Church, and even if they were not, it would have been highly prudent to go through the motions. Those who presented themselves in this way were classified as 'sponte comparentes', 'appearing of their own accord' (as opposed to those who appeared because of denunciations by others), and could look forward to more lenient treatment by the Inquisitors as a result. Nevertheless, they still had to expect their stories to be probed and tested. Thanks to the sheer quantity of such cases in the records of the Roman, Spanish and Portuguese Inquisitions, a mass of documentation was thus generated of the experiences of such Christian converts to Islam, supplying the basis for several major historical studies in recent decades.[6]

The central purpose of the questioning was to establish the degree of belief or commitment with which these people had become, and had for some time remained, Muslims. It mattered whether they had travelled to Muslim territory voluntarily or involuntarily, whether their adherence to Islam had been maximal or minimal, and so on. When, in 1592, the Archbishop of Cosenza wrote to the Inquisition in Rome, asking for advice on how to question a renegade who had asked to be reconciled to the Church, he received the following instructions: he was to tell the man to narrate the full story of his capture, to describe 'the actions, words and ceremonies they used when making him become a Muslim, and when circumcising him', to state the degree of force they used, and to say how long he stayed with the Muslims thereafter, 'whether he observed their false rites' and 'whether he ever departed in any way in his mind from the Holy Catholic Faith and adhered to the impious sect of Muhammad, and indeed whether he ever believed that anyone can be saved outside the bosom of the Holy Catholic Church'.[7] At those Inquisition tribunals where cases involving renegades were a regular occurrence, a body of standard questions was gradually assembled. In Naples, for instance, the basic questions about how the renegades had travelled there and back were supplemented from 1569 by one about whether they had eaten meat on Catholic fast days, from 1581 by more specific inquiries about the words pronounced at circumcision, about going to pray in mosques and about dressing in the Muslim way, and from 1596 by a question about whether they had believed that Islam was better than Christianity.[8]

Over time, the handbooks written for Inquisitors also made increasingly explicit allowance for degrees of coercion, whether absolute (actual torture) or conditional (threats).[9] Modern historical studies suggest that coercing Christians to become Muslims was not standard practice in Ottoman or North African society during this period; the general principle was that conversion should be properly voluntary. Some categories of captive could be exceptions to this rule, however. The most obvious one was children, whose consent was not required; others might include, for example, specialists such as armourers and shipwrights held in the North African ports, whose conversion was felt to be desirable as it might impede their return to Christendom. And, of course, in some cases ill-treatment by a Muslim master might be interpreted —if only retrospectively—as pressure to convert, even if that was not its real motive.[10] But even though the great majority of adult captives were not forced to convert to Islam, it is entirely understandable that renegades usually inserted such an element into their stories. As Lucia Rostagno has noted, most Inquisition judges in this period did work on the assumption that all renegades had converted under some kind of constraint. They assumed, therefore, that adherence to Islam was merely external unless they found clear proof of the contrary, and that the remorse was genuine in the case of any renegade who appeared of his or her own accord.[11]

One other category of people presenting themselves to the Inquisition raised a special set of considerations: Muslims, now held as slaves in Christendom, who said that they had been Christians originally, and sought to be received back into the Church. (Or, as it might be, to be received into this particular Church for the first time: some had been members of the Eastern Orthodox Church, which was a schismatic body in Roman Catholic eyes.) In such cases it was necessary to probe their memories of their earlier Christian practices, in order to establish the veracity of their accounts. Sometimes the applicant had been converted to Islam during childhood, which meant that the memories were scant at best; the Inquisitors were familiar with this problem, and did not press the matter unreasonably. A Muslim slave in a Christian land who returned (or converted) to Christianity did not thereby win his or her freedom. So long as such people had been non-Christians when enslaved, their slave-status was still secure; but they could, nevertheless, expect somewhat better treatment from a conscientious Christian master or mistress.[12] Much more fraught with practical implications were the cases of slaves who insisted that they had never been Muslims at all. If this could be proven, the Inquisition had the power, indeed the duty, to require them to be freed.

As has been mentioned already, some Inquisition tribunals built up a kind of institutional expertise in these matters because they dealt with such cases on a fairly frequent basis. Where the Roman Inquisition was concerned, the three major tribunals that were most experienced in these matters were those of Malta, Naples and Venice. These were, so to speak, on the 'front line' of human interactions—through commerce, corsairing and the slave-trade—with the Mediterranean Islamic world.[13] In the Venetian territory of Friuli, where the Inquisition was headquartered in Udine, there was much less general contact with the Islamic world, but one special factor brought some Muslims to the tribunal: the fortress-city of Palmanova (12 miles to the south of Udine), built by Venice in the 1590s as an outpost to defend them against possible attacks by

Ottoman Bosnian forces, was manned by soldiers from many parts of Europe, including some who had come originally—whether voluntarily or through capture and slavery—from the Ottoman Balkans.[14] As we shall see, a number of these would present themselves to the Inquisition for conversion or reversion to Catholic Christianity in the first half of the seventeenth century. Another place on the Mediterranean front line was Sicily, which, unlike its sister-territory, Naples, was under the Spanish Inquisition. Here the number of cases involving Islam was unusually high (732 out of a total of 2,985 recorded cases between 1560 and 1700, or 24.5 per cent).[15] Unfortunately, however, the original dossiers containing the transcripts of the trials were destroyed in 1783; all that survives, for the vast majority of cases, is the set of summary reports sent to the 'Suprema', the supreme council of the Spanish Inquisition, in Madrid. Although these give much less of the human *actualité* than the trial records would have done, they can still be informative; they have been searched thoroughly, but not in their entirety, for records of Albanians for this essay.[16] Similar searches have not been made in the records of the Spanish Inquisition elsewhere, or the Portuguese, in both of which Albanians are much less likely to feature; but the modern secondary literature produced by scholars who have worked intensively in their archives has been studied for traces of Albanians, with the result that two cases are included here.

The final question which must be asked before turning to the cases themselves is a simple one: can we be confident that these records really tell us what people said to the Inquisitors? The general answer is 'yes'. This does not mean that Inquisition records generally are flawless, non-distorting lenses through which we can stare directly at the past. Questions asked of suspected heretics might have the effect of moulding their beliefs to fit a form of heresy that pre-existed in the questioner's mind, failing to connect with those aspects of the suspect's beliefs that diverged from it. And where some folk-practices and superstitions were concerned, the educated clerical judges may have struggled to comprehend what was described to them, with similar distorting effects on the picture that emerged from their interrogations.[17] But although such issues have their analogues, in a minor way, in the questioning of converts to Islam (for example: 'Did you believe that Muhammad was God?'), such problems are much less pressing in these cases than they are in ones involving magical practices or obscure home-made heresies. In any case, the basic question about the reliability of the transcripts is very much easier to answer. The standard handbooks for inquisitors were notably clear about this. Eliseo Masini insisted that the scribe must 'write down everything that he [*sc.* the accused] answers'. He added that it was not good enough to record that accused people had replied affirmatively or negatively; it was necessary to 'have their replies, be they affirmative or negative, written down in their own words, in full detail'.[18] It does not follow, of course, that the records we now have are always the raw transcripts from the court-room; sometimes they are, but in some cases it is clear that they are fair-copy versions made at a later stage.[19] The actual wordings given may diverge to some extent from what was said, given that none of these scribes used shorthand. We can also note the recurrence of certain formulaic phrases, referring for example to returning 'to the bosom of the holy Church', which very probably reflect scribal habits and reflexes, rather than the language of the accused. But, once allowance has been made for minor details of that sort, it is still possible to agree that these tribunals were in principle devoted to what John Tedeschi has called 'the scrupulous recording of every word and gesture'. We can feel confident that, in the words of one recent study of the Venetian Inquisition, the responses of those questioned were recorded in a way that was 'more or less unfiltered'.[20] And where the documents give us the words of early modern Albanians, who are otherwise silent in almost all the records that archives can yield, such confidence is certainly worth having.

III

The first two cases to be considered here are untypical, for more than one reason. These people did not appear spontaneously. (In the second case, indeed, it is not clear whether the Albanians at the heart of the story appeared at all.) The tribunal was responding to denunciations concerning them; and the charges concerned things done outside the Albanian lands, which means that the Inquisitors had no reason to take any interest in their earlier lives. Both lack any direct quotations from the Albanians concerned, and the first is also rather uninformative because it comes from another branch of the Spanish Inquisition, the Barcelona tribunal of the Inquisition of the Crown of Aragon, where only the summary reports sent to the 'Suprema' survive. (The original dossiers were destroyed by a fire in 1820.)[21] Nevertheless, both are included here for the sake of relative completeness.

In 1590 a 26-year-old sailor named as 'Andrés' was brought before the tribunal in Barcelona. He was described as a Venetian, from a place called 'Dulsina'. This was very probably Ulcinj (Ital.: Dulcigno), the former Venetian possession on what is now the Montenegrin coast, even though the Inquisitors uncomprehendingly described it as 'near Venice'.[22] Given his age, he would have been a subject of Venice by birth; very possibly his family had left Ulcinj, taking their seven-year-old son with them, when it fell to the Ottomans in 1571. Ulcinj under Venetian rule had been both predominantly Catholic and (as it continued to be) largely Albanian-speaking, so we may guess that his name was Ndre.[23] The offence of which he was accused was sodomy—a crime which, anomalously, came under the jurisdiction of the Aragonese Inquisition, even though the rest of the Spanish Inquisition and the other Inquisitions all left it to the secular power.[24] According to the accusation brought against him, he had been in the port of Barcelona one evening when three teenaged boys approached him and asked if he could take them to Italy. He said that he could, and invited them to spend the night in a hut where he was staying. During the night he committed a sexual act on one of the boys while the others were asleep. The next day he took that boy, on a pretext, to another place and repeated the act; but the two others followed, and witnessed it. The boy was taken to a surgeon, who performed an examination and detected signs of violence; 'already the evil repute of this man was spreading through the port, because of what the boys had said about him', so he was seized and brought to the Inquisition.[25] Other witnesses then stated that he was notorious for soliciting among boys in the port of Sant Feliu de Guíxols, further up the coast. After he offered some unconvincing statements in his defence, he was subjected to 'light' torture, but during that 'he said nothing more than that he was telling the truth.' This brief account of his trial ends by saying that he was released. Without a sufficient number of adult witnesses (more than just the surgeon were needed), he could not be convicted unless he confessed, and the torture had not succeeded in making him do so.[26]

The second case comes from almost a century later, and from a very different social world. The surviving dossier, from the Venetian Inquisition, may possibly be incomplete, as it records the questioning of only one potentially guilty party in what was a more complex story. The case arose because a witness came of his own accord to the tribunal in February 1687. His name was given as 'Franciscus son of Nicolaus Pecich of Zagreb in Croatia' (so: Franjo Pečić), and he was described as living 'in the house of the Count Gegha, known in Italian as Georgius Bardi of Albania, in the Calle della Contessa, at St Martin's church.'[27] This was in a part of the Castello district of Venice, close to the Arsenal, popular with Slavs and people of other Balkan origins; the 'Scuola degli Schiavoni', a religious and social centre for Catholic Slavs, was only a few minutes' walk away.[28] Very little information is given in this document about the Albanian 'Count', whose name was presumably Gjergj Bardhi ('Gegha' here being a shortened form of 'Gjergj'). Possibly he was related to the famous Bardhi family of northern Albania which supplied priests to the Albanian Catholic Church over several generations; but that is a speculation, and one can only speculate too about the basis on which he was described as a Count. The name of the Countess was also given, Violante, and that of her brother, a Captain Andrea. The Bardhis lived in some comfort, maintaining a household that was a little microcosm of Venetian-Adriatic-Aegean world: its staff included not only the Croat Franjo Pečić, but a steward from Crete and a housekeeper from the Venetian Dalmatian town of Zadar.[29]

The story Pečić told was as follows.

My master, Count Giorgio Bardi of Albania, was seeking to recruit various soldiers from [or 'of'] this state, and the most excellent Signor Pietro Valier, one of the great *savi* of the Collegio, was opposed to this. A woman, called Catè [short for Caterina] Vicentina had come to the house, I don't know how, and through this Catè the Countess, and also Signor Count Giorgio, her husband, learned of the ability of another witch (I don't know her name, or where she lives) to bring it about that the most excellent Signor Pietro Valier would fall ill, so that he would not be able to go to the Collegio to oppose their desires. They could arrange for him to stay in bed until their request was granted. The said Count and Countess promised them 12 zecchini for doing this. And in fact the most excellent Signor Valier did fall ill soon afterwards. Some time after that, when Catè asked for the money she had been promised by the Count and the Countess, they found excuses for not giving it to her, saying that they were seeking the right to recruit two companies on the Terraferma [sc. Venetian territory on the Italian mainland], and that since they had not got that, they did not want to give her anything. So Catè said to them: 'Since you don't want to give me the money you promised, I shall get the witch to bring about the opposite of what she did.' And so soon afterwards the most excellent Signor Valier recovered and was able to go out.[30]

Pečić went on to explain the method that was used. Late in the previous year Captain Andrea, the Countess's brother, had gone to Padua, where he had arranged for two Franciscan friars (one Bulgarian, the other either Bosnian or Dalmatian) to celebrate nine Masses over a magnet. They later came to Venice and used holy oil to 'baptize' the magnet. 'And I know all these things because Captain Andrea confided in me about them. He told me that when the magnet is placed in a ring, if you touch someone's skin or clothes, whether it be a man or a woman, the person you have touched cannot fail to do what you wish.'[31] The Inquisitors did summon Caterina, who admitted merely that she knew the Count and Countess and had been at their house several times. She was dismissed with a warning, and it seems that no further action was taken against any of the parties. We learn very little, therefore, about Giorgio Bardi's life and activities; but since these events happened after Venice had joined the 'Holy League' against the Ottomans in 1684, we can at least reasonably assume that he was working as a sort of entrepreneur-condottiere, hoping to be paid a satisfactory sum per head for the soldiers he recruited.

IV

All the other cases involve apostasy from Christianity, and/or reception into the Catholic Church. In some of them, as we shall see, the Inquisitors probed the person's story, applying a whole list of standard questions. Yet people in one category received relatively cursory treatment: military men in the service of the state. The Venetian Republic, with its many connections with the Ottoman Balkans, did not exclude Muslims from the ranks of the soldiers hired by its own recruiting-officers, but was of course happy in principle if they became Christians.

To modern eyes, their adherence to Islam might seem to raise a question-mark about their loyalty to Venice in the event of a war against the Ottoman Empire; there were long periods of peace between these two powers, however, and in any case soldiers of fortune were not known for their religious devotion.

At the tribunal of Venice itself, three Albanian soldiers presented themselves on separate occasions in 1628. In June 'Paulus, son of Petrus of Shkodër, aged 20, a soldier in the armed vessels' (so: Pal, son of Pjetër) appeared and asked to be reconciled to the Catholic Church.[32] He told his story as follows.

> Roughly seven years ago I was enslaved by 'Turks' ['turchi': but the primary meaning in this context was 'Muslims'], and stayed among them for roughly six months with my feet chained. By force and threats they made me deny the holy Christian faith, threatening to cut off my head. But although I denied it with my mouth, I did not do so in my heart. And as soon as I could, I fled from them, and came here to serve the most serene Republic of Venice; I have served it for roughly six years, and still do so, living in the Catholic way, and in particular observing the vigils and fasts instituted by the holy Church.[33]

His case was processed there and then. He was told to abjure his apostasy and any other heresies or errors, and to confess his sins as soon as possible. In addition, he was to perform the penance of reciting the Lord's Prayer three times a day, and a Hail Mary three times a week, for a period of six months—an unusually light penance for the grave sin of apostasy, but perhaps a realistic maximum for someone of his way of life. Pal then made his abjuration, according to a standard formula— no doubt repeated by him as it was read out—and, 'because I don't know how to write', signed the document with a cross.[34] This was a very straightforward case. His credentials as a former Catholic did not need to be tested, as Shkodër was well known to be a major centre of Catholicism; and the fact—or, at least, claim— that he had been only thirteen years old when he converted reduced the need to probe his thinking at the time. Whether he did really experience such severe intimidation must be doubted; any slave was a commodity with a significant monetary value, and it is very hard to imagine that his master would have decapitated him merely for a refusal to change faith. But the story fits a known pattern in a more general way, in that Ottoman Muslim practice did not require boys of this age to consent to their conversion. And that was a pattern with which the Inquisitors would also have been familiar.

Three months later another soldier appeared, also aged 20. His name was recorded as 'Alexander Corbinensius, an Albanian, son of the late Joannes' (so: Lekë, son of Gjon or Gjin); he was, as the description indicated, from the small and predominantly Catholic region of Kurbin, located between Krujë and Lezhë.[35] The scribe also noted that he spoke through an interpreter, a 28-year-old soldier named as Nicolaus Tanami. Alexander's story was similar, and even briefer: 'seven years ago I was seized by Muslims, and forcefully detained by them for three weeks; by force too they made me deny the holy faith, which I did against my will. And the next morning I ran away. And because I've been a soldier for all this time, I haven't had the opportunity to present myself sooner.'[36] His case too was dealt with very swiftly; he was to confess, and as a penance he was required to say a corona of the Blessed Virgin Mary once a month for a year. (This involved a sequence of recitations of the Lord's Prayer once and the Hail Mary ten times.) The abjuration, with a note explaining that he had recited it as it was translated for him phrase by phrase, was once again signed by the penitent with the mark of a cross.[37]

The third of these soldiers appeared in December, and was recorded as 'Blasius Matagusius from Lezhë, son of the late Paulus, a soldier, aged roughly 68'. The town of Lezhë (Ital.: Alessio) was historically Catholic, though by this time there were only 170 Catholic families there, greatly outnumbered by the Muslim population.[38] This man's Christian name would have been Vlash or Vllas (the Albanian form of the saint's name); and the surname indicates that his family was originally from Mataguži (Alb.: Matagushë), a village—now a small town—on the northern side of lake Shkodër. In this case too the amount of information given was minimal. 'Having been born and brought up a Catholic, I was seized by trickery by Muslims roughly sixteen or seventeen years ago, who made me a Muslim, circumcising me and making me raise my finger. I remained among those Muslims all that time, living in accordance with their rites and performing their ceremonies, even though in my heart I always wanted to return to the holy Catholic faith and live as a Christian [or: "Catholic"].'[39] Raising the index finger of one's right hand and reciting the *shahada* (the Muslim declaration of faith) was the central component of the conversion ritual, and would have been sufficiently well known not to require any further explanation. The use of force was not even suggested by this account; yet the Inquisitors did not pause to enquire what sort of 'trickery' might have induced a man of 51 or 52 to convert to Islam, and simply decided to let him make his abjuration. His penance was to confess three times a year for two years, and to recite a corona of the Blessed Virgin Mary once a month during that period. Just one other detail of interest is provided in this brief record: the procedure was witnessed by 'Peter of Shkodër, son of the late Dominic, the *alfiere* [ensign or standard-bearer —a rank roughly equivalent to second lieutenant]'. A further note describes Peter himself as the *alfiere*.[40] This may have been the father of the 'Paul, son of Peter of Shkodër, aged 20' who had come to the Tribunal in June; in fact it is possible that in all three cases we are seeing members of the same company of soldiers, whose re-conversion may have been recommended by this particular officer. And their sequential appearance suggests that the Inquisition's policy of lenient treatment was the indeed right one, so far as encouragement to come forward was concerned.

Eighteen months later, another soldier of Catholic origin appeared; the evidence does not indicate whether he had any connection with the previous three. It was in June 1630 that 'Nicolaus, son of the late Lech [so: Nikollë, son of Lekë], from the village of Fand in Albania, a soldier, who seems from his appearance to be roughly 40' presented himself.[41] 'Fand' was Fan (often given as 'Fanti' or 'Fandi' in Italian writings), located in a district about 25 miles north-east of Lezhë which was inhabited by a strongly Catholic (and famously hard-fighting) *fis* or clan of the same name.[42] This man spoke through an interpreter, and his statement was as brief as that of any of his predecessors: 'Having been baptized a Christian, I was then enslaved by the Muslims roughly twelve years ago. I was imprisoned, and forced by them to deny the holy faith and to become a Muslim—which I did, and I observed the religion of the Muslims for all that time, and did everything that the other Muslims do. I finally came to Venice roughly one month ago, and I have always wanted to return to the bosom of the holy Church.'[43] His abjuration quickly followed. He was told to confess twice yearly for two years, and once a month to recite the Lord's Prayer once and Hail Mary five times; and he too signed the document with his mark, a simple cross.[44]

V

Another group of three soldiers appeared before the Venice tribunal in 1644–5; it is not clear whether there were any connections between them. The recorded statement of one of them is similar in style and brevity to that of the previous ones. 'Ioannes [or "Giovanni"], son of the late Nicolaus Isin of Musia in the district of Lezhë' (so: Gjon or Gjin, son of Nikollë—and the family name may have been Ishëm), appeared in February 1645. He was described as 'a soldier, aged roughly thirteen, in the company commanded by Georgius Criamchus [or: Criamchi], from Albania', and came with an interpreter, 'Marco Ise, son of the late Antonius from Merchina [*sc.* Mërqia], a soldier.'[45] To modern eyes, thirteen seems a very low age for soldiering; but there are many other references to boys of a similar age, who, attached to military units whether as trainees or as servants, were regularly described as soldiers. His story was as follows:

> After the death of my mother, Elena, a Catholic woman, and also of my father, I
> was taken nine years ago to Ishëm, a fortress of the Turks, which was under the
> power of Elez Bey, the *sancakbeyi*, in order to serve him. And since my father
> had become a Muslim because of the many taxes which the Turks imposed on
> the Christians, so he persuaded me, his son, to become a Muslim, being of such
> tender years that I did not know what I was doing. And so I stayed for six years
> in his household; after that I have been here and there in the Ottoman lands,
> always living in the way that the other Muslims do. And one of my uncles, who

is a priest, don Nicola Zigni, has given me instruction and teaching, and has persuaded me to return to the Catholic Christian religion. For even while I was living in the Muslim way, I always kept up the good intention of wanting to return to the holy Christian faith.[46]

Such assurances about the 'intention' of a young child may have seemed rather superfluous. The abjuration was quickly made; he was required to confess twice a year, and say a corona of the Blessed Virgin Mary once a week.[47]

The other two cases are a little more informative. In September 1645 there appeared 'Nicolaus son of the late Joannes Bassan of Sopot in Epirus, near Himarë, a soldier, who from his appearance is thought to be aged 55' (so: Nikollë, son of Gjon or Gjin); he used as his interpreter 'Simon Suma from Krujë, chaplain in the Order of Franciscan Friars'.[48] Suma was from a well-known northern Albanian family which supplied priests to the Catholic Church over several centuries; he himself would serve as Bishop of Sappa (a diocese to the north of Lezhë and south-east of Shkodër) from 1647 to 1673.[49] But the soldier's own background was quite different, as he explained.

My father and mother were Greek, but Orthodox, and I stayed with my father and mother until I was roughly 30, living as a Christian, but an Orthodox one. It happened that the Sultan built a town near my village; it is called Sopot, and all the area round about is called by that name, Sopot. And since the Sultan wanted to make all the Christians—not only the Catholics, but the Greek Orthodox— pay a large amount of money in tax, I became a Muslim to avoid it, as I didn't have the means to pay it. So I went to the Muslim parish priest (they call him 'hoxha' [Trk.: *hoca*], which means parish priest), in the mosque, and without circumcising me or doing anything else, they made me raise the index finger of my right hand, and made me say these words: 'la ilà, i le là, Maomet, erusulà' [*sc.* 'La ilaha illa Allah wa-Muhammad rasul Allah'], which in our language means 'God is God alone, and Muhammad is his prophet.' And he gave me the name 'Ali'. And so I lived as a Muslim, following their rite in everything, until now, when I arrived at Venice. But I never believed their doctrines, and never thought that that was the right faith; on the contrary, I lived always with the intention of returning to the Christian faith. I arrived in Venice fifteen days ago, and having had the opportunity to discuss this with Father Bartolomeo of Verona, a Capuchin, who is here now, I've been even more persuaded by his instruction to become a Catholic of the Greek rite, as is permitted by the Roman Church.[50]

The motive for conversion to Islam given here—avoiding the tax on Christians, the *haraç* or *cizye*—was the same as that attributed to Nikollë Isin by his son in the previous example. The version given here of the *shahada*, and the explanation of its meaning, were both remarkably accurate, in comparison with other such

reports by people brought up outside Islam. And the claim about not being circumcised is corroborated by other known cases of adult converts to Islam.[51]
Certainly the Venetian Inquisitors did not query this point. Nikollë Bassan was
allowed to make his abjuration (which he did, 'but in the Epirot or Albanian language, through the aforementioned interpreter'), and ordered to take Holy
Communion four times a year, and to say a corona every week for three years.[52]

The other Venetian case of a soldier in the mid-1640s involved a former
Catholic from the northern part of Albania. In August 1644 the Inquisition dealt
with 'Georgius son of the late Georgius Bastara, from Bastara [sc. Bastar], from
Krujë, which is an Albanian bishopric, and of the late Maria, his wife'; Georgius
(Gjergj) was described as roughly 24 years old, a soldier serving in the company
of Michael Illamas, an Albanian.[53] He came from a place where, as we happen to
know, Christianity was undergoing a catastrophic decline during just this period:
in the early 1640s all the Christian men in the village of Bastar converted to Islam,
leaving just 300 Catholic women.[54] Gjergj Bastar told his story as follows.

I was born in the district of Bastar, a town in Albania, of Catholic Christian
parents. My father was called Zorzi [Venetian for 'Giorgio'—so: Gjergj], and my
mother was called Maria. I lived in that place, Bastar, with my father and mother
until I was eleven. They died, and I had only two brothers, who were married; as
they were poor, they did not want the bother of looking after me. So I had to
leave my house, and I went to the Pasha's town [sc. Krujë?] in Albania, which
was one day's travel from my place, and under the rule of the Turks. And there,
while I was looking for a master in order to get a living, as an eleven-year-old, I
was seen and summoned by a Muslim called Mema. And when he asked me
what sort of person I was, I replied that I was a Christian. And then he just said
that he didn't want any Christians. But the following morning that Muslim took
me, and led me to one of their mosques, and made me convert to Islam by
force—that is, when I refused to deny my faith, he threatened to inflict special
tortures on me. He said he would have little pointed sticks put under my nails,
and would burn my hands and feet with fire, and then have me tied up to the
beams of the house and subjected to smoke. So, a poor boy, and terrified (as I've
said, I was only eleven years old), I decided to convert to Islam. This is how it
went: they made me say some words which in Italian mean 'God be praised', and
then some other devilish words that I don't remember, making me hold up the
index finger of my right hand. But they didn't circumcise me. And I stayed with
the Muslims until I was 20, living in the Muslim way, except that I didn't eat
meat on Fridays or Saturdays, as I remembered the faith which I had professed
in holy baptism. However, I never believed in the Muslim sect, and I never put
my trust in their religion and ceremonies. I always kept the holy Christian faith
alive in my heart, wanting to reunite myself with the holy apostolic Roman
Church—so much so that I found a way of fleeing from there, as I did, and I

came to the district of Sukë, where there are both Muslims and Christians. There I began to learn the craft of a blacksmith from a Muslim. I was still living as a Muslim, and I stayed with him for the space of two years. I was intending to live as a Christian, and I although I presented myself openly as a Muslim I did so because I was afraid of being burnt alive in Muslim territory; but in my heart I was a Christian. From there, after those two years, I joined the company of Captain Michael (who has already been mentioned) at the [river] Erzen in Albania. And then we came to Kotor, and once the company was completed there, we then came to Venice. Then we went into the field, and now I am serv-ing on the armed vessel here in Venice. Now, as I still maintain that desire to be welcomed again into the bosom of the holy Church, I have gone to the house of catechumens, to be instructed in matters of our holy faith.[55]

The Inquisitors allowed him to make his abjuration, and instructed him to con-fess his sins for three years, to take the eucharist four times a year, and to recite one corona each week. The text of the abjuration, which he signed with the mark of a cross, added one further point of detail: he said that 'having been baptized, but then having been made a slave of the Muslims, I denied the holy faith.'[56] Since he had not even mentioned this in his main narrative, the modern reader might almost suspect that the word 'slave' here was used in an extended, non-literal sense. Nevertheless, it probably did bear its literal meaning. For one important point that emerges from several of these narratives is that casual enslavement was a common feature of life in the Ottoman territories—as some of the cases dis-cussed later in this essay will demonstrate.

VI

During the period when those six military men presented themselves to the Inquisition in Venice, a much larger number of Muslim Albanians came before the Friulian tribunal.[57] They too were serving the Venetian state, as members of the garrison of the fortress-town of Palmanova, and their reception into the Roman Catholic Church was likewise fast-tracked by the authorities. In 29 cases they were taken to be 'native' Muslims, changing faith for the first time; these were recorded simply as baptisms, with no attempt to investigate their previous history, even though in some cases their fathers had what were clearly Christian names.[58] (Likewise, the Friulian Inquisition also recorded the transition to Roman Catholicism of six Albanian soldiers who were members of the Greek Orthodox Church.)[59] Twenty-one Muslim Albanian soldiers appeared as 'rene-gades' from Christianity, now seeking forgiveness and readmission; but the records of their interrogations are mostly much more summary than those taken in Venice. In some cases they yield very little information beyond the name, age and place of origin of the person concerned. The ways in which these men had been converted to Islam are typically glossed over in a sentence or two (or less), and frequently there is almost nothing to be gleaned about the person's life more generally. Both for that reason and because many of these documents have been presented in a modern scholarly edition, the account given here will be more selective, concentrating on the substantive details that are given in some cases.

With only one exception, all of the Muslim Albanians in these records appeared in the period 1631–45. The outlier, both chronologically and in terms of the amount of detail given, was a case of 1617. This concerned a 20-year-old soldier named as Giorgio, son of Steffano (Gjergj, son of Shtjefën). He described his place of origin as 'Rumoli, a district under the rule of the Sultan'; the scribe summarized that he was from 'Rumoli, in Albania', but it is not clear whether he was giving a particular Albanian place-name (if so, perhaps Rrumullak, a village just to the south of Peqin), or whether he was referring to Rumeli, the general name of a large part of the Sultan's Balkan territories, of which the Albanian lands formed a part.[60] His account was as follows:

> I was born in Rumoli, a district under the rule of the Sultan. My father and mother were Greek Christians, and I was raised and brought up in the Greek faith until about the age of five. Then, while I was playing with other boys in the public street, I was forcibly seized by a Muslim and put on the back of the horse of another Muslim, who was there on horseback. I was bound, taken with perhaps 500 other boys to Istanbul and put to work in a garden. And three days later I was taken to the Muslim mosque, where I was circumcised together with the others: the Muslims made me deny the Christian faith and, lifting up my finger in the Muslim way, say in the Turkish language that there was only one God and Muhammad was his prophet. After that I always lived with them in the Muslim way, eating meat every day, and doing all the things that the other Muslims did, as they were ordered to by their master. About 15 months ago, having talked with some other Christians who found themselves there as slaves, I bought a file and cut through the iron fetters that held us; then we fled together, making our way first to Tinos and then to Crete.[61]

At this point, Gjergj was made to swear on the Bible that he was telling the truth—and his interpreter, similarly, that he was translating correctly. Clearly the Inquisitors had some doubts about Gjergj's sincerity. They went on to ask him whether he had come spontaneously to their tribunal, driven only by his own conscience, or whether he was acting 'out of fear, or the persuasion of others'; but he insisted that he had been motivated all along to return to Christianity, adding that 'on two other occasions I fled in order to come and live among Christians, but each time I was caught again, until finally it pleased God to free me.' Finally, two days later, he was permitted to make his abjuration.[62] That supplementary

remark about his repeated attempts to escape helps to explain the otherwise puzzling claim that he had been kept in irons; for almost every detail of his account
suggests that he was a Janissary, and Janissaries were not normally subjected to
such treatment. His description of being taken to Istanbul with hundreds of other
boys must surely have been a reference to the *devşirme* (the 'collection' of boys for
Janissary and other official service); in theory the officers who gathered the boys
were meant to deal with their parents, but it is easy to suppose that the practice
often fell short of that. Only the age of five strikes a surprising note, though even
this is not impossible to believe. In the late sixteenth century there are references
to boys as young as eight being taken, and one Venetian bailo's report, of 1576,
gave the minimum age as six; a sturdy five-year-old might well have had his age
overestimated, and in any case Gjergj's testimony, like that of many of these
Albanians when stating their own ages, was only approximate.[63]

Where several of the other Albanian soldiers at Palmanova were concerned,
being 'taken' by the 'Turks' or Muslims at a very early age (not in the *devşirme*, but
in some entirely local and ad hoc way) was the explanation they gave for their
adherence to Islam. 'Chusain' (Hüseyin), formerly Doda, an eighteen-year-old
from 'Medua' (Shëngjin, on the coast just to the north of Lezhë), explained that
'when I was a little boy in the cradle, I was seized by Muslims and brought up by
them in that accursed sect of Muhammad; I followed it until I was told by my
relatives that I was baptized, and was born of a Christian father and a Christian
mother.'[64] 'Halli' (Ali), formerly 'Ducha' (Duka), a sixteen- or seventeen-year-old
from 'Pile, in the province of Chucci' (the village of Piluri in Himarë, roughly four
miles from Kuç), said that Muslims had taken him from his parents when he was
three, and had brought him up for the next thirteen years. 'And after this became
known to my relatives [or: parents], I escaped, and went to my father's house, in
order to take refuge. But they were afraid of being punished by the Turks [or:
Muslims], and told me that they couldn't keep a renegade in their house, and that
I should return to Christianity first. I wasn't sure which side to take, and at that
moment Captain Giambattista Stamati arrived to recruit soldiers, so I set off with
him to come to Italy.'[65] 'Giovanni', son of 'Tomaso Todero', from Shkodër, a
30-year-old, said that although all his family were Catholics he had lived as a
Muslim since he was a 'small boy', having been 'seized by Turks [or: Muslims],
and instructed in that sect by them'.[66] A seventeen-year-old from 'Gioriami' (perhaps the small Catholic village in the archdiocese of Durrës described as 'Giorai'
in one Franciscan report, or possibly the village on the coast just below Ulcinj,
called called 'Gerami' or 'Gierano'), whose name was 'Eless' (Elez), formerly
'Gregorio', explained his apostasy as follows: 'when I was a boy of five or six, the
Turks [or: Muslims] came into our house, and they began to persuade me that
their faith was good, and better than the Christian one. So, having been brought
up by them, and by their falsehood, I committed that error.'[67] In that particular
case, the circumstances of the boy's removal from his home are quite unclear.

In the cases of three soldiers (aged 18, 20 and 22 respectively), baptism as a Christian had been followed, from a very early age, by a Muslim upbringing, for the simple reason that their parents—or, at least, fathers—had converted to Islam soon after they were born. When questioned, 'Istref', baptized as 'Iuanne' (Gjon or Gjin), said: 'my father was called Hüseyin, and I don't remember my mother's name, as I was taken away when I was little and brought up by Muslims; my father also belonged to that sect, and I was baptized by a priest.' The summary report on this case, preserved in another document, clarifies this otherwise very puzzling account, describing the father as 'formerly a Christian, and now a Muslim'.[68] Similarly, the record of the interrogation of 'Allì' (Ali), baptized as 'Gianni' (Gjon or Gjin), records merely that both his parents were Muslims. Asked how he knew that he had been baptized, he replied: 'my mother told me that I was baptized at the church of St Mary in Dusda by a local priest.' The summary, however, adds the qualification that his parents were 'both now Muslims, but previously Christians'.[69] And the third such case was that of 'Curto' (Kurd), whose Christian name was given as 'Zuanne' (Gjon or Gjin), a 22-year-old whose place of origin was not stated. He explained that his father's name was Hüseyin, 'and he was a Muslim'; he did not know his mother's name, as she had died when he was a very young child. Here too the summary report adds that his father was 'formerly a Christian, and now a Muslim'.[70]

In several other cases it seems most likely that the individual's conversion to Islam took place some time before the threshold age—in the early-to-mid-teens— at which, in the view of Muslims, full consent became necessary. A nineteen-year-old called Mustafa, formerly Gregorio, from 'Marsen in Albania' (perhaps Masnë or Mashnë, a village in the Spaç region, four miles to the west of Kçirë), explained: 'When I was left at home without my father or my mother, and with no other relative, a Turk [or: Muslim] came and took me away, and so when I was in his service he made me deny the Christian faith by force and trickery.'[71] Asan (Hasan), formerly 'Giovanni' (Gjon or Gjin), a sixteen-year-old from Janicat in Himarë, said: 'As I was poor, I entered the service of a Turk, as is normal in that region; I committed the error [of apostasy] because I was both tempted and threatened by my master, not having any other clear understanding.'[72] Entering the service of a 'Turk' does seem to have been a common practice. Two Albanian soldiers who presented themselves to the Tribunal in 1631, 'Nicolo Trumpsi' from 'Zueme' (possibly Zhym, a village five miles south of Lushnjë), aged 18, and 'Giovanni Pelessa' from Lezhë, aged 17, told almost identical stories: each had converted to Islam during his childhood, while working as a 'serving-boy' to a 'Turk'.[73] Whether both 'force' and 'trickery' were used in these cases was not stated. Andrea, son of the late 'Zorzi' (Gjergj) Stoiani, from Lezhë, a 22-year-old, said only that when he was twelve years old he was 'tricked by the Turks' into abandoning Christianity.[74] Another Hasan, formerly Francesco (Frang), aged fifteen, from Renesi (a village roughly eight miles south-east of Shkodër), gave a very brief account of his own apostasy, alleging only coercion but referring to a time of festivities when other factors may possibly have been at work: 'When I was attending Bayram [the Islamic festival of Eid], a spahi forced me to deny the faith.'[75] And the 20-year-old Sinan, formerly 'Demetrio' (Dhimitër), from 'Pichera' (Piqeras, in Himarë), simply said that he had converted 'because of the coercion and false promises of the Muslims'. (His testimony adds, however, two interesting details about his return to Christianity: he said that he had been persuaded by the exhortations of his 'fellow soldiers', and that he had received instruction from the Capuchin friar Bartolomeo of Verona—the person who, as we have seen, would be giving similar instruction to Nikollë of Sopot four years later.)[76] Coercion of some kind is mentioned in most of these accounts, but the frequent twinning of 'force' with 'trickery' (a term which seems to have referred to positive induce-ments), albeit rather formulaic in character, does suggest that sheer compulsion was seldom claimed, even in retrospect, to have been the only factor.

In four cases a more specific historical context is given or suggested. 'Schender' or 'Scanderbe' (Skender or Skenderbey/Skanderbeg), formerly 'Giovanni' (Gjon or Gjin), who was in his early thirties in 1639, was from the village of Borsh in Himarë. Asked how old he was when he converted, he said: 'I was fourteen or fif-teen when, oppressed by the Sultan's forces, I was taken away by force and, also with violence, made to commit apostasy, because they had rebuilt a fortress, and not only I but all the people living round about were forced to deny the faith in order to become the garrison of the fortress.'[77] This presumably relates to either of two fortresses which may have been undergoing restoration in the early 1620s after one of many Ottoman campaigns to subjugate the district of Himarë: Sopot or Kardhiq. (Something of this kind was suggested, as we have seen, by the testi-mony of Nikollë Bassan at the Venice tribunal, which also mentioned an Ottoman building programme near Sopot in c.1620.)[78] Very possibly that same campaign is referred to in the cases of the other three men. In 1641 two soldiers from Himarë appeared before the Inquisition in Palmanova: Hasan, formerly 'Gin Chiurchio', a 40-year-old from Borsh, and Ali, formerly 'Nichagion Billimeila', aged 45, from 'Exculat' or 'Exalat' (Zhulat, a village to the west of Kardhiq, roughly seven miles from Borsh). They stated that approximately 20 years earlier, 'when Haderbeg [Hayder Bey] came into our region, forced by his violence, we committed that grave error, having more fear of the wrath of a barbarous earthly judge than of God.'[79] And in 1643 a 60-year-old, 'Haso' (Hasan?), formerly 'Giorgio', from 'Solette in Albania' (perhaps Zhulat again), testified that 'roughly twenty years' earlier, 'when a *sancakbeyi* came to his region, he took him away by force and made him convert.'[80] Himarë formed part of the *sancak* of Delvinë; so it seems that at some time in the early 1620s a punitive expedition was launched against it by the *sancakbeyi*, Hayder Bey, who took special measures both to quell the popu-lation of the region and to rebuild and garrison one of the local strategic strong-holds. The history of Himarë in this period is, unfortunately, poorly documented;

there is some evidence of anti-Ottoman action in 1618, leading to punitive forced conversions by the Ottoman authorities, but the details are obscure.[81]

Specific reasons for conversion to Islam were given in just two other cases. In the first of these, heard at Palmanova and involving a man who was presumably a retired soldier, the explanation was humdrum: 'Duca Gini' (his Muslim name was not given), from Borsh, described in one document as a 50-year-old and in another as a 70-year-old, had converted to Islam when he was 20 to avoid 'contributing my temporal goods and taxes to the Sultan'—in other words, paying the *haraç* or *cizye*.[82] The other case was more unusual. 'Vhisain' (Hüseyin), formerly 'Prens' (Prenk?), a 20-year-old whose parents had been Roman Catholics, was described by the scribe as 'from the city of Lezhë'; he himself said he was born in 'Arfandam, in Albania', a place (later given by the scribe as 'Derfandam') which was apparently near Lezhë, but is hard to identify. Asked why he had committed apostasy, he replied: 'My brother killed a man in that district and ran away; so for that reason the Turks came to Derfandam to carry out justice, and when they didn't find that brother of mine, they took me by force to Lezhë, and there they used violence to make me deny the holy faith.'[83] Here only speculation is possible about those aspects of the story that Hüseyin may have glossed over or omitted. Simply converting a brother to Islam, which would confer certain social advantages on him, was not obviously a way to carry out justice or vengeance against any Christian malefactor. Possibly Hüseyin was seized to be taken into servitude and, being below the threshold age, was converted without his consent. But it is also conceivable that the 'Turks' took him in order to punish him in place of his brother, and that he converted because he knew that that was the only way to save his own life.

Where the 'native' Muslims were concerned, the process seems to have been a very straightforward one; as was mentioned above, there was apparently no attempt to probe their personal stories. Places of origin are mentioned in a list of baptisms of Muslims between 1643 and 1647 which includes ten Albanians (plus one who was from Bar, described geographically as 'Bar in Albania', but who is excluded from the total given here): almost all of them were from the Himarë region, together with Dukat and Vlorë.[84] In each of these ten cases the name was recorded of the person's godfather at his baptism; sometimes the captain of the soldier's company performed this role, but local dignitaries also took part. When 'Captain Ali, a Muslim from Sopot, aged roughly 30, who has left his wife and three other sons there' was baptized together with his two eldest sons (aged 'roughly fourteen' and 'roughly twelve'), their godfathers were, respectively, Geronimo Civran, the general in command of Palmanova (in whose honour Ali took Geronimo as his Christian name), Geronimo Dandolo, the treasurer of the fortress, and Danilo Dotto, the governor of the town.[85] This followed a familiar pattern: six years earlier, when three soldiers from Vlorë, Himarë and Bastia had been baptized, the then holders of those three high offices had served as individual godfathers, while 'the most illustrious lady Beatrice dal Monte' had acted as godmother to all three.[86] The sponsoring of converts from Islam by nobles, grandees and prelates, which could also involve bestowing one's own family name upon the convert, was something of a fashion in Italy during this period; as we shall see, one such case would involve an Albanian whose godfather was none other than the Viceroy of the Kingdom of Naples.[87]

Finally, the Inquisition also handled six cases of Albanians who wanted to switch from the Orthodox Church to the Roman Catholic one. Here too the documentation was very summary, giving little more than names and places. One of the men may have belonged to the Serbian Orthodox Church: 'Giorgio', son of 'Nicolò Deplaua' from the region of Lezhë, whose family name suggests an origin in Plav, in Montenegro.[88] Of the other five, one was from the little port of Bastia, next to Sagiada on the coast of Çamëri, and four were from Himarë. All of these must have been members of the Greek Church, even though the Inquisition record in one case used the phrase 'of the Rascian [sc. Serbian] rite'—a term for the Orthodox Church that would have been in common use when dealing with Slavs from the Eastern Adriatic.[89]

VII

In July 1586 a young Albanian man presented himself to the Inquisition tribunal in Naples. He was described as 'Stradus Strayl, from the village of Maura near Vlorë, Greek Orthodox, aged 22'; his father, Dimitro (Dhimitër), was from Maura, and his mother, Marula, was from 'Treboulo'.[90] ('Maura' was probably Mavrovë, a village roughly seven miles south-east of Vlorë; 'Treboulo' is not easily identifiable, unless it was 'Dropull', the valley south of Gjirokastër, more than 40 miles away.) His story began as follows: 'Roughly ten years ago, when my father died, I left home and went to Vlorë, among the Muslims, and got a job as a servant to a Janissary, a renegade from Christianity. I obeyed him in everything that he ordered me to do, as I was then about twelve years old, and still one of the Sultan's vassals and tribute-payers.'[91] The Inquisitors then asked him how he had denied his faith.

> After about five years of persuasion by the man I mentioned, my master, and by the people of his household, and with a promise to treat me well, and other enticements, they brought me to the point of denying the holy Catholic faith— even though I always refused to deny it in my mind. And so one day, suddenly, I was seized by some Muslims and they circumcised me, according to the practice and rites of Islam; and before I was circumcised they made me say the words they use for the denial which they make Christians perform with the right index finger raised: 'ayllala yllala la mahometa resulala.' But I don't know what those

words mean. And they gave me the name 'Suleiman', and they told me that I had left the Christian faith and taken the Muslim religion.[92]

Unlike the Venetian or Friulian Inquisitors, the Neapolitan ones were not dealing in this case with someone in the military service of their state; so instead of proceeding rapidly to his abjuration, they went through the regular list of questions. After the conversion, had he then performed the observances of Islam? Yes, he had. Did he hold Muhammad to be God, or a prophet? No: 'I regarded Muhammad not as God, nor as a prophet, but only as a holy man.' Did he eat meat on the days when it was prohibited by the Church? Yes. Did he eat pork? No, never. Did he go to the mosque, alone or accompanied, and did he pray there? 'I did go into the mosque, given that I was accompanying my master, but I didn't pray, nor did I perform those actions towards Muhammad which they performed.' Did he ever pray to Muhammad? Yes: 'when I went to bed, I said the Muslim prayer, like this, according to the Muslim practice: "Cugliualla semet Iuuellet hala semet." Those are the only words I know, and I don't know what they mean.'[93] Did he dress as a Muslim? 'I went about dressed in the Muslim way, as I couldn't do otherwise.' After he reached Christian territory, what faith did he practise? 'Always, up to the present, I have practised the Christian religion, because I am a Christian, and I want to die a true Catholic Christian.' And how long ago had he arrived in Christendom? 'About four years ago I came to Christian territory from Vlorë, as I was sold to an Albanian, and then sold by him once more to another merchant at Otranto, and finally I was sold to signor Dr Carlo Borrello; I am now in his power, in his household.'[94]

Only with that very last sentence does it become clear that, at some point between the ages of twelve and seventeen, he had become a slave. Possibly this occurred when he first entered the service of his Janissary master; or perhaps there was a gradual progression from a *de facto* status to a *de jure* one. Standard accounts of slavery in the Ottoman Empire discuss the three obvious methods of enslavement: the *devşirme* or formal 'collection' of Christian boys for Janissary and other official service; capture in war; and being seized by raiding-parties outside the Empire (especially by Barbary corsairs in the Mediterranean region, and by Tatar raiders in the Polish, Ukrainian and Russian lands). But they say very little about the more casual methods of drawing people within the Ottoman Empire—mostly, but not only, children and adolescents—into slavery, which may have supplied a significantly larger proportion of the slave population than any modern study has yet acknowledged.

Those methods could take various forms. Perhaps the most obvious consisted of ordinary slave-raiding, with the sole difference that it was carried out by Muslim Ottoman subjects against non-Muslim ones within the Empire. One example of this can be found in the records of the Portuguese Inquisition. In April 1579 a man aged roughly 40 appeared before the tribunal in Lisbon; he was described as 'Gino [sc. Gjin], an Albanian born in Negroponte', and he came with 'Carlos the Armenian' as his interpreter (most likely translating from Turkish).[95] Negroponte was the Italian name for Euboea, the long island flanking the east coast of mainland Greece to the north of Athens. It had been under Venetian rule from 1390 until its conquest by Mehmed II in 1470, and during that period Venice had encouraged Albanians to go and live there, where they supervened on earlier patterns of Albanian settlement in the region.[96] The record of this case is summary, and it reports Gino's statements in the form of a brief narrative, rather than citing them directly. It begins by describing his capture: 'Eighteen years ago, when he was taking sheep to sell in Istanbul, as he was the son of a shepherd, the Turks seized him and put him on their galley, which was based at Rhodes. And he was a rower there for fourteen years, while always remaining a Christian.'[97] The dating puts his age at the time of capture at approximately 22; this was not the absorption of a young boy into a system of obligatory labour in return for protection, but rather a hostile act against an adult, no different in character from raiding in non-Ottoman territories. What makes it worse, to modern eyes at least, is the fact that not only were the captors subjects of the Sultan just like their victim, but they were also working in the service of the state. In 1574, after those fourteen years of hard labour, Gino was in the Ottoman fleet that seized the fortress of Goletta and the city of Tunis from the Italian and Spanish garrison that had been left there by Don John of Austria.[98] At some point towards the end of the campaign Gino escaped from his galley and went to Tunis; from there he was taken to Algiers. He tried to flee to Christian territory, but was recaptured and brought before the Pasha, who ordered him to convert to Islam. A 'Jewish barber' (sc. a mohel) was sent to circumcise him. After spending a little over one year in Algiers, he was taken to Morocco in the service of Abd al-Malik, the son of a former Sultan of Fez who invaded Morocco with Ottoman support in 1576 and later died at the Battle of Alcazar. All this time, Gino now insisted, he never took part in 'Muslim ceremonies', and 'always intended to escape to Christian territory'. Finally he made his way to Mazagão (modern El Jadida), a port on the Atlantic coast which had been under Portuguese control since 1502, and from there he was able to pass to Lisbon.[99]

A man with a somewhat similar geographical trajectory appears in the records of the Aragonese Inquisition in Majorca. In 1601 Alí Cola, the captain of a corsair ship from Algiers, was arraigned there, having been captured while on a raiding mission near Ibiza. He said that he had been born to Christian parents in Vlorë (described by the scribes as 'Velona in Greece'), and that his original name was 'Lucas'. He was now aged 50; he had been seized at the age of thirteen and taken to Algiers, where he had converted to Islam 'because everyone told him to become a Muslim'. He had apparently spent some time—in Morocco, it seems, though the details are not clear—as a captive of a remnant of the Portuguese army after the Battle of Alcazar, during which time he had learned some Latin prayers. He also claimed that he had helped Christian captives in Algiers; and he had bought a Christian slave woman and married her. While he insisted that he had never believed in Islam, witnesses were produced who had seen him taking part in 'the ceremonies of the Muslims'. The most damning element of his case, however, was the simple fact that he had been a corsair captain, actively engaged in the hunt for Christian prey. Since, when he was subjected to torture, he did not change his statement about his disbelief in Islam, he was allowed to make his abjuration; at the same time he was sentenced nevertheless to 200 strokes of the whip and permanent service, in chains, on the King's galleys. Precise details of his original departure from Albania are not given, but the most likely explanation is that the thirteen-year-old Luka had been seized opportunistically, perhaps on a hillside, at a secluded spot on the coast, or in a fishing-boat, and taken to be sold as a slave in Algiers.[100]

Another case involving raiding within the Ottoman Empire is to be found in the Naples archive—though whether enslavement happened as a direct consequence of that raid, or as a later development, is not clear. This is one of the very rare cases where we hear the voice of an ordinary Albanian woman. In March 1606 Theodora Tedea presented herself to the Inquisition tribunal; she was described as 'from the district of Scherpan in the province of Albania, aged about 25, daughter of Ghin [sc. Gjin] Tedea, and of Veppa of Phiginie'.[101] The two specific places mentioned here are hard to identify. From the rest of her account it is clear that she came from the southern (Greek Orthodox) part of the Albanian lands, and that she originally lived on or near the coast—which must eliminate Skrapar as a candidate for 'Scherpan'. Nor is the place to which she was then taken identifiable. Her account was the following:

I was born of a Christian father and a Christian mother, and I lived as a Christian, staying in my own district. And when my father died, and I was staying with my mother, the Turks came by sea with galleys, and at the [word illegible] of my mother they seized me, and took me to a district of the Turks [or: 'Muslims'] called Balliciauso. This happened five years ago. As I was a virgin, my master gave me to a Turk, his servant, as his wife, and for some years I stayed with that Turk, my husband, and I became pregnant. And while I was married to that Turk, a Greek [or: 'Orthodox'] man called Marino took me away from that Turk, telling me that he wanted to take me to the place where my mother lived; I was happy with that, as I believed him. He took me to Lecce, where he sold me as a slave to Giovanni Battista Moles, who brought me here. I've been here for two years, And because Giovanni Battista Moles died, I am the slave of signora Amelia Branci, his wife. Last year my mistress made me confess to a monk of Santa Maria della Speranza, who was Spanish; I told him that I had been married to a Muslim, and that I was a Christian, the daughter of Christians; he didn't make any objection, and gave me communion at the church of the Speranza. That happened last Easter.[102]

Theodora was then subjected to the usual questions. Had she venerated the Muslim faith? 'When I was in the power of the Muslims, I did not deny the religion of Jesus Christ. It's true that my master told me a hundred thousand times to become a Muslim; I said that I was a Christian, and that I didn't want to convert to Islam.' What religion did she practise when she was in the land of the Turks? 'I lived as a Christian, as I had done in my homeland, and I didn't do anything different in the land of the Turks; I just prayed to God for my soul, and said the Lord's Prayer, and the Ave Maria, as people do in my homeland, in the Albanian language.' Did she go to mosques, or baths, to say prayers? 'I never went to the Turks' mosques to say prayers, and the Turkish [or: Muslim] women don't go to mosques to say prayers but do it at home. I said my prayers as a Christian. I never went to the baths—I don't know what those baths are. I didn't enjoy living in that land, and wanted to live in my homeland.' And did she eat meat on the Catholic fast days? No, nor was she ever forced to; on Fridays and Saturdays 'I ate fish, and lenten food, and I'm telling you the truth.' Finally she added: 'When I was taken by that Greek man, I was pregnant, by my husband who was a Turk, and here in Naples I gave birth to a daughter, who has been baptized.' She then signed the document with the mark of a cross.[103]

The Inquisitors were not done with Theodora, however. Later that day they brought her back for further questioning, and recorded some details about the time-line of her story which had not been clear. It emerged that when she was seized by the 'Turks' she was 21; she stayed with them for five years, was married to the Muslim man for the last two of those, and was taken by the Greek three years previously, so she was now aged 29.[104] Four months later, on 12 July, they called her in again. Clearly they were not convinced by all her previous statements, as they began by asking her once more whether she had lived as a Muslim. (It may have seemed unlikely to them that a Muslim would marry a Christian woman and not require her to convert. This was in fact quite normal Muslim practice, but the great majority of the 'renegades' who appeared before the Inquisitors were male, not female, so their grasp of these matters may have been uncertain.) Her answer was the same. 'I led a Christian life, as an Albanian, and my husband, who was a Turk [or: "Muslim"], did not force me to lead a Muslim life. I went around dressed as a Turk, because in that place the Turks just like the Albanians dress in the same way, and from people's dress you wouldn't know who was Albanian, and who was Turkish [or: "Muslim"].' Had she enjoyed living in infidel territory? 'When I was living in the land of the Turks, and I had that husband, I was happy living there, and I lived there in a good state of mind, because I couldn't do otherwise, and because I was leading an Albanian life, and living in my own way. I went to the church of the Albanians, where the Greeks [sc.

Orthodox] said Mass.'[105] Asked again whether she had denied the Christian faith, she said no. She then signed the statement with her mark of a cross; but having done so, she then made some further comments which were recorded. 'If I hadn't fled from there, I would still be there now, as I was leading an Albanian life.' And again: 'If I hadn't come to this Christian territory, I would have continued to lead an Albanian life, living as a Greek [sc. Orthodox] person who didn't know the Catholic faith as it's known here; and that's how I would have died, because I didn't know about the true Catholic faith, as I have got to know it here, because in that place people live in an ignorant way.'[106]

Yet still the Inquisitors were not satisfied. Two days later Theodora was questioned again. How do the Muslims marry? 'I haven't seen how they do their marriages. I know well that they take the women and bring them to their home, and say that they are their wives.' When she was given by her master to his servant, 'there was no ceremony at all, he just took me for his wife, and I took him for my husband, and my master gave me three beatings to make me go and live with my husband, because I didn't want to live with him, and my husband was a Muslim and led a Muslim life.' She added: 'I am an Albanian, and when an Albanian man marries an Albanian woman, the women change their dress, they go to the church, they take the ring, the man puts the ring on the woman's finger, their relatives go to the wedding, they say Mass, and they do the usual ceremonies in the Albanian way. But when I was given to that Turk as his wife, they didn't do anything—nothing was done.' This was her final interrogation; the record of it also noted a certificate—brought in by her, apparently—from a Jesuit, Francesco Corcione, saying that she could be given the sacraments. (This was, in effect, a statement that in his opinion she was an Orthodox Christian: the Roman Catholic Church viewed members of the Orthodox Churches as in communion with it, even though they were judged to be schismatic.) And yet perhaps some doubts remained; for it was not until 22 March of the following year, 1607, that a decree of absolution was finally issued in the case of Theodora Tedea.[107]

The repeated interrogations of this woman had not confirmed the Inquisitors' suspicions about her conversion to Islam; nevertheless it is a striking fact that she shifted her ground on the question of whether she had been contented to live among Muslims. Very possibly—though she did not quite say this—her resistance to the arranged marriage had faded during the two years that it had lasted, giving way to acceptance or even affection. She had certainly learnt to accept those changes in her life over which she could have no control; and, as we shall see, arranged marriages were not at all unusual, even within one's own faith community. But to the modern historian, the most interesting aspect of her testimony is the way in which she referred to that community and to her own identity. 'Albanian' was used by her, apparently, not just to characterize the language she spoke, but also to mean Christian, and, in effect, Orthodox Christian—even though she also used the word 'Greek' or 'Greeks' to describe the Orthodox

Church and its priests. (As we have already seen, 'Greek' was the normal word for 'Orthodox', just as 'Turk' was used to mean 'Muslim'.) Yet at the same time she was very conscious of the fact that some aspects of her 'Albanian' way of life were identical with those of the people she referred to as 'Turks'. Admittedly, the situation she described would be a little clearer if the place where she lived among these Muslims, 'Balliciauso', could be firmly identified; there is no obvious candidate for it in modern Albania, or in the adjoining regions. But her statement that she went to 'the church of the Albanians', and her comment that these 'Turks' and Albanians dressed in just the same way, do make it seem likely that it was within the area that was then inhabited by Albanians in the more general sense of the term.

VIII

Eight years earlier, another young woman from the Albanian lands had appeared before the Neapolitan Inquisitors. It was on 14 March 1598 that 'Anastasia from the town of Paramythia, in Epirus, which belongs to the Turks' presented herself of her own accord; her age was estimated at 23. 'I am called Anastasia', she said, 'but I don't remember my surname. My homeland is the district of Paramythia, in the region called Albanian Epirus. My father was called George, and as for his village, I don't know, I can't remember. He died about 20 years ago. My mother was called Maria, daughter of Custa [*sc.* Kosta], and I don't know whether she is alive now.'[108] She then explained why she had come to the Inquisition. 'I am a Greek, a Christian, baptized in the church of the Madonna in that district. For a long time I knew the actual priest who baptized me. I have been regarded as a Christian, and publicly known to be one, and I want to live and die as a Christian, detesting the error which I committed when I denied the holy Catholic faith when I was under the power of the Muslims.'[109] In the narrative that follows, 'greco' is translated as 'Greek', but it is clear that the general contrast, when describing people in Paramythia, is between the 'greci' and the 'turchi'—that is, the Orthodox Christians and the Muslims. At some points, however, she may have used the term in a more specific way. As we shall see, she told the Inquisitors that she had forgotten the Greek language, as a result of living for eleven years in Italy, and gave this as the explanation of the fact that she could not remember her father's surname. The town of Paramythia (Alb.: Paramithi) is located roughly 23 miles south-west of Ioannina, in what is now north-western Greece; as her own description showed, it was then regarded as geographically part of Albanian territory, and the people of the region, known as Çams, were at that time linguistically Albanian overall. In the late sixteenth century, when the town was called Ajdonat (and Paramithi was the name of one district of it), the population was overwhelmingly Christian. Very many of the names in an Ottoman tax-register of

1583 are clearly Albanian Christian names (such as Gjon, Lekë, Pal, Dedë, Gjikë and Gjokë), but it is possible that while most of the population spoke Albanian in the home, some spoke Greek; it is also likely that there was a large degree of bilingualism.[110] Athanasia's case is included here both because she came from what can properly be described as the Albanian lands in this period, and because of its strong intrinsic interest.

First she was asked how it had come about that she committed the grave sin of apostasy. She replied:

> My mother had arranged my marriage and given me a husband, but because I didn't want that husband, I fled from my mother's house, and went to find refuge in the house of a Muslim in that same district. When that Muslim had me in his home, both he and likewise his Muslim wife persuaded me to deny my faith; they told me that if I did so, my mother would no longer be able to take me back and give me to that husband. So for that reason I willingly denied the faith, and I did it just two days after arriving at that Muslim's home. It was done like this: I stood up, with the husband and wife on either side, and they made me raise the index finger of my right hand, and made me say some words which I don't remember now—and still less did I know what the words meant when I said them. And they gave me a name which I don't remember now, as it was a Muslim name.[111]

The Inquisitors then asked what religion she had practised, and what kind of dress she had worn.

> I lived in the home of those Muslims for six months, and I observed the Muslim religion, eating meat on Fridays and Saturdays and on other vigils of saints' days which happened during that time; we ate sitting on the floor, with the table put on the floor. It's true that sometimes I ate pork secretly in the houses of the Greeks, which I used to visit sometimes. Likewise I also went to my mother's home after I had renounced Christianity; she cried because of what I had done. Nevertheless, I went around dressed in the Greek way, as I did before, when I was a Christian.[112]

Asked if she had gone to the baths, or to the mosque, and whether she had said prayers to Muhammad, she replied: 'I didn't go to the baths, nor to the Muslims' mosque, nor did I ever pray to Muhammad, still less did I regard him as a holy man or a prophet or a blessed person. On the contrary, I regarded him as a villain and a criminal, and their religion as villainous and infamous.'[113] They then asked her to explain how she had left.

During those six months that I was living under the power of those Muslims and in their home, I thought their religion was nasty. In order not to have to practise it any longer, I fled from their house, and went to another district, roughly half an hour's travel away from my home. And when I got there I was taken by those people, and sold to a Greek man, who, having kept me for about a year, sold me here in Naples. He brought me here from that district, and sold me to donna Allegra in Naples. I've been in her house for roughly nine years. Two years ago she gave me as a servant to some merchants for six years; I'm living in their house now, and at the end of the six years I shall be free.[114]

She insisted that she had been a practising Christian for all her time in Naples, sometimes going to confession in the church of S. Giacomo degli Spagnoli or the Gesù Nuovo. But, she admitted, she had never confessed the sin of apostasy; and she had never mentioned it to her mistress, 'for fear that they might take me back [to the market] to sell me again'.[115] (That seems to imply that Allegra's desire to grant her eventual freedom was linked to the idea that Anastasia was a Christian—a worthy impulse, although, if she really thought that Anastasia had always been a Christian, she should not have been holding her in slavery at all.)

On 12 October Anastasia reappeared before the tribunal, again of her own accord. She was now described as aged approximately 25. Asked the same question as before about her background, she replied that she could not remember her parents' surname 'because I've forgotten the Greek language, thanks to living in Italy for eleven years, and so I've forgotten their surname, which was Greek'.[116] Again she was asked to explain why she had renounced Christianity. She said that it all happened when she was thirteen years old and her mother (who had sole authority, as her father had died long before) chose a husband for her that she strongly disliked.

My mother forced me to take him as my husband, and made me contract a marriage with that man, who was Greek, with the involvement of the priest, and other ceremonies which the Greeks use in those parts. And although I ran away, and didn't want to make that marriage, my mother and other relatives and people forced me to do it, and when I had made the marriage, I was taken to my husband's house. I ran away from that house several times, and went to the house of my mother, who always gave me beatings to make me go back and live in my husband's house. So I decided to run away and not come back; I went and fled to the house of a Muslim woman whose name I don't remember.[117]

Once again she described the simple ceremony of conversion. She continued:

That same day, I repented of it, and during the time that I stayed in the home of that Muslim woman, which lasted about three months after my conversion, I tried to observe the Christian religion secretly. I went in secret to the houses of Greeks nearby and ate pork, but without letting the Muslims know, and because those Muslims, that is, the Muslim woman and her Muslim son, ate meat on Fridays, I did my best not to eat it, even though I ate it when I was in their presence, as I couldn't do otherwise.[118]

After those three months, she ran away:

I fled with another girl, who had had beatings from [*word illegible*]. We fled towards Corfu; our plan was to live there, where they are all Greeks and there are no Muslims. Having travelled for a day through various places, fields and woods, we came across some men—two on horseback and one on foot. They were armed with knives; I don't know where they were from or what they were called. They asked us where we were going, and we said we were going to Corfu. They said we should go with them, as they would take us to Corfu. And they took us with them for half a day overland till we got to the port, where there was a boat; they made us get into the boat, telling the sailors to take us to Corfu, and they stayed on dry land. On the way, the sailors told us that they had bought us from those men. They took us to Corfu, where we lived for about two months in the house of a man, I don't know his name or surname, but he was the person that those sailors had handed us over to, and he was Greek. He sent us to Naples, I mean, to the Kingdom of Naples, in a felucca, and we were both taken to Apulia, to Capo d'Otranto, and from there they brought us on horseback to Naples. They sold me to signora donna Allegra, I don't know her surname, and the other girl to another mistress, whose name I don't know.[119]

Here too the brutally casual nature of the enslavement is very striking—as is the matter-of-factness with which Anastasia recounted it. It should also be noted that we have no way of telling whether the three men were Muslims or Christians; and indeed this might have made little or no difference to the story.

Once again the Inquisitors asked Anastasia whether, when she renounced Christianity, she had believed in Islam. No, not in her heart, she replied; she had done it simply 'for fear of my mother'.[120] Five months later, on 31 March 1599, she was brought before the tribunal again, and asked whether she wanted to add anything to her story, or to withdraw anything; she said no. The Inquisitors returned once more to the act of apostasy, asking how old she was then, and whether she had understood what she was doing. She replied that she thought she was thirteen, but could not be sure, as 'I didn't know exactly how old I was.' As for her awareness of committing a mortal sin: 'I didn't know whether I was acting badly or acting well; I knew that I was abandoning the Christian religion, but I had no will to abandon it in my heart.'[121] Finally, on 12 April 1599, just over a year after her first appearance, she was summoned to receive the tribunal's judgment. She was allowed to make her abjuration and return to the Church; but she was required say the Creed every day and a corona every Sunday and holy day, and to confess and receive the eucharist four times per annum for three years.[122]

IX

The surviving records of the Sicilian Inquisition, which (as mentioned above) consist almost entirely of summary reports sent to the 'Suprema' in Madrid, offer four cases of people from Albania. (They do also present some cases of ethnic Albanians, 'Arbëresh', from Sicily or southern Italy, but those will not be considered here.)[123] One of the four states merely that at some point between October 1577 and December 1579 'Pedro of Casnes, born in Aterno [or: "Terno"] in Albania, a renegade Christian aged 30, came of his own volition and confessed that he had denied our holy Catholic faith and had performed some of the rites and ceremonies of the Muslims.'[124] The other three, however, do supply some significant details.

In July 1593 'Pietro Gion, born in Vlorë, in Dalmatia, which belongs to the Sultan, a shepherd, aged nineteen' (so: Pjetër Gjon), appeared before the tribunal in Palermo. He had been among a group of men captured on the little island of Pantelleria, a Sicilian possession which lies more than half-way towards the Tunisian coast; they had landed there from 'a Turkish galiot' in order to 'get fresh water'. The other captives (five native Muslims and one renegade) testified that 'he had come voluntarily under the power of the Muslims, and had himself circumcised in the previous year with the usual ceremonies, denying our holy Catholic faith and letting himself be given a Muslim name, Ali; he had dressed in the Muslim way, and they had seen him perform the ceremonies and rites of the Muslims.'[125] When questioned by the tribunal,

> he admitted that never in his life had he performed the sacrament of confession in his country, because all the time he was going out into the countryside to look after sheep, and an official of the Sultan had passed that way and had seized him and taken him to Istanbul. From there he was taken to Biserte [on the Tunisian coast], where they circumcised him. After that, he performed and observed all the ceremonies and rites of the Muhammedan sect, maintaining and believing that it was good and that his soul could be saved in it. This was despite the fact that before then, and at that time, he knew that our holy faith was better than that sect; nevertheless, persuaded by the Muslims, he believed in it until now.[126]

The Inquisition judges agreed that he could be reconciled to the Church, but under quite onerous conditions. First he was to spend one year in prison, undergoing religious instruction; then he was to spend three years rowing on a galley, after which he would return to the Inquisition for its final decision.[127] The surviving summary of Pjetër's narrative is too brief to allow us to judge what exactly had happened to him when he was taken from a hillside near Vlorë at some point in his boyhood. But the dominant impression is, once again, one of opportunistic enslavement. Even if the person who took him was an 'official' of the Sultan, it was not the job of Ottoman officials in Europe to supply manpower to corsairs on the Tunisian coast, so by far the most likely explanation is that he was sold in the slave market at Istanbul. Conversion to Islam by his new owners may have been designed to enable him to become a more active participant in their corsairing operations. This was in fact a common feature of such a career path; for it was of course known that the fact of conversion, with its visible sign inscribed on his body, would expose him to the risk of punitive treatment should he ever be captured by Christians—a truth demonstrated by the judgment of the tribunal.

Another case, also from July 1593, tells us even less about the person's original existence in Albania, but sheds some interesting light on the psychology of a convert to Islam who sought to return to Christianity. This was a young Albanian woman called Maria; the tribunal noted that 'she does not know her surname; her Turkish name is Girè, and she says she is from the country of Albania, but she was not able to say from which place in particular; she is 27 years old, and a slave of the marchese di Marineo, residing in this city [sc. Palermo].'[128] The record continues:

Last year it was attested by six witnesses (one of them a priest, the others all women, of whom one was a slave; all were from the household of the said marchese) that during the six years that they had known her in that household, she had always been held to be a real Muslim. She did not lead the life of a Christian, nor [sic—though the sense suggests: 'but rather'] that of a Muslim; they saw her eating meat on the days when this was forbidden [by the Church], and working on the days of Christian festivals. On the other hand, they had heard her say that she was a Christian, the daughter of Christian Albanian parents, and that she was happy for them to call her Maria. In September of the previous year, when she saw the celebration performed in this city at the time of the procession with [the relic of] the head of St Ninfa [a patron saint of Palermo], she said to herself that she wanted to be a Christian and to live as a Christian, and that she regretted not having done so before. This woman came to the Inquisition without having been summoned, though after the priest had supplied his testimony. And she admitted that what the witnesses said was true, and that, moreover, for six years she had performed all the Muslim ceremonies, believing that her soul could be saved in that sect, and that it was a good religion, notwithstanding the fact that she knew that it was contrary to the holy Roman Church. She had begun to abandon that religion six years before, after she was captured by Christians who were on a galiot belonging to don Pietro de Leyva; she said that

out of fear she had failed to come to reveal her Christian identity and be reconciled by the Inquisition. She said this with clear signs of repentance.[129]

Maria was allowed to be reconciled to the Church, on condition that she performed various 'spiritual penances' and agreed to undergo religious instruction
for one year.[130] This report does not record any questioning about her Christian
origins; but the Inquisition always took care to investigate such claims, and we
can be confident that the Sicilian tribunal was convinced of their truth in this
case, since it used the term 'reconciled' and not 'converted'. Nor, equally, does the
record tell us when or how Maria had become a Muslim. However, her inability to
name either her parents or the place where they lived suggests that she must have
been taken from them at a very early age. Whether that process too had involved
some form of enslavement can now only be guessed at.

The last Albanian to appear in the Sicilian records did so in 1611: 'Angela,
daughter of Nicolo, called Juli in Turkish, from the castle of Souli, near Preveza,
which is on the Adriatic, a slave of Giovanni Battista Sires in the city of Messina,
aged 30'.[131] Souli was a mountainous district in the territory of Çamëria; its
inhabitants were famous as warriors, and their main stronghold, the 'castle'
referred to here, was Kiafa, roughly seventeen miles south of Paramythia and 30
miles north of Preveza. Historic local place-names suggest that the Souliots were
originally Albanian-speaking; in this period many were probably bilingual in
Albanian and Greek.[132] The Inquisition record described Angela as 'of the Greek
nation', but that may have been a reflection of two things: her original member-
ship of the Greek Orthodox Church, and the fact that, as her interrogation
showed, she had spent a significant part of her life in the town of Preveza, which
was Greek-speaking.[133] The record stated:

> She appeared spontaneously and confessed as follows. When she was eight, her
> father died, and her mother took her and her brothers to the town of Preveza to
> stay in the house of one of her aunts (a sister of her mother). When she was fif-
> teen, a Greek called Cuzo Miti, a man of ill repute, wanted to marry her by force;
> and when he saw that she did not want him, he made an arrangement with a
> powerful Turk [or: Muslim] to make her marry him. When that Turk had called
> her to his house, and compelled her either to marry the Greek or to renounce
> her faith, she preferred to renounce her faith rather than marry the man. So the
> Turk made her renounce our holy Catholic faith in his house, by raising the fin-
> ger of her right hand and saying the usual words which the Muslims say when
> performing that deed—words whose meaning she did not know. And they gave
> her the Muslim name Juli, and once she had renounced her faith they let her go;
> she went back to her aunt's house repenting of having renounced our holy
> Catholic faith, and for three days she cried at having done so—she had done it
> out of desperation, and to avoid marrying the Greek. From then onwards, while

she lived in her aunt's house, she always lived as a Greek Christian. And having renounced the faith, she wanted to go to Venice or some other Christian territory; but she did not do so, for fear that they [*sc.* the Ottoman authorities] would burn her if they caught her. And when she was 20 she married the Turk [or: Muslim] who had made her renounce the faith, and for three years she lived with him as a Muslim in order to satisfy him; but in her mind she never believed in the Muslim sect, nor did she hold it to be good. Seven years ago she was seized by Florentine galleys in the town of Preveza with her two sons and taken to Miano [a village on the north-eastern coast of Sicily, seven miles north of Messina], where she was sold to the said Giovanni Battista.[134]

Some of the details here are quite reminiscent of the case of Anastasia of Paramythia, who was less than a decade older than Angela, and came from the same region. In both cases conversion was the desperate and/or opportunistic act of a teenage girl (thirteen in the earlier case, and fifteen here); we do not know whether Angela's mother was urging her to accept the offer of the ill-reputed Greek, but it is noticeable that in each of these cases parental authority overall had been weakened by the death of the father. The fact that Angela later married the powerful Muslim who had performed her conversion suggests that some further psychological or social factors may have been at work, if not at the time of the conversion then in the following five years; but these are entirely unstated in the record, and are now quite impossible to recover.

X

In each of the cases discussed so far, the basic fact of apostasy was clear, and only the degree of culpability was open to interpretation. But in some more problematic cases the Inquisitors had to determine what religious identity the person had had in the first place. On 23 August 1629 a Basilian monk (a member of an order which accepted the primacy of Rome, but followed the Greek rite), Father Jeremias, appeared before the Maltese Inquisition at Birgu.[135] As he explained, during the previous afternoon he had been in Valletta and had passed the place where slaves were put out for sale; some of the new ones there had been captured by Captain Musa Benca, whose ship had recently arrived at the port. Father Jeremias was accompanying a Greek from Athens, Antonio Dicio (later: 'Dicea'), whose own ship had recently unloaded a cargo of salt from Djerba.

While Antonio stopped to look at those slaves that were being sold, one of them began to bemoan his fate, saying 'look how they are going to sell me, even though I'm an Albanian Orthodox [or: Greek] Christian, and it's quite wrong of them to sell me!' Antonio told him to talk to those gentlemen [*sc.* Captain Benca and his colleagues], and said that he should not let himself be sold as a Muslim when he was a Christian. Or else, he said, he should run away and come to the Inquisition. While Antonio was telling me about this, someone or other told Captain Benca about the conversation that had taken place between Antonio and the Orthodox [or: Greek] Albanian, and I saw Captain Benca suddenly punch Antonio and hit him with a stone, shouting, 'so you're telling my slaves to run away to the Inquisition?'

At which point the officer of the port of Valletta had intervened; his constables had arrested Antonio and put him in gaol, where he now remained.[136]

On the 25th Antonio Dicea was brought to the tribunal to give his own account. Four days previously, he had met in Valletta a Jew from Salonica who told him about two 'Greek' Christians that were being sold as slaves. He, the Jew, had already helped one of them to make himself known to the Inquisition, and he asked Antonio to see if he could be of assistance to the other.

So I went to the portico where they usually sell the slaves, and while I was talking to other slaves that were on sale, an Albanian who told me that he was from a village near the city of Elbasan told me in Turkish that he was a Christian, and that they wanted to sell him. I replied that he should state his case, and that if he proved that he was a Christian they would not treat him unjustly. He replied that he had told them, and that it had not done him any good. I responded that when the sale was complete he should go to the Inquisition to prove that he was a Christian; 'if you are a Christian, stay where you are, and don't be afraid.' Then Musa di Benca, captain of the ship which had captured them, came up to me and kicked me in the back, punched me in the face, and hit me with a stone on the back, and said a great many insults.[137]

Two other witnesses to this were also produced, both of them Greeks. They also briefly described the slave in question: 'a young man aged about 30, injured in one shoulder, of reasonable height, with a blond beard, who said in Turkish that he was a Christian'; 'of reasonable height, with blond mustachios, who said he was a Christian Albanian aged roughly 28'.[138]

Later that day, the slave himself was questioned. The official record noted that he was 'a man of reasonable height, with pale skin and a beard which was blond but sparse'. Asked to identify himself, he replied: 'I am called Tole, son of the late Pietro, and of his wife Schieua, who is still alive; I am about 26 years old, I'm from a village called Vriuoli in Albania, and I am a sailor.' Antonio was then brought in to confirm that this was the man he had spoken to, and Tole also confirmed that Antonio was the person who 'spoke to me in Turkish'.[139] The Inquisitors then asked Tole to explain how he had come to Malta. 'Roughly four months ago', he said, 'when I happened to be in Salonica, I made an agreement to be a crew-member on Hasan Reis's cargo ship which was going to North Africa, and near Djerba we were captured by Captain Benca's ship and brought here to Malta.'[140]

The next questions were: is everyone baptized in your country; have you seen people baptized; and were you baptized? 'In my homeland everyone is baptized, and I have seen others baptized: the priest makes a cross on the baby's forehead, and then carries it round the church. I was told by my father and mother that I had been baptized. In my homeland there are churches, and crucifixes, and images of saints, that is, the Madonna and Saint Paul, and instead of bells they make a sound with a plank of wood. I didn't go often to churches because I was a peasant, but when I was little I went more often.'[141] Asked if he had apostatized, and what life he had led among the 'Turks', he replied: 'I have never apostatized, nor have I ever been circumcised, and on board ship I always lived as a Christian.' Were there any people on Malta who would recognize him? Yes, among the people that had been captured there was a merchant from Salonica called Mehmet, and a man from the Black Sea called Mustafa Iasagi. Did he know any prayers? 'I know only how to sign myself with the sign of the cross', Tole said, 'and to say Kyrie Eleison, Agios [sic] Maria, Agios Dimitri', whereupon he crossed himself 'in the Greek way'.[142]

Then he was asked what he did on the cargo ship; he answered that he was just serving as a sailor. Whose ship was it, and whose merchandise? 'It was a trading ship, owned by Hasan Reis, and the goods were iron, wooden planks, opium, and other such things. The goods belonged to Janissary merchants, and others who were on the ship; there was nobody else, apart from those who had a share in the goods.' What had he done during the battle? 'In the battle I was down below decks, then the captain came down with his scimitar, and make me go on deck, telling me that I had to do my bit, so I went on deck to look after the sails, and when I went on deck I was shot by an arquebus, so I went down again.' Was he the only Christian in that part of the ship? 'There was a Greek Christian boy, injured in the jaw, and two Russian Christian slave-women, and another little Russian boy, and five other Christians—I don't know where they are.'[143] (These details indicate that there was one other category of cargo on board: slaves. 'Russian' was used as a general term for Slavs captured by Tatar raiders in the area north of the Black Sea and sold in large numbers in Istanbul and other Ottoman trading centres.) Asked if there were any apostates on board, he said that he did not know. At the end of the interrogation he signed the record with the mark of a cross. The following week, Captain Benca was given the opportunity to present whatever arguments he might have against freeing this slave. But it was only eight months later, on 11 May 1630, that judgment was finally pronounced on the person now described as 'Tole or Anthony the Albanian': his status as a Christian was confirmed, and he was declared 'a free man, exempt from any yoke of slavery'.[144]

XI

A much more complex case was brought before the Inquisitors in Naples four years later. The dossier here opens with a statement of the problem, dated 12 April 1634. A man called Pietro d'Alba, a 'Greek', had been imprisoned for the last few months because of a dispute with his wife. While he was there, it was discovered (the statement alleged) that he had tricked the former Viceroy, the Duke of Alba. He had claimed to be a Muslim who wanted to convert to Christianity, and the Duke had not only sponsored his conversion but also provided maintenance for his wife and children; but later it appeared, from documentation which Pietro himself had presented, that he had already been baptized in the Levant.[145] There followed a narrative (dated 18 January 1634) which supplied further details. Roughly seven years earlier, five people had come to Naples: a man, his wife, and three children. When they told the Duke that they were Muslims who wanted to convert, 'he gave them a house with every kind of comfort, and they were baptized by him himself in the chapel of the palace; he gave the name Pietro d'Alba to the father and Anna d'Alba to the mother', with the sons christened Gennaro, Antonio and Angelo. He also endowed them with a pension of thirteen ducats a month each. But he later found out that they were Christians, and that Pietro was 'born in the city of Vlorë, 100 miles from this kingdom, where he was a shoe-pedlar.' It also emerged that his wife had recently got a license from the Neapolitan authorities to travel seeking alms, and that the purpose of this was 'to find an opportunity to go to the Levant, to become a Muslim, as her son don Antonio has already done: he went to Istanbul, promising that—in breach of the service of God and the King—he would reveal [the identities of] all the people who go there from here on secret business.'[146]

Various witness statements then followed. Serafino of Macedonia described a conversation with the wife, in which she had said that Pietro had obtained a license to beg for alms, and that he would use it to go to Vlorë; 'and I heard from various people who are Greek, and from donna Anna herself, his wife, that don Pietro, her husband, was a Christian.'[147] The next witness, Geronimo Paronda, was described as a 'Venetian'; we know from other sources that he was the son of a Cretan, and that he had worked for some time in Istanbul as an organizer of intelligence services for Spain and the Kingdom of Naples. He said that he had been acquainted with Pietro for the seven or eight years since Pietro had come to Naples. He had also learned, from 'various people here in Naples, and from letters from friends ["amici", a term used in intelligence circles for trusted informants] who wrote from the Levant', that he was a Christian from Vlorë, where he worked as a 'scarparo', a pedlar of shoes and boots. Pietro's wife was also a Christian, and so too were her three children by a previous marriage, who received thirteen scudi a month each. Her son Antonio had left Naples roughly one year previously, 'to convert to Islam in Istanbul', and to reveal the identities of 'the people whom this witness regularly sends on secret business to that city'. The fact that Paronda had got to know Pietro soon after the latter's arrival in Naples suggests that he had taken an interest in him as a potential recruit; and if Antonio did have privy knowledge of the network of couriers or agents, that probably means that Paronda had involved him in some way in his work.[148] The last two witnesses were Manuel Duca, from 'Melenique in the province of Macedonia' (Melnik, in the south-western corner of modern Bulgaria), who confirmed that the family was from Vlorë, a city 'inhabited by Greek Christians, even though Turks [or: Muslims] also live there, who are the rulers of it'; and a barber, who had been asked to examine Pietro's penis, and had found it 'in sound condition, without any lesion or circumcision'.[149]

The interrogation of Pietro d'Alba took place on 18 February 1634. First he was asked about Vlorë. He described it as 'inhabited by Greeks, Albanians, Turks and Jews', adding that 'there are churches there, and the people who are Christians live as Christians, as they are Greeks and Albanians, and whoever wants to be a Muslim, and the Jews—each person lives according to his own religion.' He said that he had left Vlorë roughly fifteen years previously. And what religion did he practise when he was there? 'He said that he lived as a Muslim, because his father was one', whereas his mother was a 'Greek Christian called Princes'. He explained that he had been 'taken to Istanbul and presented to the Sultan by his uncle, Semegiolli, who had come to Vlorë seventeen years ago as camp-master [a senior military officer], and when he went back to Istanbul he presented the accused [sc. Pietro] to the Sultan, and he lived as a Muslim, as his father (called Mamet Baxi, who died earlier) had been a Muslim, and so was Semegion his uncle'.[150] How long had he stayed in Istanbul? 'He said that he stayed in the seraglio [sc. the training centre for Janissaries], like all the other Janissaries, who are some of them Muslims by birth, and some of them the sons of Greeks [sc. Orthodox Christians], whom they circumcise; he stayed less than two years.' And did he undergo cir-cumcision at that time? 'No, he said, because he was a Muslim by birth; whereas those Janissaries who are the sons of Greeks, when they come into the hands of the Turks, are made to convert to Islam, and are then circumcised.'[151] What name did he have, and how did he leave Istanbul? 'He said that he was called Cursbam [later in these documents: "Cumbassa", "Cureh Bassa", "Basua"], and that he came away from Istanbul when he married a Greek woman, called Soltana [sc. Sultana] in Turkish and Cali [sc. Kalē] in Greek.' From a previous marriage she already had three sons, called Isuffo (sc. Yusuf), Sinan and Mamett (sc. Mehmed). As she was born a Christian, she asked him to take them all to Naples, so that the boys could be baptized and she could be reconciled to the Church. So he, 'with this zeal to become a Christian, came away from there, fleeing secretly with his wife'. The children were duly baptized as, respectively, Antonio, Gennaro and Angelo; his wife reverted to Kalē, but was formally baptized in the Catholic Church as Anna.[152]

On the way from Istanbul they had stopped for two months at Corfu, and Pietro had received a letter of safe conduct from the Archbishop of that island in November 1624. The Inquisitors asked him to explain why it described both him and his wife as 'born and baptized Christians'. He said that this was just an error: perhaps the Archbishop had thought that since his wife was born and brought up a Christian, the same must have been true of him. Then they inquired about his stepson Antonio, who had left Naples eighteen months earlier. Pietro said that Antonio had gone to Rome, and that he thought he had entered the service of a 'cavaliero' (knight, or distinguished gentleman) there, but he did not know where he was now.[153] When the Inquisitors asked Pietro whether he had planned to return to Vlorë, 'he said that for seven months, or let's say a year, he has not received any money', and that for that reason he had petitioned the current Viceroy for a license to beg for alms among Christians in the Kingdom of Naples. He had not yet received it; but he had no intention of leaving the kingdom, and certainly not of returning to the Ottoman Empire, 'because if he went to the Levant, the Turks would impale him and burn him—and here he made the sign of the cross'.[154]

At this point the record added some documentary evidence, which testifies to the seriousness with which the Inquisition went about its business. A copy was given of the entry in the baptismal register of the Castel Nuovo in Naples; this recorded the christening of Pietro (described as 'formerly called Basua') and the three boys on 29 June 1629. Then there came the full text of the laissez-passer issued by Benedetto Bragadin, Archbishop of Corfu, on 7 November 1624. It declared that 'Cumbassa' and Sultana were both born of Christian parents, and baptized, 'but lapsed into the Muhammedan sect when they were still children', and said that they wished to return to Christianity with their three sons and a maidservant.[155] Another text was a letter to the Auditor General of Naples (the chief of the military, in whose prison Pietro was now held), setting out some of the conventions of conversion to Islam. It described the devşirme system, which it said involved the forced recruitment of Christian boys, aged 10–12, every seven years: it explained that three days after their arrival at the seraglio or training-school they were all circumcised, 'because they cannot stay in those places without that circumcision, and still less can any sons of Muslims be received in those places, nor any Christians who have converted as adults to Islam'. (Whilst that comment about the sons of Muslims correctly stated the official position, the reality was quite different; reports by Venetian 'baili'—resident ambassadors in Istanbul—in 1573 and 1590 commented that many Muslim boys were joining the Janissaries, and it has been estimated that by 1666 half of the intake consisted of native Muslims.)[156] When a Muslim man married a Christian woman, this letter continued, the sons were circumcised; indeed, it was not possible for a Muslim not to be circumcised. 'And this is evident, because when the Christian navy captures any ship in the Levant, the only way they distinguish Muslims from

Christians is that they put the ones who are found to be circumcised in chains, and free the others as Christians.'[157]

Three weeks later, on 6 March 1634, another expert witness appeared; his testimony confirmed some of these details, while adding one important qualification. He was a Greek, from Nafplio in the Peloponnese (a former Venetian possession, conquered by the Ottomans in 1540); he said that he had left the Ottoman Empire 33 years earlier, having spent 20 years on and off in Istanbul, and that, after fighting for the King of Spain in Flanders, he was now a pensioner in Naples. Asked about the *devşirme*, he said that it happened every seven years; the target age-group was between ten and twelve, but boys up to sixteen were eligible if they were not yet growing facial hair; and they must have Christian parents. 'No one can stay in that seraglio without being circumcised, and still less do any sons of Muslims enter there.' If a Muslim man married a Christian woman, he said, the sons were normally circumcised and lived as Muslims; however, 'those who are poor are accepted as Muslims without circumcision.'[158]

On 12 May the Inquisitors interviewed Pietro's wife, now named as Anna Maria de Alba. 'In Istanbul', she said, 'I entered into a marriage with signor don Pietro in the Muslim way, even though I was a Christian. Pietro was a Janissary, the son of a Janissary, and practised Islam; he was then called Cureh Bassa, and was accepted as a Muslim.' They had later re-performed the marriage in a church in Naples. She knew little of his background, except that he was from Vlorë, and that his father was a Janissary—as was his uncle, whom she called 'Semer Giò'. Was she aware that only Christian boys were brought into the Janissary seraglio? 'No, I'm not, as I'm just a poor woman.' She had had him imprisoned by the Auditor General because 'he drank rather a lot of wine and spirits, and when he came back drunk he gave beatings to me and the boys'; nevertheless she testified that he was 'a good Christian', who often went to confession.[159]

On the following day Pietro himself was once more brought in for questioning. He repeated what he had said before about religious conditions in Vlorë, and about the mixed marriage of his parents (adding that his mother was a Christian from Vlorë who had been 'taken by force by my father'). 'I always lived in Vlorë', he said, 'and when I was 35 years old my uncle came to Vlorë from Istanbul on official business; when that was finished, he took me to Istanbul.' The purpose, apparently, was to get Pietro to take over some office or function that had belonged to his father. He insisted once again that there were native Muslims in the Janissary seraglio; and on the question of circumcision he said that 'not all Muslims are circumcised, one sees many who are not'—himself included.[160] After this interrogation, which added little or nothing of substance to what was already known, he was returned to the custody of the Auditor General. And there the case—or, at least, the surviving record of it—came to an end. The modern reader may find it as difficult to reach a conclusive verdict as, perhaps, the Inquisitors did. That a Muslim boy would not have been circumcised was highly unlikely, but

it was possible—especially, we may suppose, if the Muslim father in a mixed marriage had died before the boy was old enough for the ceremony. That a native
Muslim would have been allowed to join the Janissary intake was not only possible but, as we know now, quite common. But the idea that he could have done so
at the age of 35 is very hard to believe; if Pietro's story was essentially true, he
must surely have joined some other kind of training for some other role. However,
the job of the Inquisitors was not to determine the truth of every element here,
but simply to decide whether there had been an abuse of the sacrament of baptism by someone who was already a Christian. If they decided that that could not
be proven, there was nothing more for them to do.

XII

On 21 June 1771 a slave boarded an English ship in the harbour at Valletta and,
according to the initial report in the Maltese Inquisition's dossier on him, said: 'I
was a Muslim called Mustafa, I let myself be baptized, but since I was born a
Muslim, and was Mustafa, I want to die a Muslim, and to die as Mustafa.' He was
described as 'a man roughly 40 years old, short and heavily built, with large blond
or reddish mustachios; his skin is more pale than brown, and he has rather large
dark eyes and a short neck.'[161] When the tribunal began to consider his case on 12
July, a witness appeared who said that the man sold water by the barrel, mostly to
Greeks, 'and people say that he is the son of a Greek who later apostatized, but is
regarded as a Christian.' The slave was then produced, and the witness duly identified him.[162] At this point the scribe gave the slave's name as 'Johannes Petrus
Aristotelus a Costantina'; but this mishearing was in effect corrected a little further on, when the record reproduced the entry for the man's baptism at the Greek
Catholic church of Our Lady of Damascus in Valletta on 23 March 1770. That
entry described him as a 'neophyte Albanian slave, aged 23, from the district of
Saiada', and said that he had been given the names Giovanni Pietro Christodulo
and Constantino. 'Saiada' was Sagiada, a little port serving the northern part of
the territory of the Çams, less than two miles from the present Greek–Albanian
border.[163]

     The interrogation of Giovanni Pietro then followed. 'I am called Giovanni, son
of Anastasi', he said; 'I am from the Levant, from the district of Sagiada. I am
roughly 23 years old. I don't know what my parents were called, because when I
was little the Turks took me to Istanbul, and I never saw them again. Seven years
ago I was brought to this island by Captain Pietro and sold here as a slave; and
since some doubt arose about whether I was a Christian, I was baptized.' (Here
too what seems to have happened was a case of casual enslavement within the
Ottoman Empire—though the details given are too summary to make that certain.) His explanation of the recent episode in the harbour was that someone had

told him that the English ship was going to Rome—meaning, presumably, the Roman port of Civitavecchia—and had persuaded him to board it.[164]

Six weeks later he was brought in for questioning again. He insisted that he had thought the ship was sailing for Rome: 'I wanted to go to Rome', he said, 'because I had always been told that converts to Christianity there are given five carlini per day'; but he had been afraid that the Grand Master of the Knights of Malta—in effect the ruler of the island—would not give him permission.[165] There were in fact two papally funded institutions in Rome, the Casa dei Catecumeni, which prepared Jews and Muslims for conversion, and the Collegio dei Neofiti, where some of those converts underwent further training for careers in the service of the Church. Over time, a convention or even a right had developed, according to which slaves who entered these institutions were freed; this had prompted complaints earlier in the eighteenth century that many Muslim slaves were trying to escape from their masters in order to make their way to Rome.[166] As for being given five carlini a day: that may have been a considerable over-estimate (a carlino was a silver coin weighing 4 grams), but the inmates of these institutions certainly received their maintenance. So, even if the Collegio dei Neofiti was not the destination that this particular neophyte genuinely had in mind, the line of explanation he put forward here had some plausibility. When his interrogation resumed six days later, Giovanni Pietro said that he had wanted to travel to Christian territory, but that if it had turned out that the ship's destination was in Ottoman territory, he had planned to stay on the ship and work as a crewman. Naturally he would not have tried to enter Ottoman territory himself; 'I am well aware that if a Muslim becomes a Christian, and then goes back to the Muslim lands, he will be burnt.'[167]

Various other witnesses to his action in the harbour were then called. One man, who was on the ship selling goods to the English at the time, recalled that 'having got on board, he said "me be slave, me want come with you"'. ('Mi star schiavo mi voli venir con vui'—clearly an attempt to reproduce Giovanni Pietro's actual words in his southern-accented pidgin Italian.) Asked by the English sailors to explain himself, he said that he was a Greek Christian who had converted to Islam and had later declared himself a Christian; they then told him to leave the ship.[168] Another witness, Johannes Badacco (described as the son of George 'of Ioannina in Rumeli'), who knew the accused, testified on one of the key points at issue: 'I've been in Istanbul, and I know that when a Muslim who has fallen into slavery in Christian lands comes back from there as a Christian, saying that he converted to Christianity in order to escape, and that he kept up his adherence to the Muhammedan sect in an interior way, they pardon the error, and he doesn't incur any punishment. But it will be known that if a Muslim went as a Muslim to Christian lands in order to convert to Christianity, he incurs the death penalty.'[169] Another witness, Fortunato Vella, made a similar statement: 'I've been in the Muslim lands, and I know that when Muslims who have converted in

Christian lands come back as fugitives to their country, and especially if they have a document from their *kadi* [judge] saying that they converted to Christianity either because they were forced, or in order to flee, they will not be maltreated on any account in those countries of theirs.' The final sentence of the tribunal, delivered on 11 March 1772, was perhaps the most practical one in the circumstances: the degree of theological guilt in this case was not assessed, and Giovanni Pietro was simply forbidden to leave the island.[170] Nothing further is known of his life thereafter.

6

Pjetër Bogdani's *Cuneus prophetarum* (1685)

The Work and its Religious Context

The *Cuneus prophetarum* of Pjetër Bogdani, published in Padua in 1685, has long been recognized as a work of immense significance in the history of Albanian culture.[1] It was not the first text to be printed in Albanian, but it was the first substantial original prose work composed and printed in that language. Since its purpose was to give a full account of the essential elements of Christian doctrine, it ranged over many fields of thought, including cosmology and moral theory; and it drew on many sources, including classical literature, the early Fathers of the Church, and medieval theologians. The second part of the work, the Life of Jesus Christ, contains narrative passages of remarkable vividness; Bogdani was, indeed, a master of Albanian prose, and his work is a veritable treasure-house for the study of the history of the Albanian language.[2]

Bogdani's work has been carefully studied by linguists. It has also been studied by historians, who have emphasized the important part played by Pjetër Bogdani in the history of the northern Albanian lands—above all, his role as an organizer of armed resistance against the Ottoman authorities in 1689, the final year of his life.[3] But the text itself is, of course, a religious treatise; and its religious nature and religious context have not been discussed in much detail by previous writers. No doubt this was a very difficult subject for scholars to handle in Communist Albania, where religion itself was officially abolished; and the subject was not without some difficulties even in the more liberal regime of Titoist Yugoslavia. When the contents of Bogdani's work were discussed, there was a tendency to describe him in secular terms, as a philosopher and a 'humanist', rather than as a theologian.[4] There was also, perhaps, a tendency to assume that the Catholic Church was an authoritarian and intellectually reactionary organization in the seventeenth century, and that Bogdani must therefore necessarily have come into conflict with it: some modern writers argued that his reason for having the book printed in Padua, rather than in Rome, was to escape Roman censorship (though, as I shall argue, this supposition is quite unfounded).

It is not my purpose, in this essay, to attempt any general treatment of Bogdani's theology; that is a large subject, which would need careful investigation by a specialist in the Catholic theology of the period. (I would merely comment, in passing, that those modern writers who look for some special 'originality' in Bogdani's theology are approaching the work with the wrong kind of expectations: for a

Rebels, Believers, Survivors: Studies in the History of the Albanians. Noel Malcolm,
Oxford University Press (2020). © Noel Malcolm. DOI: 10.1093/oso/9780198857297.001.0001

Catholic Archbishop, writing a general explanation of Christian doctrine for his flock, the aim was not to put forward new doctrines, but rather to put forward the normally accepted doctrines in a convincing way.)[5] I should like to concentrate, instead, on the religious nature of Bogdani's project—I mean, on the question of what sort of religious book he was trying to write, for what sort of religious purpose—and on the context in which it was produced. For it seems to me that there are several rather intriguing puzzles here that need to be addressed.

One concerns Bogdani's decision to have the book produced in Padua, not in Rome. Another is the puzzle that arises over the physical nature of the book. We know that Bogdani's main purpose in writing the book was to produce a text that could be distributed among the members of his flock in the northern Albanian lands. The few other Albanian-language texts that had already been printed for such a purpose (for example, the translation by Pjetër Budi of Roberto Bellarmino's treatise *De doctrina christiana*) were small volumes that could be carried in pockets and, if necessary, smuggled or hidden; yet Bogdani's *Cuneus prophetarum* was a substantial folio volume, finely produced and elaborately ornamented. It also contained a few passages printed in Armenian and Syriac—languages of no possible use or relevance to the inhabitants of Albania, Kosovo and Macedonia. And in two entire sections of the book, all quotations from the Old Testament (the Hebrew Bible) were not only given in Latin and Albanian, but also printed in Hebrew and Arabic: again, this raises puzzling questions about the intended audience of the book and the religious purposes which it was meant to serve.

But perhaps the greatest puzzle concerns Pjetër Bogdani's treatment of Islam. Although there is no systematic handling of the topic, there are passages scattered through the work in which Bogdani makes negative comments about Islamic doctrine and about the Prophet Muhammad himself. For example, he criticizes the doctrine that each person has a fixed destiny or fate; he ridicules the popular cosmology of the Muslims; and he describes Muhammad as a 'great hypocrite' whose wild dreams were obviously false.[6] That Bogdani had these negative views of Islam is not surprising in the slightest: these were, quite simply, the normal views of any Christian theologian in this period. But what is highly surprising is that he should have expressed such an attitude so openly in a book which was intended for distribution within the Ottoman Empire. He must have known full well that the uncomfortable *modus vivendi* of Christianity within that Empire depended on the observance of certain rules, and that one of the most important rules was that Christians should not openly denigrate the Prophet Muhammad or Islam itself. That rule could be enforced in different ways. In 1628 one of the reasons why the Jesuits were expelled from Istanbul was that books had been found in their library which contained insults against Islam.[7] But those Jesuits got off lightly; more serious penalties could have been applied. In 1687, just two years after the publication of the *Cuneus prophetarum*, one of Bogdani's own priests,

Don Ndre Kalamashi, was arrested by the local Ottoman authorities at Gjakovë and strangled (as Bogdani himself reported) 'because he insulted Muhammad'.[8] Bogdani knew these conditions perfectly well; this was the world he had lived in, as a Catholic cleric, for most of his adult life. So what did he think he was doing, producing—for circulation inside the Ottoman Empire—a book in which the Prophet Muhammad was openly criticized?

The issue of Bogdani's attitude to Islam has to be studied carefully, I think, in order to reach a proper understanding of the nature of his book—even though, as I shall argue, criticizing Islam was not his primary purpose, but merely a secondary or even a tertiary one. The issue matters because it is so closely connected with the historical context in which Bogdani wrote. This was a period of major conflicts between Christian states and the Ottoman Empire: for large parts of Bogdani's adult life, the Ottoman state in which he lived was at war with one or more of the Catholic powers. Between 1644 and 1669 the conflict was with Venice; in 1663–4 there was a war against Austria; and, most importantly, from 1683 until 1699 (ten years after Bogdani's death) the Ottoman Empire was in conflict with a 'Holy League' consisting of Austria, Venice and the Papacy, as well as some other Christian states. In these circumstances it may be tempting to say that religion acted merely as a pretext or a cloak for *Realpolitik*: Austria had its own geopolitical reasons for wanting to defeat the Ottomans, and merely invoked Christianity as a motive in order to justify its policies, and to encourage other Catholic powers (especially the Papacy) to support it with men and money. But this is too one-sided an interpretation; religion served not only as a camouflage for politics, but also as a genuine motive for action. (To give just one example: the charismatic Italian Capuchin friar Marco d'Aviano, who gave stirring sermons demanding a new crusade to drive the Ottomans out of Europe, clearly had an influence on the thinking of Leopold I and the governing circles in Vienna.)[9] In the case of Bogdani himself, it would also be a mistake to reduce everything to political or secular motivation. The tendency of modern Albanian scholarship on this question has been to say that when Bogdani criticized Islam, he did so merely because Islam was the religion of the occupying power, and he aimed at the national liberation of his people. That Bogdani suffered at the hands of the Ottoman authorities, and longed to be free from their oppression, is indeed clear from many of his letters and reports to his superiors in Rome. It is also clear that he took active measures, at some risk to himself, to further the cause of liberation from Ottoman rule. Occasionally his letters included pieces of intelligence about the Ottomans' military plans, or the geography of the region, which were obviously intended to help a Christian invading force, if ever one came; and when such a force did come, in 1689, Bogdani took active measures to assist it.[10] Nevertheless, his motivation for seeking this sort of political change was not merely secular; it was religious too. If 'national liberation' from an occupying imperial power had been his only interest, he could not logically have welcomed the sort of conquest that might have led to his territory becoming part of an Austrian empire or a Venetian one. But he did dream of a conquest of that sort; and the reasons why he felt so differently about a Christian occupying power were, of course, religious. Bogdani's negative attitude towards Islam cannot be separated from its political context; but, at the same time, it cannot be reduced to a matter of politics alone.

The *Cuneus prophetarum* is a religious text, and in order to understand it we must begin by asking what religious purposes it was intended to serve. The primary purpose, self-evidently, was to provide a panoramic account of the teachings of Christianity in a form that could be understood by members of Bogdani's flock (or, at least, by those members who had learned to read). The overall organization of the book broadly imitated the arrangement of the Christian Bible, with its division into Old and New Testaments: thus the first part of the *Cuneus* described the Creation, the nature of God, the Fall of Adam, and the succession of 'prophets' whose words and deeds are recorded in the Old Testament (Moses, David, Solomon, etc.), while the second part described the life of Jesus Christ, ending (like the New Testament itself) with an account of the future coming of Antichrist and the Last Judgement. The importance of such a text, for an Albanian Catholic community which did not have an Albanian-language version of the Bible, should not be underestimated. From an early stage in his work as a Catholic cleric in northern Albania, Bogdani had emphasized, in his reports to Rome, the importance of supplying his flock with texts setting out the basic principles of Christianity; above all, he had emphasized the need to supply such texts in the language of the Albanians themselves. In one of his earliest letters, written in 1651 when he was a priest in the Gashi district of the Malësi, he requested five copies of the 'Doctrina Albanese' (the little book by Bellarmino, translated by Pjetër Budi), as well as four 'Dictionarij Albanesi' (the dictionary compiled by Frang Bardhi).[11] In a lengthy report written in 1665, when he was staying in Rome, he specified four essential texts that were needed by his missionary priests and curates 'in order to dispel, at least in part, the shadows of ignorance': the Gospels in Albanian (this has been identified, tentatively, with the Missal of Gjon Buzuku); the 'Spiritual Mirror' (a translation by Pjetër Budi of a little Italian devotional work, *Specchio di confessione*) and the Roman liturgy (printed in Latin, but with explanatory comments in Albanian by Budi: these two works were printed together under the title *Rituale romanum et speculum confessionis, in epyroticam linguam...translata*); and the so-called 'Little Christian Doctrine', a shorter version of Bellarmine's text, translated by Bernardo da Verona.[12] He also noted that all these texts needed to undergo a process of linguistic correction before they were reprinted (especially the translation by Bernardo da Verona), and offered to do this himself; but it seems that his offer was not taken up. Ten years later, when Bogdani was staying in Venice in the summer of 1675, he arranged for a new printing of the 'Little Christian Doctrine' to be made there (incorporating, presumably, his own linguistic corrections), and took the entire print-run of 500 copies with him back to Albania, for distribution to his clergy.[13]

It is probably not a coincidence that it was in that same year, 1675, that Pjetër Bogdani first announced to the authorities in Rome that he had written a religious text in Albanian—the original version or forerunner of the *Cuneus prophetarum*—and asked for permission to print it. (If that permission had been granted immediately, we may guess that he would have taken it to Venice and had it printed there; the reprinting of the 'Little Christian Doctrine' was presumably a substitute, prompted by the fact that the Congregatio de Propaganda Fide told him that it wished to see his work in an Italian translation before it would grant permission.) In his letter describing his own work, Bogdani declared that 'Albania has an extreme scarcity, almost a total lack, of books in the Albanian language', with the result that 'not only are the people therefore living, blinded by ignorance, among an infinite number of errors and abuses...but also, because this nation is situated between Turks, Greeks and Serbs, it is continually losing its language'. For those reasons, he said, he had been led to write a book 'in the Albanian language, his [i.e. Bogdani's] native tongue, about the coming of the Messiah, warding off, above all, those errors which he has found to be snaking their way among that people'.[14] Its title, he said, was 'Flavissae Prophetarum de Adventu Messiae Epirotice congestae ubi de Vita et ejus legitima potestate soli Petri tradita abunde consulitur': 'The Treasuries of the prophets about the coming of the Messiah, gathered together in Albanian, in which the life of the Messiah, and his legitimate power, handed down to Peter alone, are fully discussed'.[15] (I translate 'flavissae' as 'treasuries' here, though with some hesitancy. Modern dictionaries identify the word 'flavissae' as a mistake for 'favissae', itself a rare word used for underground storage chambers containing sacred utensils belonging to a temple; in the glossary of Philoxenus, 'favissae' is more simply translated as 'thesauroi', meaning treasuries or treasure-houses.)[16]

These details show that while Bogdani's primary aim, in writing the text that became the *Cuneus prophetarum*, was to teach Christian doctrine to his flock, he did also have a secondary aim: warding off the 'errors' which were 'snaking their way' among the people. Those errors included the claims of the Orthodox Church: the reference in the 1675 title to Christ's authority being 'handed down to Peter alone' was evidently intended to assert the Catholic position against the claims of the Greeks and Serbs. But although the text as we now have it does contain a section defending the primacy of Peter and his successors, as well as some other passages defending the Catholic position on issues contested by the Orthodox Churches (for example, Purgatory), it pays little direct attention to the 'errors' of Orthodox Christianity.[17] A much more prominent role is played by the 'errors' of Islam: not only popular beliefs (such as the idea that a 'falling star' signifies the death of a human being), but also religious beliefs which he attributed to Islam (such as the idea that washing with water would remove sins), and genuine

Islamic doctrines which threatened Christian belief (above all, the claim that Jesus had not died on the cross).[18]

The comments on these 'errors' (both Orthodox and Muslim) are hostile, but the hostility is primarily defensive, not offensive: Bogdani's main concern is to protect his flock from the sort of 'errors' which, if they went unchallenged, might eventually lead people to abandon the Catholic flock and join the Orthodox Christians or Muslims instead. As he put it in a letter of 1669, he made great efforts to teach the true Christian doctrine to his flock, in order to make them see 'the shadows of falsehood in which it is situated, because of its continual contacts with a Babylon of sects—above all, Muslim and Orthodox'.[19] In fact, during this period, there were very few conversions from Catholicism to Orthodoxy (which may explain why Bogdani pays comparatively little attention to Orthodox doctrines); the difficulties which the Orthodox Church caused for the Catholics came more at an institutional level, when the Metropolitans of the Orthodox Church claimed jurisdictional rights over all Christians in the region. But conversions to Islam were frequent. This, indeed, was one of the most important problems faced by the Catholic Church, as Bogdani's own letters and reports show. The reasons for conversion were manifold; they certainly included a general desire to improve one's socio-economic status, and, more particularly, a desire to escape taxes on non-Muslims (not only the ordinary *haraç* or poll-tax, but all sorts of extraordinary taxes which were often imposed at times when the Ottomans were at war with Christian powers). Bogdani himself commented on the role of taxation in people's decision to convert to Islam; and when one of his own priests converted (taking some of his flock with him), he attributed the decision to purely financial motives.[20] But he also noted that a major reason for such conversions was the failure of the Catholic Church to provide its flock with the most basic forms of spiritual satisfaction: because of the shortage of priests, whole communities were going without the administration of the sacraments, and without Christian burials.[21] Another reason, in Bogdani's view, was that the Catholic priesthood was poor in quality as well as quantity; their knowledge of Christian doctrine was, he said, extremely slight.[22] That, once again, provides an important part of the rationale for his book: he believed that people would not abandon the Church if they were properly taught, and a large-scale statement of Christian doctrine in Albanian was surely the ideal teaching aid. Given the low levels of literacy among his flock, we may assume that the most important category of intended readers of his book was the Catholic clergy itself.

So: if the primary aim of the *Cuneus prophetarum* was simply to teach Catholic doctrine to a Catholic community, its secondary aim was to prevent those Catholics from straying off into either Orthodoxy or Islam, by criticizing the 'errors' of those two faiths. This involved, as I have said, a kind of defensive hostility. But it is also necessary to add to the list a tertiary aim, converting people to Catholic Christianity *from* Orthodoxy or Islam; and here one might say that the strategy went on to the offensive. That Bogdani also had this sort of aim in mind is suggested by a comment he made in his letter of 1675, when he first informed Rome about his 'Flavissae Prophetarum': he wrote that this book would 'satisfy the aforementioned needs [of his flock] by providing a firm way of strengthening the Christians in the Holy Faith, and innumerable conversions of Muslim malësore [highlanders]'.[23] That such conversions did take place during this period is attested by several passages in Bogdani's letters. In 1660, for example, he mentioned that one of his own priests, Gjon Pal Roma (originally: Trumshi), was himself a convert from Islam.[24] In 1676 he referred to 'many Muslims, newly come to the Christian faith', and three years later he wrote that while he was Bishop of Shkodër he had converted a 'great quantity of infidels' to Christianity.[25] The most dramatic example of this came in the period 1672–4, after two villages of Orthodox Christians near Shkodër had been converted to Catholicism: following their example, a large group of local Muslims, amounting to roughly 200 adults, also converted. Bogdani reported that those ex-Muslims were then attacked by a detachment of soldiers sent by the *sancakbeyi*, but that the *sancakbeyi* had agreed to leave them in peace after receiving a monetary bribe—a story which suggests, incidentally, that in remote parts of the Ottoman Empire the strict official rules about apostasy from Islam could be treated with considerable flexibility.[26]

Some elements of a conversionist approach can also be found in the text of the *Cuneus prophetarum*. At one point, for example, Bogdani declares: 'It is better to be a Christian, the son of a Muslim, than to be a Muslim, the son of a Christian.'[27] (As always in Christian writings of this period, the word 'Turk' here is used to mean 'Muslim'.) And on the very last page of the work, he insists that although an unbaptized person who has led a perfectly virtuous life will go to Limbo, not to Hell, and will therefore suffer no positive punishment, the same is not true of a Muslim, 'even if he had never done anything bad in the world, even if he had done all that is good in the world'. Of course, it is difficult to make any clear separation here between arguments designed to discourage Christians from converting to Islam, and arguments aimed at encouraging Muslims to convert to Christianity: the defensive and offensive approaches will often end up, in practice, making the same points. For this reason, it might be objected that my prioritizing of the defensive over the offensive is arbitrary, and it might be argued that all of Bogdani's comments on Islam are essentially aimed at the conversion of Muslims. However, although it is true that the sources on which he drew included standard anti-Muslim theological works designed for conversionary purposes, it is a striking fact that Bogdani's book does not follow the structure of the standard anti-Muslim texts, which usually arranged their arguments in four main categories: a defence of the authenticity of the Christian Bible, a presentation of the doctrine of the Trinity, a presentation of the doctrine of the divinity of Christ, and, finally, a denunciation of the life of Muhammad and the doctrines of Islam.[28] Bogdani's book is not structured in that polemical way: its essential arrangement is that of an exposition of Christian doctrine to Christian readers.

At this point I should like to put forward a rather speculative suggestion about the ways in which Bogdani's text may have changed during the decade or so preceding its publication. As I have said, the first mention of the text was in the summer of 1675, when Bogdani asked for permission to print it and was told that the authorities would need to see an Italian translation of it first. After his return to Shkodër later that year, Bogdani reported that he was working hard at the Italian translation.[29] A few months might have been sufficient, perhaps, to complete that task, or even a year or two; yet in fact it took eight years before a full version of the work, in both Albanian and Italian, was available. (The prefatory materials to the *Cuneus prophetarum* include a statement by the author's uncle, Ndre Bogdani, that he had read and compared the Albanian and Italian texts in 1683.)[30] This suggests that, during those years, Bogdani was not only translating, but also adding significantly to his work. His early references to it (in his letters of 1676) describe it as a 'Life of Christ the Saviour', or a 'Life of Christ the Saviour, with his prophecies'; this may suggest that the original text corresponded primarily to what became, in the printed version, the second part of the work, the 'De vita Iesu Christi salvatoris mundi'—'On the Life of Jesus Christ, the Saviour of the World'.[31] Many of the passages which contain Bogdani's most vivid descriptive and narrative prose are to be found in this second part of the *Cuneus*—for example, the description of the physical beauty and moral purity of the Virgin Mary, or the dramatic passage in which Bogdani imagines Mary coming out of the Temple in Jerusalem and seeing in the distance the crowd that was escorting her son to the cross.[32] These were homiletic techniques, stylistic devices used by preachers to hold the attention of their listeners; I should like to suggest, therefore, that Bogdani's 'Life of Christ', the first element of the *Cuneus* to be composed, was to some extent put together out of the material of the sermons which, for many years, he had been preaching to his flock. In its earliest form, therefore, the *Cuneus* represented the teaching given by a Christian pastor to his own Christian community.

Whether the 'Flavissae prophetarum' consisted only of what we now have as the second part of the *Cuneus*, or whether there were already some embryonic elements of the first part, is hard to say. The life of Christ which now forms the second part of the *Cuneus* does itself contain many references to the Old Testament prophecies; so it is not clear whether, when Bogdani wrote in 1675 that he had written a 'Life of Christ the Saviour with his prophecies', he was just characterizing the life he had written, or referring in addition to some preliminary section in which those prophecies were separately discussed. If it was a preliminary section, then I would suggest that during the later 1670s and early 1680s it was significantly expanded, eventually becoming the first part of the *Cuneus prophetarum*. And it might also be suggested that it was during that process of expanding his text that Bogdani added more material relevant to his disagreements (both defensive and offensive) with Islam. Thus, after the very first 'discourse' of part I of the *Cuneus*, we find two substantial discourses on the doctrine of the Trinity—a topic which comes as an interruption to the overall narrative pattern (derived from the Book of Genesis) of the first part of the text, but which happens to have been one of the four basic categories of the anti-Muslim Christian treatises of this period. (And, as I shall also argue, some of the arguments used by Bogdani in his discussion of the Trinity were in fact derived from one of the standard anti-Muslim works.)

The idea that arguments against Islam grew in importance after Bogdani had already written the original version of his text is also supported by the evidence of his letters of 1675 and 1676, in which he asked for a copy of the three-volume translation of the Bible into Arabic which the Propaganda Fide had recently published. In his first letter about this, written just a few weeks after his request for permission to print the 'Flavissae prophetarum', he wrote that he needed it for 'his efforts to show the infidels more clearly, in their own language and script, the truthfulness and the foundations of the Holy faith'.[33] And in another letter, written at the end of 1675, he referred to his translation of the 'Flavissae prophetarum' into Italian, saying 'I am working hard at it all the time', and then continued: 'And because, in order to refute the infidels more thoroughly, it is absolutely necessary to have texts about the prophecies in Arabic, I humbly beg the Holy Congregation [de Propaganda Fide] to be so kind as to give me an Arabic Bible; it will also be useful in the peaceful discussions which the Muslims are becoming more and more accustomed to have with me about the matter of religion'.[34] It would thus seem that, during his visit to Rome in 1675, Bogdani had heard about (or seen) the great three-volume Arabic translation of the Bible which, after decades of preparation, had been produced by the Propaganda Fide in 1671.[35] Indeed, his meetings then with members of the Propaganda Fide might have given him the idea that they would be glad to see the edition put to use in the field (so to speak), and might also, more generally, have stimulated his interest in propagating the Christian faith among Muslims.

Yet although Bogdani asked for, and received, this Arabic Bible, and although passages from it were eventually printed in the *Cuneus prophetarum*, it must be doubted whether Bogdani himself had any knowledge of the Arabic language. In a letter of 1674 he wrote that he could argue against Islam 'in Turkish and Illyrian [i.e. Serbo-Croat]; I also know how to read and write in the script of the latter [i.e. Serbo-Croat], besides being able to speak the former [i.e. Turkish] perfectly'.[36] This implies that although he could speak Turkish, he could not read or write it—in other words, he had never mastered the Arabic script.[37] (Indeed, one might also wonder how many of the Muslims in his Shkodër diocese would have been able to read the Bible in Arabic: surely this would have been true of only a handful of people, the members of the local *ulema*. Most people might have been impressed by the sight of biblical passages in Arabic, but would not have been able to read them.) Certainly the occasional comments made about Islam in the *Cuneus prophetarum* suggest that Bogdani had never read the Koran. His overall knowledge of Islam seems, indeed, to have been quite hazy, and was apparently derived from a combination of printed sources written by Christian theologians and oral information from local informants, some of which he misunderstood. His most fundamental error, his claim that Muslims 'worship' Muhammad, was of course an error shared by very many Christian writers in this period.[38] But he also made the strange claim that the Muslims and the Jews 'follow the idols Muhammad, Surullah and Talmud', and in the Italian text at this point he described Muhammad, Surullah and Talmud as three 'heresiarchs', leaders of heretical sects.[39] Later in the text, listing a series of prominent individuals who had persecuted Christianity, he again gave the names of Muhammad and Surullah.[40] The most likely explanation of this puzzling name is that it is a distortion of the Arabic phrase 'Sirr-ullah', 'Secret of God'—a phrase used for Ali, the Prophet's son-in-law, in Bektashi writings.[41] Here, perhaps, we have a detail gleaned by Bogdani from his conversations with local Muslims; but it would appear that he had very little understanding of what he had been told.

Bogdani's knowledge of Islam came primarily, I believe, from the writings of Christian theologians. Two texts, in particular, can be identified as sources used by him. In 1651 he asked the Propaganda Fide to send him a copy of 'Apologia pro Christiana Religione': this was an anti-Muslim treatise published in 1631 by the Italian scholar Filippo Guadagnoli (*c.*1596–1656), who taught at the Propaganda Fide's own college.[42] And in a letter of 1674, discussing his arguments with local Muslims, Bogdani wrote that 'against the Koran I use, on many points, fathers Malvasia and Guadagnoli': 'Malvasia' here was another Italian priest, Bonaventura Malvasia, who had published a similar anti-Muslim treatise in 1628, entitled *Dilucidatio speculi verum monstrantis*.[43] Both books had been printed by the Propaganda Fide, and both had a similar origin. In 1625 an anti-Christian treatise by a learned Persian, Ahmed ben-Abdallah, had been brought to Rome, and a special committee had been formed to study it and prepare a reply; the texts by Malvasia and Guadagnoli were written in response to that treatise.[44] Since both writers were scholars of Arabic who had studied the Koran, their texts did at least contain some authentic details of Islamic belief—but their aim, of course, was to refute it.

Some traces of the influence of both writers can be found in the *Cuneus prophetarum*. For example, Guadagnoli's book includes a discussion of the popular Muslim belief that the earth rested on the horns of a bull, and that earthquakes occurred when the bull moved its head. Guadagnoli asked: 'If the earth is situated on the horn of a bull, where does that bull itself have its feet situated?' And he continued: 'Besides, the bull needs food to nourish it, since it is an animal: so what food does it have? And, as it is an animal, it must die, being subject to the fault of corruption: and so, when it dies, the earth will fall.'[45] In the *Cuneus* Bogdani makes essentially the same points, though he adds one further detail and presents the argument in the form of an anecdote in which he himself seems to feature: 'A bishop asked the *sancakbeyi* of Shkodër what the bull stood on; he answered, "On a fish". "And the fish," said the bishop, "what does it stand on?" He answered that he had not read that far. And he used the same answer to evade the questions, "What do the bull, and the fish, eat? And how do they stay alive, given that they are subject to corruption? And when they die, who will take their place?"'[46] Guadagnoli also criticizes the apparent statement in the Koran that when the Sun sets it descends into a pool or fountain. Translations of this verse (Sura 18, 'The Cave', verse 86) have taken various forms: 'a muddy spring', 'a fountain', 'a spring of black mud'; 'a dark, turbid sea'.[47] Guadagnoli's version is 'a spring of boiling water'; he ridicules this idea, pointing out that the Sun must be a celestial body located beyond the moon, since otherwise it could not undergo an eclipse.[48] Bogdani, similarly, attacks the notion that the Sun spends the night in 'a very hot spring of water', and presents explanations, with diagrams, of the eclipses of the sun and the moon.[49]

More importantly, perhaps, Bogdani's whole discussion of the nature of the Trinity seems to be strongly influenced by the writings of Guadagnoli and Malvasia. Both of those writers presented a philosophical defence of the Trinity, arguing that it followed necessarily from God's self-understanding and self-love, and using analogies drawn from the human intellect; Bogdani does the same, using the analogy of memory, intellect and will (used by Guadagnoli) and adding the analogy of the Sun, its light and its heat (used by Malvasia).[50] In particular, Malvasia emphasized, against his Persian opponent, that the generation of God the Son by God the Father was eternal, 'not from carnal intercourse'; similarly, Bogdani insisted that 'This is the eternal generation of the Son by the Father in God; and it is absolutely false, what the Muslims so insultingly suggest, namely, that our Holy faith says that God had a son by a woman.'[51] Malvasia also placed great stress on passages in the Old Testament which seemed to allude to the Trinity (for example, phrases repeated in triple form, such as 'Holy, holy, holy'); much of this material also appears in the third 'discourse' of the *Cuneus prophetarum*.[52]

Malvasia and Guadagnoli are not explicitly cited in the text of Bogdani's book. In fact only two seventeenth-century authors are mentioned there by name. One is the Italian theologian Gioseffo Ciantes, who is cited as the authority for the claim that various rabbinical writers have acknowledged the doctrine of the Trinity. The work referred to here is Ciantes's *De sanctissima trinitate ex antiquorum hebraeorum testimoniis evidenter comprobata discursus*, a little treatise in five chapters, which was published in Rome in 1667: Bogdani borrows material from the first chapter, and summarizes the second and third.[53] Ciantes, a Dominican from Rome, was famous for his conversion of Jews to Christianity during his period as 'catechist' of the Jews in that city (1626–40); after a period as Bishop of Marsico in southern Italy, he spent the last part of his life in Rome (between 1656 and 1670) devoting himself once again to the conversion of the Jews—a task which his little book was meant to serve.[54]

The other writer is the Portuguese Franciscan theologian Francisco Macedo, whose *Scholae theologiae positivae ad doctrinam catholicorum, & confutationem haereticorum apertae* (Rome, 1664), was cited by Bogdani on the subjects of Hell, Limbo and Purgatory.[55] Macedo served as Professor of Controversial Theology (i.e. the type of theology which is concerned with arguing against heretics and schismatics) at the College of the Propaganda Fide in Rome between 1656 and 1667; he then moved to Padua, where he became Professor of Moral Philosophy, and he died there in 1681.[56] His *Scholae theologiae positivae* included attacks on Lutherans and Calvinists, but its main target was the Greek Church, which it criticized on a range of issues including the Procession of the Holy Spirit, the authority of the Pope, the question of communion in both species, and the doctrine of Purgatory—on which it was quoted by Bogdani. Given the nature of Bogdani's own close connections with the Propaganda Fide, and the fact that he was himself an alumnus of its College, it seems very possible that he had made the acquaintance of Macedo during one of his visits to Rome (in 1660 or 1665); and he may have acquired a copy of the book in Rome in 1665, the year after it was published, with a view to using it in his arguments to convert Orthodox Christians to Catholicism.

Indeed, it is also possible that he may have met Ciantes in Rome during those visits. Bogdani was not active, so far as we know, in converting Jews to Christianity, but he no doubt understood that some of the arguments that could be used to persuade Jews might also be used on Muslims. It must also be significant that in 1683 the Propaganda Fide sent Bogdani (apparently at his own request) a copy of another book designed for the conversion of Jews: Giulio Morosini's *Via della fede mostrata a'gli ebrei*, which had been printed in Rome that year by the Propaganda Fide itself.[57] This substantial text was written by a Venetian Jew who had converted to Christianity in 1649 and had moved to Rome; in the Preface to the Readers, Morosini wrote that he had spent six years working on his book, and that he had received almost daily help from Giovanni Pastrizio, the Lecturer in Dogmatic Theology at the College of the Propaganda Fide.[58] This was a reference to the Dalmatian theologian and Hebrew scholar Ivan Paštrić, an influential member of the Propaganda Fide and one of the leaders of the 'Illyrian' community in Rome.[59] His brother, Jeronim Paštrić (Girolamo Pastrizio), was a canon of San Girolamo degli Illirici, the church of that community, and a close friend of Pjetër Bogdani; the letter in which Bogdani gave thanks for the copy of Morosini's book was addressed to Jeronim Paštrić, and at the end of the letter he also asked Jeronim to pass on his humble greetings to his brother Ivan, 'my dearest patron'.[60]

From this small but significant group of names, something like an intellectual and religious context for Bogdani's work begins to emerge. The common theme is conversion: Macedo aimed to convert the Orthodox; Ciantes and Morosini worked to convert Jews; Ivan Paštrić also supported that project. Bogdani may have known all these people personally. On his visits to Rome, the central institution to which he turned was the Propaganda Fide (where Paštrić worked); it was in that institution's College that both Malvasia and Guadagnoli had taught, and it is quite possible that Bogdani may have encountered Guadagnoli there during his student years. The Propaganda Fide had in fact been set up with a dual purpose: to sustain existing Catholic communities in territories ruled by non-Catholic powers, and to win new converts to Catholicism.[61] But although, in most practical ways (and certainly in numerical terms), the first of these was much more important than the second, it was the second purpose—conversion—that captured the imaginations of those who worked for the Propaganda Fide, and dominated the ethos and the mentality of that institution. So although Bogdani's own primary aim was to teach and protect his own flock, it is not surprising that he should have been influenced, to some extent, by the fervour for conversions that existed in the institution to which he was subordinate throughout his career.

If this is true of the world of the Propaganda Fide, which Bogdani would have encountered on his visits to Rome, it is even more true of the circle of Cardinal Gregorio Barbarigo in Padua, where the *Cuneus prophetarum* was finally printed. This energetic prelate, who was Bishop of Padua from 1664 until his death in 1697, had strong connections with Rome, having studied there as a young man; and it was in Rome, in 1665, that Bogdani became acquainted with him.[62] Barbarigo's family (one of the patrician families of Venice) had interests in Dalmatia, and it may have been because of those links that Barbarigo became involved with the 'Illyrian' community in Rome in the 1660s: he was appointed 'Protector of the Illyrian Nation' in 1663, and he kept up a long and very friendly correspondence with Ivan Paštrić.[63] (Indeed, we may guess that it was through the 'Illyrian' community in Rome that Bogdani came into contact with Barbarigo.) But Barbarigo's intellectual and religious energies were directed not only at the 'Illyrian' lands, but at all the territories in which either Eastern Orthodoxy or Islam played a role: for he was obsessed with the project of conversion, whether of Greeks, or Turks, or, for that matter, Jews. The existing Seminary in Padua was gradually transformed by him, during the 1670s and early 1680s, into a major institution designed not only for the preparation of local priests but also for the training of missionaries.[64] With the encouragement of the Papacy, he introduced the study of oriental languages there (Hebrew, Arabic, Turkish and Persian); his aim, he wrote, was to train priests to preach the Catholic faith 'wherever they might happen to be sent by the Holy See and the Congregatio de Propaganda Fide'.[65] In view of his eager desire to serve the Propaganda Fide, and his close connections with key members of that organization such as Ivan Paštrić, it is not at all surprising that Barbarigo was himself made a member of the Congregatio de Propaganda Fide in 1678.[66] And, just as the Propaganda Fide had its own printing-house in which it produced missionary materials in many foreign languages and scripts, so too Barbarigo developed a 'Stamparia' at his own Seminary in Padua, going to great efforts (and great expense) to acquire, or manufacture, type in Greek, Hebrew, Arabic and several other languages.[67] His aim was not to rival the Propaganda Fide, but to assist it—and it, in turn, happily assisted him, sending him matrices of Greek type from its own stock.[68]

There is therefore nothing sinister or suspicious about the fact that Bogdani's book was printed at the Seminary printing-house in Padua, rather than by the Propaganda Fide in Rome. There is no reason to suppose (as has been implied by Injac Zamputi and Dhimitër Shuteriqi) that Bogdani was thereby escaping some sort of criticism or censorship by the Roman authorities; the fact that they had originally asked to read the text in Italian translation before licensing it was perfectly natural, since they could hardly be expected to license a work they had not read.[69] Probably, in view of the many demands on the Propaganda Fide's own printing-house, the authorities in Rome were glad that this substantial work was taken off their hands. And Cardinal Barbarigo was probably also glad to take it on, because it came at a time when he had very recently acquired a range of oriental type, which he was eager to use. (In the winter of 1684–5 he obtained both a set of puncheons for the manufacture of Arabic type from the Bibliotheca Ambrosiana in Milan, and a large assortment of oriental type, including several Arabic fonts, from Grand Duke Cosimo de' Medici in Florence.)[70] The *Cuneus prophetarum* became, in effect, a show-case publication of the Paduan press: this was the first book in which the Paduans demonstrated their ability to print in a number of oriental scripts. Near the end of the second part of the book, they included a set of prophecies about Christ which was proudly described as being in 'eight languages': Latin, Greek, Italian, Albanian, Hebrew, Arabic, Armenian, and Syriac.[71] And at the very end of the book they included a tabulation of the alphabets of the unfamiliar languages, with instructions on pronunciation.[72] Although some modern scholars have supposed, on the basis of this, that Bogdani himself had a knowledge of Syriac and Armenian, there is no other evidence to support such a claim; it seems, rather, that his work had been used for the self-advertising purposes of the Paduan press. To some extent, indeed, the same may be true of the printing in this book of quotations from the Old Testament in both Hebrew and Arabic: this was, after all, the first publication in which the Paduans used their newly-acquired Arabic type.[73] As we have seen, it is very doubtful whether Bogdani was able to read Arabic at all. Where Hebrew is concerned, he may have had some basic knowledge of the language. It is possible that he had some instruction in it as a student, and his occasional comments on the etymology of Hebrew names may be evidence of some competence in the language (though they might equally have been drawn from secondary works); but his description of 'Talmud' as an 'idol' and a 'heresiarch', and his reference to 'Berescit Rabba a Jewish teacher' (*Bereshit Rabba* is the name of a text, one of the Midrashim, not a person), make it impossible to believe that he was a Hebrew scholar.[74] Given the evidence of his previous request for an Arabic Bible, it is of course possible that the idea of including biblical quotations in that language came from him; but the idea of matching those with quotations in Hebrew may perhaps have come from Barbarigo, who was an enthusiast for the conversion of the Jews. When Bogdani wrote to the Secretary of the Congregatio de Propaganda Fide in November 1685, after the book was printed, he declared that 'the prophecies are given also in Arabic and Hebrew, for the sake of two nations of unbelievers'; but, in view of the lack of any mention of converting Jews in Bogdani's reports from the northern Albanian lands, we may assume that he was merely going along with a conversionary purpose that had been imposed on the book by his Paduan host and patron.[75] To a certain extent, his book had been taken over.

Similar considerations may help to explain why this book, which had originally been intended as something that could circulate among an impoverished population in the Albanian lands, was in fact produced as a handsome folio volume: once again, the self-advertising purposes of the Seminary press came first. Of course, like any author, Bogdani may have been pleased to see his work finely produced; and in one way he was able to take advantage of these conditions, inserting several full-page illustrations. One of these depicted (as he put it in his letter to the Secretary of the Propaganda Fide) the Sibyls 'dressed in the Albanian and Serbian style, in order to encourage those poor people and console them as best I could'.[76] But it must be wondered how many copies of this book ever actually reached the northern Albanian lands. It is true that Bogdani declared, in a letter to the Propaganda Fide sent from Venice in January 1686, that 'my greatest and most ardent desire is to take it with me to my Church, so that the texts of the Holy Faith may be distributed as far as possible among those people.'[77] But two months earlier he had informed the Secretary of the Propaganda Fide that a bookseller in Venice had expressed the desire to buy all the copies of the book.[78] Although the Paduan press was never intended as a commercial venture, the degree to which its huge expenditure had to be subsidized out of diocesan funds had rapidly become a problem for Barbarigo.[79] Bogdani, who was very conscious of the debt of gratitude which he owed to the Cardinal, described the bookseller's offer as a 'miracle' and said that he was sure that it would please the printing-house.[80] He did not name the bookseller; during this early period of the press's activities, there were only two booksellers in Venice who regularly bought quantities of its publications, Pietro Orlandi and Giovanni Battista Indrich, and since the latter was from Dalmatia, he is perhaps the more likely of those two.[81] But a more plausible candidate is the bookseller Girolamo Albrizzi, who re-issued Bogdani's book in Venice in 1691. This has often been described as a new edition or a new printing; but such descriptions are incorrect.[82] It was merely a reissue, using a stock of the same printed sheets that had been produced in Padua in 1685. In 1691 Albrizzi printed a new title-page (calling the book *L'Infallibile verità della cattolica fede*, and describing it, absurdly, as written in 'lingua Italiana, e Schiava', the Italian and Slav languages); he also printed a new dedicatory epistle, from himself to Cardinal Francesco Maria de' Medici, and he omitted most of the prefatory materials that had been included in the original edition.[83] In 1702 Albrizzi re-issued the book, once again using sheets from the original printing, with a title-page bearing the new date and without the dedicatory epistle. Far from constituting two new editions that might be evidence of successful sales of the book, these re-issues are evidence that a large stock of (unbound) copies from the original printing had remained, unsold, in Venice. So it looks as if the bookseller's offer in 1685, as mentioned by Bogdani, was accepted. If the press in Padua had not spent so much time and money producing such a luxury product, Bogdani might not have felt under such an obligation to let the copies be sold in order to repay some of the costs; paradoxically, therefore, the decision by Barbarigo to take on the printing of this book—which must have seemed a wonderful stroke of good fortune to Bogdani—guaranteed that very few copies would go, in the end, to the people for whom it was really intended.

Other evidence of the ways in which Bogdani's project had been taken over by the requirements and the aspirations of Barbarigo can be found in the prefatory materials printed in the 1685 edition. Here it is necessary to bear in mind not only the Cardinal's general enthusiasm for the conversion of 'infidels', but also the sense of fervent expectation with which he followed the progress of the Habsburg-Ottoman war after 1683. He studied news reports of the war with great interest, and his own correspondence was full of references to it.[84] After the defeat of the Ottomans at Vienna, he wrote to Grand Duke Cosimo III of Tuscany that he hoped that Mass would soon be celebrated once again in the Hagia Sofia in Constantinople; and in the summer of 1684 he declared that 'I have always believed the capture of Constantinople to be extremely easy and extremely feasible'.[85] According to one of the witnesses who testified at the beatification proceedings after Barbarigo's death, he had serious hopes of being appointed 'Patriarch' of Constantinople once it was conquered by the Catholic powers.[86] Such a conquest was, he believed, really imminent, and he was in contact with many people who shared such a belief. One was a Franciscan from Lorraine, 'Nicolò Arnu' (Nicolas Arnoux, or Harnoux), who lectured on metaphysics at Padua University; one of the first things to be printed by the Seminary press was a little book in which Arnu gave his interpretations of a series of prophecies (mostly biblical, but also including a Turkish prophecy and a Sibylline oracle) demonstrating that Venice and her allies were about to conquer the Ottoman Empire.[87] Another such person was Marco d'Aviano, the charismatic Capuchin; when d'Aviano was in Austria in 1686 Barbarigo corresponded with him, having probably got to know him in Padua in 1682.[88] Fervent belief in such impending victories in the Habsburg-Ottoman war naturally carried with it some political implications, as well as religious ones: Barbarigo was strongly in favour of the Holy League, which seemed to have overcome the old hostilities between Vienna and Venice, and between Venice and Rome. In 1689 d'Aviano would describe Barbarigo as devoted to the Emperor; and two years later d'Aviano was approached by a bishop who wished to campaign for Barbarigo to become the next Pope, on the grounds that he would give the Papacy's full support to the Austrians.[89]

The Barbarigo circle's expectations of total victory over the Ottomans may even explain some of the other puzzling features of Bogdani's book. Possibly he had been encouraged to include in it outspoken criticisms of Islam, of a sort that could earn a severe punishment from the Ottoman authorities, on the grounds that within a short time those authorities would no longer exist. And it is possible that the grand format of the book was also designed with the victory scenario in mind: once the Balkans had been conquered, there would no longer be any need for the furtive smuggling of small volumes.

Those lines of explanation are, necessarily, speculative. But it can at least be said, with greater certainty, that the fervour of the Barbarigo circle, and its special enthusiasm for the Habsburg war effort, supplies the context for several of the items printed in the prefatory materials to the *Cuneus prophetarum*. They include, for example, a poem in Serbo-Croat by 'Pettar Riceiardi' (Petar Ričardi), written in Vienna; Ričardi, who was originally from Dubrovnik, had been made commander of a Croat regiment in the Austrian army.[90] This came with a short Latin poem by Pavao Ritter Vitezović, a friend and admirer of Ričardi who had joined Ričardi's regiment in 1683.[91] One of the longest contributions was an Italian poem by Dr Silvestro Antonii, who was the first Director of the Seminary printing-press in Padua: the whole poem was about the impending destruction of the Ottoman Empire, and the conversion, which Bogdani's book would help to accomplish, of all the Muslims. 'In the end,' Antonii exclaimed, 'the crescent will be turned into the cross, impious mosques will be turned into churches, and seraglios into cloisters.'[92] Once again, one gets the impression that the conversionist aims which had been, for Bogdani himself, at most a secondary consideration, had been elevated by those around him into the primary purpose of the book.

This essay has argued that Pjetër Bogdani had begun with a rather different set of priorities, and that the development of his text, from first draft to final printed edition, was a process that took place under various kinds of influence or pressure, both intellectual and religious (and, even, political). Nevertheless, it is clear that one of the elements of his original design (though only a subsidiary one, I believe) was an attempt to convert Muslims to Christianity: as he wrote in 1675, he did hope to bring about 'innumerable conversions of Muslim malësore'.[93] In conclusion, I should just like to add some brief comments on the way in which he approached that task. The phrase which I give here as 'Muslim malësore' was 'Turchi montagnoli'; but it is noticeable that in several places in the *Cuneus prophetarum* Bogdani refers simply to 'our malësore' ('i nostri montagnioli' in the Italian version). Thus at one point he said that he wrote 'in order to convince our malësore about the teachings of the Epicureans and Machiavellians'; in another place he praised 'our malësore' for the physical health and strength which they derived from their simple way of life.[94] It is possible that his word 'our' here signified Christians as opposed to Muslims; but the way of life, of course, was common to both. In his presentation of Christian theology he emphasized that Jesus had given his help to pagans as well as Jews, and that the Christian message was therefore inclusive, not exclusive.[95] He also emphasized that some of the basic truths of theology had been established by pagans (the ancient Greeks, for example).[96] And he gave special attention to the Sibyls, who had participated in Christian prophetic revelation even though they were not Christians themselves. In all these ways, he sought to establish his case not by denouncing other religions but by demonstrating areas of common ground between Christians and non-Christians—especially where his beloved malësore were concerned.

The main arguments of the book, however, were placed not at the level of human beings as such, but at the level of those human beings who accepted a common heritage of prophetic revelation. In other words, Bogdani had in mind what he thought to be the shared assumptions of Christians and Muslims (and Jews). His main method of argument involved the invocation of prophecy. He knew that many of the figures of the Old Testament also featured in the Islamic faith: at one point he referred to Muslims who invoked the examples of Abraham, David and Solomon.[97] Like many Christian writers in this period, therefore, he seems to have believed that the entire text of the Old Testament was somehow accepted as valid by Muslims, and that the task of a Christian theologian was to persuade them that the Old Testament, if correctly interpreted, pointed to Christianity, rather than to Islam. His argument was necessarily anti-Islamic, because, as a Christian, he denied that Muhammad was a true prophet. But at the same time he was framing his argument in terms that he hoped would be acceptable to Muslims—using the shared concept of prophecy, and appealing to the common heritage of two Abrahamic religions. In this way, an argument from prophecy, which was designed primarily to reassure Christian readers and to strengthen their faith, could also be used to bring into that faith those 'Muslim malësore' for whom, it seems, Pjetër Bogdani never ceased to pray.

7

The 'Great Migration' of the Serbs from Kosovo (1690)

History, Myth and Ideology

Kosovo has been fiercely contested, in modern times, by writers with di ... political and national agendas. This essay offers a historiographical case-study; it looks at an episode which is, or has been made to appear, one of the most important in the entire history of the region, and tries to account for some of the inaccuracies, exaggerations and myths that have grown up around it.

Let me begin by quoting, in turn, from three different accounts of the same sequence of events. The first is by the Serbian writer Dušan Bataković, a prominent historian who is regarded in Serbia as a leading expert on the history of Kosovo; it is from his book *Kosovo i Metohija u srpsko-arbanaškim odnosima*, published in Prishtina in 1991. This passage is about the invasion of the central Balkans by an Imperial army under Ludwig von Baden in 1689; more particularly, it concerns the smaller force which Baden sent into Kosovo and northern ... under the command of General Piccolomini, and about the conse- ... at intervention.

... ng down Skopje...Piccolomini withdrew to Prizren, where he was ... by roughly 20,000 Serbian insurgents, with whom, it seems, he made an agreement about joint fighting against the Turks. Soon afterwards, Piccolomini died of the plague, and his successors failed to prevent their troops from robbing and ill-treating the local population. Disappointed by the behaviour of the Christian army...the Serbian insurgents began to withdraw from the agreed alliance. Patriarch Arsenije III Crnojević tried unsuccessfully to establish a new agreement with the Imperial officers...Catholic Albanians, despite their promises of assistance, abandoned the Austrian army on the eve of the decisive battle at Kačanik, at the beginning of 1690. The Serbian militia, resisting the Sultan's superior hordes, retreated towards the west and north of the country. Turkish retaliation, in which the infidel *raya* were robbed and ferociously slaughtered, lasted a full three months...Fearing this brutal retaliation, the population of Kosovo and the neighbouring areas began to move towards the north with Arsenije III...At the invitation of Leopold I, Patriarch Arsenije III led the way, together with part of the high clergy and a considerable part of the refugees (ire, to the territory of southern Hungary, having obtained promises that a special political and religious status would be accorded to his people there... The Great Migration of 1690 was a major turning point in the history of the Serbian people. In Kosovo and Metohija alone, towns were abandoned and some villages were left without a single inhabitant... The worst consequence of the Great Migration was the large demographic collapse it caused, because after the withdrawal of the Serbs from Kosovo and Metohija, Albanian tribes from the mountain plateaux settled there in greater numbers, mostly by force. In the decades after the Great Migration the Albanians, who were mostly islamicized, flowed in like a destructive river, inundating the abandoned areas of the Serb lands. The plundering tendency of the Albanian tribes, thanks to their fantastic powers of reproduction, became a dangerous threat to the biological survival of the Serbs in Kosovo and Metohija...[1]

My second account—of the same sequence of events—is from the new multi-volume *Historia e popullit shqiptar*, produced by the Historical Institute of the Academy of Sciences of Albania, under the direction of Kristaq Prifti, Xhelal Gjeçovi, Muzafer Korkuti and Gazmend Shpuza. Having explained that von Baden had divided his army into two forces, this account states:

The second, led by Piccolomini, arrived in Kosovo, where it was welcomed by the Albanians. The Albanians were ready to accept the protection of the Austrian Empire. The Kelmendi Albanians did likewise. When Piccolomini came to Prishtina, the Albanians of Kosovo declared that they were for the Emperor. Six thousand Orthodox Albanians ('Albanensen') joined the Austrians. Piccolomini found the same situation at Prizren. The inhabitants of the town came out and gave him an honorific welcome. Roughly 5,000 Albanians, with their Archbishop, Pjetër Bogdani, greeted him with salvoes of gunfire... Austrian, English, and Papal sources show that Piccolomini was joined by 20,000 Albanians... After the death of General Piccolomini (in November 1689), the attitude of the Albanians changed for several reasons. The most important influence here was the attitude of Piccolomini's successors and the other Austrian officers, who began to mistreat the Albanians... The Duke of Holstein... tried to disarm the Albanians in Prizren, while in Lumë he ordered the burning down of some villages. [An Ottoman and Tatar army was advancing.] The Austrian forces and the Albanian insurgents withdrew to Kaçanik. The Duke of Holstein was obliged to organize a council of war, which decided to appeal to the Albanians who had joined Piccolomini, but it was too late. Nevertheless, the Albanians, loyal to the Austrians, took part in the war against the Tatars of the Crimean Khan. [Kosovo was reconquered by the Ottoman and Tatar forces, and the Austrian army withdrew northwards.] With the Austrian army there also

withdrew from Serbia and Kosovo many insurgents, allies of Austria. On this
fact, Serb historiography has built its thesis about the so-called 'great expulsion
of the Serbs from Kosovo and the populating of Kosovo by Albanians'. It is true
that among those who withdrew together with the Austrian army was the
Patriarch of Pejë [Peć], Arsenije III Crnojević... But the Serbs who left with him
were not so numerous as to justify talk of a great expulsion of them from Kosovo
in that year... Among the forces that supported the Austrian forces, two groups
were prominent: Albanians and 'Serbs'. From an approximate calculation of
them it appears that the number of Albanians was twice as great as the number
of 'Serbs'. According to documents of the [Austrian] military command... many
Albanians remained with the Austrians to the end. And among the expelled
people—who numbered fewer than 10,000—the Albanians were the majority.
According to one interpretation which deserves to be mentioned, the very term
'Serb', which is used in documents, stood for the Orthodox Albanians who came
under the jurisdiction of the Church of Pejë [Peć]. In which case, it must be
accepted that the insurgents of Kosovo, who accompanied the Austrians, were
almost all Albanians.[2]

My third account is more summary. It comes from Stanford Shaw's history of the
Ottoman Empire—a work which is based on Ottoman and modern Turkish
sources (especially the multi-volume history by Ismail Hakki Uzunçarşılı), and
which therefore reflects, in some ways, the views of Ottoman history held by the
Ottomans and Turks themselves.

While the Ottoman army massed in Edirne [in late 1689], good news came from
the Slavic provinces under Habsburg occupation. The strictness of the Catholic
priests in the emperor's army soon reminded the Orthodox population why
their ancestors had welcomed the Ottomans centuries earlier. From Serbia,
Wallachia, and especially Transylvania came appeals to the sultan to help restore
their political and religious freedom... the Habsburgs... were forced into a rapid
retreat... Many Serbs had assisted the Austrian advance, but many more, bitterly
disappointed by Habsburg rule, helped the Ottomans with renewed enthusiasm,
with Fazıl Mustafa [Köprülü] making a special effort to win back their loyalty
rather than punishing their previous treason. Other Serbs crossed the Danube
with the retiring Imperials in fear of punishment, and while many of these settled permanently under Habsburg rule in southern Hungary, many also returned
to their homes once their fears had been allayed by the Ottomans. Special
decrees were issued to make sure that none of the local Muslims would seek
vengeance and that the returning Serbian refugees would regain their houses
and property... Thus the Austrian appeals for a Christian uprising against the
sultan were forgotten, and efforts were made to restore that just regime that had
attr

one might say, a triangular pattern, with the Serbian and Albanian versions functioning as symmetrical opposites and with Shaw's version almost equidistant from the other two. I say almost equidistant because, although it makes no mention of the Albanians, its assumptions are radically opposed to those of both the other accounts. Indeed, what emerges rather strikingly when the Serbian and Albanian versions are looked at in tandem is how similar their stories are: the local people naturally wished to throw off Ottoman rule, and were therefore engaged in a general uprising ('ustanak', 'kryengritje'); the impetus of this was reduced by the negative policies of the Austrians; nevertheless, some element of the local forces continued to fight loyally on the Austrians' behalf; and some of the local people were later forced to flee. The differences between the two stories are, of course, that in one version only Serb volunteers play a significant role (Albanian fighters are mentioned, but only because they are thought to have deserted the Austrians at a crucial moment), while in the other the volunteers are all Albanians; in one version the Serbian Patriarch, Arsenije, is the key negotiator, while in the other it is the Albanian Catholic Archbishop, Bogdani; and in one version there is a large emigration of Serbs—the so-called 'Velika Seoba', the 'Great Migration' or 'Great Exodus'—which leads to a far-reaching transformation of the ethnic balance in Kosovo, while in the other there is a small exodus of 'Serbs', many or most of whom may have been Albanians. On these last two contested points it should be noted, however, that Bataković's claims are more modest than those of other writers in the modern Serb historiography; unlike many other historians, he introduces Arsenije only at a late stage in the dealings with the Austrians, and does not credit him with having rallied the Serb volunteers in the first place; and again, unlike many Serbian writers in the past, he gives an estimate of the number of Serbs who fled to the Habsburg lands which is both unspecific and apparently quite low ('several tens of thousands of people')—whereas, as we shall see, other writers have specified figures involving tens of thousands of families or hundreds of thousands of people.

Among non-Balkan and non-Ottoman historians, it is the Serbian version of these events that has had the largest influence. Albanian historiography is little known outside the Albanian lands; and in any case it has produced a much smaller quantity of writing on this topic. (The role of Pjetër Bogdani has been a focus of Albanian scholarship, but until quite recently Albanian historians took no interest in the 'Velika Seoba' of the Serbs; the text I have quoted is untypical in taking such a strong line on this subject.) The arguments of Serbian historians, on the other hand, have percolated throughout the West European and North American literature. To give just a few examples: in the *Short History of Yugoslavia* edited by Stephen Clissold and produced by the Cambridge University Press in 1968, the account of 1689–90 states that 'the Serbians rose with enthusiasm against the Turks', that Arsenije 'organized a great Serbian emigration northward', that 'some 30,000–40,000 families crossed the Danube to settle in southern Hungary', and that 'They had left the area around Peć, Prizren and northern Macedonia; and Albanian Moslems spread northward and eastward into the vacant lands.'[4] Peter Sugar's history of the Ottoman Balkans, published in 1977 (as part of the multi-volume 'History of East Central Europe' edited by him and Donald Treadgold) states that 'under the leadership of...Arsenije...some 200,000 Serbs moved northward with the retreating Habsburg forces in 1690...Southern Hungary gained a large number of Serbs, and Albanians filled the void in what is known today as the Kosovo-Metohija region.'[5] And in Barbara Jelavich's history of the Balkans, issued in 1983, we read that Arsenije migrated to the Habsburg territories with 'some thirty thousand families', and that this 'great emigration...contributed to the alteration of the ethnic composition of the Kosovo area...With the departure of the Serbs and the large-scale immigration of Albanians, the region acquired an Albanian majority.'[6]

If these claims about emigration and immigration are true, it follows that this episode is of fundamental importance in the development of Kosovo's modern ethnic identity. The standard Serbian claims about the nature of the 'uprising' inside Kosovo in 1689 also carry some implications about the way that ethnic identity was felt by individuals at the time—with Serbs supporting the revolt, and Albanians standing mostly to one side. As I have previously tried to show, these claims—in the strong forms which have been current in much of the historiography—are not supported by the historical evidence. But, at the same time, I have tried to show that the Albanian claims are also seriously exaggerated. In this essay I shall give a brief account of the actual events of 1689–90, recapitulating my previous findings and adding some other relevant details; my main purpose, however, is to look at how and why the exaggerated claims have arisen. Since most of the historiography has been generated on the Serbian side, most of my attention will be paid to Serb writings; but in discussing the events themselves, I shall also take notice of those points at which the evidence conflicts with Albanian claims.

II

When Piccolomini's small force entered north-eastern Kosovo in October 1689, it met with no resistance.[7] Most of the local Muslims had fled; some of the local Christian peasants had also fled, but these gradually returned to their homes. An early report noted that most of them were members of the Orthodox Church, and that they were now professing loyalty to the Emperor; an early history of the war, by Camillo Contarini, states that the local Orthodox bishops had offered the Austrians their homage. These statements are consistent with the fact that this part of Kosovo had a Serb Orthodox majority. The first large town reached by Piccolomini was Prishtina, which had a mostly Muslim population of 3,000 households (roughly 15,000 people); many of these had apparently fled, but one early account states that 'in Prishtina 5,000 Arnauts, having thrown off the Turks, and many leaders of the surrounding places ... swore fealty to the Emperor.'[8] Who were these 'Arnauts'? Although this word is normally treated simply as a synonym for 'Albanians', there are (as we shall see) some doubts as to how such apparently 'ethnic' labels were used by West European writers at this time. However, the fact that this writer clearly contrasts these 'Arnauts' in Prishtina with the people of the 'surrounding places' suggests that they were inhabitants of the town—in which case they were mostly Muslims, probably Albanian but very possibly including some Slavs.[9] When a foreign army had taken over a town, pledging loyalty to it was, after all, at the very least a way of trying to protect one's home from plunder or destruction—something that any person might wish to do, regardless of his religious affiliation. And pledging loyalty was not the same thing as enlisting as a fighter (though, as we shall see, some would do that too).

The statement in the modern Albanian history textbook (quoted above) that in Prishtina 'six thousand Orthodox Albanians ... joined the Austrians' is apparently based on a reference to 6,000 'Arnauts' in an early English account; what sources of information the author, Paul Rycaut, had is not clear (he was living in Hamburg when he wrote this text), but the figure is probably a slightly garbled version of the 5,000 Arnauts just mentioned.[10] What is quite unwarranted, however, is the phrase 'Orthodox Albanians'—something found only in the modern Albanian textbook, not in any of the early sources. The Muslim inhabitants of Prishtina may have been Albanian but were obviously not Orthodox, and the villages around Prishtina were Orthodox but not Albanian. The only way to justify this claim about 'Orthodox Albanians' in the eastern part of Kosovo is to follow the line taken by some modern Albanian writers who insist on a permanent absolute majority of ethnic Albanians throughout the history of Kosovo, and who therefore suppose that the Orthodox people with Slav names who appear in the early Ottoman records were in fact religiously and culturally camouflaged Albanians. Such claims, as I have argued elsewhere, are simply not convincing.[11]

After a brief expedition to Skopje—which, after deciding that it was not a defensible position, he burnt to the ground—Piccolomini then moved to Prizren, where he was met by the Catholic Archbishop Pjetër Bogdani. This was not their first meeting; soon after the arrival of the Austrians in Kosovo, Bogdani had gone to see Piccolomini to request that the soldiers would not molest members of his flock. No doubt their discussion at that previous meeting had included a suggestion that Bogdani rally the population of Prizren in support of the Austrians; and so it was that, in Contarini's words, 'Near Prizren, as he [Piccolomini] was approaching, the inhabitants came out to meet him with festive shouts: they were 5,000 in number and were led by their Archbishop, holding a banner with an image of the Holy Cross.' Many Serbian historians have assumed that this 'Archbishop' was Arsenije, the Serbian Patriarch; some have argued that both men were present to greet Piccolomini; but there is in fact conclusive evidence that Arsenije was in Montenegro at this time, and that he did not return to Kosovo until several weeks later, after Piccolomini's death. (The confusion was caused by an early report to Vienna, which apparently described Bogdani not only as the Archbishop but also as the 'Patriarch of the Kelmendi'—some early writers mistakenly supposed that two different people were being referred to here, and some modern historians, while assuming that only one person was involved, have taken the title 'Patriarch' as proof that it was Arsenije.)

Those who have believed that Arsenije was the ecclesiastic leading the crowd of 5,000 people at Prizren have naturally also assumed that the crowd consisted of members of his flock—Orthodox Serbs. But once we recognize that the ecclesiastic was Bogdani, the problem of identifying his followers calls for more careful attention. According to his own report just four years earlier, Bogdani's entire flock in the territory of 'Serbia' (by which he meant an area very roughly corresponding to modern Kosovo) came to approximately 1,000 households, and could yield a maximum of 3,000 fighters.[12] It is hardly likely that he had gathered all 3,000 in Prizren, and, even if he had, this would still not reach the stated total of 5,000—who, in any case, were described as the 'inhabitants' of that town. The problem is intensified when we read, in some of the early accounts, that during the three days that Piccolomini remained with Bogdani in Prizren (before Piccolomini died of the plague), it was arranged that the Austrians would be supplied with 20,000 local fighters. Count Veterani, the commander of the Austrian campaign in this part of the Balkans in 1690, wrote in his memoirs of '20,000 Arnauts reduced to loyal obedience to the Emperor by Piccolomini'.[13] An anonymous history of the war, written in Italian (and surviving in manuscript in two forms: the full Italian text in the French Foreign Ministry archives, and an extract in German translation, entitled 'Annotationes und Reflexiones', in the Kriegsarchiv in Vienna), refers to 'more than 20,000 Rascians, or Albanians' ('Rassiani, ò siano Albanesi').[14] Some other early texts, by writers who apparently had access to original dispatches and documents, specify Albanians: for example, Franz Wagner, in his history of the reign of Leopold I, used the words 'Arnautae' and 'Epirotae'—the latter being a term normally used to distinguish the Albanian language (and its speakers) from the Slav, 'Illyrian', one.[15] And one of Piccolomini's own officers, Colonel von Strasser, reported to Ludwig von Baden that Piccolomini had gone to Prizren in order to treat with 'the Albanians, Arnauts, and others' ('mit den Albanesernen, Arnauten und anderen').[16]

However, as that last quotation may suggest, there was some flexibility and haziness in the usage of these terms by West Europeans during this period. Some writers used the terms 'Albanian' and 'Serb' in a way that seems to have acknowledged linguistic and religious differences (for example, Lazaro Soranzo, in the late sixteenth century, writing of 'Albanians, who live as Catholics', and observing that Prizren was inhabited 'more by Albanians than by Serbs').[17] But others used terms such as 'Albanian' and 'Rascian' in very imprecise ways: Ludwig von Baden, for example, in his plan of operations for 1690, referred to 'all Bosnians, Albanians, Serbs, and other Rascian people' ('alle Bosneser, Albaneser, Servier, und anderes Rätz. Volk').[18] The term 'Albanian' could be used simply for the inhabitants of a geographical area; and for such purposes there were no clear lines on the map—indeed, no accurate maps in the first place. (One modern historian, Rajko Veselinović, has argued on those grounds that the 'Albanians' referred to in the early accounts of Piccolomini's dealings at Prizren were the mountain clans of Montenegro, which were Slav-speaking and mostly Orthodox; but enough independent historical evidence exists of the actions of these clans during 1689–90 to make this claim seem very unconvincing.)[19] And a further complication is introduced by the term 'Arnaut', which could be used as a synonym for 'Albanian', but tended to suggest those Albanians (in the ethnic-linguistic sense) who acted as soldiers for the Ottomans—though these, it should be noted, included Catholic Albanians as well as Muslim ones.[20] (When early reports refer to the local Ottoman forces, such as the force led by Mahmut Begolli [Mehmed Beyoğlu], pasha of Pejë, they usually state that they consisted largely of Arnauts; those Serb historians who claim that the terms 'Arnaut' and 'Albanian' did not mean ethnic Albanians, when applied to the supporters of Piccolomini, seem to have no difficulty in accepting that they did have that meaning, when applied to those fighting against him.)

With all these uncertainties about the terminology used in Austrian and Italian reports, it is not possible to make deductions with complete confidence from the mere fact that words such as 'Albanian' were used by them to describe the local supporters or volunteers. However, one unnoticed piece of evidence should be mentioned which has a rather different provenance. Among the papers of Ludwig von Baden in Karlsruhe, there is a copy of an intercepted letter, in French, written by a secretary of the English Embassy in Istanbul on 19 January 1690; it reports that the 'Germans' in Kosovo 'have made contact with 20,000 Albanians ["Albanois"], who have turned their weapons against the Turks'.[21] This may be significant, because the writer's information presumably came through Ottoman channels, and the Ottoman word for 'Albanian', 'arnavud', was not simply a geographical term, but referred to a people with a distinct language.[22]

Most of this evidence points, then, towards the conclusion that the bulk of the people who rallied to Piccolomini in Prizren—both the 5,000 who came out of the town to greet him, and the others who made up the total of 20,000—were, by our modern criteria, Albanian; but this type of evidence may still be open to some doubt. The doubt can be largely removed by considering the ethnic composition of Prizren. Prizren was a large town, estimated to contain 10,000 households in 1670. In 1681 Bogdani reported that just 30 of these were Catholic. Reports from earlier in the century stated that there were three times as many Orthodox Serb households as Catholic ones: in 1624 Pjetër Mazrreku reported that Prizren had roughly 200 Catholic inhabitants and 600 'Serviani'. But the great bulk of the population—12,000 people in 1624—were 'Muslims, almost all of them Albanians' ('Turchi, quasi tutti Albanesi'). There is no reason to think that this preponderance fell during the century; indeed, the steady Islamization of surrounding areas makes it likely that the proportion of Muslims grew. No doubt the 5,000 who came out to welcome Piccolomini did include many of the local Christians, both Catholic and Orthodox; but they can hardly have accounted for more than a fifth of that crowd. It is surely significant that one of the earliest printed accounts of these events, an anonymous text based on original documents, refers to Piccolomini being greeted at Prizren by '5,000 Arnauts, who were partly Christian Albanians and partly Muslim Albanians' ('5000 Arnauten, so zum Theil Christlich- Theils Türkischer Albaneser waren').[23] And the anonymous Italian manuscript history, which was also clearly based on dispatches and other documents kept in Vienna, says that 'There stood outside Prizren 6,000 and more Albanians, including the same ones who were previously paid wages by the Turks, and who are called "Arnauts"'.[24]

As for the fighting men who subsequently brought the total (at least in theory) to 20,000, some of these may also have been inhabitants of Prizren (which in 1670 had a population of roughly 50,000), but the evidence suggests that others were drawn from further afield. Contarini's account refers to Piccolomini, on his sickbed in Prizren, receiving 'the chiefs of the neighbouring peoples, who came to pay tribute to the Emperor with oaths of fealty'.[25] If, as seems likely, some of these chiefs had been summoned by Bogdani, we might expect them to have included the leaders of Catholic clans in the nearby parts of the Malësi; and, indeed, an Ottoman document written in February 1690 (just three months later) does refer to a large group of mostly Catholic clans from that area (including the warlike Fandi) who had allied themselves with the Austrians.[26] But the pledged total of 20,000 may well have included other Albanians from areas close to Prizren who were no longer Catholic, having been converted to Islam within the previous two or three generations—for example, the Shulla or Has region, where, as Pjetër Mazrreku reported in 1634, there had previously been 50 Catholic parishes but were now only five.[27] Mazrreku also noted that the conversion to Islam was quite superficial; in 1671 another report on this area stated that '28 years ago there were very many Christians [sc. Catholics]: now there remain 300 women and very few men, the rest having abjured their faith in order to escape impositions and taxes.'[28]

The point here is not that such people nursed a burning desire to restore, one day, their Catholic identity (this may have been true in some cases, those of the crypto-Christians, but these seem to have been few in number); rather, it is that the recent attachment to Islam may not have involved anything like religious conviction, and that it is therefore wrong to assume that such people would have felt any special duty to support the Ottoman state merely because they were Muslims.[29] What was going on in the mind of any local person when he or she decided to support the Austrians is difficult to reconstruct, and impossible to prove; but a modern approach which converts religious identities automatically into some sort of equivalent of national identities, and then expects blocks of people to have behaved along those fixed lines, is unlikely to give us a true picture of seventeenth-century provincial Balkan realities. The very small educated élite—the Christian clergy, above all—may have understood what Austria was, and what coming under its rule might mean; but ordinary people, including clan elders, probably had only the haziest idea. Their recent experience of Ottoman rule was (contrary to what is implied in Stanford Shaw's account) extremely negative. Taxes and other exactions had, as always, risen sharply during the anti-Habsburg war; and, what is more, in 1687–9 the *beylerbeyi* of Rumeli, Yeğen Osman pasha, had treated the territories under his rule as a personal fiefdom to be milked of its riches, and had employed armies of personal retainers to plunder it. That many local people might have welcomed as an alternative a largely unknown power—one that promised to respect their local rights, and one that was being promoted by a local figure, the Catholic Archbishop, whose moral authority extended beyond his own flock—should not greatly surprise us. However, when we recognize that such attitudes could cut across religious distinctions, this does not mean that we should fall back into the categories of most nineteenth- and twentieth-century Serbian or Albanian historians, with their axiomatic assumptions about a 'national' identity that always strove to throw off Ottoman rule. That many Albanians continued to serve in the Ottoman forces opposing the Austrians should not surprise us, even though we cannot reconstruct the precise combination of factors (economic interest, personal loyalty, local affiliation, codes of honour, and so on) that may have been involved. Similar considerations may apply to the case of the Slav Orthodox villagers of the Lumë region, to the south-west of Prizren, whose villages were burnt down by Holstein because he regarded them as hostile. One early account described Mahmut Begolli's army as consisting of 'Rascians' as well as Albanians; some of these 'Rascians' may also have been Orthodox Slavs.[30]

It has already been suggested that the Christian clergy were among the very few people in this region who would have understood the possible long-term implications of supporting the Austrians. In the case of the Catholic clergy, coming under the rule of a Catholic power was obviously a very positive prospect, and it is understandable that Bogdani and (after his death) his deputy, Toma Raspasani, were very active supporters of the Austrian forces.[31] But the case of the Orthodox Church was more problematic; Arsenije was well aware that the Austrians regarded his flock as 'schismatic', and that the long-term aim of Habsburg policy would be to force the Orthodox to become Uniates, accepting the authority of the Pope. Just one year previously he had sent an archimandrite to Moscow to ask for help from the Tsar; the warning given by archimandrite Isaias to the Russians was that if the Balkans came under Austrian rule 'the

Orthodox Christians will fall into a worse situation than under the Turks.' This does not mean that, by 1689, Arsenije was pursuing a pro-Ottoman policy.[32] Rather, he was courting another, potentially less oppressive Catholic power, Venice, and was compelled only by the pressure of events to return (from Montenegro, where he was in contact with the Venetian authorities) to Kosovo in December 1689 to make his accommodation with the Austrians. As was noted above, members of his flock had been expressing loyalty to the Austrians almost from the moment of Piccolomini's arrival in Kosovo; but their mental horizon probably did not extend as far as Arsenije's where Habsburg policy was concerned. No evidence has survived of any attempts by the Catholic priests who accompanied the Austrian army to force the Orthodox of Kosovo into union with Rome; this element of Stanford Shaw's account simply does not fit the case of Kosovo, even though it may have some evidentiary basis in other parts of the Orthodox Balkans.

Austrian rule in Kosovo was, in any case, extremely short-lived. After the disastrous defeat at Kaçanik on 2 January 1690 (which is attributed by some early accounts to disaffection among the 'Arnauts' on the Austrian side—though the most direct evidence we have makes no mention of this), the Austrians withdrew in confusion, and a joint Tatar-Ottoman force entered the region. Arsenije fled northwards from Pejë; also making a rapid retreat to the north were the Austrian troops, plus some 'Rascians' and Arnauts, who had been stationed in Prizren, together with the Catholic priest Toma Raspasani. As he later explained, the rest of the population stayed behind: 'Nobody was able to get out of Prizren or Pejë; they all remained there as prey to the barbarian.' The popular idea, promoted by nineteenth-century writers and still encountered in the modern historical literature, that Arsenije led a great 'exodus' of his people out of Kosovo is thus simply false. He travelled to Belgrade, and spent most of the summer there; this stronghold, still under Austrian control, was a natural destination for many Serb refugees, and those who gathered there during 1690 presumably included people from those parts of Kosovo (mainly the eastern half) from which it had been possible to escape from the Ottoman-Tatar incursion; but the majority of the refugees there were probably from other areas. (In the record of a meeting of Serb dignitaries held in Belgrade in June, the names of people from many parts of the Serb lands are specified, but, as it happens, no one from Kosovo apart from the Patriarch himself.) Finally, in the last months of 1690 (the chronology is unclear, but the process must have begun before the fall of Belgrade in early October), a mass of refugees, together with the Patriarch, moved northwards into Hungarian territory, settling in the area between Buda and Komárom (Komarno). Two written statements by Arsenije survive, specifying the number of people: at the end of 1690 he gave it as 'more than 30,000 souls', and six years later he wrote that it was 'more than 40,000 souls'. These are the most authoritative statements we have, and they clearly specify souls, not families. They tally quite closely both with news reports from the 1690s, and with other evidence of the pattern of settlement in the Buda-Komárom region, which was described to the Kriegsrat in 1693 as including 6,000 Serbs in Buda and 12–14,000 in Szentendre.[33]

Twenty-eight years after the move to Hungary, however, a Serbian monk, Stefan from Ravanica ('Daskal Jeromonah Stefan Ravaničanin'), wrote a short account of events in which he stated that the Patriarch had come to the Habsburg lands with '37,000 families'.[34] How Daskal Stefan arrived at this figure is not known, but it is so grossly at variance with the evidence just cited that it cannot be given credence by a modern critical historian. Nevertheless, his text, preserved in manuscript in the monastery of Šišatovac, has exerted an extraordinarily power-ful influence on the historiography of these events. The claim about 37,000 fam-ilies first made its way into print in 1765, in a book by Pavle Julinac, a history of the Serbs written in so-called 'ruskoslovenski' (Russo-Slav) and printed in Venice.[35] It was then repeated by the influential writer Jovan Rajić in his multi-volume history of the Slav peoples, published in Vienna in 1794–5.[36] From Rajić it was picked up a few years later by Johann Christian von Engel, who used it in the third volume (1802) of his *Geschichte des Ungrischen Reichs*; and it was thanks to this that it became established in the German-language literature.[37]

Only a few years after the appearance of von Engel's book, however, the first reference was made (by another German-language writer, Martin von Schwartner) to one of the documents written by Arsenije that specified souls, not families: as von Schwartner noted, 'I have seen an autograph memorandum by this remark-able man' in which the figure of 40,000 people was given.[38] A decade later, in 1819, Johann von Csaplovics wrote that Arsenije came 'with roughly 36,000 (some give this figure as 30,000, others as 35,000) mostly Serbian, but to a smaller extent Albanian-Kelmendi families (or perhaps, more accurately, individuals)'.[39] From this it appears that some information was also in circulation about the other document written by Arsenije, which specified 30,000 people; the figure of 35,000 is hard to account for, but 36,000 seems to be just a slightly modified version of the older claim about 37,000 families. Some doubts had now been sown, quite publicly, about whether these figures concerned families or individuals; but the doubts had little effect. (As we shall see, there were strong ideological reasons for this.) One Hungarian Serb, Aleksandar Stojačković, wrote in 1860 that the figure was 37–40,000 families, and that each family contained 15–20 people—yielding a minimum total of 555,000 and a maximum of 800,000.[40] (This was not, poten-tially at least, the highest claim ever made; in 1850 Milorad Medaković's history of Montenegro used the figure of 80,000 families.)[41] The issue could, in theory, have been laid to rest by anyone who consulted the original documents written by Arsenije. Unfortunately, the next influential writer to discuss these matters, Karl von Czoernig (in the 1850s), insisted that 'families' was correct, while at the same time referring explicitly to one of those documents (the later one—which meant that, according to von Czoernig, 40,000 families were involved).[42] Thanks to this error by von Czoernig, the 'families' argument became more deeply embedded in the historical literature; subsequent writers such as László Szalay (1861), Josef Jireček (1864) and Franz Vaníček (1875) confidently referred to '37,000 families', 'more than 30,000 families' and '36,000 families' (respectively), and the influential work by Johann Schwicker, *Politische Geschichte der Serben in Ungarn* (1880) stated that while 'tradition' said 37–40,000 families, Arsenije himself had specified 40,000 families.[43] Also influential was the generally well-researched study of the Serbs in Hungary by Émile Picot, which appeared in 1873; Picot summarized the Serb historiographical tradition, briefly noted Csaplovics's suggestion that the figure might refer to individuals rather than families, but came down in favour of 35–40,000 families. He declared that 'It is a constant tradition that this population was counted by families, not by heads', and also insisted that these were the large extended families known as 'zadruge'; so he concluded that the number of people was between 400,000 and 500,000.[44] And a similar calculation, producing the figure of 500,000 'if not more', was used, in turn, by the prominent publicist Spiridion Gopčević, whose book about Macedonia and Kosovo (1889) was lavishly subsidized by the government in Belgrade.[45]

The first authoritative rejection of these claims was made by the Serbian historian Ilarion Ruvarac in 1896: he cited Czoernig's reference to the document of 1706, and simply pointed out that the document did in fact refer to souls, not families.[46] Some other Serbian historians have repeated this correction—notably Dušan Popović, in his study of the 'Velika Seoba', published in 1954.[47] But many other writers have ignored it; the hugely influential geographer Jovan Cvijić, for example, wrote in 1918 that '35–40,000 families' came with Arsenije from Kosovo to the Habsburg lands.[48] These figures live on not only in the popular consciousness and in official sources (the website of the Embassy of the Republic of Serbia in Budapest states that in 1690 Arsenije came with 'several tens of thousands of families'); not only in quasi-scholarly works (such as the book by two Serb-American writers, Alex Dragnich and Slavko Todorovich, published in 1984, which specifies '35,000 Serbian families', or the article by the prominent émigré in Paris, Marko Marković, published in 1982 and reprinted with the writings of Atanasije Jevtić in 1991, which refers to 'around 150,000 Serbs'); but also in the scholarly literature: the standard history of the Serbs and Croats of Slovakia, for example (1976), gives the figure of 37,000 families, and a recent article on the same subject (2002) gives '36,000 Serb families' and interprets this as 'roughly 370–400,000 people'.[49] And, as we have seen, this tradition has flourished in the modern English-language textbooks by Clissold (30–40,000 families), Sugar (200,000 people) and Jelavich (30,000 families).

Once we accept that 30–40,000 individuals came to Hungary with Arsenije, however, it is still necessary to ask what proportion of those may have come from Kosovo. As has already been noted, there was no single, continuous collective journey beginning in Kosovo and ending at Buda; the starting-point of the final journey of those 30–40,000 was probably in or near Belgrade, and we know that people had been gathering there from most parts of the Serbian lands. One might expect people to have fled above all from those areas where the Austrian presence had been longest established (and where, therefore, the degree of local cooperation had been greatest)—in other words, an area stretching from Belgrade to Niš. On such grounds I previously suggested, offering a very rough estimate, that it was unlikely that more than one quarter of the Serbs who arrived in Hungary had come from Kosovo. Since then I have looked more closely at accounts of the Serb population in central Hungary after 1690. Lists survive of the heads of household of the Serb community in Buda in 1702 and 1720, which in some cases give the person's place of origin. An analysis of these by Dušan Popović gives the following totals: 70 from Serbia (excluding Kosovo); c.30 from Kosovo; c.20 from Montenegro; 11 from Bosnia; 4 from Macedonia; 1 from Bulgaria. In this sample, therefore, the Serbs from Kosovo make up 22 per cent of the total.[50] Among these people (but not included in the figures just mentioned) there were also a few individuals described as 'Arnauts'; Popović claims that this term just refers to Vlachs, but in view of the evidence already cited of Albanian support for the Austrians in Kosovo (and, indeed, much other evidence of 'Arnauts' continuing to serve in the Austrian military after the withdrawal from Kosovo in January 1690), it seems much more likely that these were indeed Albanians, some of whom may also have been Muslims.[51] However, the vast majority were Orthodox Serbs; the suggestion by the modern Albanian textbook (cited earlier) that the 'Serbs' who fled to Hungary were really Albanians is, as has already been indicated, groundless.

A full account of the movements of Serbs into Habsburg territory during this period would, of course, involve much more than just the journey of the 30–40,000 in 1690. In the period between the expulsion of the Ottomans from Buda and the expulsion of the Austrians from Belgrade (1683–90), efforts had been made by the Austrian authorities to settle large numbers of Slav people in the areas the Ottomans had vacated. In 1686–7 many Banat Serbs had moved across the Tisza into Bačka and Baranja; Serbs from Bosnia moved into Srem and Slavonia in 1688–9; during that period roughly 6,000 Serbs from the Užice area were settled in Slavonia; and in early 1690 approximately 1,500 came to Slavonia from the Tuzla basin.[52] In late 1690, when the Austrian line of defences from Smederevo to Belgrade to Sremska Mitrovica to Požega and Pakrac broke, and the Ottomans advanced as far as Osijek, many of these (and other) Serbs must also have fled northwards. The presence of large numbers of Serbs in southern Hungarian territory, in other words, does not allow us to make any deductions about the specific movement of people into Hungary from Kosovo.

Also uncertain is the scale of the later flow of people back into Ottoman territory. We know that this occurred, and that the main reason for it was the hostility of the Austrian local authorities and—above all—of the Catholic clergy, who put pressure on the Orthodox Serbs to join the Uniate Church.[53] It is also true that an

Ottoman decree of March 1690 had ordered a halt to the killing of Christians, and had offered protection to all those who had not actively joined the Habsburg forces.[54] This part of Stanford Shaw's account, even if he seems to put the Ottoman régime in an unusually favourable light, does have a firm basis in fact. But how many Serbs returned to Kosovo is not known.

Of course not everyone who had left Kosovo had ended up in Hungary. Some may have travelled shorter distances, from which return to their homes was easier; some may simply have fled from their homes into nearby forests and mountains, going back when the killing had stopped.[55] This was a pattern of behaviour which had unfortunately become quite common in recent years; Bogdani had done this with members of his flock in 1688 to escape the attentions of Yeğen pasha and his men. Early reports that Kosovo was 'abandoned' may have been quite exaggerated. Proper statistics are entirely lacking, but we do possess one detailed report by an Austrian officer who gathered information about Kosovo for General Veterani in early 1690: he wrote that roughly 360 villages in the Trepça and Vushtrri region were completely abandoned, that of a similar number of villages in the Prishtina region the greater part were abandoned, but that 671 villages in other areas (mostly in the western half of Kosovo) were still inhabited.[56] Of course, where a place was still inhabited, its population may have been reduced; of those who had stayed in their homes, some were killed by the Tatar and Ottoman forces in early 1690, and some were taken away as slaves. Epidemics also took many lives. But most of these factors could have affected all parts of the population, regardless of ethnic-linguistic or religious identity; and if the Ottomans did seek out particular groups for specially harsh treatment, they would have targeted above all the Catholics (co-religionists of the Austrians), most of whom were ethnically Albanian. (The Catholic population of Kosovo, said to be roughly 1,000 households—well over 5,000 people—by Bogdani in the early 1680s, was estimated at 2,800 people in 1693.)[57] The only major factor that might have led to a greater decline in the Serb population overall is the fact that the eastern areas, from which—as the statistics of those villages show—flight had been comparatively easy, had a population containing a higher proportion of Orthodox Slavs. But on the other hand there is evidence of a quite large drop in the population of the towns, most of which did not regain their pre-1690 levels until the nineteenth century; and the towns—of which this part of the Balkans possessed an unusually dense network—were overwhelmingly populated by Muslim Albanians. (Jovan Cvijić's claims about the departure of 35–40,000 Serb families from Kosovo were implausible not only on numerical grounds, but also because he described those families as mostly urban.)[58] When an observer such as Joseph Müller considered the small size of the Serb Orthodox population of Pejë in the 1830s—just 130 households, compared with more than 2,000 Muslim households—he attributed this sorry state of affairs to the 'Great Exoduses' of the past; but if he had been able to consult Bogdani's detailed report of 1681, he would have found that at that time the Serbs had just 100 households, and the Muslims 1,000.[59]

The larger question is whether the reduction in the Serb population created a 'large demographic collapse', leading to a 'dangerous threat to the biological survival of the Serbs' (Bataković); whether a 'void' was created that was 'filled' by Albanians (Sugar); whether 'with the departure of the Serbs and the large-scale immigration of Albanians, the region acquired an Albanian majority' (Jelavich). Given the facts we have considered, the claim that Kosovo was emptied of its Serb population would seem plausible only if that population had been remarkably small in the first place, or geographically limited to villages in the area between Trepça, Vushtrri and Prishtina. Serb historiography is reluctant—rightly—to endorse either of those views. The claim about 'emptying' is also hard to reconcile with the claim that another large exodus of Serbs took place in 1737 (though the two are sometimes blithely combined). Above all, it is difficult to reconcile with all the evidence that suggests that Kosovo did not acquire an Albanian ethnic majority until some time in the middle decades of the nineteenth century.[60] If the Serb population really was massively and disproportionately depleted in 1690, then it looks as if it must have been restored by substantial inflows of Serbs from other areas. In fact some such flows did happen, over time, from many directions; there was also a steady influx of Albanians, mostly from the nearby Malësi; but these were slow, long-term processes, neither of them involving any sudden surge of population into a vacuum. As for Bataković's claim about the Albanians' 'fantastic powers of reproduction', all the evidence suggests that where Albanian peasants and Serb peasants shared the same way of life (as they did, for example, in rural Kosovo as recently as the early 1950s) they enjoyed more or less the same birth-rate.[61] And claims about 'three centuries of ethnic Albanian genocide against the Serbs' can be taken only as expressions of a modern political position, not as a responsible comment on the past.[62]

III

I have already described some of the processes by which false claims about these events arose in the historical literature. In the last part of this essay, I should like to look at what might be called the ideological forces behind some of those processes—the ulterior interests and assumptions which may have led writers to distort their accounts of the 'Velika Seoba' in different ways, whether consciously or unconsciously. Most of this historiography developed, in the first place, in the Habsburg territories in the eighteenth and nineteenth centuries; to understand the background to it, we have to consider the position of the Serb population there, and the attitude taken by the Austrian and Hungarian authorities. Starting in April 1690, Leopold I had issued a number of proclamations and decrees concerning the Serbs. The first was a proclamation urging them to rise up in their own territory (which, it said, they should not abandon), and promising that when that territory came under Austrian rule, their traditional rights to practise their religion and to elect their own chiefs or 'vojvods' would be respected. Another decree, in August of that year, promised the Serbian Church the freedom to conduct its religious affairs, both in Hungary and Croatia and anywhere in the Balkans; this text also envisaged a speedy return to the territories that the Ottomans had recently retaken. In August 1691, however, when tens of thousands of Serbs had settled in north-central Hungary, another decree was issued, confirming the Serbian Church's ecclesiastical privileges on Habsburg soil, and offering (in rather vague terms) an element of temporal self-government too: it said that the Serbs would have their own magistrates, and that they would depend on their 'archbishop' in temporal as well as spiritual matters.[63] These and subsequent texts became known as the 'Privileges' of the Serb community.

During the Habsburg-Ottoman wars the fighting abilities of the Serbs (not just the ones in north-central Hungary, but the great mass of Serbs in the border region) were strongly appreciated, but at times of peace they became subject to pressure from both the local authorities and the Catholic clergy; most preferred, if possible, to live in the 'Grenze' areas which lay outside the civil administration and the feudal system. The decision to suppress some of these areas in the mid-eighteenth century caused huge dissatisfaction and led to the emigration of thousands of Serbs to Russia. In the latter part of that century the Serbs came under increasing pressure from the Hungarians, who were trying to complete the process of reincorporating the Grenze areas into Hungarian civil territory; a political dynamic developed in which the Serbs appealed to the Emperor, and more generally to the Austrian authorities, to defend or strengthen their rights vis-à-vis the Hungarians. (Such appeals often made reference to the Privileges accorded to the Serbs by Leopold I.) This dynamic was intensified in 1848, when Kossuth's hostility to any notion of Serb self-administration unleashed a wave of popular anti-Hungarian feeling. At a mass meeting in Karlovci in May 1848, the Serb Metropolitan Rajačić read out the Privileges of 1690 and 1691, demanding that they be restored and insisting on the creation of a distinct Serb territory (something which those documents had not specified); the crowd then elected him 'Patriarch', and elected a local commander 'Vojvod'. At the end of the year, after prolonged fighting between the Serbs and Hungarian forces, the new Emperor Franz Joseph confirmed those elections, and in the following year a distinct territory, the 'Vojvodina', was created. It was, however, placed under the administration of an Austrian general, and came under various pressures to Austrianize in the 1850s; and in the 1860s, when the new 'Dualist' system of Austria-Hungary was worked out, this territory remained part of Hungary.[64] By the last decades of the nineteenth century, with the growth of an active intelligentsia in Belgrade, it was possible to envisage a more radical solution to the problems of the Vojvodina: eventual incorporation in a larger Serbian state.

Against this background, it is easy to see how the story of the 'Great Migration' might be invested with a special significance. The early Privileges were constantly cited, and were often given a meaning they did not really bear. One of the most influential texts was written by the Austrian statesman Johann Christoph von Bartenstein in 1761, when he presided over the 'Illyrian Deputation' (a group that was meant to represent the interests of the Serbs to the Habsburg court); he argued that the migration of the Serbs to Hungary in 1690 had taken place 'per modum pacti', by means of a treaty, and that the rights of the Serbs were therefore stronger than those that might arise from a mere grant of concessions to a group of supplicant refugees.[65] This implied that Leopold's first proclamation had been a positive invitation to move to Hungary; in line with this interpretation, some later writers altered the text of that document, changing the key phrase from 'do not leave' ('non deserite') to 'leave'.[66] But the most important implication was that Arsenije, throughout his dealings with the Austrians, had been acting as a political leader and representative of his people; in the Serb congress of 1861 one speaker, Djordje Stojaković, insisted that Leopold's proclamation of April 1690 was an international agreement between the Hungarian crown and the Serb people.[67] In the 1890s Kamenko Subotić developed this argument further: for him, the fundamental 'treaty' had been the one agreed between Arsenije and Piccolomini in November 1689, and he deduced from the mention of 'vojvods' in the April 1690 proclamation that 'in the discussion between Piccolomini and Crnojević there was talk of a vojvodina.' His conclusion was that 'the Serbian people was, by the nature of its Church, an organized society—true, a society without a territory, but a political entity', and that 'autonomy' had been requested in a formal negotiation between that political entity and the Austrian sovereign.[68] For anyone who held these views—which had an obvious political attraction to Serbs in nineteenth-century Hungary—it was natural to emphasize several aspects of the seventeenth-century story: that Arsenije had taken a leading role from the moment the Austrian troops arrived in Kosovo; that he had organized in their support a large fighting force of Serbs; and that he had led his people (not just an ad hoc collection of refugees gathered together later and fleeing as best they could, but the great mass of his people, in one great purposive movement) to the Habsburg lands.

Some aspects of this were in tune with a simpler and more traditionally Austrophile attitude, which celebrated the loyalty of the Grenzer Serbs and their many sacrifices in the service of the Habsburgs. In 1854 the Croatian writer Andrija Torkvat Brlić (who had been closely associated with Ban Jelačić in 1848) published, in Vienna, a collection of historical documents about the support given by Serbs and Croats to the Habsburgs in the Habsburg-Ottoman wars, including much material about the events of 1689–90. His preface stated that ever since the Serbs came 'under the Austrian battle-flag', they had 'stayed under it, loyally and honestly, up to the present time, so that one can say that it is a fundamental law of Serbian national policy to remain on intimately friendly terms with Austria. This precept of national interest is deeply rooted in the hearts of the Serbs.'[69] As the century wore on, however, others took a less rosy view—especially those whose hopes lay in the development and expansion of the Serbian state. In the 1860s and 1870s a group of Serb writers, led in Belgrade by the nationalist historian Panta Srećković, began to take a very different attitude to the 'Great Migration', seeing Arsenije's actions not as confirmatory of Serb quasi-statehood but as hugely damaging to the Serb people and the Serbian lands.[70] As the historian Stojan Novaković put it, 'The alliance with the Austrians against the Turks is the only thing that one can approve of to some extent. Everything else is hard to understand; and the migration is the most unfortunate thing of all.'[71] These views were naturally combined with strong hostility towards the Austrians: in the words of Svetozar Niketić, the only things that could account for the disaster of the 'Velika Seoba' were 'the deceitful promises of Austria, and the stupidity of Arsenije'.[72] To these writers, it no longer seemed so desirable to emphasize the military cooperation of the Serbs with the Austrian forces. By the early part of the twentieth century, when Serbia saw Austria-Hungary as one of its main geostrategic enemies, nationalist Serb historians could quite happily argue that the Serbs in 1689 had resisted the Austrians; and a reason for such resistance was easily found—the imposition of Catholicism. Thus a popular history of the Serbs written in 1910 by an émigré calling himself Prince Lazarovich-Hrebelianovich stated: 'As the Austrian arms progressed, the ground occupied was annexed and German administration set up, the main immediate result of which was a stern suppression of the Orthodox Faith and attempts to forcibly convert the Orthodox Christians to Roman Catholicism. Those acts roused the Serbs to courageous resistance.'[73]

Such an anti-Austrian version of history was understandably popular during the First World War; and Harold Temperley's history of Serbia, published just after that conflict, strikes a very similar note: 'The plumed helmets of the Kaiser's soldiers and the black robes of the Jesuits who came with them soon became as hateful in their [the Serbs'] sight as the turbans and the muezzins of the infidel. Thus it was that the Serbian auxiliaries melted away in the winter of 1689.'[74] In Lazarovich-Hrebelianovich's words, the Serbs who travelled to Hungary found there 'an even deeper misery than any they had ever known before'.[75] Curiously, therefore, this Serb nationalist view bears a considerable similarity to the Ottoman view encapsulated in the account by Stanford Shaw.

For anti-Austrian writers in this tradition, there was on the face of it no reason to talk down the scale of the disaster: the greater the exodus, the greater the harm to Serbian national interests for which Austria was ultimately to blame. Some of these writers also emphasized that, as a result of these events, Kosovo was now dominated by an alien people: Gavrilo Vitković called Kosovo the Serbian 'father-land', 'which today is being set alight and burnt down by the Albanian, the fierce Albanian'.[76] But by the time of the First Balkan War, in which most of Kosovo was conquered by Serbian forces, the traditional notion that the 'Velika Seoba' emp-tied Kosovo of its Serb population had become rather an embarrassment. Great efforts were now being made by Serbian publicists to talk up the proportion of the Kosovan population that was Serb; ethnic irredentism depends, after all, on the actual existence of a significant unredeemed population. And so it was that in the most influential work on Kosovo published at this time, Jovan Tomić's *Les Albanais en Vieille-Serbie* (1913), the whole argument about the scale of the emi-gration was thrown into reverse. Tomić explicitly attacked the idea that the west-ern half of Kosovo was emptied of its Serbs: 'the Serb population', he explained, 'did not evacuate the areas bordering Albania proper, but, having been subju-gated, it was forced to undergo accelerated islamization and albanianization.'[77] Among the proofs he offered that the Serbs had not fled was the example of the Orthodox Serbs in the Lumë villages, who, he said, had actively resisted the Habsburgs; here the anti-Austrian historiographical tradition had prepared the way for what must otherwise seem a remarkable divergence from the usual ten-dency of Serb nationalist historians, which had been to characterize the events of 1689 as a general Serb uprising against the Turks. As for the local people who did promise support to Piccolomini, Tomić was willing to say that these were Serbs; the more important point to make was that they did not include Albanians. So, he explained, Piccolomini was welcomed by the Orthodox and Catholic Serbs of the Prizren area, and the islamicized Serbs of Prizren itself; but 'on the other hand, the Muslim Albanians had joined *en masse* the pasha of Pejë, Mahmut Begolli, and had withdrawn with him to the south.'[78]

Despite all the ideological pressures of Serb nationalism, a number of serious scholars in the inter-war years (such as Aleksa Ivić and Mita Kostić) did continue to maintain what the early sources had always suggested—namely, that the people supporting the Austrians in Kosovo in 1689 included Albanians as well as Serbs. This view may itself have received some ideological support in the period after 1945, when it chimed with the notion of 'bratstvo i jedinstvo' ('brotherhood and unity') between Serbs and Albanians. Thus the historian Rajko Veselinović was able to state confidently in 1949 that 'Only the Serbs and the Albanians rose up voluntarily against the Turks' in 1689.[79] (By 1960, however, Veselinović had radic-ally altered his position, and was now arguing that the allusions to 'Albanians' in the early sources could be explained as geographically based references to Orthodox Slavs.) But in the 1980s, when the situation in Kosovo became a matter of public controversy, one of the main complaints by Serb activists was that Serbs were being driven out of the territory; the theme of an 'exodus' thus took on a renewed importance in political debate. (In the 'Memorandum' prepared by the Serbian Academy in 1985–6, for example, prominence was given to the false claim that 200,000 Serbs had emigrated from Kosovo in the previous two decades.) It was in reaction to a revival of the old exaggerated claims about the 'Velika Seoba'—including a programme on Belgrade Television which stated that 400,000 Serbs had left in 1690—that the Kosovar historian Skënder Rizaj published the first explicit attack, from an Albanian point of view, on the Serb historiography of these events: while accepting that some Serbs did support the Austrians, he argued that the great majority of Piccolomini's 20,000 volunteers were Albanian. And although the detailed breakdown of that total which he gave seems to have been quite speculative, his argument was based on a larger knowledge of the ethnic and demographic situation in seventeenth-century Kosovo, derived from Ottoman sources.[80]

Overall, the position adopted by Rizaj seems to have been substantially correct; it is unfortunate that the modern Albanian textbook, while taking over his conclusions, adds further claims (asserting that the Serbs were really Albanians) that have no basis in fact. Each of the three accounts presented at the start of this essay is misleading in some ways: false claims about the ethnic identity of the emigrants are made by the Albanians; Shaw gives an exaggerated account of resistance to the Austrians and contentment with the Ottomans; and Bataković (while correctly avoiding exaggerations of the size of the exodus, and drawing a veil over the issue of a meeting between Arsenije and Piccolomini) almost eliminates the Albanians from the story, falsely states that the Serbs were 'invited' to Hungary, and grossly overstates the long-term consequences of these events. But I do not want to end by giving the impression that all nationalist versions are equivalent, or—still less—that an adequate history of these matters can be created simply by mixing together elements drawn from two or three nationalist historiographical traditions. What is needed is history written on the basis of the evidence alone; and nationalist preoccupations and presuppositions are precisely the things that prevent historians from seeing what that evidence contains.[81]

8

Ali Pasha and Great Britain during the Napoleonic Wars

Until the beginning of the nineteenth century, contacts between the British and Albania were minimal—very slight at the personal level, and non-existent at the official one. All of that changed dramatically because of the impact first of the French Revolutionary wars and then of Napoleon. After 1798, when Napoleon briefly conquered Ottoman-ruled Egypt (or at least an Egypt that was under Ottoman suzerainty), it was clear that the geopolitics of the warring European states would draw in the Ottoman Empire willy-nilly as a friend of some powers and an enemy, or a potential target, of others. At various times the possibility of a French conquest of the Ottoman Empire was something that all parties, not only the Ottomans, had to take seriously. Where the westernmost part of that empire was concerned, the French had now become near neighbours. In 1797 France took possession of Corfu and the other formerly Venetian islands to the south of it; it would lose them two years later, but regain them in 1807. By that date Napoleon was also in control of Dalmatia, having been ceded it two years earlier by Austria in the aftermath of the Battle of Austerlitz. After another decisive defeat for Austria, the Battle of Wagram (1809), France gained much of Croatia and Slovenia too (with some other territories), merging them with Dalmatia as a new entity, the 'Illyrian Provinces', in which French troops were stationed. This was the potential springboard for a large-scale military assault on the European parts of the Ottoman Empire. And while there was more than one possible route for a French invading army to take, one of the most likely strategies would have been to use the fortress and harbour of Corfu as a launching-point for an eastwards march across northern Greece.

This would have involved French troops passing through the territories controlled by Ali Pasha of Tepelenë—who, either directly or through his two elder sons, governed almost all of mainland Greece, the southern part of Albania, and a large part of Macedonia. Given the relatively poor roads and rugged landscape, armed resistance—on the scale that such a ruler could organize—would seriously impede a French advance, whereas assistance by such a locally powerful figure would be hugely advantageous. Napoleon was well aware of this, and made various efforts over many years to keep Ali Pasha on his side—by courting him, appeasing him or intimidating him. The British were no less aware of it, and made their own persistent attempts to win him over. And whilst a French invasion was

Rebels, Believers, Survivors: Studies in the History of the Albanians. Noel Malcolm, Oxford University Press (2020). © Noel Malcolm. DOI: 10.1093/oso/9780198857297.001.0001

the most dramatic scenario to consider, there were other potential large-scale developments that had to be borne in mind: the political conditions of the Ottoman Empire (especially in its European territories) were so unstable during this period that the possibility of a complete internal collapse was taken quite seriously by the Western powers. In that event, Ali Pasha would emerge as the single most powerful territorial ruler in the region.

Even without any such large-scale changes in mind, it was necessary for both the French and the British to devote attention to Ali Pasha, for much more local reasons. Corfu and the other Ionian Islands depended on the mainland territories under his rule for significant elements of their food supplies. When the British blockaded the French garrison on Corfu, the success of the British strategy required Ali's cooperation. There were territorial complications too, relating to a handful of coastal towns on the mainland which had belonged to Venice, not to the Ottoman sultans, and which were now claimed both by Ali Pasha and by the French. And the ultimate prize, from Ali's point of view, was possession of the Ionian Islands themselves: this was a reason for either opposing those islands' foreign occupiers or trying to gain their trust. That whole issue became much more complicated for him after the autumn of 1809, when the British took over most of the islands, while the French remained in control of Corfu.

For all these reasons, then, Britain had to maintain good links with Ali Pasha. British officials, from the Foreign Secretary downwards, corresponded with him; ad hoc envoys and military officers went to visit him; British representatives stayed at his court in Ioannina for months or years at a time. And as this relationship developed, the British discovered that Ali Pasha could also be of use to them—and, sometimes, vice-versa—in the politics of the imperial court and government in Istanbul, where Ali's personal agent was a significant player in the political game. The connection with Ali Pasha thus became an important aspect of Anglo-Ottoman relations more generally.

As a consequence of all this, there is a mass of documentation in British archives relating to Ali Pasha during this period: official reports by envoys, consuls, ambassadors in Istanbul, military officers and officials on the Ionian Islands and elsewhere, and also some personal correspondence written by several of the key figures involved. Only a fraction of this has previously been put to use by modern scholars. The best study, and almost the only one to make original use of such documents, is John Baggally's *Ali Pasha and Great Britain*, a little book (with 81 pages of narrative text, of which only 52 discuss the Napoleonic period) published as long ago as 1938.[1] Baggally's work was judicious and very reliable, but he had to treat some issues quite summarily, and he used only some of the documents in the National Archives (then the Public Record Office), the British Library (then the British Museum) and the personal papers of the envoy William Leake (then in the possession of Leake's descendants, later deposited at the Hertfordshire Record Office, now Hertfordshire Archives and Local Studies).

One recent book, Katherine Fleming's *The Muslim Bonaparte* (1999), quotes from some of these documents, but cites only passages already quoted by Baggally.[2] More recently, Irakli Koçollari has published an interesting selection of 59 letters from the British archives in Albanian translation, with a commentary (and with nine of the original texts reproduced photographically in an appendix).[3] But there is much more that can be said, on the basis of the full range of available materials.

The essay which follows is an attempt to say it. It does not in any way aim at giving a full account of Ali Pasha's life, activities and policies during this period; an in-depth biographical study would have to discuss other issues and consult many other sources too, above all in the Ottoman administrative archives in Istanbul. Nor does it try to cover fully Ali Pasha's relations with the French at this time; I have looked at many documents in the Foreign Ministry Archives in Paris and the Diplomatic (consular) Archives in Nantes, but have done so mostly in order to establish the background to Ali Pasha's dealings—and, especially, his double-dealings—with the British. Nevertheless, the details that emerge may shed some additional light here and there, not only on his relations with France, but also on his position within the complex internal power-relations of the Ottoman Empire itself.

II

By the time that the British began their official contacts with him, Ali Pasha was already fully established as a powerful regional ruler. Born in or near the little town of Tepelenë (to the north of Gjirokastër) in around 1750, he came from one of the small number of families that had ruled most of the Albanian lands for generations. His own family may have been one of the more recent among them, and it was certainly one of the least powerful during the period of his youth, but it still had the status of a family of pashas or *beys*—people who, for example, would marry only other members of equivalent families, not members of the general population.[4] Standard modern accounts of his early life describe him as having gained local power in southern Albania by means of his activities as a 'bandit' or 'brigand chief'; but to those unfamiliar with conditions in the Ottoman provinces at that time, this may be very misleading—especially if it conjures up images of a peasant upstart leading bands of outcasts from society. Conditions in the Western Balkan provinces in the eighteenth century were often violent, and local power rested in the hands of those who commanded large numbers of armed men. The governing families warred frequently between themselves; raising forces for this purpose required negotiating with others in their territories and around them, and for an ambitious member of the local ruling class the best way to expand one's power and influence was to become known and feared as a commander of men. An attack on another pasha might well be denounced by the authorities in Istanbul, who could then use the very general Ottoman term, *eşkıya*, which may be translated as 'brigand' or 'bandit'; but if the power-grab was successful, and the person who carried it out showed that he could supply taxes and, when required, soldiers to the Ottoman state, the new situation would be regularized with official approval.[5]

Ali first rose to prominence as a commander in the service of the powerful ruler of Berat, Kurd Ahmed Pasha; when Kurd Ahmed was dismissed from his office of *derbendler başbuğu* of Rumeli (Guardian of the Mountain Passes—an important role, as it involved controlling a far-flung network of armed men) in 1778, Ali was installed as his successor's deputy—and, *de facto*, as holder of the post. After a short time in that office he had extended his own power-base in the region to the point where he could mount a serious challenge to Kurd Ahmed Pasha; years of conflict followed, until the authorities in Istanbul decided in 1784 to buy Ali off by appointing him *mutassarıf* (administrator) of the town and *sancak* of Delvinë. Two years later he was *mutassarıf* of Trikala, in northern Greece; then, in 1787, he was made both *derbendler başbuğu* of Rumeli in his own right, and *mutassarıf* of Ioannina.[6] It is a sign of his quickly acquired diplomatic skills, and his appreciation of the role of foreign influence in Istanbul, that he got significant support from the Venetian authorities for this last appointment.[7] The city of Ioannina, an important centre of communications as well as trade, would remain his administrative base for the rest of his career.

Once installed in Ioannina, Ali devoted himself to consolidating and extending his own power. He gradually built up, by fair means or foul, a huge portfolio of *çiftliks* (privately owned agricultural estates); eventually he would possess 403 in the Epirus region, and another 477 elsewhere, and it would be estimated that his income from these alone came to 4 million piastres (at least £200,000 sterling at the time).[8] But he had various other income streams, including the farming of taxes for the central government; in 1807 one estimate put his total income at three times that amount.[9] Much of the wealth of the region was generated by local Greek and Vlach merchants, members of Epirot families that had been trading in Ancona, Venice and further afield for generations.[10] Ali was adept at extracting money from this source. There are many reports of him unjustly confiscating property, or imposing himself as principal heir when a merchant died, and it was also said that he forbade merchants to take their entire families abroad, obliging them to leave at least one relative as a hostage.[11]

And yet the bulk of this community did remain in Ali's territory, not just residing there but trading actively through it, and they did so for two reasons. One was the fact that he took care to treat the Greek Christians in an even-handed way, positively cultivating the support of the Orthodox Church (by, for example, permitting the use of church bells and the building of new churches, and even subsidizing an Orthodox school).[12] The other reason was the most important general benefit supplied by Ali's rule: public security. From his time as acting *derbendler başbuğu* he understood that there was more than one way of using armed force to generate political power. In the unsettled conditions of the eighteenth-century Ottoman Empire, any local ruler who could guarantee public safety, in towns and villages and also on the roads between them, was assured of much genuine support, which could outweigh the individual hostilities caused by particular acts of oppression. Admiring comments on this recur again and again in contemporary writings. The first Englishman to visit Ali Pasha in Ioannina, the geologist and antiquary (and, at the time, enthusiast for revolutionary France) John Hawkins, who was voyaging in the region and went there briefly in 1795, was struck by the relative security of travel in Ali's territories.[13] The next, and the first to visit Ali in an official capacity, was William Hamilton, who reported in 1803: 'He has... established the most perfect tranquillity, & security of Persons & Property throughout his dominions, whose Inhabitants, Greeks and Turks, are richer, happier, more Contented, & less oppressed, than in any other part of European Turkey.'[14] Henry Holland and Thomas Smart Hughes would make similar points, and Frederick Douglas, who visited Ioannina in 1811, would write that many people from the Peloponnese had been migrating into Ali's territory, 'where the tyrant, though naturally as cruel and avaricious as his son [Veli, then governor of the Peloponnese], is rendered more tolerable by superiority of genius and security of possession. The Greek finds that he may carry on the vast inland commerce that passes through his territory, certain (to use the image of Montesquieu) that though the fruit be plucked the tree will be left to produce again.'[15] Even the French officer Guillaume de Vaudoncourt, who devoted pages of his account to dissecting Ali Pasha's many vices, felt obliged to add: 'With regard to the security the people enjoy, the religious toleration accorded to the Greeks much more in his dominions than in the rest of the Ottoman empire, and the privileges he grants to those same Greeks by employing them indistinctly [*sc.* without distinction] near his person, or in subaltern commands, his government is moderate and equitable.'[16]

While Ali built up his own personal wealth and influence during the first decade or so of his rule in Ioannina, he also sought ways of extending his territorial power. In 1789 and again in 1792 he tried to subdue the small but fiercely independent-minded mountain district of Souli, and in the latter year he also attacked the *sancakbeyi* of Delvinë and that man's allies (and nominal subjects), the inhabitants of the coastal district of Himarë.[17] One year later Ali willingly responded to the Sultan's call for troops to attack the rebellious pasha of Shkodër, Kara Mahmud Bushatli, taking that opportunity to occupy the *sancak* of Ohrid, which he hoped (in vain) to be allowed to retain thereafter.[18] In 1796 he annexed the *voyvodlık* (tax district) of Arta, thereby pushing the southern boundary of the Ioannina *sancak* all the way to the Gulf of Arta (or Ambracian Gulf). In 1798 a major campaign brought him victory, at last, over both the *sancakbeyi* of Delvinë, Mustafa Pasha, and the warring confederation of villages of Himarë.[19] Other attempted land-grabs would follow, as we shall see, and in 1803 a final campaign against Souli would end in victory there too.

Some of Ali's efforts of this kind, such as his seizing of Ohrid and his later conquest of Albanian territories to the north of the Ioannina *sancak*, can be seen as pure expansionism, aimed at changing the local regional balance of power and gaining new resources, revenues and manpower. But in several cases there were more specific motives, relating directly to the security and prosperity of his core lands. Like several other mountain districts in the Balkans where local agriculture could barely support the population, and where the require-ments of a largely self-policing society had set a premium on fighting skills, both Himarë and Souli produced bands of armed men who could either engage in raiding expeditions on their own account or serve those who had the money to hire them. Henry Holland was told that the warriors of Souli 'were the terror of the southern part of Albania; and the descent of the Souliotes from their mountain-fastnesses, for the sake of plunder or vengeance, was a general signal of alarm to the surrounding country'; his informant was one of Ali's officials, but other sources corroborate this.[20] Ali Pasha's concern was not only with the areas that generated raiders and robbers, but also with the places that could serve as their refuges; as he gradually extended his power over the former, he became more exercised over the latter—which, as we shall see, would supply him with an extra reason for coveting some of the nearby islands to the west. As for the Arta district: seizing this gave him more control over the trade of the region. From the little port of Salaora, which served Arta, there were exports of olive oil, tobacco and cotton, as well as up to 30 shiploads a year of timber; and the customs dues levied there, which in principle belonged to the Sultan, were treated by Ali as his own income.[21] Small though it may have been, this was for some time the only significant port to which Ali had direct and undisputed access. Several other coastal towns—including the ones that had belonged his-torically to Venice—lay outside his domains; and the overland routes to the ports to the west of Ioannina (Igoumenitsa and Sagiada) passed through the district of Çamëri, which was closely linked to the pashas of Delvinë and often allied with them, and/or the Himariots, against Ali Pasha.[22] When one considers Ali's unrelenting efforts to subdue his local enemies on the western seaboard and to take over the remaining ports and pockets of land there, it is important to understand that this was not the mere reflex of an obsessive accumulator determined to leave no gaps on the map; rather, he was following a strategy that was intimately connected with the methods of rule—guaranteeing security, encouraging trade and extracting financial advantage from it—on which his overall success depended.

III

France conquered Venice in May 1797, and Corfu was occupied by French forces in the following month. Under an earlier secret agreement, France had pledged all the Ionian Islands under Venetian rule (Corfu, Paxos, Lefkada or Lefkas (Ital.: Santa Maura), Ithaca, Cephalonia, Zakynthos (Ital.: Zante) and Cythera (Ital.: Cerigo)), together with Venice's other possessions in the eastern Adriatic, to Austria; but in October of that year the Treaty of Campo Formio, signed by Napoleon Bonaparte as commander of the forces of the French Republic in Italy, transferred the islands to France. General Gentili, who managed the French take-over of the islands in June, was quick to assert French rights also to the four Venetian-ruled places on the coast of the mainland: Butrint, Parga, Preveza and Vonitsa. He had a formal meeting with Ali Pasha in August, at which Ali prom-ised friendship and cooperation but also made a series of requests and demands: for the right to sail his own ships through the Corfu Channel (something the Venetians had always denied him), for military assistance, especially the loan of some skilled artillery experts, and even for the right to establish an outpost of his own at Butrint.[23] Thus was the basic pattern of Ali's dealings with such foreign powers quickly established: courtesy and benign promises on the one hand, and demands—always pushing beyond the limit of what was likely to be granted—on the other.

That request to take over, in effect, the little Venetian fortress at Butrint (oppos-ite Corfu) was denied. In November 1797 Napoleon wrote to Gentili from Milan:

> You did very well, Citizen General, to refuse Ali Pasha's demands. Nevertheless, while preventing him from encroaching on our territory, you should favour him as much as you can. It is in the interests of the Republic that this pasha should enjoy a great increase in power and defeat all his rivals, so that he can become a prince with sufficient power to be able to serve the Republic. The possessions we have are so close to him that he will never cease to have an interest in being our friend. Send engineers and staff officers to spend time with him, so that you can be informed about the conditions, population and way of life of all Albania; commission geographical and topographical studies of all this area, which is now of such interest to us, from Albania to the Peloponnese; and make arrangements to become well informed about all the intrigues that divide these people.[24]

Here too some of the themes of the future French relationship were laid down at the outset: resistance to Ali's territorial demands, balanced with the idea that he was both pro-French in principle—though that impression would be subject to change—and the most important person to do business with in practice; but also, at the same time, an interest in fishing in the troubled waters of Ottoman Albania and Greece, with a view to encouraging anti-Ottoman actions more generally among the population. Earlier that year Napoleon had written to Talleyrand, the French Foreign Minister, that 'it would be pointless to try to prop up the Ottoman Empire; we shall see it fall in our time... The fanatical love of liberty, which is already beginning to arise in Greece, will be more powerful there than religious fanaticism.'[25] Ali Pasha was no religious fanatic, but this aspect of French policy could only be worrying for him.

For several months, Ali encouraged the French as amicably as he could. Gentili's successor, General Chabot, sent his chief of staff, Adjutant-General Nicolas Roze, to negotiate; Ali agreed to send large quantities of supplies to Corfu (for which he was never paid), and honoured the all-too-easily flattered Adjutant-General to the extent of arranging his marriage to a famously beautiful local bride. In the summer of 1798, when Napoleon invaded Ottoman Egypt, Ali was absent from Ioannina. He had been summoned by the Sultan in late 1797 to take part in the campaign against the rebellious pasha Osman Pasvanoğlu in Bulgaria, and devoted himself to that task with energy and efficiency over the next six months.[26] The French on Corfu hoped that Ali would see the invasion of Egypt as the first stage in a break-up of the Ottoman Empire from which he stood to benefit; but they were not sure of Ali's position until he returned in the autumn—and, even then, not for a while. In October Roze blithely accepted an invitation to a meeting with Ali, who promptly arrested him and another French officer, and then demanded as the price of their return not only the payments he was owed but also the ceding of Butrint, Parga, Preveza and Vonitsa. When these demands were rejected, he sent Roze in chains to Istanbul (where he would die in prison), and overran the garrisons of Butrint and Preveza, capturing more than 100 French soldiers at the latter. Vonitsa was taken without a fight soon afterwards.[27] Allegedly, Ali made his French prisoners strip the skin from the heads of their dead comrades, so that trophy-heads could be sent to Istanbul. (This was an Ottoman custom. As a British agent at Ali's court would later explain, 'the heads sent to Const[antinople] in pickle are nothing but the skin stuffed with straw— they are moistened to improve their looks before they are presented to the Grand Vezir or Kaimakam.')[28]

These actions gained Ali Pasha much credit with the Sultan, who was now at war with France. But Ali's loyalty to his imperial ruler was tested almost immediately by the arrival of a joint Russian–Ottoman fleet, under the primary command of the Russian Vice-Admiral Ushakov, tasked with driving the French out of the Ionian Islands.[29] Russia was a traditional enemy of the Ottomans, having fought two major wars against them in Ali's lifetime, in 1768–74 and 1787–92; and, in contrast with the case of France, it was clear that Russia had long-standing ambitions to take territory permanently from the Ottoman Empire. Although Ali Pasha had played a delicate double game in 1791, opening his own line of communication to the Russian commander Prince Potemkin, his general position was one of deep suspicion towards Russian designs.[30] It did not help, either, that the fleet arrived just in time to take possession of two other targets of Ali's own ambitions: the stronghold of Parga, and the island of Lefkada, where many of Ali's most rebellious subjects had taken refuge. As the siege of the main French garrison in Corfu lasted through the winter and into the spring of 1799, Ali tried out various tactics: refusing to let the Russians recruit men from his territory, offering help in return for being given eventual control over the island, and asking the French to hand over Corfu to him in return for safe passage.[31] In the event, Chabot surrendered to Ushakov on honourable terms in March 1799, and Corfu lay once more beyond Ali's reach. After much negotiation between Moscow and Istanbul, a Russian–Ottoman convention was drawn up in 1800 under which the seven Ionian Islands were declared a separate, self-governing state, the 'Septinsular Republic'. This was theoretically under Ottoman suzerainty, but predominantly under Russian military control; much complicated juggling for power would take place between the two governments, with the Ionian islanders cannily making use of both to further their own interests. The four ex-Venetian coastal possessions were not included in this republic. The three towns, Parga, Preveza and Vonitsa, were granted a kind of municipal self-government, each with the presence of an *ağa* or Ottoman officer as its symbolic governor on the Sultan's behalf. As their populations were entirely Christian, it was agreed that they would have all the privileges currently allowed to Moldavia and Wallachia, and that no Muslim (other than the Ottoman governor) would be allowed to own property or even reside there; Ali Pasha's troops were therefore withdrawn. Meanwhile Butrint—which was not a town, merely a historic site with a village and a small fort commanding a valuable harbour and rich fishing-grounds—remained under its governor's authority *de jure*, but under Ali's *de facto* control, manned by his soldiers.[32]

The first signs of any significant connections between the British authorities and Ali Pasha date from this troubled period. Since 1798 Britain had been a formal ally of Russia, and this led to some new British involvement in the area; in 1799–1800, for example, a British officer, Lieutenant-General William Villette, spent time on Corfu trying to recruit a regiment of Albanian troops. (This took place with the blessing of the Sultan, who ordered Ali to supply 2,000 soldiers to the British, but it caused some friction at the local level, as the Russian authorities there were opposed to extending British influence in this way.)[33] But the key figure was a native of Zakynthos, Spiridion Foresti (Spuridōn Phorestēs), who had served as British Consul there since 1789. Held by the French on Corfu in the summer of 1797, he was released and allowed to go to Venice in August 1798; he later spent some time with Ushakov's fleet, before being reinstalled first as Consul on Zakynthos and then, from September 1799, as Resident Minister—i.e. diplomatic representative of Britain—on Corfu.[34]

It seems that the first high-level communications were between Ali Pasha and Lord Nelson, the acting commander-in-chief of the British fleet in the Mediterranean. On 19 November 1799 Ali sent a letter (in Latin) to Nelson, which began: 'In other letters to you, I have already expressed my love for your most famous nation; moreover, I have also fulfilled, very precisely and very speedily, all the demands of your consuls, and also of your envoy', and ended with the words 'I remain your perpetual, loyal and sincere friend.'[35] The 'consuls' were probably Foresti and Nicholas Strane, British Consul in the port of Patras; the 'envoy' was most probably an officer sent specially by Nelson to congratulate Ali on his defeat of the French at Preveza in 1798.[36] Two months later Ali wrote another letter to Nelson, again in his most florid complimentary style: in view of 'your glorious deeds against the common enemy', and 'the alliance formed between your King and my Emperor', Ali could 'scarcely refrain from expressing to your Excellency my Zeal and reverence towards your illustrious nation, as I testified to the illustrious Lord Hoken...a traveller, in my country...with whom I talked of diverse matters' (a reference to the visit by the geologist John Hawkins in 1795). Ali had also sent representatives to meet Lieutenant-General Villette during his recruiting mission to Corfu, 'expressing the readiness with which I would assist him as a good neighbour in any thing which could be useful to him', and he now told Nelson that 'I assure you that whatever is in my power and can be useful to you shall never be denied.' He sent this message via Foresti—who was reporting regularly to Nelson—and enclosed with it some tokens of his esteem: 'A gold hilted sword of the workmanship of these parts; a gun of the same workmanship and a silver Ewer for water; all which are the product of our country, which though simple as they come from a sincere friend you will accept.'[37]

It was Ali's policy to seek powerful external sponsors, and no doubt he felt especially attracted to a foreign power which seemed unlikely ever to have designs on his own territories. Nelson had demonstrated very dramatically the effectiveness of British sea-power at the Battle of the Nile in August 1798 (news of which may have helped persuade Ali to turn against his French neighbours a few months later). This had completely altered the balance of power in the Mediterranean, leading to—among other things—a long but eventually successful siege of the French forces in Malta by the British; and in 1801 a British expeditionary force defeated the remains of the army which Napoleon had abandoned in Egypt. So on the one hand it was prudent of Ali Pasha to seek good relations with this newly established Mediterranean power. On the other hand, however, there was not much of a practical nature that he could actually expect the British to do for him. During the next couple of years Ali's own energies were mostly focused on fighting his internal enemies, with renewed campaigns against Mustafa Pasha of Delvinë and the final assault on Souli in 1803. And from March 1802 to May 1803, in any case, Europe was at peace, under the Treaty of Amiens.

In the late spring or early summer of 1803, as that period of peace drew to a close, relations between Ali Pasha and the British government were resumed; this seems to have been at his own initiative. It was in early May that the 25-year-old William Hamilton, who had served as private secretary to Lord Elgin, the British Ambassador in Istanbul, went to see Ali Pasha in Ioannina. Hamilton was on his way back to England; presumably this visit had been solicited by Ali, as it was a considerable diversion from the route home. Addressing the Foreign Secretary (Lord Hawkesbury)—as he explained, at Ali Pasha's request—from Ioannina on 6 May, Hamilton wrote: 'A few days ago We received here the Rumour of an Approaching War between Great Britain and the French Republic... [Ali Pasha] invited me this Morning to a Secret Conference, and repeated, in the most forcible language, the fairest sentiments of a strict friendship towards our Government.' According to Ali, reports indicated that Russia would enter into an alliance with France; 'he assured me that the Russians had always acted as his enemies, & that he never could look upon them as friends. That he had been unwilling to commence hostilities with the French during the late War, but that he had been forced to act against them, by their Treachery & Intrigues; and that he had always been an Admirer of the English Character, & looked forward to form with our Government the strictest Union.' He offered the British the use of the little bay of Porto Palermo, a sheltered spot overlooked by a fortress at the southern end of Himarë, where ships of the Royal Navy could be 'supplied with Provisions, Water, Wood, &c', suggesting also 'that we might make a disembark-ation of Troops there to garrison the Castle, or to improve the Fortifications; that there they might be supplied with sufficient Timber to repair Ships; and in time, after the Necessary Preparations to construct others'. Indeed, he said he was will-ing to do this 'even in case hostilities should not commence.' He hoped that 'this would prove an Introduction of a Trade between England & this part of Albania.' And, remarkably, he would be happy to help the British in all these ways 'what-ever might be the disposition or conduct of the Porte [sc. the Ottoman govern-ment]', even if it were to declare war on Britain. So he asked for the commander of the Mediterranean fleet to send to Porto Palermo, 'without delay, three or four intelligent Persons to examine the position, & to give in a Report of what would be Necessary for the Improvement of the Fort, & for making additional Conveniences to the Harbour'; and he also asked 'that some Englishman might be appointed to reside at Jannina, on the part of the English Government'.[38]

Ali Pasha, who did his best to be well-informed about all political develop-ments that might affect his own position, had accurate news of the coming hos-tilities between Britain and France, but his information about Russian intentions was faulty. Tsar Alexander had become increasingly irritated by Napoleon's breaches of various promises during the previous year; although it would be another two years before he joined an anti-French coalition with Britain and Austria, there was very little chance during that period of his taking the side of

France. Ali's animus against Russia is one of the most striking features of Hamilton's account, and its immediate cause is not hard to guess: his growing frictions and disagreements with the Septinsular Republic and its Russian over-lords. From 1799 onwards he had been lobbying the Russians for the return to his territories of fugitives (rebels or bandits) who took refuge on the islands. Ushakov had issued a proclamation to that effect, and further formal agreements had fol-lowed, but the problem persisted, and attempts by the local authorities to hide these people could not escape the vigilance of Ali's agents.[39] It did not help that, in appealing to the inhabitants of the islands for their support and loyalty, Russia had made use of the fact that Greeks and Russians were fellow-members of the Orthodox Church; many of the rebels against Ali were Greek Orthodox, includ-ing the warriors of Souli. In 1802 the Tsar appointed an official whose family came from Zakynthos, Count Geōrgios Mocenigo, as his minister plenipotentiary in the Septinsular Republic. (Mocenigo himself was born in Russia; his father had fled there after being punished by the Venetians for joining a Russian-sponsored revolt against the Ottomans in the Peloponnese in 1770, and had later served as Catherine the Great's representative in Tuscany.) Geōrgios Mocenigo combined a very active devotion to Russian prestige with the hostility to Ali Pasha that was common to most of the Greek inhabitants of the islands, and it seems to have been with his encouragement that representatives of Souli sent a grand petition to the Tsar in February 1803, begging for help. At the end of the year, after another such petition, Mocenigo authorized sending assistance from Corfu; but by then it was too late to save the Souliots.[40] In 1804 Mocenigo also forwarded to Moscow petitions from the inhabitants of Parga, Preveza and Vonitsa, asking to have their towns incorporated in the Septinsular Republic; and in June of that year he organ-ized a formal alliance of the *beys* of Çamëri and the pashas of Delvinë and Berat, and promised them ammunition and supplies if they would fight against Ali. Meanwhile many of the Souliots were given refuge on Corfu and the other islands; by early 1805 Mocenigo had persuaded the Tsar to permit the recruitment—mostly from these men—of an Albanian corps, under Russian command; he promised a total of 2,000 men, and this would later rise to over 3,500.[41]

In the light of all these developments and tendencies, it is clear that the motiv-ation for Ali Pasha's approach to the British in May 1803 was not essentially anti-French (as he openly admitted to Hamilton), nor primarily pro-British. (Indeed, there is some evidence that later in 1803 he also made a secret approach to a French commander in Italy, Lieutenant General Saint-Cyr.)[42] Rather, it was anti-Russian. Harder to judge is the degree to which it was also anti-Ottoman. While he enjoyed the Sultan's favour, Ali had been appointed in 1802 *beylerbeyi* of Rumeli; but he was dismissed from the post in mid-June 1803—and, given his assiduous cultivation of contacts in Istanbul, he is very likely to have had some advance notice of that. A *de facto* alliance between Ali and the British, with a permanent envoy from London at his court and a Royal Navy base on the coast of his territory, would strengthen his standing vis-à-vis not only the Russians, but also the Sultan, and indeed Ali's recently conquered subjects on the western side of his domains, whose lasting loyalty could not be assumed.

IV

It seems to have been only partly in response to Ali's invitation that, in late 1803, the British government made new plans to send agents to Greece and Albania; the main concern was with reports that the French were already active in Greece, assessing the chances of insurrection there and looking for possible invasion sites. In November 1803 the Foreign Office in London interviewed a young military officer, Captain William Martin Leake, who had recently been in the Levant; they discussed sending him on a mission to Greece, but this idea was taken no further at the time.[43] Two months later, however, formal instructions were issued to another young man with even stronger Levantine credentials: John Philip (known as 'Jack') Morier. He had been born and brought up in Smyrna, where his father— a British subject, of Swiss-French Protestant stock—was a merchant; after school-ing in England, Jack returned to Smyrna and then spent some time in Lord Elgin's service in Istanbul, before applying for a consular position.[44] Well-connected (with an aristocratic uncle) and fluent in several languages, including Turkish, he was chosen in January 1804 to be 'Consul General in Albania, the Morea, and the adjacent Territories of the Ottoman Empire'. His instructions explained that his most important task was 'impressing upon the Governments of the Morea and Albania the indispensable expediency of employing every Exertion in their Power to be prepared for resisting with effect the Designs which the French Government entertain with respect to those Provinces', and urging them to be 'upon their Guard against the designs of the numerous French Emissaries who...are most actively employed in the different European Provinces of the Ottoman Empire for the purpose of exciting disaffection and revolt'.[45]

The 25-year-old Jack Morier set off, with his 20-year-old brother David as his secretary, in February; they arrived in Patras in late April, and spent a month touring the Peloponnese, trying to assess the chances of a French-led insurrection there, before travelling to Ioannina in June. (As they entered the city, David was impressed by its overall air of prosperity, noting that 'The Houses are higher than the generality of those I have yet seen, and built of regularly cut, dark Stone in the principal Streets which are of a tolerable breadth & well paved.')[46] Writing to the Foreign Secretary on the 30th of that month, Jack described the warm welcome he had received, and Ali Pasha's assurance of 'his entire devotion to the Interests of His Majesty's Government'. But he also recorded Ali's complaint: 'He appeared rather disappointed at my not having brought him an answer to the Offer he had made through Lord Nelson, which he desires me now to renew.' What exactly the 'offer' was is not recorded. Very likely it repeated the one made to Hamilton in the previous year, and indeed Jack Morier's report went on to reiterate those terms, with the addition of a proposal about recruiting soldiers: 'He added that proper Persons might be sent to examine his Forests and that we might cut Timber wherever we thought proper;—That the Ports were open to all Our Vessels for Supplies, That he would furnish Us with Three or Four Thousand Men if we wanted Them and that such was his entire Devotion to England that if ever She quarrelled with The Porte his Assistance even then would be at our disposal.'[47] Earlier in 1804 Ali had in fact written twice to Nelson: in January he had asked for two artillery officers, and in May he requested 'eight thousand Shot and Shells, of various diameters, according to an accompanying Scale.'[48] The identity of the intended targets was made clear to Morier: not the French, but the Russians, with whom Ali seems to have been obsessed. He urged Morier to tell the British Government about 'the danger to which he sees the Ottoman Empire exposed by the preponderance of the Russian influence at The Porte'; he said that he would oppose any attempt by Russia, even if authorized by the Sultan, to occupy Preveza, Parga, Vonitsa and Butrint, adding revealingly that 'The Porte by permitting The Russians to establish Themselves on this Side wished to reduce his Power.' It was in this context that he now repeated his request for arms, raising it as he did so to include artillery pieces, a total of seven artillery experts, and two or three British cruisers to patrol his coasts.[49]

Jack Morier was clearly impressed by Ali, writing admiringly that

> with the least support his Power will rise, upon the Ruins of that of the Sultan, over the rest of European Turky and will form a Bullwark there against the hostile Views of the Christian Nations. As far as I can judge from the Conversations I have had with Him he feels himself perfectly secure against the Effects of the Jealousy of his Sovereign but he foresees that the Provinces which only form part of a disjointed Empire must sooner or later fall a Prey to it's powerful Neighbours and consequently his aim now is to court the Protection of some great Nation by whose Influence he may obtain from Others the Acknowledgement of a degree of Independence (perhaps similar to that of the Barbary States) which he hopes may save his Power from the common Wreck of The Turks.[50]

And in another despatch, penned on the same day, he commented: 'To a most warlike & restless disposition, he joins so much perseverance, that opposed to the tardy & irresolute measures of the Porte, it is probable that if he lives, his influence will extend over all Albania & Roumelia. His mind though wholly untutored possesses an uncommon degree of natural sagacity, which shews itself especially in his management of the Porte.'[51]

Returning to the key point of his mission, Morier observed that a French invasion through Ali's territories was unlikely: from northern Albania all the way down to the Gulf of Arta, wherever they landed they would have to march 'through a broken country, overrun with woods and intersected with defiles and steep precipices, over which there are no roads but for the wary footsteps of a mule, & where, even if cannon could be conveyed, it would be useless against the ambushes of an enemy composed of the most active and hardy mountaineers'.[52] This information had the effect of downgrading Ali's importance in British eyes, which is perhaps not what the somewhat star-struck Morier intended; in a later despatch, sent from Athens in July, he partly retracted what he had said about the impenetrability of the area, saying that 'The greatest difficulty... would arise from a want of horses and perhaps of provisions' and now nominating the Gulf of Arta as the most likely place for a French invasion. At the same time, he reported on Ali's continuing conflicts with the Çams of Paramythia and Margariti, 'warlike tribes of Albanian Turks [sc. Albanian Muslims]' in the area just to the north of the Gulf.[53]

While Morier was in Athens, another agent was preparing to visit the region, also at the behest of the Foreign Office but with a more narrowly military purpose: William Martin Leake. His official instructions, drawn up in July 1804, were concerned primarily with studying the defensibility of the Albanian and Greek coastline against a French attack, advising the local Ottoman commanders, and making surveys. Ali Pasha was mentioned only in the sixth of his listed tasks: 'You will repair to Ali Pasha or the Beglerbeg of Roumelia, and offer your opinion and advice, upon the general plan of defence for their territories.'[54] Leake sailed from Plymouth, and by early October he had joined Nelson's fleet of Cape St Sebastian; Nelson showed him the two letters from Ali Pasha, and also commented critically on 'the assistance and encouragement, which Count Mocenigo, and the Russian Commanders have given to the Sulliotes and the Agas, who are at war with Ali Visir of Joannina'. (This information came from Nelson's own sources, no doubt including Spiridion Foresti, the forwarder of Ali's second letter.) Nelson had already formed a very favourable opinion of Ali Pasha. In the previous year he had commented, in a letter to Spiridion Foresti: 'I am really much interested for Ali Pacha; for he has always been a stanch friend to the English, and most particularly kind to me; and if I ever should go to Corfu, I shall certainly, if he is within a few days' reach, go and see him.' Now he was in favour of giving Ali the ammunition he had requested, on the grounds that 'nothing should be neglected, that may tend to cultivate the friendship of a person, upon whom the Defence of the Grecian frontiers of Turkey must principally depend', and Leake duly echoed this opinion.[55]

Leake reached Corfu in December, where he learned that Ali Pasha had left Ioannina to visit his northern territories; so on 20 December 1804 Leake crossed to Sarandë and began the overland journey via Delvinë to Tepelenë, arriving at the end of the month.[56] There he met Ali, who had just returned from supervising the building of a new fortress at Përmet. Ali was pleased to learn that Leake was a military man, and, as Leake reported, 'wished me in particular to suggest to him any Ideas which might occur to me, respecting the Passes leading from the Coast to the Capital, and the interior of his Province, as well as respecting the formation and improvement of the Roads between the principal Towns'—military security (though not exclusively against the French) and the improvement of trade being two of his most important interests.[57] As for the main business of the meeting: although Leake brought Ali Pasha a friendly letter from Lord Nelson, Ali he said he was surprised that he still had not received any reply to his earlier request to Nelson 'to purchase by His Lordships assistance a small vessel for the protection of his Coast'. He also referred to 'the propositions he made to the Government about two years ago through the medium of Mr Hamilton, & shewed considerable peevishness and impatience at not having received any answer to them'. All he wished for, he said, was a reply; if it was negative, he would accept that, 'and should still continue to receive the English, as the nation whom he most esteems. But, that if his propositions were accepted, he should be happy to engage with all the forces he could spare, in any expedition against the enemies of England, as far as Naples & Malta to the southwards, and to the north, as far as the frontiers of Russia.'[58]

Beneath this rather extravagant rhetoric there lurked some much more practical concerns. Ali's main request was 'to be allowed to appoint the Governor of the Ex-Venetian Towns, & to be responsible for the preservation of the privileges of those places'; adapting his argument to the British point of view, he said that the officials appointed by Istanbul, 'not having that interest in the defence of the frontier that he has, are more open to French intrigue'. He hoped that the recently appointed British Ambassador to Istanbul, Charles Arbuthnot, would intercede with the Ottoman government about this; Arbuthnot was expected to stop at Corfu on his way to Istanbul, so Ali had written a message requesting a meeting to discuss it. (This was the first of several occasions on which Ali would seek diplomatic support of this kind.) Finally, Leake noted that 'He is desirous of having two small vessels to cruize upon the coast, and make Palermo their place of rendezvous. But he partly confessed to me, that as well in this as in his former applications concerning Palermo, one of his principal objects in desiring us to occupy that port, is that he may then be enabled to attempt the reduction of the yet unsubdued Khimariots with a better prospect of success.' Overall, Leake concluded, it would be a good to grant Ali his wishes for the ex-Venetian places, as this would undoubtedly 'strengthen the Albanian Frontier'.[59]

By the time Leake wrote those words he was back in Corfu, spending time with the Morier brothers (to whom, as it happened, he was distantly related). Both he and Jack Morier had formed views broadly sympathetic to Ali Pasha, and in this they had the valuable backing of Lord Nelson. But British policy was more circumspect. A new set of instructions, sent to Morier in October, told him that in view of 'the present agitated state of Greece' he should 'impress upon the Turkish governors, the propriety of their treating the Greeks with greater lenity than they have hitherto been accustomed to exercise'; the fear here was that discontent anywhere on the Greek mainland might lead to pro-French insurrection, and although Orthodox Greeks fared better under Ali than under most other pashas, his vindictive treatment of the defeated Souliots had become an awkward issue. The instructions also ordered Morier to 'abstain most carefully from taking any part whatsoever in the Disputes, which subsist between Ali Pacha, and the Agas, unless you should learn that your interposition would be acceptable to both parties, and would be likely to effect the restoration of tranquillity'. And if Ali demanded once again to know the answer to his proposals, Morier was to say that he had not received any, but that he thought it likely that Ali's disputes with the Sultan and with Russia 'may have caused the delay, and that we may not choose to enter into engagements with him, till he is reconciled to our friends.'[60]

In the larger scheme of things it was of course important for Britain to maintain good relations with Russia, which had not yet become a formal ally against the French. (That would happen in April 1805.) But this raised problems for Jack Morier, given the active hostility to Ali Pasha of the Russian plenipotentiary Count Mocenigo. In late January 1805 Morier met with Mocenigo to discuss the possible scenario of a French invasion of the Balkans. Since Napoleon would no doubt make promises of future independence to Ali Pasha in return for his help, there seemed to be just two policies that could be pursued towards Ali: 'either to crush him, with the consent of the Porte, or to gain him over by ensuring his independence'. Mocenigo was in favour of the former, and suggested making use of the Russian forces on the Ionian Islands; Morier countered that it would take a long time (whereas a French invasion might happen quite soon), and it would also alarm the other pashas, making them pro-French. In his report to London, Morier expressed the hope that Britain and Russia might together overcome 'the Scruples of the Porte' about permitting Ali to become an autonomous ruler of his territories; and he ended by asking to be told what the Foreign Office's policy was on this, 'As I cannot avoid paying Ali Pasha another visit at Yanina', and he would not know what to say to him. At the same time he also urged Mocenigo to desist from encouraging Ali's subjects to rebel against him.[61] The difference of opinion here was sharp; during this period Mocenigo complained to the Russian government about both Morier and Spiridion Foresti, and in the second half of 1805 the Russian Foreign Minister would ask London either to recall Morier or to restrain his activities.[62]

Fears of a French invasion were suddenly intensified in early February 1805, when news reached Corfu that the French fleet, which contained eleven battleships, had just left the port of Toulon. Its destination was unknown (in fact it was heading for the Atlantic, to assist a planned invasion of England, though its actual course would take it first to the West Indies, and then, fatefully, to Trafalgar); but an attack on Ottoman Greece seemed a real possibility. On hearing this news, Leake set off on a trip which he had already planned to the Peloponnese, to assess the political and military situation there, and Jack Morier travelled with his brother to Ioannina, struggling along roads turned to thick mud by heavy rains, and arriving on 13 February.[63] In response to a letter from Jack, Ali Pasha hurried back from Tepelenë with a force of 3–4,000 men; he also sent orders to reinforce key points in mainland Greece, such as Missolonghi and Corinth, and said he would quickly increase his own force to 10,000. Jack Morier was impressed by Ali's speed of action, and also by his assurance that he was doing this only for the British: if the Russians alone had asked him, Ali said, he would not have bothered. But, as always, Ali Pasha's cooperation came with further requests attached. The three main ones, as Morier summarized them, were: '1.º That the Sulliotes be sent to any other part of Europe, at a distance from his territories. 2.º That no protection be given by the Republic of the Seven Islands to culprits flying there from his justice. 3.º That the defence of Prevesa & the other Ex-Venetian towns be entrusted to him.' More generally, he told Morier that he wanted Britain to obtain 'the sanction of the Porte to all his measures & thus to be enabled to transmit his power to his children'. In his report to London, Morier commented that the suppression of the Souliots had benefited peace in the region, 'for they were marauders against Greeks as well as Mahometans', and they had also entered into relations with the French. He recommended acceding to all three of Ali's requests. That they were all, directly or indirectly, anti-Russian did not escape him; he told Ali that Britain's friendship with Russia was solely for the purposes of resisting France, and in his comments to London he observed that the Russians were merely up to their old tricks, 'creating parties, for the purpose of being called in to restore order'.[64]

Nevertheless, Jack Morier could not avoid fulfilling the one part of his instructions that was more in tune with Russian policy: asking Ali to act with 'more lenity' towards his Greek Orthodox subjects. Given Ali's suspicions of the Greek–Russian links established in recent years, Morier wrote, 'it required much prudence' to raise this. 'He said very little to me on that subject, except that he thought the present moment unfavorable to any innovations. But to his confidential Greek who is a bishop, he expressed much surprize at what I had said to him.'[65] Morier followed this, in his report, with a broadly sympathetic but quite penetrating account of the nature of Ali's rule:

> The great expence which the state of warfare the Vezir is almost constantly engaged in with the Albanians, occasions a defficiency in his revenues of several hundred purses. It is more to supply that defficiency, than from a real spirit of extortion that he oppresses the Greeks with taxes; but they on the other hand, enjoy in their persons a security which at present is unknown to most of the

wretched inhabitants of Roumelia. There, the weakness of the Government has reduced most of the male population to have recourse to robbery & plunder for subsistence; here indeed the nature of the country which is wholly mountainous, & the fierce disposition of the inhabitants makes them follow the same course. In endeavouring to subdue them, Ali Pasha has a double object in view, that of insuring the safety of the peaceable part of his subjects; and in the next place of forcing those turbulent people to a more pacific mode of life. He has been known to bring together two Chiefs inimical to each other, to upbraid them with the inhumanity of revenging private quarrels by secret assassination, and to lament that his own example has not led them to prefer cleanliness and domestic comfort to their filthy & savage habits & customs.

Wherever he cannot overcome by his arms, he follows the maxim of 'divide et impera', & thus by gradually weakening each party, he hopes one day to rule over all. I firmly believe that the fierce nature of the people he is endeavouring to reduce into order, rather then his own disposition obliges him sometimes to be cruel. The shocking inhumanities committed by the bands of robbers upon his subjects, compel him to make as cruel examples of them, & sometimes he prevents further disorders by taking those very offenders into his pay.

The lenity whether natural or affected of his temper may be argued from his taking no notice of the sarcasms & abuse cast upon him in the popular ballads sung by the Greeks in his own hearing.

There is some appearance of enlightened policy in the principles by which he is guided, but so little union is there yet in his system, that it is probable, in case these provinces are threatened with general danger, the Albanian method of defence of every man going home to protect his own possessions would be resorted to.[66]

By the time the Morier brothers left Ioannina on 6 March 1805, Ali had assembled a force of 6,000 men. (Jack reported that he could raise 15,000 in total, including 6,000 from Çameri and 4,000 from Gjirokastër, Tepelenë and Kardhiq; but in normal circumstances he employed 1,500, mostly to guard Souli '& other important passes'.) Recommending that Britain, Russia and the Porte should combine to give Ali 'some mark of approbation' for his prompt reaction to the French threat, he enclosed a list of ammunition that Ali had requested: 6,000 lb of gunpowder, and 6,500 shells of different sizes. He noted that Ali had said he would pay for it, but suggested that it be sent to him as a gift instead.[67] This request was repeated in a letter from Morier to Nelson, written on the same day.[68] In June Jack Morier was back in Ioannina, where he would stay until mid-September. His general attitude was still favourable to Ali: conveying the pasha's response to a letter from Charles Arbuthnot in Istanbul, which had mentioned Russian criticisms of his conduct and had demanded that he stop harassing the people of the ex-Venetian towns, Morier added that in his own opinion much of the trouble was caused by Russia's officials in the area, who had soured the attitude of the Russian government towards Ali Pasha.[69] In a report to London at the end of July, Jack proudly announced that he had persuaded Ali to improve the conditions of the Souliot prisoners in Ioannina, who 'had been till the other day kept chained in bodies of twenty and thirty together, to do hard work in the town'; Ali had now sent them 'with their wives and children to the neighbourhood of Tepeleni, and distributed among the Greek villages there.'[70] However, on a visit to Përmet and Berat in the second half of September, he was shocked to find that this claim was not true: in a letter of complaint to Ali Pasha, written from Salonica a month later, he said that he had found the prisoners 'compelled to hard labor in the fortress of Permetti, under the severe lash of your Albanians, chained together at night' and 'so neglected, that many have fallen victim to sickness.'[71]

Captain Leake joined the Morier brothers in Ioannina on 28 June 1805, having spent time travelling through Vonitsa, Preveza, Arta and Parga and preparing a detailed map of the area. In a long report to London he summarized his views (based on these and his previous journeys) about the practicalities of a French invasion—and, once again, the conclusions were favourable to Ali Pasha. The best place for the enemy to land was Preveza, because there, and in the other ex-Venetian places which Ali Pasha was forbidden to garrison, 'the Beys appointed by the Porte have not the same personal interest in the preservation of the frontier, and the few Greeks who form the Garrison would probably hail with pleasure the arrival of their deliverers.' However, most of the mountain passes on the routes from the coast towards Thessaly could easily be held; and 'With such advantageous Passes, and such active and hardy Troops as the Albanians to defend them, it would seem that little more than vigilance is necessary for the security of the Coast from Avlona [Vlorë] to Prevesa.' The risk was greater to the south of Preveza; many Greek peasants did have muskets (he estimated a total of 30,000), and most of them would join the French invaders. Ali could raise 12,000 men at short notice, but he could not keep them at the ready for long, as their chiefs demanded payment for twice the number of men they actually supplied; nevertheless, 'a much larger force' could be assembled in the event of a foreign invasion. And in that scenario, 'the indiscipline, which generally renders the disposal and effect of an Albanian Force, a matter of uncertainty' would not matter. 'They would unite with the utmost cordiality in the protection of their native Country. Their mode of warfare is peculiarly adapted to the defence of their strong Passes, and they would be equally expert in harrassing the Flanks and Rear of a regular Army, in cutting off his communications and supplies, and rendering his Progress a work of continued danger and fatigue.'[72]

Both Morier and Leake were becoming more aware, during this period, of the various intra-Albanian conflicts in which Ali Pasha was involved. Generally they took his side in these matters, on the principle that since he was the only significant power that Britain could do business with in the region—and a dynamic and well-disposed one too—it would be better if his power were strengthened. Having noted in April that 'The reduction of Sulli has greatly contributed to consolidate his power; but the work remains incomplete till he reigns uncontroled in the whole district of Chamuria', Jack Morier wrote in September that Ali had succeeded in stirring up fighting between rival Çam leaders.[73] More significant was the conflict that had developed between Ali and the powerful pasha of Shkodër, Ibrahim Bushatli. Ibrahim was the brother of Kara Mahmud, the northern Albanian ruler whose defiance of the Sultan had led to two major Ottoman campaigns against him; as we have seen, Ali Pasha had participated in the campaign of 1793. When Ibrahim succeeded in 1796, the Sultan made his peace with this local dynasty which he was unable to remove; Ibrahim's nephew Mehmed was made governor of the *sancak*s of Ohrid and Elbasan, and ruled them thereafter until his death in 1802. But since Mehmed's son was then only ten years old, the Sultan granted Elbasan to another pasha, Ibrahim of Vlorë.[74] This Ibrahim governed a territory including the rather ramshackle port-town of Vlorë itself—passing by in December 1804, Leake noticed 'a tolerable wharf, with an apology for a fort, in the shape of a square inclosure with ruinous walls'—and the central Albanian town of Berat, with its imposing citadel.[75] (Having married the daughter of Kurd Ahmed Pasha of Berat, he had in effect inherited Berat and its territory when Kurd Ahmed died.) His regional authority had been under constant pressure from Ali Pasha, with the steady erosion of his lands, and it was for essentially defensive purposes that he had consented, in 1794, to marry two of his daughters to Ali's two elder sons, Muhtar (Ahmed Muhtar) and Veli (Veliuddin).[76]

Over many years Ibrahim of Vlorë had been a sponsor of resistance to Ali by their near neighbours the pasha of Delvinë and the Çams. But in 1805, unusually, his relationship with Ali seemed to turn to his own advantage. After much lobbying from Ibrahim Bushatli, the Sultan had just reassigned the Elbasan *sancak* to the Bushatli family; Ali, seeing an opportunity to extend his own influence there, encouraged Ibrahim of Vlorë to send a small army to retake it, and contributed 2,500 men. The town of Elbasan was overrun in May, and in the following month Ali's son Muhtar took up residence in Berat.[77] But the conflict between Ibrahim Bushatli and Ali Pasha continued; Ali had established *de facto* power over part of Macedonia, including the town of Ohrid itself, from where Ibrahim Bushatli now sought to dislodge him. Muhtar went to reinforce the garrison there, and further fighting took place between the forces of the two pashas. In the end Ali retained his Macedonian possessions, while the Elbasan *sancak* reverted to Ibrahim Bushatli, who was riding high in the Sultan's favour; the only loser was Ibrahim of Vlorë, who, without any real gain in territory, had become more dependent on Ali Pasha.[78] Both Leake and Morier visited Ibrahim of Vlorë in Berat in the autumn of 1805. They found him a rather disconsolate figure and, as they came from Ali Pasha, received only a cold welcome; Leake described him as 'a person of a weak and indolent character, very much inclined to peace and repose, but often drawn into the quarrels of his unquiet neighbours of Ioannina and Scutari'. In the same report, Leake lamented the way in which the Albanian pashas were spending resources on these 'private Quarrels' (which did indeed supply a simple explanation of Ali's recent requests for ammunition), when they should have been making preparations for a French invasion. But, he added, Ali Pasha assured him that he had made 'an alliance with the other two Vizirs of Albania with a View to such an Event', and that they would all come together to oppose the invader.[79]

Leake left Ioannina in November 1805. Despite lingering weakness caused by a severe attack of malaria in Berat, he spent the next year tirelessly pursuing his military intelligence mission in Greece (and, briefly, Montenegro).[80] And since Ali Pasha's power extended, directly or indirectly, to most of mainland Greece, he continued to ponder the man's intentions. In a despatch from Tripolitsa, in the Peloponnese, in March 1806 he gave a cautious assessment of them. He noted that when the Russian army had been advancing on Istanbul in 1791, Ali had made great efforts to cultivate Potemkin, 'with a view of retaining his independence, notwithstanding the disasters, which might befall the Sultan'; and similarly he had cultivated the French, when their star was rising. 'That he has been sincere in his offers to the British Government is hardly to be doubted: That he would gallantly repel all attempts on the Coast of Albania, and sacrifice his Life in preserving his own Territories, I think I am sufficiently acquainted with his Character to be able to assert...and that he would heartily co-operate in case of an attack of the French upon Egypt or the Morea, supposing it unconnected with any other movements of the Enemy to the North of Turkey.' But those were outlying provinces, vulnerable to British sea-power. Leake suspected that Ali's conduct might have been very different if the French army in Egypt had been able to march through Syria to Istanbul. Indeed, it could yet turn out to be different, if French forces were to move from Dalmatia to Istanbul (via Bosnia). 'He might then perhaps shew a tardiness in collecting his forces, quite the reverse of that alacrity which he manifested last Winter at the time of the sailing of the Toulon fleet'; and if the enemy made successful progress, he might withdraw allegiance from the Sultan altogether.[81] This was a rather cooler judgement than the one expressed by Jack Morier in his despatches, and probably a more accurate one too.

V

Relations between the Great Powers were shifting to and fro during this period. In December 1804 Napoleon, irritated by Sultan Selim's refusal to recognize him as Emperor, broke off relations with Istanbul. During the following nine months Russia tried hard to persuade Selim to join it in a formal alliance. There were various reasons for Ottoman reluctance. Russia was a historic enemy, having fought two major anti-Ottoman wars in the previous 40 years. It was an expansionary power, which had conquered the Crimea (formerly under Ottoman suzerainty) as recently as 1783. It had evident ambitions to control the fertile and strategically important Romanian principalities of Moldavia and Wallachia, which formed part of the Ottoman Empire; recently it had intervened to ensure the appointment of Russophile princes there. Its interest in encouraging or stirring up the Sultan's discontented Orthodox subjects in Greece was well known, and since the summer of 1804 there had also been friendly contacts between the Russian authorities and the leaders of the revolt in Serbia—a disturbance that seemed minor at first, but grew in seriousness with almost every month that passed. During the treaty negotiations in 1805, the Sultan had to refuse Russian requests to be given powers to intervene on behalf of all his Orthodox subjects, and even to occupy the two Romanian principalities as a pre-emptive move against France. But finally the treaty of alliance was signed in October 1805.[82]

It was quickly overtaken by other events, however. In that same month, Napoleon defeated Austria decisively at Ulm; and in early December he inflicted another heavy defeat on both Austrian and Russian forces at Austerlitz. By the end of the year Napoleon had obliged the Holy Roman Emperor to sign a separate peace, taking Austria out of the war and handing over large territories, including Istria and Dalmatia, to France. A French diplomatic offensive then began in Istanbul, with blandishments including a promise to restore the Crimea to the Ottomans. Within a short time Selim broke off discussions with the British ambassador; in late February 1806 he recognized Napoleon as Emperor and sent an ambassador to Paris. He also ordered a large campaign (under the command of Ibrahim Bushatli) against the Serbs, and—with obvious anti-Russian intent—the disarming of Christians in the Romanian principalities. In May Napoleon nominated a new French ambassador to the Porte, his old friend and fellow-Corsican General Horace Sébastiani, who already had some diplomatic experience in the Levant; he would prove a highly effective representative of French interests, helping to push the Ottoman government further in an anti-Russian direction. And meanwhile other French agents, at consular or vice-consular level, were fanning out across the Ottoman territories in Europe, to counter Russian influence wherever they found it.[83]

Two of them were sent to Ali Pasha. This was a plan that had been formed as early as September 1805, before the Sultan's shift towards France, so the original idea had been simply to cultivate Ali as an independent ruler hostile to Russia; but of course the change in Ottoman policy made their mission easier. Both men had previous experience of Ottoman conditions, and one of them knew Ali well. He was Julien Bessières, a first cousin of one of Napoleon's marshals, and the other was François Pouqueville, a former priest turned medical practitioner. Both had been members of the large scientific commission which accompanied Napoleon's expedition to Egypt in 1798. In November of that year they had boarded a ship, with some other French officials, to return to France, but had been captured by a Muslim corsair. Pouqueville was handed over to the Ottoman authorities, and was employed for a while as a physician in the Peloponnese before languishing for two years in the notorious prison of the Seven Towers in Istanbul. Bessières was sold to Ali Pasha, and spent more than a year in Ioannina, where he was made to direct the construction of new fortifications. During that time he got to know Ali, and even wrote a policy paper for him, advising him to march on Istanbul, force the Sultan to abandon his alliance with Russia, 'have himself declared sovereign ruler of Albania, and obtain the cession of Egypt to France, which, in recognition of that service, would guarantee his independence'. Bessières then escaped to Corfu, but was transferred from there to Istanbul, where he joined Pouqueville in captivity. After their return to France, Pouqueville graduated MD and published an account of his adventures, with much topo-graphical description, entitled *Voyage en Morée, à Constantinople, en Albanie, et dans plusieurs autres parties de l'Empire Ottoman pendant les années 1798, 1799, 1800 et 1801*. The book caught the attention of Napoleon—to whom it was dedi-cated—and helped ensure Pouqueville's employment on this new mission. Bessières's role now was to establish friendly relations with Ali Pasha, and see if he would be willing to have a permanent French representative at his court; if Ali accepted, Pouqueville was to be that representative.[84]

The instructions given to Bessières were, in effect, that he should tell Ali Pasha exactly what he wanted to hear: that the Russians were the real enemy, that they were planning to invade Greece and raise a revolt among the Orthodox popula-tion there, and that Ali should say what help he required in order to fend them off. As for the longer term, Ali was to be told that Napoleon did not mind how much or how little authority the Sultan had over the 'Muslim princes' in his European territories, 'but what matters to France is that there should be a Muslim power in Europe, and that the Sultan's subjects should not sell their country to foreigners.'[85] When the two Frenchmen met Ali Pasha just outside Ioannina on 7 February 1806, he in turn was keen to tell them what they longed to be told: he said he was thrilled and delighted to know that Napoleon had been thinking of him. Within a few days he was insisting on retaining Pouqueville as a 'consul' at Ioannina with or without the agreement of the Sultan, announcing that 'I now hope that the Emperor of the French will protect me, like the rest of his subjects, and then I would have no more fears about Russian intrigues, and would regard my political existence as completely guaranteed.' When Bessières left, four weeks later, Ali Pasha gave him a note in which he described Napoleon as 'my sovereign and my master' and pledged all his forces to assist any French attack on the Russians in Corfu. If Napoleon then entrusted Corfu to him, he would hold it on the Emperor's behalf, and keep out the Russians and the English; but he magnani-mously declared that he would serve the French even if Napoleon had other plans for the island. All he wished for was that 'my independence will be guaranteed, and I hope that he will raise me to the rank of European sovereigns.'[86] Since

Bessières brought back to Paris a glowing image of Ali's devotion to France and an exaggerated one of his power (claiming that he could raise 60,000 men), it seems fair to conclude that Ali's ability to 'play' the French envoys was significantly greater than their ability to play him. And the subsequent reports sent back by Pouqueville from Ioannina maintained the same tone, while building up the idea that Ali could quickly take command of a large part of the Ottoman Empire in Europe: on 21 April 1806 he wrote that Ali planned to seize all the southern Balkans as far as Salonica, crush the *bey* of Serres (who controlled much of Macedonia and Bulgaria) and the pasha of Shkodër, and then lead a large army to put down the revolt of Russia's protégés the Serbs.[87]

Just two days later, Jack Morier returned to Ioannina. Alarmed by the news that a French agent had arrived there, he had put off a trip to the Peloponnese and hastened back from Salonica to assess this new situation. (The journey across northern Greece was made more unpleasant for him and his brother David by an unseasonal heatwave, in which lead melted on the roofs of mosques and birds fell lifeless from the sky.)[88] Ali's talents for embroidering the truth were quickly put to use: he insisted that he remained utterly loyal to Britain, assured Morier that Pouqueville's arrival was just a French initiative, said that he had come for purely commercial purposes, and claimed to have refused to accept him as consul until the Sultan had given his approval. In another conversation he did let slip that the French had asked for his cooperation in an attack on Corfu; when Morier questioned him more closely about this, he allowed the young Englishman to conclude—as if he had cleverly wormed a secret out of Ali—that Napoleon had actually offered Corfu to him as the reward for his help. (This was a typical gambit by Ali Pasha; but the French authorities would soon be working on his ambitions in this area, sending him a studiously ambiguous message which said that if Napoleon did acquire Corfu, he could think of no better person to whom to entrust its defence than Ali.)[89] At the same time, Ali renewed his complaints at the lack of any definite response to the requests which he had previously sent to London. The consequence of these tactics was that in each of his reports Morier advised that further concessions should be made to Ali Pasha. He should be given military help 'for the placing of the hostile tribes of Chamuria in absolute dependence upon him', and he should be granted his three demands: moving the exiled Souliots to some distant Russian territory, stopping all incursions by bandits who had taken refuge on the islands, and placing the three ex-Venetian towns under his control.[90]

One further test of Ali's diplomatic skills came two weeks later, in the form of a visit by George Flory, the Russian consul at Arta.[91] When Flory reproached him for inviting French agents, he admitted that he had sent an invitation, after receiving several requests from Paris, but insisted that he had made no promises: 'I've been trying to humour them ["les amuser"], while I wait for the situation to improve, and for the political conditions to reach a dénouement.' To the Russian authorities on Corfu he offered an exchange, on favourable terms (the sending to him of a few Muslim bandits, in return for 150 relatives of the exiled Souliots); he requested that the Russians cease arming the Çams against him, and permit his ships to pass through the Corfu Channel; and he declared rather airily that one day he would be happy to join Russia in a war against the Sultan (explaining that 'I am a Muslim, but not a fanatic; I hate my government and its administration; I feel how it is declining, and foresee its fall; I want to live honorably in this little territory that I govern, and to die as its ruler'). He ended with a warning: if you refuse my offers, 'I shall be angry, and shall be obliged to turn elsewhere. Since everyone is at war, no doubt I shall find an ally; I shall say no more than that.' And once again Ali's tactics worked: in the letter accompanying the report of this conversation, Flory too advised the Russian authorities to give him at least some minor concessions.[92]

Count Mocenigo, who was the most senior Russian official in the region, nevertheless remained implacably hostile to Ali Pasha. When David Morier went to Corfu at his brother's request to plead for a more lenient approach, he was sharply rebuffed: Mocenigo defended the policy of helping the fighters who had fled from Ali's domains (even though, as Jack noted, their incursions were 'a source of the most grievous vexation to the poor Rayahs'), and in response to Ali's well-grounded complaint about Russian support for the rebel Çams he simply accused Ali of lying.[93] Mocenigo's personal preferences, in favour of the Greek Orthodox population on the islands and the mainland, were now running counter to the strategic logic of the situation. With France taking over Dalmatia in the early months of the year, and then swallowing up the little Ragusan republic in May, Russia urgently needed to strengthen its defensive position by improving relations in this part of the Balkans with both Ali Pasha and Britain; but the pleas of the rather junior British representative were ignored, and the hostility to Ali Pasha continued—thereby more than justifying the game of wait-and-see that Ali was now playing, via Pouqueville, with the French. In his last despatch before leaving Ioannina in June, Jack Morier noted the occupation of Dubrovnik (Ragusa) and a recent French attempt to land men at Vlorë, and reported Ali's fear that France would 'probably assemble a Force on the Coast near Chimara [Himarë], among whose Inhabitants he suspects the French to have a Party.'[94] William Leake, meanwhile, had paid a visit to the one Russian-held stronghold further up the coast, the port of Kotor, but had found the Russian commander uncooperative. Soon after his return to Corfu he wrote that if the French succeeded in taking Kotor, they would probably 'invade Turkey by advancing a corps to Elbasan, and across the ancient Ignatian Road [the Egnatian Way, which ran across central Albania from Durrës to Elbasan to Ohrid]', with another force advancing through Bosnia and Serbia.[95] Apart from sending warnings of this kind, there was little more for the English agents to do. Leake kicked his heels on Corfu for the rest of the summer, before embarking on a tour of the Ionian Islands and other parts of Greece. Jack Morier, having sent his brother back to England, moved first to Patras, then to Trikala, and finally to the island of Zakynthos.[96] He calculated, surely correctly, that there was little or no useful work for him to do in Ioannina; what with Russian intransigence, Sultanic Francophilia, the blandishments of Pouqueville and, most troublingly, the continuing failure of the British government to give any proper response to Ali's requests, his presence there would serve only as a reminder of British unreliability. Following the departures of Morier in June 1806 and Leake three months later, no British representative would have any face-to-face dealings with Ali Pasha until the final months of the following year.

VI

The second half of 1806, meanwhile, saw some dramatic developments in both the external relations of the Ottoman Empire and its internal politics. In July a Russian envoy went to Paris and obtained Napoleon's signature on a provisional peace treaty between France and Russia. A few weeks later the new French Ambassador, Horace Sébastiani, arrived in Istanbul with a copy of the treaty; he told the Ottoman government that it released them from their previous promises to seek Russian approval for the appointment of the voivods (princely rulers) of Moldavia and Wallachia, and persuaded them to dismiss the pro-Russian ones who were then in post. It then emerged that the Tsar had refused to ratify the treaty. Riding high on his initial diplomatic successes, Sébastiani now demanded that the Ottomans stop Russian ships from passing through the Bosphorus. The British and Russian ambassadors—Sir Charles Arbuthnot and Count Andrei Italinsky—closed ranks, and many weeks of threats, cajolings and diplomatic brinkmanship followed. News of the formation of the Fourth Coalition against Napoleon in October 1806, an alliance that included Britain, Russia and Prussia, just tipped the balance; the Sultan promised to reinstate the Russophile voivods, and refused the French demand about the Bosphorus. But soon afterwards the two ambassadors' efforts were undone, when a Russian army under General Michelson invaded Moldavia in November; and by this time it was known that Napoleon had won a crushing victory over the Prussian army at Jena in mid-October and had occupied Berlin.[97] With the first news of the Russian invasion, Sébastiani immediately became the dominant foreign influence on Ottoman policy. Italinsky departed; Arbuthnot remained for a short time, but his position had become almost untenable. As he later wrote, it was 'unfortunately the necessary policy of our Court to alienate & disgust the Turks by our unreserved support of Russia'.[98]

Even worse damage to Anglo-Ottoman relations followed, however. At the end of January 1807 Arbuthnot received information that he was about to be arrested.

He slipped out of Istanbul by boat in the middle of the night, and joined a British squadron in the northern Aegean. That squadron, under Admiral Sir John Duckworth, then sailed to Istanbul in mid-February, trained its guns on the city, and demanded full acceptance of three demands: renewal of the Anglo-Ottoman alliance, the cessation of hostilities against Russia, and the removal of the French Ambassador. Fatefully, Arbuthnot then paused to parley with the Ottomans, and this gave the ever-active Sébastiani enough time to organize the city's defences. According to some observers, a small show of force at the outset might have carried the day; the Austrian Ambassador thought that 'a few shells fired at random' would have sufficed, commenting that 'I believe the Ottoman government would be quite willing to submit to those conditions, but it doesn't know how to set about calming the frenzy of the people, who have risen up under arms.' Arbuthnot's demands were rebuffed, and Duckworth was obliged to sail away, fearing that he would become trapped by the reinforcement of artillery positions on the Dardanelles. The only result of this action—apart from the serious damage to his ships which those guns did then inflict—was the collapse of British prestige in Istanbul and a correspondingly huge boost to Sébastiani's power.[99]

Arbuthnot could be forgiven for trying his luck, nevertheless, as the whole process of Ottoman policy-making had become more than usually unstable and unpredictable. As he later put it in a letter to a friend:

> The Turkish Government is so perfectly disjointed that the Governors, or Pachas, of the different Provinces, so far from holding friendly intercourse with each other, are, upon their own authority & for their own objects, not unfrequently in a state of open war; and indeed they never agree in anything except in uniform resistance to the orders of the Porte. This state of things prevails so generally & to such an extent, that I do not hesitate in declaring that beyond the walls of Constantinople, the Grand Signior has not more power than you or I have.[100]

During the summer of 1806 an almost total breakdown had occurred in Sultan Selim's relations with some of the most powerful governors of his European territories. Selim was a reformer, who keenly felt the disadvantages of relying either on the military power of his semi-autonomous pashas, or on that of the Janissary corps, which had its own institutional interests and agendas. But his attempt to set up a 'New Army', raised by conscription and controlled by his loyal officials, met with insuperable hostility. This was led by Ismail Aga Tirsinikli-oğlu, governor of a large part of Thrace and eastern Bulgaria, who at one point threatened to march on Istanbul; when he was assassinated in August 1806 the leadership of this opposition movement was taken over by his charismatic deputy, Mustafa Pasha Bayraktar. The Sultan managed to play off Mustafa Pasha against some of the longer-established pashas in the region, but the situation remained extremely fluid until the Russian invasion of Moldavia in November finally presented a common enemy—whereupon Mustafa's position was regularized by the Sultan, as he was a very effective military commander.[101]

While these turbulent events were taking place in the eastern Balkans, Ali Pasha stayed largely aloof. He had long enjoyed what Bessières called 'a perfect understanding' with Tirsinikli-oğlu, who came to some kind of agreement with him while preparing his revolt in the first half of 1806.[102] But, with intra-Ottoman conflicts as well as external ones, Ali's preferred strategy was to temporize and keep in, so far as possible, with all sides; and in any case the close proximity of the Russians on the Ionian Islands, together with all the uncertainties about French policy, meant that he was reluctant to divert any forces of his own to the eastern Balkans. (To conserve his strength and reinforce his own position, he put an end to his current campaign against the Çams of Paramythia in September, and formed an agreement with the pashas of Berat and Elbasan in October.)[103] For Ali's purposes, the only decisive change was the move to war against Russia in November 1806. He had some forewarning of the Russian invasion, thanks to his active intelligence network in Istanbul, which was monitoring the Russian ambassador. By the time General Michelson entered Ottoman territory on 24 November, Ali had already raised 10,000 men and taken them to Arta, with a view to occupying two of the ex-Venetian towns, Preveza and Vonitsa, as well as the Russian-occupied island of Lefkada. The first two were taken on 6 and 14 December; Ali had hoped to seize the fortress of Parga too, but 900 Russian soldiers were quickly sent there to prevent that. Although his actions were in breach of the Russian–Ottoman agreement of 1800 on the ex-Venetian possessions, he acted with the blessing of the Sultan, who was keen that these places should not fall into Russian hands; for good measure, he also arrested the Russian consul in Arta, George Flory, holding him in captivity until the following September.[104] Over the next few months Ali built up his military positions on the coast just opposite Lefkada (the two are separated only by a narrow channel), and in March 1807, using cannons and artillery officers sent to him by the French, he began a heavy bombardment of the Russian positions there.[105]

While Ali's assault on Lefkada continued for several months, opposition to Sultan Selim's reformist policies was growing in Istanbul. In late May 1807 large numbers of Janissary auxiliaries marched on Istanbul; supported by the *ulema* (Muslim clergy) and other elements in the establishment there, they demanded, and obtained, first the dissolution of the New Army and then the deposition of Selim. He was replaced by his cousin Mustafa IV, and was taken into captivity within the Topkapı Palace. Mustafa Bayraktar worked hard to preserve the Ottoman armed forces from a general collapse of discipline. Offended when he was denied the post of Grand Vizier as a reward for his labours, he now became an enemy of the new regime.[106]

Ali Pasha had no direct involvement in these events, though it seems that the fall of Selim did give him some satisfaction.[107] Throughout these months he was pursuing with unusual single-mindedness his policy of attacking the Russians—primarily for his own local advantage, but also to gain prestige in Istanbul—and aligning himself with the French. That his own interests came first was made clear when in late March he sent his secretary on a diplomatic mission to Napoleon; the main purpose was to get assurances that Ali would be put in charge of any territories—especially the islands, and above all Corfu—that were gained from the Russians. (Having sent lavish gifts to the French Emperor via Bessières, and buoyed up by Pouqueville's encouragement, Ali Pasha seems genuinely to have believed that Napoleon looked on him with special favour. This was a rare case of insufficient cynicism on his part. In a letter to his brother Joseph Bonaparte in May, commenting on one of Ali's requests for arms, Napoleon wrote: 'The pasha of Ioannina is an enemy of the Russians, but he is duplicitous ["faux"]. If you sent him some help, there's nothing wrong with that, but you shouldn't take it too far—fine words will be enough.')[108] Ali's envoy, known as Mehmed Efendi, was well qualified for the task; originally an Italian called Marco Guerini, he had worked for the Inquisition on Malta before joining Napoleon's expedition to Egypt in 1798, after which he too—together with Bessières and Pouqueville—had been captured on his return. Having been sold to Ali, he had converted to Islam, and had become a much-valued secretary and translator.[109] Mehmed Efendi left Ioannina with a French officer and reached Vienna in mid-June; he finally caught up with Napoleon at the town of Tilsit, in East Prussia, in early July, and was granted an audience in which he made the case for installing Ali Pasha as governor of Corfu. The Emperor listened politely, and pretended that he had no power to give Ali an island that he did not possess. But in fact the request could not have come at a more irritating time, as Napoleon had just finalized his negotiations with the Tsar over a general peace agreement, which did indeed involve handing over Corfu, and the other Ionian Islands, to France.[110] This agreement, signed on 7 July 1807 and known as the Treaty of Tilsit, would have far-reaching effects on Ali's policies, eventually driving him back into the arms of the British.

VII

Under the terms agreed at Tilsit, Russia agreed to hand over the Ionian Islands and Kotor to the French. It also promised to sign a truce with the Ottomans, and committed itself to removing its forces from the Romanian principalities once a general peace with them was established; and France undertook to act as mediator for such a settlement between Russia and the Ottoman Empire. However, it was secretly agreed that if that mediation failed, France would become a co-belligerent against the Ottomans, and arrangements would then be made for

Russia and France to divide between them some of the Sultan's European territories. (The details were not specified, though the region of Istanbul itself was
excluded.)[111] The rather vague and open-ended nature of this last provision shows
that taking territory from the Ottoman Empire was not one of Napoleon's primary policy goals. His attitude on that issue varied over the years, the only constant being his determination that Russia should not get Istanbul and thereby
gain control over the passage from the Black Sea to the Mediterranean. From time
to time, however, he did consider seizing some territory in the western Balkans.
While he was at Tilsit he sent a message to the military governor of Dalmatia,
asking for information about conditions in the Albanian lands and the possibility
of conquering them. An officer was duly despatched to the region, and his eventual report recommended invading the north of Albania, gaining the support of
the Christian population there, and then using their help to move southwards
and subdue Ali Pasha.[112]

The hand-over of the islands took place very promptly. On 8 August 1807 a
French general, César Berthier, arrived at Corfu; he came with 500 troops, and a
larger force arrived soon afterwards. (He also took over the 'Albanian Regiment'
formed there by the Russians; by the end of the year this would have a strength of
3,254 men.) Ali Pasha immediately sent Mehmed Efendi to congratulate him, and
to obtain his agreement to the occupation by Ali's men of Parga (from which the
Russians were now withdrawing). Keen to be on good terms with a local ruler
who controlled much of the food supply to Corfu, and considering that the fort of
Parga would be of little military importance to the French, Berthier agreed in
principle, and it was only at Pouqueville's insistence that the matter was referred
back to Paris. When it finally reached Napoleon's desk the Emperor reacted very
sharply. He instructed his minister of war to tell Berthier 'that he must take great
care in his dealings with Ali Pasha, and that it is absurd to allow any uncertainties
about whether I should give him Parga or not; it is not the business of my generals
to give away anything. Tell him not to be fooled by Ali Pasha's trickery, and not to
indulge in any diplomatic negotiations.'[113] On receiving these instructions,
Berthier sent 300 French soldiers to occupy Parga; and at the beginning of
December he wrote to Ali Pasha, saying that Napoleon also wanted an artillery
position, manned by French soldiers, to be established at Butrint (one of the other
three ex-Venetian places that Ali still controlled).[114] Ali had evidently foreseen
that a long struggle with the French over such territorial questions lay ahead, and
had already begun to put pressure on Berthier by obstructing the supply of food
to the islands: in early November the French Ambassador in Istanbul, Sébastiani,
made a formal complaint to the Sultan about this.[115]

As his relations with the French became increasingly confrontational, and with
France's former enemy, Russia, removed from the game, it was natural that Ali
should think again about Great Britain. Gradually, but only very gradually, the
government in Istanbul would move in a similar direction. To the Ottoman

authorities Tilsit had come as a shock, not least because of the treatment of the Ionian Islands, whose status up until then had been that of a republic under the theoretical suzerainty of the Sultan; and there were real fears that Russia and France would make further territorial agreements to the disadvantage of the Ottomans.[116] However, since Russian troops remained in the Romanian principalities, and Napoleon's situation in Europe seemed stronger than ever, the Ottoman government was wary of offending this new Franco-Russian axis. A British diplomat, Sir Arthur Paget, had been sent out to try to repair relations with the Sultan earlier in the summer. News of Tilsit reached him while he was in the Mediterranean, greatly simplifying his task, and when his ship anchored off the Dardanelles in August 1807 he began a friendly exchange of messages with the Ottoman Foreign Minister. But Sébastiani's hostility to this initiative proved too powerful, and the negotiations ended inconclusively more than two months later—despite Paget's having told the Ottomans of the secret agreement between Napoleon and Tsar Alexander over a possible division of Balkan territories between them.[117] With that scenario in mind, the government in London had sent a message to Paget instructing him 'to ascertain whether, in the event of the Ottoman Government being expelled from their European possessions, any of the Governors of the European dependencies of Turkey had the will or the means to maintain their independence against France and Russia, especially the Pashas of Smyrna or Janina'. While Paget was on his mission, news reached London that William Leake was being held under close arrest in Salonica, where he had been detained in February in response to Admiral Duckworth's actions; so in October Paget interceded with the Ottoman authorities for Leake's release, in order to employ him, once again, as an envoy to Ali Pasha.[118] Picked up by a British sloop-of-war, Leake was swiftly transported round the coast of Greece; he arrived at the little port of Sarandë in early November.

Paget's instruction to Leake was, on the face of it, straightforward:

you will proceed to the residence of the Pacha of Janina; & having establish'd an Intercourse with that Governor, you will state to Him, without reserve, your apprehension of the Fate, which awaits the Ottoman Empire in Europe; & you will find out, if possible, the intentions of that Pacha, as to the course He would pursue, in the event of the Ottoman Government being compelled to retire from Constantinople within their Asiatick Frontier. If you should discover that Ali Pacha is desirous and capable of maintaining his Independence, you will assure Him of His Majesty's disposition to support Him in His exertions, and to afford Him that assistance, of which alone He is in want, a Naval Force, sufficient to overpower any Fleets, which either France or Russia, or both combined, can appropriate to the Mediterranean.[119]

This was the first time that a British representative had been empowered to make a direct promise of military assistance to Ali Pasha. Admittedly, while the wording here stuck fairly closely to the instructions from London, it generated an ambiguity: did the promise of naval help relate only to a future scenario in which the Ottoman government had already been driven out of Europe, or would it apply to one in which Ali was defending Ottoman territory against the initial French or Russian attack, in the expectation that he would continue to fight for his 'Independence' in the event of an eventual Ottoman collapse? Nevertheless, whatever the precise circumstances envisaged by it, the psychological effect of such an offer of help could hardly fail to be positive.

When the ship bearing William Leake arrived off Sarandë on 6 November 1807, he sent a messenger to the port in a small boat flying a flag of truce. (The Sultan had made a formal declaration of war on Britain in the previous month, though it was not a conflict actively pursued by the Ottomans.) He met the *bölükbaşı* (military officer) who was in charge there, and gave him a letter to Ali Pasha, in which Leake asked if he could have confidential dealings under the cover of negotiating for the return of British captives. The *bölükbaşı*—who, Leake was pleased to hear, spoke about the French 'in a strain of the greatest hatred'— agreed to send the letter to Ali, and explained that he was then at Preveza. Leake sailed there, and on 12 November, after an elaborate deception operation designed to put Pouqueville off the scent, the two men met at night at a place specified by Ali, six miles up the coast from that town. Having observed fires lit at the appointed location, Leake was rowed in darkness to the beach and 'to my surprise found Ali Pasha wrapt in his black Albanian Cloak, with Sekhri Eff[endi] of Yanina in the same manner, sitting under a little Cliff, 15 or 20 Albanians near...Ali received me with an Embrace.' Their discussion began with Leake warning that France and Russia, and probably Austria too, were conspiring to carve up the European territories of the Ottoman Empire; the secret provisions of the Treaty of Tilsit gave Kotor to France, and from both there and Corfu Napoleon could launch an attack on the mainland. Pointedly, Leake added (as he wrote in his subsequent report) that 'the ultimate view of Bonaparte in this great design was perhaps that of placing one of his Family on the throne of Greece.' What would Ali Pasha and the Albanians do in such circumstances? Ali's answer was that 'their Maxim was to face their Enemies, wherever they appeared and that I might depend upon their unanimity in a Case wherein Albania itself was to be attacked'. In response to this, Leake gave a promise of British naval help in the event of any such invasion—thereby resolving the ambiguity of his instructions, in favour of what might be Ali's more immediate needs.[120]

As always, Ali was quick to ask for more. He requested that the British station a naval force off his coast as soon as possible, explaining that until that happened, he would be obliged to supply provisions to the Ionian Islands. He also urged them to expel the French from the islands; after that he would be able to help repel any French invasion from Dalmatia, though for that purpose he also requested artillery, ammunition and money. And then, displaying (as Leake noted) 'his aptitude at turning every political crisis to his personal advantage', he began talking insistently about the island of Lefkada, which was 'very necessary to him, because in the hands of any other Power, it continually endangered the safety of his neighbouring possessions'. The garrison of the fortress there had only 150 French soldiers; if the British conquered it and handed the island over to him, he would give any help that was required in seizing the other islands. In his report, Leake noted that there were two different policy decisions to be made here: one about conquering Lefkada, and the other about giving it to Ali Pasha. But he was happy to endorse the first of these,

> because in these Countries, where treachery and mistrust so universally prevail, it is highly necessary to remove every suspicion of insincerity on our part, and I have reason to believe Ali Pasha has not forgotten the disappointment he experienced at no notice having been taken of some trifling favours he sollicited of our Government in 1804. I allude to the Guns and Shot, and the armed Vessel for the navigation of the Gulf of Arta, which he asked for at that period through the medium of Lord Nelson.

Overall, Leake argued that Ali's professions of pro-British feeling were credible because they were 'founded upon the solid basis of his own interest'. That was a reasonable judgement, but his next comment suggests that he had become a little too susceptible to Ali's beguiling rhetoric: 'He does not covet any of the Islands, except Santa Maura [*sc.* Lefkada], having often declared that Albanians are not calculated for the conquest and defence of Islands.' Leake concluded: 'His wish must therefore be, to see these places in the hands of a Power, which he does not suspect of any ambitious views on the Continent of Greece.' After his lengthy travels in the region, Leake felt able to say that Britain was quite popular with the Greek people—an important point in relation to any future British occupation of the Ionian Islands. However, looking ahead to a possible future in which Greece gained its independence and Ali Pasha became a 'sovereign power', he warned that for Britain to have close links with Ali would damage 'the confidence of the Greeks' unless the British had sufficient influence with him 'to persuade him of the impolicy of his cruel conduct towards them'.[121]

As soon as William Leake reached Messina, on 20 November 1807, he wrote a letter to Vice-Admiral Collingwood, commander of British naval forces in the Mediterranean, describing his meeting with Ali and declaring that 'it is therefore with the greatest earnestness, that I beg leave to urge to your Lordship the propriety of complying with (at least) a part of a request, which he made to me'—viz, sending a small naval force both to blockade the French and to seize the fortress of Lefkada. Leake was doing little more than echoing his instructions from Paget when he emphasized 'the Great advantage of acquiring the confidence of a Person, become so powerful as Ali Pasha now is, and who will be so very necessary to us, in the event of the partition of European Turkey'.[122] But Collingwood was not easily moved. When Leake met the Vice-Admiral at the port of Siracusa three weeks later, he found him 'not very favorably impressed with regard to Ali Pasha's sincerity and good intentions'; Collingwood said he thought Britain had no interest in attacking the islands, and was content with deploying a few cruisers to cut off supplies to Corfu.[123] Writing to London on 9 December, Collingwood said that he thought it would be wrong to divert any soldiers from the defence of Sicily, and in a letter to Ali Pasha, written on the same day, he made the same point: 'The British army is at present so engaged, that troops cannot be sent.' But he also told Ali that so long as the presence of the cruisers prevented the French from reinforcing the island of Lefkada, 'I think your Albanians would possess themselves of it in a few days.'[124] Although Ali did not realize this, the Vice-Admiral was setting up a test of his resolve; and Collingwood's downbeat remark to Leake about Ali's 'sincerity and good intentions' suggests that it was a test which he expected Ali Pasha to fail.

While it is true that Ali did not launch any attack on Lefkada, his relations with the French were becoming more and more strained. By early January 1808 Pouqueville was writing that English officers had made secret visits to Ali Pasha; most or possibly all of the contacts he reported over the next few months were imaginary (in May he became convinced that Leake was living incognito in a small fortress near Preveza), but his basic complaint that Ali was conspiring with the British was not wide of the mark.[125] In a letter to César Berthier in late January Ali flatly denied that he was seeking British support of any kind: 'it is impossible', he wrote, 'that I should abandon my loyalty to the French and seek the friendship of those who are enemies of my sovereign.' But that was not the only charge from which he had to defend himself; in the same letter he also referred to Berthier's accusation about 'the obstruction of provisions from these places to the islands'.[126]

Another cause of tension between Ali Pasha and the French was the desire of the latter to establish an overland route between their new possession of Kotor and the coast opposite Corfu. In early January 1808 General Marmont, the commander of French forces in Dalmatia, sent an agent to act as French consul in Berat, with the special purpose of opening a line of communication from Kotor to Corfu.[127] Just a few days later Napoleon told his Foreign Minister to write to Sébastiani in Istanbul, instructing him to request permission for a force of 4–5,000 French soldiers to pass through Albanian territory; fearing that the British would attack Corfu at some time in the coming year, Napoleon was eager to strengthen the garrison there, as he saw the fortress and harbour of Corfu as a place of huge strategic importance. (Within a month he would write to his brother Joseph that 'you should view Corfu as more important than Sicily', adding: 'mark my words: given the present situation in Europe, losing Corfu would be the worst

thing that could happen to me.')[128] Sébastiani's request was opposed by Halet
Pasha, the *reis efendi* (Ottoman Foreign Minister), who was a supporter of Ali
Pasha and indeed a recipient of large private payments from him; Halet told the
divan (imperial council) that the entry of French troops would be the first step
towards the conquest of Albania and Greece. The government's initial rejection of
Sébastiani's request aroused such severe threats from him that Halet Pasha was
dismissed on 22 February, but many who shared Halet's views—including
Janissaries and members of the *ulema*—then caused serious unrest in Istanbul.[129]
In March Sébastiani got formal permission from the Ottoman government for
the passage of 4,000 French troops overland, as well as a promise to ensure the
provisioning of Corfu for the next three years; the Austrian Ambassador, reporting this development, wrote that 'I have been confidentially assured that the government is merely seeking to humour Sébastiani, and that it is determined not to
give in to any of his demands.' Indeed, the Ottoman official charged with taking
this imperial decree to Ali Pasha was instructed to tell Ali privately that he was
not obliged to obey it.[130] It is understandable that the authorities in Istanbul were
reluctant to allow foreign armies to cross their territory; but in addition they may
have been alarmed both by the threat made rather casually by Napoleon in late
1807 to invade the lands governed by pashas such as Ali if they did not cooperate
with the French, and by Ali's claim (which may have been fictitious) to have intercepted three couriers in February 1808 carrying secret messages exhorting the
Greeks to prepare for a revolt against Ottoman rule.[131] Hostility to the transit of
foreign troops through the Albanian lands was felt by the local population too.
Two French officers who took 136 barrels of gunpowder overland from Kotor to
Vlorë were abused and spat at throughout their journey; and in mid-March, when
three of Marmont's officers arrived at the city of Bar (just south of Kotor) and
imprudently responded to a jeering crowd by drawing their swords, they were all
killed.[132] While this episode did new damage to Franco-Ottoman relations, it may
well have caused some satisfaction to members of the government in Istanbul.

Covert governmental approval was also a factor in Ali Pasha's responses to
French demands for the little ex-Venetian port of Butrint, which occupied a strategic position on the Corfu channel. As early as December 1807 César Berthier
was asking Ali to hand over Butrint; in January Napoleon wrote to Berthier to say
that the Ottoman government had ceded it to France, and that 'it is my intention
that you should take possession of it immediately, to fortify the headland and set
up a good artillery position there.'[133] In early March Julien Bessières, who had just
arrived in Corfu as an imperial commissary, began corresponding with Ali on
this subject. Told by Bessières that the Sultan had ordered the handing over of
Butrint, Ali replied that he had not received any *firman* (sultanic decree) to that
effect; the French had been told that the *firman* was sent out on 1 January, but Ali's
temporizing was clearly in line with the real policy of his government.[134] At the
same time, Ali ramped up his own rhetoric, referring in one of his letters to

Bessières to 'Butrint, Parga, Preveza and Vonitsa, for the defence of which the whole of Albania too is willing to shed its blood'.[135] When Berthier sent an ultimatum threatening to occupy Butrint by force, Ali passed this to Istanbul as evidence of aggressive French intentions; he showed Pouqueville a letter from his agent there which reported that the ultimatum had alarmed the members of the *divan*, who were now saying that if France demanded Butrint today, tomorrow it would want Preveza, and then the Peloponnese.[136] Over these months Pouqueville received consistently hostile treatment from Ali; in his reports to French officials he wrote that local people were forbidden to give him information, and that he was kept under a kind of house arrest. At the same time he also noted that, unusually, Ali received deliveries of arms and ammunition from the Ottoman government.[137]

Napoleon's hostility to Ali Pasha continued to grow. In April 1808 he sent a formal complaint about him, calling him a 'brigand'; in May he assumed that Ali was implicated in the killing of the three French officers at Bar; and in June he ordered that the French chargé d'affaires in Istanbul (Pierre Ruffin, who was standing in after Sébastiani's departure in late April) should tell the Sultan to declare Ali Pasha a rebel. In the same message he instructed Bessières, his commissary on Corfu, to 'stir up against Ali Pasha the minor pashas, his neighbours, who are discontented with him, and to weaken him by all possible means, giving arms and money (but doing so secretly) to all his enemies'.[138] Within less than a year of taking possession of the Ionian Islands, Napoleon's policy towards Ali had thus become a near-replica of the one previously adopted by the Russians. That Ali Pasha had local enemies was still true; but in February he had taken care to end a conflict with Ibrahim Pasha of Vlorë (in which, unusually, he had been losing—he had been forced to abandon Elbasan in January).[139] He was confident, however, that the other pashas would agree with him on the need to repel any French invasion. As he had told Leake during their conversation on the beach near Preveza, referring both to the Albanian pashas to the north and to Ismail of Serres, 'we shall fight together with you, we shall fall together with you.'[140] In April a senior Ottoman official was sent to urge all three Albanian pashas to put aside their disputes and collaborate against the French; he came back to Istanbul in early May, reporting that all had agreed to do so.[141] The only potential weak link here was Ibrahim Pasha of Vlorë; he was receiving advice both from the newly installed French consul at Berat and also from his own physician, the Francophile Corfiot Giōannēs Liperakēs, who had been encouraging the French on Corfu to stir up opposition to Ali Pasha since December. But in a letter to César Berthier in March, Ibrahim explained apologetically: 'What stops me from obeying you is the fear of the people. It's true that previously I gave you to believe that letting French troops pass through here would be easy. But now, seeing the whole of Albania put into a state of alarm for the same reason, I cannot make any agreement that goes against the opinion of these barbarians and the other viziers [*sc.* Ali Pasha and Ibrahim of Shkodër].'[142]

VIII

Ali's mounting hostility towards the French thus had some support from Istanbul. Just how much support he could count on from London, however, must have remained unclear to him for quite a long time. Sheer distance was part of the problem. When William Leake returned to Britain at the end of January 1808, he found that his long report on his conversation with Ali, sent in mid-November, had not yet arrived; he handed over a copy, but was too ill (with, probably, a recurrence of his malaria) to meet the Foreign Secretary in person.[143] Reports from David Morier, who was now on Malta, relating news of Ali's anti-French activities from January to April, seem to have elicited no reaction from London.[144] In April Ali Pasha sent a letter to Vice-Admiral Collingwood. That text does not survive, but Collingwood's reply to it, written in late June, conceded only that Ali might use his own money to buy arms from the British on Malta, and that British ships would try to give support to 'any operation which you may undertake against the enemy'; we may assume that both points fell short of what Ali was requesting. Before he received that reply, Ali wrote again to Collingwood in early June, politely but a little plaintively: 'I spoke to Mr. Leake of what I thought most necessary at present, and I hope he has mentioned it to your Excellency.' And in early August Ali asked once more for 'a sufficient naval force, of which the senior officer should receive full powers to concert and co-operate with me in all that is necessary', pointedly adding that he could do nothing without British help.[145]

By this time, Ali Pasha's efforts to gain such British help had started down a second track: he had sent his own personal envoy to King George III. The opportunity to do this arose from the fact that the government in Istanbul, recognizing that he had channels of communication with the British, had sent him a letter to transmit to London. (This was not the first time that Ali had been used in this way; the previous *reis efendi*, his friend and client Halet Pasha, had sent a letter via Ali soon after Leake's visit in November.)[146] As relations between the Sultan and Napoleon deteriorated, the Ottoman government had begun to regret its cold-shouldering of Sir Arthur Paget, and was now actively seeking a peace agreement with Britain; the letter it sent via Ali was an instruction to that effect, addressed to its resident chargé d'affaires in London, Sıdkı Efendi. Rather than just hand the letter to a passing British naval vessel, Ali ordered an agent of his own to take it to London; whether he was asked to do so by his government (as he later claimed), or whether this was his own initiative, is not clear. The man he chose, Said Ahmed, left Ioannina in April; by May he was in Malta, where he met David Morier.[147] In early July, off the Bay of Biscay, the ship that was carrying him encountered another British ship, which was taking Sıdkı Efendi from London to the Ottoman Empire in the company of a diplomat, Sir Robert Adair—who, in response to a further message from the Ottoman government, had been sent out with plenipotentiary powers to negotiate a peace settlement. Adair continued on his way, but Sıdkı Efendi returned to London with Said Ahmed.[148]

On his arrival there later that month, Said Ahmed presented Ali's personal letter to King George, which William Leake then translated from the Greek. In the words of his draft translation, it began: 'Sir, With a veneration the most profound, and a love, which is deeply rooted in my heart, & mixed with my blood, I presume to address your Majesty…ready to execute your commands.' The letter's main aim was to boost Ali's status in the eyes of the British by emphasizing his vital role as not just an intermediary with, but also an influence upon, the government in Istanbul. 'At the time, Sir, that your late Ambassador was sent to Constantinople, I wrote to the Government exhorting it to make peace', Ali wrote; as a consequence, he declared, 'My request has been complied with.' The Ottoman government had 'deputed' Ali to send his own envoy, and he had chosen Said Ahmed because he knew Ali's 'most intimate counsels' and would be able to explain Ali's requests in detail. For good measure, he added that 'Capt Leake, Your Maj servant & my friend received Sr in person the like intimation of all my wishes, & has undoubtedly made Your Majesty acquainted with them.'[149] The precise nature of Ali's 'requests' and 'wishes' is not recorded, but one of them does clearly emerge, as we shall see, from a later document: he asked for the help of the British in taking control over the ex-Venetian fortress (now garrisoned by the French) of Parga.

While Said Ahmed was representing his master to the British as someone who could influence or even direct the policy of the Ottoman government, that government was undergoing some dramatic changes. During the first half of 1808 Mustafa Bayraktar had strengthened his position as the leading military and political authority outside Istanbul. As commander of the forces that were still fighting the Russians (who had not abandoned their positions in Wallachia and Moldavia), he was also pursuing his own foreign policy, offering peace terms to the Tsar in an attempt to split the Franco-Russian alliance. At the same time he was assembling a broad coalition of leaders opposed to the governing circle in Istanbul.[150] Powerful local governors such as Ismail of Serres promised him their full backing; Ali Pasha was much less closely involved, though he did give Mustafa a general promise of support, and sent his son Muhtar to a meeting of Balkan notables at Edirne in June 1808 where Mustafa discussed taking the army to Istanbul in order to effect a change of regime.[151] That march on Istanbul (the real purpose of which was cleverly concealed from the authorities) took place in mid-July. Within a week, Mustafa had ejected or assassinated several key figures in the government; but then the Grand Vizier, discovering that Mustafa's final aim was to restore to the throne the former Sultan Selim III (who was held captive in the imperial palace), had Selim killed. Mustafa arranged for Selim's son, Prince Mahmud, to become Sultan, and was himself appointed Grand Vizier. Within a month, he began to summon all the powerful local rulers of the Balkans—or their representatives: Ali Pasha sent one of his grandsons—to a meeting in Istanbul, for a formal discussion of the governance of the Empire; in late September they drew up a so-called 'Deed of Alliance', in which they pledged to accept some military reforms in return for an acknowledgement by the central authority of their own local rights. But Mustafa's new quasi-constitutional settlement was not to last. In November discontented Janissaries besieged his house, and he died when an ammunition store there exploded. His rule had not been popular in Istanbul; the new sultan, Mahmud II, a much more decisive figure than his two predecessors, declared that Mustafa's reforms were at an end, and took more power into his own hands.[152]

Sir Robert Adair, who was on his way to conduct peace negotiations with the Ottomans, first heard of the 'revolution' in Istanbul when he was in Sicily in mid-August. While stopping at Malta in early September he spoke to Spiridion Foresti, who had recently received a letter from Ali Pasha; this revealed that Ali was 'uncertain as to the footing on which he stands with the new Government', which made Adair decide against using Ali as a channel for his forthcoming negotiations.[153] The promise of support which Ali had given to Mustafa Bayraktar earlier in the year was, it seems, just an example of his general policy of keeping in with all those who held power. His reaction to the coup was essentially negative, most likely for the simple reason that he had enjoyed a comfortable relationship with the previous regime: it had supported him in his conflict with the French, key members of it (such as the *reis efendi*) accepted payments from him, and its anti-reformist attitude suited his general wish not to be interfered with. Rather strangely, Ali's initial reaction to the news of Mustafa Bayraktar's march on Istanbul in July was to denounce him as a tool of French policy: he wrote to Collingwood on 2 August that Mustafa 'has been instigated to commit these acts by the insidious arts of our enemy'. When William Leake had a chance to discuss Ali's attitude with Spiridion Foresti later in the year, he would comment that whilst it was 'evidently Ali Pasha's policy to make us believe, that Mustafà Bairaktar was a Partizan of the French and Russians', the truth was that the sheer accumulation of power in Mustafa's hands had made him the object of Ali's 'jealousy and Enmity'.[154]

The nature of the change of regime cannot have been known in London when, in August 1808, a significant alteration occurred in British policy towards Ali Pasha. The Foreign Secretary wrote to Adair, informing him that artillery and ammunition would be sent to Ali, and that Collingwood was to receive 'a general instruction to appoint a sufficient naval force to guard the Coasts of Albania, & to cooperate with A. P. in any enterprize against the french in that quarter which may appear necessary for the security of his territory & which may be within the reach of naval cooperation' (with the proviso that 'Land force or money is not intended to be promised').[155] Although that instruction to Collingwood did not go much beyond what the Vice-Admiral himself had envisaged, the fact of its being decreed as official policy did make a difference; and the gift of military supplies was an important new development. The quantity of supplies was quite substantial, including 30 cannons and ten smaller artillery pieces, and a ship was chosen to take them from England in September.[156] In the following month George Canning gave a new set of instructions to William Leake in London. His essential task was to 'enter into communication with Ali Pacha of Joannina, in consequence of the application of that Chieftain for His Majesty's Assistance against the French.' He was to proceed first to Malta, to learn the state of Adair's peace negotiations with the Ottomans. 'If it shall appear that Ali Pacha is determined to attack the French in his Neighbourhood, or to defend his Territories against them, although Peace between Great Britain and the Porte shall not have been concluded, You are still at liberty to communicate with him.' On meeting Ali, Leake was to give him a list of all the arms and ammunition that were on their way, and ask him to 'make use of his Influence for uniting the other Albanian Chieftains against the French, especially for persuading the Vizir, Pacha of Scutari, to act offensively against the French Troops bordering upon his Province'. And if he did agree to open hostilities against them himself, he should know that Collingwood 'has been instructed to employ his Ships on that Station, in effecting, if practicable, the Reduction of the French Garrison in the Town of Parga. Which Instruction you will represent to have been given in consequence of Ali Pacha's request to [sic] the Seid Achmet, and with the view of putting him in possession of a Port, which he has represented as so important to the Security of his Country; and as a fresh Proof therefore of His Majesty's Friendship and Attention to Ali Pacha's Interests and Wishes.'[157] This move in British policy would eventually enable Ali to argue that he had been promised possession of Parga—an argument that would resonate in his dealings with Britain over many years, with, eventually, fateful consequences for the Parganots.

Said Ahmed was taken back to the west coast of Greece on a British ship. He was accompanied by a young Englishman, Anthony St John Baker, who was going out to serve as a secretary to Sir Robert Adair. When they arrived at Preveza at the beginning of November 1808, Ali Pasha sent a message insisting that Baker come and talk with him in Ioannina. In Baker's account of their subsequent conversation, Parga also looms large. Ali argued that it should be given to him 'as a proof of the sincerity of the professions of friendship made to him by Great Britain'. Cannily, he suggested that the seizure of this stronghold would cause a serious rift in Franco-Ottoman relations: since the French 'would not fail to address themselves to the Porte to obtain restitution of it and as his Highness [sc. Ali Pasha] is most firmly determined, when once in possession of it, never to restore it to the Enemy, the French would probably attribute their not obtaining it to the little regard which the Porte was inclined to pay to their representations upon the subject, which feeling might eventually lead to a coolness between the two powers, and therefore tend to favour the renewal of amicable relations between Great Britain and Turkey'. The effects on the local balance of power were also adduced: the conquest of Parga 'would greatly distress the Enemy, as it is by means of this town that a correspondence and connection is kept up with the Independent Albanians who furnish provisions to Corfu and adjacent Islands, and who would soon be reduced under the power of the Pacha was it not for the support and countenance they derive from Parga'. And, finally, the prospect was held out of more military cooperation with Britain: 'The Pacha would likewise be enabled to spare a considerable force which is at present employed before this place, and in keeping the mountaineers in check, either more effectually to prevent provisions from being sent into Corfu, by stationing bodies of troops along the Coast, or for any other more active service which might be undertaken in conjunction with the English.'[158] This account gives us a sense of the skill and resourcefulness with which Ali was capable of pressing his demands. On the question of Parga, as on all other specific requests made by Ali, the formal letter written by George Canning (on behalf of George III) which Said Ahmed brought to Ioannina was in fact studiously vague: it merely said that the 'the Objects of your Highness's desire, first laid before H. Majesty by Captain Leake, & now repeated by Said Ahmet Effendi, have engaged in an eminent degree His Majesty's attention.'[159] But that would not stop Ali Pasha from later claiming that Said Ahmed had come back from London with letters from the British government promising him both Parga and Lefkada.[160]

Once again it was Vice-Admiral Collingwood who gave the driest assessment of Ali's motives. Writing to Lord Mulgrave, First Lord of the Admiralty, in late January 1809, he commented: 'His anxiety to possess Parga is more for the purpose of controlling the neighbouring Agas, than of extirpating the French, with whom I have a suspicion that he was carrying on a friendly correspondence last year, when to us he was professing himself their inveterate enemy.'[161] (This 'suspicion' was not baseless, but neither was it accurate; Ali had indeed been corresponding with the French on Corfu, but mostly in answer to their complaints, and his disclaimers of any hostile policy towards them were transparently false.)[162] Collingwood recalled that he had frequently encouraged Ali—thus far without success—to attack the French. But if and when he did, Collingwood observed,

> he will have more than the French to oppose; for the Greeks have a much greater dread of him than of the French, and will exert themselves for the independence of their respective countries. It is difficult to form a just notion of the policy and complex interests of such a number of little Governments, ruled by Pachas and Agas, along the coast, all subject to the Porte, but all jealous of their

independence of each other; ready to oppose any invader of their Country; and most of them more afraid of Ali Pacha than of the French, and only holding intercourse with the latter, as they enable them to resist his projects.[163]

Less than a week later, however, Collingwood received from Adair the news that a peace treaty had successfully been concluded between Britain and the Ottoman Empire. (This was the so-called Treaty of the Dardanelles of 5 January, the fruit of long and difficult negotiations by Adair on board his ship, which was anchored there.)[164] One comment the Vice-Admiral made in his next letter to Adair puts Ali Pasha in a very different light: 'Indeed, from the assurance of Ali Pacha that the negociation would terminate favourably, I had little doubt of it; for that chieftain is known to have great influence at the Porte, and to be very much engaged in the politics of its internal government.'[165] Adair himself was convinced that Ali had played a significant role behind the scenes: the day after the treaty was signed, he wrote to Ali thanking him for 'your powerful exertions at the Sublime Porte in bringing about the renewal of those happy relations of peace and friendship'. That Ali had been following developments closely is also suggested by the fact that in mid-December he had jumped the gun, sending a letter to Foresti announcing that peace had just been agreed.[166] And there is further evidence that he was in favour in Istanbul: on 16 January a sultanic official arrived at Ioannina with a document confirming Ali Pasha in all his dignities.[167] Overall, there is no reason to doubt that Ali's influence (and, probably, money) had been employed in pushing the government towards a more Anglophile policy; his own position, locked into a hostile stand-off against the French, could only benefit from such a development. And it may well be that the change of governmental personnel after the fall of Mustafa Bayraktar in November had brought back some of Ali's previous clients, who were more amenable to his persuasive methods. At any rate, the larger consequence was that when Sir Robert Adair took up his role as resident ambassador in Istanbul in late January 1809, one of the assumptions on which he would work was that Ali Pasha was more than just a regional ally or protégé; he was a powerful agent of influence, who might be used to further British interests at the heart of the Ottoman state. This was another significant development in the relationship between Britain and the Pasha of Ioannina.

IX

William Leake reached Malta on Christmas Eve 1808—just two days after the ordinance ship bearing arms for Ali Pasha, which had set out long before him. Having spoken at length to Spiridion Foresti, who had been receiving regular communications from Ali throughout the year, he wrote a lengthy report to the Foreign Secretary, George Canning, on 26 December. While recognizing that Ali pursued his own interests, he said that he believed him to be well aware of French 'ambitious projects', and therefore 'sincerely attached to our Cause'. Maintaining the policy line that he had previously held, Leake wrote that 'I still think it would be advisable to indulge the Vezir's [*sc.* Ali's] ambition by assisting him to reduce the independent tribes of the Western Coast of Greece.' The French on Corfu depended on the Çams for their supplies of cattle, and on the Himariots for their grain; so, given the ability of small craft to pass quickly to and fro, a blockade of Corfu would be ineffectual unless those coastal districts, and the fortress of Parga, were under Ali's control.[168] In a later meeting with Collingwood, Leake gained the Vice-Admiral's agreement to this policy. Collingwood accepted that 'it will be of great utility to have a single powerful opponent to the French rather than several small states, divided by mutual jealousies and mistrusts'; and, as Leake reported, he sent an order to the captain commanding the British ships off the coast of Albania 'to cooperate with Ali Pasha in the design of reducing Parga, as soon as my communications with his Highness have enabled me to determine upon the most advisable time and manner'.[169]

After the news of the Treaty of the Dardanelles had reached Malta, it was decided that Leake should at last set off for Ali Pasha's territory, taking the ordinance supply ship with him. Bad weather delayed his arrival at Preveza until the beginning of March. Ali Pasha was there to greet him, and began by expressing his thankfulness for the military supplies; but later he said that he was dissatisfied by the letter written by George Canning on the King's behalf, as he had been hoping for an explicit acceptance of his offers to assist the British, and a formal statement that he was under British protection. Ali's apparent ardour for immediate joint actions against either Parga or Lefkada (or both) had also cooled, and he gave two reasons for this. One was the advice of Adair in Istanbul that he should wait until he (Adair) had had his audience with the Sultan; the other was that the French had been hardening their policy towards him. He had intercepted a letter from the commander of Corfu (General François-Xavier Donzelot, who had succeeded César Berthier in the spring of 1808) to the authorities in French-governed Dalmatia, suggesting a large-scale invasion of the Albanian lands by two armies.[170] This last claim may well have been correct; having hired an expert engraver from Malta in the previous year to make exact copies of the seals of various French officials, Ali was now in the habit of opening, reading and then resealing all French correspondence that passed through his territory.[171] And it is certainly true that Julien Bessières was sending threatening letters to Ali; on 27 February he wrote to him about the rumour that 'your Highness, in collaboration with the English, is preparing to make an attack on Parga', and warned that if he did this his life would be in danger from Napoleon's severe retaliation.[172]

Yet barely three weeks after his arrival at Preveza, Leake was being given a very different story by Ali: apparently Bessières had written to him offering not only to hand over all the Souliots who had taken refuge on the islands, but also to give him Parga, so long as he agreed to break off all his relations with the British.[173] Leake obtained a copy of the text of Bessières's letter, in which no such promise was made; indeed it was full of reproaches about 'the secret correspondences Your Highness has with the English, the gifts of cannons, gunpowder and other similar military supplies which Your Highness has received'.[174] It is hard to avoid the conclusion that, as he often did, Ali was exaggerating or inventing the offer received from one side in order to raise the bid of the other. But he was quite capable of doing this while simultaneously following a different tactic, in which he ramped up one side's threat in order to extort more of the other's assistance. In the same conversation with Leake, he discussed the scenario in which France and Russia would force the Sultan to declare him a rebel. As Leake reported: "'in such a predicament" His Highness adds "I cannot have any hopes but from my own exertions and the assistance of the English. I can raise Forty or fifty thousand Men, but I have not the means of maintaining them without pecuniary assistance.—I have constructed Fortresses in all the most important parts of my Territory, but they are only half armed with Cannon and I shall be in want of a large supply of Gunpowder."'[175] Thus, within weeks of receiving a large shipment of military supplies from the British, Ali was already asking both for more arms, and for money. And just a couple of weeks later he raised his demands still higher. On 9 April he told Leake that he planned to expel the French from all the Ionian Islands with British naval assistance, and then 'to leave one of his sons in the Government of Ioannina and to march at the head of Thirty thousand Men towards Cattaro [Kotor], Dalmatia or the Danube'. He calculated that he would need £450,000 to cover the costs of an army of 30,000 men for six months. In addition, he asked for 5,000 muskets, 50,000 lb of gunpowder, 50,000 lb of lead and 20 cannons 'of the largest Calibre for the service of his Fortresses'—plus several engineers and artillery officers, and 150 artillery men.[176]

When these proposals and requests were transmitted to Collingwood in early May 1809, he reacted with more than his usual scepticism. As he wrote to the First Lord of the Admiralty:

> Before he got the cannon, &c. which were necessary for the attack of Parga, nothing else was represented to be wanting,—his army was numerous, his power great; he waited only for our concluding peace with the Porte, to declare his alliance with England; and for the arrival of cannon from Malta, to begin his operations against the French. The peace is concluded, and he has got his cannon, and now he reveals overtures which have been made to him by the French, which he doubtless means should be considered as the cause why he suspends hostilities against them. But he makes amends for that, by proposing to extend the scale of the war. This will require an increase of aid in money, cannon, and stores; and he has now the advantage of a British Agent in his Capital, which greatly facilitates the transmission of his requests. Your Lordship, who can better

judge of Ali Pacha's political character and importance, and the dependence that may be placed in his integrity to us, will estimate these observations truly.[177]

Collingwood's misgivings were justified. And one can only guess what his feelings would have been had he known that on 21 April Ali summoned Pouqueville and proposed that, if the French agreed to give him Parga, he would expel the British, close his ports to their ships, send envoys to Napoleon and ask him for his protection, on conditions of vassalage.[178] The news had only recently reached Ali that Russia had recommenced hostilities against the Ottoman Empire, partly in response to the latter's diplomatic *rapprochement* with Britain.[179] Ali knew that Russia would put pressure on Istanbul to break its British connection; and since Russia's ability to harm was much greater than Britain's ability to help, he had some reason to keep his options open.

The British, meanwhile, still had every reason to try to keep Ali Pasha on their side. Leake was now a resident at Ali's court, and was able both to maintain communications between Ali and Sir Robert Adair, and to transmit the pasha's requests to Malta. At the beginning of May, for example, he told Captain George Eyre, the commander of the British squadron off the Albanian coast, that Ali wanted to consult a British surgeon; in July the commander at Malta, Sir Alexander Ball, wrote to Leake that he was sending 'the surgeon of my Flag Ship of whose skill and experience I have a very good opinion', adding that 'I hope this mark of attention to Ali Pacha will be well received and prove how anxious we are for the preservation of his health.'[180] (The precise nature of Ali's medical problems is not known. As Leake noted, a British naval surgeon, Mr Turner, had already attended him in April or May. Leake also commented on Ali's medical needs and requests in his diary: 'He has lately become more difficult of access, being subject to giddinesses in the head, when he applies too much to business...His great desiderata, as of all the Turks I ever knew, are a philtre for his wives and a poison for his Enemies.')[181]

During the summer, Adair continued to treat Ali Pasha as a valuable political ally. The benefits of this connection were intended to be mutual: in August, for example, Adair wrote that—following a request from Ali, transmitted to him by Leake—he had pleaded with the Ottoman government for Ali Pasha to be 'relieved from the burthen of furnishing his contingent of 8 thousand men to the Grand Vizier's army'.[182] (Throughout the long-drawn-out conflict with Russia, Istanbul made frequent demands that Ali supply large numbers of troops—orders which he usually evaded.) Conversely, Adair was keen to make use of Ali's own influence on the Ottoman government. In August he wrote to Leake about a recent agreement by the Shah of Persia to sign a treaty of alliance with Britain; this had been achieved by a dynamic official, Sir Harford Jones, whose young assistant, James Morier (brother of Jack and David) had now reached Istanbul on his way to London with a Persian representative. French diplomacy had been active in Tehran, and since the Treaty of Tilsit there had been a danger that pressure from both France and Russia (a traditional enemy of Persia, engaged in a long-standing territorial dispute with it) would turn Persia into a through-route for an invasion of India.[183] Adair asked Leake to tell Ali Pasha about this, and to explain that British diplomacy had prevented a separate treaty between Persia and Russia; as a result, those two states were now engaged in a war which was drawing Russian forces away from the Ottoman front. Since some people in the *divan*, such as the deputy Foreign Minister, were opposed to the policy of alliance with Persia, Leake should tell Ali that Adair had the power to instruct Sir Harford Jones to promote a Russian–Persian peace agreement, which would be harmful to the Ottomans. 'I entreat His Highness Ali Pacha', he continued, 'to consider deeply the matters which I here so unreservedly communicate. His Highness is the only Man in the Empire who can appreciate their importance, or give effect to the measures to which they point. Let his highness be assured that such is the present state of the Ottoman Councils, that it is only by the interposition of some powerful Mind like his own that the Empire can be saved from the mischief which awaits it, or can regain that prosperity, that Security, and that high Consideration which is once more within its reach.'[184]

The greatest benefit that Adair hoped to gain from Ali Pasha's pro-British leanings, however, consisted of direct military action against the French. But here, throughout the spring and summer of 1809, the situation did not change. Not every obstacle to action was on Ali's side. In late April the commander of the British squadron off the coast told Leake that his own instructions from Collingwood were that he should not join Ali Pasha in any offensive actions against the French without 'the sanction of the Porte'—which, as Leake complained to Adair, differed from what Collingwood had said to him on Malta.[185] Ali himself now declared that he needed authorization from his government (a condition which, as Leake reminded him, had been absent from his previous promises of action); Adair urged the *reis efendi* to provide this, and was frustrated when the latter's promise to do so turned out to be empty.[186] At the same time, Ali continued to ask for more British ships to be stationed off his coast, and he also kept up his demands for large payments. By early October Adair was writing to Leake that he could not possibly recommend 'the granting of Subsidies on any remote or speculative Contingency, or for any purpose except that of employing them directly against His Majesty's Enemies'. And a few days later, evidently irked by repeated reminders from Ali of the behind-the-scenes help he had given in Istanbul, Adair wrote somewhat tetchily: 'I see plainly what Aly Pacha would insinuate by the constant tenour of his conversations with you. He *may* have been of use to us at the Porte. I can neither deny nor affirm a fact which rests upon evidence I cannot reach. All I say is that his interference has never been made sufficiently manifest for me to judge of its Value.'[187] As these words showed, the 'honeymoon' period of Adair's relationship with Ali Pasha had by now come to an end.

While Ali was quiescent towards the French, he did embark on some military actions against his own local enemies. As early as January 1809 he had mounted a small campaign against Himarë; Ibrahim Pasha of Vlorë, who had become a loyal client of the French, wrote to General Donzelot on Corfu saying that French subsidies had helped to limit the effectiveness of this. In April Ali also sent a small force under his son Muhtar to attack the Çam stronghold of Paramythia.[188] During the following month, Ali informed Leake that Ibrahim Pasha of Vlorë had made an alliance with two of the Çam leaders, and that those powers, together with Himarë and Parga, formed a 'defensive league' against him.[189] Ibrahim was acting in accordance with French policy here, but he soon found that the support of the French was of little help when Ali invaded his territory. By mid-May Ali's army was fighting Ibrahim's troops on the outskirts of Elbasan.[190] What had probably prompted this attack was the news in March that Ibrahim's more powerful namesake, Ibrahim Pasha of Shkodër, had died leaving a five-year-old son as his successor. Ali gave his open support to a rival claimant, the boy's older cousin Mustafa, who had married one of Ali's nieces, but evidently he also saw the opportunity to extend his power northwards towards the border with the *paşalık* of Shkodër while attention there was distracted by the on-going dispute over the succession.[191] In early August Ibrahim of Vlorë sued for peace; Ali took possession of Elbasan, installing his grandson as pasha there, and began to direct his forces against the Çams. (Leake would later comment that it was a sign of how much influence Ali had in Istanbul that the Ottoman government 'reprimanded him for his conduct towards the Pasha of Berat and by the very next Messenger, conferred the Pashalik of Elbassan, of which His Highness had just despoiled Ibrahim, upon his Grandson, a youth of nine years of age'.) Yet at the beginning of October he resumed the conflict with Ibrahim, sending a force of 2,000 men to attack the district of Berat. By mid-October he had occupied the town of Berat, and only the citadel held out against him; Ibrahim would undergo a three-month-long siege there, before finally escaping to Vlorë in January.[192]

William Leake viewed these developments with a lack of enthusiasm bordering on irritation. He had, in any case, a rather jaundiced view of intra-Albanian warfare, believing that such conflicts 'last but a short time and produce no decisive results'. This was partly because of the method of fighting ('dodging behind Trees, & Stones... & firing upon one another at long distance are the usual modes'), and partly because local 'chieftains' demanded so much money for supplying contingents of fighters that the expense was prohibitively high. By late July he noted that Ali was said to have spent 1,500 purses (750,000 piastres) on his campaign against Ibrahim Pasha, and that it was necessary for him to oppose or ignore his counsellors, 'who see the folly of his present contest'. There was also the problem of 'his loss of credit at Constantinople, wch he is obliged to counteract by an additional present of money—for such is his constant policy'. At the financial level, it was of course clear where the superior power was located: 'Ibrahim Pasha whose riches are not great...begins to feel the difficulties of carrying on the contest.' But still Leake doubted the wisdom of any campaign that might try to take Berat, with its citadel high above the town: 'the fortress of Berat will certainly be a difficult job for Albanian engineering & by that time probably the purse of the Vezir or the patience of the Albanians will be...exhausted'.[193]

Nevertheless, Leake adopted a defensive tone when writing about these matters to London. At the beginning of the campaign against Ibrahim, he observed that it was not 'duplicity' on Ali's part to seek British support partly for the sake of increasing his own power locally, as Ali had never concealed the fact that that was one of his motives; and, while admitting that these 'designs of local aggrandizement' were very 'ill-timed', Leake insisted that 'The strength of the Albanian nation would undoubtedly be most useful to the common cause, in the hands of a single person'.[194] When the renewed attack on Berat took place in early October, he dropped his previous argument about its untimely nature; by now, any hopes he had previously nursed of Ali attacking Parga or Lefkada on his own initiative had faded away. In his report he did emphasize that Ibrahim, like the Çams, was supported by the French. But he could not escape the awkward fact that the military supplies given to Ali by the British for a direct attack on French positions were now being used for a very different purpose. As he put it, the citadel of Berat was expected to fall quickly, thanks to 'the superiority in Artillery, which the Vezir [Ali Pasha] has derived from the generosity of His Majesty's Government'. Defending the position he had previously taken, Leake felt obliged to write that when he originally recommended sending ordinance to Ali Pasha he had thought that 'there could be no question of the expediency of encouraging the augmentation of His Highness's power in general'.[195] He must have known full well that supporting the conquest of a rival Albanian pasha was not what he or—still less— the British government had really intended.

X

At the very time when Leake wrote that report, the greatest change in the entire relationship between the British and Ali Pasha was in the process of taking place. On 26 September 1809 a small British naval force left Sicily, carrying an assortment of troops (British, Sicilian, German, Corsican, Spanish and émigré French); the operation had been managed with great secrecy, and the soldiers' commanders were informed only on the following day that their destination was the Ionian Islands.[196] The initiative for this action came from Collingwood, who, in a letter in mid-July to Sir John Stuart (the army commander in Sicily), had proposed an attack on Zakynthos and Cephalonia, commenting that it would 'exceedingly

distract the French in their operations, and probably open the way to the reduction of Corfu'. With Stuart's somewhat reluctant agreement, the operation went
ahead, and quickly achieved its objectives: Zakynthos surrendered to the British
on 2 October, Cephalonia and Ithaca within the following week, and Cythera
(Ital.: Cerigo) on the 11th.[197] The largest of these islands were not insignificant
territories: Zakynthos had a population of 40,000 and Cephalonia of 55–60,000.[198]
But their main value to the British was strategic and political. Possessing them
made it easier to enforce the blockade of Corfu; restoring (if only notionally) the
official suzerainty of the Sultan was a sop to the pride of the Ottoman government. And there was a possible further value, as Sir Robert Adair would point out
in the following year: they would serve not only 'for the consolidation of our preponderance at the Porte while at Peace with her', but also 'for a new naval empire
if she quarrel with us'.[199]

There is no evidence that the British authorities had forewarned Ali Pasha of
this move—nor, indeed, that they hastened to inform him about the conquest of
the islands once it was under way. (Only on 15 October did Lieutenant-Colonel
Hudson Lowe, who was second-in-command of the British expeditionary force,
write to Leake that he had now sent a message to Ali Pasha with the news of the
conquest of Zakynthos and Cephalonia.)[200] Ali had left Ioannina on 30 September
and had travelled northwards to Tepelenë, in order to supervise the campaign
against Berat; Leake was in Ioannina, and evidently had no advance knowledge of
the British action.[201] He seems to have heard something about it, though not
through any official channels: on 9 October Pouqueville wrote that Leake had
spread a rumour that Zakynthos had fallen to the British. (According to
Pouqueville, who was sometimes quick to grasp at rumours, this had turned out
to be false, to the great discomfiture of Leake.)[202] Coincidentally, two travelling
Englishmen—Lord Byron and John Cam Hobhouse—arrived at Ioannina on 5
October, having sailed from Malta and arrived in the Gulf of Arta on 29
September; they travelled on to Tepelenë, but it was only on their arrival there on
19 October that they gained any definite information about the British military
action.[203] Some modern writers have claimed that they were on a special diplomatic mission to placate Ali Pasha with regard to the occupation of the Ionian
Islands, but there is no evidence for this, and it seems extremely unlikely that the
British authorities would have used these casual visitors for such a purpose in
preference to their highly experienced agent William Leake.[204]

In one important way, this seizure of power by the British in the majority of the
Ionian Islands cannot have been welcome to Ali Pasha. He must have understood
that if and when the French were driven out of Lefkada and Corfu, it was now
much less likely that those places would be handed over to him; the British could
simply add them to their own possessions. But on the other hand the establishing
of a permanent British presence within such a short distance of his own territories proffered some clear advantages. In recent months he had been occasionally

fearful about the prospect of a new rupture between Istanbul and London, caused by the effects of Napoleon's ongoing victories in Europe on the impressionable (and already partly pro-French) *divan*; in early September he had even threatened to detain Leake as a hostage, in the event of Britain withdrawing its support.[205] Abandonment by the British would now seem a much more unlikely scenario. They were tightening their blockade of Corfu, and for that purpose they would still depend on Ali's help. Their policy of support for, or at least indulgence of, his attempts to crush local rivals on the mainland had not changed. And one major geopolitical development had actually increased Ali's importance in their eyes: after Napoleon's overwhelming defeat of the Austrian army at Wagram in July 1809, the Treaty of Schönbrunn (14 October) obliged Austria to transfer to French rule large swathes of territory in Croatia, Slovenia and southern Austria. These areas were then united with Dalmatia to form a new French possession, the 'Illyrian Provinces'. Fearing an imminent French invasion from that direction, Leake wrote to the military commander Sir John Stuart in mid-November that the presence of the French in Corfu prevented Ali Pasha from 'turning his atten-tion to the protection of the Northern frontier, where a mountainous and difficult Country, and a numerous population of the most hardy, warlike and independent habits, would otherwise present a formidable barrier against the Invader'; for that reason he recommended making speedy plans for the conquest of Corfu. Writing at the same time to the Foreign Secretary in London, he observed that the expan-sion of French power on the borders of Bosnia was a very serious development for the Ottoman authorities, and that this required the British to 'keep up their [*sc.* the Ottoman government's] confidence by every means in our power', espe-cially by completing the takeover of all the Ionian Islands.[206] British commitment to the area was likely to become more entrenched, and this was part of a larger strategy in which Ali Pasha was seen as a potentially important ally.

Where one particular matter was concerned, Ali's relations with the British occupiers of the islands did quickly fall into the same pattern as his previous ones with the Russians and the French: he demanded that they should not give refuge to 'robbers' from his mainland territories. In early November the commander of the British forces on the islands, Brigadier-General John Oswald, responded to this by telling Leake to give Ali his assurance 'that in none of the Isles under our Protection shall Shelter be given to any Person committing acts of Violence against the Persons or Properties of His Highness's Subjects'.[207] Some of these men may well have been robbers (though Lefkada was, traditionally, the preferred base for those who regularly raided the mainland); but some were Souliots or other local enemies whose hostility to Ali was essentially political. In order to gain leverage over them, Ali also demanded the return to the mainland of their families. A month after receiving this assurance from Oswald, Ali sent a detailed list of such families then resident on Cephalonia and Ithaca (plus some on Zakynthos); he specified, for example, the relatives of Alē Pharmakēs, noting that

Pharmakës himself was now on Lefkada 'with quite a few Albanians under his command, in the service of the French.'[208] There were various issues here that could not be solved by Oswald's simple declaration; as we shall see, such requests would later become a major source of friction between Ali Pasha and the British.

At the same time, one form of cooperation between them was developing quite smoothly. In the spring of 1809 William Leake had sent a report to the Navy Office on the possibility of acquiring timber for ship-building from Ali Pasha's domains; evidently Ali had renewed the offer he had first made to William Hamilton in 1803. An expert was sent from the Arsenal in Malta in September to look at suitable sources of timber, and in December he sent back a positive report on no fewer than seven different forests.[209] By then an experienced British contractor, John Leard, had already got involved; a former British consul in Dubrovnik, he had previously been obtaining timber from Dalmatia and Croatia, but was forced out of each in turn as they fell under French rule. In November he left Rijeka [Ital.: Fiume], which was now passing to the French, and sailed to the port of Durrës. As he later reported, he arrived there on 3 January 1810, and quickly established that the nearby forests contained 'a considerable quantity of Oak timber'; so he wrote to Ali Pasha in Berat, who, at his request, asked the local governor, Kapllan Pasha, to permit 'the exportation of Timber for H.M. service'. A large quantity was felled, and when it reached Malta in June it was found to be 'of a most excellent quality'; three more shiploads arrived, and the whole cargo was sent on a transport ship to London at the beginning of August.[210] Before the end of the Napoleonic war, therefore, some British warships would be made, at least in part, of Albanian oak.

During the first three months of British rule in the Ionian Islands, Ali Pasha's energies were mostly occupied by the campaign against Berat. Only in early January 1810 did the citadel there fall to his forces. Even before that siege began in October, he had told Leake that he was 'tired' of the conflict, not only because of its great expense (Leake would eventually attribute the victory to his use of fighters from northern Albania, who were more effective than the southerners, and correspondingly more expensive to hire), but also because he knew that it incurred the displeasure of the Ottoman government.[211] On this last point, his connection with the British was advantageous to him. Ali took care to maintain good relations with the British Embassy in Istanbul; writing to Leake in early December, he asked him to assure Sir Robert Adair of 'my willingness to do all those things that will give service and satisfaction to your nation'.[212] And when, in early February, the French chargé d'affaires there made a fierce complaint about Ali to the *reis efendi*, we may suspect that it was partly thanks to British influence that the latter adopted a very defensive attitude. To the accusation that Ali had acted illegally in evicting Ibrahim Pasha from Berat, the *reis efendi* replied that whilst it was true that this had not been ordered by the Ottoman government, Ibrahim had governed so badly that he deserved to be deposed: Ali had acted, he said (presumably keeping a straight face as he did so), in response to popular discontent, 'to avoid greater evils'.[213]

The French chargé's other main complaint was that Ali was now building a fort for artillery opposite Lefkada, in order to assist an imminent British assault on that island. (The *reis efendi* blithely replied that Ali Pasha was a faithful servant of the Ottoman government who respected its policy of neutrality, and that anyway the fort was on Ottoman territory, and therefore of no concern to France.)[214] A full-scale British attack on Lefkada began with a naval bombardment on 21 March; on the following day the island was invaded by a force of 4,000 men, consisting mostly of British, Sicilian, Corsican and Greek troops. After an energetic siege of the fortress, the French commanding officer, General Camus, finally agreed to surrender on 16 April.[215] During the first half of this brief campaign, Pouqueville felt satisfied that Ali Pasha was remaining neutral; he was able to report, for example, that on 5 April Ali met a French colonel who had been sent from Corfu on a mission to General Camus, and helped to arrange his safe passage. But within a few days Pouqueville was denouncing Ali for 'treason', and by the 14th he was accusing him of openly assisting the British.[216] Subsequently, Pouqueville would allege that Ali had supplied Brigadier-General Oswald with 800 soldiers in disguise; but there is no evidence for this in the British sources, and Oswald himself would later flatly deny it. Although Ali's amicable relations with the British—who clearly had the upper hand in military terms—were not concealed, he did try to keep up at least the rudiments of a continuing relationship with the French, and the reason for this is not hard to grasp. On the very day that Pouqueville reported the surrender of Lefkada, he also noted another demand by Ali that the French transfer Parga to his control—with the suggestion, no doubt, that this was the only way to keep it out of the hands of the British.[217]

The importance of gaining power over both Parga and Lefkada remained fundamental to Ali Pasha's thinking. On 8 April, just at the time when Pouqueville had the impression that he was shifting decisively towards the British, he sent a long, passionate letter to William Leake, setting out his fears about a future scenario in which Britain and Russia became allies again, and in which the former would then hand over its Ionian possessions to the latter. He emphasized that having control over Lefkada and Parga would be 'the most important means for strengthening the security of my rule over these territories and my peace of mind, and for freeing me from all kinds of dubious eventualities', and begged Leake to consider 'our agreement and your promise' in these matters.[218] When that letter was written, he was aware that Leake had gone to Malta; presumably he thought that Leake was consulting with the authorities there, and that, as an accredited representative of the British government, he would have more influence on policy-making than the military officers with whom Ali now had to deal *in situ*. What he did not know was that Leake would never come back to Ioannina. (Informed of this later in the month by Hudson Lowe, he expressed, as Lowe put it in a letter to

Leake, 'some surprize at your sudden and unadvised Departure for England'.)[219] William Leake returned to London; thereafter, following a short period as military attaché to the Swiss cantons, he would lead a retired life as an author, publishing the fruits of his very detailed topographical researches in Greece and Albania.[220] Evidently Leake felt that the arrival of senior British officers on, so to speak, Ali Pasha's doorstep had decisively changed the situation, reducing the importance of his own role; but he had also been badly unsettled by Ali's threat to detain him as a hostage in September, and it seems that his confidence in the pasha had never fully recovered from that.

XI

Ali Pasha was too important to the British, however, for them to abandon the practice of keeping an agent at his court. In Leake's place came George (Geōrgios, Giorgio) Foresti—whose father, Spiridion, had accompanied the British military expedition in September–October, and acted as Resident Minister on his native Zakynthos from March 1810. George was a young man, probably now in his late 20s; he did not lack ambition, and had been angling for such a position for some time. Four years earlier he had written to George Hamilton-Gordon, Earl of Aberdeen: 'There is a great probability of M.ʳ Moriers removal to Valachia, and, in that event, the Consulship of Albania will be vacant. I know no situation more suitable for me than this. I speak the Greek and a little of the Turkish language, which, with my fathers influence in those parts, will enable me to serve advantageously there'.[221] (Clearly he had worked for Aberdeen in some capacity during the latter's tour of the Mediterranean, Greece and the Levant in 1803–4; it is very likely, in fact, that he had accompanied him on a visit to Ali Pasha in November or early December 1893, though direct evidence of this is lacking.)[222] Twice more, in 1808 and 1809, George Foresti had written to Aberdeen asking for help in gaining such an appointment either at Ioannina or on the Ionian Islands (if and when they fell into British hands).[223] But it was most probably through his respected and well-connected father, for whom he had been working during the previous two years in Malta, that he finally got the position he had been seeking.

George Foresti had already been dealing with Ali Pasha on behalf of the British before he was formally employed in this way. Leake was absent from Ioannina, on one of his topographical tours of northern Greece, from mid-November 1809 until mid-January, and during that period Foresti seems to have been tasked with bearing messages to Ali Pasha from the British military authorities on the islands. In a report to Lieutenant-Colonel Lowe from Përmet in early January 1810, he commented on some recent threat—of an unspecified but serious nature—made to him by Ali, apparently in response to criticism of Ali's improper sending of an emissary to the Ionian Islands.[224] Despite this bumpy start, however, he was still keen to act as Leake's replacement when the latter departed in mid-February. George Foresti landed at Preveza on 9 March 1810 to begin his new job, and would remain continually in post for five years. His appointment was, in the first instance, the initiative of General Oswald on Zakynthos; a few months later it was accepted and regularized by Sir Robert Adair in Istanbul. (Sir Robert's formal letter told Foresti that he would have the same job as Leake, but did not actually specify the same level of pay. He would be shocked to discover, when settling accounts in 1815, that his services were valued at less than half Leake's rate.)[225] Oswald had chosen well. Thomas Smart Hughes, who got to know George Foresti when visiting Ioannina in 1814, would later write about him admiringly: 'wary, cautious, and indefatigable in labour, intimately acquainted with the character of the vizir [*sc.* Ali Pasha], he never ceased to penetrate his designs, avert his indignation, and keep him constant in that line of policy which ultimately contributed to preserve Europe from the degrading yoke of French tyranny.'[226] Whilst he did not always cause such admiration in the minds of his superiors (as we shall see), his energy and devotion to British service would never falter.

One contentious issue was already causing friction before George Foresti took up his post in Ioannina. In late February 1810 Oswald wrote to Hudson Lowe, evidently in response to more demands from Ali Pasha for the surrender of 'robbers': 'The fact is that the Albanian Captains are ancient enemies of Ali Pacha & that he desires to get possession of their persons upon any pretence whatsoever. I have told Captain Leake that if the Officers of the Pacha can prove that any one living under our protection has, since that was granted to him, been concerned himself or instigated others to acts of violence against the persons or property of the Subjects of the Vizir [*sc.* Ali Pasha] that person shall immediately be given up.'[227] (Lowe was currently the governor of Cephalonia and Ithaca; he would move to Lefkada after the siege, and in consequence would often be engaged with this issue.) In late April Ali Pasha wrote directly to Lowe, asking for the return of one of his subjects who, he claimed, had fled with his family because he owed Ali money. Prudently, Lowe asked for documentation of the debt; Ali's reply, which promised to supply it, also included a more general admonition: 'For the sake of the friendly and neighbourly good relations that exist between us, you should not give refuge and protection to people who abandon their homeland and their natural obedience. I ask you to remedy this where it has happened in the past, and not to allow further emigrations to take place in the future.'[228]

Another source of friction arose in May 1810, when the British noticed that Ali Pasha was building a substantial artillery fort on the coast directly opposite Lefkada. He had previously notified the British authorities, and shown them a plan of what was intended; but the site where the actual building work commenced was not the one on the plan—which, lying further inland, and involving only a barrack for soldiers, would have posed no potential threat. The sheer scale of this work (involving up to 2,000 men), and the fact that any artillery placed there would be able to bombard the fortress of Lefkada, caused real alarm to the inhabitants of the island. Hudson Lowe wrote to Ali's local governor, Süleiman Bey, about this, warning that it could damage 'the perfect friendship and harmony that reign between our governments'.[229] The matter was also raised directly with Ali Pasha by George Foresti in early July. Addressing Ali (as his report put it) in strong terms, Foresti told him that 'Scarcely a Day past that he thought proper to change his Intention and instead of a Barrack to be raised at a Distance of nearly 2 miles from the Coast He orders a regular Fort to be errected upon a Position which completely commands the Entrance of Ships into the Porte of Santa Maura [sc. Lefkada] and menaces the Tranquillity and Security of that Island.' Somewhat chastened, but also playing for time, Ali suggested writing to London to ask if the British government wanted the fort to be demolished.[230] On receiving an account of this conversation from Foresti, Hudson Lowe wrote to Oswald with a rather similar suggestion: 'Viewing the progress the Vizir has made and his determination to persist, the best plan to pursue is perhaps to endeavour to limit him to this Work alone and prevent his bringing Cannon to it until a reference to the respective Governments can bring about a decision, whether the Work is to be suffered to exist in any shape at all.' He noted that Foresti himself favoured a more hard-line approach: 'M[r]. G. Foresti hints at Intimidation and a direct line of Policy with his Highness. If however he proved obstinate we must send to destroy the Work and this might bring in a War.' A tactic of direct military confrontation would, he felt, be 'a very painful one to adopt with a Man whose dispositions in other respects have appeared so friendly & with whom it is so much our interest to continue on an amicable footing'.[231] Somehow, it seems, the disagreement was resolved; the issue does not recur in subsequent correspondence. But it must have served as a reminder—if any were needed—to these new British authorities in the region that Ali's straightforward cooperation could never be taken for granted.

One reason why Ali would, in the end, have been willing to give way to British wishes on this issue was that he was under pressure at Istanbul from the French chargé d'affaires there, Florimond de Faÿ de La Tour-Maubourg (who had served as second secretary under Sébastiani, and succeeded Pierre Ruffin as chargé); he felt very much in need of British support there. La Tour-Maubourg had handed in a fierce letter of complaint, accusing Ali of breaching the neutrality of his government during the siege of Lefkada—the Ambassador repeated Pouqueville's claim about the loan of 800 soldiers—and demanding that he be punished as a rebel. Ali obtained a copy of this and transmitted it, in mid-June, to Oswald, requesting British help in the matter as 'my government is very angry with me.' Oswald then sent it on to Adair in Istanbul with his own comments on the complete falsity of the French claims.[232] Since Sir Robert Adair left Istanbul for London on 14 July, it was his 23-year-old assistant, Stratford Canning (a cousin of the former British Foreign Minister), who, taking over as chargé d'affaires, had to deal with the matter. Four days later, as he recorded in his diary, Canning received a visit from Ali Pasha's Istanbul agent, who told him that the French were still fiercely denouncing Ali for his actions, and were also complaining of his failure to send provisions to Corfu. 'His Master was apprehensive of an attack from the French, at the same time that he might be deprived of the aid of the Porte by their intrigues. In that case what should he do? I answered that we must try to stop the mischief in the beginning, by setting Ali Pasha right with the Porte. And then if the French were to attack him he would be entitled to the assistance of the English as being a part of the Turkish Empire. The Agent agreed with me.' On the following day Canning sent the Ottoman government a copy of Oswald's letter about Ali's non-involvement in the siege of Lefkada, and asked them to issue a formal document commending Ali for his correct conduct. 'This the Reis Effendi refused for the present, because Ali Pasha had offended the Sultan by his attack upon the Pasha of Avlona [*sc*. Vlorë], but he promised to give me one when that affair is finished.' Within a day, however, the *reis efendi* had changed his mind, and promised to send Ali a letter of commendation.[233] At some point in late July an Ottoman official was despatched to Ioannina to investigate not only the French charges against Ali, but also Ali's own formal complaints against Pouqueville; his eventual report was in favour of Ali Pasha. And at the beginning of September Canning was 'positively assured' that another French demand for a condemnation of Ali's behaviour during the siege had been firmly rejected.[234]

The 'affair' of Ali Pasha's hostility against Ibrahim Pasha of Vlorë was far from finished. On 25 July 1810 a messenger from Istanbul arrived at Ioannina with a *firman* (sultanic decree) proclaiming that Ali's son Muhtar had been appointed pasha of Vlorë and Berat; Ali was happy to let it be known that he had achieved this thanks to the help of the English. Within a few weeks, however, Pouqueville was reporting that the *firman* was a forgery. Given the *reis efendi*'s comment in mid-July about the Sultan being offended by Ali's attack on Ibrahim, that might well seem a plausible explanation. Yet a few months later George Foresti would comment on 'the final Decision of the Porte, which not only sanctioned an Act that the Sultan just before had declared so unjust [*sc*. the conquest of Berat], but added to his usurped Acquisition the joint Pachalik of Avlonna', and would explain that 'Aly Pacha has stated to me that he paid Five thousand Turkish Purses to manage this Affair at Constantinople.'[235] As it was a central feature of Ali Pasha's *modus operandi* at Istanbul to get his way by making large payments to senior officials, this account is entirely credible.

In any case, one thing is clear: the *firman*, whether real or fictitious, was a product of Ali's own initiative. It is very likely that he hoped thereby to provoke Ibrahim into making the first move in a new military conflict; and in this he was successful. Possibly Ibrahim was buoyed up by Napoleon's decision, in June, to give him not only a financial subsidy but also arms, ammunition and the use of some military engineers.[236] During August Ibrahim gathered his forces, and called for the assistance of those who had joined his alliance against Ali Pasha. In September they marched on Berat; Ali's forces—which were inferior in number—engaged with them two miles outside the city, and inflicted a heavy defeat, with 300 killed and 400 taken prisoner. (Foresti also reported that 'Among the Prisoners taken from Ibrahim Pasha, two were French Artillery Men dressed as Albanians.') Ali himself, who had been visiting his son Veli at Trikala, quickly gathered 3,000 men and set off for Berat.[237] Commenting on what he took to be the impending final defeat of Ibrahim Pasha, George Foresti wrote to Stratford Canning: 'The good Effects that will result by the complete Reduction of Ibrahim Pasha and his Party are Innumerable, but the immediate and most forcible Consequences are—the Destruction of the only Remnant of French Influence in Albania, and by leaving to Aly Pasha no possible Antagonist in the Country, he is enabled to destroy at Once the System of Intrigue practised by the Natives, to remove the Cause of Internal Commotion and Weakness.'[238] Thanks partly to the French policy of active support for Ibrahim Pasha, Foresti's advice thus perpetuated the line of argument previously established by both Jack Morier and William Leake.

When Ibrahim Pasha retired to the port-town of Vlorë in mid-September Ali instituted a blockade of it by sea, using his own flotilla of small ships, one of which was armed with 22 cannons. This was combined with a further tightening of the screw on Corfu, when Ali made the Çams promise that they would cease supplying the island with food. A peace agreement between Ali and Ibrahim in early November did not lead to any relaxation of the blockade where supplies to the French were concerned, and by mid-December Foresti was reporting serious shortages on Corfu, with grain prices rising there by 40 per cent in one month.[239] During November and early December French officers were twice sent to hold talks with Ali; the ostensible topic was his detention of some Himariot officers in French service, whose boat had been captured by his men, but the supply situation was surely the dominant one.[240] Discussing these visits with Foresti in January, Ali said that he was offended by the fact that while the French made such attempts to renew friendship with him, their ambassador in Istanbul was all the while trying to poison the minds of government ministers against him. He also claimed that the second mission had brought a proposal from Donzelot on Corfu that, in return for his full cooperation, he could take over Parga immediately; his reply, he said, was that 'as to Parga He considered it now of so little Importance to Him that he never thought about it.'[241] Since the last part of that claim was patently untrue, we are entitled to assume that the first part was another of Ali's fictions, designed, as always, to encourage the British to forestall the French by seizing Parga and giving it to him themselves. Less than three months before, Foresti had reported Ali's bitter complaint that 'although a year has elapsed since the British have arrived in his neighbourhood nothing has been done for him;

that on the contrary they permit the French to occupy Parga in preference to himself'.[242]

Despite all such complaints, the British had good reason to think that Ali was broadly on their side during this period. The French strategy of rallying and subsidizing his local enemies had helped to ensure that; and all the while Ali was still fearful of a possible invasion of the Albanian lands by a French army. (In such a scenario, Foresti observed, Ali would need ordinance and ammunition; he would ask first of all for money, but this was not necessary, as he was estimated to have the equivalent of £5 million in his treasury at Tepelenë. Foresti also thought that the Albanians would prove effective fighters in their own terrain, and made a comparison with the harrying of the French in Spain by what would soon become known as 'guerrilla' forces.) Ali told Foresti that the presence of the British with their ships off his coast was a vital protection for him; his greatest fear was that pressure from France and Russia would force the Ottoman government both to break off relations with Britain, and to permit a French army to march through Albania to attack Lefkada and the other British-ruled islands.[243] And yet, although it was clearly in Ali's interests to cultivate the government in Istanbul, his main way of doing this was to make payments to individual officials there: as Foresti put it, 'my Residence in this Country has enabled Me to ascertain, that He has Hitherto succeeded by Bribery & Corruption to render the Ministers of the Porte subservient to Him.' Foresti urged him to contribute the thousands of soldiers that Istanbul was constantly calling on him to supply for its continuing war against Russia. If he had taken 20,000 men to Sofia, as the Sultan had requested, he would have 'animated the Whole Albania in Common Exertion. The Pacha of Scutari with twenty thousand Men—the Bey of Dibra with Fifteen thousand mostly Cavalry—And the Bey of Seres (near Salonica) with Fifteen thousand Men more would have all felt Themselves bound to have joined, or to have followed Him.' But, Foresti continued, instead they had 'remained behind, to protect their Possessions from the Intrigues and Encroachments of each other, but more of Aly Pacha, who, on account of His superior strength, Ability and all-grasping Disposition, is looked upon as the Terror of Albania'.[244]

XII

After the kaleidoscopic shifts of the previous few years, the situation in 1811 was a comparatively unchanging one. Friction between Russia and France had become serious in the previous year, and in the first half of 1811 each of those powers was making plans for war against the other; but both were still officially locked in the agreement drawn up at Tilsit. The Russian–Ottoman war continued, with little significant change in the front line. Although the Tsar reduced his forces there, in preparation for a war against France, his talented commander, General Kutuzov, was still able to inflict a heavy defeat on the Ottomans in the autumn, trapping the Grand Vizier's army on the northern bank of the Danube.[245] Tentative peace talks, based in Bucharest, were already under way, but the sheer scale of Russian territorial demands meant that no agreement would be made until the following summer. Napoleon, meanwhile, was increasingly preoccupied with the war in the Iberian Peninsula, which was beginning to turn against him by the end of the year. Nevertheless his commitment to the strategic importance of Corfu did not change, and more than once in late 1810 and early 1811 he was able to send reinforcements there from Italy; in the month of January alone, according to Pouqueville, the garrison was strengthened by 2,000.[246] The increase in the number of troops was exaggerated by French propaganda; it was claimed that they had as many as 16,000 on the island, but in the summer of 1811 George Foresti wrote that the total had never been higher than 12,000, and that it was now reduced by desertion to 8,500, plus a similarly diminished force of 1,200 'Albanian' (i.e. mostly Souliot) troops.[247]

Such numbers were still sufficient to make Ali Pasha wary of possible offensive actions by the French. In early March he sent a messenger to Spiridion Foresti on Zakynthos, expressing his concerns; as Hudson Lowe reported, the message indicated not only that Ali was 'much alarmed at the augmentation of Troops, Stores &c which the French are almost daily receiving at Corfu', but also that he seemed 'excessively anxious, and disappointed about not receiving any replies from our Government to his various demands and communications'.[248] (The main demands referred to were, presumably, the ones for more arms and ammunition, and the request for help in taking Parga.) A week later George Foresti wrote from Ioannina to one of the military commanders on the islands, saying that the reinforcing of Corfu, together with a reported build-up of French troops further up the Adriatic coast, made him fear an imminent attack on Preveza. Taking that port would give the French 'not only the sure Means of penetrating at Pleasure into the heart of Aly Pacha's Country, but of supplying Corfú with Provisions, and eventually of attacking Santa Maura [sc. Lefkada]'. So he proposed, as the best way of helping Ali, driving the French out of Parga. This could be done by 'a trifling Force of British Soldiers', and would have very positive effects: 'if Englishmen do in fact occupy this commanding Position on the Albanian Frontier not only Aly Pacha will be enabled to carry all His Forces to other Quarters, but the occupation of It, in a relative Point of View, must furnish a fresh Basis of mutual Interest and Freindship between us and the Pacha.'[249]

Expanding on this theme in a letter to Lowe on the following day, Foresti wrote that Ali was taking active measures, gathering up to 8,000 men to place on the coast opposite Corfu, and that he was not despondent. But he added:

I must not conceal from you however that this state of His affairs has drawn from him the severest Reproaches against us for having brought him to so desperate a Conjuncture without giving him the means of successfully resisting His Enemies—He does not hesitate to say to me that the Enemy had foretold him that the English would abandon him and that his Connection with them would bring Destruction upon him and upon his Family—You know enough of me to feel certain how embarrassed and overwhelmed I was going to add at hearing and seeing all this.

The suggestion then immediately followed: British forces should seize Parga, in order to prove to Ali Pasha that they were capable of supporting and protecting him.[250] While Ali certainly had some worries about a French attack, it is once again hard to avoid the conclusion that he was playing rather expertly here on the feelings of his interlocutor. Fears of being 'abandoned' by the British were highly exaggerated (even more so now than in his previous outburst to Leake); and the idea of placating Ali by expelling the French from Parga was surely not a spontaneous thought in George Foresti's mind, but something planted there, in these emotionally heightened circumstances, by Ali himself. True, Foresti's suggestion was that the British should take Parga and hold it themselves; but Ali would have seen that as at least a step in the right direction.

Hudson Lowe was sufficiently concerned by the prospect of a French offensive to write to Oswald about it. However, he was also cautious enough to distinguish between France attacking the Ottoman Empire as such, and its merely fighting against Ali Pasha. In the latter case, the requirements of Ottoman neutrality vis-à-vis France meant that 'the card we shall have to play may become extremely delicate'; political decision-making at a higher level would be needed. And he was no less cautious about taking any military action that might lead to Ali gaining possession of new territory.[251] Nevertheless, when he wrote again to Oswald on 8 April he supported the idea of seizing Parga, and at the same time emphasized the value, for British strategic purposes, of Ali Pasha's predominance in the region: Ali's ability to check the power of Ibrahim Pasha of Vlorë was, in Lowe's view, 'perhaps the only cause why the whole of Albania is not at the present moment in a state of Revolution against the Porte and the French designs triumphant'.[252] Eventually, word came in May from Stratford Canning, the chargé in Istanbul, that the British squadron blockading Corfu was authorized to assist Ali in the event of a French attack; he also wrote that several British gunboats were being transferred from Messina to the Ionian Islands.[253] But by then the crisis had passed. In fact the French had not been planning to attack the mainland; the only change was that in early April, possibly in reaction to news of Ali's attempt to incite a British assault on Parga, that fortress received a reinforcement from Corfu of 600 Albanian troops.[254] And there was one corresponding change on Ali Pasha's side: in May he began to strengthen the defences of Preveza, ordering thousands of the local peasants to dig a sea-moat, nearly three miles long, between the two small fortresses that protected its port.[255]

During the first half of 1811 Ali was extending and consolidating his power along the coast. In mid-January George Foresti reported that the territory controlled by Ibrahim Pasha was rapidly shrinking: 'Every Town round Avlonna [sc. Vlorë] has surrendered.' Within a month, the people of nearby Himarë had signed an agreement, submitting to Ali's terms; he soon set to work installing forts and garrisons in their territory.[256] He continued to extend his power over the coast of Çamëri, until, at the beginning of June, Pouqueville informed the French Foreign Minister that Ali held sway, for the first time, over the entire coastline (only excepting Parga itself). Within a couple of weeks Ali was already planning to build a new fortress of his own, at the Çam port—now at last under his control—of Sagiada, to the north of Igoumenitsa.[257]

Given the degree of Ali Pasha's cooperation with the British at this time, the main effect of this consolidation of power was to restrict even more thoroughly the supply of food to the French on Corfu. Both Pouqueville in Ioannina and the Ambassador, La Tour-Maubourg, in Istanbul complained constantly about this. In early January 1811 Pouqueville wrote to Mathieu de Lesseps, Bessières's successor as imperial commissary on Corfu, that it was Ali's intention to starve the French troops there. As always, Ali was in pursuit of an ulterior purpose: later that month Pouqueville explained, in a despatch to the Foreign Minister, that since November Ali had been offering Donzelot large quantities of grain if he agreed to a number of conditions, which included handing over to him all the people from his domains who were then on Corfu and giving him the fortress of Parga.[258] Widespread shortages during the winter led the Ottoman government to issue a general prohibition of the export of grain, but in late February La Tour-Maubourg persuaded the Grand Vizier to make an exception for Corfu. An order was sent to Ali Pasha, who quickly assured the French that he would open all his ports to them. Soon afterwards he told Pouqueville, conspiratorially, that he had been instructed to make the export of grain as secret as possible, to avoid antagonizing the British. A month later Pouqueville was complaining that he had allowed only a very small quantity to pass, at a high price; and in May he protested that the grain was mouldy.[259] Ali was playing, as skilfully as ever, his game of cat and mouse, and the severe shortages of food on Corfu continued.

Nor was he the only person on the Ottoman side who was playing games with the French. The government in Istanbul, bombarded with complaints and threats by La Tour-Maubourg, would from time to time make its own gestures of compliance. The apparent capitulation of the Grand Vizier in February seems to have been just one instance of this. In December 1810, for example, La Tour-Maubourg had been pleased to learn that Ali Pasha was being stripped of two of the *paşalıks* that were under his general control: Trikala, which was governed by his son Veli, and Elbasan, which, as we have seen, had been awarded to Ali's nine-year-old grandson. This might have looked like decisive evidence of a punitive attitude towards Ali Pasha at the highest level; according to Pouqueville, Ali himself was deeply troubled by it.[260] Yet by early March the new pashas appointed to Trikala and Elbasan had still not set foot in those places, and Ali was displaying (as Pouqueville despondently reported) a new mood of confidence. The situation was the same in mid-April; and a month later Ali told Hudson Lowe that he continued to exercise jurisdiction over those *paşalıks*, his ejection from which (however theoretical it turned out to be) he blamed squarely on the French.[261] Very probably he also fortified his case at Istanbul by making large payments to suitable people. If he did, however, he was pushing at a door that was already more than half-open. In early June he gave George Foresti a copy of a letter he had received from the *kaymakam paşa* (the senior minister who deputed for the Grand Vizier in the latter's absence from Istanbul). It informed Ali that the French Ambassador had presented a formal note about 'the innumerable outrages which Your Highness has committed, and is committing, against the French government during a period when the Porte has written to you so many times telling you not to do such things'. The letter explained that the Ottoman government had denied the truth of the Ambassador's claims; and in the next section it gave Ali Pasha instructions to 'make in secret all the preparations that will be needed for driving out the French if they make any move against you'. Whilst this would have made heartening reading for Ali, the underlying reason for such governmental support was not one of personal admiration, still less one of approval for his semi-detached attitude to the Ottoman Empire and its central government. As the letter openly admitted, the government's great fear was that if France did invade Albania, it might attract the support of many of the 300,000 Christians who lived there.[262]

The French denunciations came thick and fast. In March 1811 the Foreign Minister sent a message to Pouqueville informing him that Napoleon, 'tired of the outrages committed by Ali Pasha, and of his constant resistance to supplying Corfu, is determined to suffer his insults no longer. It is his intention to declare war on Ali Pasha, if the Porte fails to oblige him to do his duty.'[263] Pouqueville did not receive this until June, but the same message seems to have reached La Tour-Maubourg in April, when he did indeed startle the Ottoman authorities by telling them that Napoleon was threatening war against one of their regional governors. When in late June Ali Pasha learned of another such intervention by the Ambassador, again invoking the wrath of Napoleon, he turned on Pouqueville defiantly: 'I assure you that my government will not abandon me, and that I shall not separate myself from it. If Napoleon wants war, he can declare it; let him act openly, like a man of honour, without trying to do things in roundabout ways.'[264]

Finally, in early July, La Tour-Maubourg's patience snapped. He had been nervous of issuing an ultimatum, waiting cautiously in the hope that the situation might improve; but all such hope was extinguished by the stream of reports from Corfu and Ioannina. His continuing fear was that Sultan Mahmud II would react badly to being put under such pressure. As he explained in a letter to the Foreign Minister, he worried that his action might make the Sultan 'change his position towards a rebel whom he hates and wants to destroy, making him see him as someone henceforth worth preserving, in order to defend the frontiers of the Empire.[265] Overcoming these doubts, he handed in a note that was, by the diplomatic standards of the day, exceptionally severe. It listed the various outrages committed by Ali Pasha: the maltreatment of French subjects, the help given to British corsairs (i.e. local armed vessels given letters of marque by the British to attack French shipping), the blockade of Corfu, the close relations between Ali and Britain, and so on. If the Porte did not act quickly to give the French satisfaction on all these points, they would have only one option left: the use of military force.[266] To the Ambassador's surprise, the ministers of the Ottoman government were at first quite unyielding; they described Ali as a loyal vizier, and said that if the French touched the least of Ali's officials, that would lead to a formal rupture of relations between the Empire and France. Pretending to know nothing about Ali's misdeeds, they offered to mount an enquiry into the allegations about them—while also insisting that Pouqueville must be removed from his post before that could take place. La Tour-Maubourg's response was to threaten to leave Istanbul. After a week the Ottoman government changed its tune; the *reis efendi* was dismissed, and promises were made that Ali Pasha would be reined in and that the full trade in grain and cattle with Corfu would resume. In addition, a senior official would be sent to Ioannina, and his instructions would be co-drafted by the French Ambassador.[267]

That official, Celal Efendi, left Istanbul at the beginning of September, equipped with various *firmans* instructing Ali to stop obstructing the French, and reached Ioannina by the end of the month. La Tour-Maubourg had full confidence in him; he described Celal as 'austere and independent', a person who would resist 'all the seductions of the English and Ali Pasha'. Ali himself was quite untroubled by Celal's arrival, however. He told George Foresti that the man's mission was 'meant only to pacify the French'.[268] Gradually it emerged that Celal had no authority to order Ali Pasha to send supplies to Corfu; his job was merely to hear Ali's responses to the *firmans*. Ali managed to spin out the discussions for nearly seven weeks, and to persuade Celal (as Ali put it in a letter to his agent in Istanbul) that the whole dispute had been concocted by the 'Malignity' of Pouqueville. One characteristic method of persuasion was reported by Pouqueville himself: he wrote that Ali had given Celal 40 purses (20,000 piastres—roughly £1,000 at the time).[269] Yet again, Ali Pasha was off the hook, and the situation of the French in Corfu had hardly changed.

During these months, Ali had continued to extend his power over some of the nearby territories on the mainland. Here too he was countering, successfully, French policy; in June La Tour-Maubourg had sent a Greek agent called Diopoulos to visit all the local leaders who were opposed to Ali and persuade them to form another 'league' against him.[270] But Ali was steadily prising away the few remaining allies of Ibrahim Pasha. In July he persuaded the region of

Dukat (to the south of Vlorë, just north of Himarë) to come over to his side. And at the beginning of August he finally seized the city of Vlorë; Pouqueville reported that this was achieved without a shot being fired, as all of Ibrahim Pasha's key supporters there had been bribed and suborned.[271] The strongest remaining opponents of Ali Pasha were located in parts of Labëri—the district extending inland from Vlorë down to the city of Gjirokastër. Foremost among these were the hardy fighters of Kardhiq, a small highland district centred on its own historic fortress. Ibrahim took refuge with them; but opposition to Ali Pasha did not necessarily equate with support for Ibrahim, and after a few weeks—during which Ali wooed them with presents and promises—Ibrahim was handed over.[272]

Pouqueville commented despairingly that this change in the regional balance would open the way for Ali to extend his power over northern Albania: already the pashas of Elbasan, Tirana and Krujë had come to pay their respects to him, as well as the commander of Durrës, the beys of Myzeqe (Musachia) and the chiefs of Dibër. (Such fears were in fact shared by Mustafa Pasha of Shkodër, who, after the fall of Vlorë, wrote to the Sultan that Ali was now aiming to take control over his territory too.)[273] Nevertheless, the French had remained active in encouraging resistance to Ali Pasha: in September, for example, George Foresti reported that a French officer had brought money and gunpowder to Gjirokastër, and had per-suaded the people there to rise against Ali.[274] A new alliance—led by the chiefs of Kardhiq and Gjirokastër, but also including the leaders of Delvinë—mustered its forces, and in October the men of Gjirokastër inflicted a heavy defeat on Ali's troops. Ali Pasha was now drawn into a longer campaign. In late November George Foresti was able to report that 'the Inhabitants of Argirocastro, dreading the Vengeance of Aly Pasha, surrendered themselves to him and received his Troops into their Town and Castle. 8 Pieces of French light Artillery with some ammunition was found concealed in Argirocastro, which the Inhabitants con-fessed to have received from Corfu.' But the resistance of Kardhiq would be both fiercer and more prolonged, and Ali's revenge, after it eventually fell to him in February 1812, would be all the more terrible.[275]

While all these developments during the second half of 1811 had the inevitable effect of strengthening Ali's quasi-alliance with the British, that relationship itself was far from problem-free. The main bone of contention, once again, was the issue of so-called 'robbers' taking refuge on the islands under British control. In August Ali Pasha sent a grandiloquent letter to Hudson Lowe, claiming that Lowe had previously promised him that if fighters from Ali's territory abandoned his service—he was thinking primarily of Souliots now on Corfu, but he may also have had in mind some of the men who had joined the regiment of 'Greek Light Infantry' which had been formed on the Ionian Islands—the British would not give refuge to their families. 'Yet I see nothing done about it', he complained, 'which fills me with justified grief and astonishment'. (He added rather extrava-gantly: 'all the sacrifices I have made, and shall make, for your love, I make utterly whole-heartedly, as if I were doing things for my own personal benefit.')[276] Ali wrote again in August and twice in September, and in the last of these letters he supplied a list of the 'robbers' he wanted, and of where they lived; clearly his many agents had been busily employed on the islands.[277] Hudson Lowe was feeling increasingly rattled by this. As Brigadier-General Oswald had returned to England, it was to his temporary replacement, Colonel Havilland Smith, that Lowe wrote in October to express his worries. He explained that Ali Pasha had always returned to the Ionian Islands any deserters he found from the British army; so if these cases had merely involved deserters from Ali's forces, there would have been no difficulty in reciprocating. But this was the first time the Pasha had asked for individual 'robbers'—'or rather their Chiefs many of whom have long lived in a state of open war with him.'[278]

Ali's requests were supported by George Foresti; but this did not strengthen them in the eyes of Hudson Lowe, whose opinion of Foresti was taking a distinctly negative turn during this period. At the end of September 1811 Foresti sent him a letter describing the new league against Ali, saying (correctly) that the French were involved in promoting it, and stating that he had been urging Ali to attack both Gjirokastër and Kardhiq.[279] On receiving this report, Lowe wrote with evident irritation to Colonel Smith; he thought that the claims of French financial support were just invented by Ali, and he also disagreed with George Foresti's whole approach to the conflict. 'Of the grand policy of encouraging the Vizir in his efforts to subdue & oppress the small Pachalics & Governments that have hitherto preserved themselves in a manner independent of him, I have my doubts', Lowe commented. 'Those he is now about to attack are very warlike States...and if we are supposed to be his advisers in attacking them (as M.ʳ G. F. states himself to be) it cannot but render the British name odious to them. Some conciliatory plan to unite & reconcile the jarring higher & lower powers, it appears to me would be more judicious.' (This was a significant departure from the view Lowe had expressed just six months earlier, when, as we have seen, he wrote that Ali's ability to exert superior force against Ibrahim Pasha was 'perhaps the only cause why the whole of Albania is not at the present moment in a state of Revolution against the Porte and the French designs triumphant'.)[280] In another letter to Smith, written a week later, Lowe's criticism of Foresti on the issue of the robbers was even harsher; he suspected him of encouraging Ali Pasha's 'sentiments of mistrust' towards the British, and concluded that Foresti 'in short is on this, as he has been in other cases, more a servant of the Vizir, then of the British public'.[281]

The problem, as Lowe saw it, was that a reasonable promise he had previously made was now being misinterpreted. As he wrote to Colonel Smith, the pledge he had given to Ali was that if the robbers 'did not join their families [sc. on the islands] but continued to rob on his Territory & keep their families here, the Families should be delivered up to him, giving the Robbers a sufficient notice & a

Choice to lead a quiet life, if they did not chuse to expose their Families to this alternative'. This had been transformed in Ali's mind into a general promise to hand over all robbers, and Lowe blamed George Foresti for the misinterpret-ation.[282] Towards the end of October he summoned him to Lefkada; there fol-lowed several long discussions, during which (as he told Smith) Lowe tried hard to treat Foresti 'amicably', but found it 'extremely difficult'. Lowe's complaint remained the same: as he put it to Captain Rowley, 'He is here as the Representative of Ali Pachà, than as an Agent of the British Government.'[283]

Now, however, Spiridion Foresti entered the debate, on the opposite side of the argument from his son. He addressed a formal letter, with numbered points, to Colonel Smith, giving reasons why none of the fugitives should be returned to Ali Pasha at all; Smith passed it on to Lowe, who added his own responses. When Spiridion said that some were refugees from 'dispotic [sic] Government' and others had fought against Ali 'to vindicate the blood of their Parents and Relations', Lowe replied: 'All this may be very true, but what have we to do with the internal disquiets of the Turkish Empire?' To Spiridion's claim that 'the General Law of Nations...does not admit of delivering up delinquents of another Dominion, as every Individual must be received whereever he goes', he responded: 'The Exceptions to the General Law of Nations are all in the Visirs favor. Are not Murderers & Robbers a Risk to Society?' And when Spiridion argued that hand-ing over the men would harm British interests, by alienating the local population which was providing 'an Albanian Regiment of Greeks', Lowe observed that this was insignificant 'when the Visir offers you the Service of 30,000 Men, to be employed for the Defence of Sicily or in any other Part of the Mediterranean.'[284] The elder Foresti acted as a statesman-like figure for the people of islands, espe-cially those of his native Zakynthos, and here he was expressing the deep hostility felt by them towards Ali Pasha; the idea that some respect must be paid to such feelings had been a significant strand of British policy even before the conquest of the Ionian Islands. But Lowe stood his ground. In the long letter he wrote to Smith, accompanying his responses to Foresti senior, he wrote that it would be 'highly unpolitic' to give protection to those who have rebelled against Ali. Yet at the same time he continued to criticize 'the too accommodating system of M.ʳ G. Foresti which would lead the Vizir to expect that he had a right to demand the delivery up of every Individual to him and would not allow any hesitation on our part in acquiescence'.[285]

In the end this was a dispute which Hudson Lowe was happy to abandon. Disappointed not to have been made Oswald's successor, he had been applying for leave, which was finally granted at the end of 1811. He departed in early February, never to return.[286] Meanwhile, in December, Major-General George Airey arrived to take the place (which had been temporarily filled by Smith) of Brigadier-General Oswald as overall commander in the Ionian Islands. Spiridion Foresti now had a new opportunity to press his case. In late December Airey wrote to the acting commander of British forces in the Mediterranean, Lieutenant-General Frederick Maitland, saying that he had heard that Ali Pasha was trying to send a message about this issue to Maitland himself. Airey enclosed a letter from Spiridion Foresti, arguing strongly against handing over any of the fugitives, and explained that these were not robbers in the usual sense of the term. Rather, 'They are individuals of Certain Tribes of People, who from some Cause or other and indeed from the Nature of the Government are almost always at Variance with the Vizir. They possibly in their sort of Predatory Wars have had their Villages burnt, are living in the Woods; and some few when hard pressed take refuge in the Neighbouring Islands.' Airey also made the point that giving them up to Ali Pasha might harm 'our Interest with the Greeks'.[287] In February, when Ali presented another demand, Airey told Maitland that on Spiridion Foresti's advice he merely gave Ali 'an Indefinite Answer'. But it seems that Ali Pasha was not pushing hard on this issue. In the same letter to Maitland, Airey noted that 'He is very anxious also for Gunpowder; which (if it could be spared) It might be perhaps adviseable to send him.'[288] Ali Pasha was now in the final stage of his siege of the fortress of Kardhiq, and had more important matters to think about.

The issue seems to have remained largely dormant until mid-April 1812, when Major-General Airey issued a proclamation ordering every 'Armatolò' (fighter) to register with the authorities; a copy was sent to Ali Pasha by Spiridion Foresti, with a covering note referring confidently to the continuation of 'good harmony and sincere friendship' with him.[289] In a letter to the commander of British forces in the Mediterranean, Lord William Bentinck (on whose behalf Maitland had acted at the end of the previous year), Airey explained the background to this. Where bandits and outlaws were concerned, he wrote, the British policy had always been to refuse them entry to the islands, and to expel them if they were found to have entered clandestinely. 'The only delicacy that We have ever observed towards them, is the not delivering up those people to the Pascia himself. This is what he demands, and what We have always warded off. His Vengeance would be extreme; and our national Character would be implicated.' Since Airey's arrival, Ali had asked for a few men who were enrolled in the Greek Light Infantry regiment; Airey had had no hesitation in refusing. Ali had also demanded the handing over of 'two or three old Women who have been for many years perfectly domiciliated at Santa Maura [sc. Lefkada]. These Women he wished to have in his power, as Pledges for the Good Conduct of one of their Relations. But to have given them up to him would have been a Great Cruelty; and an order was sent to them to remove from S.ta Maura to such part of the Continent, as they wished themselves; to prevent further discussion upon the Point.'[290]

In fact, further discussion of this whole issue does appear to have become very muted from this time onwards. One reason for that may be that in March 1812 Ali badly over-played his hand, by organizing the assassination of an alleged 'robber' on Lefkada in broad daylight. The two assassins, arrested by the British, said that their orders had come from Ali Pasha; Ali denied this, while interceding with Airey for their release; and Airey, while pretending to Ali Pasha that he was shocked by their claim about his responsibility—he wrote that they deserved severe punishment both for the murder and for 'such a false, black and abominable calumny against Your Highness'—put them on trial, and resisted implacably all of Ali's further attempts either to plead for clemency, or to get them returned to him for punishment at his own hands.[291] After this episode, it would have been impossible to argue that the safety of fugitives returned to Ali Pasha's territory was in any way guaranteed. The British knew that; and even Ali Pasha, for all his rhetorical resourcefulness, might have been at a loss for an argument to persuade them otherwise.

XIII

On 8 April 1812 a new Ambassador to the Ottoman Empire set off from England: Sir Robert Liston, an experienced diplomat who had already served as Ambassador in Istanbul in the mid-1790s (and subsequently as British Minister to the United States). He was the successor to Sir Robert Adair—whose place had been filled, in the mean time, by the young workaholic Stratford Canning—and his appointment had in fact been announced in the previous spring; but no provision had been made for his travel until Castlereagh took over again as Foreign Secretary in March 1812.[292] A draft set of instructions, composed shortly before Liston's departure, included the following. 'Sir, It appears that one of the most essential Duties of your Embassy to the Porte will be a careful Attention to the Management of His Majesty's Interests on the Western Coast of Greece, but more especially in the Province of Albania.' It commented that Ali Pasha had become 'a determined Enemy to the French', and that he saw the promotion of British interests as 'intimately connected with his own Security and Aggrandizement'. Unfortunately he had recently been complaining of neglect by Britain, so Liston was encouraged to stop at Zakynthos and arrange a meeting with him. While he was there, the instructions said, he might also inquire into the 'unfortunate Quarrel' between Foresti senior and George Foresti, and 'judge of the eventual necessity of removing this young Man, and appointing a proper Person in his place'.[293] Liston's ship did not in the end stop at Zakynthos, and the 'young Man' remained in his post.

On the face of it, there was no reason for the British to feel doubtful about Ali Pasha's loyalty to, or at least alignment with, their cause. Those occasional complaints of neglect, together with the previous badgering about fugitives on the islands, were the only signs of discontent. In April Ali wrote a gracious letter to Lord William Bentinck, thanking him for a recent supply of gunpowder, and proclaiming once again his pro-British 'zeal and devotion'.[294] Certainly Lord

Castlereagh had some confidence in Ali Pasha: responding to yet another report of a possible attack by French forces, he wrote to Ali in May that 'I can have no doubt you will take every proper Measure to support the Independence of the Territories you command, and to assist the Exertions of His Britannick Majesty's Officers in counteracting the designs of our Common Enemy.' He told him, furthermore, that he had instructed Bentinck and the naval commander in the Mediterranean, Vice-Admiral Edward Pellew, 'to pay particular Attention to the Wishes and Wants of Your Highness in all Measures which may be for the common Interest against the Enemy'.[295]

Also on the face of it, Ali's strength and security in the region had grown, with the elimination of the last and most determined component of the French-sponsored league against him. In December the men of Kardhiq had offered to surrender, on condition that they be allowed to emigrate to Corfu; Ali had refused, and his siege continued until the fall of Kardhiq on 21 February 1812. At least 300 defenders were killed in the final assault.[296] Worse was to happen, however. Ali Pasha bore a deep grudge against the people of Kardhiq; it was said that in his childhood, after the death of his father and the sudden decline of his family's local power, his mother had been captured by them, raped, and humiliated by being forced to walk through the streets with a man on her back.[297] Now Ali took his revenge. On 15 March he ordered that nearly 800 of the captives be taken to a roadside *han* (inn for travellers) with a large courtyard, a few miles from Gjirokastër. Some were selected to be taken away for slavery in other parts of Albania, but the great majority were gunned down in cold blood. When Henry Holland passed through the area exactly one year later, he found Kardhiq a dead town, with empty streets, and the courtyard of the *han* choked with human remains.[298] This final conquest strengthened Ali Pasha's political position vis-à-vis the rest of Albania, where he had in any case been steadily extending his influence; Pouqueville reported in late February that he now controlled, directly or indirectly, the ports on the Albanian coast all the way up to Lezhë.[299] And Ali's recent gains in territory and power had economic consequences too. Pouqueville calculated that he would receive an income of 3 million francs from the estates of Ibrahim Pasha and the beys of Vlorë whom he had dispossessed, plus half as much again from the customs of Vlorë and other tax revenues. (At this time one franc was worth one piastre.) He also supplied a characteristic detail of how Ali squared things with Istanbul: whereas in the past the ports of Çamëri had sent no customs dues at all to the Ottoman government, Ali was now extracting customs, keeping most of the revenues for himself, but sending a certain amount to Istanbul, and gaining credit there for doing so.[300]

Nevertheless, despite these increases in his local power, and despite the generally positive attitude of the British, Ali Pasha continued to feel real doubts about his own geopolitical prospects. He followed as closely as he could the long-drawn-out negotiations between the Russians and the Ottomans at Bucharest, fearing the consequences of an eventual settlement. If Russia renewed friendly relations with the Sultan, and broke off its connection with France (as seemed increasingly likely anyway), it might end up in some sort of triple alliance with both the Ottoman Empire and Great Britain; in those circumstances, Ali thought, it would demand to be restored to power in the Ionian Islands. And although the French troops on Corfu were a small and beleaguered force, no one could deny that France was still by far the most successful and intimidating military power in the whole of western and central Europe. (That impression would be changed only by the collapse of the Grande Armée during the retreat from Moscow in November 1812.) It is not surprising that Ali sided generally with the British after the arrival of their soldiers in 1809 and the increase in their naval presence locally. But at the same time it should not surprise us that he still made efforts, from time to time, to keep up a positive connection with the French. In December 1811 Pierre Joseph Guès, who had been serving as French vice-consul in Vlorë, passed through Ioannina on his way to Corfu. He had a long meeting with Ali Pasha, who proclaimed his friendship with France, his desire to renew good relations with Napoleon and his wish for French protection against the English.[301] At Donzelot's behest Guès went back to Ioannina in February and stayed there for at least two weeks, having many conversations with Ali; the professions of loyalty to France were repeated, together with an assurance that in the event of the dissolution of the Ottoman Empire, Ali would take the side of France. (Guès also made arrangements to buy an entire forest for timber; it belonged to Ali's long-term enemy Mustafa Pasha of Delvinë, who surrendered at Kardhiq, and whose estates Ali was already expropriating.)[302] Little seems to have come of these tentative diplomatic manoeuvrings at the time. But Ali Pasha was still keen to keep this potential line of policy open two months later, when he summoned the chief medical officer on Corfu to Ioannina for a consultation; this, as the doctor reported, was merely a pretext for a meeting in which Ali earnestly enquired about the attitude of the French government towards him.[303]

Ali Pasha's main concern, as so often, was with Russia. In January 1812 Stratford Canning reported that Ali claimed to have received 'Intelligence' that General Kutuzov was requesting, as part of the Russian demands in the peace negotiations at Bucharest, the restoration of Russian rule in the Ionian Islands. Canning checked with the reis efendi, who denied that the Russian negotiators had asked for any such thing, and added that the Ottomans would be very reluctant to grant it.[304] Where these slow-moving negotiations between Russia and the Ottoman Empire were concerned, Ali's relationship with the British was a rather complex one. Promoting peace between those two states was a high priority for British foreign policy: it would eliminate the possibility of a joint Franco-Russian partition of the Ottoman Empire, help to normalize British–Russian relations, and enable the Tsar to return forces to Russia for what seemed increasingly likely to be a coming war against France. Although Ali had no interest in such a peace, he was reluctant, as always, to contribute large forces to the Ottoman army for the war against Russia, and benefited from Canning's interventions with the Porte to excuse him from such demands. (From the British point of view, a continuing military stalemate was greatly preferable to a new Ottoman offensive, as it would not disrupt the peace negotiations; and Ali's armed force was best concentrated in his own domains, as a bulwark against any possible French invasion there.) During the spring of 1812 Stratford Canning became closely involved in the nego-tiations, putting pressure both on the Ottomans and, through his own confiden-tial agent, on the Russians.[305]

In mid-March 1812 George Foresti took the unusual step of travelling to Istanbul in order to discuss Ali Pasha's position with Stratford Canning in person. Soon after his arrival there he wrote a memorandum on his recent conversations at Ioannina. He described how Ali had summoned him for a discussion after receiving a letter from the Grand Vizier; the letter said that since the Russian demands were exorbitant and could not be accepted, Ali was ordered to bring a large number of troops to the front for a new offensive campaign. Ali told Foresti that he suspected that this request had been engineered by the French in order to make Ali's territories vulnerable to attack. When Foresti asked why he thought that the Ottoman government was inclined to act in the interests of the French, Ali referred to 'the Orders sent to Him to cultivate them underhand, to comply with their Demands, to allow Provisions to pass to Corfu'. Where the Grand Vizier's order was concerned, Ali said that he felt 'perplexed how to act between the Force of His Duty and His real Interest'. Foresti continued: 'He assured me that he desired nothing so much as to see His Country united with England and Russia against France, that whenever that Day arrived he would willingly go to the farthest corner of the World to find the French and to fight them, without which, He said that he could not die satisfied'. Ali explained that he was willing to go to the front and 'by a secret Concert of Measures with the English' bring about a peace agreement with Russia which he could then 'dispose the Sultan to accept'; but if there was no certainty of British support for such a move, 'He would rather remain quiet at Ioannina and let Affairs take their own Course'. Fearing that his couriers might be intercepted by the government, he asked Foresti to go to Istanbul in person in order to convey this message. Foresti himself was 'not a little astonished at this Proposition'; as he wrote, 'A Moment's Reflection on his former Conduct and Character' might have made him suspect Ali's sincerity. Nevertheless, knowing how dependent Ali was on the good will of the British, he could not see what reason he would have to deceive Canning on this issue. Foresti's only remaining doubts were phrased rather carefully: 'I would not risk to say, that he may not have other Views to satisfy in desiring so earnestly these Negotiations'—the most obvious 'View' being Ali's determination that the Russians should not be restored to power over the Ionian Islands.[306]

This was indeed a very strange initiative on Ali Pasha's part, and the sincerity of some elements of his argument must surely be doubted. It is extremely hard to believe that he really desired 'nothing so much as to see His Country united with England and Russia against France'; and his extravagant phrase about going to the farthest corner of the world to fight the French was, by its very nature, almost transparently false. That Ali wanted, once again, British support for his refusal to lead a large force to the front is easy to believe; and he may have relished the opportunity to slip in some self-exculpatory details about instructions from Istanbul to permit supplies to be taken to Corfu. (Commenting on this in a later report to London, Canning wrote that after a strict enquiry 'I do not find that the Porte has ordered Ali Pasha to allow Provisions to pass to Corfou, but simply not to give the French any just Cause of Complaint.')[307] But neither of those points was so unusual as to require a personal visit to Istanbul by Foresti in order to make them. Possibly Ali hoped to learn some secret details of the state of the peace negotiations and of the British involvement in them; offering to play a key role himself in the British interest, of a kind that his influence over Ottoman government ministers entitled him to suggest, might have been expected to encourage the British to confide in him more freely. But since we know that he remained deeply hostile to the Russians and feared an agreement with them, it is necessary to consider an even more Machiavellian strategy. Perhaps he really did hope to gain a key position as a secret negotiator, and then to use that position to bring about the collapse of the talks in such a way that the Russians would take the blame. On the other hand it is possible that he did not have a worked-out plan at this stage and just wanted to become involved, to see what advantages he could then draw from the situation; for he was, after all, a master of improvisation and opportunism, and he was also familiar with the power of gold to influence the outcome of official dealings of all kinds.

Stratford Canning's reply, given to Foresti in writing, was intended to be both reassuring and non-committal. On matters of high policy he said that he must consult London first. The Porte's request to Ali to bring troops had now been suspended, so no further action there was needed. The peace negotiations seemed close to completion; any attempt by Ali to interfere at this stage might be counterproductive, but Canning hoped that he would use his influence to lobby 'through his confidential agents' in Istanbul and at the army headquarters for a speedy peace, and for continued vigilance against France. Foresti was to remind Ali of the great advantages he got from the presence of the British off his coastline, and to urge him to maintain the blockade of Corfu. And he was to assure him—but only orally, without committing anything to writing—that His Majesty's Government had no intention of allowing the Russians back in the Ionian Islands.[308] Equipped with these instructions, Foresti left Istanbul on 13 May 1812. Just three days later, the Treaty of Bucharest was finally signed. And only six days after that, when the details of the agreement were still not public knowledge,

Canning wrote to Foresti to say that the Russians were offering not just a peace agreement but an alliance, with better terms for the Ottomans. 'You will urge the Pasha to employ his influence in order to bring about the acceptance of this proposal', he instructed, while again insisting that Foresti should not put anything in writing.[309] Whatever doubts Canning may have had about Ali Pasha's good faith and reliability, he continued to treat him, as Sir Robert Adair had done before, as a valuable 'agent of influence' in Istanbul.

On 18 May 1812, two days after the signing of the treaty, while Foresti was on his way back to Ioannina, Pouqueville wrote a long report of his own most recent discussion with Ali Pasha. Unusually, he set it out in dialogue form. Pouqueville had begun by asking whether Ali was happy with the fact that Russia was at war with his country. 'Yes, very happy, because France will help us by making a powerful diversion.' (This was a reference to the widely expected French invasion of Russia.) Would he go to war himself? Yes, he would take 10–12,000 men to fight the Russians. How did his friends the English see this war? They disliked it, and wanted peace; but the Ottoman Empire would 'never' make peace 'without French agreement'. But what about the two British officers who had recently visited Ioannina, on their way to Istanbul, who said openly that you had told them to promote peace? 'I told them everything they wanted to hear, but I warned the Grand Vizier not to listen to them. I shall trick the English to the end, and make them think that I am their friend.' Ali then told Pouqueville that after 'the first cannon shot fired in Poland'—in other words, the opening of Napoleon's campaign against Russia—the Sultan would declare war on Britain within three months. So although Ali personally was eager to take his troops to launch an offensive against the Russians, the Sultan wanted him and his son Muhtar to stay in their domains, 'to defend our country and the Peloponnese from any invasion by the English, and so that we can fight together, Mr Consul, to expel them from the Ionian Islands'.[310] However odd some of the contents of Ali's recent proposals to Foresti may have been, what he said in the last part of this conversation with Pouqueville went some way beyond them in improbability.

Just two weeks later Pouqueville was reporting that Ali had renewed his 'intrigues' with the British. On 22 June 1812 he wrote that Lord William Bentinck himself had visited Ioannina, accompanied by fourteen heavily laden mules; he was convinced that they carried a large payment from the British, and that this was the reason for all 'the difficulties and obstacles which I encounter in my negotiations'.[311] (That Britain sent large subsidies to Ali Pasha was a constant refrain in Pouqueville's reports. There is no trace of any such payments in the British records—which do, on the other hand, contain Adair's clear refusal to countenance such subsidies in 1809. Most probably Ali dropped hints referring to such large but imaginary payments from time to time, in order to stimulate the French to make equivalent but real ones.)[312] Nevertheless, Ali Pasha had not abandoned his attempts to convince the French that he was devoted to their cause. When the news came on 8 July 1812 that the Russian–Ottoman treaty had been ratified, he told Pouqueville: 'This peace will complete the ruin of my country. Your Emperor will be justly indignant with us. God is my witness that I did everything I could to stop it from being brought to completion.'[313] And three days later Lesseps wrote from Corfu to the French Foreign Minister, summarizing a message that Ali had recently sent him, 'secretly and orally': Ali had said 'that he revered, feared and loved His Majesty the Emperor Napoleon, and that he would submit blindly to his orders.'[314] Some French officials were more immune to Ali's persuasion than others, however. At roughly the same time, La Tour-Maubourg was writing to Pouqueville from Istanbul, commenting that Ali's reaction to the peace agreement with Russia was to assume that it would lead to a rupture between the Ottoman Empire and France; La Tour-Maubourg believed that Ali had therefore offered to lend the British 6,000 men for the siege of Corfu, on the condition that they would take Parga and give it to him.[315]

After the signing of the Treaty of Bucharest and the withdrawal of Russian forces from Wallachia and Moldavia (just in time—Napoleon's invasion of Russia began on 24 June), the mood in Istanbul changed rather quickly. In a diplomatic counter-move, France and Austria offered to guarantee the territorial integrity of the Ottoman Empire if the Sultan broke off the treaty and joined them in the war against Russia, and to many in Istanbul this seemed a tempting prospect. Sir Robert Liston, who arrived there at the end of June, found his task very difficult. As he wrote in December to his friend Lord Tyrconnell (who had volunteered to serve in the Tsar's army): 'the Turks have thought they made a bad peace prematurely and without necessity. They have been ever since in a state of sullen dissatisfaction with themselves, of extreme ill-humour with England for having *advised* the conclusion of the treaty, and, above all, of rancorous enmity towards the Russians.'[316] The only thing that could alter this state of affairs was news of a French defeat; and no such news was available during the summer and autumn of 1812.

Ali Pasha's own calculations proceeded, evidently enough, on the same basis. His dealings with the British were mainly concerned with seeking protection and assistance. In July he warned of a possible French invasion, with news of 18,000 troops ready to be shipped from Toulon to Corfu; in September he wrote to Bentinck about sending him a confidential agent (presumably to request arms or other assistance); and soon afterwards he arranged for one of his secretaries to travel to Istanbul for discussions with Sir Robert Liston. When that man went back to Ioannina in late October, Liston also gave him a letter to take to George Foresti, in which he wrote: 'I have frankly told him that, as an Enemy of Bonaparte, as a Bulwark of the Ottoman Empire, as a friend in fact of the independence of nations and consequently of the good cause, I think Great Britain bound, if his Master were attacked by France, to come to his assistance with fleets, armies, supplies of every kind, in short, to defend him to the utmost of Her power.'

Furthermore, if French intrigues persuaded the Sultan to go to war against Ali Pasha, 'it would then become my Duty to exert every nerve, to employ representations, remonstrances and protestations... in short, to leave nothing untried to avert the storm.'[317]

At the same time, uncertain of the military outcome in Russia, Ali still tried to keep some options open with the French. That his general policy of pressure and obstruction, where Corfu was concerned, did not change is unsurprising, both because of the presence of British ships enforcing the blockade, and because Ali always hoped to use such leverage to obtain concessions (above all, the handing over of Parga). Pouqueville's reports for August, September and much of October contain the usual litany of complaints about Ali's uncooperative behaviour.[318] In the second half of October, however, as news of the successful French campaign came in, Ali began to talk about a falling-out between him and the British. He told Pouqueville that in late May, soon after the signing of the Treaty of Bucharest, a British ship had arrived with 7 million piastres in cash, which was offered to Ali in return for an immediate declaration of war by him against the French. 'I refused the subsidy', he told Pouqueville, 'and from that moment onwards the English have hated me.'[319]

Despite his years of experience at Ali's court, Pouqueville fell for this piece of utter fiction, and was soon reporting to his Foreign Minister that there was an opportunity to profit from the 'division' between Ali and the British: as you know, he wrote, 'we must forget the past, or at least pretend to... in the end we must make use of Ali Pasha just as he is.' In a subsequent report he listed the various advantages that would flow from having Ali fully aligned with the French cause: food for Corfu, timber for ships (he included a list of eighteen suitable forests), and so on.[320] It was from Ali that he learned, on 1 November, of Napoleon's entry into Moscow in mid-September; the news came from a Turk who had travelled to Ioannina from Bender (in Bessarabia), but it made no mention of the almost immediate burning of the city by the Russians, and falsely claimed that the Grande Armée had then marched on St Petersburg. Napoleon's victory thus seemed almost complete. When Ali talked to the English traveller Henry Holland a few days later, he seemed 'discomposed', and 'spoke with little disguise of the probable designs of Napoleon, alluding to Turkey as one of the first objects of his [sc. Napoleon's] future career.'[321] It now seemed prudent to take a pro-French turn; so in mid-November Ali told Pouqueville that he was forbidding all export of grains to the British in Malta and Spain, and made 'the most fervent declarations of his desire to serve His Majesty [Napoleon]'.[322] But on 28 November Ali learned, from the Russian Ambassador in Istanbul, of what was described as a great victory over the French, involving the abandonment of Moscow and a retreat to Lithuania. Within three days, Pouqueville was complaining that Ali's devotion to the French cause was like the faith of a neophyte, 'very wavering and uncertain'; and on 7 December he wrote despairingly that there was now a 'new coalition' between Ali and the British: 'one false piece of news received by him, or one whim, is enough to destroy the wisest and best-made plans.'[323] However, at this stage reports from Russia were confused and unreliable, and Ali was still inclined to hedge his bets. At the beginning of January he had another meeting with Pierre Joseph Guès, and gave him a set of proposals to take to Paris: in return for Napoleon's protection, he undertook to cooperate fully with French forces, offering to supply up to 60,000 men for the reconquest of the Ionian Islands. (Just one extra condition was added, though not in writing: he wanted the French to give him Parga.)[324] But this was the last initiative of its kind. The sheer scale of the French disaster would become clear to Ali Pasha in mid-February 1813, when a bulletin written in Vilnius on 26 December arrived—via the Russian Ambassador in Istanbul—at Ioannina. It recorded that of the 450,000 soldiers sent into Russia by Napoleon, only 25,000 had returned.[325]

XIV

Although there were times when this was not at all obvious to the participants in the war, the retreat from Moscow marked the beginning of the endgame for Napoleon. Austria's alliance with France ended in February 1813; Sweden and Prussia declared war on France in March; and Austria joined them in August. These powers, together with Britain, Russia and a few others, formed the 'Sixth Coalition' which would bring about Napoleon's downfall. Meanwhile in Spain, the British and their local allies inflicted a heavy defeat on the French at the Battle of Vitoria in June 1813; from then on the French were fighting a defensive campaign there, with depleted numbers. Napoleon did make huge efforts to raise new troops. But despite winning significant victories in Germany in May and August, he was eventually forced, after his defeat in October at the 'Battle of the Nations' near Leipzig, to make a final strategic withdrawal into France.

From the early spring of 1813 onwards, therefore, the likelihood of an offensive French campaign against Ottoman territory was very close to zero. This was a period when troops were being recalled from both Spain and Italy to fortify Napoleon's army in the Central European arena. In early February George Foresti wrote to Bentinck that the French were planning to reduce the strength of the garrison on Corfu; a month later his father was able to report that 2,000 had recently left; and at roughly the same time an analysis by a Russian agent on Corfu said that the garrison was down to c.7,000 French troops, plus '2,000 Albanians, who are more inclined to serve the cause of humanity, if the stronghold is attacked, than to defend the French'.[326] Nevertheless, a report on the situation in Corfu in late January noted that the French still had large quantities of light artillery there, and enough of some categories of foodstuffs to last another two years.[327] So although Corfu seemed militarily less important, it was not easy to see how or when it would actually fall.

From Ali Pasha's point of view, the need for protection against French attack had more or less evaporated. If any protection were required, it was against his own sovereign, Sultan Mahmud II. In February 1813 George Foresti obtained copies of some messages which had passed in the final months of 1812 between the new French Ambassador in Istanbul, General Andréossy—who had replaced La Tour-Maubourg in the summer of that year—and Donzelot on Corfu. 'For a long time the Sultan has had the intention of destroying Ali Pasha', Andréossy wrote. 'He had abandoned this plan several times, but is reviving it now.'[328] (If Foresti read these messages, we can be confident that Ali did so too. As Foresti would later explain, when claiming for 'secret Expences': 'Aly Pacha being in the Habit of intercepting all Correspondence passing through his Territories, occasionally shewed to Me, what he stated to be copies of such Parts of the Dispatches as turned to his Account. This Confidence put me in the Way of employing the same People that He did, and, by this Means, I succeeded to obtain, *for above two Years,* nearly the whole Correspondence, between the French Ambassador Andreossi, General Donzelot, and M.ʳ Pouqueville.')[329] Ali Pasha's very existence as a quasi-autonomous ruler of Ottoman territory, capable of resisting with impunity—as he had done, repeatedly in recent years—urgent orders to bring troops to the Ottoman army, was a sufficient reason for the Sultan to seek his removal; Mahmud's programme of restoring power to the centre of the Empire was pursued with great persistence, and would indeed bring about Ali's defeat and death nine years later. In March 1813 Ali once again ignored the call to supply soldiers for the Sultan's campaign against the rebellious Serbs. On being ordered to reinstate Ibrahim Pasha, he not only refused but had Ibrahim transferred to a prison cell in Ioannina, to prevent his possible release and render him more easily disposed of. And in response to rumours of a planned campaign against him by the Ottoman army, he began strengthening the castle at Gjirokastër and stocking it with provisions.[330] When Airey's successor, Lieutenant-General James Campbell, took over in the Ionian Islands in the summer of 1813, one of his first reports said that Ali Pasha's apprehension of 'the hostile disposition of the Porte towards him' had led him 'not only to desire, but to court the protection of Great Britain'. (Campbell noted at the same time, however, that it was necessary to keep 'a watchful eye upon this powerful and crafty Chief, who knows no other Policy, but his own interest'.)[331]

One particular issue that troubled Ali Pasha at this time concerned the future of the three ex-Venetian places on the mainland which he still held: Preveza, Vonitsa and Butrint. The first of these was the largest and most important; he had occupied it, and Vonitsa, as a pre-emptive measure against the Russians when they invaded Ottoman territory in 1806. With relations between St Petersburg and Istanbul normalized, it was to be expected that the Sultan would want to

restore the previous state of affairs, which had been set up under a Russian–
Ottoman convention; this would mean removing Muslims from those three
places, each of which would once more be put under the supervision of an individual Ottoman official. As we have seen, Ali had already taken great trouble to
make Preveza easier to defend against any attack. He had also been trying to
change the character of the population there: in 1809 he had seized 300 houses,
which he gave to Muslims, and in July 1812 Pouqueville reported that he ordered
all the Christian inhabitants to leave. (Most, it seems, had done so by October of
that year, when Henry Holland visited the town; he wrote that its population had
fallen under Ali Pasha's rule from 10–12,000 to 3–4,000, and that Ali had 'substi-
tuted the Albanian peasant or soldier for the industrious Greek inhabitants.')[332]
From mid-December 1812 Ali spent nearly three months in Preveza, accompanied by 4,000 troops. No dramatic changes were made while he was there, but he
continued to enforce his policy of irrevocable change: as Spiridion Foresti
reported in February 1813, 'he endeavours by various kinds of vexations to make
the christian inhabitants of Prevesa abandon it, and replaces them by Albanians
in order to make it entirely a Turkish [sc. Muslim] town.'[333]

Even more important in Ali Pasha's eyes, however, was the one ex-Venetian
place on the mainland that he did not control: the town and fortress of Parga.
Early in 1813 he sent his dragoman and confidential agent, Colovo (a man
described by Henry Holland as fluent in Italian, French and German, and 'of
extreme sedateness of manner'), to discuss Parga with Sir Robert Liston in
Istanbul. Liston suggested that he talk to Lord Bentinck, so in late February
Colovo took a ship from Preveza to Malta, in order to travel from there to
Bentinck's headquarters at Palermo. Reporting on his departure, Foresti correctly
assumed that Parga would be the main topic of discussion, and with that in mind
he sent a background paper of his own, discussing the history of the issue. He
noted that the refusal of the French to give the stronghold to Ali had caused in
him 'a Spirit of Disrespect, Enmity and Revenge' towards them, and he commented that Parga remained useful to the French, both as a port and as a potential
bargaining chip with Ali Pasha. If the British took it, Ali would of course expect
them to transfer it to him, but that would weaken support for the British among
the Greeks, and would also offend the Russians, who still felt that they had an
interest in the matter (as signatories of the 1800 convention). The best solution,
Foresti advised, would be for the British to seize it and hold it until they were able
to take possession of Corfu as well, by which time they would have 'sole
Arbitration of it'.[334] A later memorandum by Ali Pasha confirms that when
Colovo did meet Bentinck, he did raise the question of Parga, and received some
rather predictable advice for his master: he was told to be patient.[335]

Realizing that the British were unlikely to hand over Parga to him even if they
did take it, Ali began to develop a different strategy. In August 1813 he sent a force
of 8–900 soldiers to occupy the village of Agia, which was just inside the

north-western edge of Parga's small territory (a semi-circle extending inland from Parga, with a radius of barely three miles). This move was energetically resisted by the Greek commander of the Parga garrison, Nicholas Papasoglu, who rallied his forces and managed to drive Ali's troops back after a gunfight that lasted for nine hours. Ali then disavowed the operation, saying that his men had acted without authority; nevertheless, this was a foretaste of military action to come.[336]

The second half of 1813 was a period of relative calm in the region. Rumours of Ottoman preparations for military action against Ali came to nothing, not least because Sultan Mahmud had to focus his attention on the renewed revolt of the Serbs.[337] Where the French on Corfu were concerned, the stand-off continued unchanged; and the rarity of any mention of Ali Pasha in the reports of Liston in Istanbul and Campbell in the Ionian Islands shows that there was likewise little alteration in his relations with the British. This situation changed only in early 1814, when Ali's attention focused once again on Parga. By now Ali had clearly decided that he could strike at the French with relative impunity; when the travel-ler Thomas Smart Hughes spoke to him on 14 April, Ali 'seemed well aware of the tottering power of the French emperor'. Two weeks later Ali wrote from Preveza to Lieutenant-General Campbell, saying that since the French had occupied 'his' village of Agia it had become a base for Souliots and other people he had ban-ished from his territories, who committed 'innumerable thefts and other out-rages'. He now wished to stop this, and requested support from British ships; Campbell replied that he had no power to order any such naval action.[338] Evidently Ali was keen to act as quickly as possible: even before he received this response, he sent first George Foresti and then his trusted agent Said Ahmed to explain his case to Campbell.[339] From these meetings it would have become clear—if it were not already—that Ali's aim was seize control not only of Agia, but of Parga itself.

Campbell remained deeply sceptical about the desirability of encouraging, or even allowing, such action. As he wrote on 14 March 1814 to the Secretary of State for War and the Colonies, Earl Bathurst:

> I confess myself to be considerably influenced by the dictates of common Humanity in my desire to prevent the little interesting Greek Community of Parga from falling under the Dominion of their sanguinary and relentless neigh-bour, whose rancour in regard to its Population is such, that I am convinced he would exterminate them by a general and indiscriminate Massacre, and so well aware are they of it, that failing of support and protection on our part, they have prepared themselves for the most desperate and determined resistance.

Campbell estimated that there were roughly 5000 inhabitants of Parga; letting them be killed would be 'considered an indelible stain upon our National Character by the Greek Nation at large'. Pointedly, he quoted from the instructions he had been given by Bathurst when he took up his post in the Ionian Islands: he was ordered to 'omit no opportunity of cultivating the most friendly understanding with the Greek People' and to 'avoid every thing which may have the appearance of dread or unbecoming Subserviency to Ali Pacha, holding towards him a firm and a decided tone, tho' temperate and friendly'.[340]

Meanwhile, Ali had already seized Agia and begun constructing a fort there. According to a later memoir by the British officer (of Swiss origin) Charles Philippe de Bosset, most of the inhabitants of Agia tried to flee from the territory by boat; Ali stationed his own ships off the coast to intercept them, and many were either drowned, or captured and then killed. The people of Parga sent a deputation to Captain Garland, the commander of a British force which had only recently taken over the nearby island of Paxos. They told him that they had inter-cepted a letter from Ali to the commanding officer of the French garrison in Parga, Nicholas Papasoglu, offering him a large payment in return for its surren-der, and they begged for British help. Garland reported this to Campbell, who sent a detachment of soldiers to Paxos on board two frigates. Captain Hoste, who commanded one of the frigates, told the Parganots that he did not have authority to attack Parga directly, but that he would land his men there if they hoisted a British flag at the fortress. On 22 March the flag was smuggled in by a widow under her voluminous dress, and an armed group of Parganots then rushed the garrison; as soon as the flag was raised, the British detachment of Greek Light Infantry, commanded by Major Sir Charles Gordon, landed at the port and took control.[341] When he heard this news, Campbell wrote to Bathurst saying how glad he was that Parga had been 'rescued from the impending Ferocity of its powerful and relentless Neighbour'. He emphasized that this action greatly strengthened the credentials of Britain as the friend of the Greek nation, which, he said, 'may lead to the happiest consequences'.[342] In a further report, written on the following day, Campbell noted that although Ali Pasha had been extremely eager to take Parga, 'the desperate courage of the Parguinotes repelled his formidable assault on the land side, while the operations of his Flotilla before it were frustrated by the timely interference of the Naval Officers Commanding the Squadron before Corfu, who could neither permit the limits of the Blockade to be violated, nor the cruelties practised by the Vizier's Cruizers on the Parguinotes to remain unchecked.'[343]

Ali's feelings on having this prize snatched from him at the last moment are not hard to imagine. Nevertheless, as a veteran politician and diplomatist, he was used to having to play a long game. Writing to Campbell immediately after the event, he pretended that he had only ever wanted to take the village of Agia. Soon afterwards, however, he tried a different tack, sending a long letter to Sir Robert Liston in Istanbul; no doubt Ali was aware, from his agent there, that Liston was relatively well-disposed towards him. On 14 April 1814 Liston wrote to the Foreign Secretary about this approach, asking for instructions. He began by praising Ali,

noting that 'I have had former occasions to mention to Your Lordship the eminent abilities and the political importance of this extraordinary man.' On the
issue of the ex-Venetian possessions, Liston explained that 'He has all along
entertained the hope, indeed he affirms that he had the positive promise, that
when any of those places fell into our hands they should be made over to him as a
mark of our friendship or as the price of his cooperation; and he was disappointed
at not getting possession of Santa Maura, to the capture of which he claims the
merit of having contributed.' Ali had asked the government in Istanbul for permission to attack Agia, but had not received any clear reply; therefore 'he had
resolved to leave the matter in suspence, when the complaints of the innocent
inhabitants of the adjacent hamlets, who came in hundreds to throw themselves
at his feet and to implore his protection against the daily outrages of the Banditti,
determined him to do his duty by expelling them from their den. He accordingly
assaulted Aya, but finding that the people of Parga came out to defend the crim-
inals, he resolved to attack the town also'—whereupon he found to his surprise it
was occupied by Major Gordon. His letter to Liston was written ostensibly just to
seek his advice, 'but in fact—as I learnt from his Agent here—in the hope that I
would write to General Campbell to deliver up the place to him.' Liston's reply to
Ali was that this was an issue for the government in London. And his respectful
advice to Lord Castlereagh was that if he did decide to give Parga to Ali Pasha, he
should consider 'that the conveyance ought not to be unconditional, for that
many innocent men have sought an asylum in those places, whom it would be
unhandsome and inhumane to leave at his mercy'. He should also bear in mind
that this would be, in theory at least, an addition to the territories that were under
the direct rule of the Sultan—an alteration for which Britain should naturally seek
a *quid pro quo*.[344]

When Liston wrote those words, he would have been aware that the armies of
the Sixth Coalition had carried the fight onto French soil. But he did not yet know
of the rapid collapse of Napoleonic power. Russian, Austrian and Prussian forces
began attacking Paris on 30 March 1814, and it surrendered on the following day.
Napoleon, who was with his army to the south of the city, was obliged to offer his
unconditional abdication six days later; and the Treaty of Fontainebleau, under
which he ceased to be Emperor and would leave France for Elba, was signed on 11
April. As always, news took several weeks to pass from western Europe to
Istanbul, so it was not until 9 May that Istanbul learned of Napoleon's fall. Sir
Robert Liston reported that this caused 'astonishment and dejection' among the
members of the Ottoman government, who had 'continued all along in a state of
infatuated credulity'.[345] The news had already reached the Ionian Islands, where
negotiations over the surrender of Corfu began in late April and continued
throughout May. A small French naval force left Toulon, under General de
Boulnois, who was 'commissaire royal' (that is, acting under the orders of the
newly established King Louis XVIII), and arrived at Corfu on 6 June. After ten

days of final negotiations between him and Lieutenant-General Campbell, the British took possession of the island on 17 June.[346]

Ali Pasha's chances of gaining power over Corfu were now more remote than ever. But the possibility that Parga might be transferred to his control could only become greater with the end of the Napoleonic Wars. (For Ali and the region around him, those wars did end in 1814; the return of Napoleon for his 'Hundred Days' from March to July 1815 would have no effect in this part of Europe.) So, once again, he applied himself to the task of persuading the British. In August or September he put to Liston the idea of sending a personal envoy to London; Liston dissuaded him, saying that a written message would suffice. The letter which Ali then sent, to Castlereagh in late September, misleadingly declared that Parga 'passed under the Treaty of 1802 to the absolute rule and sovereignty of my government [sc. the Sultan], which later ceded it to me as feudatory ruler of it'. Liston also received a copy of this letter. Commenting on Ali's request for Parga, he began by praising him as pro-British, reminding Castlereagh 'that He was instrumental in bringing about our Peace with Turkey; that as far as it was possible, without an open breach with France, and without bringing on Himself the consequent Vengeance of His own Government, His Power in the province has, during that latter years of our conflict with France, been exerted in our favour; that His Influence at the Seat of Government is still great; and that He has it in His power either to do us essential mischief or to render good service'. Nevertheless, on this particular issue Liston had 'taken care to give Him very slender hopes of success'. He had written to Ali that if the British gave Parga to anyone, it would be to the Sultan. At the same time he had pointed out that it was normal, after a war, to reward those who had actually taken part in the war, 'and that the Ottoman Government had contributed nothing to the victories gained; that it might rather be accused of showing partiality to the common enemy; not to speak of its unfriendly Conduct towards the Ministers of some of the Allied Courts residing at Constantinople'. These barbed remarks, he explained to Castlereagh, were made 'Knowing that the Pasha has a regular and confidential Correspondence with the Capital'.[347] Ali's influence in Istanbul was once more being presumed on by the British, but not to effect the sort of outcome that Ali himself desired.

Ali Pasha wrote another letter to Castlereagh in October 1814. Replying to it in January, from Vienna, the Foreign Secretary assured Ali of Britain's desire 'to give to Your Highness every Proof of sincere Friendship', but on the question of Parga he could only say that 'it is not in my Power to give to you at present any answer. The fate of the Ionian Islands and of their dependencies still awaits the decision of the Congress assembled here'.[348] George Foresti left Ioannina in early 1815 and travelled to London via Vienna, from where he wrote to Ali Pasha, apparently giving him—though we have only Ali's later word for this—'some favourable Hints...with regard to His obtaining Possession of Parga'. So in April Ali wrote another formal letter to the British government, and in the following month his trusted diplomatic agent Said Ahmed, bearing that letter, set off once again for London.[349] At roughly the same time, Lieutenant-General Campbell was inform- ing the British government that ever since his forces had occupied Parga, 'the Vizir has perseveringly employed every Means, short of actual Force, to obtain the Possession of that Rock, with its Brave, Independent, and Peaceful Population'—means that included forging petitions from the inhabitants, and making bogus complaints about British encroachment on his own territories. (A later memoir by a British official would describe Ali's methods as follows: 'by bribing some, by intimidating others...by stopping their supplies, by sowing dis- sentions among the inhabitants, by harassing all their communications, & by every means likely to break down their spirit'.)[350] Campbell also sent instructions to the commander of the garrison there, about how to deal with Ali Pasha and his officials: 'you will preserve a civil but firm demeanour, shewing yourself desirous of keeping up a good understanding and neighbourhood, but no way disposed to give way in the smallest degree to any Incroachments which they in their Caprice or haughtiness may attempt'.[351] When Said Ahmed arrived in London in late September, he was told that it was not the practice of the government to accept diplomatic approaches from any except those accredited by their sovereigns, but that, exceptionally, he would be allowed to submit Ali's letter via the Ottoman chargé d'affaires in London. This was done, but the reply that was then written to Ali was entirely to be expected: the fate of both Parga and the Ionian Islands was 'now under Discussion by the Ministers of the Allied Powers assembled at Paris'.[352]

What finally ensured the abandonment of Parga by the British was not Ali's persuasive rhetoric, nor the frequent probing and pressure of his actions on the ground, but rather what might be called the legal and diplomatic logic of the situ- ation. The Congress of Vienna agreed to place the Ionian Islands, as defined by the convention of 1800 (i.e. the territories of the 'Septinsular Republic'), under British protection. Since Parga and the other three ex-Venetian coastal places had not been included in those territories, it was now felt that they reverted automat- ically to the Ottoman Empire. Britain stipulated that all those Parganots who wished to leave should not only be allowed to do so freely, but also be compen- sated for their property; and when, after a long delay, it became clear that the Ottoman government was unwilling to pay an adequate sum, the suggestion was made that if Ali Pasha were prepared to pay it he could incorporate Parga in his own *paşalık*. Even longer delays followed, as British and Ottoman commissioners reached conflicting valuations of the properties (with the Ottoman ones hugely undervaluing them, for Ali's benefit), and Ali haggling over both the sums involved and the conditions. Eventually, in April 1819, the exodus took place of 3,000 Parganots—the whole of the remaining population—carrying the icons from their churches and the bones from the graves of their ancestors.[353] The issue of Parga had become a major obstacle to good relations between London and

Istanbul, so the British were relieved to see it brought to an end, albeit on terms that were widely seen as a stain on the honour of British foreign policy. But at the same time Ali's relations with the Sultan were deteriorating, and in the following year a *firman* was issued deposing him from his *paşalık* and declaring him a rebel. Less than three years after his triumphal entry into Parga, Ali Pasha's forces were heavily defeated by the Sultan's army. The whole fabric of rule which he had laboured throughout his adult life to construct was swept aside, and on 5 February 1822 he himself was killed.

XV

From this survey of Ali Pasha's relations with Great Britain during the Napoleonic period, some conclusions emerge quite clearly. Britain's interest in cultivating Ali Pasha was always primarily concerned with countering French power. The greatest fear was of a French invasion of Ottoman territory, which might lead to the expulsion of the Sultan from Europe. Napoleon's long-term strategy in this regard was unknown—and indeed unknowable, as he did not have one; at different times he toyed with various ideas for invasions or possible joint partitions, but the military planning never got beyond the stage of elementary reconnaissance. Nevertheless, the fears of the British were reasonable. Nor was it only the coast of Epirus or Albania that formed the possible target for a French invasion. Both Jack Morier and William Leake spent some of their time studying the terrain, and the political situation, in other parts of the mainland down to the southern Peloponnese. The fact that during most of this period Ali had control or influence, through his sons, over these territories too was another reason for making efforts to align him with British interests. At the same time, however, British policy-makers were conscious of the fact that if Napoleon did invade, he would appeal to the local people as a liberator, calling on them to shake off the yoke of Ottoman rule. Associating British power and prestige with the fortune of one notoriously exacting Ottoman governor was therefore a policy with potential drawbacks. That is why the initial instructions to Morier ordered him to urge Ali and other local rulers to treat the Greeks with greater 'lenity', and why Leake, commenting in 1807 on the broadly pro-British feelings of the Greek population, warned that close links with Ali might be damaging unless he could be persuaded to see 'the impolicy of his cruel conduct towards them'.[354] British cooperation with Ali thus involved, in principle at least, not merely seeking his support in military or logistical matters, but also trying to change his behaviour. Yet the agents who were sent to deal with him were provided with very little in the way of either carrots or sticks with which to bring that about.

The presence of the French on Corfu, from 1807 until the end of the war, was another case of an apparently simple reason for the British cultivation of Ali

Pasha that carried with it some more complex implications. Maintaining the blockade—which, to be effective, required Ali's cooperation—was the relatively simple task. But this gave the British an interest in supporting Ali's strategy of expanding his control over the coastal areas of north-western Greece and southern Albania, since Çamëri, Himarë and Vlorë were the main sources of foodstuffs and other provisions reaching Corfu. Britain was thus drawn, to some extent, into an involvement in a range of local political and territorial disputes. A foretaste of this had already occurred in 1805, when Jack Morier found himself at odds with Count Mocenigo, the Russian minister on Corfu, over the Russian policy of supporting resistance to Ali Pasha on the mainland. That posed in some ways a more awkward political problem, as Russia and Britain then enjoyed friendly relations; when the French took up the same policy, subsidizing Ali's local enemies and supplying Ibrahim Pasha with weapons and artillery officers, the appropriate British response may have seemed on the face of it much more straightforward. Yet from late 1809 onwards, when the British occupied the majority of the Ionian Islands, involvement in these local political disputes became more problematic. The 'robbers' whose extradition from the islands Ali demanded so insistently were, as the British came to realize, in some cases his political opponents; and it was not a coincidence that they had sought refuge on the islands, as the local populations there were strongly hostile to Ali too. During the first period of British contacts with Ali Pasha, the general pattern was that the agents who dealt with him directly recommended supporting his local expansionism against such enemies as the Çams (as Morier did in 1806, and Leake in 1808), while higher authorities, who were further away, expressed uncertainty or caution (as Collingwood did in early 1809). In the later period, the higher authorities were senior officers on the Ionian Islands; as we have seen, some of them took a sceptical attitude, and one of them (Lowe in 1811) not only doubted the wisdom of supporting Ali in his Albanian conflicts, but accused the British local agent, George Foresti—who continued the Morier-Leake line in these matters—of being 'more a servant of the Vizir, then of the British public'.[355]

In addition to his ability to act against the French, there was, from the British point of view, one other significant aspect of Ali Pasha's power that made him a person worth cultivating: his influence in Istanbul. The first person to claim that he used it in a pro-British way seems to have been Ali himself, in the letter to George III which Said Ahmed brought to London in 1808: 'At the time, Sir, that your late Ambassador was sent to Constantinople, I wrote to the Government exhorting it to make peace...My request has been complied with.'[356] Soon afterwards the claim was accepted by both Collingwood and Adair; and although the latter would eventually characterize it as unverifiable, he had no hesitation in appealing to Ali for help over the Ottoman government's policy towards Persia in 1809: 'Let his highness be assured that such is the present state of the Ottoman Councils, that it is only by the interposition of some powerful Mind like his own that the Empire can be saved from the mischief which awaits it.'[357] In 1812 Stratford Canning wanted Ali to use his influence in Istanbul to gain acceptance for the terms of the Treaty of Bucharest, and as late as 1814 Sir Robert Liston was still reminding London 'that His Influence at the Seat of Government is still great; and that He has it in His power either to do us essential mischief or to render good service.'[358] No doubt Ali's influence was stronger or weaker at different times, according to the composition of the Sultan's *divan*; so there is no contradiction involved in the fact that, conversely, he sometimes appealed to the British to use their influence in Istanbul for his benefit. As we have seen, in his first meetings with Leake at the end of 1804 he expressed the hope that the new British Ambassador, Sir Charles Arbuthnot, would ask for Ali to be given power over the ex-Venetian places on the mainland; and soon afterwards Morier was transmitting not only that request, but also Ali's wish that the British would obtain 'the sanction of the Porte to all his measures & thus to be enabled to transmit his power to his children.'[359] In later years he would benefit from interventions by the British Ambassador in Istanbul, either persuading the Ottoman government to suspend its order to Ali to bring troops to the front, or countering the vigorous efforts of the French Ambassador to undermine him.[360]

One aspect of this mutual relationship has not been discussed above, and deserves brief notice here: the flow of news and information. Ali Pasha had a voracious appetite for international news. Pouqueville wrote in 1811 that 'he informs himself in minute details about the state of Europe'; when Henry Holland first met him in November 1812 Ali immediately asked for news of the French army in Russia, and 'it was evident that the information we gave, was not new to him.'[361] Much of his information came from the far-flung network of Epirot merchant families, whose members, as Holland noted, were located in places such as Germany, Moscow and Istanbul; Vienna was another such trading centre; and one month before Holland's visit, Pouqueville complained that Greek merchants in Venice, Trieste, Rijeka and Dubrovnik were sending 'scandalous' reports about French military misfortunes.[362] Sometimes the information could be of value to the British, either because it reached them sooner by this route, or because Ali had news from sources (in the government in Istanbul, or at the Russian–Ottoman peace negotiations) that were not otherwise accessible to them. And at the same time, Ali Pasha was constantly asking the British for news and information; in a letter to Collingwood in June 1808, for instance, he wrote: 'I beg of your Excellency to favour me with any news you have.'[363]

The British were happy to oblige, not only because this was part of maintaining good relations with Ali Pasha, but also because it gave them an opportunity to pass on news of Allied military successes and French reverses—information which could then be sent by Ali to his own contacts in Istanbul. In September 1808, for example, the Austrian Ambassador reported that Ali's agent there had passed on to the *reis efendi* a letter to Ali from Spiridion Foresti in Malta,

containing much news of French defeats in Spain.[364] Spiridion Foresti was not the
only person writing to Ali from Malta at that time; David Morier was also giving
him news of French military setbacks, and according to Pouqueville Ali had his
own agent in Malta, 'Mefoud Effendi', who sent him English news every two
weeks—extracts from which were then sent by Ali to Istanbul.[365] One year later
Ali Pasha told William Leake that he had orders from the Ottoman government
to send them any intelligence he received about events in Europe; he said that he
sent them Leake's news reports unchanged, but modified the ones he received
from Pouqueville. The British were thus well aware of Ali's potential value to them
in these matters, and continued to feed him with suitable information. In March
1812, for example, Ali thanked Airey for sending him a 'gazette' with news of
Wellington's victory (on 19 January) at Ciudad Rodrigo.[366]

That the relationship between Ali Pasha and the British was a reciprocal one,
involving varying degrees of mutual benefit, is clear at almost every level. Ali's
military importance to them was significant, though mostly in the realms of
potentiality: the key assumption was that he would raise many thousands of
troops in the event of a French invasion of the mainland. For Ali, on the other
hand, the military importance of the British was more practical, ranging from the
supply of arms, ammunition and gunpowder, which he requested so frequently
and received twice, to the actual presence of British warships off his shores. As we
have seen, he told George Foresti in 1810 that the British naval presence was a vital
protection for him, and as late as the autumn of 1812 he was seeking promises of
British assistance in the event of a French attack; this was when Liston felt obliged
to assure Ali's secretary that 'if his Master were attacked by France ... [Britain
would] come to his assistance with fleets, armies, supplies of every kind, in short,
to defend him to the utmost of Her power.'[367] An underlying sense of mutual
need and mutual benefit was what maintained the essential stability of the relationship between Ali and the British, despite all the causes of irritation and friction that arose—the long-running British failures to respond to requests of
various kinds, the refusal by them to hand over Lefkada or Parga, Ali's building of
the fortress opposite Lefkada (where, in the end, British pressure seems to have
faced him down), the contentious issue of the fugitive 'robbers' (on which, again,
Ali had to accept defeat), and so on. While it is certainly true that the extent of
Ali's double-dealing with the French was never fully appreciated by the British,
they did have some inklings of it, not least because of George Foresti's intercep-
tion of French correspondence. But they were able to discount it, for the simple
reason that, where the basic alignment of interests was concerned, they knew
that—unless and until Britain itself underwent a general defeat by France—Ali
had more to gain from British support and British protection.

The most recent study to consider these matters, Katherine Fleming's *The
Muslim Bonaparte* (1999), comes to a very different conclusion. This study
deserves some comment here, as it is the only recent full-length work on Ali by a

Western academic, and has been both widely acclaimed and influential. Professor Fleming writes that 'In the case of Ali…France and Britain felt, if anything, a sense of threat, and clearly they perceived that he had the upper hand in diplomatic dealings for the better part of a quarter century.' She also remarks that 'By 1811, Ali had managed to establish a position of geographic, psychological, and strategic dominance over the British in the region of the Ionian Islands.' She continues: 'British concern over the tenuousness of their position had nothing to do with the Ottoman government but was based entirely on Ali's obvious strength and superior position.' No evidence of such feelings of 'threat', 'dominance' or 'concern' is presented. Readers who have followed the detailed account given above, which was based on a study of the original documents, will be aware of various different interests and preoccupations at work at different times, but not of anything that could possibly serve as the basis of such a characterization.[368] The only justification put forward by Fleming consists of a long quotation from the report written by William Hamilton, the very first British diplomatic official to visit Ali Pasha, in 1803.[369] This gave a very positive description of Ali's power, ability and influence; but it expressed no sense of 'threat' or 'concern' (quite the contrary, as it was boosting his credentials as an ally), and cannot in any case be used as evidence of how the British experienced their relationship with Ali Pasha, which it preceded. This quotation is immediately followed, in Fleming's account, by the comment, 'If in 1803 the British were worried by Ali, by 1811 they were positively fearful'; but again no evidence is offered for such a very puzzling claim.[370]

Fleming's interpretation serves a larger purpose, however. It is part of a more general account, framed by the argument set out in Edward Said's *Orientalism* (1978), of how and why Western writers used negative terms to describe Ali's personal character or his method of government. She explains:

> descriptions of Ali's 'cruelty' and 'despotism' were ubiquitous, indeed de rigueur features of any account of him. As the British position in the Adriatic vis-à-vis Ali became increasingly tenuous, weak, and dependent, this denigrating, formulaic description was retained and heightened. It seems that it functioned almost as a compensatory device with which the British swept away their own insecurities in relation to Ali and heightened his otherness, portraying him in increasingly pejorative, Orientalist terms…Subsequent Western accounts, both diplomatic histories and biographies of Ali, have retained this heightened Othering while downplaying or eliding entirely the relative strategic weaknesses of the European powers in relation to Ali.[371]

Two subsequent chapters of her book are then devoted to 'Orientalist strategies' and 'Orientalist themes'; here writings by those who knew Ali and the local conditions very well, such as Leake, are intermingled with those of travellers who made brief visits to Ioannina, as well as much later bellelettristic authors with no direct experience at all. Leake is dismissed more than once as merely a typical Orientalist, and his very scholarly interest in classical geography (which led him to identify on the ground numerous ancient sites in northern Greece for the first time) is also presented as just another example of 'the mechanisms of othering'. As Fleming observes, 'The lack of any imperial/colonial control over Ali's lands, coupled with his primacy in the region, demanded an alternative basis for a European sense of dominance over him. The romantic ideal of ancient Greece provided Europe with a surrogate imperialism, whereby Ali's lands could be ideologically and philosophically claimed, controlled, and colonized.'[372]

To this general account of 'Orientalizing', which is broadly familiar insofar as it fits a Saidian template, Fleming does however add one surprising twist: the claim that 'Ali came to be intimately familiar with the Orientalist vision of him and...cleverly manipulated it to his advantage.' The rationale of this manipulation lay in his 'realization that it was perhaps in his best interests to be seen as weak, silly, and fundamentally nonthreatening'; in this way 'it was less likely that he would be perceived as a viable military competitor and targeted for systematic suppression.'[373] In Fleming's view he was highly successful in this: a 'clever and cynical manipulation of his European visitors' (a category that includes Morier and Leake) was taking place, and 'Ali's visitors...could not afford to entertain the possibility that this was the case.' Yet there is a strange internal tension in Fleming's argument. While supposing that this tactic made him seem weak and unthreatening, she also writes that his 'erratic behavior' and 'much advertised cruelties' were all 'intentionally heightened and designed by Ali to confirm the West's view of him as the quintessential Oriental Despot'; a very cruel and unpredictable despot was surely just the sort of character that might have seemed thoroughly threatening, and indeed it was an essential part of Fleming's claim about the diplomatic relations of the British with Ali (as quoted above) to say that they did feel threatened by him.[374]

Another tension in the argument arises from the fact that at the same time, in Fleming's words, Ali 'adjusted his behavior so as to appear more European to his guests'. Much more could be said about Ali's interest in Western European ways of doing things, which extended far beyond the carpets and ornaments he installed in his palaces (the evidence considered by Fleming); one might mention, for instance, his eagerness to question Henry Holland about the latest developments in telescopes, microscopes and electricity, or his plan to send his youngest son, Salih, to be educated in Western Europe. Holland himself noted that 'A comparative freedom from Turkish prejudices was one of the most obvious and striking circumstances in the conversation of this man', and was particularly struck by the fact that, unlike the many haughty Ottomans he encountered, Ali Pasha displayed a 'constant seeking after information, which might enable him to remedy the deficiencies under which he laboured'.[375] But Fleming's main focus is on her concurrent and contrary theory about Ali's deliberate intensifying of his own image as an 'Oriental Despot'; this, in the end, becomes the master-theme of her book. She discusses two cases of his cruel and despotic behaviour: the massacre at Kardhiq, and the notorious drowning in the lake at Ioannina of several young women, one of whom was said to have been wooed and/or seduced by Ali's son Muhtar. Both of these actions were shocking, and were intended to be so: they were minatory displays of power, addressed to the wider population. But Fleming gives no example of Ali 'intentionally heightening' the horror of these particular events in conversations with Western visitors—or, indeed, discussing them at all. Her only evidence is a statement by Leake that whereas Ali clearly hoped to make a favourable impression on foreign visitors, 'Nevertheless, he has little scruple in alluding to those actions of his life which are the least likely to obtain such favour, though he generally endeavours to give such a colouring to them as shall make them appear less criminal.'[376] Leake's perception, then, was that whilst on the one hand Ali was not so ashamed of his ill-deeds as to forbear to speak about them altogether, on the other hand, far from 'heightening' them, he tried to give explanations that would at least mitigate, if not justify, the wrongs he had done. It is hard to find any comment by Ali, in the voluminous reports of Morier, Leake and Foresti, that consists of boasting about or seeking to exaggerate his killings and oppressions; and these three men, between them, spent a huge amount of time in his company.

In fairness, two comments (unmentioned by Fleming) from the reports of Pouqueville should be cited here. He did note that Ali had said to him, when leaving Ioannina in March 1812 to deal with the defeated men of Kardhiq: 'I have shed so much blood, I dare not look back!'—perhaps more a rueful comment on the necessity of his situation (as he saw it) than a boast. And one month earlier Pouqueville also recorded Ali's statement to him that over the years he had arranged the assassinations of many rival *bey*s, and that the serving-boys at his court all had relatives who had been killed by his order.[377] The reference to the serving-boys needs to be understood in context (these youths were not a random selection of the population—their presence derived from the local tradition of hostage-giving by prominent families, above all, ones in relations of enmity); but the comment was still a serious admission of ill-doing. What it was not was a typical statement by Ali to one of his foreign 'visitors'. On the contrary, it was an exceptional remark, confided to someone who had by now been at Ali's court for six years; it cannot be used as evidence of a regular *modus operandi*. In the end, it may be that the carefully balanced and qualified depiction of Ali by Leake—who spent years in Ioannina, had innumerable conversations with Ali Pasha, travelled widely in the region and spoke Greek with complete fluency—is a better guide to understanding him than any newly devised adaptation, however original and intriguing, of the theory of Orientalist discourse.

Finally, a few brief observations on Ali's own methods, policies and aims. It is surely impossible to consider the whole story of his diplomatic relations with Britain and France, as presented above, without admiring both his skill and his stamina. Ali's ability to play off the two sides, saying utterly contradictory things to them (plus, perhaps, a third contradictory thing to Istanbul), and dropping hints to each that the other might be making a more tempting counter-offer, was extraordinary, even if it did not often achieve the practical results that he sought. His professions of loyalty, when experienced, so to speak, cold on the page by the modern reader, may often seem exaggerated and insincere; but such claims, when made by him in person, were persuasive enough to convince experienced officials such as Bessières, Guès and even, despite repeated disillusionments, Pouqueville. And his sheer persistence was perhaps the most impressive thing of all. When courting the British, Ali was prepared to wait for years for a positive response, uttering only occasional plaintive comments on the silence he experienced; each time he was directly rebuffed, above all over the possession of Lefkada and Parga, he adopted once again a strategy of patience, knowing that he would gain more in the long run from maintaining friendly relations than from breaking them off in a display of wounded pride. Ali thought and planned for the long term. He also acted at long distance, projecting his own diplomacy far into the world of 'Great Power' politics: he sent one envoy to London (twice), and another to follow Napoleon all the way to Tilsit. The first mission to London did reap a positive reward for him; and the failure of the other two came about through no fault of his own.

Ali Pasha was, then, a very accomplished player of the game. But to what end was he playing it? What were the prime motives and aims of all his complex diplomatic manoeuvrings? At the minimum—this at least can be taken for granted—he aimed for sheer survival, involving if possible the preservation of his rule over all the territory he controlled. Beyond that, as the survey given above has demonstrated again and again, his main preoccupation was with the ex-Venetian territories, both on the mainland and off the coast. The basic rationale for this was mentioned at the start of this essay, and bears repeating here. This was no mere acquisitiveness for more square metres of land; these places had a special value in terms of both commerce and security. The Venetians, after all, were canny assessors of those two things, and there were good reasons why they had held these territories tenaciously until the final overthrow of their republic. The islands—especially Corfu, with its fine harbour and near-impregnable citadel—were of huge importance for trade up and down the Adriatic coast; and Preveza had been described by a British visitor in 1795 as 'the port of exportation for much of the produce of Romelia'.[378] Of the four places on the mainland, two—Butrint and Parga—helped to guarantee the security of Corfu, and the other two—Preveza and Vonitsa—controlled the Gulf of Arta. (The guns of the fort of Preveza overlooked the narrow entrance channel itself; Vonitsa was only a very minor port,

but, as the French military engineer Guillaume de Vaudoncourt noted, possession of it by a hostile power would have 'closed against him [*sc.* Ali Pasha] the
only practicable road that goes round the gulf of Arta.') As for Ali's own security
interests: de Vaudoncourt wrote that Parga was 'of infinite importance, owing to
the connections its inhabitants then did and still continue to keep up with the
Paramithians, the Souliots, and the other independent clans... This was one of
the principal seats of the insurrectional movements which agitated the Epirus,
and a secure asylum for the enemies of Ali Pacha.'[379]

There were thus strong intrinsic reasons why Ali should wish to take over these
places. But their occupation by distant foreign powers, neither Venetian nor
Ottoman, introduced some new, extrinsic factors into the situation. For most of
the period we have been considering, the key external powers were France and
Russia. Ali was naturally suspicious of both, not just because they were unwelcome interlopers in the area, but because their intervention took place in a context of European war, where an annexation of Ottoman territories in Europe by
either or both of them was a real possibility. Generally, Russia seemed the more
serious threat. It had long-standing ambitions to take over the Ottoman Danubian
provinces; it had stirred up a Greek revolt in 1770, and was now sponsoring the
rebellion of the Serbs; its historic desire to control Istanbul and the Bosphorus
was well known; and it was also developing a kind of Orthodox irredentist ideology, presenting itself as the natural leader of all Eastern Christians. The relations
of the Russians with Ali Pasha were essentially antagonistic almost from the
moment that they took power in the Ionian Islands, and they were made even
more hostile by the instincts and preferences of Count Mocenigo. Nevertheless,
Ali was still prepared to present himself to them as sympathetic when he thought
some advantage might come of it. (We have seen one example of this, his friendly
conversation with George Flory in 1806; in August 1809 he sent a message to the
Russians, offering to become a 'faithful vassal' of the Tsar; and in 1814–15 he was
still asking for Russian good will and help in relation to the question of Parga.)[380]

The French too might pose as liberators of the Ottomans' Christian subjects,
but their status as 'atheists and not Christians' (as Ali described them to Leake)
reduced their appeal to the Orthodox population.[381] Even on ex-Venetian Corfu
their popularity as rulers sank quite rapidly. French policy was, to begin with,
more pragmatic and positive towards Ali Pasha; a strategy of cooperation with
them would have seemed to him, at first, more likely to yield the territories he
hankered after, even as he resisted every French blandishment or ultimatum over
Butrint. And all the while there was Napoleon's extraordinary and continuing
record of military success to think about: until a very late stage, Ali still had to
keep open some option of alignment with the French, even after it had become
clear that he would be better protected locally, and have a better chance of making
the territorial gains he sought, if he gave his primary support to the British.

Finally, there is the question of Ali Pasha's relationship with the Ottoman government—an issue which has not been a primary concern of this essay, but still
invites some brief reflections. There has long been a temptation for Albanians to
look on Ali Pasha as a kind of proto-nationalist. He has sometimes been presented as intent on building something like an independent Albanian state
(although the majority of its inhabitants could not be described as Albanians in
modern ethnic-linguistic terms); and even without adding this special Albanian
dimension to the issue, it may still be tempting to look on him as someone who
worked consistently to break away from the Ottoman Empire.[382] But some caution is needed in handling such claims.

That Ali was, in almost all practical respects, the autonomous ruler of his territories was a fact that struck all observers. This in itself was not unusual, however.
There were quite a few other such provincial rulers in the European territories of
the Ottoman Empire; as we have seen, Sir Charles Arbuthnot, on returning to
England after his stint as Ambassador in Istanbul, would tell a friend that 'I do
not hesitate in declaring that beyond the walls of Constantinople, the Grand
Signior has not more power than you or I have.'[383] We have also seen Ali's request
for British help in getting the Sultan's agreement to a hereditary succession of
power from him to his children.[384] That may seem like a radical departure from
the Ottoman system, in the direction of independent statehood; but in fact some
kind of familial succession was the rule rather than the exception where most of
the Albanian *paşalık*s were concerned. Only the formal concession of such a
privilege would have been unusual; for the power to replace a refractory governor
was understood to be a basic right of the Sultan, even though in practice it was
also clear that this might be limited by an inability to dislodge the offending pasha
by force of arms.

There was undoubtedly a more general tendency, already well under way at this
time, towards what has been called 'the dynasticization of provincial elites' within
the Ottoman Empire. The most valuable recent study of how the structure of the
Empire was changing during this period has posited a range of competing models.
Sultan Mahmud's centralizing and bureaucratizing principle represented one of
these, but there was an opposing model or 'order' favoured by the provincial
notables, in which, while they enjoyed the opportunity to entrench and dynasti-
cize their local power, they also used that power to act as 'administrative, fiscal,
and military entrepreneurs, whose relations with the Ottoman establishment
were based on ongoing deals, negotiations, and a process of give and take.'[385]
Although Ali Pasha was very obviously an enemy of the centralizing programme,
he can hardly be described as an active exponent or advocate of the 'order of notables'. As we have seen, he gave only the most nominal support to Mustafa
Bayraktar's attempted re-ordering of the Empire, with its 'Deed of Alliance'
expressing the principles of the 'order of notables' in a quasi-constitutionalist way.
From the early 1800s onwards, Ali Pasha's preferred method of dealing with the

government in Istanbul was not to bargain with it as an administrative-military contractor, offering services in return for local power; rather, it was to act as he wished, and then to buy confirmatory support for his actions, or to pay off those who were inclined to punish him. The huge income which he was able to extract from his territories was what made such a *modus operandi* possible, and this in turn must have strengthened his desire to gain new rents, or larger customs revenues, by extending his power on the ground. Not every problem in Istanbul, admittedly, could be solved by these means; his requests for British diplomatic support, mentioned above, were clearly genuine. But sheer financial power was the primary engine of Ali's political activity in the capital, and compared with that, all else was secondary.[386]

In this way it is surely right to see Ali Pasha as more independent-minded than most—perhaps all—of the other great 'notables' of Ottoman Europe. But does that mean that he was actively seeking independence in the modern political sense? At various times he may have said things to his foreign interlocutors that did give that impression. Pouqueville confidently asserted in 1806 that Ali was planning to carve out a personal territory that would stretch as far as Salonica; five years later he wrote that Ali's aim was to gain independent power 'to counterbalance the authority of the Sultan'.[387] Even if we assume that these comments were based on things that Ali had said, we still need to bear in mind the context of such remarks. At a time when the possibility of a French invasion and partition of the Empire was to be taken seriously, he would have wanted to seem, in French eyes, a potential participant in that process, a man who could be installed as a powerful vassal ruler, free of any residual loyalties to the Sultan.

A clear statement of what Ali Pasha's preferred long-term goal might have been if there had been no European war and no prospect of the collapse of the Empire is not available. Nor, during this whole period of conflict, might there have been any such idea in his head, to be stated clearly or otherwise; all the evidence which we do have is the product of the circumstances that actually obtained. Thus as early as 1804, as we have seen, he told Jack Morier that 'he foresees that the Provinces which only form part of a disjointed Empire must sooner or later fall a Prey to it's powerful Neighbours and consequently his aim now is to court the Protection of some great Nation by whose Influence he may obtain from Others the Acknowledgement of a degree of Independence (perhaps similar to that of the Barbary States) which he hopes may save his Power from the common Wreck of The Turks.'[388] This was a plan both reactive and defensive, involving the 'Protection' of a European power, and the model he had in mind was of *de facto* independence, like that of the rulers of Algiers, Tunis and Tripoli, under *de jure* suzerainty. The idea that some sort of independence would be made necessary by an Ottoman collapse remained with him; but if the kind of independent entity he envisaged turned gradually into something more like a regular West European state, that may have been because of the promptings of the West Europeans themselves. One of the few points on which Jack Morier did agree with Count Mocenigo when they met on Corfu in early 1805 was that if Napoleon invaded the Ottoman Empire, he would offer independent statehood to Ali Pasha. The key question which William Leake was tasked with putting to Ali when he renewed contact with him in late 1807 was whether, in the event of an Ottoman collapse, he would have 'the will or the means to maintain...independence against France and Russia'. That question might in theory have concerned just a temporary state of affairs before the restoration of sultanic rule; but Leake's first report on his meeting with Ali on the beach north of Preveza referred to the prospect of Ali becoming a 'sovereign power'.[389] When the young Greek statesman Ioannēs Kapodistrias (then in Russian service) composed a long memoir on Ali Pasha in 1812, he wrote that in the event of a dissolution of the Ottoman Empire, Ali hoped to obtain a 'kingdom of Epirus and Albania'—again, a phrase that conjures up a European-style state.[390]

What Ali Pasha most clearly wanted was to exercise full control over a large area of territory, extracting from it the money and men that he needed. In itself, the Ottoman Empire was not an obstacle to that; indeed, the decentralized and by some standards dysfunctional system that prevailed during this period was well suited to his attaining such a goal. To a governor in his position independence and autonomy were not absolutes, but ranges of a spectrum, and there was probably enough room, in principle, within the existing Ottoman system for the satisfaction of Ali's fundamental desires. However, the wars unleashed by the French Revolution destabilized that situation, as they disrupted so much else. The collapse of Venetian power immediately set off a new dynamic in the region; the threat of Napoleonic invasion changed things too; and the reality of a renewed Russian–Ottoman war also had large consequences. Ali Pasha concentrated his thoughts and energies on benefiting as he could from all these changes; but at the same time the new circumstances put Ottoman power in much greater danger, and his repeated refusal to contribute an army to its defence, while he still opposed any prospect of a Russian–Ottoman peace agreement, placed him in an uncomfortably exposed position. Eventually, in the aftermath of the Napoleonic wars, his acquisition of Parga did mark the final consolidation of his territorial power on the mainland. But that was of little avail when the military strength of a centralizing Sultan was finally turned against him. His own power had been very great while it had lasted, however; and it is testimony to his extraordinary skill that he had sustained it, in one of the most internationally contested areas of the Ottoman Empire, through all the twists and turns of a major European war.

9

British Diplomacy and the League of Prizren, 1878–1880

The 1870s and 1880s were an unusual period in the history of British diplomacy in the Balkans—unusual because, for several years, Britain played a leading role. It was thanks to the reaction of the British Foreign Secretary, Lord Salisbury, to the proposals contained in the Treaty of San Stefano that the Great Powers agreed to come together at the Congress of Berlin. Salisbury's 'Circular', which subjected each provision of San Stefano to strenuous criticism, and which was sent to all the Great Powers on 1 April 1878, has been described as 'one of the greatest State Papers in British history', and it certainly laid the foundations of the Congress's work. But Salisbury also went further than that, designing much of the structure that was built on those foundations: by means of three secret bilateral agreements with the Ottoman Empire, Austria-Hungary and Russia, he had 'made the great issues of the Berlin Congress foregone conclusions even before it was officially summoned'.[1] The transfer of Cyprus to British rule gave Britain a much closer interest in the affairs of the Middle East; her diplomacy played a key role in the years immediately following the Congress, as British policy revived the idea of a 'Concert of Europe'—in other words, of co-ordinated action by the Great Powers, used in this case to put pressure on the Ottoman government to fulfil its new Treaty obligations.[2]

This activism on the part of the British government reflected the importance which the whole issue of 'Turkey-in-Europe' had acquired in British political debate during the previous few years. Protests against Ottoman atrocities (first in Hercegovina in 1875, then in Bulgaria in 1876) had attracted mass support in Britain; it was his campaigning on this issue in 1876–7 that relaunched the political career of the elderly Gladstone. But on the other hand the declaration of war by Russia against the Ottoman Empire in 1877, and the prospect of a Russian conquest and occupation of Istanbul, had caused considerable alarm in British political circles. Thanks partly to its recent advances in Central Asia, Russian expansion was seen as a geopolitical threat to British rule in India; the idea of Russia dominating the eastern Mediterranean (and thus, perhaps, controlling access to the Suez Canal) was especially worrying. While the Liberal ex-Prime Minister Gladstone championed the Bulgarians and Serbs, whom the Russians supported, the Conservative Prime Minister Disraeli proclaimed the overriding interest of the British Empire. By 1878 public opinion was on Disraeli's side, and

Rebels, Believers, Survivors: Studies in the History of the Albanians. Noel Malcolm,
Oxford University Press (2020). © Noel Malcolm. DOI: 10.1093/oso/9780198857297.001.0001

the idea of going to war against Russia in defence of Turkey did not seem so strange to a country which had done precisely that—in the Crimea—just under a quarter of a century before.

However, although British political opinion was thus polarized into anti-Ottoman and pro-Ottoman elements, it would be wrong to see this division simply as a matter of humanitarianism versus imperial *Realpolitik*. There were those on Disraeli's side who had moral and humanitarian objections to the Russians (the Catholic press, for example, constantly reminded its readers of Russian atrocities in Poland); such feelings were strengthened in 1878 by news of the mass expulsions and mass killings of Muslims (by Russians, Serbs and Bulgarians) in several parts of the Balkans. And on the Gladstonian side there were also many who thought that propping up the Ottoman regime was false *Realpolitik*, and that a more realistic policy required the creation of new national states as the building-blocks for any future stability in the region.[3]

These geopolitical debates included, it must be said, remarkably little discussion of Albanian issues.[4] Indeed, in some ways the terms of these debates tended to exclude the Albanians from consideration: they simply did not fit the pattern of these arguments. The Gladstonians talked constantly about the national rights of the 'Christians' in the Balkans; although there was some awareness of the existence of Catholic and Orthodox Albanians, the Albanians in general were thought of as a Muslim population, and when 'Arnauts' were mentioned at all, they were often associated with the Ottoman forces carrying out repressive measures against the Christians. On the other hand, the Disraelians were seeking to defend or strengthen the territorial integrity and administrative viability of the Ottoman Empire. They regarded the Albanian lands as a key component of that Empire in Europe; the idea that the Albanians might also seek self-government was alien to them, and they continued to regard the maintenance of Ottoman rule over the Albanians as a condition of stability, not as a source of instability.

There was thus no particular guiding doctrine, no dominant line, to determine British diplomacy towards the Albanians. Various different interpretations were possible, and the interests of the Albanians were always likely to be subordinated to the interests of other populations, or of some or other of the Great Powers. In addition, it is worth remembering that no country during this period had an absolutely monolithic diplomatic machine. Modern historians tend to talk of the preferences and demands of 'Whitehall', 'the Quai d'Orsay' or 'the Ballplatz', as if each were of only one mind; in most cases, closer inspection will reveal an internal debate in which many different interests and attitudes were at work. British policy towards the Albanians during this period furnishes, I believe, a classic example of this phenomenon.

Let us begin with the 'men on the ground'—the British consular officials in Prizren and Shkodër. Consul Charles Louis St. John arrived in Prizren in the autumn of 1879; his special responsibility, in accordance with the provisions of the Treaty of Berlin, was to investigate the situation of the Christians in the Prizren region, but of course he was also expected to furnish information about the general political situation. From the moment of his arrival there, he regarded the League as a Muslim organization—and, therefore, as a hostile and dangerous one. He reported to Lord Salisbury that 'my arrival has caused the greatest satisfaction to the Christian community, numbering at Prizrend about 5,000', but that 'the Mussulman population, numbering about 25,000...look upon me as a spy'; and, commenting on the fact that all real power was now in the hands of the League, he remarked that 'your Lordship will observe how completely the fate of the Christian population and the maintenance of public security now depends, not on the authorities appointed by the Porte...but on a set of lawless fanatics.'[5] He was in fact one of three consuls there, the others being from Austria (the power which had recently occupied Bosnia and sent troops into the Sancak of Novi Pazar) and Russia (the power which had sent an army into the Balkans in the previous year); that local Albanians felt some suspicions about the arrival of such a consular corps is easily understandable. St. John appears to have depended to a large extent on his consular colleagues, not only in acquiring specific information, but also in framing his general interpretation of the situation. Both Austria and Russia were suspicious of Italian interests in this part of the Balkans; it is surely not a coincidence that within a few weeks of his arrival there, St. John was sending despatches to London full of warnings about Italian manoeuvrings, the sending of Italian 'propaganda' via Italian missionaries, and even a rumour that the League was hoping to turn its territory into an Italian protectorate.[6] St. John did in fact develop a particularly close friendship with his Russian colleague, Ivan Yastrebov, and his entire interpretation of the Albanian issue was coloured by Yastrebov's prejudices. Thus in 1880 he argued, on the basis of information supplied by Yastrebov, that the Prizren region belonged to Serbia both historically and ethnically; he argued that half of the Albanians in Kosovo were not real Albanians but merely Albanianized Slavs, and he even claimed that 'the Albanian dialect [is] only used by the tribes inhabiting the mountains west of the longitude of Prisrend'.[7] His views were promptly dismissed by the more senior British diplomat Lord Edmond Fitzmaurice, who remarked that they were 'almost peculiar to himself'; Fitzmaurice's own information about the region came from one of the leading Albanian intellectuals in Istanbul, Kostandin Kristoforidhi, who told a very different story.[8] Overall, St. John's opinions do not seem to have had any strong influence on the formation of British policy. He serves, rather, as a reminder of the fact that the man 'on the ground' might sometimes be even more restricted in his sources of information than others who were further away.

The other most important man on the ground was Consul William Kirby Green, in Shkodër. His case is in some ways similar to St. John's; he too seems to have been heavily influenced by another member of the consular corps. But unlike St. John, Kirby Green did have a real influence on policy-making: it was he who persuaded the British Government to adopt the cession of Ulcinj (Ulqin, Dulcigno) as the solution to the territorial dispute which had triggered the creation of the League.

The person who exerted decisive influence on Kirby Green's thinking was Ritter Ferdinand von Lippich, the consul-general of Austria-Hungary in Shkodër. Von Lippich was a Slovene, from Gorizia; he had been in the region for more than a decade, and had served as consul in the *vilayet* (Ottoman administrative province) of Kosovo.[9] His experience clearly carried great weight: Kirby Green disagreed with him about almost nothing, and became, in effect, an active supporter of Austrian policy in the region. Such support was not especially out of keeping with general British diplomacy in the period during and just after the Congress of Berlin, which depended heavily on cooperation with Austria. Nevertheless, Austria did have its own particular interests to pursue, especially where the Albanian lands were concerned. Heavily committed as they were to the occupation of Bosnia and Hercegovina, the Austrians could not envisage taking full responsibility for Albania too; but they were fearful of Italian ambitions to annexe Albania, and felt that any movement towards the unification of the Albanians might lead eventually towards their seeking some kind of Italian protectorate. As the official protector of the Albanian Catholics, Austria also disliked the idea of a unified Albania because the Catholics would be a minority in it. The preferred policy, therefore, was to emphasize differences between the Muslim and Catholic Albanians, and to work gradually towards the separate establishment of a northern Albanian Catholic territorial unit—while, at the same time, guarding against either unnecessary friction with Montenegro, or any unnecessary strengthening of Montenegro (which might encourage Montenegrin territorial ambitions towards Hercegovina).[10]

Accordingly, Kirby Green's assumptions were that the only Albanians who had any serious autonomist tendencies were the Roman Catholics; that the League of Prizren was essentially a Muslim organization; that the League was therefore incapable of practising any real cooperation with Catholics; and that the League was little more than a tool of the Ottoman government, called into existence only to obstruct the cession of territory required by the Treaty of Berlin. The most he would accept was that the League was a creature of the government which had run somewhat out of control; he used this argument to threaten the governor of Shkodër with an Austrian invasion, on the grounds that it was a similar loss of governmental control in Bosnia that had necessitated the Austrian occupation of that territory.[11] In Kirby Green's mind, the only possible motive forces were either Ottoman policy, or the innate tendency of Albanians towards anarchy and violence: commenting on the title 'League of National Safety' used by the League of Prizren, he wrote that if the Ottomans did not reassert their authority, 'the tactics of the turbulent in North Albania will get the upper hand, and the pillage of rich and defenceless districts will commence, for the only meaning attached by these people to "national safety" is licence.'[12] He somehow managed to maintain this view even in the face of many reports which noted that conditions of public safety (and, for that matter, the treatment of Christians) greatly improved when areas came under the full control of the League.

Similarly, Kirby Green resolutely maintained his opinion that there was no 'national' dimension to the League's activities or ambitions. On 30 September 1878 he reported: 'I am only disposed to attach importance to the League as an organization of the localities directly affected by the territorial concessions made by the Treaty to Montenegro, and not as one embracing in any strong body the rest of Albania'; coincidentally, this interpretation was contradicted by a report written on the very same day by Consul Blunt in Larissa, who noted that many of the Albanian soldiers who had deserted to the League were Tosks from Epirus.[13] Six weeks later Kirby Green insisted that 'the term "national" must not be taken to mean even the shadow of a desire for separation from the Sultan's rule.'[14] During subsequent months he had many opportunities to observe support for the League among the Catholics of the Shkodër region, and to hear expressions of interest in autonomy or even eventual independence; yet he continued to treat cooperation between Christians and Muslims as an anomaly, and to assume that only the Catholics could possibly wish for full self-government. Thus in April 1880 he wrote: 'For the moment the Mahommedans and Christians of this province are undoubtedly working together. If the Porte permits them to continue much longer in this course, the approaching struggle...will probably result in the determination of the Christians to break away from Ottoman rule, and it will then be too late for the Mahommedans, who are the minority, to remember their allegiance to the Sultan.'[15] A week later he was obliged to remark: 'the enthusiasm which exists to a most remarkable degree among the Roman Catholic Albanians is not solely developed by a determination to prevent any of their country falling into Slav hands, but...it is also aroused by a secret conviction that a favourable opportunity has presented itself for shaking off the Ottoman yoke; and I have observed, much to my surprise, that this feeling is not unknown to the Mussulman Albanians.'[16]

Kirby Green's closeness to Austrian policy is the key to understanding the most significant intervention made by him in the diplomatic history of these territories: his advocacy of the ceding of the town and coastal district of Ulcinj. The plan seems to have been worked out by Kirby Green and Captain Sale (an officer of the Royal Engineers who was a member of the frontier commission); but it was Kirby Green who ensured its acceptance by the British government.[17] Writing to London on 29 May 1880, he declared: 'I have fully discussed with M. Lippich, the Austrian Consul-General, the question of a cession of territory to Montenegro to the west of Lake Scutari, in lieu of territory defined in the Convention...On not one single point have M. Lippich and I differed.'[18] In a subsequent despatch he set out the advantages of this new plan (as opposed to both the original provisions of the Treaty of Berlin, for the cession of Gusinje (Guci) and Plav (Plavë), and the so-called 'Corti Compromise' of April 1880, which would have ceded the Catholic Albanian areas of Hoti, Gruda and Kelmendi); all the arguments he set out here coincided, implicitly or even explicitly, with the dictates of Austrian policy. Thus he argued that it was absolutely necessary to find some Albanian-inhabited territory to hand over to Montenegro, on the grounds that 'when it is admitted that no compensation is obtainable on the Albanian side, it may be sought on that of the Herzegovina. The contemplation of the difficulties which such an attempt at such a solution would bring upon Austria-Hungary has attractions for those who are not well-wishers of that Empire which it is unnecessary to describe.' He went on to point out that the Corti Compromise would have fatally weakened the Catholic element in northern Albania: 'The incorporation of the Gruda and Hotti tribes with Montenegro would be a death-blow to the hope of a North Albanian autonomous province.' He claimed that giving extra coastal territory to Montenegro would reduce the influence of the highland Montenegrins on that country's policies, and would 'make the Principality amenable, in some degree, to the influence of the maritime force of the Western Powers' (the nearest such maritime force being, of course, the Austro-Hungarian navy). And he concluded: 'For these reasons, from a North Albanian point of view, it is of vital importance that the Roman Catholic tribes should remain intact, whilst the retraction of the frontier to the mouth of the River Bojana, and the loss of a small outlying town, would be more of an advantage than otherwise.'[19] What he called a 'North Albanian' point of view was very much an Austrian view of a North Albanian point of view.

In his long report of 29 May 1880, Kirby Green not only argued for this new territorial concession, but also expressed his ideas about the implementation, in the Albanian lands, of the proposals for administrative reform set out in the Treaty of Berlin. 'I share M. Lippich's opinion', he wrote, 'that it would be premature and unnecessary to attempt to extend the reforms in the administration to much beyond the present limits of the Vilayet of Scutari.'[20] In other words, he was keen that in this way too the predominantly Catholic area of northern Albania should be hived off from the other Albanian *vilayet*s and receive exclusive treatment. On this point, Kirby Green met with strong resistance from the Special Ambassador of Britain in Istanbul, George Goschen, who protested to the Foreign Secretary, complaining that the overall policy towards both northern and southern Albania was not a matter to be entrusted to a mere consular official, and setting out his own view that a united Albania was greatly to be preferred.[21] Kirby Green did not, in the end, determine long-term policy towards the whole of Albania; but he did play a significant part in sealing the long-term fate of the Albanians of Ulcinj.

We have seen, then, that British diplomats could be influenced by either Russian or Austrian policies. One other country exerted a powerful attraction on British minds: Greece. As suffering Christians, the Greeks had attracted strong

Gladstonian sympathies; as the supposed heirs to ancient Greek civilization, they were capable of catching the interest of any British person who had enjoyed a classical education. Philhellenism was a strong current in British political culture, with a long and honourable history. While the diplomats on the ground do not seem to have been particularly affected by it, there was at least one senior figure involved in British diplomacy who had been a very active philhellene: Charles Dilke, who became Under-Secretary of State for Foreign Affairs in 1880, and was the new government's spokesman for foreign affairs in the House of Commons. Influenced by his close friend Lord Edmond Fitzmaurice (who shared Goschen's views on the Albanians), Dilke was prepared to work for a united Albania, but on one condition—and it was a condition that virtually negated any idea of genuine Albanian statehood. His proposal was for an Albanian province which would enjoy not only autonomous status within the Ottoman Empire, but also a 'personal union' with Greece: in other words, it would be ruled, in a personal capacity, by the King of the Hellenes.[22] He discussed the idea with Goschen, who evidently thought it unrealistic, but wanted to encourage him to continue to think in terms of Albanian autonomy. 'I have given a great deal of thought to the Albanian question', Goschen wrote. 'Albanian autonomy with personal union to Greece would be a very valuable solution for Europe, but the Turk will struggle hard to outbid the Greeks, & the Albanians are very strong in the Palace, and are trusted all over the Empire, it seems. But autonomy I think they will & must have in some shape.'[23] Later that year, Dilke discussed his pet project with the Greek chargé d'affaires in London, who sought the views of his government; but, not surprisingly, nothing ever came of it.[24] Dilke was still putting forward this proposal seven years later, when he wrote his book *The Present Position of European Politics*; the only thing that had changed was that he was now advocating pushing the Greek border as far north as possible, so that the 'autonomous' Albania attached to it would in any case be little more than a rump of Albanian territory.[25]

Elements within the British diplomatic machine were thus supporting Russia (or at least, by implication, Russia's protégés, the Serbs); Austria; and Greece. No one, on the other hand, was directly supporting the Ottoman Empire: the government of Disraeli and Salisbury, which had been so keen to prevent the destruction of Turkey-in-Europe at the hands of Russia, had to devote its energies after the Congress of Berlin to putting pressure on the Ottomans to fulfil their unwelcome obligations. Perhaps the closest thing to a pro-Turkish element in British diplomacy at this time was represented by the Ambassador in Istanbul, Sir Henry Layard, who had got to know the Ottoman world well during his previous work as an archaeologist. Layard was widely regarded as having 'gone native'—in other words, as having learned to see things through Ottoman eyes—and it was no surprise that when Gladstone and the Liberals returned to power in the spring of 1880, Layard was replaced. A reading of Layard's despatches, however, suggests not that he was in the grip of a pro-Turkish agenda, but merely that he was capable of a certain objectivity and even-handedness. His response to the murder of Mehmet Ali pasha (the senior official sent by Istanbul to persuade the Kosovars to accept the provisions of the Congress of Berlin) at Gjakovë furnishes a typical example of this: he attributed it to 'the resentment of those who appear determined to dispute the right of Europe to hand them over, without consulting their wishes and interests, to a foreign Power'. And he continued:

> the present warlike attitude of the Albanians may be attributed to the fact that in the new territorial distribution of Turkey in Europe, the existence of the Turkish and Mussulman populations has been, to a great extent, forgotten or overlooked. The Porte is held responsible for a resistance which any proud, independent and warlike people would naturally make to their transfer to a foreign Power, alien to them in religion, in laws, and in customs, and suspected of a design to deprive them of their liberty, their property, and their ancient rights.[26]

The person who replaced Layard in the summer of 1880 was in many ways the most impressive of all the diplomats under discussion here. George Goschen was the son of a German immigrant; he had had a dazzlingly successful career in finance, becoming a Director of the Bank of England at the age of 27, and was one of the rising stars of the Liberal Party. But although he enjoyed the trust of both Gladstone and the new Foreign Secretary, Lord Granville, he had sided with Disraeli rather than Gladstone on the Russo-Turkish war, and was regarded with deep suspicion by the more radical wing of the Liberal Party—the wing which had been most fiercely anti-Turkish during the 'atrocity' agitations of the 1870s. Goschen's main task as Special Ambassador was to put pressure on the Sultan to carry out his obligations under the Treaty of Berlin; this task he performed energetically, above all during the crisis over the cession of Ulcinj. (Queen Victoria even complained that he was excessively anti-Turkish.)[27] But he was also deeply concerned to develop a long-term policy for the stability of the entire region, and it was in this context that he turned his mind to the Albanian question. He was assisted and supported by Lord Edmond Fitzmaurice, who was a member of the international commission on Eastern Roumelia, and had taken a serious interest in the Albanian territories. Fitzmaurice had also been a Liberal MP, and in the stormy debates of 1876 he had argued in favour of granting 'the benefits of self-government' to all the insurgent provinces of Turkey-in-Europe.[28] Together, it seems, Goschen and Fitzmaurice developed a position on these issues which might be described as 'liberal realism': they were in favour of self-government not only as a good in itself, but also because they thought that only the creation of a number of mutually balancing or counteracting national states could bring long-term stability to the region. This made Fitzmaurice, in particular, amenable to the idea that there might be some nascent national consciousness among the

Albanians—in contrast to Consul St. John, with whom, as we have seen, he openly quarrelled.

Goschen set out his case in a long despatch to Lord Granville, written on 26 July 1880. It was organized on two main bases: fairness or justice on the one hand, and utility or *Realpolitik* on the other. On the side of fairness, he pointed out that

> the Albanian movement is perfectly natural. As ancient and distinct a race as any by whom they are surrounded, they have seen the nationality of these neigh-bouring races taken under the protection of various European Powers, and gratified in their aspirations for a more independent existence...Meanwhile, they see that they themselves do not receive similar treatment. Their nationality is ignored, and territory inhabited by Albanians is handed over in the north to the Montenegrins, to satisfy Montenegro, the protégé of Russia, and in the south to Greece, the protégé of England and France.

He emphasized that any people would object to such treatment; and on that basis he argued that even if the League of Prizren had received some tacit encourage-ment from Istanbul, it could not be 'passed over as a mere manoeuvre conducted by the Turks in order to mislead Europe, and evade its will'. He then turned to the argument from geopolitical utility. 'The Albanian nationality', he insisted (using a phrase which St. John and Kirby Green would hardly allow to have any meaning) 'is an element which ought not to be overlooked in any future political combin-ations. On the contrary, I believe it may be utilized with much advantage to gen-eral interests, and accordingly I should deprecate any partial measures which would be likely to impede the formation of one large Albanian province.' If such a major part of the remaining Ottoman territories in Europe were to slip from the grasp of an enfeebled Istanbul, then it would be best to see Ottoman sovereignty replaced not by a power-vacuum but by a viable independent state. This, he believed, would not only be good for the internal stability of the region; it would also reduce the chances of foreign intervention.

> If a strong Albania should be formed, the excuse for occupation by a foreign Power in the case of the dissolution of the Ottoman Empire would be greatly weakened. A united Albania would bar the remaining entrances to the North, and the Balkan Peninsula would remain in the hands and under the sway of the races who now inhabit it...I consider that, in proportion as the Albanian nationality could be established, the probability of European intervention in the Balkan Peninsula would be diminished.[29]

This was undoubtedly the most carefully considered general proposal for the long-term future of the Albanian lands to be put forward by any British diplomat during this period. It may not have been directly caused by the activities of the

League of Prizren; nevertheless, it depended on the assumption that the Albanians too were entitled to have political goals of their own, and it was principally the activities of the League that had demonstrated that many Albanians did already have such goals. For a very brief period, the idea of creating such a 'unified province' was in fact accepted by the Ottoman government; this temporary change of mind on the part of the Ottoman authorities cannot, however, be attributed to Goschen's influence, as the key decisions were taken at meetings of the Ottoman cabinet on 25 and 30 May 1880, while Goschen arrived in Istanbul only on the 28th of that month.[30] And when the Ottoman government later abandoned that plan, Goschen was not in a position to demand its reinstatement, as he never received any proper support for his proposal from his own government in London. At most, in a rather paradoxical turn of argument, Gladstone was willing to threaten the Ottomans with the prospect of Albanian independence if they failed to restore their own authority and enforce the hand-over of Ulcinj: he thus saw the unification and autonomy of the Albanian lands not as a constructive step but rather as something which the Ottomans should be more strongly motivated to avoid.[31] Whatever the currents of British diplomatic opinion may have been in Prizren, Shkodër or Istanbul, the fact remained that the final decisions were made in London. Goschen's official task was to ensure the enforcement of the provisions of the Treaty of Berlin, and he performed it with considerable efficiency. Thereafter, his political masters were relieved to be free of their Balkan entanglement, and simply had no wish to entangle themselves any further.

10

The First Albanian Autobiography

Autobiography, like some other literary genres, came relatively late to the Albanian lands. In most of the well-known early cases the stimulus for writing was political or historical: during the first decade or so after the declaration of Albanian independence in 1912, several leading politicians wrote autobiographical narratives, both to justify their own conduct and to contribute to the record of events. Thus we have the full-length memoirs of Ismail Qemal Bey Vlora, written with the help of the British journalist Somerville Story and published posthumously (in English) in 1920; the brief autobiographical account by Myfit Bey Libohova of his political activities in the period 1916–20, which came out in 1921; and the pamphlet-length narrative of the 1912 uprising by Hasan Bey Prishtina, also printed in 1921.[1] A substantial text of this kind was written in the 1920s in Ottoman Turkish by Syrja Vlora, and has recently been published in Albanian translation; also significant is the political-autobiographical work by Ismail Strazimiri, written in 1931 and published nearly 80 years later.[2] Other contributions to this genre, likewise mostly describing events from the early part of the century, would later include the political memoir by Ibrahim Temo (with a first chapter on his family background and education) written in Ottoman Turkish and published in the year of his death, 1939; the memoirs of Sejfi Vllamasi, which cover the period 1899–1942; the posthumously published memoirs of Tafil Boletini; the voluminous political autobiography of Spiro Kosova, written in the 1960s; and—what is surely the richest narrative of them all—the autobiography of Eqrem Bey Vlora, which was also published posthumously, in 1968–73.[3]

Very different in character from all of these was the book *Daughter of the Eagle: The Autobiography of an Albanian Girl*, written in English by Nexhmie Zaimi when she was a student at Wellesley College (after she had emigrated from Albania), and published in 1937. This was a much more private and personal account, unconcerned with high political or military events, and reflecting the experience of an ordinary member of society as she grew from early childhood to youth. It is doubtful, however, whether this work could really be classified as an autobiography. While it clearly incorporates childhood memories and impressions of various kinds, its whole style is novelistic, with much detailed dialogue of a sort that could only have been re-invented or imagined. And whereas the heroine of this book is described as being brought up in a village near Vlorë, we know that Nexhmie Zaimi was born in Preveza and brought up in Tirana.[4] The superbly atmospheric account of a childhood in Gjirokastër given by Ismail Kadare in his

Rebels, Believers, Survivors: Studies in the History of the Albanians. Noel Malcolm,
Oxford University Press (2020). © Noel Malcolm. DOI: 10.1093/oso/9780198857297.001.0001

Kronikë në Gur (*Chronicle in Stone*) is probably closer to being a direct representation of the author's early life; yet we naturally classify Kadare's book as a novel,
not an autobiography.[5]

If we eliminate Nexhmie Zaimi's work from the competition, the field of early
Albanian autobiographies of a purely personal (as opposed to politico-historical)
nature may seem very sparse. One contender might be the memoirs, written in
English and surviving in typescript in the National Library of Albania, of the edu-
cator Sevasti Qiriazi Dako, which were apparently completed in 1938.[6] In terms of
the period covered by the narrative, the memoir of childhood and youth composed by Mustafa Kruja (who was born in 1887) would certainly count as early;
but that text was not written until after the Second World War.[7]

The first personal autobiography—indeed, the first autobiography of any
kind—to be produced by an Albanian is, rather, an entirely unknown work. It
survives, in an autograph fair-copy manuscript, in the provincial library of the
Capuchin order in the northern Italian town of Trento.[8] Written in Italian and
entitled 'My Life in Albania' ('La mia vita in Albania'), it is a substantial work,
long enough to form a short book—even though, just like Zaimi's text, it discusses
only the early part of the author's life. The manuscript is in four fascicles, of which
the last two are dated December 1881 and May 1882 respectively. Each begins with
list of contents of the whole work; while 33 chapters are listed in the first fascicle,
the list undergoes some subsequent revision, and in the last fascicle the final two
chapters are presented only as chapter-headings, with blank pages under them. So
it seems that the author gave up the task when, with 31 chapters fully written, it
was very close to completion. Although the contents of the text do not supply any
definite explanation for its abandonment, they do give the reader a sense of some
of the concerns, both psychological and spiritual, that troubled its author. The
personal drama that lies at the heart of the narrative is the story of someone who
set himself up with high aspirations and was then forced to contemplate his own
failure to fulfil them; sadly, it appears that the aspiration to appear before the
world as a published author became another one of these. At the time when he
ceased writing this work, the author was only 20 years old.

His name was Lazër Tusha (or Tushë)—or, as he gave it in Italian, Lazzaro
Tuscia. In the chapter entitled 'My Birth', he stated that he was born in the city of
Shkodër on 15 October 1861, adding: 'I was given the name "Lazzaro" in accordance with the practice of some Albanians, who give two or three names...My
father, Antonio, son of Lazzaro Tuscia, from the Giolalla family, was a civilized
person, comfortably off, enjoying the reputation of an honest man. My mother,
Cristina (Ziu) was from the Duoda family, which was rich and well-known in the
city. As I was the first-born, I had the privilege of being named after my grand-
father.'[9] His father was in fact—though it takes quite a long time for this detail to
emerge in his narrative—a tailor, with a shop in the city's bazaar, specializing in
the expensive, elaborately decorated clothes worn at weddings. Lazër Tusha was

thus born into a relatively prosperous family of the Scutarine Catholic artisan and business class.

The phrase just quoted about 'the practice of some Albanians' sets the tone for much of the explanatory material that is woven into Lazër Tusha's narrative. Self-evidently he was writing for outsiders: the choice of the Italian language is itself an indication of that (even though there may well have been other more psycho-logical factors, involving cultural self-presentation, at work in that decision). Throughout this text, although the essential story he has to tell is an extremely personal one, Tusha addresses potential readers who may stand at quite a distance from him and his life-circumstances, having no direct knowledge of Albania or Albanians. He takes evident pleasure in describing and explaining the minutiae of customs, dress and (albeit with a touch of theological disapproval) folk-beliefs and superstitions; what might almost be called an ethnographic strand runs through some parts of his account. A more general sketching of the background is also undertaken at the start: the reason why his birth does not take place until chapter 4 is that he begins with three broad introductory chapters, of which the first is on 'ancient Albania'—a discussion of Illyrians and others, which estab-lishes his credentials as a serious reader, referring to works by Vasa Effendi (Pashko Vasa), Kristoforidhi and other authors.[10] The second, 'Albania in its pre-sent condition', runs briefly through topics such as religion, agriculture and the methods of Ottoman government, before concluding that 'Albania still lies in a barbaric and uncivilized state, in extreme misery. People live there as in the Middle Ages, and the life they lead in the countryside is like the pastoral life led by the ancients in the Old Testament.'[11] And the third, 'Description of Shkodër', gives a concise account of the city, tinged here and there with some local or con-fessional pride. Shkodër, he declares, is 'a delightful city, the capital of Albania, the commercial centre, and the number one city for its wealth, natural beauty and good climate'. He estimates that it has a population of 9,000 'Christians' (i.e. Catholics), and notes that the Muslims have their houses a little 'set apart from the Christians'.[12] The Catholic houses are 'more beautiful, and in particular one street, called Paruzza [Parruca], has begun to show the influence, to a slight extent, of modern progress.' The Jesuits already have 'a great seminary', and the Franciscans are in the process of constructing 'an extremely beautiful friary'.[13]

Naturally, when an autobiography includes a whole chapter on the author's birth, the material of that chapter does not consist of memories. Lazër Tusha takes the opportunity to launch into a loving description of the customs of the Scutarines, using the privilege of his own notional presence at the centre of the scene to insinuate himself into a very female occasion. When the women heard the news of my birth, he writes, they came to visit my mother with a special sweetmeat. 'This sweetmeat is called "ysemerii" [yshmeri] and is made of flour, butter and sugar; the woman eats roughly one kilogram at this stage.' He continues:

Having received the happy announcement of my birth, roughly fifteen or 20 women gathered, relations of my mother's family, and came *en masse* to visit her. Each one brought a given number of eggs (which, according to recent rules, were meant to be four, or six at the most), and, looking at the baby, they rubbed his face with those eggs. After that, each one put some piastres under my mother's pillow; that money was to be given to the 'thirzs' [thirrës], or messenger. In view of the fact that I was her first child, my mother's face was covered by a large, fine oriental handkerchief ('scamii ciubuke' [shami çubuke]), and when the women expressed their traditional compliments she made no reply, and did not say anything, but merely gave them her hand—that is a sign of modesty, given that I was the first-born.

Even at this very early stage in his narrative, Tusha cannot quite conceal the fact that he has developed, as the son of a luxury tailor, a special taste for fine materials: 'My mother lay on a broad mattress which was spread out on the floor; she was covered with a beautiful and luxurious eiderdown, and her head rested on a long pillow with a red covering; and as the sheet was also red and white, and the eiderdown was of silk or gold thread, they made a fine sight.'[14]

On the second day of his life he was baptized. There followed many visits from female friends and relatives, bringing gifts to his mother—especially fruit, but also raisins from Salonica, coffee, sugar and milk. During his first week no man entered the room; often, Tusha observes, even the husband will not do so. His mother stayed in bed for six weeks, and then went to church, where, accompanied by another woman, she placed an offering of a few piastres on the altar. (He explains that this was called 'me hi nen urat', meaning literally 'for entering into prayers'; this was a symbolic version of the 'churching of women', a ceremony of thanksgiving with some overtones of ritual purification, after which the mother would re-enter the ceremonial life of the Church.) After this the parents hosted a banquet, which was more solemn than usual, since he was their first child, and had arrived after four full years of marriage. Then, he writes, it was the custom among both Catholics and Muslims that after some weeks the baby boy would be taken to the mother's father, whereupon the mother's brother would give the baby a dress, called 'luteri', a fez, and a gold coin, which would be attached to the little fez as an ornament.[15]

There follows a chapter on his early childhood and schooling. For some years he was the only child in the house. 'After my mother, it was my paternal grandmother who particularly looked after me; she raised me in her room for the first two or three years.' It is at this point that the flow of genuine memories begins. 'Although it is in the nature of Albanian boys never to remain still, in the house or anywhere else, I nevertheless became gentle-natured.' He continues: 'I was a good boy, thanks to the great care taken over me by my parents and my grandmother. They seldom let me leave the house, and most of the time I remained shut up indoors, unlike our boys generally, who spend all day on the streets, playing and getting muddy. I always loved quietness, peace and retirement.' He took great pleasure in playing with quoits, or with knuckle-bones, piling them up in little columns and then trying to knock them down with one bone, the 'Koc' (kockë), thrown from a distance. 'Often I played with "asciiki" [ashiki] or little bones and bits of the joints and knees of animals: these bones are sometimes coloured red, and it is the favourite boys' game.'[16]

At the age of seven Lazër Tusha underwent the ceremony of confirmation, at the hands of Archbishop Karl Pooten, and said his first confession. He records that he used to say the rosary at Mass, as is the Albanian custom; and he proudly states that on one occasion he said it nine times, during a sung Mass in the cathedral. (Ominously, he adds: 'How happy I was then! When I think of the happiness I felt at that age, I feel the onset of tears, as I compare it with the present time.') His first schooling took place at the age of eight, when he was sent to a private teacher, 'Signor Marco, from Venice, an educated and gentlemanly person, now dead'. For two years he attended his little school—he notes that his father paid 10 piastres a month in the first year, and 15 in the second—learning reading, writing, arithmetic and Italian. After this his parents sent him to 'a certain Nicoletta', also a private teacher, with whom he spent just four months; then to 'Filippo Cioba, an Albanian', for one year (the Çoba family was prominent in Shkodër, well-known for its intellectual interests); and then to 'an Italian Garibaldian, whose surname was Battaglia', for 25 piastres a month. But the young Lazër Tusha had already set his heart on becoming a Catholic priest; so, after just two months, he persuaded his parents to send him to the Jesuit secondary school. This was the predecessor of the much better-known school dedicated to St Francis Xavier (known as the Xaverianum or 'Kolegja Saveriane'), which would be founded in 1878; it had begun in 1868 with one Jesuit giving grammar lessons to a small group of boys in a private house, and grew rapidly until, after a few years, the Jesuit authorities decided to suspend the project until they could find proper accommodation for it. But Lazër Tusha spent only a short time there. Finally, at the age of eleven, he achieved his ambition of being accepted at the 'Collegio Ponteficio Albanese', the seminary of Shkodër.[17]

This was a great turning-point in his life. Like a good novelist, he steps aside at just this point, to occupy the reader's attention with other things. He comments on schooling more generally in Shkodër and the wider region: Shkodër itself has a Franciscan school as well as a Jesuit one; in the villages the only teacher is the parish priest, but there are foreigners who work as private teachers in Durrës, Bar (Tivar), Prizren and some other cities. Wednesday is the day off for schools in Shkodër, as it is the market day, and fathers take their sons to the market to learn their trade; only the Jesuit school has Thursday as its day off. As for female education: generally this is non-existent, so that the girls 'grow like animals without education, and no sooner are they grown than they are locked up at home'. But in

Shkodër 'there were always some private schoolmistresses, or nuns; and now there are the Stigmatine Sisters [a recently founded tertiary order of Franciscan nuns, who developed elementary schools and orphanages in Albania], who give free lessons, and have roughly 300 female pupils.' You can see boys and girls taking little lunch-boxes of bread with them to school every day, 'and the sons of the rich are usually accompanied to school by their servants.'[18]

Those observations are followed by three whole chapters giving further background information: on the Albanian language (where he explains the extra symbols which had become standard in the writing and printing of the Scutarine Catholics, and comments on differences in pronunciation between the city-dwellers of Shkodër and the people from the surrounding villages); on 'the paternal home' (with a long description of Albanian houses and their interior decoration); and on 'Albanian furniture' (including various kinds of utensil).[19] Only then does he resume his personal narrative.

For three years he had been badgering his father for permission to enter the seminary; he had even complained to the Archbishop about his father's 'obstinacy against the will of God'. (His mother, on the other hand, was supportive.) Once, to prove his dedication, he had walked up Mount Tarabosh and then proceeded almost all the way to the village of Shirokë, reciting the rosary non-stop; he had also informed the Jesuits that if they did not give him a place in the seminary he would drown himself in the river Bunë. Many parents, he says, did not want their sons to become seminarians, thinking that the treatment of the students was too austere and harsh. (The sheer length of the training, one assumes, must also have put them off.) But eventually his father capitulated. On a fine sunny day in February Lazër got up early 'and, dressed for the last time in Albanian clothes, took myself to the seminary, escorted by a great crowd of relatives and well-wishing friends'. He was presented to the authorities there by his father and his uncle Giovanni, while his mother and grandmother gathered in the public chapel of the seminary with many other female relatives. Lazër also recalls that his uncle Marco, who thought he would not persevere in his calling, promised to give him a gold Napoleon if he stayed there longer than six months. (With a touch of bitterness he notes that, in the event, Uncle Marco never made good his promise.) At last he put off his secular clothing and donned the ecclesiastical dress of the seminarians—he lists the various items of clothing in some detail—while his father handed over the fee of 900 piastres. He was, Lazër solemnly records of his eleven-year-old self, 'the happiest man in the world'.[20]

This seminary was a recent foundation, of huge potential importance to Catholic life in Albania. Previously, Albanians who wished to become priests had received their training in Italy, Dalmatia or Austria. The creation of this seminary (known at first as 'Kolegja Shqiptare', 'the Albanian Seminary') in 1861 made it possible at last to train for the priesthood on Albanian soil. It was under the supervision of the 'Propaganda Fide' organization in Rome, which acted through a local 'apostolic delegate', and its basic funding came from Austria, the country which enjoyed special status as the protector-power for Albanian Catholicism; but the actual running of the institution was entrusted to the Jesuits of Shkodër, who were drawn from the Venetian province of their order. In 1862 it was raised to the special status of 'Kolegja Papnore Shqiptare', 'the Pontifical Albanian Seminary'—the first of only three seminaries outside Rome to receive this special Pontifical title. It began with a teaching staff of nine, and fifteen students; the number of the latter quickly rose to 20, and would reach its official limit of 30 by 1880. Since the maximum age at entrance was fourteen—and some, like Lazër Tusha, were significantly younger than that—it had to offer a full secondary education, lasting six years, after which the pupils would study philosophy for two years and theology for four.[21]

The general tone of Lazër's account of the seminary is very appreciative; he was no doubt aware that this was the best education available in the Albanian lands. He gives respectful mention to the Rector, Father Buffoli, but reserves his special praise for the Spiritual Director, Father Giuseppe Sacchi, whom he describes as 'a real servant of God—a contemplative man, perfect in all the virtues'. During the first six years there was a strong emphasis on Latin, but the seminary also taught Greek, history, arithmetic, geometry, physics, astronomy, geography, poetry, music and the ceremonies of the Church. Whilst Albanian was spoken on Thursdays and Sundays, the general language of the institution was Italian; not surprisingly, when Lazër writes that his special love was for 'fine literature' and classic writers of 'eloquence and poetry', it is Italian authors that he has in mind. There were two months of holidays each year, but the pupils underwent a gradual process of detachment from their families: parents were allowed to visit every week during the first year, every other week in the second, and once every three weeks during the third. At one stage, struck down by intermittent fever (probably malaria) after a trip to Italy, Lazër was sent home for six months, and then taken to Ulcinj to recuperate, but otherwise his health was good; he notes that the students went for walks in and around the city every day.[22]

The next chapter begins with a visit to the village of Troshan, which is located well to the south of Shkodër, about eight miles north of Lezhë. In the village there was a small Franciscan friary—one of only three remaining at that time in northern Albania, out of the 30 or so that that order had once maintained there.[23] It was during the autumn vacation of 1876 that the acting Rector of the seminary, Father Lombardini, decided to take the boys to stay with the Franciscans; Lazër recalls that on their arrival at Troshan, late in the evening, they were greeted by festive lights and pistol-firing from all over the village. From there they had many fine excursions, walking to the nearby village of Kallmet, where the Bishop of Lezhë had his residence, and, beyond that, climbing to the summit (which stands at 1,170 m) of Mount Velë to admire the superb view. It was only on their return to Shkodër on 9 September that Lazër Tusha was informed that his father had died, four days earlier; Father Lombardini had been given the news, but had decided to conceal it from him. The full title of this chapter is therefore 'A country holiday in Troshan; the death of my father; description of the funeral'.[24]

The account of the funeral arrangements is so detailed that the reader might well assume that it is an eye-witness narrative, were it not for the fact that Lazër inserts a delicate reminder that all this took place in his absence. Whereas the account of his own birth just seized an opportunity for a general description of customs and traditions, this account carries, understandably enough, a stronger emotional charge, which can only have been intensified by the feeling that he should have been allowed to participate in an event of such importance to him. After his father's death, Lazër writes, there was much grieving, with the clapping of hands, a 'sign of extreme grief'. His father's body was washed, and then clothed in a silk shirt and a xhamadan (decorative waistcoat); his fez and his watch were placed upon him, his head was bound with a silk handkerchief and he was put in the centre of the room. A hundred female relatives gathered to cry; Lazër's mother and the household servants stood at the head of the deceased, receiving the mourners. Lazër explains that his father had been a member of three societies ('Compagnie') which organized and paid for the burial:

> All the members of these societies, when they were informed of the death by the elders, were obliged to come to bury him, paying two piastres each for his soul. All his relatives and friends also came to bury him; it made a gathering of roughly 300 Scutarines. There also came all the priests who were in Shkodër (given that we clerics were on our country holiday). The six Jesuits came, and the six Franciscans; roughly 20 came into the room where the body was, and sang a 'De profundis'; and then they arranged themselves in procession, two by two, singing psalms.

The women accompanied them, and the coffin, to the front door, but no further; only the men went to the burial itself, though all the mourners would later return to the house for a funeral banquet. Lazër then gives an extended account of the weeks and months of mourning that followed. The customs of the Catholic city-dwellers were, he suggests, more dignified (and less superstitious) than those of the villages, where 'they tear at themselves and draw blood, and heavily beat their chests'. The village women, he notes, do go to the burial, and sometimes they will enter the grave and cry there; 'in some places their custom is to smash a large pot when the dead person leaves the house, saying that all evils are shut up in that pot, and that when they smash it the evils evaporate.'[25]

The next two chapters lighten the tone by giving brief descriptions of periods spent away from Shkodër. In August 1878 Lazër accompanied one of the Jesuits, Father Enrico Legnani, on a trip to the latter's family in Milan; as he notes, this was a rare privilege, as it was not normal for the seminarians to travel. They went first to Lezhë, where Lazër fell ill (was this, perhaps, his first bout of malaria?), and then passed by boat from the port of Shëngjin to Dubrovnik, Split, Zadar, Trieste and Venice. From there they went via Padua and Verona to Milan, where, during their week-long stay, he was treated by a doctor; the return trip was via Florence, Rome (where they stopped for four days) and Ancona, with a ferry journey from there to Ulcinj.[26] For the young Lazër, who was already so much in love with the world conjured up for him by Italian literature, the experience of visiting these famous cities may well have added to a certain sense of internal alienation from the humdrum experience of Scutarine town life.

The next trip, in the following summer, was arranged (as he has previously explained) for the benefit of his health. He was sent to stay in Ulcinj, and in the village of Salč, which lies just four miles to the north of it; his host, 'Paolo Sciantoja' (Pal Shantoja), was the parish priest of Salč and the ecclesiastical 'administrator' of Ulcinj. As Lazër explains, there were only nine or ten house-holds of Catholics in Ulcinj—he estimated the total population at 20,000, 'all Muslim'—but they did have a fine church, recently built and dedicated to St Joseph: it was located on a hillside ten minutes' walk outside the city, as the Ottoman authorities would not give permission for one in the city itself. Ulcinj, which he described as only seven hours on horseback from Shkodër (or a day's journey if you took a boat down the river Bunë), had been badly sacked by Montenegrin forces in the previous year, but the surrounding countryside pleased him greatly: 'it is an extremely healthy district, and the gentlemen of Shkodër and other districts go every year to have country holidays there, and to take baths, i.e. to wash themselves in the sea'. Salč, a Catholic parish with 300 households in it, was also a very pleasant place. Accompanying the priest to different villages on their festive saint's days, he noted that the local people made brandy (raki) out of figs, and also from mulberries. 'There were tortoises there in plenty, and that was our favourite food in Salč; but the Albanians don't pay any regard to them, and don't know how to prepare them'. Altogether, he concluded, this area would be extremely prosperous, 'if it had not been sacked by the Montenegrins, who are more barbarous than the Turks'.[27]

That last sentence sets the tone for a much more sombre chapter, entitled 'The consequences of the war'. Lazër writes that Montenegro, having gazed greedily for a long time at the fertile land of the Albanians, decided to take advantage of the Russian–Ottoman war to seize it by force; so it began 'a relentless war against the Ottomans, and against those peasants themselves who, even though they were fed up with the Ottomans, nevertheless resisted the Montenegrins'. The people of the district of Krajina (Alb: Kraja; on the southern side of Lake Shkodër) fled to Shkodër as the Montenegrins burnt down their villages. These sturdy hillsmen—Lazër calls them 'tough people, and tireless workers'—were reduced to selling their flocks there for a pittance; you could buy a sheep for as little as 7 piastres. The same happened to the people of the neighbouring district of Ana Malit (between Lake Shkodër and Lake Šas). Both of these populations, he notes, were mostly Muslim, whereas the people of Shirokë, who were also forced to flee, were all Catholic (with the exception of three or four houses), and had many Scutarine family connections; people in Shkodër opened their houses to them, but after some days they were able to return to Shirokë.[28] The Muslims of Podgorica also fled *en masse* to Shkodër. As Lazër unsympathetically puts it: 'full of Muslim fanaticism, they preferred to leave their houses, lands and real property peace- fully as a gift to Montenegro, and, for the sake of their false religion, they reduced themselves to extreme misery.' Another reason for his disapproval quickly emerges: the refugees from Podgorica soon 'involved themselves in all our crafts and businesses' and spoiled the trade by undercutting the locals, 'selling things at low prices, for little profit'. The end-result was that 'for roughly the last five years, in the words of people here, trade in Shkodër has been dead'—not only because of this unfair competition, but also because the Montenegrin conquests had ruined several previously thriving commercial cities (Ulcinj, Bar and especially Podgorica) with which the people of Shkodër had traded.[29]

The following chapter is simply entitled 'Return to the lay world'.[30] It describes the next great turning-point in Lazër's life, and, as it does so, casts a pall of gloom over the narrative. Not only gloom but an element of mystery too, as he steps back, at first, from the task of explaining the real reason for this move, and then gives a notably limited and formal account of it. Here the precise nature of the relationship between writer and reader seems more problematic than in any other part of this text.

He begins by explaining that at the end of 1879 he abandoned his ecclesiastical status, having completed six years of study within the seminary. (Rather puz- zlingly, he also states that the Archbishop, Karl Pooten, had promised him a lodg- ing in the archiepiscopal residence, but that when he went there 'he did not recognize me any more and broke his promise; he did not want to have me.') Many people urged him to continue his training for the priesthood, including 'Monsignore Radoja' (Ëngjëll Radoja, a prominent Scutarine priest, the published author of several theological and homiletic works in Albanian), the Italian consul, and a merchant called signor Simoni who was married to one of Lazër's aunts; nevertheless, he cryptically writes, 'I had to expiate old sins with a new penance.' He left the seminary on his name-day, the feast of St Lazarus (17 December), and on 22 December he went 'to the bazaar, to my shop, which was bequeathed to me by my father, and I began to take care of the family business; that is where I still am today.'[31] Various friends and relatives came to offer him their consolation and advice, encouraging him to take on the responsibility of being the breadwinner for his family. They said he should think no more of the priesthood, 'since it had not been—as they put it—"kismet"'.[32] According to some, he had left for health reasons; others said it was in order to seek pleasure, or because of misconduct in the seminary, or because he was not good enough at his studies; many said he had left in order to look after his family. But Lazër said nothing, thinking of the proverb 'Dica il mondo quel che vuole, alla fine son parole'—'let the world say whatever it wants to, in the end those are only words.' He writes that he did indeed love the ecclesiastical life, and felt great sadness when it came to an end:

> I did whatever I could to avoid leaving it (even going against the wishes of the authorities); but God did not will it, since I was unworthy of it, because of my sins. I made some effort later, too, but got nowhere, and am still in the same situation. What I wish for is different from the life I lead. I run a business, against my will. As for the future, it is in the hands of God; nevertheless I hope that He will look favourably on me in a holy undertaking for which I am preparing myself.

He does note that a doctor had warned him to abandon his life of study because he was developing tuberculosis; but that, he says, was just a 'pretext' for leaving the seminary. The real reason was a 'lack of vocation'. To the modern reader, any talk of a vocation may seem to concern a purely subjective state of mind; but it seems that in this case he was informed that, as a matter of objective fact, he lacked the priestly calling. After his second stay in the countryside near Ulcinj, he records, the Rector of the seminary summoned him and declared that he was not suited to becoming a priest. Had he transgressed in some way, or revealed a character trait that was fatal to his ecclesiastical ambitions, during that stay? Or was this simply the end-point in a process of judgment upon him carried out by the authorities at the seminary over many years? Lazër's brief reference to the 'old sins' for which he had to do penance may suggest the latter; but his whole account is so guarded that no clear answer to those questions is possible.[33]

There follow five chapters of more general description of the conditions of life and ways of behaving of the people of Shkodër; these are pages rich in colourful detail. The first is simply entitled 'My clothes'; it begins with the fact that, on leaving the Seminary, he had to order a complete new set of lay clothes for himself, at a cost of 500 piastres. As the son of a tailor and, willy-nilly, a tailor himself, Lazër has of course a very precise knowledge of the various items of clothing, and he now goes through them in loving detail, beginning with the components of the standard male outfit (xhamadan, jelek, and 'braghe' or britches) and then turning to the items worn by women. But he also has a keen sense of the social symbolism of clothes, and of the nuances of identity expressed through them. He comments on the importance of clothes for the Albanians, explaining that 'the system is oriental, with Asiatic luxury tempered by the poverty of the country', and notes the special value placed on fine embroidery done by hand. As for the difference between the Muslims and the Catholics in Shkodër: 'the Muslim townsmen dress like the Catholics, with some small differences; in the Muslim dress the colour white is given prominence, while the Catholics use black and red. Instead of britches, the Muslims wear a sort of white petticoat down to the knee, which they call a "fistan"; it is very wide, and as white as snow, and confers grandeur and gravitas on the person who wears it with its innumerable pleats.' He also describes the dress of the village Muslims and Catholics, and that of the townspeople of Prizren, Gjakovë and Pejë. And he gives a special account of the clothes worn by Catholic priests and Muslim *hoxha*s (commenting also on the latter's hubble-bubbles, through which they smoke 'tymek', strong tobacco which has been cooked with honey).[34]

In a chapter on 'The Albanian market' he writes that he was amazed by the first Wednesday market-day that he witnessed in Shkodër; there follows a long account of the bazaar, the shops in it and the huge range of products sold there, and a bravura description of the bustle, the noise, the many languages, and the press of men, women, children and animals. Haggling over prices is the standard method: 'you often hear people referring to the "Jewish market", the Jewish double system for selling things [i.e. with two different opening positions, of the buyer and the seller, which eventually converge], and seldom do people use the so-called "Elbasan market" or "Salonica market", the method involving selling at a fixed price. In Shkodër almost nothing has a fixed price, except for the bread sold by the bakers, who are mostly Orthodox, apart from a few Muslims.'[35] The next chapter, 'An invitation to a wedding', describes in some detail the ceremonies and festivities involved in the wedding of his relative Rosa to a 'signor Nicolò'; as a Catholic wedding it took place on a Monday (Muslim weddings were on Thursdays), and he notes with some pride that there were roughly 300 guests.[36]

There follows another richly detailed chapter, on 'Superstitions'. He writes that he has observed 'many errors, many prejudices, many fears and precautions, which prevail everywhere in Albania among both the Muslims and the Catholics'. They are all obsessed with the idea of 'kismet' or destiny: 'they say that when any-one is born, the Lord writes on his skull all the events that will happen to him during his life, so that when any misfortune occurs they say that it was already decreed and written by God from eternity.' The Muslims take this further than the Christians; when they go off to fight, they believe that whether they live or die has already been decided, and 'this fanaticism makes them hardy in warfare.' At the same time they are 'extremely curious' to know the future, and will pore over a bone from a hen or cockerel in order to learn about it: 'they look at the back of the bone, and predict wars, armies, peace, deaths in the family, deaths in the neigh-bourhood or among relatives, and many other things. If the bone has a little hole at the top, it is certain that the head of the house will die very soon. If, looking at the bone, you see red marks, rivers of blood will flow in our land; if it has white marks, they indicate tombs, and a member of the household will die'—and so on. These bones are better at predicting the future if the hen or cockerel was born or brought up at your own home, or has at least eaten your salt. The tone Lazër adopts in this passage may be disapproving (after this passage he goes on to discuss 'other terrible superstitions'), but the disapproval is not in any way based on scepticism. For, as he emphasizes, 'the most remarkable thing is the certainty and precision with which they predict these things, which do then happen, for the most part. So I am convinced that, in reality, the Devil still maintains the dominion which he has always held in our land: for he really does play a part in these things.'[37]

While Lazër never associates Islam directly with the Devil, he does blame the prevalence of many of these superstitions on the influence of the Muslims; one example he gives—though his reasons for thinking that this practice has a Muslim origin are not stated—is that of killing a cockerel and sprinkling its blood on the foundations of a new house. Various other superstitious practices are mentioned, such as predicting the future from the behaviour of birds, or observing Friday as a day of ill omen. (It is believed that anyone who has his hair cut or even combs his hair on that day will suffer from a headache.) But all of these, he says, are minor and harmless matters 'in comparison with those greater superstitions which fully prevail among our Catholics.' The main one is belief in 'shitim', a state of being bewitched by spirits. As Lazër explains, when Lucifer rebelled against God, the angels formed two parties, one following Lucifer and the other following the Archangel Michael. But some were uncertain which party to join, and held back; God punished those ones by putting them on earth, where they must live until the Day of Judgment. Being both male and female, they procreate; but their sole job on earth is 'to torment and tempt human beings'. Sometimes they gather to sing and amuse themselves, and some of them are very beautiful. A human being who comes across them by chance is punished by them with the loss of reason, or health, or the use of a limb, or life itself. Normally they are invisible, and only the person who has been 'shituar' (bewitched or dumbstruck) can see them. Again, Lazër solemnly concludes that 'in my opinion, the Devil truly does make these things happen in our lands.'[38]

Magic, Lazër observes, is 'extremely commonly practised' in Albania. To give an example, he launches quite matter-of-factly into the story of the death of a younger brother—a person whom, up to this point, he has not mentioned at all in his narrative.

When a little brother of mine, called Nicolò, was found dead one morning with his mouth full of blood, they attributed such sudden death to the magical practices of witches, because the lamp also went dim by itself. It was easy, after that, to find the witch. The first poor man or poor woman who came to beg alms that morning would be the person who had brought these acts of witchcraft about, so long as he or she refused to spit on the ground, as a person who did spit would not be the one who was responsible. Sure enough, that morning an old woman came to beg. We asked her to spit, and promised her plentiful alms, in cash. She, suspecting some joke, absolutely refused to spit, and went away; she was held to be the person who had caused the death of my brother.[39]

On some points, Lazër seems to accept that the prevalence of superstitions can be explained, at least in part, in instrumental terms: thus, discussing the 'kulshedër' or dragon, he says that grown-ups will stop little boys from going too near a well by telling them that a kulshedër lives at the bottom of it. 'Yet', he insists, 'people certainly do believe in the existence of kulshedërs, sphinxes, and certain indescribable beings which live in deserted places and cast spells on travellers.'[40]

Even where the practice of Christianity is concerned, he writes, an element of superstition has crept in. Much faith is placed in talismans—prayers or holy words written on little pieces of paper by priests. (And, he notes, some Christians obtain similar talismans from the Muslim *hoxhas*.) Lazër's tone becomes quite unsettled here; the supernatural effects are undoubted, but there is room for serious doubt about their origins. 'Certain priests have the gift from God (or from elsewhere) of performing similar benefits with talismans—for example, curing illnesses, expelling devils, restoring the full use of the senses or of the limbs. They use talismans also for animals, and here the superstition of the "evil eye" comes into play. And in this matter the Devil has a role, as these are not natural things.'[41]

The next chapter is devoted to blood-feuds. Lazër begins by recommending Alessandro Manzoni's *I promessi sposi* as the best introduction to the psychology of these vendettas: from his pages you will learn about 'the force and the overwhelming—almost despotic—power of the cut-throats of that time, their murders, their vanities, their fights, and about how, from father to son, the memory was passed down of vendettas that had to be pursued for ancient insults and almost forgotten murders'.[42] When someone kills another man, regardless of his motive (or lack of it) for so doing, vengeance becomes a strict obligation for the victim's relatives; and each new killing gives rise to another. 'Thus there is a chain of murders in Albania, especially in the mountain areas.' Even the cities are not free of this formalized violence: quite often such a murder takes place in Shkodër, 'in the middle of the marketplace', with the perpetrator fleeing on foot and the Ottoman zaptiehs (guards) arriving 'half an hour later'.[43] Both the *hoxhas* and the Catholic priests do their utmost to stop this practice; entire families are excommunicated, and yet the vendettas continue. At best, pacification can be achieved by means of a large payment. Lazër notes that the current price is fixed at 3,000 piastres; rich families pay more, and the cost of any such peace-making is increased by extra expenses for gifts, visits, meals, fees to adjudicators, and so on. Yet even when solemn pledges of peace have been made, and fulfilled for some time, it often happens that a father on his deathbed will urge his sons and grandsons to take up the vendetta again, in order to restore the family's honour. If any man is impelled 'either by his nature or by his faith' to offer forgiveness without revenge and without a payment, he is treated with contempt: 'to this despicable person, the highlanders at their gatherings pass the glass of raki under their knees, sitting as they do in the Turkish fashion with their legs crossed. So, by dishonouring him, they drive him to carry out the vendetta—and the longer it is delayed, the more cruel it turns out to be.'[44]

After this grim account, the following chapter comes as welcome relief: entitled 'Friendships in Albania', it is both more positive and more autobiographical. Lazër Tusha gives a passionate description of the depth of loyalty that is to be found in Albanian friendships. 'For his friend, an Albanian would drown himself, throw himself into the flames, fall from a high precipice, or condemn himself to perpetual imprisonment, to hunger, privations, the loss of all his property, and of his own life. And if the Albanians are wanting when it comes to obeying the other commandments of Our Lord, I believe that they perfectly fulfil the one that says "love your neighbour like yourself"—given that, frequently, they love their neighbour more than they love themselves.'[45] Lazër explains that he has had many friendships, especially among ecclesiastics; he also likes the friendship of foreigners, 'especially if they are Italians'. Among his ecclesiastical friends he singles out the late Monsignor Radoja, the present Rector of the Seminary, the Jesuits Jungg, Legnani, Vasilicò, Pasi and Crociolani, and many Franciscans, including Father Pietro, the present Superior of the order in Albania. Relatives with whom he has had especially friendly relationships include his uncle Marco (despite, one may recall, the failure to pay the promised gold Napoleon), his cousin Nicolò Cioba (Nikollë Çoba), and Antonio Summa, with whom Lazër corresponded frequently during the time Antonio spent studying in Venice. But here a small shadow—connected in some way, perhaps, with the thwarting of his ambitions for a career in the Church?—falls across Lazër's account. 'Now, however', he writes, 'I have abandoned that intimate way I had of trusting everyone, without distinction of persons; for experience taught me that I was deluding myself, and I have begun to experience a certain amount of distrust towards some people, having fallen into the traps set by others.'[46] Among Albanians he has 'much friendship and familiarity with people who come to my shop, and with good peasants, and also with honest Scutarines, and with those who love virtue and the study of literature, and who think and judge matters clearly and without prejudice'. Cautiously he admits that 'there are also impure friendships, which are all too frequent, especially among young people'; however, generally speaking, 'Albanians love one another—and hate one another—intimately, without carnal motives, and not out of self-interest, but rather in a way that is heartfelt and honest.'[47]

The autobiographical narrative is now resumed, with a chapter entitled 'False vocation'. Lazër explains that he twice applied to the Provincial of the Jesuits in Albania, Father Vioni, and was twice turned away. Feeling impelled by 'an interior voice, an interior desire, an interior vocation towards another religious order', he did not realise that this was 'a false vocation, an illusion'. Eventually the Franciscans agreed to take him; so, ignoring the wishes and advice of his mother and other relatives, he decided to join them. Abandoning his shop, he set off for Lezhë, accompanied by Father Mariano of Palmanova (who was Prefect of the mission of the Observant Franciscans, based in Lezhë and Troshan) and Marco Gojani of Mirditë, in order to become a Franciscan novice. For six miserable weeks, in October and November, he lived in the Lezhë friary, enduring the cold, the poor food and the many hardships, and beginning to discover that he lacked the spirit of St Francis. Then he returned to Shkodër to spend time in the friary there. He applied to be sent to Koper (Capodistria) for training; again his family tried to dissuade him, but he was obdurate. And so, in late December 1880 (one year ago, he writes), he went back to Lezhë in order to embark on a boat that would take him up the Adriatic coast. Since his friend Father Mariano had not yet arrived, he was obliged to stay one week in the hateful room he had occupied in the friary, subject to the unpleasant treatment meted out to him by Fra Leonardo; and it was there that 'the unhappiness, combined with the privations, the mal-treatment, and the ridicule, gave the coup de grâce to my imaginary vocation.'[48]

In the next two chapters Lazër gives a description of the town of Lezhë and an account of his friendship with another ecclesiastic, Father Leonardo Martini dei Greci, whom he describes as a linguist, a poet and a very cultured man.[49] There follows a chapter on 'My business', which describes in some detail the nature of the trade conducted in the family's shop in the marketplace. As Lazër explains, in the time since his father's death they had been lucky to have the services of a good agent, Antonio Milla, from whom he had been able to learn how the trade worked. 'Our whole business consists of buying cloth from the signori [meaning, presumably, prominent tradesmen in the city], making clothes from it, and then selling them to the peasants; the name of this art, which has come down from ancient times, is "boimalii".' Lazër estimates capital assets of his business at 100 'purses' (i.e. 50,000 piastres), consisting of his stock of 'coarse cloth, woollen cloth, silk and gold' and the payments owed to him at any given time. The fur-nishings of the shop are worth 400 piastres, and he pays an annual rent of 1,000 piastres. Above all, the shop specializes in wedding costumes, sold to 'Muslim peasants, who are honest, good people, and our very good friends'. The standard cost, for both bride and groom, is 2,000 piastres, and the father of the bride will spend 1,500 on other items. As the peasants are unable to pay this sort of sum up front, they hand in a formal contract drawn up by their hoxha, which states the future date by which payment will be made—typically, the grain or maize harvest. For this reason, at any given time, 'most of our wealth consists of credit.' Proudly, Lazër notes that the peasant families have been buying from the Tusha shop for generations. 'We do business with the richest villagers, and they are all well-disposed towards me. And when I went to visit them for Bajram they treated me like a great signore, because almost all the villages around Shkodër owe me money—and not a small amount, as one family may owe me 2,000 piastres, another 3,000, or even up to 4,000 for a single family.' In one of the most detailed sections of the entire work, he lists the names of prominent villagers with whom he has done business; he also itemizes the many smaller items of clothing and adornment (handkerchiefs, combs, etc.) that can be purchased from his shop.[50]

Overall, Lazër Tusha calculates that his business makes an annual return of between 15 and 20 per cent on its capital; that is 'pure profit, after paying all the agents, the shop-boys, the tailors, and the rent for the shop'. In addition, he notes, the family has 'various pieces of land, two houses, three vineyards, a meadow with a vineyard and a cabin at Barbullush, a productive piece of land at Gur i Zi, some private credit, and money at interest; and my mother and grandmother have money from which they get 10 per cent interest per year, as is normal among Christians in Albania, whereas the Muslims give, and receive, 15 per cent.'[51] All of the family's assets are looked after by Lazër's uncle (his mother's brother) Giovanni Duoda. At the time of writing, Lazër notes, there are seven people working in the family business. There is the agent, Antonio Milla, who gets a salary of 2,000 piastres per annum and has declared his wish to become a partner in the business during the following year. Then there is Lazër himself, the owner of it 'or, as people here would say, master of the shop'. The third is an old man who has been a partner for 50 years but has fallen on hard times; he comes to the shop every day and is paid three piastres per diem for doing a little sewing, but the Tusha family and the Society of SS Peter and Paul have a lien on his house because of the money he owes. The fourth is Giacomo, son of Nicolò Tusha, a first cousin of Lazër's father, who is a good tailor and earns seven piastres a day; he is also paid to travel round the villages 'to shake down those who owe us money', as he is, fortunately, 'very friendly and well-acquainted with the villagers'. Then there is the tailor Marco Scirgi, who is paid on a piece-work basis; the shop-boy Antonio Sciapercata, who sews, serves customers, and opens and closes the shop; and finally the junior shop-boy Antonio Sciegeri, who performs menial tasks and a little sewing, and is paid 75 piastres a year. The boys seldom stay longer than one year; Lazër explains that the commercial year in Shkodër begins on St George's day, 3 May, so that is when they come and go.[52]

The final chapters of Lazër Tusha's autobiography are more miscellaneous. One, entitled 'A trip to the mountains', describes visits to Kallmet (just to the south of Troshan) and to the Mirditë region. Another, 'Festivities in Albania', concentrates mainly on the festivals of the Catholic Church. The most important one in Shkodër, he writes, is that of 'Our Lady of Good Counsel', commemorating of the famous painting of the Virgin Mary which, 'at the coming of the barbarian Turks, was carried through the air by angels, and put down at Gennazano, where it is still venerated, miraculously suspended in the air, with nothing supporting it over the niche of the rich altar.' (This belief in the supernatural voyage of the painting was widely held, though the idea that it still hovered in the air could not be shared by those who had actually visited the Augustinian church in Gennazano, to the south of Rome, and viewed this early-fifteenth-century fresco.) In what sounds like a strong expression of the desire that Ottoman rule would come to an end, Lazër goes on: 'And the Scutarines continue to hope, in their hearts, that this blessed image of their Protectress will soon come back to the Albanian lands.' In passing here, he notes that there is a 'Congregation' or confraternity of 300 young men in Shkodër, dedicated to the Annunciation of the Virgin Mary, 'which does quite a lot of good, and I am a member of this congregation, and have a medal from it'.[53] As for profane festivities: these, Lazër says, are 'few, and rather paltry'. During the Carnival people put on masks and 'go round the city, shouting and yelling' to the sound of musical instruments. He explains that there are no orchestras or bands in Albania, with the sole exception of the municipal band in Shkodër; rather, the Albanians have their own traditional music, played on the violin, the cymbalom, 'a sort of guitar', a small guitar and 'çapare' (finger cymbals or castanets). These form the background, at weddings and other celebrations, to 'paid singers, and much drinking of raki, and indescribable dances and songs'. Popular festivities of an essentially non-religious nature include the eve of St John the Baptist's day, when people light fires and jump across them; the annual celebration of the Austro-Hungarian Emperor's name-day (by the Albanian Catholics, whose Church came under his protection) has a secular origin but a religious form, with Masses and prayers for the Emperor's health. Lazër also notes the propensity of Albanians to fire into the air with their rifles, not only at celebrations, but also at eclipses (when they beat drums too): 'for they say that the dragon is devouring the moon, and that they are scaring it away, and killing it.' For a similar reason, he says, they fire their guns when about to cross a fast-flowing river.[54]

By this point the directly autobiographical impetus of the work seems to have been more or less spent; Lazër Tusha has, after all, brought the story of his life up to the year in which he is writing. In one chapter he describes a little trip he took in the summer of 1881 to Bushat (a village to the south of Shkodër, on the way to Barbullush). The next is about the 'Madonna di Scutari', returning to the subject of the miraculous image and the cult of the Virgin Mary as the patron saint of the city. There follow three more general chapters, on Albanian food, on Lake Shkodër, and on Skanderbeg.[55] But there the surviving text ends. Two more chapters are given their chapter-numbers (32 and 33) and their titles: 'True divine vocation' and 'Entry, and perseverance' – the latter meaning, presumably, entry into a religious order or some other form of ecclesiastical life. The second of these is described as 'the 33rd and last chapter'. In both cases, after a few mottoes or epigraphs, the text consists of the simple statement 'This chapter will describe that which the Lord has inspired us to do, when we have obtained it'; the rest is blank.[56]

Whatever it was that the Lord intended and effected for his would-be faithful servant remains, today, unknown. Other traces of Lazër Tusha's life are lacking; his date of death is not recorded. Given the references to his bouts of illness, and the doctor's diagnosis of tuberculosis, the possibility must be considered that he died while still in his twenties, perhaps not long after the writing of this text. Nor is the full story known of the subsequent history of his manuscript. But one key link in that chain is evident. On the front cover of the second fascicle there is an annotation signed by 'G. de Rada', which states: 'This interesting narrative should be printed, for the sake of its ingenuous truth, so long as it is made shorter, corrected where the language and spelling are concerned, with the [non-Italian] words written out clearly, with notes explaining if they are Albanian or Turkish, and so long as the angry anti-Muslim tone is softened.' Another note, at the end of the last fascicle, confirms that this was none other than Girolamo De Rada, the Arbëresh poet and intellectual who was the leading figure in the nineteenth-century revival of interest in Albanians and the Albanian language in Italy. In the pages following his blank final chapters, Lazër Tusha had jotted down various extracts from Italian poems which he intended to use as epigraphs to the individual chapters of his work. For chapter 31 he gave five lines of poetry attributed to De Rada; against them, De Rada has written 'This is not by me.' So it appears that someone—perhaps one of Lazër's ecclesiastical friends in Shkodër—had obtained the manuscript and had sent it to De Rada in the hope that he would recommend, or even arrange, its publication. Since De Rada's main comment contains no suggestion that the author himself could be involved in revising the work, and since the manuscript in its present state is unfinished, with those two remaining chapters yet to be written, it must seem likely that De Rada's involvement happened after Lazër's death. And this in turn implies that he did not have a long life, as De Rada himself died in February 1903, when Lazër would have been only 41 years old.[57]

By the time the reader reaches the all-too-provisional end of Lazër's text, he or she will have gained quite a strong sense of this author's character—despite, and also because of, the touches of obliquity and psychological reticence that cast their shadows over the narrative here and there. This was an unusually thoughtful and observant young man, whose upbringing had given him a partial entrée into two shining worlds that he wanted to inhabit more fully: that of Italian literature and high culture, and that of the Catholic Church and its religious orders. Both of these, in actuality or in prospect, endowed his mental and spiritual life with deeper meaning. Yet at the same time both made him feel disaffected—alienated, even—from the quotidian existence as a businessman to which he had been predestined by his family, however prosperous and respected that position may have been in its local context. His desire to serve God as a priest or friar was, we have to assume, never to be fulfilled. But his love of literature, and his interest in descriptive writing (both outwardly and inwardly directed), achieved something remarkable: by his pen he bequeathed to future generations an account which is not only one of the most vivid early descriptions of ordinary life in Albania, but also the first to be put in an autobiographical form. Let us hope that by this means Lazër Tusha did, in the end, redeem himself from oblivion.

11

Ernesto Cozzi (1870–1926)

A Neglected Figure in Albanian Studies and in the History of Albania

Although Ernesto Cozzi is a little-known figure today, he was, at the time of his death in 1926, a person of national significance in Albania, the most important and most authoritative figure in the Catholic Church. He was the man who had planned and supervised the reform and recovery of the Church during the previous six years, after the severe disruptions of the First World War. That Albanian historiography ignored him during the second half of the twentieth century is not surprising; the history of the Catholic Church was almost a taboo topic for historians in Communist Albania, and the vital contributions made by Catholic priests to the social, intellectual and cultural life of the country were systematically down-played or ignored.[1] But it is disappointing to find that, even today, he remains largely unknown to writers on Albania.[2] For Ernesto Cozzi was, in addition to being a tireless servant of his Church, a remarkably knowledgeable 'Albanologist', whose writings on the life, customs and beliefs of the villagers of northern Albania can easily stand comparison with those of much better-known figures such as Edith Durham and Franz Nopcsa. He did in fact write a full-length book, which, if only it had been published, would have secured his reputation as an authority in this field. Sadly, the plans for this publication were overtaken by the Balkan Wars and the First World War, and never resumed thereafter. Yet a significant part of the book does survive, in the form of a series of articles, printed both during Cozzi's lifetime and after his death. The purpose of this essay is twofold: to draw attention to these fascinating texts, and to shed some light on the career of their no less remarkable author.

II

Ernesto Cozzi was born in Trento on 6 July 1870; the Cozzi family spoke Italian in the home, though Trento was in the Südtirol, then an integral part of Austria. He studied in that city, first at the episcopal college and then at the theological seminary, being ordained a priest in 1894. During the next four years he served successively in two local parishes, Ala and Levico Terme, before becoming the parish priest of the Italian community in Bolzano.[3] But this was not quite the vocation to

Rebels, Believers, Survivors: Studies in the History of the Albanians. Noel Malcolm,
Oxford University Press (2020). © Noel Malcolm. DOI: 10.1093/oso/9780198857297.001.0001

which he felt himself drawn. From an early stage, Ernesto Cozzi wanted to become a missionary—'for which', in the words of an obituary published by the Jesuits of Shkodër, 'God had graced him with a special aptitude, and with strength of mind and robust health'.[4] According to the same source, he also studied foreign languages, and acquired some of the practical expertise that a missionary would need; no specific details are given, but he seems to have undergone medical training at this time, and it is also possible that he did some service as an army chaplain.[5] His application to be sent to Africa was unsuccessful; but in 1901 the Bishop of Trento accepted a request by the Bishop of Pult (or 'Pulat'), in Albania, that Ernesto Cozzi should be allowed to move to his diocese as a missionary.[6] The Bishop of Pult, Nicola Marconi, was a Franciscan who had started work as a parish priest in Albania in 1878, and had been appointed bishop in 1891; Marconi was himself from Trento, so it seems likely that some personal or family connection was the catalyst for this decisive change in Ernesto Cozzi's career.[7]

Little is known of Cozzi's early years in Albania. At the outset much of his time must have been spent in learning the Albanian language, of which, before long, he became a fluent speaker. According to one of his obituaries, he served as a parish priest first in Xhan and then in Sumë.[8] Cozzi himself would later record that he was at Sumë from 1901 to 1903; so the period in Xhan was presumably very brief—perhaps just a few months of apprenticeship with another priest.[9] The parish of Sumë had just been re-instituted by Bishop Marconi, and Cozzi was the first priest to reside there for a long time.[10] For someone whose pastoral experience had been acquired in the sleepy parishes of the Trento district, life in this Albanian village must have come as a challenge; the term 'culture shock' would hardly be out of place. As he would later write in his essay on the blood-feud, on one occasion 'because of a single insulting expression, I saw five highlanders gunned down at the door of my church in Sumë'.[11] Another incident he recalled from his time there involved a Muslim girl who was made pregnant by a young man (also Muslim) to whom she was neither married nor betrothed. The girl's father gave a cartridge to one of his nephews, who duly shot the girl in the chest, with the bullet passing through her right lung; 'treated by the author', Cozzi wrote, 'she quickly recovered, and is now a married woman in Montenegro'. Her seducer was shot at the door of his own house by her father and one of her brothers.[12] Sumë was unusual, in the diocese of Pult, in having a mixed Catholic–Muslim population: in 1920 it was reported to have 374 Catholics and 240 Muslims (the only other mixed parishes being Mërtur, which had 20 Muslims, and Nikaj, which had 5).[13] So it was probably here that Cozzi began to acquire his knowledge of Islamic folk-beliefs and practices.

After leaving Sumë, Cozzi appears, according to one of his obituaries, to have served for just over a year in the parish of Kodhel, to the south of Shkodër.[14] Another obituary states that he spent some time as secretary to the Bishop of Sapë, Lazër Mjeda; as Kodhel is in the diocese of Sapë, it seems likely that these two positions were combined.[15] Then, in 1905, Cozzi moved northwards to become the first priest of a new parish which included the villages of Reç and Lohje, inland from Koplik on the eastern side of Lake Shkodër.[16] He was transferred to the nearby district of Rrjoll in early 1909.[17] In both of these parishes Cozzi's knowledge of Muslim village life would have been further strengthened, as the Catholics were a minority: in 1920 the figures for the parish of Reç and Lohje were 490 Catholics and 1200 Muslims, while those for Rrjoll were 360 of the former and 1200 of the latter.[18] Cozzi would remain at Rrjoll, though with some interruptions, until the outbreak of the First World War. At some point during this period (the exact date is not known, but it was between mid-1910 and mid-1912) he also became secretary to the Archbishop of Shkodër.[19]

All the evidence suggests that during these years in the western tip of 'Malësia e Madhe' Cozzi was a hard-working and conscientious parish priest.[20] Edith Durham, who visited him in Reç in the early summer of 1908, recorded: 'On Sunday the sick and the afflicted flocked from an early hour. The priest had had several years' medical training, and cares for the bodies as well as the souls of his people. His church is always well filled. A crowd of out-patients waited at the door on Sunday.'[21] Clearly, Cozzi's character and intelligence impressed both his colleagues and his superiors. A Jesuit report of 1909 commented on his tireless zeal, the affection in which he was held by all, his mastery of the language, and also his physical energy: in Reç, it said, he had built a new church with his own hands.[22] In that same year, when Bishop Marconi asked Rome to supply him with a coadjutor or auxiliary bishop, Cozzi's was one of the names put forward. His candidature was supported by Jak Serreqi, who had succeeded Mjeda as Bishop of Sapë. Cozzi's name was on the final short-list of two, but eventually the other candidate (Bernardin Shllaku) was chosen, as he was a Franciscan and the diocese of Pult was served almost exclusively by that order.[23]

During this process a question-mark was raised against Cozzi's name; but the question concerned politics, not religion. The Austro-Hungarian authorities took an active interest in all such appointments in Albania: the Catholic Church in that country fell under their protection, in a formal arrangement (the so-called 'Kultusprotektorat') under which Austria-Hungary helped to fund the Church and had official status as its guardian. This arrangement was valued by the Austro-Hungarian authorities for reasons of political interest, as it gave them a special standing in the country unlike that of any other Christian state. As a general rule they were keen to promote priests who were Austro-Hungarian subjects, and Cozzi satisfied this requirement. But in 1907 the Austro-Hungarian Consul General in Shkodër, August Kral, complained that Cozzi was receiving money from the 'Associazione nazionale italiana per soccorrere i missionari italiani all'estero' ('Italian National Association for the Support of Missionaries Abroad'); this was a bona fide religious organisation, but Kral suspected it of being a vehicle for Italian influence over Albanian affairs.[24] In 1909, when Cozzi's candidature for the auxiliary bishopric was under discussion, Kral began his account of Cozzi by stating that he should be the preferred choice, 'because of his excellent level of culture and undeniable proficiency, and also in consideration of his popularity'. He continued:

> Don Ernesto Cozzi is from Trento, a former military chaplain, who has been in this country since 1901, speaks German, and has learned the Albanian language thoroughly. The only black mark concerning him might be that two years ago he was so politically imprudent as to enter into excessively close relations with Don Nicolò Ashta, and, through him, he came into indirect contact with Aladro and Schiaparelli.[25]

Nikollë Ashta was an Albanian who served for many years as the parish priest of Shkreli, and published some path-breaking articles on the 'Kanun', the code of Albanian customary law.[26] Ernesto Schiaparelli was the organizer of the 'Associazione nazionale italiana per soccorrere i missionari italiani all'estero', of which the Austro-Hungarians were so suspicious. As for Juan de Aladro y Pérez de Valasco, who had adopted the name 'Gjin Aladro Kastriota', this was an altogether more colourful figure. Originally a Spanish diplomat, he had adopted the Albanian nationalist cause, proclaiming himself a descendant of Skanderbeg's sister (and thereby openly aiming at a future Albanian throne); since 1899 he had issued a stream of appeals and manifestos, calling for Albanian autonomy and/or independence. Although he did attract some support in the Albanian diaspora, several of the leading figures who were at first drawn towards him—such as Faik Konica—were quickly alienated.[27]

In January 1910 an official at the Austro-Hungarian Foreign Ministry sent an enquiry about Cozzi to that country's Ambassador in Istanbul; the official believed that Cozzi was suitable for promotion to a bishopric, but wanted to know whether he had been in conflict with the Ottoman authorities. The reply he received was that the Ottomans had mistrusted Cozzi for the last two or three years, on the grounds that he had had too many contacts with priests who were known to be agents of either Aladro or another agitator and would-be King of Albania, Prince Albert Ghika.[28] In particular, the Ambassador wrote, Cozzi had become an object of suspicion after meeting Aladro's secretary in Montenegro in the autumn of 1907; and, at about that time, he had been suspected of giving shelter to Aladro himself, with the result that Cozzi's residence was searched by the authorities. (Nothing incriminating was found.)[29] How far Cozzi had become involved in political schemes or activities is hard to judge; he was never a political activist in the full sense of the term, but he did develop a strong desire for the liberation of Albania from Ottoman rule—as would become apparent within a few years. What is clear is that if, in 1907, he was involved in any way with the plans of these agitators and pretenders, such conduct would have been very unwelcome to the Austro-Hungarian authorities. They had a delicate relationship to manage with the Ottoman Empire (a relationship which would be severely strained in 1908, when they annexed the territory of Bosnia-Hercegovina), and the last thing they wanted was to see a sudden unravelling of Ottoman power, uncontrolled by them, in ways that might give new geopolitical advantages to rival states such as Italy.

III

Cozzi's intellectual life during this period was dominated, in any case, not by politics but by a long-term project of his own devising: writing a detailed study of the way of life, laws, customs and beliefs of the inhabitants of the Albanian highlands. According to Giuseppe Valentini, the outstanding Jesuit Albanologist whose time in Shkodër overlapped with the last four years of Cozzi's life, Cozzi began to write this work after he had completed two years of service in Malësia e Vogël; we may guess, therefore, that he began it during his final months at Sumë, and worked on it while he was a Kodhel in 1904. 'From the draft of his great, massive manuscript, calligraphically perfect and with no revisions, one can deduce', Valentini later wrote, 'that he thought this was the final version.'[30] But (again, according to Valentini) Cozzi later became dissatisfied with the work, and went on to add a huge quantity of corrections and additions—tentative ones in pencil, and definitive ones in ink. Some of these involved putting in new material gleaned in Malësia e Madhe; others arose from changes of mind, or from information gathered from his wide reading.[31] Altogether, the book comprised fifteen chapters; and from Valentini's description of the manuscript (which, very sadly, no longer survives), it would seem that Cozzi never abandoned the idea that it might one day be issued as a single work.

The earliest surviving description of this project by Cozzi himself comes in a letter which he sent in 1909 to the Austrian scholar Carl Patsch (1865–1945). One of the key figures in German-language Balkan studies in this period, Patsch was an archaeologist who had been based for nearly 20 years in Sarajevo; appointed Director of the Provincial Museum there in 1898, he had set up the 'Bosnisch-Herzegowinisches Institut für Balkanforschung' ('Bosnian-Hercegovinan Institute for Balkan Research') in 1904, and was the general editor of a series of short monographs entitled 'Zur Kunde der Balkanhalbinsel' (roughly: 'Studies on the Balkan Peninsula').[32] As an expert on the Illyrians he also had a special interest in Albania, and had written a study of the district of Berat.[33] Replying in March 1909 to a letter which Patsch had sent to him two months earlier, Cozzi wrote:

For several years now I have collected, according to my abilities, much material about the way of life and traditions of the highlanders of northern Albania (in particular, the highland tribes of the *vilayet* of Shkodër); but unfortunately I have not yet put these notes in order. Besides, I should like to make a comparison between the way of life and traditions of Malësia e Vogël and those of Malësia e Madhe, where I am active at present, thereby supplementing the small study I have written. As a missionary, however, I unfortunately have too little time for doing so. I must also mention that I have written my essays in my native language (Italian). In consideration of these circumstances you will, I am sure, bestow on me your kind forgiveness for the fact that I cannot accept your offer.[34]

From this it would appear that Patsch had solicited a text from him for publication; no doubt he had heard something about Cozzi's ethnographic interests, and was hoping to garner another item for his monograph series.

Any reader of this letter to Patsch would assume that Cozzi's work was, in 1909, still at a very rough stage. Yet within weeks of writing that letter he was in fact preparing one of its chapters for publication; possibly an existing commitment to publish a part of it in this way was another reason, albeit an unspoken one, for declining Patsch's offer. Altogether, during the period 1909–14 Cozzi had five chapters of his work printed as articles in learned journals; and he also arranged for one of the most important chapters—the opening one, on the 'tribes' of northern Albania and their social and political organisation, containing a wealth of information about the 'Kanun'—to be issued as a separate volume. (Details of this venture, which reached the stage of galley-proofs but was then overtaken by the outbreak of the First Balkan War, will be given below; the text was later edited and published by Giuseppe Valentini.) When preparing to submit these chapters as articles, Cozzi no doubt made some changes or additions. Evidence of this can be found, for example, in the first of them to be published, where one sentence begins: 'Just as I was writing this article (on the 29th of March 1909), I was called out to visit a fifty-year-old woman...'.[35] But the fact that these separate publications consisted essentially of chapters extracted from the book is confirmed not only by Valentini's account, but also by internal evidence: they sometimes refer to themselves as 'chapters' ('capitoli'), and some of them have cross-references to other 'chapters' of the same book. In this way, at least, less than a half but more than a third of Cozzi's great work was preserved for posterity. (The original manuscript of that work passed, on Cozzi's death, to Francesco Genovizzi, a senior Jesuit in Shkodër; Giuseppe Valentini would later speculate that it had subsequently passed from Genovizzi to the great Jesuit scholar Fulvio Cordignano, but there is no trace of it among those papers of Cordignano that survive today.)[36]

The first article to be printed, on the sombre subject of 'Illnesses, Death and Funerals in the Mountains of Albania', appeared in the Viennese ethnographical journal *Anthropos* in 1909. Three others would be published by the same journal:

on 'The Blood-Feud in the Mountains of High Albania' (1910); on 'The Albanian Woman, with special regard to the Customary Law of the Mountains of Shkodër' (1912); and on 'Beliefs and Superstitions in the Mountains of Albania' (1914).[37] How and why Cozzi had first made contact with this journal is not known.[38] The choice was a significant one; for *Anthropos* represented an important new initiative in ethnographic studies, with a character that was both scientific and religious. Its founder was a German Catholic priest, Wilhelm Schmidt (1868–1954), a brilliant linguist who had worked on Melanesian languages and had written a study of the Mon-Khmer people.[39] As a researcher, he was aware that the science of ethnography and social anthropology was very undeveloped, often relying on source-materials of dubious value; and as a member of a recently founded missionary order, the 'Societas Verbi Divini', he felt that the worldwide network of missionaries could be used to supply ethnographic information in a much more systematic and reliable way. In the prospectus for his new journal he observed that most ethnographic researchers who visited distant cultures could not provide anything like an exhaustive description of their subjects, because of 'the brevity of their stay (in most cases) and their inadequate knowledge, or complete ignorance, of the languages of the peoples concerned'.[40] He continued:

> Here the situation of the missionary seems to be uniquely fortunate. Because of his calling as a missionary he has already had to gain a thorough knowledge of the language of the people among whom he works...He does not stay with the people for only a couple of days or weeks, but for years and decades on end, and so he does not see the life of the people merely in bits and pieces—rather, it is played out in front of his eyes in its full extent, in its regular pattern as well as in its changing details...[41]

The prospectus also explained that there would be a subscription of 12 Marks per year; missionaries would pay half that amount, and contributors would receive, in addition to 25 offprints of each article, payment at the rate of 3.20 Marks per printed page.[42] (If this promise was kept, Cozzi should have received a total of 345.20 Marks between 1909 and 1914.)

One of Schmidt's underlying purposes, no doubt, was to strengthen the credentials of Catholic scientific research.[43] And at a deep level he did believe that ethnographic studies of this kind would provide vital evidence for a universal history of mankind, in which a pattern of development from an original monotheism would become clear: his own articles in *Anthropos* between 1908 and 1912 became the first volume of what was to be his huge, lifelong study of 'the origin of the idea of God'.[44] But in his instructions to contributors, Schmidt emphasized that the purpose of the journal was the scientific collection of data: they must concentrate on 'Tatsachen', matters of fact, and avoid theorizing. In particular, he said, they must never diminish or suppress any facts for religious-apologetic reasons.[45] As an appendix to the prospectus he provided an 'Introduction to Ethnographic Observations' listing the various categories of subject-matter that needed to be recorded, including illnesses, dwellings, diet, ornaments, clothes, weapons, hunting, agriculture, family relations, honour and the position of women, social organisation, war and peace, laws, moral values such as honesty and chastity (where the key issue, he wrote, was what the people themselves thought about these), and finally religion, death, burial and belief in an afterlife.[46] By the time copies of this prospectus were distributed in 1905, it seems that Ernesto Cozzi had already written much of his own work, in its initial version. If he read the prospectus (as seems likely: 100,000 copies were printed, in several languages, and widely distributed through Catholic missionary networks), or indeed if he saw some of the early issues of *Anthropos*, he must have felt that Schmidt was a kindred spirit, as the ethos of this journal chimed so perfectly with the approach which he himself had taken to his Albanian subject-matter. It is not at all surprising, then, that within a few years he was publishing some of his material in its pages.

What may seem a little surprising, on the other hand, is that after his first article was published in *Anthropos* in 1909, his next publication was in the pages of a rival journal: his chapter on agriculture appeared as 'The State of Agriculture in Albania, with special regard to the Mountains of Shkodër' in Arnold van Gennep's *Revue d'ethnographie et de sociologie* in 1910.[47] The French ethnographer van Gennep (1873–1957), whose classic work on *Les Rites de passage* was published in 1909, was an opponent of Schmidt, with a distinctly anticlerical cast of mind; but he had been so impressed by *Anthropos* that he started his own journal, in 1908, in emulation of it.[48] The most likely explanation of Cozzi's participation in van Gennep's *Revue* is that the French editor, having seen his article in a recent issue of *Anthropos*, wrote to him and asked him to contribute. Cozzi would no doubt have felt flattered by such a request, while knowing little or nothing about the background to van Gennep's project.

The last of Cozzi's chapters to be published has been briefly mentioned already: the one on the social and political organisation, and customary laws, of the Albanian highlanders, which was eventually edited and printed by Giuseppe Valentini, long after Cozzi's death.[49] In March 1912 Cozzi sent a letter to Carl Patsch, describing his plan to publish this text. 'Since it is likely that a general revolt will break out in Albania', he wrote, 'I have quickly composed a work in Italian describing the social and political organisation of the highland tribes of northern Albania, and I should like to have it printed immediately.'[50] He had approached the printer and publisher Daniel Kajon in Sarajevo (whom Patsch himself employed to print some of the works in his monograph series), and Kajon had given him a quotation for the cost of printing 200 or 500 copies. But Kajon was not willing to take on the work as one of his own publications, as he had no links with Italian booksellers and therefore could not distribute it properly; so

Cozzi was obliged to pay for the entire printing himself. What he now requested was that Patsch's 'Bosnisch-Herzegowinisches Institut für Balkanforschung' might place an advance order for 100 copies (at 3 Kronen each), thereby underwriting a significant part of the printing costs.[51] Patsch's reply does not survive, but it seems likely that he gave a positive answer, since the printing by Kajon did go ahead—at least as far as the production of a set of proofs. But then the First Balkan War intervened, and the project went no further.

In his preface to the version of the text that was eventually published (in 1944), and in a later short account Cozzi's work, Valentini explained how he had been able to reconstruct it. The proofs which Cozzi received from Kajon were later deposited by him, albeit in an incomplete form (lacking the opening and closing sections), in the archive of the Xaverian College in Shkodër, together with part of his original draft. Using the draft, it was possible to supply the missing material at the beginning of the proofs. The missing final section—minus its 'statistical appendix', which has not survived in any form—was supplied by a different source: a long article by Cozzi which had been published in the newspaper *Il Trentino* on 24 December 1913, and which bore exactly the same general title as the overall text. From these materials Valentini was able to reconstitute Cozzi's work, giving primacy to the version in the proofs, but also recording significant divergences in the draft. (As he noted, however, he did make one significant change. He added book-, chapter-, section- and paragraph-numbers throughout, which gave the text the appearance of something codified in a systematic way, along the lines of Shtjefën Gjeçov's more famous presentation of the 'Kanun'— even though Cozzi explicitly said in his preface that he had written only a sketch, not a codification.)[52]

IV

Cozzi's statement that his account of the 'Kanun' was a mere sketch ('which does not claim to be a scientific study, something for which one would need a very extensive knowledge of the juridical sciences, which I entirely lack') was in keeping with other self-deprecating comments in these writings.[53] At the beginning of his article on illnesses, death and funerals, he wrote that it had occurred to him, as a mere 'pastime', to describe 'in an accurate and at the same time simple way whatever had seemed most interesting to me about the life of these mountain tribes'; in his article on women he described his text as 'notes written *alla buona* [unceremoniously, simply] in my rare moments of leisure'.[54] Each article has a general structure, but it is a loose one, dictated entirely by the subject-matter. There is certainly no attempt to fit the material into any preconceived pattern, and—with one basic exception, discussed below—no riding of larger theoretical hobby-horses; Father Schmidt would have been pleased by the general absence of 'theorizing' in these pages. But it is also clear that Cozzi was not an intellectual *ingénu*; he did have a wider knowledge of some relevant literature. Although his texts were not heavily annotated, he did refer to, among others, the writings of the criminal psychologist Cesare Lombroso; the handbook *Antropologia* (Milan, 1878) by Giovanni Canestrini, the Italian translator and popularizer of Darwin; the memoirs of the Capuchin missionary Cardinal Guglielmo Massaja, *I miei trentacinque anni di missione nell'Alta Etiopia* (Rome, 1885); Alessandro Levi's monograph on ancient Greek ideas of crime and punishment, *Delitto e pena nel pensiero dei greci* (Turin, 1903); and the multi-volume world history by Cesare Cantù, *Storia universale*.[55] (Since this last work occupied, in its most recent printing (Turin, 1883–91), seventeen volumes, we may assume that Cozzi consulted it in a well-stocked library such as that of the Pontifical Seminary in Shkodër.) He also cited a range of modern authors on the Balkans: these include Albert Dumont, *Le Balkan et l'Adriatique: les bulgares et les albanais* (Paris, 1873); *Les restes illyriens en Bosnie* (Paris, 1900), by Ćiro Truhelka, Patsch's predecessor as Director of the Provincial Museum in Sarajevo; an article by Nopcsa on death statistics in Albania; an article by the Italian writer on Albania Antonio Baldacci; Paul Siebertz's somewhat superficial work *Albanien und die Albanesen: Landschafts- und Charakterbilden* (Vienna, 1910); Karl Steinmetz's travelogue *Eine Reise durch die Hochländergaue Oberalbaniens* (Vienna, 1904), which was one of the first items published by Patsch in his series; an article by the Austrian consul and Albanologist Theodor Ippen; the classic work by Cyprien Robert, *Les Slaves de Turquie*, which Cozzi read in its German translation (Dresden, 1844); and a recent pamphlet by Gaspare Gugga, *L'Albania dei due vilajet adriatici: appunti di morfologia e d'antropogeografia nella regione albanese. I suoi rapporti commerciali con l'Italia e con l'Austria. Il suo avvenire economico* (Venice, 1909).[56] Also mentioned were Giuseppe Jubany's Italian-language collection of Albanian songs and poems, *Raccolta di canti popolari e rapsodie di poemi albanesi* (Trieste, 1871), and the epic poem by Cozzi's colleague Gjergj Fishta, *Lahuta e malcis*, of which he had apparently read the first two parts in the form in which they were published in Zadar in 1905 and 1907.[57]

The one underlying argument in these writings that might be regarded as a kind of theorizing was Cozzi's assumption that the mentality and way of life of these Albanians preserved some of the features of archaic societies. This approach arose from what was an almost universal assumption among ethnographers in this period: for many (including Wilhelm Schmidt), the most fundamental reason for engaging in the study of 'primitive' people was that it would give the researcher access, at the present time, to mankind's distant past. In the case of the Albanians there was also what might be called an ideological tradition, developed in the nineteenth century and actively adopted by intellectuals such as Faik Konica, that identified various aspects of ancient Greek culture as stemming from an even more ancient autochthonous Albanian population; 'archaic' features of

Albanian culture could, if they corresponded to ancient Greek ones, be invoked in support of this view.[58] Cozzi does not seem to have been an active supporter of this argument; he did make comparisons with aspects of ancient Greek life, but the correspondences he noted hardly went beyond those that might have occurred to any western European with a classical education, and he made no attempt to draw tendentious conclusions from them. Thus, for example, he compared the 'pleq' or elders who formed the governing body of the *fis* (clan or tribe) to the 'gerontes' of ancient Greece; discussing the tendency of men pursued by blood-feuds to leave their own clan and seek hospitality in another clan's territory, he cited a line of Homer that described virtually the same phenomenon; writing about the simple iron-tipped plough with no wheel that was still in use in these mountains, he noted that it was just like the ploughs described by Hesiod.[59] His strongest statement of this theme came in his discussion of the lamentations for the dead which were sung by the women of the family for many days after the burial:

> There is in these highland funeral chants a brutality of grief which we find it hard to understand, and the sight of which is almost unbearable. The picture is indeed an archaic one, which we find among the earliest Greek poets; it is often represented in the figurative arts, but above all in the first epochs of those arts. In our museums we have black-figured vases and terracotta plaques which are accurate portrayals of these Albanian ceremonies. The men of the fifth century BC, and their predecessors, were in this matter just like the Albanians.[60]

However, the point Cozzi was making was a more general one. In several cases, he mentioned the ancient Greeks only as components of a wider picture: describing the custom of killing a sheep or goat immediately after a person's death, 'in order to free the spirit of the deceased', he noted that traces of this practice could be found among the Etruscans, Greeks and Romans; discussing the funeral banquet in honour of the dead, he referred to Greeks and Romans, suggesting that this custom belonged to 'a part of the Indo-European family'.[61] When he wrote about the 'fatalism' of the Albanians, he rejected the claim that this was something introduced into their culture by Islam, and emphasized the parallel with ancient Greek thought; but then he quoted a modern author who argued that it was a feature of antiquity as such—oriental and Hebraic as well as Graeco-Roman.[62] The practice of the groom's family paying a bride-price ('mërqir'), as opposed to the payment of a dowry by the bride's family, was, he observed, described by Aristotle as a feature of primitive societies, and was still common among various peoples in Asia, Africa and America; and the custom of marrying a young widow to a brother or nephew of her late husband was also found among the ancient Egyptians and Hebrews, and among the Copts.[63] This was not the only point on which he drew parallels with the Old Testament: for example, discussing the contempt felt by Albanians for those who accepted monetary compensation for a murdered relative (instead of avenging his blood with blood), he referred both to Homer and to the ancient Hebrews.[64] At its most basic, Cozzi's argument was simply that these Albanians were 'closer to the primitive state of nature'. As he put it, rather strikingly, in his account of their attitude towards surgical operations:

> When an Albanian is ill, he does not fear death at all; instead, he is quite fearful of pain. In my medical practice among these highlanders I had extensive grounds for convincing myself of this fact. One can hardly believe what emotion and ill-concealed anxiety the highlander feels before an operation, even of the simplest kind; and yet at the moments of greatest pain he can bear it heroically. Nor is this a contradiction. The Albanian is closer to the primitive state of nature than we are, and for him there is no shame in openly showing that pain is unwelcome and worrying [sc. in prospect], just as Homer's heroes did not shrink from showing it too.[65]

These assumptions about the 'primitive' nature of the Albanian highlanders might lead the reader to conclude that Cozzi adopted a lofty or superior tone in his writings about them; but that is certainly not the case. While his aim was always to give a truthful and objective account, he clearly felt that the real nature of these people's beliefs and practices could be grasped only if one understood those beliefs and practices from (so to speak) the inside. The inwardness which he had gained, through his many years as their pastor, confessor, adjudicator and medical practitioner, imparts a sense of empathy to many of these pages. This is particularly evident in his long article on the place of women in Albanian highland society. Almost from the outset, he disagrees with those writers who have portrayed the Albanian woman as a sort of household slave, and complains about foreigners who pass briefly, 'like a meteor', through this territory and then publish their superficial impressions. It is true, he observes, that 'all Albanian men, in public, affect a great indifference towards the female sex, and especially towards their own wives; but this is more a matter of appearance and of customary usage.' The fact that women are regarded—in a society that put such a premium on martial valour—as the weaker sex also gives them privileges, such as immunity from blood-feuds; 'in reality the weaker sex is treated lovingly and with respect, and there is nothing more touching than the relationship between brother and sister, and between sons and mother.' Only at special celebrations, and in church, is there a strict segregation of the sexes; otherwise, for example, 'these proud inhabitants of the Albanian Alps do not scorn the company of the weaker sex when they are travelling; they converse with them in a genial way, but always observing propriety in their words and deeds.'[66] While custom requires a public show of indifference by a husband towards his wife, conjugal life within the family presents an utterly different picture; but you need to enter their houses and live there for a long time in order to know about the loving relations that exist between husband and wife. I always remember the words spoken to me by one highlander who was my friend: 'Nuk kee bes, zotníi, saa dashtnii kena per graat t'ona, e saa fort rúhena, qi mos t'a diin kushi', that is, 'You cannot believe, Sir, what love we have for our women, and what effort we make to ensure that nobody knows it.'[67]

Later in this article, Cozzi remarked with unusual asperity on statements made by two recent foreign travellers in the region. The claim by Karl Steinmetz that the main cause of blood-feuds was marital infidelity by women was, he wrote, 'absolutely false'; such cases were in fact very rare, and in the last 30 years only six had occurred in the whole of Malësia e Vogël.[68] And he added an even more scornful comment on a passage in Paul Siebertz's book where, embroidering on Steinmetz's account, the author declared that ideas of conjugal fidelity among the highland women were 'of an excessively lax nature'. 'Making one journey from Shkodër to Prizren is not a sufficient basis for letting fly such criticisms... every honest person who has some knowledge of the private life of these people is bound to agree that such a claim is a mere calumny.'[69] Lest these comments by Cozzi seem almost too defensive in tone, it should be said that he made no attempt to deny that some real problems did arise in this area of social life. In the same article he discussed the customary rules concerning cases where wives fled from their husbands; this usually followed 'serious maltreatment of their persons', and was regarded as legitimate if the husband had drawn blood.[70] Other motives (though non-legitimating ones, according to custom) included infidelity by the husband, and the fact that the husband was 'ill with some secret disease'. That rather delicate reference should perhaps be understood in the light of the frank account of syphilis given in Cozzi's article on illnesses, death and funerals, where he noted the inroads it had made in the population of Malësia e Vogël.[71]

Nowhere is Cozzi's willingness to enter into the mental world of his subjects so striking as in his long account of the blood-feud. Although he never seeks to diminish the harmful effects of this practice—he endorses, naturally enough, the Church's long-standing efforts to eliminate it, while admitting that they have been entirely ineffectual—he takes special care to dispel some of the misunderstandings that prevail among Western writers. 'One should not judge the blood-feud as negatively as some authors do; nor should one think that the frequent killings which take place in Albania happen because the Albanians hate one another and because love and harmony cannot exist among them.'[72] Rather, it must be understood as an institution that has arisen 'naturally, as it were', in circumstances where neither religion nor government has been strong enough to restrain the shedding of blood.[73] The practice functions, he says, as 'an effective restraint' on acts of cruelty, especially robbery and murder; without it, the level of violence would be much greater in a society with a warlike ethos, where all men go armed, and where there is no enforcement of justice by a superior authority. He notes in passing that western Europeans, 'who so often like to call these Albanians barbarous and cruel', see many brutal crimes committed in their own countries, and would no doubt witness a much higher level of brutality if their own police and justice system were entirely removed. The Albanian blood-feud is not, as these people imagine, the product of fierce and bestial natures; 'no—for the Albanian, the blood-feud is a feeling of indignation, idealized, as it were, into a religious and moral duty'.[74] At its heart lies a concept of honour; and it is the extreme nature of the highlander's sense of honour that leads to the sometimes appalling sequences of deaths that a blood-feud can entail. Cozzi gives details of some of the worst cases he has experienced, such as an episode in Lohje in 1907 when damage by two oxen to a few maize plants led first to the owner of the plants shooting the oxen, then to the owner of the oxen shooting that man's brother, and later to eight more human fatalities.[75] But he also takes care to correct the false impression given by some previous writers, who had claimed that between 50 and 70 per cent of all deaths were caused by blood-feuds; Cozzi sets out detailed statistics for the male Catholic population of the Malësi over the previous 25 years, showing that in most *fises* the figure was somewhere between 12 and 25 per cent.[76]

It is this attention to fact and detail that so distinguishes Cozzi's writings, and makes them such a valuable resource. From his chapter on illnesses we learn, for example, that the Albanian highlanders treat intestinal wounds with pellets of butter and hare-skin, and snakebites with a mixture of tobacco, onion and salt; that they have women who are extremely skilled in the use of massage to treat abdominal illness, colic, pleurisy, ascites, oedemas and rheumatism; and that itinerant surgeons from Epirus visit the mountains and perform cataract operations using an archaic method (which Cozzi describes).[77] The chapter on women includes a detailed account of the preparations for a wedding, specifying the various gifts, payments and purchases of clothes and ornaments, and a list of all the items of clothing worn by the bride, with comments on the differences of design and terminology between Malësia e Madhe and Malësia e Vogël.[78] Cozzi also provides valuable information about the so-called 'sworn virgins', emphasizing the right of inheritance to property as a major reason for this phenomenon, and also noting that very few of the sworn virgins (a total of three in Malësia e Vogël and four in Malësia e Madhe) actually dress as men and carry weapons; he writes that the sworn virgins do mix more with men, and engage in some male occupations and pastimes such as working in the fields and smoking tobacco, but he corrects Franz Nopcsa's mistaken assertion that they enjoy the full range of masculine rights, including the right to take part in blood-feuds.[79] The article on superstitions is a rich source of information about popular belief in supernatural beings such as the 'kulsheder' [kulshedër, kuçedër], the 'drague' [dragua] or 'dragon', the 'ora' [orë] and the 'zâna' [zanë]; about witches, the evil eye, and magic spells; and about divination, especially using the shoulder-blades of sheep.[80] In his chapter on agriculture, Cozzi makes a detailed analysis of the causes of agricultural backwardness in the region, including the disastrous practice of borrowing at high rates of interest (which could be between 30 and 50 per cent) from Muslim money-lenders in Shkodër, and gives a precise account of how the system is further rigged against the borrower by the practice of valuing the repayments (made, naturally, in kind) at artificially low rates.[81] And his account of the 'Kanun', while much more summary than the full-length codification of it by Gjeçov, contains some points of detail—and some conceptual distinctions, such as the division of the term 'guest' into three different categories—that are not given in Gjeçov's version.[82]

Cozzi's role as a Catholic priest is not concealed in these pages. On several occasions he describes, and endorses, the efforts of the missionaries to stop particular practices among their flocks: not only the blood-feud, but also mourners clawing at their own faces until they bleed, the taking of a second or third wife if a first wife fails to produce a son, and the convention that a child born to a widow more than nine months after her husband's death—even as late as two or three years after that event—is regarded as the legitimate child of the deceased man.[83] He describes, evidently from personal experience, the slow and painstaking process of negotiation by which a priest may eventually succeed in ending a blood-feud; and in a footnote he awards high praise to the Jesuits of Shkodër who, visiting remote parishes on their 'travelling mission', pacify innumerable blood-feuds and eliminate many 'abuses'.[84]

While Cozzi's knowledge was, of course, most directly derived from the Catholic population, it is clear that he was also well acquainted with the customs and beliefs of the highland Muslims. In his article on illnesses and death he describes the final profession of faith made by a Muslim on his or her deathbed (noting that if the dying person is unable to speak, raising the index finger of the right hand is sufficient); he also gives a detailed account of how the washing of the corpse by the imam or *hoxha* (Islamic religious teacher) follows the same pattern as the ritual ablutions performed before prayer.[85] When rejecting the accusation that the highland women are treated like slaves, he emphasizes that the position of the Muslim women is just the same as that of the Christian ones.[86] Discussing the use of amulets or talismans, he describes first the ones made for Muslims using verses of the Koran or 'cabalistic words' and then the ones issued by the missionary priests to the Christians, containing the words of a prayer—and explains that the priest has to do this 'because, if he refused, the Christians would undoubtedly turn to the ministers of Islam' for amulets of the Muslim variety.[87] In several of his articles Cozzi quotes, with respect, verses from the Koran; and in one of them he refers to a local *hoxha* as a personal friend.[88]

But although Cozzi's relations with local Muslims were evidently good, his hostility towards the Ottoman administration shines through on several of these pages. In his account of the blood-feud he writes that the Ottoman officials have an interest in allowing this practice to continue, as they supplement their income with the fines which are levied for homicide; indeed, he claims that when a previous governor of Shkodër had succeeded in reducing the level of feuding for a while, the practice was revived at the instigation of Ottoman officials, who wanted the flow of fines to resume.[89] At the end of his article on agriculture in the highlands he lists the elementary measures that are needed to improve its 'miserable and deplorable state', such as laws to protect forests, the introduction of better tools, the development of better roads and the creation of agricultural credit institutions, and then concludes: 'but...we are in Turkey, a country whose carelessness and neglectfulness have become proverbial. Not only has Turkey failed to do anything, ever, for its subjects; it has allowed even what was there before to deteriorate.'[90] Most strikingly of all (and, in the circumstances, most daringly), in a footnote discussing the willingness of the highland women to supply, support and encourage their menfolk in battle, Cozzi observes: 'I am also prompted to write this note by the war à l'outrance which is now (April 1911) being fought in these mountains between the government troops and our highlanders who are already tired of the tyrannical regime of the Young Turks. The energy, daring and courage displayed by the women of Malësia e Madhe are beyond any praise.'[91]

V

The 'war à l'outrance' which raged in northern Albania in the spring of 1911 was in some ways a consequence of the great revolt which had taken place in Kosovo during the previous year. The Ottoman army under Şefket Torgut pasha which quelled that revolt had marched through the northern Albanian mountains to Shkodër; there, in July 1910, Şefket Torgut pasha declared martial law and imposed a strict policy of disarmament on the population of the Malësi. No action could have been better calculated to turn every malësor against the Ottoman regime than this mass confiscation of guns (of which, it was stated, 147,525 had been collected by September of that year).[92] Many Albanian rebel leaders took refuge in Montenegro, and from that country a steady flow of smuggled weapons poured back into the Malësi. (King Nikola of Montenegro was keen to promote a future uprising in Albania which could be coordinated with a Montenegrin campaign against the Turks, with the aim of incorporating much of northern Albania into the Montenegrin state.) In the spring of 1911 many of the Catholic Albanian leaders returned to Albania and began—with Montenegrin encouragement—a new revolt, which soon spread to the Mirditë territory. However, the revolt failed to gain support in other areas, and the local Muslim Albanians, fearful of Montenegrin ambitions, did not take part; by August 1911 the Catholic highlanders, who had suffered some military defeats and many punitive actions against their villages, were obliged to accept the peace conditions imposed on them by the Ottoman regime.[93]

Some glimpses of Ernesto Cozzi's life during this period are afforded by the diaries and notebooks of Edith Durham, who made repeated visits to Shkodër from 1908 onwards. She had first met Cozzi in the summer of that year when, as we have seen, she visited his parish of Reç. 'The priest of Rechi', she wrote, 'a keen student of Albanian custom, was full of information both about Rechi and Pulati, where he had spent several years'; she then recorded, over several pages, information he had given her about local beliefs and practices.[94] A few months later, when the new Ottoman constitution was celebrated in Shkodër on 10 August, she was present when the Catholic highland clans, each led by its *bajraktar* and its priest, processed grandly into the city. (A *bajraktar* was the leader of a *bajrak*, an Ottoman territorial unit which could coincide with the area of a small *fis*, or function as a subdivision of a large one.) 'It was a day of days for the missionaries', she wrote. 'For the first time in the land's history they were entering the capital triumphant, with their flocks...Each well-known figure was hailed as he passed. There was...the priest of Rechi, soldierly, erect on his white horse, with his big hound following.' At first, a *hoxha* and two Turkish officials read the Ottoman proclamations, inaudibly, to the assembled mass of people. 'But the priest of Rechi sprang to the platform, and, in a stentorian voice that rang clear everywhere, roared an impromptu speech, and cried "Rrnoft Constitution! Rrnoft Padishah! Rrnoft Schyptarii!" ["Long live the Constitution! Long live the Sultan! Long live the Albanians!"]'[95] (A photograph of Cozzi riding his splendid white horse, annotated by her 'Dom Ernesto', is preserved in the notebook that she kept during that trip.)[96]

When Edith Durham returned to the city in the spring of 1910, she was again in touch with Cozzi: a diary entry for 12 May recorded 'Visit from Don Ernesto. Was very pleased with the scalpels.'[97] She came back to Shkodër in the late summer of 1911, just after the suppression of the Catholic revolt, and several entries for October of that year relate to the efforts Cozzi was making on behalf of his destitute parishioners: 'Visit from Dom Ernesto—promised him stuff for 12 houses for shirts'; 'Bought lots more stuff—all the flannel left—gave out 24 pieces to Dom Ernesto'; 'Dom Ernesto asks for wood as he has only 10 houses to roof'; 'Gave out 200 planks & 60 battens to Rioli. Paid 56 piastres to aid carriage of same. Wrote Don Ernesto.'[98] On 7 November she had a visit from Cozzi and one of his colleagues, who discussed the continuing preparations for further conflict: 'Don Ernesto & the Padre of Traboina called in evening. Rioli & Lohja have asked for arms & promised 1 Martini per house. Don E. is sticking out for one per man...The insurgent Maltsori have been offered Turkish Mausers instead of their Montenegrin ones & asked to remain where they are & act as frontier guards. They've replied they've enough Monte: weapons & prefer them as they bought them with their blood.'[99] And on 15 January 1912 she received another visit from

Cozzi, and had an 'Interesting talk re Moslems': from what Cozzi told her, she wrote, 'It appears they are uniting with Xtians—at any rate at Lohja.' The diary entry continues with a comment which demonstrates the personal *rapport* that was beginning to develop between these two people, but which is also highly untypical of Edith Durham's writing in its use of British colonialist language: 'Chaffed Dom Ernesto—the only white man with whom I can raise a laugh.'[100]

On that occasion, the main aim of Cozzi's visit to Shkodër must have been to plead with the Ottoman authorities to supply the people of his parish (both Christian and Muslim) with maize to ward off starvation. The State Archive in Tirana preserves a formal statement, in Cozzi's hand, written just one week earlier, which describes itself as a 'document drawn up in the *bajrak* of Reç' in the presence of the *bajraktar* (Nuz Sokoli), the *hoxha* (Molla Mehmeti) and 'Don Ernesto Kozzi' himself. Written in response to an offer of grain from Nedim Bey, the Vali or governor of the *vilayet* of Shkodër, it explains that the people of Reç were unable to plant maize in the previous year because of the fighting, and that they are now suffering from 'extraordinarily great distress and poverty'; 171 families are listed (by the name of the head of the family, with the number of adults in each family also specified), plus eight more who represent less extreme cases, out of the total of 212 families (1,529 souls) in the Reç bajrak.[101] An accompanying letter from Cozzi explains that the *bajrak* includes 'the two tribes of Reç and Rrjoll'.[102] Whether this request for grain was successful must, however, be doubted; a later comment by Cozzi, recorded by Edith Durham (and quoted below), suggests that the desperately needed maize was never supplied.

In the following weeks and months conditions continued to deteriorate, and all observers felt that it was only a matter of time before northern Albania was engulfed in another large uprising; as we have seen, Cozzi wrote to Patsch on 4 March 1912 that 'it is likely that a general revolt will break out in Albania.'[103] Less than three weeks earlier, Edith Durham had been sitting one evening in her lodgings in Shkodër when, as she noted in her diary,

Gurashi & his assistant came in with the jemadans I'd ordered—in wild excitement saying 'It has begun! There is a battle. Dun! dun! dun!—we heard the shots. Everyone is running about! &c &c' We all ran downstairs to door. Crash came down the iron shutters & doors. Mičić already fortifying.

I dodged under the 'portcullis'. A crowd was rushing up the street but no shots audible. Dom Ernesto rushing along with his boy, skipped over gutter, crowded me back into the entrance & whispered hoarsely in great excitement 'I believe it is some of my people—Rechi. Oh yes—lots of shots—Over by Kiri. I told the Vali some time ago that if he wouldn't give the Moslems of Rechi maize there'd be trouble & he mustn't say I hadn't warned him. And that I was not responsible. I don't *know* but I feel pretty sure it's the Rechi Moslems. They are very angry. Don't tell anyone here!'[104]

This particular incident turned out to be a false alarm.[105] But the political tensions continued to increase; on 14 March, when she met Cozzi again, he told her that the *fis* of Kastrat was 'furious' after its leaders had been personally threatened by the governor of Shkodër.[106]

On 4 April 1912 Edith Durham noted that 'Dom Ernesto came & was delighted to receive medicines'; and one month later, she and her faithful guide, Marko Shantoja, went to visit him in the parish of Rrjoll.[107] This brief visit forms one of the happiest episodes in her diaries of this period. They arrived at Rrjoll in the afternoon of 4 May: 'D. Ernesto most hospitable. Fed us like fighting cocks. Told many interesting customs about Pulati.' On the following day, which was a Sunday, she noted: 'D. E. went to Reci to read mass there & got back in time to read mass at Rioli before noon. Two hours tramp there & back & fasting all the time. Wonderful man.' Their conversation that day turned to medical matters, and Cozzi told her the following story: 'In winter two boys were chopping frozen snow. One unluckily stooped as other swung his hatchet; it fell on his skull & chopped it thro'. Boy was brought for dead to D. E. who found a large piece of skull quite loose. Raised it & saw brain uninjured. Raised two small pieces that pressed on brain & dressed with iodoform. Sent boy down to hosp & he came back well in 15 days!' On the Monday she travelled back to Shkodër with Cozzi (she on horseback, he on foot), passing the remains of the medieval town of Balesium or Balecium (Balez, Baleç):

> Saw site of Balesium on hill. D. E. says it is very difficult to visit as the Moslems there suspect everyone of treasure hunting. He took an entomologist into a cave there 4 years ago—to hunt for beetles. After that the natives took it in turns to watch the cave all night for over a week lest the stranger should return & carry off gold. They are very stupid he says, find many things & smash all that are not coins or precious metal. Smashed a lot of amphorae lately & threw away the bits of a bronze sword.[108]

It was probably soon after this visit that Edith Durham recorded some of the information Cozzi had given her about Albanian customs and beliefs:

> In Pulati, says Dom Ernesto, it is generally believed that the soul on quitting the body is not at once judged but must first retrace every step it has made in life—visiting each place in turn.
>
>   Marko says when he was young everyone in Scutari believed this & also that before starting on the journey the soul had to walk three times round the body it had just left.
>
>   Dom E: says that in Pulti the soul is believed to haunt the hearth stone & that it is very common for a place for departed souls to be left at the table on feast days.

He says that great ceremony is observed when the fire is for the first time kindled in the hearth of a newly built house. The Zoti i Shpis [master of the house] must enter alone, stark naked, while the rest of the family wait outside. The fire has already been laid on the hearth & into this the Zoti i Shpis fires his revolver thus lighting it.

He then goes out & dresses & all enter & take possession of the house. He says that the first time a new pair of oxen are yoked together their master must also strip naked to yoke them. Marko had never heard either custom. D. E. says both are very frequent in Pulti but he believes do not exist in Maltsia e madhe.[109]

One element here, the detail about leaving a place for a dead person at a feast, had in fact already been mentioned by Cozzi at his first meeting with Edith Durham in 1908. On that occasion he had also told her that 'at Pulati he had found traces of a belief in two powers, one of light and one of darkness, and thought that the sun- and moon-like figures found as a tattoo pattern are concerned with this.'[110] Now, in 1912, they reverted to this topic, and her notes recorded:

> The Pulati people are still strongly under the influence of pre-Xtian beliefs. That the world is influenced by the 2 powers Kolshedra & Drangoni—good & evil. This I suggested to Dom E. is the remains of Bogomilism. He took up the idea.
>
> He says the Pulati people consider tattooing disgraceful, as a pagan custom & that it is therefore less there now than in Maltesia e madhe. But that it is dying out rapidly everywhere now.
>
> He agreed that the sun & moon belongs to the old religion,—prob. Bogomil.[111]

This exchange shows that the flow of ideas and information was not entirely one-way; the role of Bogomilism as a vehicle for pre-Christian dualist ideas, together with the supposedly Bogomil character of patterns and images (from the Roman period to the present) found in Bosnia-Hercegovina, Montenegro and Albania, was one of Edith Durham's intellectual hobby-horses.[112] But it is clear that the flow was mostly from Cozzi to Durham; he was one of her most trustworthy sources of information, and details derived from him—such as the belief that a person's ghost or shadow ('hije') retraces all of that person's lifetime travels after death—can be found in several of her books.[113] What is very surprising, however, is that nowhere in her writings did she make any reference to his publications. Thus, for example, the section on 'Magic, Medicine, Soothsaying' in her final work of synthesis, *Some Tribal Origins, Laws, and Customs of the Balkans*, makes no use of the information contained in Cozzi's two highly relevant articles.[114] Paying tribute to him in that book, which was published two years after his death, she wrote that his passing was 'a loss not only to the tribesmen but to science, for his pile of MS. notes on tribal customs was destroyed in the war years, and his probably unrivalled knowledge died with him'; it seems that the existence of his published articles was simply unknown to her.[115] As she evidently had at least a reading knowledge of Italian (she cited Minucci's *Historia degli Uscocchi* in that book), the most likely explanation for this ignorance would seem to be the modesty of Ernesto Cozzi himself, who had apparently not even mentioned his publications to her during their years of mutual acquaintance.[116]

VI

During the summer of 1912 the crisis in the Albanian provinces of the Ottoman Empire gathered pace. A revolt which had begun in the western districts of Kosovo in the spring quickly spread throughout that territory, and by the end of July the rebels were in control of Prishtina, Mitrovicë, Vushtrri, Ferizaj and Prizren. Tensions continued to grow in the Malësi; there was much discontent over the failure of the Ottoman government to implement promised reforms, and a widespread expectation that Montenegro would begin full-scale hostilities against the Ottomans before the end of the year. On 27 July Edith Durham, who was now staying in Podgorica, received a visit from one of the leaders of the Malësi, Nikollë Mirashi of Kastrat:

> Kol Miriashi called... Vows Monte: is about to move & that Alb: will not accept Monte: rule at any price. Says the scheme is to annex as far as the Drin— Scutari—Dukagini, Pulati or Maltsia e madhe. Sokol. B: [Sokol Baci, a leader of the *fis* of Grudë] is in favour of this. Kol & his party are against. Says that Monte: has offered his fam: house & land to fall in with this scheme. But Alb: means now to play for autonomy. Turkey is rotting rapidly & by waiting till Turkey falls to pieces Alb: can get liberty. It is only a matter of a few years. Sooner than accept Austria or Monte Alb: will support Turkey till the moment for liberty comes. But as things now stand Alb must rise. They must get in their blow before Monte: starts so as to show Europe they are independent.
>
> Kosovo vilayet has begun & is holding its own. Therefore Maltsia e madhe must strike too. The rising must be general.[117]

For many, however, Albanian autonomy seemed an unobtainable ideal under the present conditions. And many Catholics—both in the Malësi and in the important territory of Mirditë—would, in any case, be nervous about becoming part of an Albanian political entity dominated by a Muslim majority population. The Ottoman authorities were trying, with some success, to motivate the local Muslims to defend the territory against a possible Montenegrin war of annexation, and this had the effect of widening the gap that existed, in some areas, between Muslims and Catholics. For most of the latter, political plans were dominated by two scenarios: Austrian intervention to impose some kind of protectorate, or a Montenegrin invasion, supported by the Catholic highlanders on the condition that their rights and freedom of religion would be respected.

On 3 September Ernesto Cozzi left Shkodër for Vienna; details of this trip are given in the one surviving volume of his manuscript diary, which covers the vital period from September 1912 to May 1913.[118] The aim of his journey was, ostensibly, to represent Jak Serreqi (Archbishop of Shkodër since 1910) at the 'Eucharistic Congress' in that city.[119] But its real purpose was to lobby the Austro-Hungarian Foreign Ministry: Cozzi was instructed by Serreqi to 'plead the Albanian cause', and to warn that if Austria did not offer immediate support, 'all the mountains above Shkodër' would turn to Montenegro for help.[120] He was not the only Albanian heading for Vienna at this time. When he reached Trieste he met both Lazër Mjeda (who was now Archbishop of Skopje and Prizren) and Prenk Bib Doda, the hereditary leader of Mirditë, who wanted Austrian support for an autonomous Mirditë principality. On 9 September Cozzi had a meeting in Vienna with Alfred Rappaport, a former vice-consul in Shkodër who was now head of the Albanian section at the Foreign Ministry; Rappaport (who refused to see Prenk Bib Doda) assured him that Austria-Hungary would not abandon the Albanians. Five days later Cozzi, Mjeda and Archbishop Primo Bianchi of Durrës were received at the Imperial Court; Bianchi implored the Emperor to protect the Catholics of Albania, but Franz Josef merely nodded and walked away, without giving a proper reply.[121] On 17 September Cozzi, Mjeda and Prenk Bib Doda had lunch in Vienna with August Kral, the former consul at Shkodër who was now consul-general in Salonica; Baron Nopcsa also joined them at the end of the meal. Kral was sympathetic to the plan for a Mirditë principality, and Nopcsa favoured using the threat of Montenegrin action to force Vienna's hand; but these were just private opinions.[122] A few weeks later, when Cozzi discussed these experiences with Edith Durham, she noted down the following succinct summary: 'D. Ernesto...told me behind scenes of affairs. Archb'p gave Austria ultimatum some time ago—situation intolerable. Zambauer [the Austro-Hungarian consul in Shkodër] told him wait: Ab'p said—if Austria won't, call in Montenegro. Z said "wait a little & you'll be an Austrian Archb'p." When revolt began Arbp. was in difficulty as Monte: was not ready...Sent D. Ernesto to Vienna Sept 10 & Euch: Congress to give last word—that Albanian Caths could not wait so chose Monte: assistance.'[123]

Cozzi may or may not have been aware that during his absence from Albania the Catholic authorities there were negotiating directly with the Montenegrin government, drafting a treaty—between the 'religious leaders' and 'leaders and bajraktars' of the vilayet of Shkodër on the one hand, and Montenegro on the other—for a 'military and political union' between the vilajet and the Montenegrin kingdom. According to this draft treaty, the Albanian territory would 'preserve its Albanian ethnic identity' and would enjoy 'an administrative autonomy altogether similar to that enjoyed by the most privileged nations in the Austro-Hungarian

Monarchy'.[124] Two versions of the draft survive, one in Italian, the other in very poor French; the former, presumably drawn up by the Church authorities in Shkodër, contains various attempts to fortify the rights of the Albanians (such as an elected legislature, and a guarantee that Albanian would be the official language) that are omitted from the latter, which must surely represent a revision of the text by the Montenegrin government.[125]

After a brief visit to his family in Trento Cozzi returned to Albania, arriving in Shkodër on 29 September 1912. A week later he noted in his diary that the Ottoman commander, Hasan Riza bey, was gathering his forces in Shkodër, and that the mountains were now in open revolt, well supplied with arms by Montenegro. He decided to go to his parish, Rrjoll (despite the advice of both his Archbishop and the Austro-Hungarian consul, who said it was too dangerous to travel).[126] There he was told that a number of malësor leaders, including the *bajraktar* of Kastrat, Nikollë Doda, had visited Podgorica in the third week of September and had subsequently drawn up a formal document, addressed to King Nikola, asking to be incorporated into Montenegro; on delivering this, they were assured that the Montenegrin advance would begin within 20 days. Montenegro duly declared war on the Ottoman Empire on 8 October; Cozzi learned of this on the following day. Almost immediately, he noted, the Catholics of Kastrat, Shkrel, Reç and Lohje attacked the Muslims of Koplik, Grizhë and other nearby areas, burning their houses and driving them out. Those Muslims then went to Shkodër to join the Ottoman forces.[127]

An odd episode occurred a few days later. On 11 October Cozzi was visited in Rrjoll by a mysterious Italian, calling himself Vito Giovanni Lombardo, who said that Montenegro's plans should be resisted, as both Italy and Austria wanted Albania (or, at least, the *sancak* of Shkodër) to become an independent principality. Two days later, just after midnight, a bomb went off under the refectory window of Cozzi's residence. 'I was alone in the house and was sleeping peacefully. When the explosion happened—which reduced the whole area to a mass of rubble, breaking in all the doors and shattering all the windows—I leapt from my bed and rushed into the courtyard with my revolver in my hand, for fear of some further explosion.' But nothing further happened, and he was left wondering who had done this, and why; perhaps, he thought, it was 'an attack by Esad Pasha [Toptani] in response to the message from Vito Lombardo'.[128] A few days later, however, when he described this experience in a letter to the Austro-Hungarian consul, he wrote that the main suspect was the *hoxha* of Repisht (a small Muslim *mahallë* of Rrjoll), who was 'a well-known spy of the Ottoman government'.[129] On further reflection, he recalled a Turkish journalist telling him that he (Cozzi) was regarded with hostility by the new Ottoman government, and that Hasan Riza bey had organized an assassination attempt against that journalist; many people assumed, he noted, that Montenegro's attack was supported by Austria, and

Cozzi's own trip to Vienna was widely believed to have been a political mission.[130]

On 16 October Cozzi went with four other priests to Podgorica, and on the following day he was granted an audience by King Nikola. Cozzi declared his support for Nikola, and said he hoped that Albania would enter 'a new era of peace, tranquillity, progress and civilization'; the King, in return, assured him that he would 'not make any religious distinctions, that being a completely private matter.'[131] A few days later Cozzi returned briefly to Rrjoll, before going down to the Montenegrin army units at Koplik to offer his services to the wounded, 'whether as priest or as doctor'. In his diary he recorded that he was shocked by the deficiencies of the Montenegrin medical service, and also disappointed by the poor quality of the Montenegrin troops; this is the first sign of what was to become a rapid process of disillusionment with the invading power.[132] Edith Durham arrived at Koplik at the same time, and formed a similar impression. On 23 October, she later wrote, 'I went with Dom Ernesto to the headquarters of the General Staff...I asked Plamenatz [Jovan Plamenac, Minister of the Interior] how I could best help with the wounded, and found no arrangements of any kind had been made.'[133] On the following day Cozzi was badly stunned and bruised by a horse which kicked him on the head and thigh, and had to stay in bed for seventeen hours. ('Very unlucky', noted Edith Durham. 'He is the best of all the lot.')[134] But within a few days he was hard at work treating the wounded men; Edith Durham's diary entries for 30 October read 'No aid at all for wounded. Don E. used all his material last night on ten.' 'Not a bandage to be got. Dom. E. wants me to go & get some tomorrow.'[135]

Meanwhile, troubling news was beginning to arrive. On 27 October Cozzi learned that the Catholic highlanders were looting not only abandoned Muslim houses, but also the Muslims of Lohje, Reç, Rrjoll, Zagorë, Drisht and other places 'who had declared their solidarity with the Christians and had therefore stayed in their houses'.[136] The Montenegrin authorities were, it seemed, encouraging the Catholic Albanians to attack their Muslim neighbours, and Montenegrin troops were engaged in much looting themselves.[137] Cozzi was increasingly troubled by what he saw as the cynical manipulation of the Albanians by Montenegro, and as early as 30 October, just three weeks after the start of the fighting, his diary entry recorded: 'I secretly urged the leaders of the highlanders not to give their help to the Montenegrins, who desire nothing better than that the highlanders should occupy the most exposed positions, where their lives are most at risk.'[138] On 3 November the men of Hot, Grudë, Kastrat, Shkrel, Reç, Lohje and Rrjoll got permission to go home. They were fed up, Cozzi noted, with Nikollë Mirash of Kastrat, who had been given control of the distribution of provisions by Plamenac, but they were also 'tired' of the Montenegrin authorities 'who seek only to exploit them as best they can and to lead them by the nose with their false promises.'[139] A week later, when Montenegro summoned a gathering of those Albanian malësor leaders who were still loyal, Cozzi wrote bitterly: 'The Montenegrin government wants to have at least these chiefs, who are loyal to its cause, among its troops, so that it can influence European public opinion by means of false information—viz, that the Albanian mountain people are making common cause with it, and desire to be ruled by it. But if the Albanians did at the beginning throw themselves into Montenegro's arms, driven by desperation, now they have become aware of "how bitter the bread is that King Nikola gives them", and are making new prayers for the victory of the Turk...and hoping.'[140]

By this stage the siege of Shkodër had already begun, with the increasingly frequent bombardment of the city by the Montenegrin artillery. When Cozzi noticed, on 14 November, that Montenegrin shells were landing on the Christian quarter of the city, he asked the artillery commander to adjust his aim.[141] A week later he met an Italian journalist who had come disguised as a medical worker (because the Montenegrin authorities would not allow any journalists at the front, apparently for fear of their reporting 'acts of cruelty and looting'); from him he learned, for the first time, that both Italy and Austria were demanding an independent Albanian state.[142] This news must have powerfully reinforced his hostility to the Montenegrin war effort. On 1 December he chanced to meet King Nikola, who was visiting the front, and, unfortunately, when he spoke briefly to the King he was filmed doing so; as he wrote in a later note inserted in his diary entry for that date, 'the film was then shown in other countries with the caption "Homage to King Nikola by the Catholic Albanian missionaries". Poor homage! And poor public, bamboozled by King Nikola's propaganda.'[143]

Cozzi spent much of December in Rrjoll, laid low by fever and a large abscess, which was eventually lanced by a doctor from the Italian Red Cross; but in January 1913 he returned to the army camp at Grizhë. He found a place to stay close to the Italian Red Cross unit, where spent much of his time working with the doctors.[144] Cozzi's distaste for the Montenegrin authorities, and especially for the royal family, continued to strengthen: he commented that 'here in Grizhë there is a continual orgy, in the full sense of the term', and that Prince Peter had a succession of highland women brought to his tent.[145] In early February, when an imminent assault on Shkodër was planned, he recorded that the high command issued a public order of the day to the Montenegrin army not to sack Shkodër or to act with cruelty towards the defeated, in order to show the world that the Montenegrins were a civilized people; 'whereas', he noted, 'to our highlanders, in order to ensnare them, it was said that the Montenegrin government had given them permission to loot Shkodër for three days, and that out of deference to them! Oh, the wretched "civilization" of King Nikola!'[146] A few days later he wrote that he was beginning to be viewed with 'coldness' by the Montenegrin authorities, who suspected him of advising the highland Albanians not to fight for them; the suspicion, he observed, was quite correct.[147] Another reason for criticizing the Montenegrins was their appalling treatment of Turkish prisoners, who were cruelly overworked and forced to eat pork.[148] Such was Cozzi's disillusionment, in fact, that by the second week of March he was identifying wholeheartedly with the defenders of Shkodër. Noting that the Montenegrins were now aiming their artillery at the cathedral there, on the grounds that it was used as an ammunition store by the Ottoman forces, he wrote that this was just a 'pretext' and that the real reason was their loathing of 'the hated Albanians who are defending themselves heroically'.[149] At the beginning of the war Montenegro had openly shown its intention to destroy everything that was Muslim, 'but now it is changing, or a change has taken place: all the anger and hatred of the Montenegrin authorities is directed against the Catholics, and they curse the promise-breaking Archbishop of Shkodër, the Albanian clergy, and the highlands...'.[150] As an example of Montenegrin hostility towards the Catholic clergy, he noted on 17 March that the priest of Sumë, Lazër Boriq, had been arrested and imprisoned in Podgorica merely because 'he had gone to see Miss Edith Durham, the benefactress of the Albanians, to ask for charity from her.'[151] But worse news than that quickly followed. The Montenegrins, he learned, were forcing 'all the Muslims and Catholics of High Albania to abjure their faith and become Orthodox'; examples mentioned by Cozzi included not only the notorious case of the Catholic priest Luigj Palaj [Alojzije Palić] in Gjakovë, killed for resisting conversion, but also 'a friend of mine, Hysen Shyti of Vonthai' who was 'barbarously gunned down merely because he refused to convert to Orthodoxy'.[152]

On 7 April 1913 Cozzi went to Virpazar, on the north-western shore of Lake Shkodër, in order to travel to Bar, where he hoped to meet the Austro-Hungarian consul. Knowing that Austria-Hungary was putting pressure on Montenegro to halt the campaign, he wanted the consul to tell him what course of action he should advise the Albanian highlanders to take if Montenegro continued with its siege of Shkodër. In Virpazar he was arrested by Montenegrin gendarmes and confined to a hotel for the night; he told them to send a telegram to Prince Danilo or General Vukotić, who could vouch for him, and eventually they let him go. But when he proceeded to Bar he noticed that he was being followed, and so gave up the idea of calling on the consul. Instead he went to Stari Bar (the old city of Bar, located several miles inland) to visit the Catholic Archbishop of Bar, Nikola Dobrečić, who invited him to stay the night. Eventually Cozzi plucked up the courage to ask Dobrečić why he had issued a public denial that the Montenegrin forces were committing atrocities; the Archbishop said that he had denied only that forced conversions had taken place in the town of Ulcinj, and that his statement had then been distorted into a general one by the Montenegrin authorities.[153] On his return to Bar the next day, Cozzi met the local agent of the Lloyd Austriaco shipping company, who gave him a message from the consul: if Montenegro did not abandon the siege, it would be necessary to organize an anti-Montenegrin uprising in the highlands.[154]

That the Montenegrin authorities were suspicious of Cozzi—an Austro-Hungarian subject as well as a critic of their policy—was only to be suspected; what is surprising is not that he was arrested at Virpazar but that he was released so soon. But attitudes were hardening quite rapidly. Less than two weeks later, at Gruemirë (near the front line), he was told by an Albanian acquaintance that Montenegro had paid some agents to assassinate him. On learning this, he decided to take refuge at his parish house in Rrjoll. When he got there on 21 April, however, he found two Montenegrin soldiers waiting for him, who said that they had orders from Brigadier Bećir to escort him first to Bećir's camp at Boks and then to General Vukotić's headquarters outside Shkodër. Cozzi parleyed for time, and they agreed to take him the following morning; but as they were leaving, one of them told him privately, in German, that he was the subject of an indictment or accusation on the part of the Montenegrin military.[155] So, in the middle of the night, Cozzi slipped quietly out of Rrjoll. He went first to Shkrel, then to Kastrat, and then to Rrapshë; it was there, on 23 April, that he heard that Esad Pasha had surrendered Shkodër to Montenegro. Two days later Cozzi went, accompanied by highlanders 'all armed to the teeth', to visit the Italian Red Cross unit at Dobre in order to learn more. Finally, after several more days waiting in Kastrat and Shkrel, he set off for Shkodër on 1 May, 'not without fear of being arrested'.[156] On entering the city he found the conditions less terrible than he had feared, and was delighted to find that all his old friends there were alive.[157] Cozzi then returned to Rrjoll. Revisiting Shkodër on 13–14 May, he encountered Brigadier Bećir, who greeted him with a threat: he said that it was well known that Cozzi and the other Catholic clergy had been working against Montenegro, and that he should tell his Archbishop that if the highlanders or the city population did anything to oppose the Montenegrin forces, he—the Archbishop—would be held directly responsible.[158] However, Bećir's power in Shkodër came almost immediately to an end. On the afternoon of the 14th the international troops arrived, and the city was handed over to their commander, Vice-Admiral Burney. Cozzi's diary—one of the most vivid personal documents of the First Balkan War—ends at this point, sounding, almost for the first time, a note of expectation and hope. 'The Muslim political and religious slavery faded away for ever; the Montenegrin incubus vanished; and on the horizon a better future is starting to dawn. *Fiat!*'[159]

VII

The next six years of Cozzi's life are much less well documented. Presumably he worked once again, during the rest of 1913 and the first half of 1914, to help his parishioners rebuild their lives, their houses and their communities. But the advent of war in August 1914 changed everything: Cozzi's duties now lay elsewhere, as a loyal subject of the Austro-Hungarian Empire. He volunteered his services as a military chaplain, and by November he was serving with the seventh infantry division of the Austro-Hungarian army.[160] This division was sent to the Eastern Front, where Russian forces had penetrated deeply into Galicia and the Carpathian region in the first six months of the war; during 1915 a combined Austro-Hungarian and German army pushed the Russians back through the territories of so-called Russian Poland and Volhynia. Cozzi served throughout this campaign, and, in the words of one of his obituaries, 'was often to be found right up against the enemy, among the forward-most trenches'.[161] But when, after the defeat of Serbia, Austro-Hungarian forces entered Albania in 1916, Cozzi returned to Albania (also in the capacity of a military chaplain); according to the same obituary, he was based mostly in Orosh, which was the ecclesiastical centre of the Catholic territory of Mirditë.[162] Details of how he spent his time have not survived; Edith Durham's report (quoted above) that 'his pile of MS. notes on tribal customs was destroyed in the war years' is so chronologically vague as to leave open the possibility that he was still collecting material for his ethnographic work during this period.[163] Presumably he left Albania with the departing Austro-Hungarian troops in late 1918 (which is one point at which the destruction of his work might have occurred). In 1919, nevertheless, he returned to Albania and was once again installed as a parish priest, this time in the village of Obot, just to the south of Shkodër.[164]

Although northern Albania had been, during the latter part of the war, in the hands of the European power that was the traditional protector of the Catholics, the state of the Catholic Church there had deteriorated quite badly. In December 1918 the Jesuit Francesco Genovizzi sent a depressing account to the Secretary of the 'Propaganda Fide' Congregation in Rome. Genovizzi, who had been in Albania for 25 years and had become the Superior of the Jesuits' 'travelling mission', was an energetic man and an Albanophile, who had long campaigned for a greater role for the Albanian language in the educational and other activities of his order in Shkodër; his strongest desire was to see a vigorous local Church in Albania, run by an Albanian hierarchy. But he had very little that was positive to report. The travelling mission had been unable to go outside Shkodër in 1915; in 1916–17 it had visited the Catholic parishes in Montenegro, and in 1917–18 the diocese of Sapë, but large areas remained untouched. The Archbishop of Durrës was so old and mentally incapacitated that he was unable to govern his archdiocese, which was 'rather decayed'; and 'I would have many other things of a similar nature to say, all of them necessary for the moral good of Albania, but that could be done only in speech', not in writing.[165] Six months later, in mid-June 1919, Genovizzi sent another long text; it seems that he had been persuaded to set out the predicament of the Church in writing after all, and the text, which is headed 'The State of Religion in Albania and Montenegro', has the nature of a general report rather than a personal letter.[166] Its contents are almost entirely negative, beginning with some jaundiced comments on the episcopate. The process of creating indigenous bishops had been embarked on too soon in Albania; Lazër Mjeda (Archbishop of Skopje) was the best of the bishops, but the others were 'almost worthless so far as apostolic activity is concerned'. A list of their failings followed, beginning with the fact that 'they usually waste the day in prolonged chit-chat'.[167] As for the secular clergy: 'one would say that half of the Albanian clergy are priests for reasons of material advantage; inertia and avarice are their leading characteristics; they usually spend their days smoking tobacco, chatting and lazing around'. And the same applied to a large part of the regular clergy.[168] Towards the end of the report, Genovizzi made a positive proposal:

> Send to Albania as soon as possible an Apostolic Visitor who is a man of experience, and of excellent character, to travel slowly through each diocese. Also, he should not be too old, as otherwise he would not be able to cope with the difficult journeys which need to be made. I would suggest, moreover, that he be a foreigner and not an Albanian, because the Albanians, accustomed as they are from infancy to the sight of their ecclesiastical abuses, are not so bothered by them...Someone who would be suitable for this weighty office, for example, would be the Reverend Don Ernesto Cozzi, who was born and ordained in the diocese of Trento, and who has lived for roughly 15 years as a voluntary missionary in Albania.[169]

If the Church authorities preferred an Albanian, then he would suggest Lazër Mjeda, or Pjetër Gjura (a Jesuit-trained Albanian who had become the parish priest of the city of Shkodër).[170] Gjura's name was mentioned again in a final section of the report, on the need to reinvigorate the episcopate; but here too Genovizzi gave special emphasis to the qualities and merits of Ernesto Cozzi:

> As suitable people to be appointed as bishops, I would again suggest the aforementioned Don Ernesto Cozzi and Don Pjetër Gjura, who are both roughly 40 years old and who have always shown themselves to be particularly zealous and active in Church matters. They are both endowed with more than average learning, and, besides, know several languages. Although Don Ernesto Cozzi is not Albanian, he does indeed enjoy the sympathy and trust of all the Albanians; he speaks their language well, he has a profound knowledge of the customs of this nation, and he is no less capable than Don Pjetër Gjura of putting into effect the reform that is looked for here in Albania.[171]

VIII

Genovizzi's advice appears to have been decisive. At some point during the next six months (the surviving records do not supply the precise date) the Pope appointed Cozzi 'Apostolic Visitor' to Albania; the task assigned to him was to examine the conditions in every parish and draw up a detailed report, with specific recommendations. The energy and thoroughness with which Cozzi set about this were exemplary. In the lengthy report which he eventually submitted there is a 'diary of expenses', in which every sum disbursed en route was minutely recorded: from this we learn that his travels began on 20 January 1920, when he paid for a rowing boat to transport his possessions from Obot to Shkodër, and continued non-stop until 3 September, when he took the ferry from Shëngjin (San Giovanni di Medua) to Bari. From there he travelled first to Rome and then to Trento, where he stayed with his sister from 12 September to 28 October, writing up his report; on 30 October he paid for a typed copy of the first part of it, which was entitled the 'Relazione'.[172]

Altogether, the report was divided into four parts. The 'Relazione' gave a general account of the conditions of the Church and of the Catholic population in Albania; at the head of it, Cozzi placed seven typescript pages of conclusions in which he summarized all the main points. The second part set out the comments and complaints put to him by the individual members of the clergy in each diocese. The third consisted of statistical tables, listing the property of the parishes and the number of souls (both Catholic and Muslim) in them. And the fourth gave the replies of the parish priests to a printed questionnaire which Cozzi had sent to them, asking about such matters as whether Sundays were properly observed in their parishes, whether there were any lay confraternities, and whether there were people living publicly in sin (for example, as usurers, or with concubines). The primary version of the entire report remains in the archive of the Propaganda Fide; the typescript copy of the 'Relazione' is now in the Vatican Archives.[173]

Almost as striking as the thoroughness of Cozzi's work is the uncompromisingly negative nature of his overall conclusions. Beginning with the bishops, he wrote that Lazër Mjeda was the only one to enjoy positive respect, and that Bernardin Shllaku, the Bishop of Pult, was at least not charged with either political manipulations or the pursuit of self-interest.[174] Otherwise, Cozzi declared, all of them were accused of '1) engaging, sometimes disastrously, in politics; 2) excessive love of money, and embezzling Church property; 3) nepotism, or an unreasonable use of patronage; 4) excessive negligence concerning liturgical matters, Church discipline, the guidance and correction of the clergy, pastoral visits...'.[175] Jak Serreqi, Archbishop of Shkodër, was not only 'condemned to sloth by his obesity and his ailments'; he was also accused of financial greed, maladministration and favouritism, as well as political meddling which had led to 'grave disorders and numerous killings'.[176] The Bishop of Lezhë, Luigj Bumçi, was too fond of worldly life and showed an utter negligence towards Church property; the Archbishop of Durrës, Primo Bianchi, was in a feeble state, both physically and intellectually, and was accused of meddling too much in politics; and so on, and so on.[177] Only when he came to the currently vacant Abbacy of Mirditë (at Orosh) did Cozzi strike a positive note: 'the current administrator, Don Giuseppe Gionli [Zef Gjonali], is the *only* priest in Albania who is described by everyone as exemplary and capable of governing a diocese.'[178] Turning to the ordinary clergy, he noted that their abuses included 'excessive attachment to their personal interest, and extreme avarice, especially where expenses relating to religious worship are concerned; exploitation of the people...excessive familiarity with laymen and with women, from which there often arise very serious scandals; and political tendencies, which often are ill-regulated and cause serious harm.'[179] As for the Catholic population: 'generally, the people still retains a spirit of faithfulness and of attachment to religion; but religious indifference is growing all the time. The religion of the people is, moreover, superficial and a matter of outward appearance, taking on almost the character of superstition.'[180]

For any reader who has studied Cozzi's ethnographic writings, much of the interest of the main text of the 'Relazione' lies in its account of the conditions of life of the ordinary Catholic population. Many of the practices which he had previously discussed as a social anthropologist were now addressed—and condemned—from a strictly pastoral point of view; at the same time, more specific details emerged, and the replies to his questionnaire provided some new statistical data. Thus, for example, when he wrote about what he called 'concubinage' (i.e. levirate, the quasi-marriage of a widow to her dead husband's brother) in the dioceses of Pult, Sapë and Mirditë, he observed that 20 years earlier it seemed to have died out, but that the practice was now rapidly growing: the replies to his questionnaire revealed a total of 173 cases. And there were 32 cases of bigamy— that is, the practice of taking a second wife if the first one had failed to produce a male child.[181] Bride-seizing was quite rare, he noted, but the practice of betrothing daughters to Muslims, which seemed to have died out previously, was now growing again in Nikaj and Mërtur (in the diocese of Pult) and in some parts of the Archdiocese of Durrës.[182] Other customs, such as cohabitation before marriage, the refusal of betrothed girls to go to church (for fear of meeting their fiancés, which was strictly forbidden by Albanian tradition), and the practice of attributing a widow's children to the dead husband even when they were born long after his death, were also described and condemned.[183] The account Cozzi gave of the 'sworn virgins' was, on the other hand, not directly condemnatory (nor could it be, since he did criticize the lack of female consent in the normal arrangement of an Albanian marriage). On the one hand he emphasized that the 'virgin' status of these women had nothing to do with a religious principle of chastity, and he commented that their frequenting of male company raised some doubts about their personal morality; but on the other hand he noted that a number of these virgins had moved to Shkodër, where they dressed in black 'like real nuns' and generally led 'a truly edifying life'. It was a pity, he observed, that no one had set up a religious association for them, on the model of the Italian society of the 'Figlie di Maria' ('Daughters of Mary').[184]

In some places, the overlap between this text and Cozzi's previous ethnographic writings is very clear: for example, discussing the deplorable habit of Catholics going to *hoxha*s to obtain talismans and amulets, he made exactly the point he had previously made about how the Catholic priests were obliged to provide Christian equivalents.[185] And where some of these practices were concerned, he did make an effort in the 'Relazione' to explain what they meant to the practitioners: he stressed, for instance, that concubinage occurred not as a result of sexual passion, but only out of a desire for sons, and he added that those sons were then given the same rights as the offspring of ordinary marriages.[186] Overall, however, the emphasis in this text was on the causes of these 'abuses' and the measures that might help to end them. The underlying cause, he wrote, was 'the great attachment they have to the traditions, superstitions and customs of their ancestors; their customary law forms the only rule of their public and private life, and at the same time it is itself the only obstacle to the moral and social development of this people.' In addition there was 'the lack of government, while every tribe rules itself, even now, almost independently, according to its own laws and traditions', as well as 'the spirit of moral and political independence which animates these peoples'.[187] The blood-feud, he wrote, was regarded as a national institution, and was therefore something extremely hard to change, 'the Albanian being conservative *par excellence*'. Blood-feuds had been suspended in the period 1916–18, thanks to the general disarmament of the population by the Austro-Hungarian authorities; but now they were raging more fiercely than under the Ottomans. This phenomenon could not be eliminated, Cozzi thought, without 'an inexorable military government which would know how to administer justice, impose laws and execute them effectively'; but above all, what was needed was 'to develop the intellectual and religious culture [of the population] by means of schools'.[188] Education—both the spiritual teaching provided by priests through sermons, catechizing and personal instruction, and the regular teaching given to the young in schools—became a major theme in Cozzi's recommendations for the general improvement of conditions of life in Albania.

His primary task in this document, however, was to recommend measures for the reform of the Albanian Catholic Church and the elimination of its manifold failings and abuses. Cozzi's final conclusion was that the most urgently needed measures were the following. There should be a complete reordering of the episcopate, and the Archbishops of Shkodër and Durrës should be either removed or given coadjutors to do their work for them. A new Abbot of Mirditë should be nominated, and the Franciscan province reformed. The clergy should be given spiritual exercises to perform, and a National Council summoned, at which measures would be taken for the proper administration of Church property, the maintaining of proper archives, the provision of schools and the teaching of the catechism, and so on. Churches and residences should be repaired. Lastly, to make all of this happen, Cozzi recommended that the Pope should nominate a permanent Apostolic Delegate who could at the same time be either Archbishop of Shkodër or Primate of Albania.[189]

IX

Was that final recommendation a self-interested one? Everything we know about Ernesto Cozzi's character suggests otherwise. The fact that he was the ideal candidate for the role of Apostolic Delegate would surely not have motivated his recommendation; nevertheless, it was a plain fact, and the thoroughness and efficiency of his work as Apostolic Visitor must have made it very plain indeed to the relevant authorities in Rome, beginning with Cardinal Willem Marinus Van Rossum, the Prefect of the Propaganda Fide. So it is not surprising that in November 1920, less than two months after the submission of his report, Ernesto Cozzi was appointed Apostolic Delegate to Albania by Pope Benedict XV; in the following month he was also appointed to a titular archbishopric (of 'Philippopolis'—the Latin name for the Bulgarian city of Plovdiv). On being nominated as Apostolic Delegate, he made a public declaration which was later printed by the Jesuit magazine *Lajmtari i Zemres së Krishtit* in Shkodër: 'The nomination of a Delegacy is concrete proof of the love and care which the Holy See, and especially Pope Benedict XV, have always had for the complete freedom and real progress of Albania...I shall devote my life to the flourishing of this country, Albania, which is, at the same time, my second homeland.'[190]

On 28 January 1921 Cozzi arrived in Shkodër.[191] The next day, he wrote his first official document as Apostolic Delegate, a letter to the Archbishop, Jak Serreqi, emphasizing his own sense of humility when he contemplated the task ahead of him and reassuring the Archbishop that, during his audience with Benedict XV, the Pope had expressed to him 'feelings of paternal affection and special benevolence...towards the episcopacy, clergy and people of Albania'; at the same time, he asked Serreqi to publicize throughout his archdiocese the new role and authority of the Apostolic Delegate.[192] While Cozzi treated the Archbishop (whose secretary he had once been) with decency and respect, however, he remained convinced that Serreqi must go. Only fragments of the relevant correspondence have survived, but they suggest that the Archbishop came under unrelenting pressure. In April, for example, Cozzi wrote to him asking for a detailed listing of all the essential building and restoration works that were needed by the churches and priest's houses in his archdiocese, and in July he demanded that he start work on the restoration of the cathedral in Shkodër, which was in a 'deplorable condition'.[193] Such pressure had an effect. In November 1921 Cozzi was able to write to Serreqi informing him of a letter from the Propaganda Fide of 23 October which accepted Serreqi's resignation and appointed Cozzi as 'Apostolic Administrator' of the archdiocese.[194] At the same time, he pointed out, the Propaganda Fide asked him to remind Serreqi that 'your resignation does not relieve you of the serious duty of giving a complete and detailed account of your administration'; a surviving summary does show that the archdiocesan finances were in an appalling state, with many large unpaid debts.[195]

On receiving Serreqi's resignation in mid-October, the Vatican had moved swiftly to follow another of Cozzi's recommendations: on 19 October it nominated Lazër Mjeda as the new Archbishop of Shkodër, and he moved to that city in February 1922.[196] Other changes were also made during this period. In late August Zef Gjonali, whose work as Administrator of the Abbacy of Mirditë Cozzi had previously praised, was appointed Abbot there; he also received a titular bishopric in November.[197] The process of replacing Primo Bianchi as Archbishop of Durrës was also under way: an Italian Franciscan, Francesco Melchiori, was nominated to a titular bishopric in late September, and in May–June 1922 he took over from Bianchi in Durrës. (This transition did not go smoothly, however: supporters of Luigj Bumçi, who felt that he should naturally have succeeded to the archbishopric, campaigned against Melchiori and made it impossible for him to live in Durrës; Cozzi would not bend on this issue, and the tension remained unresolved, despite Mjeda's best efforts to mediate.)[198]

By the autumn of 1922, with his preferred candidates now installed in several of the most important positions in the Church, Cozzi was able to begin a series of diocesan synods and bishops' conferences, at which many of the issues raised in his 1920 report were addressed: improving the conditions of worship, the state of repair of buildings, the discipline of the clergy and the maintenance of archives and proper financial records; financing a seminary for priests; increasing the provision of Catholic schools, and so on.[199] Cozzi's enthusiasm for these tasks clearly had a very positive effect on the Albanian Catholic Church. Unfortunately much of the work involved is now difficult or impossible to trace, since his personal archive, containing all the records of his Delegacy, was later destroyed by the Communists.[200] Only some fragments survive, in what remains of the archdiocesan archive of Shkodër (now in Tirana), and in a small collection of papers relating to the Delegacy in the Vatican Archives (a collection which has remained curiously unexplored by scholars). Each of the documents issued by Cozzi in his official capacity was assigned a number; 'Protocollo no. 1' was the letter to Serreqi of January 1921 quoted above, and by April 1925 he had issued 'Protocollo no. 1950'.[201] This at least gives some idea of the tireless industry with which he performed his duties.

One issue of special concern to Cozzi has left some trace in the archives: the question of relations with other forms of Christianity in Albania. In his 1920 report he had commented on the new threat posed by Protestant 'propaganda' in Shkodër, where American missionaries had founded a boarding-school, handing out bread and clothing to the boys who went there.[202] He returned to this topic in another report to the Propaganda Fide in June 1921. The initial focus here was on the threat posed by Protestant schools (at a time when the Albanian government was in fact inviting Albanian Methodists to help organize higher education in the country); the obvious response to this challenge was to strengthen the Catholic educational system. But Cozzi also had a larger strategy in mind, which was that the Catholic Church should 'regain' the Orthodox Albanians, and thereby establish itself as the national Church of Albania. (He was also worried by the thought of Protestant conversions among the Orthodox population.) Fan Noli's creation of an autocephalous Orthodox Church was a sign, he observed, that Orthodox Albanians wanted to detach themselves from Greece; and Cozzi felt that Noli himself had some sympathy with the idea of union with Rome. In his 1921 report he gave examples of Orthodox Albanians who, he believed, would be willing to accept papal primacy: these included priests such as Archimandrite Visarion Xhuvani and leading laymen such as Aleksandër Xhuvani and Lef Nosi, as well as the Orthodox population of the Myzeqe plain in south-central Albania. He recommended a number of measures, aimed especially at helping a pro-Catholic Orthodox congregation in Elbasan, which had seeking for some time to be brought under the Catholic Church: he suggested paying for the repair of their chapel (for which he had already raised 12,000 lire), bringing in Basilian monks (Greek-rite Catholic Italo-Albanians) from Italy, and setting up schools in Elbasan for Orthodox children, to be run by Basilian monks and nuns.[203] Most of Cozzi's recommendations were not taken up, but in 1924 the authorities in Rome sent two prominent Albanian friars, Shtjefën Gjeçov and Vinçenc Prennushi, to explore the situation in Elbasan; reporting to Cozzi in October of that year, Gjeçov wrote that enthusiasm for union with Rome was mostly confined to a few leading figures (including Simon Shuteriqi, a professor at the teachers' training school there); converting the general Orthodox population would be a very long-term task.[204]

The background to all Cozzi's work in these years was the unstable political situation in the country as a whole. In his first report to Van Rossum, written not long after his arrival in Shkodër in early 1921, he commented that it was 'a source of anguish that this small nation, which has such an extreme need of peace, tranquillity and the combined effort of all forces for its constitutional, economic and social development, is so often made a victim of internal wars, with enormous costs in blood and money'. Internal and external problems went hand in hand, he observed:

> even though Albania as an entity has been recognized as an independent state, nevertheless, considering that its borders have been fixed by the European powers without any principle of equity or justice, and that they certainly do not correspond to ethnographic and topographical needs, nor to the economic and

strategic interests of the country, there have accumulated too many reasons for hatred and envy between the Albanians and their Yugoslav and Greek neighbours for intrigues ever to cease.[205]

Cozzi seems to have reported regularly on the political situation, and the comments made in his surviving letters to Rome make depressing reading. In May 1924 he wrote that 'it is very difficult to make predictions in Albanian affairs, because of the impulsive and changeable character of the people, and because of foreign influences, which in no other country make themselves felt as strongly as they do in Albania.'[206]

A particular question that troubled him was the degree to which the Church should involve itself in political affairs. In the summer of 1921 the authorities at the Propaganda Fide wrote to him that they had received reports criticizing Serreqi, Bumçi and some others for their conduct in the recent elections: apparently they had tried to impose candidates of their own choosing, who were of poor quality, and they had even used illicit methods to get them elected.[207] In April 1923, at a gathering of Albanian bishops, Cozzi issued instructions of a general nature, saying that the clergy could not be indifferent to political affairs that impinged on spiritual matters, but that they should do nothing against the judgement and direction of the Church authorities; it was recommended that the clergy should make efforts to ensure that candidates were elected who 'enjoy the reputation of being good Christians' (i.e. good Catholics), and who would promote and defend the interests of religion.[208] In November of that year the Propaganda Fide actually recommended that some priests be allowed to stand as candidates; but by April 1924 it was complaining that Lazër Mjeda had 'taken too active a role in the elections, publicly working for the victory of one of the parties', and in June it reproved him for 'taking part in recent political demonstrations, especially on the occasion of the funeral ceremonies for the death of the young Muslim who killed Esad Pasha'.[209] By January 1925, after Ahmet Zogu's armed takeover of the country, Cozzi was reporting to Rome that Mjeda had forbidden priests to stand as candidates for parliament; Zogu was now saying that he wished to make two priests (Nikollë Sheldija and Nikollë Deda) members of parliament, but these were dubious characters in Cozzi's opinion, 'leading figures in his party and former refugees in Belgrade', so he recommended upholding Mjeda's prohibition.[210] In this report, written at a time when Zogu's seizure of power had been swiftly followed by acts of violence committed by his followers against Catholic institutions in Shkodër, Cozzi penned what were perhaps his darkest comments of all on the political prospects of the Albanian people:

Already, Catholics, Orthodox and Muslims are disheartened and humiliated on seeing their country overrun by foreign armed bands (Russian and Montenegrin); and they call out for a liberator. No one believes any more that

Albania, with its utterly deplorable economic situation and the resulting instability of its internal politics, with the various succession of short-term governments; with the deep, incurable resentments and hostilities of the parties, which prevent any collaboration; with the parasitism and favouritism of those in power—no one believes that it can establish itself, organize itself and prosper, without foreign help.[211]

This was a far cry from the words of hope that he had written less than twelve years earlier, at the end of the siege of Shkodër: 'on the horizon a better future is starting to dawn. *Fiat!*'[212]

X

Cozzi's report of January 1925, which contains those despairing words, is one of the last surviving documents from his pen. There is very little further information about his activities during the last year of his life.[213] In the second week of February 1926 he fell ill; after a few days he was confined to bed, unable to move without assistance. The doctors in Shkodër, and others who were called in from Durrës and Cetinje, diagnosed an inflammation of the spinal cord, and recommended that he be taken to Rome for specialist treatment. Cozzi had already had a presentiment of his own death, and had told his sister (who lived with him as his housekeeper): 'I shall never get up from this bed again.' But in order to satisfy her and others, who pleaded with him to go, he agreed to travel. Accompanied by his faithful servant Kola, Dr Prela from Shkodër, and Father Genovizzi (the Jesuit who had initially recommended him to the authorities in Rome), he was taken by boat to the little port of Shëngjin and put aboard a steamer for Bari. Ernesto Cozzi died as the steamer was a couple of hours away from that port, at 12.15 a.m. on 23 February 1926.[214]

On the evening of the 27th Cozzi's body was conveyed to Shëngjin and taken to the Catholic church in Lezhë. The next day, it was brought to Shkodër for burial in the Jesuit church. A newspaper report records that on its arrival in that city it was greeted first by Genovizzi, Cozzi's servant Kola, Archbishop Mjeda and Bishop-Abbot Gjonali, and then by the civil and military authorities, the clergy, and a great mass of people, Muslim as well as Catholic, who had gathered to pay their respects. 'Albania greeted the body like that of an adopted son.'[215]

The obituary published by the Jesuits of Shkodër—written, we may suspect, by Father Genovizzi—paid warm tribute to Cozzi's personal character. 'He was very devout, zealous, patient, affable, gentle, lovable, generous, and easy for anyone to get on with (so much so that small children spoke with him just as they did with their own parents). He was very honest, loyal, indefatigable and steadfast in fulfilling his duties.'[216] The obituary printed in the *Corriere della sera* emphasized his work as Apostolic Delegate: 'in a little more than five years, he was able to over-come innumerable obstacles and difficulties, calming people's feelings, ending abuses, denying privileges, and demanding that the clergy act in a genuine and holy apostolic spirit.'[217] No one who has studied Ernesto Cozzi's life would have any reason to disagree with these tributes to both his character and his work. It is necessary only to add a third tribute: his writings on the ordinary lives of the highlanders of northern Albania constitute one of the richest bodies of 'Albanological' work of the first half of the twentieth century—a veritable treasury of information which has remained all too sadly neglected until this day.

12

Myths of Albanian National Identity

Some Key Elements, as Expressed in the Works of Albanian Writers in America in the Early Twentieth Century

'ANCIENT ILLYRIANS IN ENTENTE: AFTER 2,000 YEARS OF SOLITARY STRUGGLE ALBANIANS JOIN FORCES WITH SOLDIERS OF DEMOCRACY—DUSK OF A PICTURESQUE NATION.' This was the headline that greeted readers of the *New York Evening Sun* one day in September 1918. One could hardly wish for a better example of the mythic mentality at work: two millennia of history are essentialized in a single phrase, and the 'ancient' and contemporary worlds are brought into immediate conjunction in a way that implies the existence of an almost timeless Albanian 'nation', its identity standing behind or beyond history itself.

I found this *New York Evening Sun* article reproduced in the first issue of *The Adriatic Review*, a monthly journal produced by the Pan-Albanian Federation of America, 'Vatra'.[1] As the First World War drew to a close, the activists of Vatra—at that time, as much a lobbying organization as a cultural body—were evidently pleased to see their homeland receiving such attention in the American press; indeed, the mythopoeic reference here to 'Ancient Illyrians' may have reflected the influence of Vatra's own publications, and those of other Albanian writers in America, whose activities in the first two decades of the century represented an extraordinary efflorescence of Albanian image-making and consciousness-raising.

Vatra had been formed in 1912 out of a number of Albanian associations in different American cities; its headquarters were in Boston, which possessed one of the oldest and largest Albanian communities in the United States. Thanks partly to the proximity of Harvard University, Boston attracted some of the leading Albanian intellectuals in the first decades of the twentieth century—above all, Fan Noli and Faik Konica. Noli took his BA degree at Harvard, and Konica also studied there for some time; another Harvard graduate was Kostandin Çekrezi (Constantine Chekrezi), who published his own magazine *Illyria* in Boston during 1916, before taking over the editorship of *The Adriatic Review* from Noli in 1919. Also active in Boston during the same period was Kristo (Christo) Dako, who became editor of Vatra's weekly paper *Dielli* in 1913; Dako was also a major contributor to another semi-monthly magazine, *Ylli i mengjezit*, published during

Rebels, Believers, Survivors: Studies in the History of the Albanians. Noel Malcolm,
Oxford University Press (2020). © Noel Malcolm. DOI: 10.1093/oso/9780198857297.001.0001

the years 1917–20.[2] Although of lesser stature than Konica and Noli, these two writers and editors would also play an important part in presenting Albania to the world: Çekrezi's *Albania Past and Present* (New York, 1919) was the first book about Albania to be written in English by an Albanian, while Dako's *Zogu the First, King of the Albanians* (Tirana, 1937) would be the first work on Albanian history and politics to be published in English in Albania.

The writings of these four men, and other articles contained in the journals they edited, do not form an utterly homogeneous body of materials. Even in the early years there were differences in emphasis and approach, and during the interwar period some strong political divisions would open up between them.[3] Nevertheless, their writings on the central issues of Albanian history and Albanian identity do exhibit a strong common stock of themes and arguments—particularly in the crucial period 1912–21. Those were the years in which the existence of an Albanian state was first accepted by the Great Powers, and then so thoroughly undermined by the war that the Albanians and their spokesmen had to argue all over again to re-establish the principle of Albanian statehood in the post-war settlement.

As has often been observed, Albania came very late to national statehood, and had only a short space of time—essentially the period 1878–1921—in which to build the sort of national consciousness and national ideology that, in most other European countries, had been developing since at least the first stirrings of the Romantic movement. Also, more than in the case of any other country, Albania depended for the development of its national ideology on intellectuals who lived outside the Albanian lands. This was mainly a consequence of the Ottoman policy of hostility to Albanian-language education; but it was also a reflection of the fact that the crucial battle for Albania's independence had to be fought not in the mountains and plains of the Balkans, but in the hearts and minds of Western politicians, within whose gift it lay. Two activities which can sometimes be distinguished in the history of other countries—nurturing national self-consciousness among the home population, and presenting national claims to the outside world—were thus, in the Albanian case, virtually fused into one.

The writings of the Albanian-American publicists of the early twentieth century played, I believe, a significant part in that two-in-one process. I do not claim that the arguments they used were original to them: in virtually every case it is possible to trace their themes and motifs back to earlier writers, both Albanian (or Arbëresh) and non-Albanian. But, given the belated development of Albanian nationalist ideology and the crucial importance of the second decade of the twentieth century for the creation and survival of an Albanian state, this body of writings does take on a special importance. The purpose of this essay is to explore these writings, picking out some of the characteristic mythic arguments they contain. I do not use the terms 'myth' and 'mythic' to imply that everything so labelled is false or absurd; some of these myths rested on serious historical arguments, elements of which are still accepted by modern scholars. Rather, the term 'myth' is used to suggest the symbolic, emotional and talismanic way in which such ideas have functioned, both as components of identity and as weapons in a war of conflicting political and historical claims.

Albanian Myths of National Identity: Four Categories

Myths of identity are usually historical myths: they make assertions about identity over time. But they are also ahistorical: they claim a kind of permanence and solidity outside time, in an attempt to establish an identity that is not vulnerable to flux, development or decay. (Those processes are presumed to apply to other people or peoples, who lack this special, myth-fortified identity.) Looking at the whole range of Albanian national myths, we can distinguish four major categories: the myth of origins and priority; the myth of ethnic homogeneity and cultural purity; the myth of permanent national struggle; and the myth of indifference to religion. Of these, the first is directly historical, concerned as it is with establishing a chronological priority over other peoples. But it also underlies the other myths: it provides the identity of the Ur-Albanian people whose unchanging characteristics (ethnic homogeneity, cultural purity, national struggle and religious indifference) are then exhibited throughout Albanian history.

The Myth of Origins and Priority

'It is generally recognized today', wrote Kostandin Çekrezi in 1919, 'that the Albanians are the most ancient race in southeastern Europe. All indications point to the fact that they are the descendants of the earliest Aryan immigrants who were represented in historical times by the kindred Illyrians, Macedonians and Epirots.' Those 'earliest Aryan immigrants' were identifiable, he claimed, as 'Pelasgians'.[4] Kristo Dako agreed; two years earlier he had written that the Albanians were 'the result of the combination of the ancient Illyrians, Macedonians and Epirotes, who were all descendants of the more ancient Pelasgians. These Pelasgians were the first people who came into Europe.'[5] This 'Pelasgian' theory, which gave the Albanians a kind of racial superiority over every other people in south-eastern Europe—or perhaps in Europe tout court— was the foundation stone on which rested all the other components of the myth-charged account of Albanian identity.

Questions about origins are perfectly valid historical questions, even if the full range of evidence needed to supply a conclusive answer may not always be available. In the case of the Albanians, modern scholarship recognizes a strong balance of probabilities in favour of the view that they are indeed descended from the ancient Illyrians. The evidence for this is primarily linguistic; its significance has become clear only with the development of the modern (twentieth-century) science of historical linguistics.[6] Long before this, however, versions of the 'Illyrian' theory of Albanian origins developed in competition with other hypotheses, of which the most influential was the one that identified the Ur-Albanians with the inhabitants of an area in the Caucasus also known (to classical geographers) as 'Albania', and supposed that they had migrated from there to the western Balkans in the late classical or early medieval period.

This Caucasian theory was first expounded by Renaissance humanists (such as Enea Silvio Piccolomini) who were familiar with the works of the classical geographers and historians; it was developed in the 1820s by the French diplomat and influential writer on the Balkans François Pouqueville; and in 1855 it was presented in a polemical response to the work of Johann Georg von Hahn by a Greek doctoral student at Göttingen, Nikolaos Nikoklēs.[7] By the late nineteenth century this theory was in retreat, thanks to the work of linguists who had demonstrated that Albanian was definitely Indo-European, not Caucasian.[8] One last attempt to salvage the theory, however, was made by an Arbëresh writer, Francesco Tajani, who suggested that the Ur-Albanians were Scythians who spoke an Indian language but whose place of residence, before they moved to Albania, was in the Caucasus. With delightful ingenuity, Tajani derived the word 'shqiptar' (Albanian) from the Sanskrit 'kship', meaning 'to fight', and 'tär', meaning bow—thus demonstrating, to his own satisfaction at least, that the original Albanians were Scythian archers.[9]

In retrospect, it seems obvious that the proponents of the Caucasian theory were engaged in little more than wishful thinking, with their selective use of classical authors, their bizarrely fanciful etymologies and, in some cases (such as the work of Nikoklēs), their transparently political motivation. Yet it must be pointed out that even those writers who were developing the 'correct' (Illyrian) theory of Albanian origins were not always free of those same faults. Although the first major exposition of the Illyrian theory, published by the German scholar Johann Thunmann in 1774, was both tentative and based mainly on historical evidence, subsequent writers incorporated this theory into a much more mythopoeic frame of argument, identifying the Ur-Albanians with the Pelasgians—a quasi-mythical population, referred to by Herodotus, of non-Greek and pre-Greek inhabitants of the Balkan peninsula.[10]

The key move here seems to have been made by the French geographer (of Danish origin) Conrad Malte-Brun; his interest in the Albanians had been aroused by the Arbëresh scholar Angelo Masci (Ëngjëll Mashi), whose Discorso sull'origine, costumi e stato attuale della nazione albanese (Naples, 1807) he reissued, in French translation and with his own critical annotations, in his multivolume compilation Annales des voyages.[11] Masci argued that the languages spoken by the Illyrians, Epirots and Macedonians in classical times were substantially the same, and that this was the source of the Albanian language; he did not, however, identify this *Ur*-language as Pelasgian. That step was taken by Malte-Brun himself in a later publication, albeit in a somewhat confused way. According to Malte-Brun the Albanians were descended from Illyrian tribesmen who had spoken a language 'affiliated' to that of the Pelasgians, Dardanians, Greeks and Macedonians. However, while identifying the Albanians as 'Illyrian' and their language as basically 'Pelasgian' ('the Albanian language is an ancient, important and distinct link in the great chain of Pelasgo-Hellenic languages'), Malte-Brun described Pelasgian as a primitive version of Greek, and distinguished it from Illyrian, which he regarded as a branch of the Thracian language.[12] These ambiguous invocations of a Pelasgian origin were repeated in turn by another influential Arbëresh writer, Giuseppe Crispi (Zef Krispi), in his *Memoria sulla lingua albanese*.[13]

The author who removed these confusions and finally established the Pelasgian theory in what was to become its classic form was the great Albanologist Johann Georg von Hahn, in his *Albanesische Studien* of 1854. Von Hahn reverted to Masci's original classification of Illyrians, Epirots and Macedonians as a single linguistic group (constituting the *Ur*-Albanian language), and added to this theory Malte-Brun's identification of the *Ur*-Albanians as Pelasgians: this meant that the language spoken by the Pelasgians was not a version of Greek, but something different and perhaps more ancient.[14] The theory quickly established itself among Albanian writers: one of the first Albanian weekly papers (printed in Albanian and Greek, and published in the Greek town of Lamia in 1860–1) was entitled *Pellazgu*; Pashko Vasa devoted the opening pages of his influential pamphlet *The Truth on Albania and the Albanians* (1878) to the Pelasgian story; and another magazine called *Pellazgu* was published by the Albanian community in Cairo in 1907.[15]

The primary function of this Pelasgian theory was, of course, to establish a claim of priority. In Kristo Dako's words, the Albanians were 'the autochthonous inhabitants of the Balkan Peninsula, which they have ruled for thousands of years before the Barbarians ever crossed the Danube.'[16] By identifying with Pelasgians, Albanians could claim that they were present in their Balkan homeland not only before the 'barbarian' invaders of late Roman times (such as the Slavs), not only before the Romans themselves, but also, even more importantly, before the Greeks. As Fan Noli put it in an article written in 1916, 'The Albanians are the only lawful owners of Albania. They have possessed that land from time immemorial, long before the Greeks and Slavs had come into the Balkan Peninsula.'[17] Dako too emphasized the theme of 'ownership': the Albanian, he wrote, 'is the descendant of the original owners of the soil.'[18] Albanian political leaders had felt territorially threatened by Greece ever since 1881, when a large part of the Ioannina *vilayet* was ceded to the Greek state. Their fears were strengthened by the transfer of Ioannina itself to Greece in 1913, and would be intensified in 1918 when news leaked out about the Allied powers' secret treaty of 1915, which had promised a large part of southern Albania to Greece. Although the idea of basing present-day political claims on theories about ancient Balkan tribes must strike the modern reader as bizarre, the emotional attraction of such theories for Albanians at that time is not hard to understand.

However, the implications of the Pelasgian theory went further than mere claims of 'historic right' to territory. It also enabled its proponents to claim that some of the most famous elements of ancient Greek culture and history had a Pelasgian, and therefore an 'Albanian', origin. 'Let it be known', announced Kristo Dako, 'that Philip and his son Alexander the Great as well as all the Macedonians were not Greeks but the forefathers of the Albanians.'[19] Çekrezi, similarly, could refer confidently in passing to 'Alexander the Great, whose Illyrian-Albanian origin cannot be disputed'.[20] The greatest expansion of Hellenic civilization and rule thus occurred thanks to an 'Albanian', not a Hellene.

A similar but more subtle insinuation of an 'Albanian' element into Greek civilization was prompted by Herodotus' comment that the Greeks had learned the names of many of their gods from the Pelasgians.[21] Taking up this hint, Malte-Brun and Crispi had devised Albanian origins for various ancient Greek names: Thetis (one of the Nereids, mother of Achilles) was derived from 'det', 'sea', the goddess Hera from 'erë', 'wind', Deucalion (the man who repopulated the earth after the Flood) from 'dhe ka lënë', 'he has left the earth' (referring to his embarkation during the Flood), and so on.[22] This etymology game was also played by von Hahn (Chronos from 'krujë', 'source'; Deucalion from 'dhe', 'earth', and 'kalli', 'ear of corn'), and by Pashko Vasa (Chronos from 'kohë', 'time'; Chaos from 'has', 'eaten'; Mousai, the Muses, from 'mësoj', 'I teach').[23]

Such arguments were taken up enthusiastically by the Albanian publicists in America: Çekrezi referred to 'the Albanian Zeus', whose memory survives even today in the appellation of God as 'Zot' by the modern Albanians, while Dako reproduced almost the whole list of derivations, however dubious, proposed by Pashko Vasa.[24] As Dako explained, 'Until lately it was believed that the mythology taught in schools as "the Greek mythology" was of Hellenic conception. The Albanian furnishes enough material to prove that this is not so.'[25] Another, slightly more practical use to which this method of argument could be put was to derive the Greek names for Albanian-inhabited areas from Albanian words, in order to reinforce the claim about ancient ownership of the territory: thus, according to Çekrezi, 'the historical names of what we now call Southern Albania or Epirus were "Thesprotia", i.e. the land of the sack-bearers, as it is very plainly expressed in Albanian, or "Molossia", i.e., "the Land of the Mountains"'.[26] Similarly, in a pamphlet published in England in 1918 and reproduced in *The Adriatic Review*, Mehmet bey Konica derived Emathia (an ancient Greek name for Macedonia) from 'e madhe', 'the great', and Illyria from 'liria', 'freedom'.[27]

Such derivations, almost all of which would be rejected by modern scholars, exhibit some of the classic features of a mythic style of thinking. They elide the difference between the ancestral past and the present, identifying the ancient Pelasgians as 'Albanian' (rather as if one were to refer to the ancient inhabitants of Britain as 'English', or to ancient Gauls as 'French'), and assuming that they spoke a version of the modern Albanian language. Etymology, instead of illuminating the nature of long processes of change over time, is thus used to imply an eternal present. What is more, a kind of intentionality is built into the past: classical names are treated not as products of chance and change, but as riddles and rebuses, cleverly devised by an Albanian-speaking, Albanian-thinking mind.[28] And, where the connections with the Greeks are concerned, these arguments do something very characteristic of mythic thinking: exploiting the ambiguous status first given to the Pelasgians by Malte-Brun, the Pelasgian theory implies, simultaneously, both that the Greeks were quite distinct from the Albanians (being mere alien immigrants to the Albanians' ancestral lands) and that they were somehow derived from the Albanians, culturally or even linguistically. (According to Dako, scholars were 'convinced that the Albanian language is the most ancient language of Europe, the mother of the Greek and the Latin'.)[29]

The Myth of Ethnic Homogeneity and Cultural Purity

Closely linked to the myth of origins was the myth of a pure, homogeneous ethnic identity: in addition to claiming that the Albanians had always lived in the same place, it was necessary to show that they had always remained pure Albanians, untouched by any intrusion, admixture or dilution by foreign elements. Although some of the other myths of Albanian identity may have contained an important element of historical truth, this one is hardly defensible at all: modern scholars know that no Balkan population has remained in a watertight compartment, and that all have undergone ethnic interminglings of many different kinds. In the case of the Albanians, the added ingredients would include Romans (themselves of various ethnic origins), Slavs (especially during the early middle ages, when Bulgarian Slav settlers penetrated much of Albania), Greeks and (in much smaller numbers) Turks. And, just as the gene-pool of the Albanians contains many different elements, so too their language, culture and way of life reflect the many influences they have absorbed, such as the linguistic legacy of Latin and Slavic vocabulary and the strong cultural imprint of the Ottomans.

The myth of ethnic homogeneity and cultural purity, however, dictated otherwise. As Kristo Dako explained in 1917, 'the Roman conquest seems to have wrought little change in the social condition of the Albanians. They still retained their language and their national manner and usages, and still remained a distinct and peculiar people.'[30] Two years later Kostandin Çekrezi wrote: 'In the course of her long history, Albania has been invaded by various civilised, half-civilised, and barbarian races. The Gauls, the Romans, the Goths, the Slavs, the Normans, the Venetians, and, finally, the Turks…So many invasions and influences have left hardly any appreciable traces, least of all on the national characteristics, traditions, customs, and language of the Albanians people.'[31] That Albanian writers felt the need to argue in this way was easily understandable at a time when Greek propagandists were claiming that the Albanians were not a proper people at all, that their language was just a mish-mash of other languages, and that any Albanian member of the Greek Orthodox Church was 'really' a Greek. At the same time, Slav publicists were insisting either that the Albanians of Kosovo were 'really' Slavs, or that they were 'Turks' who could be 'sent back' to Turkey. It is not surprising, then, that Çekrezi argued with particular vehemence that the Turks had not made even the slightest cultural impression on the Albanians: 'the despised Turk has been utterly incapable of exercising any kind of influence on their national characteristics, language, customs and traditions.'[32]

It was Faik Konica, however, who extended this argument from the cultural level to the ethnic or genetic. In one of his posthumously published essays he defined the Albanian race as 'a group of men who, having lived together for many centuries, speaking the same language, having led a secluded life, constantly intermarried, and until now successfully fought large settlements of invaders, present certain unmistakable similarities in physical appearance and in temperament.'[33] Konica himself thought there were two physical types in Albania, 'the tall man with clear eyes and light hair, and the shorter man with brown eyes and dark hair'. Nevertheless, he went on to cite approvingly the findings of the German anthropologist Paul Traeger, who claimed that 'the Albanians on the whole were a homogeneous racial group', and the French professor Eugène Pittard, who observed that 'It is difficult to find a population whose skull characteristics are more clear-cut.'[34] The explanation of this remarkable ethnic homogeneity was supplied by Kristo Dako, who imputed a kind of permanent 'national consciousness' and national pride to the *Ur*-Albanians and Albanians: 'While the Macedonians, Epirotes and Illyrians intermarried among themselves, they never did so with the Greeks.'[35] The fact of permanent identity was thus founded on the permanent consciousness of, or belief in, identity; in this way, the myth enlisted all the Albanians of past centuries as believers in the myth itself.

The Myth of Permanent National Struggle

From the myth of permanent consciousness of national identity, it was only a short step to the myth of a permanent struggle to defend that identity against outsiders. Çekrezi referred to 'struggles with the Romans, the Galles [*sic*], the Slavs, the Turks and with all the powerful hordes of invaders who poured from time to time into the Balkan Peninsula', concluding in his book that 'The Albanian has always been noteworthy for his dogged endurance in resisting the consummation of foreign conquest and occupation of his native soil.'[36] Here the myth had much genuine historical evidence to draw on: from Illyrians resisting Roman conquest to Albanians fighting under Skanderbeg, there were many examples of active resistance to invasion or foreign rule. However, modern scholars would be much less willing to assume that the thinking and motivation of the resisters were dominated in every case by a 'national consciousness' of the modern sort. Modern historians would also think it necessary to refer to the many examples of cooperation (sometimes to mutual advantage) between inhabitants of the Albanian lands and their foreign rulers—above all, in the case of the Ottomans, with their innumerable soldiers and officials of Albanian origin (including more than 40 Grand Viziers).

For Albanian publicists in the late nineteenth and early twentieth centuries, however, the most important aspect of the myth of permanent national struggle was the fight against the Ottomans. The reasons for this, in the political context of that period, were obvious: as the Ottoman Empire was eroded and finally broken up, there was a danger that the West would regard only the Christian states of the Balkans as the historic practitioners of a national anti-Ottoman struggle, and therefore see them as the sole legitimate claimants to ex-Ottoman territory. In addition, the status of Ottoman Turkey as an enemy power during the involvement of the United States in the First World War made it particularly necessary for the Albanian publicists in America to dissociate themselves from it. Thus we find Fan Noli and five other Orthodox Albanian priests submitting a 'Memorandum' to President Woodrow Wilson in November 1918, in which they declared: 'Of all the Balkan nations, they [sc. the Albanians] were the last to surrender to the Turk but never acknowledged his rule and never bowed to him. While all the other Balkan races were utterly crushed, the Albanians... still defied the Turk early in the nineteenth century.'[37] Interestingly, the picture of eternal enmity between Albanians and Turks supplied by these writers, who were active outside Albania, was considerably more extreme than that provided by Albanians commenting from a viewpoint inside the Albanian lands. Ismail Qemal Vlora gave what was perhaps a more realistic account of the Albanians' relations with the Ottoman regime when he wrote:

> Since that time [sc. the death of Skanderbeg], although the Albanians have never given up their passionate desire for independence, they have been the only Balkan people really attached to the Ottoman Empire, always ready to support it, always happy to help strengthen it and to profit by its strength. But whenever the Albanians have become aware that, instead of growing stronger, Turkey had weakened herself, and hurried to her ruin, they have risen in an effort of

self-preservation with the unanimous cry, 'Let her commit suicide if she wishes; we intend to survive.'[38]

A similar picture could be derived from the writings of Eqrem bey Vlora, or indeed from the comments of Isa Boletin reported by Aubrey Herbert.[39]

One explanation of this divergence of views would simply be that the publicists stationed outside Albania had a much stronger sense of the political needs of the day, so far as the policy assumptions of the Great Powers were concerned. But the full explanation goes deeper, surely, than that. Writers such as Konica, Noli, Çekrezi and Dako were responding not just to immediate political requirements, but to the dictates of their whole mythical pattern of thinking itself. The underlying line of thought was most directly expressed by Faik Konica in the first issue of his journal *The Trumpet of Croya*, published in St Louis, Missouri, in 1911: 'I wish that I could break every connection between Albania and Turkey, obliterate as far as possible the results of the conquest, and connect the present with the past by making it possible for my country to resume her natural evolution just where it was interrupted by the alien invaders.'[40] One could hardly wish for a more explicit statement of the mythic approach to time: half a millennium of human history can simply be erased, and what remains on either side of it can be 'connected' as if nothing at all had happened in between. This is possible not in the real world of human time, but in the timeless (mythical) world of essences, where identity is supposedly located.

The Myth of Indifference to Religion

Among the essential and timeless characteristics imputed to the Albanians, one other deserves special mention: religious indifference. Once again, it should be emphasized that to call this a 'myth' is not to imply that there was no truth in it at all. By the early decades of the twentieth century, when these Albanian publicists in America were writing, it was quite common for even the leading 'Muslim' families of Albanian *bey*s to be almost completely unconcerned with religion in their daily lives.[41] But, on the other hand, it is clear that the Albanians have produced many devoted believers, Muslim and Christian, over the centuries, and it would be absurd to suggest that these people were somehow less Albanian by virtue of possessing genuine religious beliefs.[42] When modern writers refer in general terms to the religious indifference of the Albanians, they are often mixing together various phenomena which need to be more carefully distinguished: these include the syncretism of folk-religious practices, the tolerance (and doctrinal syncretism) of the Bektashi, the much rarer phenomenon of crypto-Christianity (both Catholic and Orthodox), the social system of the northern Albanian clansmen (for whom loyalty to their *fis* or clan would take priority over any division of that *fis* into Catholic and Muslim branches), and the perfectly normal practice of Muslim men taking Christian wives without requiring their conversion to Islam. These are all different factors, too easily blurred into a single syndrome of 'indifference' by casual outside observers.

One such observer was Lady Mary Wortley Montagu, whose comments in a letter from Istanbul in 1717 became the *locus classicus* for Western writers: 'These people [*sc.* Albanian soldiers]...declare that they are utterly unable to judge which religion is best; but, to be certain of not entirely rejecting the truth, they very prudently follow both, and go to the mosques on Fridays and the church on Sundays, saying for their excuse, that at the day of judgment they are sure of protection from the true prophet; but which that is, they are not able to determine in this world.'[43] In his posthumously published work Faik Konica shrewdly analysed this passage, commenting that Lady Mary 'failed to perceive the dry humor of her informants. What those soliders told her can still be heard daily in Albania: it is an ironical and nonchalant way, almost a cliché, with the Albanians when they want to keep out of a religious controversy.' He also unpicked the claims of the Rev. Thomas Hughes (in his *Travels in Sicily Greece and Albania* of 1820), who had adduced as evidence of Albanian religious indifference the fact that Albanian Muslim men would marry Christian women: Konica noted the Western ignorance of Koranic law in these matters, and concluded that this was 'the key to the whole misunderstanding.'[44] Here at least Konica appeared as a dismantler, not a builder, of myths. Elsewhere, however, he quoted with approval Hobhouse's famous comment about the fellow-feeling of the Albanians being based on nationality, not religion—a comment which may be substantially true about the modern period, but which becomes more questionable the further back into the past the modern concept of 'nationality' is projected.[45]

Other writers of Konica's acquaintance were more willing to build up the popular image; nor is this surprising, given the political importance at that time of emphasizing that the Albanians were a single nation with a claim to a single statehood. Thus Çekrezi wrote in 1919: 'The truth is that the Albanian is not fanatical; on the contrary, it may be said that, *au fonds* [*sic*], he is indifferent in religious matters.' While making this an essential characteristic of the Albanians, Çekrezi also attributed the climate of religious tolerance to the special influence of Bektashism. Cleverly adapting his language to his American readership, he described the Bektashi as 'the Protestant element of Islamism', and declared that the rise of this sect had represented 'a liberal reaction against the fanaticism and rigorous rules of the faith of Mohammed'.[46] However, some confusion remained in Çekrezi's account; it was not altogether clear whether Albanian religious tolerance was the consequence of Bektashism, or whether the growth of Bektashism among the Albanians was the consequence of their own innate tolerationist tendencies.

Even more confusing was his deployment of another standard argument, using the evidence of syncretistic folk-religion to suggest that the Albanian commitment to Islam was only superficial: 'The Albanian Moslem has never forgotten...his former religion to some of the saints of which he still pays tribute, such as St George...and...St. Demeter.'[47] This argument (understandably popular among Catholic and Orthodox Albanians, but, in view of the use made of it by Slav and Greek propagandists, a dangerous one for Albanian interests) raised a potentially awkward question. If the Albanians had been so devoted to Christianity (which was at one stage their national religion), why had so many of them converted to Islam? This question becomes even harder to answer if one assumes that, as Çekrezi sometimes seemed to imply, the Albanians' religious tolerance or religious indifference was largely a consequence of Bektashism—in which case they must have been more committedly Christian before the Ottoman period.

The commonest way of answering this question was to invoke the most important element in the essentialized Albanian identity: the desire for freedom and independence. Kristo Dako put forward three main reasons for Albanian conversions to Islam. The first was that the Orthodox Church refused to preach the Gospel in the Albanian vernacular: this made the Albanians think of it as a foreign Church, to which they could feel little attachment. The second was the 'love of wearing a sword, symbolizing power, which is one of the greatest characteristics of the Albanian people'. And thirdly, 'Another reason why the Albanians embraced Islam was because this pledge gave special political rights for their country'—a somewhat dubious historical claim, but one which usefully brought the focus of the argument back to the central issue of national political rights.[48] Similarly, Çekrezi observed that 'Whenever life became intolerable under the Turkish regime, the Albanians found a way of escaping their miserable lot by an outward adoption of the religion of the conqueror. The Albanian is too zealous in the cause of liberty and independence to be a fanatic in religion.'[49]

Of all the comments on this question, however, the most revealing of the mythic pattern of thought I have tried to describe in this essay was the one made by Tajar Zavalani, a friend and at one stage political colleague of Çekrezi, whose explanation of the conversion of Albanians to Islam was as follows:

> Without wishing to minimize the importance of the historical factors which caused the spread of Islam among the Albanians, we must emphasize that their racial characteristics also played a part. For it is evident that Albania developed under Ottoman rule in a completely contrary direction to the one taken by the other Balkan peoples. The reason may be that the Albanians were formed spiritually under the influence of Roman paganism, which was added to the pagan traditions of the Illyrians. For the Illyrians, the development of a national consciousness was not channelled through the acceptance of Christianity. Thus, from ancient times, the thinking and social activities of the Albanians were characterized by a clear separation between religion and nationality.[50]

With this argument, the mythic pattern becomes complete, its components mutually sustaining one another. According to this interlocking set of beliefs, the choice between Christianity and Islam did not greatly matter for the Albanians, because their national identity existed independently, rooted in its ancient Illyrian past. The Albanians had preserved the traditions and the 'racial characteristics' of the Illyrians, among which—as all Albanian writers were understandably keen to stress—a desire for freedom and independence, expressed through permanent national struggle, was the most important feature. It can easily be agreed that some elements of historical truth were woven into this mythic pattern of thought; but it is also one of the proper tasks of historians to enable present-day Albanians to understand the ways in which the pattern has operated, not as the product of historical science, but as talisman, symbol and myth.

Notes

Preface

1. As I found when I published a history of Kosovo in 1998, the 'textbook view' of some issues, which was derived from Serbian national—and nationalist—historiography, exerted such an influence on the minds of some Western writers that they were predisposed to dismiss any evidence that contradicted it. See N. Malcolm, 'Response to Thomas Emmert', *Journal of Southern Europe and the Balkans*, 2 (2000), pp. 121–4, and cf. ch. 7 of this book.

Chapter 1

1. One modern study presents materials from pilgrim narratives relating to Istria and Dalmatia: S. Graciotti, *La Dalmazia e l'Adriatico dei pellegrini 'veneziani' in Terrasanta (secoli XIV–XVI): studio e testi* (Venice, 2014); but it has only a brief discussion (pp. 175–8) of a few of the texts that comment on Albania.
2. For an overview see D. Webb, *Medieval European Pilgrimage, c.700–c.1500* (Basingstoke, 2002).
3. J. G. Kohl, ed., *Pilgerfahrt des Landgrafen Wilhelm des Tapferen von Thüringen zum Heiligen Lande im Jahre 1461* (Bremen, 1868), pp. 69–74; R. Röhricht, *Deutsche Pilgerreisen nach dem Heiligen Lande*, 2nd edn. (Innsbruck, 1900), pp. 142–55 (Albrecht).
4. See H. F. M. Prescott, *Friar Felix at Large: A 15th-Century Pilgrimage to the Holy Land* (New Haven, CT, 1950), pp. 39–41. The basic price ranged from 30 to 40 ducats; various taxes and dues added 10–15 ducats, and there were some other expenses (see G. Pinto, 'I costi del pellegrinaggio in Terrasanta nei secoli XIV e XV (dai resoconti dei viaggiatori italiani)', in F. Cardini, ed., *Toscana e Terrasanta nel medioevo* (Florence, 1982), pp. 257–84, at p. 268).
5. C. Horstmann, 'Ratschläge für eine Orientreise (aus MS. Cotton Append. VIII, f. 108ff.)', *Englische Studien*, 8 (1885), pp. 277–83, at pp. 279–80.
6. G. Williams, ed., *The Itineraries of William Wey, Fellow of Eton College, to Jerusalem, AD 1458 and AD 1462; and to Saint James of Compostella, AD 1456* (London, 1857), p. 4.
7. Kohl, ed., *Pilgerfahrt*, p. 81(n.) (brought to land).
8. C. Hippler, *Die Reise nach Jerusalem: Untersuchungen zu den Quellen, zum Inhalt und zur literarischen Struktur der Pilgerberichte des Spätmittelalters* (Frankfurt-am-Main, 1987), pp. 71–5 (upper classes); M.-C. Gomez-Géraud, *Le Crépuscule du Grand Voyage: les récits des pèlerins à Jérusalem (1458–1612)* (Paris, 1999), p. 263 (family tradition).
9. On curiosity see Hippler, *Die Reise*, pp. 77–9; for evidence of humanist interests, see the comments on de Rochechouart, Ariosto and da Crema, below.

10. See B. Dansette, 'Les Pèlerinages occidentaux en Terre Sainte: une pratique de la "Dévotion Moderne" à la fin du Moyen Age? Relation inédite d'un pèlerinage effectué en 1486', *Archivum franciscanum historicum*, 72 (1979), pp. 106–33, 330–428, at pp. 111–12.

11. D. R. Howard, *Writers and Pilgrims; Medieval Pilgrimage Narratives and their Posterity* (Berkeley, CA, 1980), p. 18. On the desire to create a record for one's family see Hippler, *Die Reise*, pp. 191–5.

12. Cf. U. Ganz-Blättler, *Andacht und Abenteuer: Berichte europäischer Jerusalem- und Santiago-Pilger (1320–1520)* (Tübingen, 1990), pp. 164–5.

13. See the valuable study by K. Beebe, *Pilgrim and Preacher: The Audiences and Observant Spirituality of Friar Felix Fabri (1437/8–1502)* (Oxford, 2014).

14. On the illustrations see E. Ross, *Picturing Experience in the Early Printed Book: Breydenbach's Peregrinatio from Venice to Jerusalem* (University Park, PA, 2014).

15. See Gomez-Géraud, *Le Crépuscule*, pp. 305–8. Beebe notes that Fabri took a copy of Tücher's work with him to the Holy Land (*Pilgrim and Preacher*, p. 85).

16. J. Richard, *Les Récits de voyages et de pèlerinages* (Tournhout, 1981), p. 43 (de la Broquière: 'en ung petit livret'; and author of *Voyage de la Saincte Cyté*). The 14th-century pilgrim Nicolò da Poggibonsi, who was widely read in the 15th and 16th centuries, explained that he carried two wax writing-tablets on which to make immediate notes: Ganz-Blättler, *Andacht und Abenteuer*, pp. 111–12.

17. The writer was Ambrosius Zeebout, who may have been a Carmelite resident in the friary of that order in Ghent: see A. Zeebout, *Tvoyage van Mher Joos van Ghistele*, ed. R. J. G. A. A. Gaspar (Hilversum, 1998), pp. xliv–xlviii.

18. See the edition of Capodilista's text in S. Brasca, *Viaggio in Terrasanta 1480*, ed. A.-L. Momigliano Lepschy (Milan, 1966), pp. 161–237, and R. da Sanseverino, *Viaggio in Terra Santa*, ed. G. Maruffi (Bologna, 1888). See also U. Baldini, 'Capodilista, Gabriele', *Dizionario biografico degli italiani* (Rome, 1960–), xviii, pp. 635–8.

19. See R. Röhricht and H. Meisner, eds., *Das Reisebuch der Familie Rieter*, Bibliothek des Litterarischen Vereins in Stuttgart, clxvii (Tübingen, 1884), pp. 36–149; the description of Albania (pp. 44–5) is virtually identical to Tücher's.

20. Beebe, *Pilgrim and Preacher*, pp. 83–92; E. Neeffs, 'Un Voyage au XVᵉ siècle', *Revue catholique*, 9 (1873), 268–91, 321–36, 425–51, 553–81, at p. 332 (Aerts on Albania).

21. Anon., ed., 'Journal de voyage à Jérusalem de Louis de Rochechouart, évêque de Saintes (1461)', *Revue d'Orient latin*, 1 (1893), 168–274, at p. 231 ('Interrogatis sapiencioribus, novi quod tota nocte navigaveramus inter Albaniam et Ciciliam').

22. C. Schefer, ed., *Le Voyage de la Saincte Cyté de Hierusalem fait l'an mil quatre cens quatre vingts* (Paris, 1882), p. 39 ('Et nous dirent les marinniers qu'il y avoit grosse garnison des gens dudict Turc en ladicte ville').

23. N. Le Huen, *Le Grant Voyage de Jherusalem* (Paris, 1517), fo. 12r ('vne aultre cite appartenant au turc anciennement grande & puissante et en bie[n]s habundante: comme on nous dict').

24. A. Denke, ed., *Konrad Grunembergs Pilgerreise ins Heilige Land, 1486: Untersuchung, Edition und Kommentar* (Cologne, 2011), p. 332 ('nit ver vom mer das selbs, sagten uns die marner, ligen Duratzo, ain gros zerstört stat'); cf. R. Herz, ed., *Die 'Reise ins Gelobte Land' Hans Tüchers des Älteren (1479–1480): Untersuchungen zur Überlieferung und*

kritische Edition eines spätmittelalterlichen Reiseberichtes (Wiesbaden, 2002), p. 356 ('nit weyt vom mere do ligt ein grosse zustorte stat, Duratzo genant').

25. E. Henrici, 'Beschreibung einer Seereise von Venedig nach Beirut im Jahr 1434', *Zeitschrift für deutsches Altertum und deutsche Literatur*, 25 (1881), pp. 59–70, at p. 66.

26. F. Fabri, *Evagatorium in Terrae Sanctae Arabiae et Aegypti peregrinationem*, ed. K. ['C'] D. Hassler, 3 vols. (Stuttgart, 1843–9), i, p. 89; N. Chareyron, *Pilgrims to Jerusalem in the Middle Ages*, tr. W. D. Wilson (New York, 2005), pp. 42–3. The rule about foreign ports was frequently bent, however, to permit a landing at Dubrovnik.

27. P. Tucoo-Chala and N. Pinzuti, eds., 'Le Voyage de Pierre Barbatre à Jérusalem en 1480', *Annuaire-Bulletin de la Société de l'Histoire de France*, for 1972–3 (1974), pp. 74–172, at p. 117 ('on voit les haultes montaignes d'Albanie et la sont grandes neiges car on les veoit bien de XXX ou XL lieues').

28. P. Walther, *Fratris Pauli Waltheri guglingensis itinerarium in Terram Sanctam et ad Sanctam Catherinam*, ed. M. Sollweck (Tübingen, 1892), p. 75 ('venimus ad terram et montes Albaniae, que terra cum suis confiniis et montibus totaliter sibi Thurcus subiugavit preter unam civitatem, que vocatur Duratze, que est Venetorum').

29. [D.-C.,] marquis de Godefroy Ménilglaise, ed., *Voyage de Georges Lengherand, mayeur de Mons en Haynaut, à Venise, Rome, Jérusalem, Mont Sinaï & Le Kayre, 1485–1486* (Mons, 1861), p. 93 ('du costé à la main senestre nous voyemes grandes roches et montagnes; et nous fut dit que au delà d'icelles c'estoit pays d'Albanie, et de l'obéissance du Turcq').

30. Zeebout, *Tvoyage*, p. 58 ('dit voorseyde land van Albanien es een zeer steerc landscip van ghebeerchten, van stranghen passaigen, van steercken steden ende casteelen ende van goede rivieren; daer in woonen vele vromer lieden, vele bosch daer in ende goet vruchtbaer land').

31. F. Geisheim, ed., *Die Hohenzollern am heiligen Grabe zu Jerusalem, insbesondere die Pilgerfahrt der Markgrafen Johann und Albrecht von Brandenburg im Jahre 1435* (Berlin, 1858), p. 210 ('das Lannd...das heist Albania'); Brasca, *Viaggio*, p. 170 ('le montagne di Dalmatia', 'le montagne de Albania'); F. Strejček, ed., *Jana Hasišteinského z Lobkovic putování k Svatému Hrobu* (Prague, 1902), p. 26 ('zemie, gijez rziekagij Albania').

32. On Venetian Albania the classic work is O. J. Schmitt, *Das venezianische Albanien (1392–1479)* (Munich, 2001). See also D. Sferra et al., *L'Albania veneta: la Serenissima e le sue popolazioni nel cuore dei Balcani* (Milan, 2012).

33. Herz, ed., *Die 'Reise'*, p. 356 ('Do endet sich das landt Slafonia vnd hebt sich an Albania').

34. W. Kreuer, ed., *Tagebuch der Heilig Land-Reise des Grafen Gaudenz von Kirchberg, Vogt von Marsch/Südtirol im Jahre 1470: Bearbeitung und Kommentierung des von seinem Diener Friderich Steigerwalder verfassten Reiseberichts* (Paderborn, 1990), p. 95 ('Ain schloss, genanndt Buda. Unnd höbt sich daselbs An daz lannd, gepürg unnd sprach Allwania').

35. J. Heers and G. de Heyer, eds., *Itinéraire d'Anselme Adorno en Terre Sainte (1470–1471)* (Paris, 1978), p. 376 ('Ab ibi conspeximus montes Albanie provincie quae in situ et circumferentia satis parva est, non dives, sed pravissima gens, linguam habens propriam. Hec fere tota, preter aliquas civitates que Venetorum sunt, Turci Magni est').

Unusually, he included both Kotor and Bar in his description of Dalmatia (p. 379). Adorno was from a branch, long established in Bruges, of a well-known Genoese merchant family.

36. E. von Groote, ed., *Die Pilgerfahrt des Ritters Arnold von Harff* (Cologne, 1860), p. 65 ('dese stat lijcht in Albanijen dae sij ouch eyn eygen spraiche haynt, der man nyet wael geschrijuen en kan, as sij geyn eygen litter in deme lande en hauen').

37. Fabri, *Evagatorium*, iii, p. 354 ('homines ferocissimi', 'Ab his gentibus venit olim exercitus in Peloponnesum et diffusi per littus maris regionem illam etiam Albaniam vocaverunt').

38. See e.g. G. Botero, *Relationi universali*, 2 vols. (Vicenza, 1595), ii, fo. 50r; G. A. Magini, *Geografia, cioè descrittione universale della terra*, tr. L. Cernoti (Venice, 1598), fo. 121v.

39. An account of a 1494 voyage by an anonymous pilgrim (who may have been Ludwig, Freiherr von Greifenstein) says, at the relevant point in the return journey, that it gave much more information about Budva in its description of the initial journey, but that part of the manuscript does not survive (see T. Schön, 'Ein Pilgerfahrt in das heilige Land im Jahre 1494', *Mitteilungen des Österreichischen Instituts für Geschichtsforschung*, 13 (1892), pp. 435–69, at p. 466); M. M. Newett, ed., *Canon Pietro Casola's Pilgrimage to Jerusalem in the Year 1494* (Manchester, 1907), p. 183 (about to land).

40. Zeebout, *Tvoyage*, p. 57 ('Zij seilden ooc voor bij eenen propren stedekin, over de zelve slincke hand gheleghen in Albanien, ghenaemt Dulsinjon, ligghende up eene steenrotse met eenen becke ter zee waert in loopende, zeer steil, recht oft met beetels ende grooten aerbeide afghehauwen ware, ende up trechte pointkin es de zelve stede ghefondeert, bijcans omrijnct vander zee. De zijde ten lande waert es zo steerc bemuert dicke, ende heeft zo diepe, wijde graven inde rootsen ghehouden, datse onmoghelic ware van winnene; heeft een zeer goet poort ende havene voor scepen ende galleyen').

41. A. Ariosto, *Itinerarium (1476–1479)*, ed. F. Uliana (Alessandria, 2007), p. 12.

42. Brasca, *Viaggio*, p. 170 ('se ritrovono ad un castello...nominato Dulcigno, ed ad uno altro chiamato Ludrino, terre de la Albania, dove è uno pessimo colpho chiamato colpho de Ludrino...dove volentieri haveriano preso porto se gli fusse stato receptaculo per la galea, ma non essendogli, bisognò stare in mare a la misericordia de Dio; a cossè costezando tuto el dì dito castello'). Roberto da Sanseverino's account omits the words from 'terre' to 'colpho de Ludrino' (*Viaggio*, p. 38): this might be a case of eye-skip while copying from Capodilista's text.

43. Zeebout, *Tvoyage*, p. 57 ('Niet verde van desen voorseyden stedekin zo leit een schoon poort ende havene, ooc ter luchter hand, ter welker plecken eene schoone riviere inde zee comt ghevallen, ghenaemt Labajona, onttrent der welker zeere vele ghebeerchs ende wonderlicke vele boschs es. Zij leden ooc voor bij eender goeder steden in Albanien gheleghen, ghehauden vanden Torck, ghenaemt Allijssio, daer onttrent dat oec zeer veel boschs es. Niet verre van daer zo comt ooc eene schoone riviere inde zee ghevallen, ghenaemt Loudrijn, maer en es gheen zonderlinc watere zomen daer seit').

44. Ibid., p. 57 ('zo quamen zij anckeren in een poort ende havene van eender goeder stede, over de luchter hand oec in Albanien gheleghen, ghehouden vanden kerstenen...ghenaemt Durassen').

45. Brasca, *Viaggio*, pp. 170–1 ('più volta feceno prova de redursi a terra, ma la forza del vento teneva la galea come serata', 'deliberò lo patrone ad ogni modo andar a Durazo,

e lì far scala, acciò li peregrini che erano tuti lassi et afflicti potesseno prender qualche quiete', 'sopravene la galea de la guardia de la illustrissima Signoria de Vinezia, la qual per custodia del dicto colpho ne tiene continuamente xv armate. E de la predicta galea era patrone miser Alexandro Contarino; e proximandose e cognoscendo nostra galea esser di peregrini, longi uno miglio comenzorono rabasar la vella e l'arbore e fare riverentia segondo lor usanza. Poy aproximata una galea a l'altra, cognosutosi li patroni uno cum l'altro, comenzò el comito nostro dimandar di novelle').

46. Williams, ed., *Itineraries of William Wey*, p. 56. Despite a few small discrepancies, Wey's dates of arrival at various destinations coincide closely with those of Capodilista and Sanseverino. The reference to Belgrade is puzzling; the Ottoman defeat was at its failed siege of that fortress in 1456. So too is the reference to Euboea, which the Ottomans would not besiege until 1470. Sultan Mehmed II's campaign in the spring and early summer of 1458 was mostly in the Peloponnese; he did go to Euboea in the late summer, but as a visitor, not a military aggressor (see F. Babinger, *Mehmed the Conqueror and His Time*, tr. R. Manheim, ed. W. C. Hickman (Princeton, NJ, 1978), p. 161).

47. da Sanseverino, *Viaggio*, p. 44 ('gli feze mille careze et offerte et acompagniato dicto Sig.re Ruberto et compagni, inseme con prefato don Alexandro, ad la chiesia di sancto francischo, doue haueuano deliberato stare quella nocte. Ma non hauendogli trouato locho che se facesse per loro, se partirono de dicta chiesia et andarono ad alogiare ad sancto dominicho, doue trouarono megliore alogiamento per tuta la compagnia, la quale con grande caritate fu da quelli frati receputi et seruita de alogiamento'). The Dominican friary was probably the richest conventual body in Durrës; it had close connections with the noble Thopia family, and its friars were active in the salt trade, enjoying a special freedom from customs dues (see Schmitt, *Das venezianische Albanien*, pp. 136–7).

48. Brasca, *Viaggio*, p. 171 ('cenato che hebbeno, deliberò vedere quella antiquissima cità, chi già fu magna, e nel presente è molto ruinata et disfacta, edificata suxo colline apresso lo litto de lo mare et circundata da tre canti de muri grossissimi; et montati suxo dicti muri trovorono una statua di bronzo, cioè uno cavallo cum uno imperatore suxo, et qual si raxona esser stato Constantino imperatore; et dicta statua sta cum una manu levata, guardando verso Thesalia. Da quello loco si vedeva le mure che fece fabricare Cesaro quando perseguitava Pompeyo, ne quale lo introcluse per assediarlo, le quale son grossissime. Vedevase etiamdio la Emathia che hè una parte de la Albania, dove fo roto lo exercito de Pompeyo da Cesaro, quando esso poy fugite in Egipto dove da Ptolomeo fu decapitato. In quelli campi che sono proximi a Durazo cercha meglia xii si raxona che si trova arrando pezi de arme, tanta fu la strage de li homeni che rimase in dicti campi, apresso li quali fu una cità chiamata Thesaglia, la quale al presente è ruinata e destructa et quasi inhabitata come Durazo, ne la qual habita pochissima gente et antiquamente se chiama Epirro').

49. Ariosto, *Itinerarium*, p. 13 ('urbem, olim amplissimam et ingentem ruinis nunc collapsam'); B. von Breydenbach, *Sanctarum peregrinationum in montem Syon... opusculum* (Mainz, 1486), unfoliated, between 4 and 12 June ('iam pridem destrúcta'); for Tücher and Grunemberg's comments, see above, n. 23.

50. On the earthquake see R. Elsie, *Early Albania: A Reader of Historical Texts, 11th–17th Centuries*, Balkanologische Veröffentlichungen, xxxix (Wiesbaden, 2003), pp. 12–13. It

is sometimes suggested, on the basis of 16th-century descriptions, that the ruined state of the town was the consequence of the Ottoman conquest (see e.g. S. Yerasimos, S., *Les Voyageurs dans l'Empire Ottoman (XIVe–XVIe siècles): bibliographie, itinéraires et inventaire des lieux habités* (Ankara, 1991), p. 26); the pilgrim narratives show that Durrës was already 'ruined' in the previous century.

51. von Groote, ed., *Die Pilgerfahrt*, p. 65 ('eyn groysse verstoerde stat van deme Turcken, yetzont vnderworffen den Venecianeren').

52. Geisheim, ed., *Die Hohenzollern*, pp. 210–11 ('dieselb stadt Durazo vnnd Constantinopel vnnd Rana hat erhöht und bekehrt Constantinus'); Anon., ed., 'Journal de voyage à Jérusalem de Louis de Rochechouart, évêque de Saintes (1461)', *Revue d'Orient latin*, 1 (1893), 168–274, at p. 231 ('olim Constantini magni urbem'). The identity of 'Rana' is unclear.

53. Herz, ed., *Die 'Reise'*, pp. 356–7 ('Dieselben stat hat der keiser Constantinus angefangen zu pawen jn maynung, Constantinopel vnd seinen palast dohyn zu richten. Aber als er sich nachuolgend anders bedacht, gevil jm die art des lands doumb nit. Vnd zog furter an das ende, do yecunt Constantinopel stet, die er jm zu einer keÿserlichen wonung pawen liess').

54. Fabri, *Evagatorium*, iii, 355; von Breydenbach, *Sanctarum peregrinationum*, unfoliated, between 4 and 12 June ('propter sterilitate[m] et glebe inepcia[m]'); Zeebout, *Tvoyage*, p. 58 ('Het deedze eerst maken de keyser Constantinus, ende zoude ghesijn hebben Constantinopolen, maer de lucht ende aert van daer onttrent en beviel hem niet, uuten welken hij daer niet meer en wrachte, ende dede Constantinopolen maken ter plecken daer zij noch staet').

55. I am very grateful to Dr George Woudhuysen for his advice on this. He informs me that various accounts of the founding of Constantinople (in works by the Anonymous Continuator of Dio, an anonymous chronicle, Cedrenus, Glykas, a poet in the Greek Anthology, Manasses, Sozomen, Theophanes, Zonaras and Zosimus) did mention that Constantine considered other places for it; those they specified included Chalcedon, Ilion, Salonica and Sardica, but none mentioned Dyrrachium.

56. Anna Comnena, *The Alexiad*, tr. E. A. S. Dawes (Cambridge, Ontario, 2000), XIII.2, p. 231 (saying that it was on 'the gate that opens to the East'); Ciriaco of Ancona, *Epigrammata reperta per Illyricum a Cyriaco Anconitano apud Liburniam* (n.p., n.d), p. xxii, no. 147.

57. D. Malipiero, *Annali veneti dall'anno 1457 al 1500*, ed. A. Sagredo, Archivio storico italiano, ossia raccolta di opere e documenti finora inediti o divenuti rarissimi risguardanti la storia d'Italia, vii (1843), p. 94 ('Adesso l'è quasi deshabità per la mala qualità dell'aere: ha molti vestigii de statue antiche, tra iquali è un Imperador a cavallo; alguni dise che l'è Theodosio, alguni Costantin').

58. [S. Feyerabend, ed.,] *Reyssbuch dess heyligen Lands, das ist ein grundtliche Beschreibung aller und jeder Meer und Bilgerfahrten* [sic] *zum heyligen Lande* (Frankfurt-am-Main, 1584), fos. 30v–47r, at fo. 46r ('als man sag / Durazzo ist ein hübsche Statt / vnd Constantinus / S. Helene Sohn / hat sie lassen bawen / vnd daselbst vor dem hohen Stifft stehet Constantini form oder gestalt / auff einen grossen ehern Pferd / vbergüld / vnd hat in seiner Hand ein Zettel / lautend: *Haec est via, &c.*').

59. Zeebout, *Tvoyage*, pp. 57–8 ('es een zeer oud ghestichte, rontomme bemuert met ghebacken steenen zomen hier inden landen useert. Daer staet oec een zeer schoen

steerc casteel over de zijde ten lande waert, ende leit an wat hoochden; ronts omme deser voorseyder stede eist meest al neringhe oft sompe linghe ware, datmer nauwe met paerden, karren oft oec te voet an en mach alst ghereghent heeft. Men seit dat Pierus, de zone van Achilles, coninc was vander zelver steden, ende dat dlant van Eperien oft Epieren daer an leyt. Item ande poorte vander voorseyder stede die te lande waert staet, zijn twee viercandtte colommen, die ghenouch onderhouden tverwelf vander zelver poorten, breet onttrent onderhalven voet over elke zijde, ende moghen lanc zijn onttrent vier vademen, dwelc al te wonderlic een weerc es om sien. Dese zijn van diversschen colueren zeere blinckende; men siet daer in ligghen sticken van meinschen beenen, als knetkins van handen ende voeten, sticken van hoefden, van caecbeenen, tanden, ende sticken van aerm pijpen oft been pijpen, datmer bescheedelic binnen inde beenen siet, zomen doet de blommen in dese glasen appels, bijden welken wel te gheloevene es dat in ouden tijden de colommen, diemer vele inden landen van over zee vindt van diversschen colueren, ghemaect zijn bij misterien, ende niet alle uutghehauden uut steenrotsen. Item up de poorte zo staet een paert met eenen mensche daer up sittende, van wonderlicker grootten, beede van metale, daer ghestelt teender ghedinckenessen zoot te bemoedene es. Dese voorseyde stede heeft tanderen tijden in een heylant ghestelt ghezijn, ende teertrijcke duer dolven zo diepe, datter dwater van eender zijde ter ander duer liep, maer es nu al vervult ende heffen zo datmer wel alomme over rijdt').

60. See, for example, specimens nos. 163, 220–5, 268–73, 415–17 in the Corsi collection: http://www.oum.ox.ac.uk/corsi/

61. A. Gutteridge, 'Cultural Geographies and "the Ambition of Latin Europe": The City of Durres and its Fortifications, c.400–c.1501', *Archeologia medievale*, 30 (2003), pp. 19–65, at p. 22.

62. Ibid., pp. 20–31; M. Kiel, *Ottoman Architecture in Albania, 1385–1912* (Istanbul, 1990), p. 94; S. Santoro, 'Lo stato degli studi sull'urbanistica di *Epidamnos-Dyrrachium*', in M. Buora and S. Santoro, eds., *Progetto Durrës: l'indagine sui beni culturali albanesi dell'antichità e del medioevo: tradizioni di studio a confronto* (Trieste, 2003), pp. 149–208, at pp. 160–2.

63. See Gutteridge, 'Cultural Geographies', pp. 48–9 (pre-1436), and Kiel, *Ottoman Architecture*, p. 95 (post-1501). Note also that Capodilista and Sanseverino referred simply to walls on three sides.

64. Schmitt, *Das venezianische Albanien*, pp. 537–42.

65. See Santoro, 'Lo stato', p. 162.

66. Anon., ed., 'Journal de voyage', pp. 231–2.

67. Ariosto, *Itinerarium*, p. 13.

68. A. da Crema, *Itinerario al Santo Sepolcro, 1486*, ed. G. Nori (Pisa, 1996), pp. 12–13 (on motivation), 43–4 (text).

69. da Sanseverino, *Viaggio*, pp. 43–4 ('se dicea ch'el douea andare in la morea, che è vna prouintia di grecia, parte de la quale è de la Signoria di Vinegia et parte de vno Signore di grecia; pur fin a quella hora non se diceua gli fusse andato, et che se diceua anchora ch'el faceua grande apparato de exerciti per venire a croya, città in albania, siue castello del signore Scanderbech, o vero per andare ad nigraponte').

70. Zeebout, *Tvoyage*, pp. 58–9 ('den meesten deel vanden steden ende casteelen ligghende ten lande waert up heeft de Torck alle in handen, als Petrella, Croeya,

Scouterij, Drijvasto ende vele meer andere, te lanc om noumen. De Torck en hads nemmermeer ghecreghen, hadde dlant in hem zelven eendrachtich ghezijn, maer daer waren diverssche heeren de welke dlant van Albanien beheerden, die eeuwelic in gheschille waren ende in oorloghen deen jeghens den anderen, mids welken ghescille de Tuerc te eer ende te bat zijnen wille ghecreech over tvoorseyde land; emmer wasser een heere, ghenaemt Scanderbec, dat al te vroom een kerstin was die altoes den Toorck vromelic wederstont, zo dat de Tuerc noynt in zijnen levene an tselfs Scanderbecx deel yet gheraken conste, maer doodde in zijnen tijt zo vele Toorcken zomen daer ghemeenlic seit, als halvelinghe nu leven, ende naer zijn doot zo ghinc dlant al verloren, uutghedaen eeneghe steercke steden die als noch kersten zijn, zo hier vooren gheseit es').

71. [Feyerabend, ed.,] *Reyssbuch*, fo. 36v ('Auch was mein G. H. [sc. Gnädige Herr] gewiesen / ein hoher Berg auff die lincke seiten / darauff hatten sich in kurtzer zeit davor versammlet / zehen oder zwölff tausent Albaneser / wartend der zukunfft dess Königs von Franckreich den Türcken zubekriegen / Nach dem dass der jetztgenannt König von Franckreich das Königreich von Neapolis gewonnen hat / vnnd da der Türck gehort hat / wie der König von Franckreich wider hindersich gezogen were auss dem Königreich von Neapolis / hat er sich auff gemacht / vnd die jetzigen Albaneser alle oder mehrertheils todt geschlagen').

72. See P. Durrieu, 'Valona, base d'une expédition française contre les Turcs projetée par le roi Charles VIII (1494–1495)', *Comptes rendus des séances de l'Académie des Inscriptions et Belles-Lettres*, 59 (1915), no. 2, pp. 181–90, and K. M. Setton, *The Papacy and the Levant (1204–1571)*, ii, *The Fifteenth Century* (Philadelphia, 1978), pp. 180–90.

73. On the siege see M. Barleti, *The Siege of Shkodra*, tr. D. Hosaflook (Tirana, 2012); on the ending of it, O. J. Schmitt, *Südosteuropa und die Adria im späten Mittelalter* (Bucharest, 2012), pp. 397–8.

74. Fabri, *Evagatorium*, iii, p. 354 ('Civitas, quae est caput totius Albaniae, dicitur Scodra, quae Venetorum fuit, sed anno Domini 1478 eam civitatem Turco dederunt in confoederatione. Hanc nos in vulgari nominamus Scultur. Ad eam bene venissemus pro celebratione festorum, sed jam nec cultus nec festa in ea sunt...').

75. von Breydenbach, *Sanctarum peregrinationum*, unfoliated, between 4 and 12 June ('vna cu[m] quoda[m] munitissimo castro Tornesij cognominato').

76. Strejček, ed., *Jana Hasišteinskeho putování* ('hrad a miesto welmi pieknee a pewnee a lezij na Insuli, a Czysarz tureczky Stary, tohoto nynieyssijeho otecz, dluhy czas, yako sem zprawen, geho dobywal A niekolikrat k niemu Ssturmowati dal. A nikoli geho dobyti nemohl...su w niem Statecznij lidee byli a mnoho Tisycz Turkuow ze su zbili w ssturmu, kdyz k nim Ssturmowali, ze Czysarz s hanbau od nich musyl odtrhnuti...Mohli su ti wssiczkni tehoz miesta Sskutery obywatele tu przi swych Statczych zuostati, A Czysarz gich miel przi gich wierze nechati. Ale nechtiel zadny z nich tu zuostati, Ale wssiczkni tahli do benatek wssech Statkuow swych krom, czo s sebu nesti mohli, se odwaziwsse pro wijeru krzestiansku').

77. Ariosto, *Itinerarium*, pp. 13–14 ('confecta nuper (hoc est Christi anno milessimo quadringentesimo septuagesimo [nono]) cum Turco, Christianorum hoste truculentissimo, a Venetis pace, qua illi Scodrae castellum, Staliminis insulam et Maini brachium in Peloponeso situm oppidis quidem hominibusque refertum traddidere, atque in tantis reipublicae Christiane periculis pollicentibus etiam quinqeginta triremibus

armato milite completis opem ei auxiliumque ferre petenti, uber hic sane deplorandi locus nobis ingeritur et ingens Christiane religioni dolor offertur, quandoquidem nobis summopere verendum sit ne tali teterimo foedere hostem nobis in exitium extremum penitus armaverint et excursionibus, vastitatibus, incendiis, eversionibus conficiamur a Turcis'). Ariosto was probably a native of Ferrara; he served in the Bolognese province of the Franciscan order (see R. Pratesi, 'Ariosto, Alessandro', *Dizionario biografico degli italiani* (Rome, 1960–), iv, pp. 166–8). On the terms of the peace treaty (which did not include any such pledge of military assistance) see Babinger, *Mehmed the Conqueror*, p. 369, and Setton, *Papacy*, p. 328.

78. On the development of Vlorë in the early Ottoman period see M. von Šufflay ['Shuflay'], *Qytetet dhe kështjellat e Shqipërisë, kryesisht në mesjetë*, tr. L. Malltezi (Tirana, 2009), pp. 63–4.

79. See A. Esch, 'Gemeinsames Erlebnis—individueller Bericht: vier Parallelberichte aus einer Reisegruppe von Jerusalempilgern 1480', *Zeitschrift für historische Forschung*, 11 (1984), no. 4, pp. 385–416 (with a comparison of their accounts of the passage past Vlorë: pp. 398–400). This was Fabri's first pilgrimage, about which he wrote only a brief narrative; his main account describes the pilgrimage of 1483.

80. Schefer, ed., *Le Voyage*, p. 39 ('vismes toutes les montaignes d'Albanye et plusieurs villes appartenantes au Turc entre lesquelles y en a une grande et forte nommée Vallone qui souloyt estre aux Veniciens. Et nous dirent les marinniers qu'il y avoit grosse garnison des gens dudict Turc en ladicte ville et avoyt sur le port de la ville grant quantité de navires et gallées audict Turc'). Vlorë had not in fact belonged to Venice.

81. Tucoo-Chala and Pinzuti, eds., 'Le Voyage', p. 117 ('on disoit que le Turcq avoit une grande partie de son armee en ladite ville de Waronne, et que pres de la avoit plus de cent velles'); Brasca, *Viaggio*, p. 30 ('cento vele').

82. von Breydenbach, *Sanctarum peregrinationum*, unfoliated, between 4 and 12 June ('ciüitas eqüide[m] firmissima. iuxta qua[m] in flümine quoda[m] Turcus [i[m]pe[rator] ingente[m] solet habere classem nauiu[m] vt com[m]uniter quadringentaru[m]').

83. Kreuer, ed., *Tagebuch*, p. 99 ('Ain schloss genanndt Tanina, das lag Auf ainem hohen perg. Das hat der Türckh Innerhalb drey oder vier Jar Auferpawt, unnd Enthalb des geschloss bey drey meylen ligt ain stat genanndt velana, unnd is mit Tirkhen Unnd albasanern [*sic*] besötzt und hört auch den türken Zue').

84. See A. Baçe, 'Qyteti i fortifikuar i Kaninës', *Monumentet*, 7–8 (1974), pp. 25–54.

85. Zeebout, *Tvoyage*, p. 58 ('zo leden zij voor bij een groot colf ende schoettinghe vander zee, al over de slincke hand gheleghen, up dwelc eene schoone, groote stede ghestaen es, ghehouden vanden Tuerck, ghenaemt Lavalona, ombemuert, maer es wat omrijnct met dijcken, dounen ende staeckijtsel van haute ende van eerden; daer staet oec een zeer schoon, steerc casteel, dat al waert dat de stede ghewonnen ware, men tselve casteel wel hauden zoude, want tes ghenouch onwinlic').

86. Strejček, ed., *Jana Hasišteinskeho putování*, p. 26 ('A tu lezij przi brzehu morskem geden hrad na wrchu a pod nim miesto dobrze welikee. A rziekagij temuz miestu a hradu walona. A gest tyz zamek Czyesarze Tureczkeho. A tyz Czyesarz ma tu przi tom zamku mnoho lodij, gimz rziekagij Subtile Galege a ffusty'). A 'galea sottile' or light galley was the standard military galley, as opposed to a 'galea grossa', a broader-hulled galley used for commerce; a 'fusta' was a foist, a small galley-style vessel.

87. von Groote, ed., *Die Pilgerfahrt*, p. 65 ('off die lyncke hant van deser portzen an deme lande lijcht gar eyn schoin groyss dorff, hait wael tzwey dusent fuyrstede, Velona geheysschen. dyt dorff vermaich dem turckschen keyser zo dem kreych brengen seuen hundert peert, ain die zo voysse. item boeuen desem dorff lijcht eyn schoin berchsloss, Kano geheysschen, dar off hait der turcksche keyser eynen amptman sittzen').

88. Kiel, *Ottoman Architecture*, pp. 271–2.

89. Kreuer, ed., *Tagebuch*, p. 99. Venice had occupied Sazan in 1372, returning it to the local ruler of Vlorë on a quasi-feudal basis in 1389 (Schmitt, *Das venezianische Albanien*, pp. 221, 227); but no attempt was made to assert Venetian ownership after the Ottoman takeover of Vlorë.

90. Zeebout, *Tvoyage*, p. 58 ('een cleen heylandekin, hem toeghende met drien plompen pointen...up twelc woont ghemeenlic een caloeyer, dats een Griecx monic').

91. Strejček, ed., *Jana Hasišteinskeho putování*, p. 26 ('A nezda mi se, by byla osazena lidmi, pokud sem widieti mohl').

92. von Groote, ed., *Die Pilgerfahrt*, pp. 65–6 ('dyt Saseno is gar ein kleyn insell des Turcken. item hie off lijgen gar kleyne tzwae grece capellen, die eyne zo vnser lieuer frauwen, die ander so sijnt Nyclais genant. in deser tzijt hait der groisse here van Turckijen gar vill suuerlicher henxt weyden gayn off deser insulen').

93. Anon., ed., 'Reise des Ritters Hans Bernard von Eptingen nach Palästina, im Jahr 1460', *Der Schweizerische Geschichtsforscher*, vii (Bern, 1828), pp. 313–402, at pp. 329–30 ('da sahen wir zwischen einer Insel und einem hohen Gebirg hin, dem wir nacher und unser fuhren, dasselbig Gebirg war fast felsechtig und voller Schnees, so ruch, dass wir keine Bäum da sahen noch gesehen möchten, dann hin und her Rosmarin, Salben und dergleichen Gestäud. Item wir sahen auch einen Wasser-Runs von dem Gebirg in's Meer gahn und fliessen, das war gar frömbd zu sehen, und darnach in der Gegend uf dem dürren und scharfen Gebirg sahen wir viel grosser langer Feuren, die sich alle zusehentlich mehrten, und da fragte ich, was Feuer das gesein möchte, da sagten ein Theil: es wären Wortzeichen der Türken; da sprach ein Theil: man brannte Eisenerz; als da meynten ein Theil: es wären Hirten-Feuer, aber es war in allem ungleich, sunder das Gebirg so rauh, dass Leut noch Vieh sich also nit enthalten möchten, so wären auch fast wohl sichtbarere und höhere Berg da gewesen, daruf Wortzeichen zu geben, so wurden die Feuer je grösser und je länger, auch dann hin und her brennen, also dass da nit wohl könnte Eisenerz gebrennt oder geläutert werden; und hatten auch die Berg solche Gestalt, dass Niemand daran kommen möchte oder daruf, darzu so war auch ganz kein Holz da, aber ein Theil, die über-schlugen, dass es solche Berg wären, die von ihnen selbst brennen, mit denen hielt ichs allervestig').

94. Tucoo-Chala and Pinzuti, eds., 'Le Voyage', p. 117 ('et vers le soir deulx ou troys heures devant soleil couché fusmes en mer et estoit le vent contraire tellement que nous con-vint gesir en mer devant une isle et chasteau en Turquie nommee Waronne; et la au soir apersumes III feux sur les montaignes, car la coustume des paisans est de faire feu sur les mons au soir quant ilz voyent venir barques, navez ou galeez sur mer affin que ceulx des villes et cités se guardent').

95. Schefer, ed., *Le Voyage*, p. 40 ('Après soleil couchant, avoit sur une grant montaigne dessus ladicte ville plusieurs grans feux que faisoyent lesdictz Turcz; à cause de quoy, nous fusmes bien esbahis et fusmes toute la nuict en grant peur et danger; et firent les

pellerins le guet avecques les galiotz toute la nuict, craignant que lesdictz Turcs venissent assaillir nostre gallée').

96. P. Walther, *Fratris Pauli Waltheri guglingensis itinerarium in Terram Sanctam et ad Sanctam Catherinam*, ed. M. Sollweck (Tübingen, 1892), p. 76 ('multi ignes in diversis montibus et presertim circa civitatem Velonam. Et dixerunt patroni, quod pagani fecissent istos ad honorem sancti Johannis Baptistae, cuius vigilia erat ipsa dominica').

97. For the custom see above, p. 272.

98. R. Röhricht, 'Die Jerusalemfahrt des Heinrich von Zedlitz (1493)', *Zeitschrift des Deutschen Palästina-Vereins*, 17 (1894), 98–114, 185–200, 277–301, at p. 291 ('auf die rechte handt, do sindt wir die nacht bey gefaren, do habenn die Turcken viel grosser Feuer die Nacht auff Iren gebirge gemacht').

99. [Feyerabend, ed.,] *Reyssbuch*, fo. 36v ('als die Albaneser wonhafft auff den hohen Bergen daselbst / sahen vnser Galee vorfahren / machten sie vil Fewer / vnd wardt vns gesagt dass sie solche Feuwer machten / auss freuwde dass vnser Galee alldar kommen wer / vnd dass wir das H. Land besuchen wolten / dann dieselben Albaneser seind gute Christen').

100. H. Holland, *Travels in the Ionian Isles, Albania, Thessaly, Macedonia &c. during the Years 1812 and 1813* (London, 1815), pp. 522–3. Holland also cites references to this phenomenon (at a place in the region of Apollonia, probably in this area) in Strabo, Plutarch and Dio Cassius. On the production of pitch in the early modern period see below, p. 349, n. 72.

101. Anon., ed., 'Journal de voyage', p. 231 ('terram fertilem gleba, vino, oleo, olive et pomis orangie dulcibus; tonsa jamque erant omnia blada').

102. Brasca, *Viaggio*, p. 59 ('gran copia di grano').

103. Zeebout, *Tvoyage*, pp. 59–60 ('vischt men dicwilt vele scoens coraels dwelc zeer goet ende fijn es, maer nieuwer naer zo groot noch zo steerc van brancken als tcorael datmen vischt up de costen van Barbarien'). More than 300 years later François Pouqueville would comment on the coral 'which carpets its [sc. northern Himarë's] underwater rocks', suggesting that an entire coral industry could be developed there: *Voyage dans la Grèce, comprenant la description ancienne et moderne de l'Épire, de l'Illyrie grecque, de la Macédoine cisaxienne ... et du Péloponèse*, 5 vols. (Paris, 1820–1), i, pp. 260–1 ('qui tapisse ses rochers sousmarins').

104. Zeebout, *Tvoyage*, p. 59 ('een zeer groot ghebeerchte ... ghenaemt Lasimara, in welc ghebeerchte woonen eene maniere van lieden, kersten zijnde, de felste ende quaetste diemen daer yewers onttrent vindt, ende en hebben gheenen heere noch en houden van niemende niet, ende hoe dicwilt de Tuerck met al zijnder macht ghecommen heeft int voorseyde ghebeerchte, mids den steercken passaigen ende wildernessen die daer onttrent zijn, en conste up hemlieden noynt niet of lettel ghewinnen, maer trac altoes onghecust van daer ende lietse over zulc dat zij waren, zo zij als noch zijn').

105. Röhricht, 'Die Jerusalemfahrt', p. 113 ('haben wir gelassen ein gros gebürge, do sindt Ir aigen hernn, vnd der Torck hat ir nicht megen gewinnen, wen sie gar ein fest gebirge Inne habenn vnd geben auf Niemanden nichts').

106. Strejček, ed., *Jana Hasišteinskeho putování*, p. 27 ('A po lewe rucze nam asa X mil wlaskych tyz den byli nam hory welike, gimz rziekagij Czimera. A teez hory Czimera negsu Insule, nez Czela zemie welmi hornata a kamenita, pokudz sme widieli.

A przilezij k Czyesarze Tureczkeho zemi. A taaz kragina Czimera gest Sto mil wlaskych wuokol a LX mil z Sfirzij. A lidee w tee kraginie gsu sami swogi pani A nechtije byti zadnemu poddani...A magij w teez kraginie mnoho wsy, mnoho dobytka, wobilee y wina...welmi vzkymi czestami skrze welikee skalee. A kdyz se czeho obawagij, tehdy ty czesty a klauzy osazugij a branije gich, ze zadny k nim nemuoz. Tijz lidee a obywatelee tee kraginy, komuz mohu czo wzyeti, wssem naporzad beru: krzestianom, pohanom y Turkom a nawijecze Czysarzi Tureczkemu a geho poddanym przekazegij berucze gim, czoz mohu... ze pro gich takowee kradeze a lupeze ze Czysarz Tureczky byl se na nie welmi Sylnie sebral chtie ge pod se podmaniti...ze k nim nemohl, A niektery Tisycz drahnie lidij gemu zbili, A ze prostie s weliku sskodu a hanbu odtrhnuti musyl od nich. A w temz kragi Czimera tento obyczey a zpuosob ti obywatelee zachowawagij, Yakoz w czechach pohrziechu take ten obyczey gest, ze wierzij, kto chcze, yak chcze, y teez ti Albanazarowe mnoho rozlicznych wier mezy sebu magij...Take magij plnu swobodu wssem okolnim swym Susedom brati, lupiti, krasti, mordowati, A proto se zadny netrescze. Take dielagij mezv sebu ffalessnee zlattee y teez ginu minczy na rozlicznee razy a gsu toho swrchowanij mistrzi nad ginee'). What was meant here by 'pagans' is not clear. The statement about a religiously mixed population presumably derived from more general comments Hasišteinský had heard about conversion to Islam in the Albanian lands. Islamicization seems to have taken place very slowly in Himarë, beginning in the 16th century (see F. Duka, 'Aspekte social-ekonomike dhe demografike të Himarës gjatë sundimit osman (shek. XV–XVI)', in L. Nasi et al., eds., *Himara në shekuj* (Tirana, 2004), pp. 52–95, at p. 70).

107. L. Conrady, *Vier rheinische Palaestina-Pilgerschriften des XIV. XV. und XVI. Jahrhunderts* (Wiesbaden, 1882), p. 97 ('eyn grote stat geheisen Cente quarante, went daer so veel kirchen stonden, die wilche um eirre fonden wil vordeliet syn, vnd en is itson nicht wan eyn hauen').

108. Zeebout, *Tvoyage*, p. 60 ('zoe lijdtmen voor bij wat colfs, ooc ligghende ter luchter hand, up twelke eene schoone stede plach te stane, wel alzo groot als Akers int lant van beloften, ghenaemt Ayjos Seranda, maer es zo te nieuten ende ghedestrueert, datmer als nu anders niet af en siet dan de fundamenten ende hoepen van steenen').

109. Kohl, ed., *Pilgerfahrt*, p. 87 ('ein hübsch Schloss Bottintra, das ist der Venediger. Davor sind die Türken zwei Mal gewest, es zu gewinnen').

110. Conrady, *Vier rheinische Palaestina-Pilgerschriften*, p. 174 ('geliken in vnsen lande deit in den meyde vnde mut so wast seer lustich daer to wesen int dat lant of int velt, went dat gras daer wt begost to springen gelychen in vnsen lande indem somer. Hier bleef die galeye alre zelen dach al den dach').

111. Zeebout, *Tvoyage*, p. 60 ('eer men comt ter zelver steden zo lijtmen noch voor bij een cleen colfkin, ligghende over de slincke zijde te Griecken waert datmen nu Tuerckien seit, crom ende slom ten lande waert in loopende, up thende vanden welken staet een steerc casteel up eene ronde, steile steenrotse, bicans rontomme inde zee ligghende, ende es daer onttrent al marrasch, zo datmer nauwelic met paerden noch halvelinghe met scepen ende qualic te voete an gheraken can, ende es ghehouden vanden kerstenen; de Torck heefter dicwilt voren ghesijn, maer altoes schiet hij van daer met grooter scaden ende es ghenouch eene onwinlicke plaetse. Men vancter vele goets visch onttrent, zonderlinghe twee manieren, deen ghenaemt cyvales ende dandre mauvrachis, van wiens kijten men daer maect de beste boterghen diemen ter weerelt

vindt, dwelc eene zonderlinghe spijse ende provande es diemen daer in dien landen zeere useert; het zijn alle meest visschers die daer woonen ende zeer vrome lieden. Daer onttrent leyt zeere veel goets bosch, meest al van lauwerier boomen, ende leit rontomme in planuren, maer daer bij achterwaert leyt een zeer hooch ghebeerchte. Dit voorseyde casteel es ghenaemt Buventroo'). Kephalos (mugil cephalus) is flathead mullet; mavraki (mugil capito) is thin-lipped grey mullet; botargo or bottarga is dried and salt-cured roe. On Butrint in this period see A. Crowson, *Butrinti venecian: Venetian Butrint* (London, 2007), esp. pp. 60–9 on the fisheries.

112. Brasca, *Viaggio*, p. 59 ('levossi lo sirocho et apparseno due vele de turchi uscite da la ditta Valona, per la qual cosa tuti stessimo con qualche timore et non senza cagione, eo maxime perchè in la pace fatta per el Turcho con venitiani parmi che alcuno non se intenda securo s'el non è del paese loro; et apresso hanno capitulato insieme che ogni hora che li navilij de venetiani sono richiesti de calare le vele per parte del Bassaa sive capitaneo de l'armata del Turcho, elli siano obligati calare, chè una mala cosa per forestieri che intrano in loro navilij').

113. Schefer, ed., *Le Voyage*, pp. 39–40 ('Et environ soupper, vismes une gallée saillir devers la ville et cuidions qu'elle vint à nous; et à celle heure, nous faillit le vent et ne pouvoyt aller nostre gallée ne avant ne arriere'), 41 ('furent fort esbahys de nostre venue. Et disoient que se n'eust esté le grant miracle evident que Dieu nous fist quant il nous envoya ung vent contraire le vendredy et samedy dernier passé, nous estions tous perdus et prins des Turcz qui passerent nostre chemin par ou nous venismes et en passa par devant le port de Corphol environ quatre vingtz navires qui s'en alloyent pour mettre le siege à Raguze dont nous estions partis le mercredy dernier').

114. Fabri, *Evagatorium*, iii, p. 355 ('nec progredi nocte licebat propter maris illius petrositatem, nec in tutum portum Albaniae intrare v[o]luimus propter inhabitantes Turcos, alia autem loca importuosa erant', 'portuosum…sed desertum, juxta quod nec homines nec bestiae morabantur').

115. J. Schmid, ed., *Luzerner und Innerschweizer Pilgerreisen zum Heiligen Grab in Jerusalem vom 15. bis 17. Jahrhundert* (Lucerne, 1957), p. 34 ('So was das mer als voll Türggen vnd vnsicher').

116. Horstmann, 'Ratschläge', p. 284 ('never have the excessive boldness of voyaging in little vessels on any of the coasts of the heathen, for fear of the sort of corsairs that have been mentioned already, both the Christian ones and those not of our faith, in every part of the sea').

117. G. Ghinassi, ed., 'Viaggio a Gerusalemme di Nicolò da Este, descritto da Luchino dal Campo, ed ora per la prima volta messo in luce', in *Miscellanea di opuscoli inediti o rari dei secoli XIV e XV* (Turin, 1861), pp. 99–160, at p. 109 ('dubitando non fusse nave di corsari').

118. Anon., ed., 'Reise des Ritters', p. 329 ('dess so rüsteten wir uns zur Wehr, mit Büchsen und andern Dingen').

119. See M. P. Pedani, *Dalla frontiera al confine*, Quaderni di Studi Arabi, Studi e testi, v (Venice, 2002), p. 32.

120. Röhricht, 'Die Jerusalemfahrt', p. 291.

121. Schön, 'Ein Pilgerfahrt', p. 465 ('da kam gar ein wunderlich grausams weter mit plitz und dönrren, das vast erschreckenlich was, und thet die grösten schleg, als ich sy mein lebtag nie gehört hab').

122. Johannes von Frankfurt, *Opuscula: itinerarius, arenga, collatio*, ed. M. L. Bulst-Thiele (Heidelberg, 1986), p. 55 ('superuenit talis et tanta tribulatio, quod patronus et omnes naute de vita desperauerunt implorantes dei misericordiam et sanctorum suffragium, quia mare galeam subintrauit, et iam vicina erat totali submersioni').

123. Kreuer, ed., *Tagebuch*, p. 101.

124. Brasca, *Viaggio*, p. 170 ('lo patrone molto si meravegliava vedendo tal fortuna, la qual al dir suo haveria bastato di genaro, et non vedendo altro rimedio lo patron fece scriver molti nomi de sancti in breve e ponerli in una beretta e disse ad alguni peregrini…che ogniuno cavasse uno de dicti breve e facesse voto a quel sancto ch'el trovaria scripto suso, che come fosse in terra ferma gli fariano dire una messa a suo honor e riverenzia, e getaseno li brevi in mare, e cossì fu fato. E come a Dio piacque la sera comenzò la pioza, el vento, el mare abonazarse').

Chapter 2

1. F. Nopcsa, *Die Stammesgesellschaften Nordalbaniens: Berichte und Forschungen österreichischer Konsuln und Gelehrter (1861-1917)*, ed. F. Baxhaku and K. Kaser (Vienna, 1996), p. 210.

2. M. E. Durham, *Some Tribal Origins, Laws and Customs of the Balkans* (London, 1928), p. 22.

3. Nopcsa, *Die Stammesgesellschaften*, p. 83.

4. See R. Veselinović, 'Die "Albaner" und "Klimenten" in den österreichischen Quellen zu Ende des 17. Jahrhunderts: historisch-geographische und ethnographische Abhandlung', *Mitteilungen des Österreichischen Staatsarchivs*, 13 (1960), pp. 195-230; for a disproof of Veselinović's identification of this 'Patriarch of the Kelmendi' with the Serbian Orthodox Patriarch, see N. Malcolm, *Kosovo: A Short History* (London, 1998), pp. 146-8, 155-6.

5. P. Bartl, 'Die Kelmendi: zur Geschichte eines nordalbanischen Bergstammes', *Shêjzat (Le Pleiadi)* (1977), pp. 123-38; F. Zefiq, *Shqiptarët Kelmendas në Hrtkovc e Nikinc (1737-1997)* (Zagreb, 1997). I am very grateful to Prof. Zef Mirdita for his help in obtaining a copy of this book for me.

6. H. Hecquard, *Histoire et description de la Haute Albanie ou Guégarie* (Paris, 1858), p. 177.

7. M. von Šufflay, *Srbi i Arbanasi (njihova simbioza u srednjem vijeku)* (Belgrade, 1925), p. 7.

8. See especially S. Pulaha, 'Formation des régions de selfgouvernment [*sic*] dans les Malessies du sandjak de Shkodër aux XVe-XVIIe siècles', *Studia Albanica*, 13 (1976), no. 2, pp. 173-9, and K. Kaser, *Hirten, Kämpfer, Stammeshelden: Ursprünge und Gegenwart des balkanischen Patriarchats* (Vienna, 1992), pp. 107-11.

9. Hecquard, *Histoire et description*, pp. 183-4, 190.

10. M. E. Durham, *High Albania* (London, 1909), p. 85; Bartl, 'Die Kelmendi', p. 124; Nopcsa, *Die Stammesgesellschaften*, p. 216.

11. J. N. Tomić, ed., 'Gradja za istoriju gornje Arbanije', *Spomenik Srpske Kraljevske Akademije*, 42 (= ser. 2, vol. 37) (1905), pp. 51-77, at p. 55.

12. M. Jačov, ed., *Spisi tajnog vatikanskog arhiva XVI-XVIII veka* (Belgrade, 1983), p. 136.

13. S. Pulaha, ed., *Defteri i regjistrimit të sanxhakut të Shkodrës i vitit 1485*, 2 vols. (Tirana, 1974), i, pp. 431–4.

14. See K. Luka, 'Pamje mbi ekonominë dhe topografinë e viseve të Hotit, të Kuçit, të Piprit dhe të Kelmendit në fund të shek. XV', *Studime historike* (1980), no. 4, pp. 219–52, esp. pp. 219–21. Another Ottoman document, a summary of the 1497 appendix, was published by Branislav Djurdjev in his *Iz istorije Crne Gore, brdskih i malisorskih plemena* (Sarajevo, 1954): this supplies details of the sections on Hoti and Kuçi which are lacking from the otherwise fuller text published by Pulaha.

15. Luka, 'Pamje mbi ekonominë', pp. 229–33.

16. Pulaha, ed., *Defteri*, i, pp. 431–3.

17. Durham, *High Albania*, p. 85; Jačov, ed., *Spisi tajnog arhiva*, p. 136; J. G. von Hahn, *Albanesische Studien*, 3 vols. (Jena, 1854), i, p. 184.

18. Jačov, ed., *Spisi tajnog arhiva*, p. 136.

19. Durham, *High Albania*, p. 43, and *Some Tribal Origins*, pp. 45–6. See also the comments of Antonio Baldacci in his *Nel paese del Cem: viaggi di esplorazione nel Montenegro orientale e sulle Alpi albanesi* (Rome, 1903), pp. 19–29, at p. 24.

20. Pulaha, ed., *Defteri*, i, pp. 431–4; cf. Luka's comments on the place-names of the *nahiye*: 'Pamje mbi ekonominë', pp. 243–4.

21. J. N. Tomić ['I. Tomitch'], *Les Albanais en Vieille-Serbie et dans le Sandjak de Novi-Bazar* (Paris, 1913), pp. 61–2.

22. S. Pulaha, *Popullsia shqiptare e Kosovës gjatë shekujve XV – XVI (studime dhe dokumente)* (Tirana, 1983), p. 644.

23. S. Pulaha, ed., *Qëndresa e popullit shqiptar kundër sundimit osman nga shek. XVI deri në fillim të shek. XVIII: dokumente osmane* (Tirana, 1978), pp. 69–70.

24. L. Soranzo, *L'Ottomanno* (Milan, 1599), p. 167 ('E questi sono quelli, che per hauer sito forte, & esser di natura ferocissimi, non acora [sic] si son lasciati ben soggiogare dall'armi del Turco'). [On this work, and on the author's main source of information about Albania, see above, pp. 38, 42–3, 53–4.]

25. F. Lenormant, *Turcs et monténégrins* (Paris, 1866), p. 331; J. M. Floristán Imízcoz, ed., *Fuentes para la política oriental de los Austrias: la documentación griega del Archivo de Simancas (1571–1621)*, 2 vols. (Leon, 1988), i, pp. 434–5, 486.

26. Lenormant, *Turcs et monténégrins*, p. 316.

27. Luka, 'Pamje mbi ekonominë', pp. 222, 229–30; cf. also S. Shkurti, *Der Mythos vom Wandervolk der Albaner: Landwirtschaft in den albanischen Gebieten (13. –17. Jahrhundert)*, ed. K. Kaser (Vienna, 1997), pp. 60–1.

28. Pulaha, ed., *Defteri*, i, p. 434.

29. The best study of *derbend* status in the Balkans is A. Stojanovski, *Dervendžistvoto vo Makedonija* (Skopje, 1974). On this collective treatment of the *haraç* tax see C. Cahen, P. Hardy and H. İnalcık, 'Djizya', in *The Encyclopaedia of Islam*, 2nd edn., ed. H. A. R. Gibb et al. (Leiden, 1960), ii, pp. 559–66, at p. 563. Elsewhere, İnalcık comments on this grant of *derbend* status to the Kelmendi, giving the date '1486' but apparently referring to this 1497 appendix to the 1485 defter: 'Timariotes chrétiens en Albanie au XVᵉ siècle d'après un registre de timars ottoman', *Mitteilungen des Österreichischen Staatsarchivs*, 4 (1951), pp. 118–38, at p. 136(n.).

30. Luka, 'Pamje mbi ekonominë', p. 239.

31. I. Zamputi, ed., *Relacione mbi gjendjen e Shqipërisë veriore e të mesme në shekullin XVII*, 2 vols. (Tirana, 1963–5), i, p. 198.

32. Jačov, ed., *Spisi tajnog arhiva*, p. 36.

33. Zamputi, ed., *Relacione*, i, p. 298.

34. D. de Gubernatis and A. M. de Turre, *Orbis seraphicus: historia de tribus ordinibus a seraphico patriarcha S. Francisco institutis* [...] *tomus secundus*, ed. M. A. Civetia and T. Domenichelli (Quaracchi, 1886), p. 406. Cf. Bolizza's comment in 1614 that the Kelmendi had 650 fighters of their own, but could raise a force of 5,380 men: Zamputi, ed., *Relacione*, i, pp. 272–8.

35. Bartl, 'Die Kelmendi', pp.127–31; see also L. Ugolini, 'Pagine di storia veneta ai tempi di Scanderbeg e dei suoi successori (con due documenti inediti)', off-printed from *Studi albanesi*, 3–4 (1933–4), p. 27 (for the plan of 1616); and I. Zamputi, 'Bashkimi i maleve shqiptare në fillim të shekullit të XVII-të: ekspedita e Vuco Pashës mbi Kelmend me 1638', *Buletin për shkencat shoqërore* (1957), no. 3, pp. 63–95 (for the plans of 1614 and 1620).

36. Jačov, ed., *Spisi tajnog arhiva*, p. 136.

37. See, for example, the report of 1638 by Frang Bardhi, quoted in Zamputi, 'Bashkimi i maleve', pp. 89–90.

38. Tomić, ed., 'Gradja za istoriju', pp. 56–7.

39. R. Tričković, 'U susret najtežim iskušenjima: XVII vek', in R. Samardžić et al., eds., *Kosovo i Metohija u srpskoj istoriji* (Belgrade, 1989), pp. 115–26, at p. 120.

40. Veselinović, 'Die "Albaner" und "Klimenten" '.

41. See Malcolm, *Kosovo*, pp. 146–8, 155–6.

42. Ibid., pp. 148–51.

43. De Gubernatis and de Turre, *Orbis seraphicus*, p. 567.

44. I. Zamputi and S. Pulaha, eds., *Dokumente të shekujve XVI–XVII për historinë e Shqiperisë*, iv (Tirana, 1990), pp. 128–31.

45. Ibid., p. 153 (contacts with Austrian envoy); J. Tomić, 'Patrijarh Arsenije III Crnojević prema Mlečićima i ćesaru 1685–1695', *Glas Srpske Kraljevske Akademije*, 70 (= ser. 2, vol. 43) (1906), pp. 66–161, at p. 94 (*provveditore*).

46. F. Ongania, ed., *Il Montenegro da relazioni dei provveditori veneti (1687–1735)* (Rome, 1896), pp. 49–52.

47. Archivio di Stato, Venice [hereafter: 'ASVen'], Provveditori da terra e da mar, filza 529, report of interview with 'Nicon', 7 Oct. 1689 (quoted with various inaccuracies in Tomić, 'Patrijarh Arsenije', p. 106).

48. Zamputi and Pulaha, eds., *Dokumente*, iv, p. 247 (report from Istanbul); Biblioteca Nazionale Marciana, Venice, MS IT VII 1068, fo. 160v (report from Vienna).

49. ASVen, Provveditori da terra e da mar, filza 530, Molin report, 5 Mar. 1690.

50. ASVen, Provveditori da terra e da mar, filza 529, Zmajević to Molin, 22 Nov. 1689.

51. ASVen, Provveditori da terra e da mar, filza 530, Molin report, 5 Mar. 1690.

52. Istituto per la storia della società e dello stato veneziano, Fondazione Cini, Venice, microfilms of Archivio Segreto Vaticano, nunziatura di Venezia: microfilm 136, fo. 168r (report of 22 Apr. 1690).

53. Zamputi and Pulaha, eds., *Dokumente*, iv, p. 342.

54. Tomić, ed., 'Gradja za istoriju', pp. 58–9.

55. P. Bartl, ed., *Quellen und Materialien zur albanischen Geschichte im 17. und 18. Jahrhundert*, 2 vols. (Munich, 1975–9), ii, pp. 139–40.

56. Tomić, ed., 'Gradja za istoriju', p. 60 (1707); A. Theiner, ed., *Vetera monumenta slavorum meridionalium historiam illustrantia*, 2 vols. (Rome, Zagreb, 1863–75), ii, p. 241 (1711).

57. Archivio Segreto Vaticano, Vatican City, Visitationes ad limina, 728, items 1 (Karadžić report, 12 Dec. 1713) and 9 (Karadžić report, 12 June 1716).

58. Pulaha, ed., *Qëndresa e popullit shqiptar*, pp. 311–12.

59. Jačov, ed., *Spisi tajnog arhiva*, p. 246.

60. M. Kostić, 'Ustanak Srba i Arbanasa u Staroj Srbiji protiv Turaka 1737–1739 i seoba u Ugarsku', *Glasnik Skopskog Naučnog Društva*, 7–8 (1930), pp. 203–35; Zefiq, *Shqiptarët Kelmendas*, pp. 32–7. See also J. Langer, 'Nord-Albaniens und der Herzegowina Unterwerfungs-Anerbieten an Österreich, 1737-1739', *Archiv für österreichische Geschichte*, 62 (1881), pp. 239–304. For a brief account of the events of 1737 see Malcolm, *Kosovo*, pp. 168–70.

61. Jačov, ed., *Spisi tajnog arhiva*, p. 136. The arrival of the Franciscans in 1641 is recorded by de Gubernatis and de Turre, *Orbis seraphicus*, p. 449.

62. Sh. Gaspari, 'Nji dorshkrim i vjetës 1671 mbi Shqypni', *Hylli i Drítës* 6 (1930), pp. 377–88, 492–8, 605–13; 7 (1931), pp. 154–61, 223–7, 349–55, 434–47, 640–4, 699–703; 8 (1932), pp. 48–50, 98–104, 208–10, 265–7, 310–14 here at 6, p. 608.

63. Durham, *High Albania*, p. 86.

Chapter 3

1. L. Soranzo, *L'Ottomanno* (Ferrara, 1598), pp. 113 ('Antonio Bruni...nel suo Trattato del Bellerbegato di Grecia'), 117 ('De gli Albanesi Latini scriue lo stesso Bruni lor co[m] patriota nel Trattato allegato di sopra...').

2. Biblioteca Apostolica Vaticana, Vatican City, MS Barb. Lat. 5361, fos. 200r–207r; Biblioteca del Museo Correr, Venice, MS Wcovich Lazzari 25, busta 9. (It is of course possible that other copies survive, as yet unnoticed, in other collections.) I am very grateful to both libraries for letting me study these items; similarly, I wish to thank all the other libraries and archives mentioned in the notes below.

3. For details of all these individuals, and of other members of this extended family, see N. Malcolm, *Agents of Empire: Knights, Corsairs, Jesuits and Spies in the Sixteenth-Century Mediterranean World* (London, 2015), *passim*.

4. Archivio del Collegium Germanicum et Hungaricum, Rome, MS Hist. 145 (G. Nappi, 'Annali del Seminario Romano'), fo. 39r. (Hence the deduced date of birth.) In the brief account of Antonio Bruni's life which follows here, I give references to original sources; but in most cases further information will be found in Malcolm, *Agents of Empire*.

5. Archivio del Collegium Germanicum et Hungaricum, Rome, MS Hist. 145, fo. 39r (departure, Aug. 1577); Archivio Segreto Vaticano, Vatican City, Segr. Stato, Legaz. Avignone, 12, fo. 47r (letter from G. Bruni to Cardinal Como, Jan. 1581, saying that Antonio had left Perugia and that Gasparo hoped he would transfer to Padua), and Segr. Stato, Legaz. Avignone, 15, fo. 191r (letter from Gasparo to Como, saying Antonio had arrived in Avignon).

6. Archives départementales de Vaucluse, Avignon, MS D 36 (University of Avignon, 'Livre concernant les noms...des primiciers, docteurs...et gradués'), fo. 105r. He was described there as 'Antonius Brunus dioces. Olciniensis' ('of the diocese of Ulcinj'), which seems to imply that that was his place of birth.

7. G. Vida, *De' cento dubbi amorosi di Hieronimo Vida iustinopolitano*, ed. A. Vida (Padua, 1621), fos. 66v–68r (contribution to literary debate; on the dating, see Malcolm, *Agents of Empire*, p. 310).

8. Soranzo, *L'Ottomanno*, 42 ('Tale è l'informatione, ch'io hò hauuto da quelli, c'hanno veduti i libri della Moldauia, e della Valacchia').

9. Archivio di Stato, Trieste, microfilm of Archivio municipale di Capodistria, MS 550, fo. 58v (reel 688, frame 149).

10. A. Theiner, ed., *Vetera monumenta Poloniae et Lithuaniae gentiumque finitimarum historiam illustrantia*, 4 vols. (Rome, 1860–4), iii, p. 209 ('Ex litteris tuis atque ex sermone dilecti filii Antonii [Bruni], cui eas litteras et mandata ad nos dederas, cognovimus, quam praestanti voluntate sis, quibusque de causis cupias ad nos venire. Fuerunt illa omnia nobis iucundissima'); Theiner mistranscribes 'Bruni' here as 'Bruti'; E. de Hurmuzaki et al., eds., *Documente privitóre la istoria Românilor*, 19 vols. (Bucharest, 1887–1938), iii(2), p. 387 does so as 'Shuni'.

11. Tiroler Landesarchiv, Innsbruck, MS O. Ö. Geheimer Rat, Selekt Ferdinandea, Pos. 86, fo. 85r ('Cum Sancto Papa habemus familiaritatem Bonam...Et D[ominu]m quenda[m] ex aula n[ost]ra habebam, nomine Brutus, sepius nam [*sic*: for "eum"?] ad Papam mittebam'); 'Brutus' was probably used here because Antonio was known to Petru as a nephew of Bartolomeo Bruti. These travels 'quite often' between Moldavia and Rome would help to explain Antonio's familiarity (exhibited in his treatise) with places such as Constanța and Vlorë.

12. G. Chivu et al., eds., *Documente și însemnări românești din secolul al XVI-lea* (Bucharest, 1979), pp. 178, 183.

13. See de Hurmuzaki et al., eds., *Documente*, xi, pp. 346–7, 358 (interpreter), 774 (7 months).

14. Biblioteca Ambrosiana, Milan, MS S 102 sup. ('Relatione della potenza del Turco et in spetie delle cose d'Vngaria Di Lazaro Soranzo'), fo. 44v ('com' io trattai con sua S.^tà d'ordine suo, et per opera di Antonio Bruni gentilhuomo Albanese').

15. See the letters sent in 1594 to Archduke Ferdinand by his agent in Venice, Bernardino Rossi, in Tiroler Landesarchiv, Innsbruck, MS O. Ö. Geheimer Rat, Selekt Ferdinandea Pos. 86, fos. 356r (29 Aug.), 358r–359r (2 Sept.), 360r–361v (10 Sept.), 437r (1 Oct.) and 515r–518v (4 Nov.), and the letter from Bruni to Rossi of 20 Oct. (fos. 519r–520v).

16. de Hurmuzaki et al., eds., *Documente*, xi, p. 533 ('col nome suo solo et con la segretezza necessaria in tali maneggi, Sua Maestà Cesarea potria riceverne singularissimo servitio, et in Moldavia, et altrove').

17. Ibid., xi, p. 477; Malcolm, *Agents of Empire*, p. 388.

18. F. Patrizi, *Paralleli militari* , 2 vols. (Rome, 1594–5), ii, p. 87 ('se noi smontassimo in Albania, ci si accosteriano tutti gli Albanesi, gente valorosa, e da Turchi già tanto temuta, e per l'antica memoria della gloria loro sotto Scanderbego, e per l'odio fierissimo presente').

19. Archivio Segreto Vaticano, Vatican City, Fondo Borghese, ser. IV, MS 229, fo. 49r ('Hor poiche V. S. mi scriue, che da Roma li uiene acennato, che così fatta

informatione al' Illmo suo Patrone non saria discara, uado entrando in openione [*sic*], che da lei sia stata rapresentata molto maggiore di q^ello, che è in effetti…Che io a la fine mi risoluo d'appigliarmi al suo prudentiss.^{mo} et amoreuoliss.^{mo} conseglio, acciò el Sor Card.^{le} sappia, che da me le sarà mandata la scrittura col mezo di V. S. mio singulariss.^{mo} patrone'). On the likely origins of Ingegneri's acquaintance with Bruni see Malcolm, *Agents of Empire*, p. 431.

20. Soranzo, *L'Ottomanno*, sig. 3†1r (Ischia, Venice); Biblioteca Ambrosiana, Milan, MS S 102 sup., fos. 410r–465r. Soranzo sent the work to Mantua via Lelio Arrigoni, the Duke's ambassador in Rome (*L'Ottomanno*, sig. 3†1r); Arrigoni left Rome in Jan. 1597 (see Archivio di Stato, Mantua, Archivio Gonzaga, busta 968, fos. 669–77).
21. Soranzo, *L'Ottomanno*, pp. 113, 117–18.
22. Ibid., pp. 27 (tribute), 32 (taxes), 62 (Polish relations), 105 (geographical terms).
23. Ibid., pp. 38 (timber), 40 (biscuit), 56 (Sinan), 58–9 (ports), 120 (Ulcinj etc.), 122 (Gasparo). On Sinan's relation to the Bruti family see Malcolm, *Agents of Empire*, pp. 263–4.
24. See F. de Vivo, *Information and Communication in Venice: Rethinking Early Modern Politics* (Oxford, 2007), pp. 57–63.
25. M. Pozzi, *Filippo Pigafetta consigliere del principe*, 2 vols. (Vicenza, 2004), ii, pp. 203 ('discorso del Beglierbei della Grecia delle genti che ha sotto sé'), 205 ('Mando…una relazione dello stato d'Europa del Gran Turco, fatta da un valent'uomo che lungo tempo, essendo natio albanese, dimorò in quelle contrade').
26. On the Venetian attempt see G. Sforza, 'Un libro sfortunato contro i Turchi (documenti inediti)', in C. Cipolla et al., *Scritti storici in memoria di Giovanni Monticolo* (Venice, 1922), pp. 207–19; on the northern Italian editions see J. Balsamo, '*Il Turco vincibile*. Un "corpus turc" à la fin du XVIe siècle: La Noue, Naselli, Soranzo, Esprinchard', in Gruppo di studio sul cinquecento francese, *Scritture dell'impegno dal rinascimento all'età barocca* (Fasano, 1997), pp. 205–16, at p. 213; the Naples edn., correctly describing itself as the 4th edn., was printed by Costantino Vitale.
27. J. Esprinchard, *Histoire des Ottomans, ou empereurs des Turcs, iusques à Mahomet III*, 2nd edn. (Paris, 1609) (referring to a Geneva, 1600 edition, which I have been unable to locate).
28. See the revised edn. of this translation, *Ottomannus: von Zustand, Macht und Gewalt, auch anderen verborgenen heimlichen Sachen des Ottomanischen Türkischen Reiches*, ed. H. Hattenhauer and U. Bake (Frankfurt-am-Main, 2009), p. xxiv (n. 28).
29. L. Soranzo, *The Ottoman of Lazaro Soranzo*, tr. Abraham Hartwell (London, 1603).
30. L. Soranzo, *Ottomannus…sive de rebus Turcicis liber unus*, tr. J. Geuder von Heroltzberg (Hanau, 1600); L. Soranzo et al., *Turca nikētos, hoc est, de Imperio Ottomannico evertendo, et bello contra Turcas prospere gerendo consilia tria* (Frankfurt-am-Main, 1601); Anon., ed., *Turcici imperii status* (Leiden, 1630), pp. 226–74 (2nd edn., Leiden, 1634, pp. 221–66); H. Conring, ed., *De bello contra Turcos prudenter gerendo* (Helmstadt, 1664).
31. For the original Italian text, see N. Malcolm, 'An Unknown Description of Ottoman Albania: Antonio Bruni's Treatise on the *beylerbeylik* of Rumeli (1596)', *Revue des études sud-est européennes*, 53 (2015), pp. 71–94, at pp. 79–92. This English translation appears here for the first time.

32. The province governed by the *kapudan paşa* (admiral of the Ottoman navy), created in 1533-4, contained the *sancak*s (administrative districts) of Gallipoli, Euboea (which included, as Bruni says, a large part of the mainland, from Volos down to Cape Sounion but excluding Athens), Mystras (in the southern Peloponnese; some sources merge this with the *sancak* of Nafplio, while others treat the latter as a separate *sancak*, also in the *kapudan paşa*'s province) and Lepanto (in addition to islands such as Rhodes and Chios, and some Anatolian coastal territories). Most sources also include in it the *sancak* of Karlieli, which Bruni places within the *beylerbeylik* of Rumeli (see below, at n. 58). (See İ. Bostan, 'The Establishment of the Province of *Cezayir-i Bahr-i Sefid*', in E. Zachariadou, ed., *The Kapudan Pasha: His Office and His Domain* (Rethymno, 2002), pp. 241-51; İ. M. Kunt, *Sancaktan eyalete: 1550-1650 arasında Osmanlı ümerası ve il idaresi* (Istanbul, 1978), pp. 152-3; A. Birken, *Die Provinzen des Osmanischen Reiches* (Wiesbaden, 1976), pp. 57, 101-8.)

33. The territory of Feodosiya (Caffa, Kefe) had been a *sancak* of the *beylerbeylik* of Rumeli until 1586, when it was raised to the status of a province (Birken, *Die Provinzen*, p. 56).

34. Bruni refers to Slav Catholic villages in the Skopska Crna Gora (Malet e Karadakut), of which the most prominent, Letnica, retained its Catholic population until the 1990s.

35. The title 'Primate of Serbia' had belonged historically to the Archbishops of Split, but by the early 16th century it had been transferred (for reasons which remain unclear) to the Archbishops of Bar (see S. Ritig, 'Primacijalni naslov splitske i barske metropolije', *Bogoslovska smotra*, 11 (1923), pp. 89-95, esp. pp. 93-4). Bruni's uncle Giovanni Bruni was Archbishop of Bar from 1551 to 1571.

36. Bruni may refer here not only to Protestantism (predominantly of the Swiss Reformed type) but also to Antitrinitarianism, which was present in Ottoman-ruled Hungary (in Pécs and the surrounding districts of Baranya and Tolna) at this time (see S. K. Németh, 'Die Disputation von Fünfkirchen', in R. Dán and A. Pirnát, eds., *Antitrinitarianism in the Second Half of the 16th Century* (Budapest, 1982), pp. 147-55).

37. The Paulicians were an early Christian sect, originally from Armenia but transplanted by Byzantine emperors to the Balkans, with what may have been a dualistic theology (hence the common association with Manichaeism). They were strongly targeted by Roman Catholic missionaries from the 1590s onwards. See D. P. Hupchick, *The Bulgarians in the Seventeenth Century: Slavic Orthodox Society and Culture under Ottoman Rule* (Jefferson, NC, 1993), pp. 77-82. Giovanni Botero wrote that there were 15,000 Paulicians living in 12 villages on the Bulgarian side of the Danube: 'They speak Bulgarian, and partly follow the heresy of the Manichaeans, with many other errors' ('Parlano Bulgaro, e seguono in parte l'heresia de' Manichei, con molti altri errori'): *Relationi universali*, 2 vols. (Vicenza, 1595), ii, fo. 49v). The charge of Arianism arose over their Christology, which may have been adoptionist; the reason for the charge of Donatism is less clear.

38. The Roman province of Moesia covered much of modern Serbia and northern Macedonia ('Moesia Superior'), and northern Bulgaria with part of the Romanian Black Sea coast ('Moesia Inferior').

39. Alaric, leader of the Visigoths (d. 410), spent some time in Epirus in 397. The Goths spoke a Germanic language, unlike the Alans (with whom they were not closely associated), who spoke an Iranian one. The idea that the Goths were the ancestors of the Slavs was (thanks partly to the influence of the medieval 'Chronicle of the Priest of Dioclea') commonly held in this period: see for example M. Orbini, *Il regno de gli Slavi hoggi corrottamente detti Schiavoni* (Pesaro, 1601), p. 97. Bruni's suggested identifications of the ancestors of the Albanians with Goths or Macedonians were untypical, given that the standard Renaissance view was that the Albanians were descended from a population which either was driven out of Asia by Scythians, or was itself Scythian and was driven out of Asia by Tatars (though the Alans were sometimes regarded as Scythians). (See e.g. J. Zuallart ['G. Zuallardo'], *Il devotissimo viaggio di Gierusalemme* (Rome, 1587), p. 80; Botero, *Relationi universali*, ii, fo. 50r; G. A. Magini, *Geografia, cioè descrittione universale della terra*, tr. Leonardo Cernoti (Venice, 1598), fo. 121v.)

40. Bastia was a small port just to the north of Igoumenitsa. A report of 1566 described it as 'a disinhabited place' ('un loco dissabitato') with an Ottoman customs official, situated below the village of Sagiada which, with 30 households, was 'also inhabited by Albanians' ('habitato puro de albanesi') (J. M. Floristán Imízcoz, 'Los contactos de la Chimarra con el reino de Nápoles durante el siglo XVI y comienzos del XVII', *Erytheia: revista de estudios bizantinos y neogriegos*, 11–12 (1990–1), 105–39; 13 (1992), 53–87; at 13, p. 76).

41. On the extensive settlements of Albanians in Greece, and especially in the Peloponnese, see P. Topping, 'Albanian Settlements in Medieval Greece: Some Venetian Testimonies', in A. E. Laiou-Thomadakis, ed., *Charanis Studies: Essays in Honor of Peter Charanis* (New Brunswick, NJ, 1980), pp. 261–71; V. Panagiōtopoulos, *Plēthusmos kai oikismoi tēs Peloponnēsou, 13os–18os aiōnas* (Athens, 1985), pp. 59–100; Sh. Raça, *Shtegtimet dhe ngulimet e shqiptarëve në Greqi shek. XIII–XVI* (Prishtina, 2004).

42. Aurelian (r. 270–5) decreed the abandonment of the Roman province of Dacia, resettling people from it on the southern side of the Danube.

43. 'Čiči' was a name for Vlachs used in Istria and the region of Trieste (see e.g. I. della Croce, *Historia antica, e moderna, sacra, e profana, della città di Trieste* (Venice, 1698), pp. 334–5). Some writers claim that they migrated there only in the 16th century (e.g. G. Vassilich, 'Sull'origine dei Cici: contributo all'etnografia dell'Istria', *Archeografo triestino*, ser. 3, 1 (1905), pp. 53–80; 2 (1906), pp. 209–47; D. Darovec, *Breve storia dell'Istria*, tr. M. Rebeschini (Udine, 2010), p. 111); but the name also appears in records from the 14th and 15th centuries (see S. Puşcariu, *Studii istroromâne*, 3 vols. (Bucharest, 1906–29), ii, pp. 23–30).

44. 'Zalicanac' is perhaps based on a scribal misreading of some term derived from 'Balkan' (the normal Turkish name)—possibly 'Balkan daği', meaning the Balkan mountain range.

45. Of the four clans or tribes named here, the Kelmendi (on the Albanian side of the modern border) were Albanian-speaking Catholics [see above, pp. 26–37]; of the others (on the Montenegrin side), the Kuçi were also Abanian-speaking and Catholic at this time, but later became mostly Slav-speaking and Orthodox (see M. E. Durham, *Some Tribal Origins, Laws and Customs of the Balkans* (London, 1928), pp. 51–2;

F. Baxhaku and K. Kaser, eds., *Die Stammesgesellschaften Nordalbaniens: Berichte und Forschungen österreichischer Konsuln und Gelehrter (1861–1917)* (Vienna, 1996), p. 270), and the Piperi and Bjelopavlići were Slav-speaking and Orthodox. These four were closely associated. In 1565 the Kelmendi, Kuçi and Piperi jointly rebelled against the Ottomans (S. Pulaha, *Qendresa e popullit shqiptar kundër sundimit osman nga shek. XVI deri në fillim të shek. XVIII: dokumente osmane* (Tirana, 1978), pp. 69–70); in 1614 a document appealing for Western help for an anti-Ottoman rising, written at a meeting of Balkan chiefs in Kuçi territory, declared that the Kelmendi, Kuçi, Piperi and Bjelopavlići 'have lived in freedom for the last thirty years, and do not pay tribute to the Sultan' ('già sono trenta anni che vivono in libertà e non pagano tributo al Gran Signore': F. Lenormant, *Turcs et monténégrins* (Paris, 1866), p. 331).

46. The title of Patriarch of the Serbian Orthodox Church had fallen into abeyance in 1463. Mehmed Sokolović (Sokollu), who was *beylerbeyi* of Rumeli (1551–5), then a vizier (1555–65), then Grand Vizier (1565–79), revived it in 1557 and appointed his own close relative, Makarije, Patriarch.

47. The *nahiye* (sub-district) of Pejë (Peć) was in fact in the *sancak* of Shkodër; the north-eastern tip of the *sancak* of Dukagjin extended as far as Gjakovë, roughly 25 km to the south of Pejë (S. Pulaha, 'Krahinat e Sanxhakut të Dukagjinit gjatë shekullit XVI', *Studime historike*, 27 (1973), no. 3, pp. 3–51, at pp. 4–5). In this period Pejë was a small town with an overwhelmingly Muslim population: an Ottoman tax register of 1582 lists 158 households, of which only 15 were Christian (S. Pulaha, *Popullsia shqiptare e Kosovës gjatë shekujve XV–XVI (studime dhe dokumente)* (Tirana, 1983), pp. 476–7).

48. The Yürüks were a semi-nomadic pastoral people of mixed Asiatic origin in Anatolia, many of whom were settled by the Ottomans in the Balkans (see Ć. Truhelka, 'Über die Balkan-Yürüken', *Revue internationale des études balkaniques*, 1–2 (1934–5), pp. 89–99; M. T. Gökbilgin, *Rumeli'de Yürükler, Tatarlar ve Evlâd-ı Fâtihân* (Istanbul, 1957)). On their production of felt see H. İnalcık, *The Middle East and the Balkans under the Ottoman Empire: Essays on Economy and Society* (Bloomington, IN, 1993), pp. 25, 116.

49. 'Zechelle' here was Shahkulu, the charismatic leader of an anti-Ottoman revolt in the Teke region of southern Anatolia in 1511. (He was therefore known as 'Tekeli', given as 'Techellis' in some Western writings, e.g. P. Giovio, *Historiarum sui temporis tomus primus* (Venice, 1566), fo. 95r–v.) Shahkulu was not himself from Persia, but the rebel movement was pro-Persian, as Shahkulu's followers were *kızılbaş* (Shiites: hence Bruni's reference to the veneration of Ali). (See Ç. Uluçay, 'Yavuz Sultan Selim nasıl padişah oldu?', *Tarih dergisi*, 6 (1954), no. 9, pp. 53–90, at pp. 61–74; H. Sohrweide, 'Der Sieg der Safaviden in Persien und seine Rückwirkungen auf die Schiiten Anatoliens im 16. Jahrhundert', *Der Islam: Zeitschrift für Geschichte und Kultur des islamischen Orients*, 41 (1965), pp. 95–223, at pp. 145–56.)

50. After the defeat of Shahkulu many of his followers were deported to the Balkans. Those who came to eastern Bulgaria and the Dobrudža supervened there on groups of previously deported Shiites or quasi-Shiites (see F. F. de Jong, 'The Kızılbaş Sects in Bulgaria: Remnants of Safavi Islam?', *The Turkish Studies Association Bulletin* 9, no. 1 (Mar. 1985), 30–2; L. Mikov, *Izkustvoto na heterodoksnite miusiulmani v Bŭlgariia (XVI–XX vek): Bektaši i Kŭzŭlbaši/Alevii* (Sofia, 2005), pp. 22–3). In the early 16th century roughly 200 groups of Yürüks were settled in Dobrudža (see R. Kovačev

['Kowačev'], 'Register aus dem osmanischen Archiv in Konstantinopel für die Stadt Varna und ihre Umgebung (zweite Hälfte des 16. Jh.)', *Bulgarian Historical Review*, 31 (2003), 29–68, at p. 61), many of whom were apparently followers of Shahkulu. A mid-16th-century register of the district of Varna shows Yürüks named 'Shahkulu' (see Gökbilgin, *Rumeli'de Yürükler*, pp. 214–16; on Yürüks in Dobrudža, and devotion to Shahkulu there, see also A. Kayapınar, 'Dobruca yöresinde XVI. yüzyılda gayr-i Sünni İslam'ın izleri', *Alevilik-Bektaşilik araştırmaları dergisi*, 1 (2009), 85–102, at pp. 88, 93, 99).

51. This reference to tithes ('xme, *sc.* 'decime') is ambiguous, but seems most likely to mean the *devşirme*, the collection of Christian boys for Janissary (and other) service.

52. The general validity of Bruni's account here can be judged in the light of Ferhad Pasha's attempt to assemble an army in northern Bulgaria for the Wallachian campaign of 1595: of the 40–50,000 men summoned, only 4–5,000 appeared (see R. Murphey, *Ottoman Warfare, 1500–1700* (London, 1999), p. 140).

53. On the exiled Voivod Petru Şchiopul, and Bruni's involvement in his law-suit, see above, p. 40. This conversation with Archduke Ferdinand, at which Bruni acted as interpreter, took place at the castle of Ambras, near Innsbruck, on 3 Aug. 1593 (see de Hurmuzaki et al., eds., *Documente*, xi, p. 358).

54. The use of Belgrade (and Buda) for the wintering of Ottoman forces between campaigns was a significant feature of this war (see C. B. Finkel, 'The Provisioning of the Ottoman Army during the Campaigns of 1593–1606', in A. Tietze, ed., *Habsburgisch-osmanische Beziehungen*, Beihefte zur Wiener Zeitschrift für die Kunde des Morgenlandes, xiii (Vienna, 1985), 107–23, at pp. 117–19).

55. The Sultan's standing force of cavalry (the 'spahis of the Porte') was divided into four regiments: the *sipahioğlanlar* ('sons of spahis'); the *silahdarân* ('sword-bearers'); the *ulufeciyân* ('paid troops'); and the *gureba* ('foreigners'). The last two were each divided into two separate troops, giving a total of six. (See A. H. Lybyer, *The Government of the Ottoman Empire in the Time of Suleiman the Magnificent* (Cambridge, MA, 1913), pp. 98–9; and the entries in G. Bayerle, *Pashas, Begs and Effendis: A Historical Dictionary of Titles and Terms in the Ottoman Empire* (Istanbul, 1997).) The term *sipahioğlanlar* was commonly applied to all of them; as Lazaro Soranzo explained, 'because the number of *sipahioğlanlar* exceeds that of all the others, they are all called *sipahioğlanlar* indifferently' (*L'Ottomanno*, p. 13: 'perche il numero de' Spahoglani è maggiore di tutti gli altri, indifferentemente sono chiamati tutti Spahoglani').

56. *Azab* was a general term for an auxiliary soldier employed in a garrison; *beşlü* had a similar meaning (from *beş*, 'five', referring to a system of recruitment in which every five households had to supply one man).

57. Bruni's account is corroborated by Ottoman payroll documents, which show that in most Hungarian garrisons in 1596–7 Janissaries (who were better paid than *azab*s) received between 5½ and 7 *akçe*s per day (see C. Finkel, *The Administration of Warfare: The Ottoman Military Campaigns in Hungary, 1593–1606* (Vienna, 1988), p. 76.) Until the debasement of the silver content of the *akçe* in the mid-1580s, there had been 40 *akçe*s to a thaler; Bruni's statement here implies a rate of between 60 and 75.

58. This *sancak* was more commonly known as Karlıeli. Its seat of administration was Angelokastro, but its most important towns were Preveza and Arta. (See Birken, *Die*

Provinzen, p. 55, where it is described as belonging to the province of the *kapudan paşa*.)

59. Turahan Bey, who died in *c.*1456, inherited large land-holdings in Thessaly from his father, Yiğit Bey, a prominent Yürük commander; Turahan's son and grandson endowed many charitable foundations in Thessaly, and their descendants retained a strong connection with the town of Larissa until the nineteenth century (see F. Başar, 'Osmanlı devletinin kuruluş döneminde hizmeti görülen akıncı aileleri: III: Turahanoğulları', *Türk dünyası tarih dergisi*, no. 65 (May 1992), pp. 47-50; M. Kiel, 'Das türkische Thessalien: Etabliertes Geschichtsbild versus Osmanische Quellen. Ein Beitrag zur Entmythologisierung der Geschichte Griechenlands', in R. Lauer and P. Schreiner, eds., *Die Kultur Griechenlands in Mittelalter und Neuzeit: Bericht über das Kolloquium der Südosteuropa-Kommission 28.-31. Oktober 1992* (Göttingen, 1996), pp. 109-96, at pp. 145-52). Yürüks and others from Anatolia were settled in Thessaly, and the family's political power in the 16th century may have derived from the fact that they continued to supply *akıncı* forces (irregular cavalry) to the Ottoman army, drawn from that population (see, e.g., the order of Mar. 1565 to the 'Turhanlu'ya tabi' in İ. Binark, ed., *6 Numaralı Mühimme Defteri*, 3 vols. (Ankara, 1995), iii, p. 6). That this *sancak* belonged to the family is, however, not recorded in other sources.

60. Gastuni (on the north-western corner of the Peloponnese) does not feature in other listings of *sancaks* for this period; Birken notes it as a *sancak* only in the 18th century (*Die Provinzen*, p. 63).

61. The territory of Bender (Tighina) was part of the *sancak* of Akkerman (Bilhorod-Dnistrovskyi, Cetatea Albă) until 1570, when it became a separate *sancak*; both, however, were transferred from the *beylerbeylik* of Rumeli to the newly formed *beylerbeylik* of Özü (Ochakiv) in 1593 (see Birken, *Die Provinzen*, pp. 52-3).

62. Bruni's figures may be compared with those given by an Ottoman register of spahis of 1605-6 (the last year of the Habsburg-Ottoman war), and by the writer Ayn-i Ali (who combined both contemporary and historical data) in 1609. For Kiustendil the figures were, respectively, 866 and 1,065; only one other *sancak*, Sofia, had more than 800 (1,423 and 2,045); the former document listed 4 *sancaks* as between 369 and 517, the latter 5 as between 312 and 517; Skopje and Prizren were not listed, but Dukagjin was given as 49 and 62; Shkodër as 108 and 254; Çirmen as 55 and 150. (See V. P. Mutafčieva and S. A. Dimitrov, *Sur l'état du système des timars des XVIIe—XVIIIe siècles* (Sofia, 1968), pp. 13-14.)

63. Bruni correctly translates *kul kardaşı*; the word *kul*, meaning a male slave, was generally applied to Janissaries and spahis of the Porte, but the use of this phrase for a type of militia is not recorded in other histories of this war.

64. The *akıncı* ('raider') troops were irregular cavalry forces. On their conditions of life and service (including exemption from taxes) see M. Alkan, 'The End of the *Akıncı* Corps in the Ottoman Empire', in *IBAC 2012:2nd International Balkan Annual Conference: The Balkans at a Crossroads*, ed. B. Çınar, 2 vols. (Istanbul, 2013), ii, pp. 492-501, at p. 496; cf. also Finkel, *Administration of Warfare*, p. 47.

65. The *gönüllü* ('volunteer') soldiers served without salary, for plunder or the possibility of a reward (e.g. a timar estate). However, some did receive salaries to perform garrison duties, and from the end of the 16th century some *gönüllü* units were recruited as salaried auxiliaries to the Janissaries (see the entry in Bayerle, *Pashas, Begs*).

66. The Mihaloğulları were descendants of Köse Mihal (d. 1340), a Greek convert to Islam who became a famous Ottoman military commander; members of this family were influential in Bulgaria and the Dobrudža region, where they commanded *akıncı* forces, some of whom were Yürüks. See F. Başar, 'Osmanlı devletinin kuruluş döneminde hizmeti görülen akıncı aileleri: I: Mihaloğulları', *Türk dünyası tarih dergisi*, no. 63 (Mar. 1992), pp. 20–6; M. Kiprovska, 'The Mihaloğlu Family: *Gazi* Warriors and Patrons of Dervish Hospices', *Osmanlı araştırmaları*, 32 (2008), pp. 193–222; Kayapınar, 'Dobruca yöresinde', p. 92.

67. Bruni refers to the 'Valu lui Traian' ('Trajan's rampart'), a combination of three fortification systems, a stone wall and two earthen walls, running eastwards from near Cernavodă to Constanţa, which was traditionally attributed to the emperor Trajan. Romanian archaeologists have dated it to the 10th or 11th century, but recent work suggests that it may indeed have a Roman origin (see W. S. Hanson and I. A. Oltean, 'The "Valu lui Traian": A Roman Frontier Rehabilitated', *Journal of Roman Archaeology*, 25 (2012), pp. 297–318, esp. pp. 298–9, 306–16). Karasu ('Carasui' in Bruni's text) was a village, on the site of which (to the south-east of Cernavodă) the modern town of Medgidia was founded in the 1850s (see K. H. Karpat, *Studies on Ottoman Social and Political History: Selected Articles and Essays* (Leiden, 2002), pp. 202–5).

68. The term *cebelü* or *cebeli* ('armed man') normally referred to an armed retainer who was equipped and maintained on a military campaign by his spahi.

69. Bruni refers to Herodotus, *Histories* IV.3.2, which mentions a trench dug between the mountains of Tauris and the Sea of Azov. Perekop is the town on the isthmus of that name which joins the Crimean peninsula to the mainland. The name comes from a Slavic word meaning 'to excavate across'; a defensive trench was dug across the isthmus in 1540 (see S. R. Grinevetsky et al., eds., *The Black Sea Encyclopedia* (Heidelberg, 2015), p. 605).

70. On these two *sancak*s see above, n. 61. The Polish name for Bender is Tehinia.

71. Kiliya (Chilia), a former Moldavian port which was now located in directly ruled Ottoman territory on a branch of the Danube close to the Black Sea, was an important trading centre during this period.

72. Pitch (bitumen) was a major export from Vlorë, sent mostly to Ottoman territory or Dubrovnik (see V. Vinaver, 'Dubrovačko-albanski ekonomski odnosi krajem XVI veka', *Anali Historijskog Instituta u Dubrovniku*, 1 (1952), pp. 207–31, at pp. 208, 211; V. Miović, *Dubrovačka republika u spisima Osmanskih sultana* (Dubrovnik, 2005), p. 56). That it was mined by Slavs in the Vlorë region is a detail not supplied by any other source.

73. That the original Muslim population of Vlorë consisted of deported *kızılbaş* (Shiites) is not recorded in any other source. Yet it helps to explain an otherwise puzzling comment in the travelogue of Evliya Çelebi, who visited the city in 1670 and observed that the young men of Vlorë habitually invoked Ali, and were 'devoted to the Prophet's family'—a code-phrase for strong Shiite tendencies (see *Evliya Çelebi in Albania and Adjacent Regions (Kosovo, Montenegro, Ohrid)*, ed. and tr. R. Dankoff and R. Elsie (Leiden, 2000), p. 145; on devotion to the family of the Prophet see M. Moosa, *Extremist Shiites: The Ghulat Sects* (Syracuse, NY, 1988), pp. 78–87). Although the population register of 1583 records no Muslims in Vlorë other than the members of the garrison, other evidence testifies to a Muslim community engaged in a range of

civilian activities: see J. Luetić ['Luetiq'], 'Lundruesit detarë, marina tregtare dhe vep-rimtaria e porteve të Vlorës, Durrësit e Lezhës dhe lidhjet nautike-komerciale të shqiptarëve me dubrovnikasit në vitet 1566–1584', *Gjurmime albanologjike*, ser. shk. hist., 14, for 1984 (1985), pp. 111–36, and G. Veinstein, 'Une source ottomane de l'histoire albanaise: le registre des *kadi* d'Avlonya (Vlorë), 1567–1568', in Ch. Gaspares, ed., *Oi Alvanoi sto mesaiōna* (Athens, 1998), pp. 371–84.

74. The two instances of 'etc.' in the text are puzzling; possibly the scribe of an earlier ver-sion had found two passages, containing names, hard to read. Athanasios Riseas, Archbishop of Ohrid, led a revolt in Himarë which began in late July 1596; on 10 Aug. his men overran a recently built Ottoman fort, raising the Spanish flag there, before the Ottomans swiftly re-took it. Athanasios had previously made contact with the Spanish authorities in Naples, where he had received some general encouragement but very little practical help. See P. Bartl, *Der Westbalkan zwischen spanischer Monarchie und Osmanischem Reich: zur Türkenkriegsproblematik an der Wende vom 16. zum 17. Jahrhundert* (Wiesbaden, 1974), pp. 124–7; J. M. Floristán Imízcoz, ed., *Fuentes para la política oriental de los Austrias: la documentación griega del Archivo de Simancas (1571–1621)*, 2 vols. (Leon, 1988), ii, pp. 430–2; I. Zamputi, ed., *Dokumente të shekujve XVI–XVII për historinë e Shqipërisë*, ii (Tirana, 1990), pp. 114–15, 132–3, 142–3, 152–6; A. Pippidi, *Byzantins, Ottomans, Roumains: le Sud-Est européen entre l'héritage impérial et les influences occidentales* (Paris, 2006), pp. 126–31.

75. In a letter to Rome in 1581 the leaders of Himarë listed 38 villages (including many outside the Himarë district in the strict sense) and said that from these and the neigh-bouring areas they could immediately raise 10,000 men (N. Borgia, *I monaci basiliani d'Italia in Albania*, 2 vols. (Rome, 1935–42), i, pp. 18, 21). For Himarë in the strict sense, the Ottoman tax register of 1583 listed 13 villages; the largest, Himarë itself, had 130 households, Vuno had 100, and most others had between 40 and 80 (F. Duka, 'Aspekte social-ekonomike dhe demografike të Himarës gjatë sundimit osman (shek. XV–XVI)', in L. Nasi et al., eds., *Himara në shekuj* (Tirana, 2004), pp. 62–95, at pp. 75–86).

76. The village of Dukat, lying outside Himarë (to the north-west), had cooperated with the Himariots in earlier anti-Ottoman initiatives; a document of 1566 described it as having 1,800 households (but only 200 potential anti-Ottoman fighters, perhaps because many had converted to Islam). (See Floristán Imízcoz, 'Los contactos de la Chimarra', pp. 133, 137–8.) It took part in the revolt of 1571 (İ. Binark et al., eds., *12 Numaralı mühimme defteri*, 3 vols. (Ankara, 1996), i, pp. 263–4), and joined Himarë in planning a rising in 1581 (Borgia, *I monaci basiliani*, i, p. 21). The identity of Piri Pasha is unclear; he may perhaps have been the Piri who served before 1589 as *kethüda* (chamberlain) to Doğancı Mehmed Pasha, the *beylerbeyi* of Rumeli, and became *san-cakbeyi* of Silistra by 1593 (de Hurmuzaki et al., eds., *Documente*, xi, p. 770), or the Piri who was *sancakbeyi* of Salonica in 1594–5 (Selaniki Mustafa Efendi, *Tarih-i Selaniki*, ed. M. İpşirli, 2 vols. (Istanbul, 1989), ii, pp. 423, 452). Orikum, on the south-western side of the Bay of Dukat (below the Bay of Vlorë), is close to the site of the Illyrian and Roman port of Oricum.

77. Mount Scardus is normally identified with the Sharr Mountains (whose name is derived from it), which straddle the border of Kosovo and Macedonia, to the south of Prizren. Bruni extends the term to cover the entire northern Albanian mountain

range; this was shared between the *sancak* of Dukagjin, which extended south-westwards from Gjakovë to Lezhë, and the *sancak* of Shkodër, which covered the arc of mountain country to the north of it, from Pejë to Shkodër. The name 'Dukagjin', which is now limited to one area (to the north-east of Shkodër), was commonly used as a general term for the northern Albanian highlands.

78. In addition to the term 'Monte Negro' (Crna Gora, Karadağ, Mal i Zi) which has become the name of the modern country, Bruni probably also has in mind the Skopska Crna Gora (Malet e Karadakut), the hill-country to the north and north-east of Skopje.

79. Nikollë Bardhi (Nicolò Bianchi), who came from a famous Albanian Catholic family (he was the uncle of the author and bishop Frang Bardhi) became Bishop of Sapë in 1594 (C. Eubel, *Hierarchia catholica medii aevi*, iii (Munich, 1910), p. 310). The diocese of Sapë (Sappa), on the south-eastern side of Lake Shkodër, was united with that of Sardë (Sarda), which included the town of Danj (Dagno).

80. Nikollë Mekajshi (Nicolò Mechaisci) became Bishop of Benda in 1592; this diocese, which was located on the southern side of the Mat district, to the east and north-east of Tirana, was often described as united with (or perhaps equivalent to) the diocese of Stefani (or 'Shtjefni'), the precise location of which is unclear (see P. Bartl, ed., *Albania sacra: geistliche Visitationsberichte aus Albanien*, ii: *Erzbiözese Durazzo* (Wiesbaden, 2011), pp. 18–19).

81. Innocentius Stoicinus (Stojičić? Stojković?) became Bishop of Lezhë in Aug. 1596 (Eubel, *Hierarchia catholica*, iii, p. 116). He was apparently a friend of Bruni's: according to a denunciation of Stoicinus by Mekajshi in 1603, Bruni had once intervened in Rome to save Stoicinus from punishment for immoral behaviour (see Malcolm, *Agents of Empire*, pp. 310–11). Bruni describes him here as a former Franciscan ('Zoccolante'); the ecclesiastical historian Daniel Farlati (*Illyrici sacri*, 8 vols. (Venice, 1751–1819), vii, p. 391) wrote that he was a Benedictine.

82. Further details about this episode are not known, but Mekajshi continued to take an active part in anti-Ottoman initiatives in subsequent years. In 1601 he sent a detailed plan for an anti-Ottoman rising to Rome, and in 1602 he took part in a meeting of Albanian leaders in Mirditë which sent Nikollë Bardhi to Venice with a proposal for a pro-Venetian revolt (Bartl, *Der Westbalkan*, pp. 92–3).

83. Bruni may have had in mind the text by Feliks Petančić (Felix Petantius), *De itineribus in Turciam libellus* (Vienna, 1522) (later known as *Quibus itineribus Turci sunt aggredi-endi*, and re-published in 1543, 1550 and 1561), which was in fact copied from a manu-script work by Martino Segono, Bishop of Ulcinj (see A. Pertusi, *Martino Segono di Novo Brdo, vescovo di Dulcigno: un umanista serbo-dalmata del tardo Quattrocento* (Rome, 1981), pp. 60–6).

Chapter 4

1. See J. G. von Hahn, *Albanesische Studien*, 3 vols. (Jena, 1854), i, p. 36; R. L. N. Mitchell, 'A Muslim-Christian Sect in Cyprus', *The Nineteenth Century and After*, 63 (Jan.–June 1908), pp. 751–62; F. W. Hasluck, *Christianity and Islam under the Sultans*, ed. M. M. Hasluck, 2 vols. (Oxford, 1929), ii, pp. 469–74; R. M. Dawkins, 'The

Crypto-Christians of Turkey', *Byzantium*, 8 (1933), pp. 247–75; K. Amantos, *Scheseis Ellēnōn kai Tourkōn apo tou endekatou aiōnos mechri tou 1821* (Athens, 1955), pp. 193–6; R. Kiszling, 'Glaubenskampfe in Albanien um die Jahrhundertswende', *Mitteilungen des Österreichischen Staatsarchivs*, 12 (1959), pp. 426–32; S. Skendi, 'Crypto-Christianity in the Balkan Area under the Ottomans', *Slavic Review*, 26 (1967), pp. 227–46; A. Bryer, 'The Crypto-Christians of the Pontos and Consul William Palgrave of Trebizond', in his *Peoples and Settlements in Anatolia and the Caucasus, 800–1900* (London, 1988), item XVII; K. Photiadēs, *Oi exislamismoi tēs Mikras Asias kai oi kruptochristianoi tou Pontou* (Salonica, 1993); G. Andreadis, *The Crypto Christians: Klostoi: Those who Returned; Tenesur: Those who have Changed* (Salonica, 1995).

2. D. de Gubernatis and A. M. de Turre, *Orbis seraphicus: historia de tribus ordinibus a seraphico patriarcha S. Francisco institutis deque eorum progressibus per quatuor mundi partes* [...] *tomus secundus*, ed. M. a Civetia and T. Domenichelli (Quaracchi, 1886), p. 492b.

3. G. Valentini, ed., *La legge delle montagne albanesi nelle relazioni della missione volante 1880–1932* (Florence, 1969), p. 129; M. Krasniqi, *Lugu i Baranit: monografi etnogjeografike* (Prishtina, 1984), p. 44, with examples from Kosovo.

4. Valentini, ed., *La legge delle montagne*, p. 205.

5. M. Barjaktarović, 'Dvojerske šiptarske zadruge u Metohiji', Srpska Akademija Nauka, *Zbornik radova*, vol. 4 (Etnografski Institut, vol. 1) (1950), pp. 197–209, at pp. 204–6.

6. Ibid., pp. 200–8.

7. F. Siebertz, *Albanien und die Albanesen: Landschafts- und Charakterbilder* (Vienna, 1910), p. 107; Valentini, ed., *La legge delle montagne*, p. 24; C. Libardi, *I primi moti patriottici albanesi nel 1910-1911-1912, specie nei Dukagini*, 2 parts (Trento, 1935), part 1, p. 33; C. S. Coon, *The Mountains of Giants: a Racial and Cultural Study of the North Albanian Mountain Ghegs* (Cambridge, MA, 1950), p. 36 (giving examples from the Nikaj and Merturi clans in 1929).

8. L. Mihačević, *Po Albaniji: dojmovi s puta* (Zagreb, 1911), p. 10; see also A. Dumont, *Le Balkan et l'Adriatique: les bulgares et les albanais; l'administration en Turquie; la vie des campagnes; le panslavisme et l'hellenisme*, 2nd edn. (Paris, 1874), p. 289.

9. J. G. von Hahn, *Reise von Beograd nach Salonik* (Vienna, 1861), p. 48 (Sveti Prohor); G. Muir Mackenzie and A. P. Irby, *Travels in the Slavonic Provinces of Turkey-in-Europe*, 3rd edn., 2 vols. (London, 1877), ii, p. 88 (Deçan); Mihačević, *Po Albaniji*, p. 30. The *bula* is a female Muslim religious teacher who also officiates at ceremonies for women.

10. Hasluck, *Christianity and Islam*, i, pp. 31–6; de Gubernatis and de Turre, *Orbis seraphicus*, p. 588b; G. Stadtmüller, 'Das albanische Nationalkonzil vom Jahre 1703', *Orientalia christiana periodica*, 22 (1956), pp. 68–91, at p. 71; S. Vryonis, 'Religious Changes and Patterns in the Balkans, 14th–16th Centuries', in H. Birnbaum and S. Vryonis, eds., *Aspects of the Balkans: Continuity and Change* (The Hague, 1972), pp. 151–76, at p. 174; Mitchell, 'A Muslim-Christian Sect', p. 752.

11. Archivio della Sacra Congregazione de Propaganda fide, Rome (hereafter: 'ASCPF'), SOCG 895 (report of 1791), fo. 75r ('certa curiosa malatia donesca'); SOCG 872 (report of 1785), fo. 130r ('visitare i loro malati, ed anche nell' escorcizare, e benedire i loro animali').

12. ASCPF, SOCG 482, fos. 288v–289r ('ivi tutta la notte se la passano, con Tamburi, Siffare, balli, e Canti. Passata la mezza notte principiano una confusa Processione Turchi, Serviani, e Greci con candele di cera accese a misura della propria vita longhe. Circondano la Cima del più alto monte per spatia di tre hore a piedi scalzi alcuni de turchi principali a cavallo').

13. N. Clayer, *L'Albanie, pays des derviches: les ordres mystiques musulmans en Albanie à l'époque post-ottomane (1912–1967)* (Berlin, 1990), pp. 22, 171 (Sarı Saltık); B. Nušić, *S Kosova na sinje mora: beleške s puta kroz Arbanase 1894. godine* (Belgrade, 1902), p. 35 (Pantaleimon). On Sarı Saltık more generally see H. T. Norris, *Islam in the Balkans: Religion and Society between Europe and the Arab World* (London, 1993), pp. 146–57.

14. de Gubernatis and de Turre, *Orbis seraphicus*, p. 590a–b ('Addebant autem impii parvam esse differentiam inter ipsos et Christianos; habemus enim, dicebant, omnes unum solum Deum; vestrum Christum ut Prophetam et Sanctum colimus, Sanctorum vestrorum plures festivitates vobiscum celebramus, vosque nobiscum festivum diem Veneris agitis: Mahometes et Christus fratres sunt...Eo hic error attigerat, ut ex eadem familia alius Christum sequeretur, alius Mahometem, et alius schisma'). The Catholics did celebrate Fridays because of the Muslims, and their bishops had promoted the cult of 'Sancta Veneranda' in order to assimilate this practice (p. 591a).

15. I. Zamputi, ed., *Relacione mbi gjendjen e Shqipërisë veriore e të mesme në shekullin XVII*, 2 vols. (Tirana, 1963–5), ii, p. 398 ('predicandoli li Turchi, ch'ogn'uno nella sua fede si puo saluare'). A 17th-century German author also noted that those who live among Muslims and observe their daily piety and good works 'will come to think that they are good people and will very probably be saved': T. W. Arnold, *The Preaching of Islam: a History of the Propagation of the Muslim Faith*, 3rd edn. (London, 1935), pp. 165–6.

16. ASCPF, SOCG 792, fo. 153r ('fine arti, ed astuzie').

17. The document, in the state archives in Tirana, is discussed in P. Thëngjilli, *Renta feudale dhe evoluimi i saj në vise shqiptare (shek. XVII–mesi i shek. XVIII)* (Tirana, 1990), p. 96, and N. Limanoski, *Islamizacijata i etničkite promeni vo Makedonija* (Skopje, 1993), pp. 137–8.

18. I. Zamputi, ed., *Dokumente të shekujve XVI–XVII për historinë e Shqipërisë*, iii (Tirana, 1990), pp. 50–1 ('ritenere nel cuore la fede cristiana').

19. M. Jačov, ed., *Spisi tajnog vatikanskog arhiva XVI–XVIII veka* (Belgrade, 1983), p. 38 ('Maumetanam Sectam estrinsece profitentur...in corde tantum Christianam fidem retinendo: quo et[iam] presuposito, frustra coram Archiep[iscop]o in visitationib[us] illis insteterunt pro decreto, ut sibi a parochis secreto sacramenta penitentiae, et eucharistiae, ministrarentur').

20. D. Farlati, *Illyrici sacri*, 8 vols. (Venice, 1751–1819), vii, pp. 120–3.

21. Zamputi, ed., *Relacione*, ii, pp. 440–2 ('Alcuni dicono, et sono moltissimi, che con il cuore siamo christiani, solamente habiamo mutato il nome per non potere pagare li datii impostici dagli Turchi; per questo dicono...caro reverendo, venite a confessarme e communicarme occultamente; io questa cosa non ho fatto in sino adesso...ne anche mi pare che si deve fare').

22. Sh. Gaspari, 'Nji dorshkrim i vjetës 1671 mbi Shqypni', *Hylli i Dritës*, 6 (1930), pp. 377–88, 492–8, 605–13; 7 (1931), pp. 154–61, 223–7, 349–55, 434–47, 640–4, 699–703; 8 (1932), pp. 48–50, 98–104, 208–10, 265–7, 310–14; here at 8, p. 100 ('vengono chiamati

con nomi turcheschi in presenza delli Turchi, mangiano della carne e cibi prohibiti dalla nostra santa fede, quando però non sono visti dalli Turchi vanno in chiesa a sentir messa, confessarsi e communicarsi da un certo prete D. Martino Politi, che va alle volte in detta terra, permettendo il prelato, che a questi tali chiamati da lui christiani occulti si possino amministrare li santi sacramenti').

23. Farlati, *Illyrici sacri*, vii, p. 136 ('infidelitati').

24. See Arnold, *Preaching of Islam*, pp. 188–9; de Gubernatis and de Turre, *Orbis seraphicus*, pp. 564–6.

25. Zamputi, ed., *Relacione*, ii, pp. 97, 440; Gaspari, 'Nji dorshkrim', 6, p. 386.

26. Zamputi, ed., *Relacione*, ii, p. 442 ('non vogliano pigliare per moglie la turca, ma la christiana dicendo, che non si morsi affatto in casa mia il nome di Christiano').

27. E. Albèri, ed., *Relazioni degli ambasciatori veneti al senato*, 15 vols. (Florence, 1839–63), ser. 3, i, p. 454 ('Pigliano anco i Turchi le mogli cristiane indifferentemente, perchè la loro legge lo tollera. Il figlio maschio, ad instanza del padre, vien fatto turco, le femmine, ad instanza della madre, cristiane; ma tuttavia le femmine sono introdotte nella legge maomettana, secondo la volontà del padre').

28. Archivio Segreto Vaticano, Vatican City, Processus consistoriales, 114, fo. 617r ('Domicilia fidelium sunt 237 et animae fidelium 4695, et multae aliae animae fideles sunt dispersae inter domicilia turcharum et sunt a nobis administrate sacramenta').

29. Farlati, *Illyrici sacri*, vii, p. 146. I am not sure whether this is identical with the decree referred to by L. Rostagno and dated by her to 1628: 'Note sulla simulazione di fede nell'Albania ottomana', in G. Calasso et al., *La bisaccia dello sheikh: omaggio ad Alessandro Bausani islamista nel sessantesimo compleanno* (Venice, 1981), pp. 153–63, at p. 156.

30. On the theories see P. Zagorin, *Ways of Lying: Dissimulation, Persecution and Conformity in Early Modern Europe* (Cambridge, MA, 1990), pp. 153–220; J. P. Sommerville, 'The New Art of Lying: Equivocation, Mental Reservation, and Casuistry', in E. Leites, ed., *Conscience and Casuistry in Early Modern Europe* (Cambridge, 1988), pp. 159–84.

31. Farlati, *Illyrici sacri*, vii, pp. 147, 148, 158; on this synod see also Stadtmüller, 'Das albanische Nationalkonzil'.

32. Rostagno, 'Note sulla simulazione', p. 157.

33. ASCPF, SC Servia 1, fo. 318r.

34. Ibid., fos. 317r ('professano interiormente la fede Christiana, ma tanto nascostamente, che tavolta il Padre non si palesa ai Figli, ne i Figli al Padre, e nell'estremo si mostrano, e fanno credere per turchi…Le Mogli di essi sono per lo più publicamente Christiane, purchè non siano Figlie di Christiani occulti, o di turchi e convertite poi in casa de loro Mariti Christiani'), 330r ('mantengono occultamente la Fede Christiana').

35. Zagorin, *Ways of Lying*, p. 56.

36. Farlati, *Illyrici sacri*, pp. 172–6, 188–9.

37. ASCPF, SOCG 792, fo. 147v.

38. Ibid., fos. 145v–146r ('come per esser abbandonati da noi Missionari, assolutamente abbracciano il Mahometanismo, e questi tali ci portano un'incredibile odio, aversione, et esecrazione, e la più grande persecuzione da essi patiamo, che dalli veri, et antichi Turchi').

39. Ibid., fo. 149v.

40. ASCPF, SC Servia 4, fos. 238v–240r.

41. E. Wiet, 'Mémoire sur le pachalik de Prisrend', *Bulletin de la Société de Géographie*, ser. 5, vol. 12 (1866), pp. 273–89.

42. R. H. Davison, *Reform in the Ottoman Empire, 1856–1876* (Princeton, NJ, 1963), pp. 36–45.

43. H. Kaleshi and H.-J. Kornrumpf, 'Das Wilajet Prizren: Beitrag zur Geschichte der türkischen Staatsreform auf dem Balkan im 19. Jahrhundert', *Südost-Forschungen*, 26 (1967), pp. 176–238, at p. 181.

44. ASCPF, SOCG 922, fo. 333r–v (Krasniqi report, 1820). In Sept. 1820 Rome began a 'processo informativo' on the Rugovë martyrs (fos. 314r–315v).

45. All these details are from ASCPF, SC Servia 4, fos. 172r–173v (report by Fra Dionisio d'Afragola; fo. 172v: 'perchè i Fantesi non sono stati mai disturbati nei loro affari di Religione?', 'dispersi tra i Villaggi tutti Turchi'), and fos. 178r–180v (report by Gaspër Krasniqi).

46. ASCPF, SC Servia 4, fos. 209r–210v (letter from Archbishop Bogdanović), 237r (visitation report by Bogdanović giving the figure of 158 people); G. Gjini, *Ipeshkvia Shkup-Prizren nëpër shekuj* (Zagreb, 1992), pp. 190–3; Gj. Gjergj-Gashi, *Martirët shqiptarë gjatë viteve 1846–1848* (Zagreb, 1994), pp. 61–5, 82–92 (with 148 names and other statistics).

47. ASCPF, SC Servia 4, fos. 350r–352v, 368r–370v (Bogdanović reports, 1849, 1850).

48. Davison, *Reform*, pp. 55–6; text in A. Šopov ['Schopoff'], *Les Réformes et la protection des chrétiens en Turquie, 1673–1904* (Paris, 1904), pp. 48–54 (p. 51: quotation).

49. von Hahn, *Reise von Belgrad*, p. 83 (noting 17 families who had declared themselves recently at Letnicë (Letnica)); Archbishop Bucciarelli, report of 1872 (ASCPF, SC Servia 5, fo. 589v).

50. The Serbian writer and vice-consul Milan Rakić stated that it was common knowledge: Rakić, *Konzulska pisma 1905–11*, ed. A. Mitrović (Belgrade, 1985), p. 239. Bejtullah Destani tells me that he has received confirmation of this claim from a member of Idriz Seferi's family. On the kaçak rebellion see N. Malcolm, *Kosovo: A Short History* (London, 1998), pp. 272–8.

51. L. Freundlich, *Albaniens Golgotha: Anklageakten gegen die Vernichter des Albanervolkes* (Vienna, 1913), p. 27.

52. A. Urošević, *Gornja Morava i Izmornik*, Srpski etnografski zbornik, vol. 51 (Naselja i poreklo stanovništva, vol. 28) (Belgrade, 1935), p. 112; on the coming out of crypto-Catholics in the 1920s and 1930s see Gjini, *Ipeshkvia*, p. 153.

53. G. Duijzings, 'The Martyrs of Stublla', unpublished typescript. I am very grateful to Ger Duijzings for letting me see this work. [*Additional note*: This was subsequently published in G. Duijzings, *Religion and the Politics of Identity in Kosovo* (London, 2000), pp. 86–105; on Gnidovec see pp. 101–2.]

Chapter 5

1. See, for example (though it is a highly untypical example), the members of the Bruni and Bruti families discussed in N. Malcolm, *Agents of Empire: Knights, Corsairs, Jesuits and Spies in the Sixteenth-Century Mediterranean World* (London, 2015).

2. See L. Peirce, *Morality Tales: Law and Gender in the Ottoman Court of Aintab* (Berkeley, CA, 2003), pp. 101-6 (noting that the apparent recording of first-person statements in these records may often have been a stylistic convention rather than a matter of direct quotation).

3. These records are currently being edited, in an exemplary fashion, by Peter Bartl: see the references to his *Albania sacra* (Wiesbaden, 2007-), below.

4. One exception to this statement consists of documents generated by Muslim Albanians when applying for conversion to Christianity at the 'Casa de' Catecumeni' in Venice—though the formal narrative statements were usually brief and seem to have been scribally composed. See A. Vanzan, 'La Pia Casa dei Catecumeni in Venezia. Un tentativo di *devshirme* cristiana?', in A. Destro, ed., *Donne e microcosmi culturali* (Bologna, 1997), pp. 221-55 (referring on p. 221 to 'laconic' statements ('laconiche')); P. Ioly Zorattini, *I nomi degli altri: conversioni a Venezia e nel Friuli Veneto in età moderna* (Florence, 2008), pp. 75-90; D. Lappa, 'Religious Conversions within the Venetian Military Milieu (17th and 18th Centuries)', *Studi veneziani*, 67 (2013), pp. 183-200.

5. For a general institutional overview of the three Inquisitions see F. Bethencourt, *The Inquisition: A Global History, 1478-1834* (Cambridge, 2009). On the Roman Inquisition the best surveys are G. Romeo, *L'Inquisizione nell'Italia moderna*, 2nd edn. (Bari, 2004) (p. 37: shift from 1570s); A. Del Col, *L'Inquisizione in Italia, dal XII al XX secolo* (Milan, 2006); C. Black, *The Italian Inquisition* (New Haven, CT, 2009) (p. 132: shift from late 1560s).

6. The major studies are: L. Rostagno, *Mi faccio turco* (Rome, 1983); B. Bennassar and L. Bennassar, *Les Chrétiens d'Allah: l'histoire extraordinaire des renégats, XVIᵉ-XVIIᵉ siècles* (Paris, 1989); A. Gonzalez-Raymond, *La Croix et le croissant: les inquisiteurs des îles face à l'Islam, 1550-1700* (Paris, 1992); and I. M. R. Mendes Drumond Braga, *Entre a Cristandade e o Islão (séculos XV-XVII): cativos e renegados nas franjas de duas sociedades em confronto* (Ceuta, 1998). See also G. Fiume, *Schiavitù mediterranee: corsari, rinnegati e santi di età moderna* (Milan, 2009); G. Boccadamo, *Napoli e l'Islam: storie di musulmani, schiavi e rinnegati in età moderna* (Naples, 2010). Many of the issues which will strike readers of the testimonies presented in this essay—for example, the emphasis on food or dress as a marker of religion—are discussed in depth in this secondary literature. The purpose of this essay is not to explore those issues, but rather to present specific cases.

7. Bibliothèque nationale de France, Paris, MS lat. 8994, fos. 252r-266v (case of Jacobus Gerardus), at fo. 255r-v ('li modi, parole, et ceremonie che ritennero per farlo rinegare, et circoncidere', 'et se habbia osseruati li loro falsi riti', 'se mai si sia discostato in alcun modo con l'animo dalla S.ᵗᵃ Fede Cat.ᶜᵃ ed aderitosi alla empia setta di Mahumetto, ouero se habbia mai creduto che alcuno si posse saluare fuora del grembo della Santa Chiesa Catholica').

8. Rostagno, *Mi faccio Turca*, pp. 55-6.

9. Ibid., pp. 21-2. On the questions, cf. also the detailed list of points in one of the major handbooks, E. Masini, *Sacro arsenale ò vero prattica dell'officio della S. Inquisitione ampliata* (Rome, 1639), pp. 241-3.

10. See Bennassar and Bennassar, *Les Chrétiens d'Allah*, pp. 275, 321, 338; Gonzalez-Raymond, *La Croix et le croissant*, pp. 204-9. Discussing Algiers in the early 1720s,

Jacques Philippe Laugier de Tassy wrote that generally masters made no effort to convert their Christian slaves, since this would lower their value in the market, but that they converted children up to the age of 12, as this was seen as a meritorious act (*Histoire du royaume d'Alger, avec l'état présent de son gouvernement, de ses forces de terre & de mer, de ses revenus, police, justice politique & commerce* (Amsterdam, 1725), pp. 86-7). Mendes Drumond Braga gives examples of some accounts of coercion which, she judges, are 'too realistic to be false', a judgement that is necessarily very subjective: *Entre a Cristandade e o Islão*, pp. 78-81 (p. 81: 'realistas demais para serem falsas'). More generally, she does note the widespread use of 'a discourse of self-exculpation' among those questioned by the Inquisition (p. 131: 'um discurso de desculpabilização').

11. Rostagno, *Mi faccio Turca*, p. 22. The 'sponte comparentes' were also treated more mildly by the Spanish Inquisition (Gonzalez-Raymond, *La Croix et le croissant*, pp. 88-9) and the Portuguese (Mendes Drumond Braga, *Entre a Cristandade e o Islão*, pp. 131-3).

12. See S. Bono, *Schiavi musulmani nell'Italia moderna: galeotti, vu' cumprà, domestici* (Naples, 1999), p. 255; G. Wettinger, *Slavery in the Islands of Malta and Gozo, ca. 1000-1812* (San Gwann, 2002), pp. 463-6.

13. For a general account of the Maltese Inquisition see A. Bonnici, *Medieval and Roman Inquisition in Malta* (Rabat, 1998); for the Neapolitan see L. Amabile, *Il Santo Officio della Inquisizione in Napoli* (Castello, 1892); for the Venetian see Del Col, *L'Inquisizione in Italia*, pp. 342-94.

14. On the Friulian Inquisition see Del Col, *L'Inquisizione in Italia*, pp. 374-91; on Palmanova and its Muslim soldiers see G. Minchella, '*Porre un soldato alla inquisitione': i processi del Sant'Ufficio nella fortezza di Palmanova, 1595-1669* (Trieste, 2009) (and cf. Ioly Zorattini, *I nomi degli altri*, pp. 267-74).

15. J. Tedeschi, *The Prosecution of Heresy: Collected Studies on the Inquisition in Early Modern Italy* (Binghamton, NY, 1991), p. 104 (figures). On the Inquisition in Sicily see F. Renda, *L'Inquisizione in Sicilia* (Palermo, 1997). On cases there involving Islam see pp. 341-75 of that work, and W. Monter, *The Frontiers of Heresy: The Spanish Inquisition from the Basque Lands to Sicily* (Cambridge, 1990), pp. 171-3.

16. These reports are held by the Archivo Histórico Nacional, Madrid, which, where four out of the five bound volumes are concerned, allows consultation only of microfilms (the fifth has been digitally photographed). The difference between the writing on the surface of a page and the 'show-through' of ink on the other side is perceptible when one looks at the original, but not in a microfilm, where the black-and-white photography homogenizes everything that appears as black. As a consequence, hundreds of pages of these documents are now illegible, and have thus been excluded from the scope of historical research.

17. See the classic essay by Carlo Ginzburg, 'L'inquisitore come antropologo', in R. Pozzi and A. Prosperi, eds., *Studi in onore di Armando Saitta dei suoi allievi pisani* (Pisa, 1989), pp. 23-33, and the comments in A. Del Col, 'I criteri dello storico nell'uso delle fonti inquisitoriali moderne', in A. Del Col and G. Paolin, eds., *L'Inquisizione Romana: metodologia delle fonti e storia istituzionale* (Trieste, 2000), pp. 51-72.

18. Masini, *Sacro arsenale*, pp. 41 ('Scriuasi tutto ciò, che risponderà'), 43 ('Habbiasi consideratione di fare scriuere le risposte de' Rei, ò affermatiue, ò negatiue ch'elle si siano, con le loro proprie parole distesamente').

19. See Del Col, 'I criteri dello storico', p. 61, and N. S. Davidson, 'The Inquisition of Venice and its Documents: Some Problems of Method and Analysis', in A. Del Col and G. Paolin, eds., *L'Inquisizione romana in Italia nell'età moderna: archivi, problemi di metodo e nuove ricerche* (Rome, 1991), pp. 117-31, at pp. 123-4.

20. Tedeschi, *Prosecution of Heresy*, p. 132; J. Seitz, *Witchcraft and Inquisition in Early Modern Venice* (Cambridge, 2011), p. 9.

21. J. Riera i Sans, *Sodomites catalans: història i vida (segles XIII–XVIII)* (Barcelona, 2014), p. 521. For a summary history of the Barcelona Inquisition see J. Badia Elias, *La Inquisició a Catalunya (segles XIII–XIX)* (Barcelona, 1992).

22. Riera i Sans, *Sodomites catalans*, p. 260 ('cerca de Venecia').

23. On the fall of Ulcinj see Malcolm, *Agents of Empire*, pp. 140-6.

24. On this anomaly see Monter, *Frontiers of Heresy*, pp. 276-83; V. Lavenia, *Un'eresia indicibile: Inquisizione e crimini contro natura in età moderna* (Bologna, 2015), pp. 20-2.

25. Riera i Sans, *Sodomites catalans*, pp. 260-1 ('Ya por la marina se extendía la mala fama deste hombre por lo que los mochachos havían dicho').

26. Ibid., p. 261 ('no dixo más de que él dixiera la verdad'). Contrary to popular modern belief, torture was a rarity in the Spanish (or any other) Inquisition. The commonest form was the 'garrucha' (Ital.: strappado), where the accused's wrists were tied behind him and he was hoisted by them on a pulley. 'Light' here (p. 261: 'leve') refers probably to brevity of duration. A confession made under torture was not itself legally conclusive; it had to be ratified by the accused subsequently. See H. Kamen, *The Spanish Inquisition* (London, 1976), pp. 174-8.

27. Archivio di Stato, Venice (hereafter: 'ASVen'), Savi all'eresia (Santo Ufficio) (hereafter: 'SU'), busta (hereafter: 'b.') 124 (1687), fo. [1r] ('Franc.ˢ q. Nicolai Pecich de Zagrabia Crouatie, habitans Venetijs in Domo Comitis Gegha, italicè Georgij Bardi de Albania, in Calli dictj della Contessa apud S. Martinum').

28. Many Albanians lived in Castello: see S. Moretti, 'Une communauté étrangère dans la Venise des XVᵉ et XVIᵉ siècles: le cas des Albanais', in J. Bottin and D. Calabi, eds., *Les Étrangers dans la ville: minorités et espace urbain du bas Moyen Âge à l'époque moderne* (Paris, 1999), pp. 183-94, at p. 186.

29. ASVen, SU, b. 124, fo. [1v].

30. Ibid., fo. [1r-v] ('pretendendo il S.ʳ Conte Georgio Bardi d'Albania mio P[ad]rone, la leua di diuersi soldati, da q[ue]sto Pub.ᶜᵒ, perche l'Ecc.ᵐᵒ S.ʳ Pietro Valier sauio grande di Collegio, si era contrario, essendo capitata in Casa, non sò come, una tal Donna Catè Vicentina…et per mezo di dᵗᵃ Catte, fù essibito alla dᵗᵃ Contessa, et anco al Sʳ Co: Georgio suo marito, il mezo di un' altra strega di cui non sò il n.ᵉ, nè doue habiti, di operar in modo, che l'Eccᵐᵒ Sʳ Pietro Valier, si darebbe am[m]alato, oue non hauerebbe potuto andar in Collegio ad opporsi à lor brame e l'haurebbero fatto star à letto sino tanto hauessero sortito il lor intento, p[er] la qual operat.ⁿᵉ li sud.ᵗⁱ Conte e Contessa li promisero 12. Cecchini…Et in fatti de li à poco tempo si am[m]alo l'Eccᵐᵒ Valier sudᵗᵒ, e de li à qualche tempo ricercando la sud.ᵗᵃ Catte il promesso danaro da' dᵗⁱ Conte, e Contessa, q[ue]sti trouorno scuse p[er] non dargelo [*sic*], dicendo che

pretendeuano hauer la leua di due Compagnie in terra ferma, e che non hauendo ciò ottenuto, non uoleuano darli cosa alc.ᵃ. Perciò la d.ᵗᵃ Catte le desse: Già che non uolete darmi il danaro promesso, farò che la strega operi al incontrario di q[ua]nto hà operato. E così di là à poco l'Ecc^mo Sr Valier si ricuperò et uscì di Casa'). The 'savi' were members of senior committees in the Venetian government, and belonged to the 'Collegio', the body with overall executive authority. A zecchino was a gold ducat; a soldier's salary in this period might be four ducats per month.

31. Ibid., fo. [1v] ('E tutte q[ue]ste cose sò p[er]che d.ᵗᵒ Cap.ⁿ Andrea me le hà confidate, Dicendomi che toccando con d.ᵗᵃ Calamita posta in un' An[n]ello sù la Carne, ò Veste de qualche persona, ò homo, ò donna, la persona toccata non può far di meno à corrisponder à q[ua]nto si brama'). The use of baptized magnets was a fairly well-known magical practice, used especially in love-magic: see E. Reeves, 'Occult Sympathies and Antipathies: The Case of Early Modern Magnetism', in W. Detel and C. Zittel, eds., *Wissensideale und Wissenskulturen in der frühen Neuzeit* (Berlin, 2002), pp. 97–114, at pp. 102–3.

32. ASVen, SU, b. 86 (1628), fasc. 1, unnumbered item, 23 June, fo. [1r] ('Paulus filius Petri de Scutari, aet an. 20. miles in cimbis armatis'). There was a strong Venetian tradition of using Albanians as fighters on the ships that patrolled the northern Adriatic. Cf., for example, Captain Marco Gini [Gjin], described in the 1590s as 'commander of eleven, and then six, armed vessels with 300 Albanians, serving the Venetians against the Uskoks [*sc.* pirates]' (ASVat, Fondo Borghese, ser. III, MS 128 (F. Patrizi, notes on Albania, 1590s), fo. [7v]: 'gouernatore di xi e poi sei barche armate con 300 Albanesi di Ven.ⁿⁱ contra Scochi').

33. ASVen, SU, b. 86 (1628), fasc. 1, unnumbered item, 23 June, fo. [1r] ('già 7. anni in c.ᵃ fui fatto schiauo de turchi, fra quali dimorai 6. mesi in c.ᵃ con la catena alli piedi, et per forza et minaccie mi fecero rinegare la s.ᵗᵃ fede Xp[ist]iana, minacciandomi di tagliarmi la testa. et se bene rinegai con la bocca, non la rinegai però col core. Et quanto p.[rim]ᵃ potei fuggi[re?] da loro, et me ne ueni à seruire la ser.ᵐᵃ Rep.ᶜᵃ di Venetia, quale hò seruito questi 6. anni in c.ᵃ et seruo ancora, uiuendo catolicam.ᵗᵉ et in particolare osseruando le uigilie et digiuni instituti da s.ᵗᵃ chiesa'). Here and subsequently, the letters 'xp' represent the Greek chi and rho, the first two letters of 'Christos'. Note that in Roman Catholic usage in this period, 'cristiano' typically meant not merely Christian, but Catholic; Orthodox Christians were called 'scismatici'.

34. Ibid., fo. 1r–v (fo. 1v: 'per non saper io scriuere').

35. ASVen, SU, b. 86, fasc. 1, unnumbered item, 13 Sept. 1628, fo. [1r] ('Alexander Corbenesius Albanensis f. q. Jo[ann]is'). A report by a Catholic priest in *c.*1685 said: 'Kurbin, which pays tribute to the Sultan: there are Muslims and Christians together, the Muslims form one third of them; it is the residence of the Archbishop of Durrës' (P. Bartl, ed., *Albania sacra: geistliche Visitationsberichte aus Albanien*, i: *Diözese Alessio* (Wiesbaden, 2007), p. 141: 'Corbini sotto tributo al G. Sig.re. Sono Turchi, e Christiani insieme, la 3.a parte è turca, è la residenza di Mons.r Arciv.o di Durazzo').

36. ASVen, SU, b. 86, fasc. 1, unnumbered item, 13 Sept. 1628, fo. [1r] ('già 7. anni sono fui preso da turchi, et trattenuto da loro p[er] spatio de tre settimane per forza mi fecero rinegare la s.ᵗᵃ fede et per forza, come fece contra mia uolontà. et la matina seguente me fugi uia. Et perche in q.° tempo son stato sempre soldato in diuerse parti, non hò hauuto commodita di p[rese]ntarmi più presto').

37. Ibid., fo. [1r–v].
38. ASVen, SU, b. 86, fasc. 1, unnumbered item, 19 Dec. 1628, fo. [1r] ('Blasius Matagusius de Alexio q. Pauli miles, aet an. 68. in c.ª'); Bartl, ed., *Albania sacra*, i, p. 85 (visitation report of 1629: 170 families, 'a great number' of Muslims ('gran numero')).
39. ASVen, SU, b. 86, fasc. 1, unnumbered item, 19 Dec. 1628, fo. [1r] ('essendo io nato et alleuato Christiano, già 16. ò 17. anni in c.ª fui preso da turchi con inganni, li quali mi fecero turco circoncidendomi et facendomi alzar il dedo. fra quali turchi son perseuerato tutto questo tempo, uiuendo conforme alli loro riti et osseruando le sue ceremonie, se bene haueuo sempre nel core de uoler ritornare alla s.ta fede cat.ca et uiuer da Christiano').
40. Ibid., fo. [1r–v] ('Petro de Scutari q. d[omi]nici Alphentis', 'S.r Pietro da Scutari Alfier sop[radet]to').
41. ASVen, SU, b. 87, unnumbered items, 5 June 1630, fo. [1r] ('Nicolaus f. q. Lech de Albania de Villa Fand, miles, aet an. 40. in c.ª p[ar]at ex aspectu').
42. See R. Elsie, *The Tribes of Albania: History, Society and Culture* (London, 2015), pp. 247–50; and cf. above, p. 66.
43. ASVen, SU, b. 87, unnumbered items, 5 June 1630, fo. [1r] ('Essendo io stato battiezato Xpiano, fatto poi schiauo de turchi già 12. anni in c.ª, et incarcerato, fui necessitato da loro à rinegare la s.ta fede et farmi turco, come in fatti hò fatto, et hò osseruato la legge de turchi in tutto questo tempo, et tutto quello che osseruano li altri turchi. Finalm.te uenuto à Venetia già un mese in c.ª, hò sempre desiderato ritornare al grembo di S.ta Chiesa').
44. Ibid., fo. [1r–v].
45. ASVen, SU, b. 101, unnumbered item, 21 Feb. 1645, fos. [1r] ('Jo[ann]es q[uondam] Nicolai Isin de Musia Alexij Albaniae, [a]et. an. 13 in c.ª miles societatis Georgij Criamchi? de Albania Gubernatoris', 'Marco Isè q. Antonij de Merchina Milite'), [1v] ('Gioanni'). Mërqi (Merqi, Merqin) was a village just north of Lezhë, where the Bishop of Lezhë traditionally had his summer residence: see Bartl, *Albania sacra*, i, p. 86 (report of 1629, referring to 'Merchigna').
46. ASVen, SU, b. 101, unnumbered item, 21 Feb. 1645, fo. [1r] ('Morta che fù mia m[ad]re Elena donna Cat.ca, come anco mio p[ad]re, fui condotto già 9. anni sono, ad Issimo Castel di turchi, in poter di Elisbich turco sanzacco à seruirlo, e si come mio padre per molti tributi che il turco poneua à Xriani, si fece turco, cosi indusse ancora me suo fig.lo à farmi turco, non sapendo per l'età tenera che cosa facessi, e così hò continuato per il corso di sei anni in casa del sud.to e dopo son stato anco e quà e là in turchia, uiuendo sempre come fanno li altri turchi. Et un mio Barba prete, chiamato don Nicola Zigni, dal quale son stato instrutto et ammaestrato, m'ha indotto à ritornare alla relig.e Xriana Cat.ca come sempre ho continuato con questo buon proponimento. se bene uiueua alla turchesca, di uoler ritornare alla Sta fede Xriana'). Ishëm was a fortress on the river Ishëm, north of Durrës, built by the Ottomans in the early 1570s: see Gj. Karaiskaj, *Pesë mijë vjet fortifikime në Shqipëri* (Tirana, 1981), pp. 221–4. A Venetian report of 1614 described Elez Bey as 'a leading Turk and lord of Albania': F. Lenormant, *Turcs et monténégrins* (Paris, 1866), p. 265 ('un principal turcho e sig. d'Albania nominato Elesbegh').
47. ASVen, SU, b. 101, unnumbered item, 21 Feb. 1645, fo. [1v].

48. ASVen, SU, b. 101, unnumbered item, 7 Sept. 1645, fo. [1r] ('Nicolaus q. Jo[ann]is Bassan de Sapotti in Epyro prope Cimeram, miles, [a]et. an. 55. put ex aspectu s.' 'R. P. Fr[atr]em Simeonem Suma de Croia Albaniae ordinis min. de obs.ᵃ capellanus').

49. P. Bartl, ed., *Albania sacra: geistliche Visitationsberichte aus Albanien*, i: *Diözese Sappa* (Wiesbaden, 2014), p. 12; see also pp. 165–71 (his visitation report of 1659).

50. ASVen, SU, b. 101, unnumbered item, 7 Sept. 1645, fo. [1r–v] ('Nacqui di padre e m[ad]re Greci ma scismatici, e steti con mio p[ad]re e m[ad]re sino all'età mia d'anni 30. in c.ᵃ uiuendo da Xr[ist]iano, ma scismatico. Con occ[asi]one che il turco fabricò una città, appresso la mia Villa, chiamata Sappot; e tutti quei contorni si chiamano con qᵒ nome di Sappot. e uolendo exigere il turco, come fà co[mune]m.ᵗᵉ da tutti li Xr[ist]iani, non tanto cat.ᶜⁱ quanto greci, e scismatici, grossa somma di danaro di tribunato, per non pagarlo, non hauendo commodità, mi feci turco, cioè andai dal Parocho turco che loro chiamano ogia, che uuol dir Parocho, nella Moschea, e senza circo[n]diermi ne altro, mi fecero alzare l'indice della man destra, e mi fecero dir queste parole, la ilà, i le là, Maomet, erusulà, che in lingua n[ost]ra uuol dire: dio è dio solo, e Macometo è suo profeta. E mi messe nome, Alì. E così son uissuto da turco in tutto conforme al rito loro sino adesso, che son capitato à Venetia, ma non hò però mai creduto à dogmi loro, ne che quella fosse la buona fede, anzi son sempre uissuto con quest'animo, di ritornar alla fede Xr[ist]iana. E capitai in Venetia gia 15. giorni, et hauendo occ[asi]one di descorrere col P. Barth[olom]eo Veronese Capucino quì p[rese]nte, dalle sue instructioni tanto più, mi son indotto à farmi cat.ᶜᵒ col rito greco p[er]messo dalla chiesa Romana'). The Church of the Arbëresh in southern Italy and Sicily, now called the Italo-Albanian Catholic Church, was in full communion with the Roman Church, accepting the primacy of the Pope, but retaining Greek Orthodox ritual and traditions. Sopot, at the southern end of Himarë, just to the north-west of Borsh, was the site of a medieval fortress, strengthened by the Ottomans in the mid-16th century but later demolished (see Gj. Karaiskaj, *Die spätantiken und mittelalterlichen Wehranlagen in Albanien: Städte, Burgen, Festungen und Kastelle*, ed. M. W. E. Peters (Hamburg, 2010), pp. 247–50). It is quite unclear what 'town' the Ottomans were building; the ambiguity about whether the town or the village was called Sopot is present in the original. Most likely 'town' here was a clerical error for 'fortress', and the reference was to the fortress of either Sopot or Kardhiq.

51. For garblings of the *shahada* see Rostagno, *Mi faccio Turco*, pp. 61–3; for cases of men not circumcised, Boccadamo, *Napoli e l'Islam*, pp. 116–17; cf. also Bennassar and Bennassar, *Les Chrétiens d'Allah*, p. 123.

52. ASVen, SU, b. 101, unnumbered item, 7 Sept. 1645, fo. [1v] ('idiomate ta[men] Epyrotico, siue albanense, mediante sup[radic]to interprete').

53. ASVen, SU, b. 101, unnumbered item, 23 Aug. 1644, fo. [1r] ('Georgius f. q. Georgij Bastarae de loco Bastarae, de Crua Ep[iscop]atus Albane[nsi]s, et q. Mariae Jugalium, [a]et. an 24. in c.ᵃ miles societatis D. Michaelis Illamas Albanensis').

54. Bastar is 10 miles south-east of Krujë; there was a diocese of Krujë, but Bastar was in fact in the diocese of Benda. See P. Bartl, *Albania sacra: geistliche Visitationsberichte aus Albanien*, ii: *Erzdiözese Durazzo* (Wiesbaden, 2011), pp. 16–19 (diocese), 207 (conversion).

55. ASVen, SU, b. 101, unnumbered item, 23 Aug. 1644, fo. [1r–v] ('Essendo io nato di padre e m[ad]re Xr[ist]iani Cat.ᶜⁱ, quello chiamato Zorzi, e questa Maria, nella terra di Bastara, di una città di Albania, uissi con d.ᵗᵒ mio p[ad]re e m[ad]re fino alla mia età di xi anni, nella sud.ᵗᵃ terra di Bastara. Morti che furono, hauendo solo dio miei fr[at]elli maritati, che non uolsero fastidio de fatti miei essendo poueri, fui necessitato partirmi di casa mia, e capitò alla città del Bassan in Albania, discosta una giornata dalla mia terra, commandata da turchi. E quiui cercando P[ad]rone per camparmi la uita, nell'età sod.ᵗᵃ di xi. anni, fui ueduto e ricercato da un tal turco chiamato Mema. E ricercandomi di che conditione io fossi, risposi che ero Xr[ist]iano. E lui per all'hora non mi disse altro, se non che non uoleua Xr[ist]iani. Ma la matina seguente mi prese d.ᵗᵒ turco, e mi condusse ad una delle loro moschee, e mi fece far turco per forza. cioè ricusando io di rinegar la fede, mi minacciò di farmi tormentare particolarmi [sic: for 'particolarm[ent]e'] con farmi mettere delle stecchette sotto le ongue, e darmi il fuogo alle mani et alli piedi, e poi di farmi attaccare in alto alle traui delle casa [sic], e fumigarlo di sotto, del che io poueretto spauentato, in età solo de xi anni come hò detto, mi risolsi di farmi turco, in questa maniera, che mi mecero dire alcune parole significanti in lingua Italiana, sia lodato dio, con altre poi parole diaboliche che non mi ricordo, facendomi alzare l'indice della man destra. Però non mi tagliarono ne altro. E con li turchi son stato fino all'età mia de 20. anni in c.ᵃ uiuendo allor modo, eccetto che al Venerdi e Sabbato non hò mangiato carne, ricordeuole della fede Xr[ist]iana, professata da me nel s. Battesimo. Non hò però mai creduto alla sette de turchi, ne dato fede alla loro fede e ceremonie, ma si sempre hò mantenuta nel mio core la s.ᵗᵃ fede Xr[ist]iana uiua, con desiderio di unirmi di nuouo alla S.ᵗᵃ Ap[osto]lica Rom.ᵃ chiesa, che perciò procurai di fugire come feci, e capitai alla terra di Such, doue sono e turchi e Xr[ist]iani, et li mi misi ad imparar l'arte di fabro con un turco, uiuendo ancor io da turco, col quale mi tratt[en]ei per spatio di doi anni, con pensiero di uiuer di Xriano, e se faceuo da turco scopertam.ᵗᵉ lo faceuo per paura di non esser abbrugiato uiuo in terra de turchi, ma nel core ero Xr[ist]iano. De li a d.ᵗⁱ 2. anni, capitai nella compagnia di d.ᵗᵒ Capitano Michiel in Argentea in Albania. E poi uenissimo à Cattaro doue compita la compagnia uenissimo poi à Venetia. andassimo poi al campo, et adesso seruo la barca armata qui à Venetia. Hora conseruando io pure q.ᵒ desiderio di aggregarmi di nuouo nel grembo della s[an]ta chiesa andai alli Catecumeni p[er] esser instrutto nelle cose della S. nostra fede'). Sukë was a village close to Blinisht, roughly 5 miles north of Lezhë. A report by Frang Bardhi in 1641 noted that of its two small chapels, one was 'violated by the Muslims' and the other 'completely destroyed'; but Blinisht itself had a very fine church, 1,800 Christian inhabitants and no Muslim ones. See Bartl, ed., *Albania sacra*, iii, pp. 152 (Blinisht), 157 ('violata da Turchi'), 158 ('affatto destrutto'). 'Argentea' was the Italian name of the river Erzen, which runs from south of Tirana to the coast north of Durrës: see G. Cantelli, *Albania propria overo superiore detta anche Macedonia occidentale* [engraved map, single sheet] (Rome, 1689).

56. ASVen, SU, b. 101, unnumbered item, 23 Aug. 1644, fos. [1v] (instructions), [2r] ('essendo stato battizzato, nondimeno fatto poi schiauo tra turchi, rinegai la S.ᵗᵃ fede').

57. Many these cases are printed in Minchella, 'Porre un soldato'; in what follows, I cite Minchella's edition (which lightly modernizes punctuation), correcting only significant mistranscriptions. Although I thereby highlight a few errors, I should like to pay tribute to this very valuable scholarly edition.

58. Minchella, *'Porre un soldato'*, pp. 122 (three cases), 153–4 (ten cases); Archivio storico dell'Arcidiocesi di Udine, Udine (hereafter: 'ASAU'), Curia Arcivescovile, Sant'Officio (hereafter: 'SO'), busta (hereafter: 'b.') 1348, sewn volume of summary reports, 1630–63, fos. 11v (27 Sept. 1638: Sinan, from Sopot), 13v–14r (6 Jan. 1641: list of eleven, including 'Amathe figliuolo di Nicha', 'Amath figliuolo di Gini', 'Ali figliuolo di Martin'), 16r (11 Nov. 1641: list of four, each called 'Himariot' ('Cimariotto')).

59. See above, p. 87.

60. Minchella, *'Porre un soldato'*, p. 72 ('Rumoli, in Albania', 'Rumoli, terra sottoposta al Turco').

61. Ibid., p. 72 ('Io son nato in Rumoli, terra sottoposta al Turco, di padre e madre christiani greci et da quelli nutrito et allevato nella fede greca fino all'età di cinque anni in *circa*, nel qual tempo, giocando con altri putti nella publica strada, fui per forza da un turco preso et posto in groppa d'un altro turco, che si ritrovava ivi a cavallo et, legato, fui condotto insieme con forse cinquecento altri figlioli a Constantinopoli et puosto in un giardino a lavorare. Et doppo tre giorni fui condotto nella moschea turchesca, dove fui circonciso insieme con gl'altri, facendomi loro renegar la fede christiana et, alzando il dito all'usanza turchescha, dire in quella lingua turchescha che era un solo Dio e Mahometto suo messagiero. Et doppo ho sempre vivuto con loro all'usanza turchescha, mangiando carne ogni giorno et facendo tutto quello che facevano gl'altri turchi, conforme a quanto commandava il suo patrone, sono già quindici mesi in circa; nel qual tempo, havendo conversato insieme con alcuni altri christiani che si ritrovavano schiavi, io, comprata una lima, ho tagliato li ferri nelli quali stavamo et insieme poi siamo fugiti, capitando prima a Tino et poi in Candia'). On Crete he had signed up with a captain who was recruiting men for the service of Venice.

62. Ibid., pp. 72 ('metu, seu suasione aliorum', 'due altre volte son fugito per venirmene tra christiani, ma sempre son stato ripigliato e poi finalmente piaciuto a Dio che sii liberato'), 74–5 (abjuration).

63. S. Gerlach, *Stephan Gerlachs dess Aeltern Tage-Buch*, ed. S. Gerlach (Frankfurt-am-Main, 1674), p. 314 (8); V. Vratislav ['Baron Wenceslas Wratislaw'], *The Adventures of Baron Wenceslas Wratislaw of Mitrowitz*, tr. A. H. Wratislaw (London, 1862), p. 4 (8); E. Albèri, ed., *Relazioni degli ambasciatori veneti al senato*, 15 vols. (Florence, 1839–63), ser. 3, ii, p. 142 (6).

64. ASAU, SO, b. 1302, fasc. 907 ('Doda'—an Albanian diminutive form of 'Dominic'); Minchella, *'Porre un soldato'*, p. 144, case of 1641 ('Mentre mi trovai fanciulo alla cuna, fui rapito da turchi et da loro alevato in quella setta maledetta di Maomet, la quale io ho seguitato per insino che da mei parenti mi fu datta la notizia che io fui batezzato e nato da padre et madre christiani').

65. ASAU, SO, b. 1302, fasc. 914 ('Halli'); Minchella, *'Porre un soldato'*, p. 150, case of 1641 ('Pile, provincia de Chucci', 'Et doppo che vene in cognitione di miei parenti, scapai et andai a chasa di mio padre per richoverarmi da loro. Ma dubitando loro delle pene turchesche, dicendo a me che non potevano tener in casa un renegato et che mi conveniva prima tornar alla fede et io non sapendo che partito prender, in quel tempo capitò capitanio Giobatta Stamati per far soldati et con lui m'inviai a questa volta d'Italia').

66. ASAU, SO, b. 1348, sewn vol., fo. 6r ('fanciullo', 'rubato da Turchi, e con quelli instrutto in d[ett]a setta').

67. ASAU, SO, b. 1304, fasc. 937 ('Eless', given mistakenly as 'Cless' by Minchella; in b. 1348, sewn vol., fo. 19r, it is 'Aless'); Minchella, *'Porre un soldato'*, pp. 161–2, case of 1643 ('Ritrovamdomi [*sic*] fanciullo di cinque o sei hani et capitando li turchi in casa nostra, mi cominciarno a persuadere che la loro fede era buona e miglior della christiana, dove che allevato da loro et dalla loro falsità, feci questo mancamento'); Bartl, ed. *Albania sacra*, ii, p. 282 (Franciscan report, 1744: Giorai); Malcolm, *Agents of Empire*, pp. 42, 456 (n. 12) (Gerami/Gierano).

68. Minchella, *'Porre un soldato'*, p. 161, case of 1643 ('Mio padre havea nome Husain et il nome di mia madre non mi arricordo, poiché da piccolo fui portato et allevato da turchi, essendo il mio padre dell'istessa setta, et io fui batezato da un prete'); ASAU, SO, b. 1348, sewn vol., fo. 19r ('gia Cristiano et hora turcho').

69. Minchella, *'Porre un soldato'*, p. 160, case of 1643 ('Mi fu detto dalla mia madre d'esser stato battezato a Santa Maria di Dusda un prete del paese'); ASAU, SO, b. 1348, sewn vol., fo. 18v ('ambi due hora Maumettani ma prima Cristiani'). 'Dusda' may have been Dush, a village roughly 4 miles west of Pukë, which had a church dedicated to St Mary Magdalen (see Bartl, ed., *Albania sacra*, iii, p. 111).

70. Minchella, *'Porre un soldato'*, pp. 160–1, case of 1643 ('et era turco'); ASAU, SO, b. 1348, sewn vol., fo. 18v ('gia Cristiano et hora turcho').

71. ASAU, SO, b. 1304, fasc. 937 ('Marsen'); Minchella, *'Porre un soldato'*, p. 161, case of 1643 ('Retrovamdomi [*sic*] a casa senza il padre et madre, nemeno alcuno parente, venne un turcho et mi menò via, et così alla sua servitù mi fece renegare la fede per forza et con ingano').

72. Minchella, *'Porre un soldato'*, p. 141, case of 1641 ('Essendo povero huomo, si mise a servire un turco, come per ordine si fa in quel paese dove, parte per lusinghe, parte minacciato dal padrone, non havendo altra perfetta cognitione, feci queso mancamento').

73. ASAU, SO, b. 1348, sewn vol., fo. 4r–v ('nella sua età puerile stando p[er] garzone co[n] un turcho', 'stando co[n] un turco p[er] garzone nell età puerile'). Giovanni was the son of 'Bibba' (Bib) Pelessa. Possibly these were relatives of Tommaso Pelessa, who was knighted by Venice for his services to that state in 1572 and was active as a representative of Albanian anti-Ottoman rebels in the 1590s: see V. Vinaver, 'Toma Peleš', jedan od radnika na dizanju ustanka protiv Turaka krajem XVI veka', *Istoriski glasnik*, 3–4 (1950), pp. 134–9; P. Bartl, *Der Westbalkan zwischen spanischer Monarchie und Osmanischem Reich: zur Türkenkriegsproblematik an der Wende vom 16. zum 17. Jahrhundert* (Wiesbaden, 1974), pp. 81–9; Malcolm, *Agents of Empire*, pp. 408–10. The family presumably originated from Plezhë, a village 6 miles south of Shkodër.

74. ASAU, SO, b. 1348, sewn vol., fo. 6v, case of 1633 ('ingannato da Turchi').

75. Minchella, *'Porre un soldato'*, p. 161, case of 1643 ('Ritrovandomi al Bariam, un spahi per forza mi fece renegare').

76. Ibid., p. 140, case of 1641 ('comilitonibus meis', 'Bartholomeo ordinis minorum capucinorum, Veronensi', 'Causa coactionis et illusionis Turcarum').

77. Ibid., p. 131, case of 1639 ('Havevo quatordeci in quindec'anni che, oppresso [emended here] dalle forze del Turco, per forza fui menato via et anco con violenza appostai dalla fede, perché loro havendo fatto di novo una fortezza, non solo me, ma tutti i circonvicinati violentarono alla renegatione per presidiare la fortezza'). This is from ASAU, SO, b. 1302, fasc. 886, where the interrogation is dated 21 May (calling him

Schender and giving his age as 30), and the abjuration is dated 1 May (calling him Scanderbe and giving his age as 35); Minchella presents these as two different cases, but the person is clearly the same in both, and the latter date is presumably just a slip for 1 June. Minchella also mistakenly describes Skender as a Bosniac: p. cxlvi. The summary account in ASAU, SO, b. 1348, sewn volume, fo. 12r, gives his age as 30. In the abjuration he took the name of 'Alessandro', clearly having enjoyed his previous nominal association with Skanderbeg.

78. See above, n. 48.

79. Ibid., p. 145, case of 1641 ('per l'occasione della venuta in nostro paese di Haderbeg et dalla violenza sua astretti, incoressimo nel grave mancamento, temendo più l'ira del tereno giudice et barbaro che quella di Dio'). In Minchella's transcription Gin Chiurchio is described as 'prior Cimariae'; this is a misreading of 'Pro[uincia]e Cimariae', 'of the province of Himarë' (ASAU, SO, b. 1302, fasc. 908).

80. Ibid., p. 160, case of 1643 ('Solette d'Albania', 'essendo capitato nel paese un sanzacho, lo menò per forza et lo fece renegare', 'circa 20 anni'). In ASAU, SO, b. 1348, sewn vol., fo. 18v, the place is given as 'Soles'.

81. See P. Thëngjilli, *Shqiptarët midis lindjes dhe perëndimit (1506–1750): fusha politike*, ii (Tirana, 2006), p. 218.

82. ASAU, SO, b. 1302, fasc. 884 ('Duca'); Minchella, *'Porre un soldato'*, p. 128, case of 1639 ('contribuire li beni temporali et dacij all Turcho'). (Minchella mistakenly gives 'Luca' for 'Duca', and 'dare' for 'dacij'.) The age of apostasy is stated in ASAU, SO, b. 1348, fo. 12r. He gave his place of origin as 'Orosse' in Himarë; this was a variant form of 'Borsh', appearing as 'Orasha', 'Oresha' or 'Orsha' in 16th-century Ottoman documents (see F. Duka, 'Aspekte social-ekonomike dhe demografike të Himarës gjatë sundimit osman (shek. XV–XVI)', in L. Nasi et al., eds., *Himara në shekuj* (Tirana, 2004), pp. 62–95, at pp. 66, 68).

83. ASAU, SO, b. 1302, fasc. 907 ('arfanda[m], in Albania', 'derfanda[m]' (where the 'm' is represented by a macron over the 'a')); Minchella, *'Porre un soldato'*, p. 143, case of 1641 ('della città d'Alesio', 'Avendo amazato un mio fratello un homo là in paese, se ne fugì et li turchi venero per questa ochasione a Desfandam, per far la giustitia, et non trovando predeto mio fratello, mi menorno per forza in Alesio et quivi con violenza mi fecero renegare la santa fede'). The place-names may suggest a possible connection with the Fan or 'Fandi' region, east of Lezhë; see above, at n. 42.

84. Minchella, *'Porre un soldato'*, pp. 153–4 ('Antivari in Albania'). The case of Sinan in 1638 (above, n. 58), also specifies that he was from Sopot. For details of other baptisms of Albanians at Palmanova and Udine (not processed by the Inquisition) see Ioly Zorattini, *I nomi degli altri*, pp. 268–70 (including two from Durrës and one from Krujë).

85. Minchella, *'Porre un soldato'*, p. 154 ('il signor capitanio Alì, turco di Sopoto, d'anni 30 in circa, qual ha lasciato moglie e tre altri figli al paese', 'di anni 14 incirca', 'd'anni 12 incirca').

86. Ibid., p. 122 ('l'illustrissima signora Beatrice dal Monte'). I take the place of origin given for one of them, 'Tunichio, in Albania', to be the village in Himarë, now no longer extant, listed in a Latin document of 1581 as 'Turnechei': see N. Borgia, *I monaci basiliani d'Italia in Albania*, 2 vols. (Rome, 1935–42), i, p. 21.

87. See above, pp. 103–7. On the sponsoring of converts see Bono, *Schiavi musulmani*, p. 286; W. Rudt de Collenberg, 'Le Baptême des musulmans esclaves à Rome au XVIIe et XVIIIe siècles', *Mélanges de l'École Française de Rome*, 101 (1989), pp. 1–181, 519–670, at pp. 53–71, 551–65.

88. ASAU, SO, b. 1348, sewn vol., fo. 8v, case of 1636.

89. ASAU, SO, b. 1302, fasc. 893 ('del rito Rasciano') (mistakenly given in Minchella, *'Porre un soldato'*, p. 135, as 'del rito persiano'). This Albanian is described here as Giovanni Piero, from Himarë, reconciled to the Church on 22 Apr. 1640, and is thus presumably the same person as the Giovanni Paolo, from 'Paileth' (Palasë?) in Himarë, aged 70, described as having appeared at the Tribunal on 21 Apr. 1640 in ASAU, SO, b. 1348, sewn vol., fo. 13r. For the other cases see that vol., fo. 11v (1638: Giovanni, son of Martin, of Himarë; Nicolò, son of Giovanni, of 'Sutta' (Sotirë?), Himarë); Minchella, pp. 135–6 (1640: Noan Pogato, from Himarë), 149–50 (1641: Giorgio of Bastia).

90. Archivio Storico Diocesano, Naples (hereafter: ASDN), Sant'Ufficio (hereafter: SU), filza 56.659, fo. [1r] ('Stradus Strayl de Casale di Maura de Velona grecus etatis Annor[um] xxij').

91. Ibid., fo. [1r] ('sono an[n]i circa dece che morendo mio p[ad]re me partio da mia casa et andai p[ro]prio nela Velona tra de turchi et me posse p[er] seruitore co[n] uno Ianniczoro chr[ist]iano renegato et lo seruio In tutto q[ue]llo che esso me co[m]mandaua che ero Io allora de an[n]i circa dudici et p[er] essere ancora vassallo et tributario a lo gran turco').

92. Ibid., fo. [1r–v] ('In fine de an[n]i circa cinque de p[er]suasione de lo p.[redet][to] mio p[adr]one et de la gente de sua casa co[n] p[ro]missione de me fareno [*sic*] bene et altri cariezi me redussero a far renegar la santta [sic] Cath.[ca] fede no[n] ob[sta]nte che Io sempre recusai deno[n] volere [in?] mente renegare et cossi vno di ala Imp[ro]uisa fui p[re]so da certi turchi et me circo[n]cisero alo mo[do] et rito torchesco et p[er] auante mia circo[n]cisione me fecero dire le parole quale vsano ala renegatione che fatio fare ali chr[ist]iani con deto Indice alzato de la mano destro ayllala yllala la mahometa resulala et pero lo no[n] so che voleno dire ditte parole et me possero nome soliman et me dissero che Io era vscito dela fede chr[ist]iana et pigliata la legge mahomettana').

93. Ibid., fo. [1v] ('Io mahometto no[n] lo ho tenuto p[er] dio ne p[er] profeta ma solo p[er] santto', 'Io ho andato dentro ala moschea atteso Io ac[c]ompagnaua lo mio p[ad]rone et ne fici oratione ne faceua a mahometto ne ta[m]poco quelli atti che loro faceuano', 'quando andaua a letto diceua la ora[tio]ne torchesca In qu[es]to mo[do] et la vsanza torchesca Cugliualla semet Iuuellet hala semet et no[n] ne so altre parole che q[ues]te et no[n] so che voleno dire'). The prayer was most likely a garbling of the first part of the 112th Sura of the Koran, which is used as one of the basic prayers of Islam: 'Qul huwal laahu adad, Allah hus-samad' ('Say: He is Allah, the One and the Only, Allah, the Eternal, the Absolute'). Cf. the case of a Slav convert to Islam, questioned by the Friulian Inquisition in 1666, who said he was taught 'a certain prayer called Culuvala, which is the same as the Pater noster in our language' (Minchella, *'Porre un soldato'*, p. 395: 'una certa oratione chiamata Culuvala, che in lingua nostra è l'istesso che il Pater noster').

94. ASDN, SU, filza 56.659, fo. [2r] ('Io ho andato vestito ala torchesca atteso no[n] ne posseuo fare altro', 'Io se[m]pre ho obseruato al p[res]ente la lege chr[ist]iana p[er]che

Io so chr[ist]iano et voglio morire da vero Catt.ᶜᵒ chr[ist]iano', 'sono da an[n]i circa quattro che Io so venuto dala Valona a t[er]ra de chr[ist]iani atteso Io fo venduto da vno albanese á [*sic*] da esso fui venduto vnaltra volta á vnaltro mercante Intra de otranto et finalmente so stato venduto alo S.ᵒʳ Carlo borrello dottore In potere de lo quale mi ritrouo In soa casa').

95. Instituto dos Arquivos Nacionais, Lisbon (hereafter: 'IANL'), Tribunal do Santo Oficio (hereafter: 'TSO'), Inquisição de Lisboa, proc. 8488, 24 Apr.–4 May 1579, fo. 2r ('gino natural de negroponte Albanes', 'Carlos Armeno'). This case was briefly cited in Bennassar and Bennassar, *Les Chrétiens d'Allah*, p. 334, but without any reference to the archive or the document. I am extremely grateful to Prof. Mercedes García-Arenal, who kindly located this in the Lisbon archive.

96. See T. Jochalas, 'Über die Einwanderung der Albaner in Griechenland (eine zusam-menfassende Betrachtung)', in P. Bartl, M. Camaj and G. Grimm, eds., *Dissertationes albanicae in honorem Josephi Valentini et Ernesti Koliqi septuagenariorum* (Munich, 1971), pp. 89–106, at pp. 95–9; Sh. Raça, *Shtegtimet dhe ngulimet e shqiptarëve në Greqi shek. XIII–XVI* (Prishtina, 2004), pp. 120–30.

97. IANL, TSO, Inquisição de Lisboa, proc. 8488, fo. 2r ('auera dozoito annos que leua[n]do carneiros a ue[n]der a Costantinopla por ser filho de pastor o catiuaram os turcos & cometerao em sua gallee de Rodes aonde andou ao Remo quatorze annos sendo sempre crestao'). From another document summarizing this case we learn that the Armenian's name was Simão Carlos: A. Baião, 'A Inquisição em Portugal e no Brazil', *Archivo historicao portuguez*, 7 (1909), pp. 227–40, at p. 232. Again, I am very grateful to Prof. García-Arenal for this reference.

98. On the Goletta-Tunis campaign of July–Sept. 1574 see F. Braudel, *The Mediterranean and the Mediterranean World in the Age of Philip II*, tr. S. Reynolds, 2 vols. (London, 1972), ii, pp. 1,133–9.

99. IANL, TSO, Inquisição de Lisboa, proc. 8488, fos. 2r (Tunis), 2v (conversion, 'Judeu barbeiro', Morocco, 'ceremonias de turquo'), 3r ('sempre tenea vontade de fugir per a terra de cristaos', Mazagão).

100. O. Vaquer Bennasar, *Captius i renegats al segle XVII: mallorquins captius entre musul-mans renegats davant la Inquisició de Mallorca* (Palma, 2014), p. 126 ('Velona in Grecia', 'porque le decían todos que se hiciera moro', 'las ceremonias de moros'). For other examples of 'renegade' Albanians in Algiers who became galley captains see 'D. de Haedo' [A. de Sosa], *Topographia e historia general de Argel, repartida en cinco tratados* (Valladolid, 1612), fo. 18r.

101. ASDN, SU, filza 119.1529 (1606–7), fo. [1r] ('Theodora tedea de la terra de Scherpan de la Prouincia de Albania, di anni venticinque in circa, figlia delo qᵒ Ghin tedea, et di Veppa de Phiginie').

102. ASDN, SU, filza 119.1529, fo. [1r–v] ('Io sono nata da p[ad]re et madre christiani, et Io viuendo da christiana, staua al mio paese, et essendo morto mio padre, et staua co mia matre, li turchi uennero p[er] mare co[n] le galere, et alla [*word illegible*] de mia matre mi piglaro, et mi condussero in vn paese di turchi chiamato balliciauso, et questo haueuà da cinque anni, et q[ue]llo mio padrone essendo io vergine, me diede p[er] moglie ad uno turcho, suo seruitore, et p[er] alcuni anni stettj co[n] p[rede]tto turcho mio marito, et mi ingrauidò, et mentre staua maritata co[n] q[ue]llo turcho, vno greco chiamato Marino, mè rubbò de q[ue]llo turcho, dicendomi che mi uoleua

condur alla terra mia da mia matre, et Io cosi credendo mi contentai, et p[er] nave mi condusse à Lecce, doue mi vendi p[er] schiaua à Giobattista moles, il q[ua]le mi condusse quà che sono da dui anni, et p[er]che detto Gio:battis[ta] moles è morto, sono schiaua dela S[ra] Amelia branci sua moglie, et l'anno passato la p[ad]rona mia me fece confessar ad vn monaco di S[ta] Maria della Speranza che era spag[no]lo, al quale dissi che era maritata co[n] vn turcho, et che era christiana, figlia di christiani, et no[n] me fece difficultà, è mi com[m]unicai alla chiesa della Speranza è fù la Pasqua passata'). S. Maria della Sapienza was a Dominican nunnery in central Naples; the present church (on the via Costantinopoli) was built later, in 1625–30, and the nunnery was demolished in the 19th century.

103. Ibid., fos. [1v–2r] ('Io nò haggio ringata in mano di turchi la fede di Giesu Christo, è vero che il mio p[ad]rone turcho Centomilia volte me desse che mi facesse turcha, et io diceua che ero chr[ist]iana, et non mi uoleua far turcha', 'Io faceua uita di christiani Come faceua al mio paese, et non faceua altro in turchia, solo che pregaua Dio p[er] l' anima mia, è diceua lo paternostro, è l'auemaria all' vsanza del mio paese in lingua albanese', 'Io mai andai alle moschee di turchi à fare or[azio]ne, et le donne turche no[n] vanno alle moschee à fare or[azio]ne, ma la fano di casa, et io faceua or[azio]ne come chr[ist]iana, ne [mai?] so stato alle bagni, dicens, Io no[n] sauio che cosa siano questi bagni, et no[n] mi pieaceua stare llà, et l'a[n]i[m]o mio era de stare al mio paese', 'mangiaua pesce, e cose di quatragesima, et dico la verità', 'quando fui robbata da q[u]ello greco, era grauida di mio marito che era turcho, et quà In napoli fogliai, è feci vna figliola femina che è stata battezzata'), [2v] (cross).

104. Ibid., fo. [2v].

105. Ibid., fo. [3r] ('Io faceua vita dei christiani come albanese, è mio marito che era turcho no[n] mi forzò à far vita turchesca...Et Io andaua vestita de turcha, p[er]che tanto li turchi q[ua]nto li albanesi llà vanno vestiti de vna manera, et al vestito no[n] se Conosce chi è albanese, et chi fusse turcho', 'quando staua In turchia, et hauea q[ue]llo marito, me piaceua stare llà, et ci staua di buon animo, per non poter ne fare di [manco?], p[er]che faceua la vita albanese, et viueua à mio modo...io andaua alla chiesa deli albanesi, douè li greci diceuano la messa').

106. Ibid., fos. [3v–4r] ('se no[n] mi era fuggita ancor restaria llà, p[er]che faceua la vita de' albanesi', 'Se Io no[n] veneua In queste parti di chr[ist]iani, haueria continuata di fare la vita albanese, et greca che no[n] si conosce la fede Catholica come qua, et cosi saria morta, p[er]che no[n] hauea Cognit.[ne] dela vera fede Catholica, come lhaggio hauuto quà, perche In q[ue]lle parti si uiue co[n]fusame[n]te').

107. Ibid., fos. [5r–v] ('no[n] hò uisto come si facciano li matrimonij sò bene che pigliano le don[n]e le portano In casa, è dicono che li sono moglie', 'no[n] ci furno fatte soll[enn]ità alcuna, basta che q[ue]llo mi teneua p[er] moglie, et Io teneua lui p[er] marito, et lo p[ad]rone mi dette tre volte delle bastonate accio che andasse a stare co[n] q[ue]llo mio marito, p[er]che Io non [ci?] voleua stare, et lo mio marito era turcho, et faceua vita de turcho', 'Io sono albanese, et quando vno albanese fà matr[imoni]° co[n] vna donna albanese si cambiano le veste le donne, se và alla chiesa, si pigliano le anello [sic], et l'huomo pone l'anello alla donna, et ci vanno li loro parenti, et si dice la messa, è se fanno le soll[enn]ità solite farsi all'vsanza di albanesi, Mà quando Io fui data p[er] moglie à q[ue]llo turcho no[n] ci fù fatta nessuna cosa, niente fù fatta'), [8r] (certificate), [9r] (judgment). Francesco Corcione SJ

was himself from Naples, and would serve for many years as Procurator of the Professed House (communal Jesuits' residence) there; see J. Grisar, *Maria Wards Institut vor römischen Kongregationen (1616–1630)* (Rome, 1966), p. 140(n.).

108. ASDN, SU, filza 119.1529, fo. [1r] ('Anastasia de ciuitate Paramitiae In epiro pertinen[te] turcaru[m]', 'Io me dimando Anastasia però il mio cognome no[n] lo so ne me lo ricordo, la mia patria e la p[re]detta t[er]ra de Paramethia, la quale sta nelle parte de[i] turchi doue se dice Epiro d'Albania…mio p[ad]re se dimandaua georgii, la casata del quale io no[n] la so ne me la ricordo il quale al p[re]sente è morto saran[n]o da venti an[n]i In circa…mia ma[d]re se dimandaua Maria de Custa, la quale no[n] so si al p[rese]nte viue').

109. Ibid., fo. [1r–v] ('essendo io Greca…sono chr[ist]iana battezzata nella chiesa dela Madonna di detta t[er]ra, et ho conosciuto p[er] gran tempo quello istesso prete che me battizzo…et per chr[ist]iana sono stata tenuta, et reputata, et come chr[ist]iana voglio viuere et morire detestando l'errore che ho fatta in renegare la santa fede Catt.ca In potere de turchi').

110. See F. Duka, 'Shoqëria dhe ekonomia në Çamërinë osmane: kazatë e Ajdonatit dhe Mazrakut (gjysma e dytë e shek. XVI)', *Studime historike* (2007), pp. 25–38, esp. p. 33 (names); N. Merxhushi and M. Minga, *Paramithia, qytetërimi mes tragjedive* (Tirana, 2011), pp. 38–44.

111. ASDN, SU, filza 119.1529, fo. [1v] ('mia madre hauendome accasata e dato marito, io p[er] che no[n] lo uoleua quel marito me ne fuggiuj da la casa di mia ma[d]re, et nell' istessa t[er]ra me andai a saluare In casa d'un turco, il quale turco hauendome In casa sua tanto esso, quanto sua moglie torca similm.te me Indussero a renegare la fede, dicendomi che io hauesse renegato che cosi mia m[ad]re no[n] me haueria piu possuto pigliare, et dar' quel marito, et io p[er] tal causa renegaj liberamente, et me contentaj no[n] correndocj altro In questo atto che doj giorni dopoj essere arriuata In casa dj detto turco, la quale renegatione fu In questo modo stando io allerta, et detto marito et moglie attorno a me me ferno alzare il dito endice dela man destra, et me ferno dire alcune parole che io al p[rese]nte no[n] me ne ricordo ne tampoco quando io le dissi dette parole sapeua quello che uoleano dire, et me possero un nome che Io al presente no[n] me lo ricordo p[er] che era nome turchesco').

112. Ibid., fo. [2r] ('stettj nella p[re]detta casa de turchi sej mesi, et osseruaua la legge di turchi, in maggiare carne de venerdj di sabbato et di altre vigilie de santi che corsero In detto tempo mangiando seduti In t[er]ra con la tauola posta In terra, e ben uero che alcune uolte Io mangiai carne di porco nascostam.te alle case delli grecj alle quale io soleua andare alcune uolte, cossi come anco andaj In casa de mia m[ad]re dopo detta renegatione, et lej piangeua p[er] detto atto che Io haueua fatto, però andaua uestita alla greca come andaua prima che era chr[ist]iana').

113. Ibid., fo. [2r] ('Io no[n] sono stata ne à bagni, ne à Moscheta de turchj ne ho fatta maj oratione a Magometto, ne tampoco l'ho tenuto ne p[er] santo, ne p[er] profeta, ne per beato, anzi l'ho tenuto p[er] vn tristo, e scelerato anche la p[redet]ta loro legge p[er] trista et nefanda').

114. Ibid., fo. [2v] ('per quelli sei mesj ch'io stettj In potere et casa de detti turchi detta lor legge me pareua brutta, et Io per no[n] far la piu me ne fuggiuj da detta loro casa, et andai In vn altra t[er]ra Vicino detta mia p[at]ria da circa una mezza giornata nella quale essendo arriuata fui pigliata da quelle gente, et fuj uenduta ad vn greco, il qu[a]le

greco hauendome tenuta da vn'anno In circa me Vendj qua In Nap[oli], doue me
portò da detta t[er]ra, et me vendj a donna Allegra In Napoli In casa della quale Io
sono stata da noue anni In circa, et detta donna allegra saran[n]o doi anni che me ha
data a stare p[er] serua con certj mercantj per sej an[n]j In casa deli quali hoggi sto, et
che finiti decj sei an[n]i Io stia in liberta').

115. Ibid., fos. [2v–3r] ('p[er] paura che no[n] me tornassero a vendere vn'altra uolta').
S. Giacomo degli Spagnoli is a church built in the mid-16th century in the centre of
Naples (on what is now the Piazza Municipio); the Gesù Nuovo is a church built by
the Jesuits in the 1580s and 1590s, to the west of the city centre (Piazza del Gesù
Nuovo).

116. Ibid., fo. [4r] ('p[er] che me sono scordato de la lingua greca p[er] hauere da vndcj
[sic] anni che sono In Italia, e cosi me è scordato il Cognome loro che era greco').

117. Ibid., fo. [4r–v] ('mia m[ad]re me forzo che me lo pigliasse p[er] marito, et me fece
contrahere il matr[imo]^{nio} con detto homo che era greco, con Interuento del prete, et
altre ceremonie come vsano li grecj In quelle partj, che si ben io fuggeua, e no[n]
uoleua fare detto matr[imo]^{nio}, mia m[ad]re et altre parentj et gentj me lo fecero fare
p[er] forza et fatto detto ma[t]rimonio, fui portata In casa del detto mio marito dal
quale Io me ne fuggiui più uolte, et andaj In casa de mia m[ad]re la quale sempre me
daua mazze à causa che Io ritornasse à stare In casa de detto mio marito, et cosi Io
pigliaj resolut.^{ne} di fugirmene, et no[n] ritornare, et me ne andaj, et fuggiuj In casa de
vna turca dela qu[a]le no[n] me ricordo il nome').

118. Ibid., fos. [4v–5r] ('l'istesso giorno io me ne pentiuj, et cercai p[er] lo tempo che stettj
In casa de detta turca che furno da tre mesi In circa dopo hauer renegato dj osseruare
la legge chr[ist]iana secretam^{te}, et andaua secretamente alle case delli grecj la vicino et
magnaua carne di porco, ma no[n] lo faceua saper alli turchj et p[er]che loro turchi
cioè detta don[n]a con il figlio turco magnauano carne lo venerdj, Io faceua quanto
poteua di no[n] magnarne si ben in p[re]sentia loro Io ne magnaua che non ne
poteua far altro').

119. Ibid., fo. [5r–v] ('me ne fuggiuj con vna altra figliola, la q[u]ale hauea hauuto mazze
dalla [word illegible] ce ne fuggemmo verso Corfù con Intentione di stare là doue
stando tuttj grecj, et no[n] ci stando turchj, et hauendo caminato vna giornata p[er]
diuersi lochi, campagne et poschj ritrouaimo certj huominj doj à cauallo, et vn' a
piede armatj di coltelli che no[n] so di che natione fussero, ne come se chiamano, li
q[u]alj ce dimandorno doue andauamo, et noj discemo che andauamo In corfû, et
loro dissero che andassemo con loro p[er]che ce haueriano portato à Corfù et ci portorno con loro da vna mezza giornata per t[er]ra alla marina, doue ci era vna barca,
nella q[u]ale ci fecero saglire dicendo alli marinarj che ce portassero à Corfù, et loro
rimassero In t[er]ra, li q[u]alj marinarj p[er] la uia ce dissero che ci haueuano com-
prate da dettj huominj et ce portorno à Corfù, doue stettemo da doj mesj In circa In
casa dj vno del quale no[n] so il nome ne cognome, ma ad esso ce haueano consig-
nato dettj marinarj et era greco, il quale ce mandò In Napoli cioè al regno di Nap[oli]
con vna felluca, et fummo portate tutte due in Puglia, nel capo dj ottranto, et dallà ci
hanno portato a cauallo qua in Nap[oli]. et à me hanno venduta alla sig^{ra} donna
Allegra dela q[u]ale no[n] so il cognome, et al quella altra figliola ad vn altra patrona
de la quale no[n] so il suo nome'). Paramythia is 12½ miles from the coast (as the

crow flies); a felucca was a small sailing boat; Capo d'Otranto is the easternmost point on the 'heel' of Italy.

120. Ibid., fo. [6r] ('p[er] pagura de mia m[ad]re').

121. Ibid., fo. [8r] ('no[n] sapeua p[ro]prio la età mia', 'no[n] conoscendo si faceua male, osi faceua bene però concosceua ch'io lasciaua la fede chr[ist]iana, ma con lo core no[n] hauea uolunta di lasciarla').

122. Ibid., fos. [9r-10r].

123. See for example Archivo Histórico Nacional, Madrid (hereafter: 'AHN'), Libro 898 (microfilm 2540), fo. 111r, in the summary of cases from Oct. 1577 to Dec. 1579, the case of 'Bernardino, son of Nicola, Albanian, born in the district of Airola in the kingdom of Naples' ('Bernardino de Nicola albanez natural del Reino de Napoles dela tierra de ayrola'), charged with blasphemy; Libro 901 (microfilm 2543), fo. 94r (for Mar. 1630), the case of 'Master Cola Matranga, born in the district of Piana dei Greci [now Piana degli Albanesi], and resident there' ('Maestro Cola Matranga, natural y vezino de la tierra de la llana de los Griegos'), charged with bearing false witness.

124. AHN, Libro 898 (microfilm 2540), fo. 222v ('Pedro de casnes natural de Aterno in Albania xp[ist]iano Renegado de edad de Treinta años, vino de su voluntad e confesso hauer Renegado de n[uest]ra Sta fee catholica e hecho algunos Ritos e ceremonias de moros'). The 'A' of 'Aterno' has been either roughly strengthened or cancelled by the scribe; possibly the place referred to was Tërnovë, a village a few miles east of Bulqizë, in Dibër county.

125. Ibid., fos. 575v–576r ('Pietro Gion, natural dela Belona en Dalmacia del dominio del Turco, Pastor de edad de 19. años', 'vna galeota Turquesca … p[ar]a tomar Refresco', 'se fuese a poder delos Moros espontaneamente. y que se dexo Retajar el año passado con las çeremonias que acostumaban, y que Renego de n[uest]ra Sta fee cat.^{ca} y se dexo poner nombre de Moro, llamandose Aly y se vistio [sic] ala Turquesca y que le vieron hazer las çerimonias y Ritos Mahometanos'). The reference to Dalmatia was inaccurate.

126. Ibid., fo. 576r ('confeso no hauerse confesado en su vida sacramentalmente en su pais por causa que siempre andaua en campaña guardando obejas y que passo por alli vn official del Turco y le tomo y lleuo a Constantinopla y di alli fue traydo a Viserta donde la Retajaron. y que despues aca hizo y obserbo todas las çerimonias y Ritos dela secta Mahometana teniendo y creyendo que fuese buena y que en ella se pudiese saluar el anima. No obstante que primero y entonçes sabia que n[uest]ra Sta fee era mejor que a quella secta. pero que a persuasion delos Turcos creyo enella hasta ora').

127. Ibid., fo. 576r. Rather surprisingly, in view of the perennial shortage of rowers, a marginal note records that the three years on the galley were later commuted into three years in the Inquisition's prison.

128. Ibid., fo. 554v ('no sabe el sobre nombre y en Turquesco se llama Girè y dixo ser del pais de Albania, no supo dezir en particular de que lugar, de Edad de 27. años esclaua del Marquis de Marineo Residente en esta Ciudad'). The marchese di Marineo, who had fought at Lepanto in 1571, was a leading figure in Palermo, where he served as 'pretore' (magistrate responsible for public order) twice in the 1590s: see G. Fiume, 'Marineo, Vincenzo Beccadelli di Bologna, marchese di', Dizionario biografico degli italiani (Rome, 1960–), lxx, p. 415.

129. AHN, Libro 898 (microfilm 2540), fos. 554v–555r ('l'año passado fue certificada con seis t.ᵒˢ vno sacerdote, y los de mas mugeres y vna dellas sclaua, todos dela casa de dicho Marques de que por tiempo de seis años que en la d[ic]ha casa la hauian conoçida siempre fue tenida por uerdadera Turca y que no hazía uida de xp[ist]iana ni de Turca y la veyan comer carne en dias prohiuidos y hazer labor los dias de fiestas hauiendola oydo dezir por otro cabo que era xp[ist]iana e hija de Padres xp[ist]ianos albaneses y que se acordaua la llamauan Maria y quel Mes de Septiembre proximo passado con occasion de uer la fiesta que en esta çiudad se hizo ala entrada de la cabeza de S.ᵗᵃ Ninfa, Dezia assi mismo que queria ser xp[ist]iana y uiuir como tal y que le pesaua de no lo auer hecho antes. Esta muger vino alla Inqui.ᵒⁿ sin ser llamada, pero despues de la testificaçion del sacerdote. Y confeso ser uerdad lo que los t.ᵒˢ dizen y mas que hizo todas las çerimonias Mahometanas creyendo, que en aquella secta se podia saluar el anima y q[ue] estuuo onesta creençia tiempo de seis años No obstante que sabia era contrario ala S.ᵗᵃ Romana igl[esi]a, de la qual creençia [sc. Islam] comenzo seis años hauia a salir despues que fue cautiuada de Xp[ist]ianos por una galeota de don P.º de Leyua y que por temor no hauia uenida a Reuelarse y Reconciliarse al S.ᵗᵒ Offi.º y esto dixo con demostracion de arrepentimiento'). Pietro de Leyva was general of the Sicilian galleys in the 1590s: see G. E. Di-Blasi, *Storia del regno di Sicilia dall'epoca oscura e favolosa sino al 1774*, 20 vols. (Palermo, 1847), iii, p. 104. A galiot was a small galley.
130. Ibid., fo. 555r ('penitençias spirituales').
131. AHN, Libro 899, fo. 455r ('Angela de Nicolo y en turquesco Juli natural del Castillo de Suli Junto a Preuesa en el golfo de Veneçia...esclaua de Joan bautista sires en la d[ic]ha ciudad de Mecina de edad de treinta a[ño]s').
132. See Sh. Raça, 'Disa aspekte studimore mbi Sulin dhe Suliotët', *Studime historike*, (2012), pp. 201–22.
133. AHN, Libro 899, fo. 455r ('de nacion griega').
134. Ibid., fo. 455r–v ('pareçio espontaneamente y confeso que siendo de edad de ocho años murio su padre y su madre la lleuo con sus hermanos a la ciudad de Preuesa en casa de una tia hermana de su madre y siendo de edad de quinçe a[ño]s un griego llamado Cuzo miti por mal nombre queria casarse por fuerça con ella y el uiendo que no le queria hizo diligen.ᵃ con un Turco potente para que hiciese se casase con el d[ic]ho griego, y hauiendola el d[ic]ho turco llamado a su casa, y forzado aque se casase con el d[ic]ho griego o que renegase, se contento mas presto renegar que casarse con el, y asi el d[ic]ho turco en su casa la hizo renegar de n[uest]ra sᵗᵃ fee catholica y alzar el dedo de la mano derecha, y deçir las palabras ordinarias que dicen los turcos en tal acto, las quales no sabe que quieren decir, y le puso nombre de turca Juli, y hauiendo renegado la dexo yr, y ella reuoluio en casa de la d[ic]ha su tia arepentida de hauer renegado de n[uest]ra sᵗᵃ fee catholica y lloro tres dias por hauerlo hecho, lo qual hizo por desesperacion y por no casarse con el d[ic]ho griego...y de alli adelante el tiempo que estubo en casa de la d[ic]ha su tia siempre uiuio como xrna griega, y que despues de hauer renegado deseo yrse a Veneçia, o otra t[ier]ra de xp[isti]anos y no lo hizo por temor no la quemasen. si la cogian, y siendo de edad de veinte años se caso con el d[ic]ho turco que la hizo renegar y hizo uido con el tres años como turca por darle satisfaçion mas nunca ynteriormᵗᵉ creyo en la setta de los Turcos ni la tubo por buena, y que abia siete años que fue presa de las galeras de Florençia en la d[ic]ha ciudad de

Preuisa con dos hijos suyos y trayda a Miano donde fue uendida al d[ic]ho Joan bautista').

135. Archive of the Inquisition, Cathedral Museum, Mdina, Malta (hereafter: 'AIM'), Processi, 47B, case 268, fos. 620r–631v, at fo. 620r ('p[ate]r Hieremias...Calogerus S.ti Basilij'). The small town of Birgu was the former seat of government (before the construction of Valletta), on the south-eastern side of the Grand Harbour.

136. Ibid., fo. 620r–v ('à lamentarsi dicendo uedete come mi uanno uendere tutto che io son xpiano greco Albanese, e mi uendeno per uizio e d.º Antonio gli disse che parlasse à quelli SS.ri, e che [non? *page damaged*] si lasciasse uendere p[er] turco già che era xp[ist]iano, ò che fugisse, e uenisse al [S.? *page damaged*] off[ici]o, si come mi referse d.º Antonio e no[n] so chi riferse al d.º Capitan Benca questo ragionamento che passò fra d.º Antonio, e d.º greco Albanese, et ho uisto che [di? *page damaged*] un subito d.º Capitan Benca prese di pugni e di petrate à d.º Antonio gridando, e dicendo, tu fai fugire i miei schiaui al sant'off[ici]o').

137. Ibid., fo. 621r ('allora io andai alla loggia doue sono soliti uendersi i schiaui, e mentre io parlauo con gl'altri schiaui che si uendeuano, uno Albanese che me disse esser d'una villa uicina alla Citta Elbasan me disse in turchesco che lui era xp[ist]iano, e che lo uoleuano uendere, io gli riposi che dicesse la sua raggione, e si manifestasse p[er] xp[ist]iano che non gl'hauerebbono fatto torto, lui rispose che l'haueua detto, e che no[n] gli haueua giouato niente, io gli replica che finito di uendere se ne passasse al sant'Off[ici]o à manifestarsi p[er] xp[ist]iano, che se sete [*sic*] xp[ist]iano restarete là no[n] hauerete pagura. allora uenne uerso di me musu di Benca capitano della presa, e mi diede un calce con la sua gamba nella [schena? *page damaged*] un schiaffo in faccia et un colpo con un sasso nella schena, e mi disse una quantità d'ingiurie').

138. Ibid., fos. 621v–622r ('giouane di 30. anni in c.ª ferito in una spalla di giusta statura di barba bionda disse in turchesco che era xp[ist]iano', 'di giusta statura con mustacci biondi che diceua esser Albanese xp[ist]iano di eta d'anni 28. in c.ª').

139. Ibid., fos. 622v ('homo iusta statura albi coloris barba glauca licet rara', 'Io mi chiamo Tole figlio del q[uon]dam Pietro, e Schieua uiuente iugali son d'età d'anni 26. in c.ª son d'un casale chiamato Vriuoli nell'Albania e son marinaro'), 623r ('parlò con me in turchesco'). 'Schieua', probably 'Schieva' in modern orthography, may perhaps have been a short version of the Greek saint's name Paraskevē (in Vlach: Paraschiva); this saint was very popular in the Albanian lands, though normally under the names Veneranda, Shënepremte or Prende (see R. Elsie, 'The Christian Saints of Albania', *Balkanistica*, 13 (2000), pp. 35–57, at pp. 43–4). Vriuoli has not been identified.

140. Ibid., fo. 623r ('Quattro mesi in c.ª sono trouandome in Salonich m'accordai con l'vrca di Hasan Rays p[er] barcarolo per uenir in Barbaria e sopra delli Gerbi fummo presi dal Pittacchio di d[etto] capitan Benca e fummo condotti qui in Malta'). 'Reis' meant captain. Hasan Reis's ship is described here as an 'urca', which was a broad-hulled cargo ship, developed originally in the North Sea region (Eng.: 'hulk'). Benca's ship is described here as a 'Pittacchio'; a petacchio was a small warship, two-masted and square-rigged.

141. Ibid., fo. 623r ('nella mia patria tutti si battezzano, et ho uisto battezzar altri il prete fa la croce nella fronte della creatura, e gira p[er] la Chiesa co[n] essa, e intesi dal mio p[ad]re, e da mia m[ad]re d'esser battezzato, et nella mia patria ui sono chiese e ui sono crocifissi et Immagini di santi cioè della Madonna, di san Paolo, et in luogo di

campana si sona una tauola, e p[er]che ero contadino frequentauo puoco le Chiese ma q[ua]n[do] ero piciolo più ci andauo spesso'). Instead of bells, Orthodox churches used a 'semantron', a large piece of wood struck by a mallet. This had already been a Byzantine practice, but became general in the Ottoman Balkans because of the Ottoman disapproval of church bells.

142. Ibid., fo. 623r–v ('Io mai ho apostatato ne son circonciso, e sempre ho fatto uita da xpiano nel vassello', 'Io no[n] so altro che segnarmi col segno della S.ᵗᵃ Croce e dire Kyrie leyson Agyos Maria Agyos Dimitri', 'more grecorum'). 'Iasagi' was perhaps *yasakçı*, a man who acts as a guard and way-clearer for an important person. 'Agios [for "Agia"] Maria' may perhaps have been an error committed by the Inquisition's scribe.

143. Ibid., fos. 623v ('il Vassello era di Mercantia et era di Hasan Rays, la mercantia era ferro tauole affione, et altre cose simili, e le mercantie erano di mercanti gianizzari, et altri che erano sop.ᵃ il vassello, e no[n] ui erano altre p[er]sone che quelli che haueuano parte nella mercantia', 'io allora nel combatto ero abasso sotto coperta, poi il Rays con la scimitarra uenne à basso, e mi fece salire sopra con dirmi che hauerei presa la mia parte, e p[er]ciò che andassi sopra ad hauer cura delle ueli, et andato sop.ᵃ mi uenne un' archibugiata, e tornai à basso'), 624r ('ui erano un figliolo xp[ist]iano greco ferito a la mascella due [schiaue? *page damaged*] xp[ist]iane Russiotte, et un altro figliolo piciolo Russiotto, e cinque altri xp[ist]iani quali no[n] so doue siano').

144. Ibid., fos. 624v–625r (Benca, 'Tole siue Antonij Albanensis', 'lib[rum] et ab omni iugo seruitutis exemptu[m] declaramus').

145. ASDN, SU, filza 189.2476, fo. [1r]. Antonio Álvarez de Toledo, 5th Duke of Alba, was Viceroy from 1622 to 1629.

146. Ibid., fo. [2r] ('gli diede casa co[n] ogni comodità, e da lui med.º furono battizati nel oratorio di Palazo e pose nome al Padre di Pietro d'Alua, della madre d'Anna d'Alua', 'natural della Città de Valona cento miglia de questo Regno doue la sua p[ro]fessione era di scarparo', 'trouar occasione di pasar à leuante à farsi Turco come già si è fatto suo figlio D. Antonio che è andato in Constantinopoli promettendo contra il seru.º di Dio e di Sua Maᵗᵃ scoprir tutte le persone che di qui uanno à quelle parti p[er] diligencie secrete').

147. Ibid., fo. [2v] ('et ho inteso da diuerse persone di d.ᵃ natione greca e dalla med.ᵃ D. Anna sua moglie come detto D. Pietro suo marito era christiano').

148. Ibid., fo. [3r–v] ('diuerse p[er]sone qui in nap[oli], e p[er] lettere d'amici che li scrissero da leuante', 'p[er] farsi Turcho in Constantinopoli', 'le p[er]sone che di qui esso test.º manda p[er] ordinario p[er] diligenza segreta in detta Città'). On Paronda see P. Preto, *I servizi segreti di Venezia* (Milan, 1994), p. 121. A scudo was worth five sixths of a ducat.

149. ASDN, SU, filza 189.2476, fo. [4r–v] ('Melenique della Prou.ᵃ de macedonia', 'habitata da Christiani greci, si bene ci habitano Turchi che sono li p[ad]roni'), [5r] ('sano, e senza lesione alcuna ne circo[n]cisione').

150. Ibid., fo. [5r–v] ('habitata da Greci, d'Albanesi, Turchi, giudei', 'ui sono Ecclesie, et quelli che sono Christiani viuono da tali come sono greci et albanesi e chi uuole essere turco e giudei ogni uno uiue alla legge sua', 'dixit che uiueua da Turcho sin come lo forno suo padre', 'sua madre fù greca chr[ist]iana chiamata Princes', 'portato

In Constantinopoli apprese[n]tato al gran turco da semegiolli Zio di esso dep.^{te} che dicesetti anni sono venne p[er] m[aest]ro di Campo in d.ª Città, et al ritorno in Constantinopoli presentò esso dep.^{te} al gra[n] Turcho, e faceua vita de Turco come lo era detto suo padre che morse prima nomine Mamet baxi e lo detto semegion suo zio'). The form 'Semegiolli' suggests 'Semerci-oğlu', 'son of the packsaddle-maker'; the 'Baxi' here, and also the 'Bassa' or 'Basua' element of Pietro's name later in this paragraph, might perhaps represent 'Beşe', an Ottoman military title 'common among low-level members of the [Janissary] corps by the middle of the seventeenth century' (G. Tülüveli, 'Honorific Titles in Ottoman Parlance: A Reevaluation', *International Journal of Turkish Studies*, 11 (2005), pp. 17–27, at p. 21). (I am very grateful to Prof. Amy Singer for these suggested identifications.)

151. Ibid., fo. [5v] ('dixit che stette in serraglio come tutti li altri giannizzeri che sono parti naturali, e parti figli di greci, quali figli di greci li fanno ritagliare e stette meno di doi anni', 'dixit che nò perche era già turco nat.^{le} atteso alli giannizeri figli di greci che uanno in potere di turchi li fanno rinegare, e poi retagliare').

152. Ibid., fo. [5v] ('dixit che si chiamaua Cursbam, e se ne uenne da Constantinopoli con occ.^{ne} che si casò co[n] una don[n]a greca christiana no[m]i[n]e Soltana alla turchesca et alla greca Cali', 'co[n] questo zelo di farsi christiano si ne uenne fugendo segretam.^{te} insieme co[n] d.ª sua moglie').

153. Ibid., fo. [6r] ('chr[ist]iani nati, e battizati').

154. Ibid., fo. [6r-v] ('dixit che hà sette mesi, dico un anno, che no[n] hà recuperato soldo ness.°, 'p[er]che si fosse andato in Leuante, li haueriano inpalato, e brugiato li turchi, et sic f. signum crucis').

155. Ibid., fo. [6v-7r] ('Pietro Prima detto Basua', 'in Maumetanam tamen sectam adhuc pueri lapsi').

156. Ibid., fo. [7r] ('p[er]che no[n] ponno stare in quelli luochi senza detta Circun.^{ne} ne tanpoco uiene riceuuto in detti luochi figli di turchi, ne chr[ist]iani fatti turchi di matura età'); Albèri, ed., ser. 3, i, p. 305 (M. Barbaro report, 1573); M. P. Pedani ['Pedani-Fabris'], ed., *Relazioni di ambasciatori veneti al Senato*, xiv: *Costantinopoli: relazioni inedite (1512-1789)* (Padua, 1996), p. 323 (L. Bernardo report, 1590); R. Murphey, *Ottoman Warfare, 1500-1700* (London, 1999), p. 223 (1666).

157. ASDN, SU, filza 189.2476, fo. [7v] ('E questo è manifesto p[er]che quando l'armata Chr[ist]iana fà alcuna presa in Leua[n]te p[er] riconoscere il turco dal chr[ist]iano altra dilige[n]za no[n] fà che ponere in catena quelli che si ritrouano circuncisi, e l'altri uengono liberati p[er] chr[ist]iani').

158. Ibid., fo. [8r-v] ('in detto serraglio senza detta Circu[n]cizione no[n] ci può stare nessuno ne tanpoco ui entrano figli de turchi', 'quelli che sono poueri passano p[er] turchi senza Circu[n]cisione').

159. Ibid., fos. [10r-v] ('In Constantinopoli contratti Matr. con S. D. Pietro all'usanza di Turchi, si bene io era Christiana, e S. D. Pietro era Iannizzaro figlio di Iannizzaro e faceua la legge di Turchi e si chiamaua S. D. Pietro all'hora Cureh Bassa, et era tenuto p[er] Turco'), [11r-v] ('Io no[n] lo so p[er]che sono pouera don[n]a', 'beui uino assai et acqua uita...q[ua]ndo ueniua imbriaco dava mazza a me et alli figlioli').

160. Ibid., fos. [12r-v] ('le la pigliò p[er] forza mio p[ad]re', 'Io sono stato sempre nella Vallona et quando fui di età di trenta cinque anni mio Zio venne da Const.^{li} in uff. nella Vallone finito l'uff. mi portò in Constantinopoli'), [13r] ('Non tutti li turchi si

circoncidono, che se ne uedeno molti che no[n] siano circoncisi'), [15r] (Auditor General).

161. AIM, Processi, 130, case 33, fos. 204r–255v, at fos. 204r ('Io ero Turco di nome Mustafà, mi son lasciato battezzare ma come nacquei Turco, e fui Mustafà, così voglio morir Turco, e morir Mustafà'), 205r–v ('Uomo dell'età in oggi d'anni quaranta in circa, corto e grosso con gran baffe di color giallo, o sia rossigno, di color piuttosto bianco che bruno, con ochi neri un puo grandi, e col collo corto').

162. Ibid., fos. 209r ('e del quale si dice essere figlio d'un greco e poi fatto apostata, tenuto per Christiano'), 210r (identified).

163. Ibid., fos. 210r ('Johannes Petrus...?'), 213r ('Neofito Schiauo Albanese di anni 23 dalla Terra Saiada'). Our Lady of Damascus was a Greek Catholic church, built during the original construction of Valletta in the 1570s, and housing a famous icon of the Virgin brought by the Knights of Malta from Rhodes. Like Anastasia of Paramythia and Angela of Souli, this man came from what were then described as the Albanian lands, and may have been bilingual in Greek and Albanian.

164. Ibid., fo. 214r ('Io mi chiamo Giovanni d'Anastasi sono levantino della Terra Saiada sono dell'età d'anni venti tre in circa, non so come si chiamano i miei Genitori, perchè di piccola c[ondizio?]ne i Turchi mi anno preso in costantinopoli, ne mai li ho più veduti, dopo [word illegible] sette anni sono da Cap.no Petro fui portato in quest Isola, ove sono stato venduto p[er] schiavo, e nato il dubio d'essere Io Christiano, fui battezato'), 214v (explanation).

165. Ibid., fo. 219r ('Io volevo andare a Roma, perchè sempre sentij, chè i Neofiti godono cinque carlini al giorno').

166. See Bono, Schiavi musulmani, pp. 270–2.

167. AIM, Processi, 130, fo. 226r–v ('mi è ben noto, che se un Turco si fa poi cristiano, e poi torna a Paesi de Turchi la sarà bruciato').

168. Ibid., fo. 230r ('salito su la nave disse—Mi star [etc.]').

169. Ibid., fos. 236r ('de Giannina de armelia'), 239r ('Io fui in Costantinopoli, e sò che quando un Turco caduto schiavo in Paesi Cristiani torna cola Cristiano con dire che si fosse fatto cristiano p[er] fugire, e che auesse mantenuto interiorm.te la setta Maomettana, allora gli si condona l'errore, e non incorre alcuna pena, ma si saprà che il Turco, essendo Turco si fosse portato in Paesi Cristiani p[er] farsi cristiano, allora incorre la pena di morte'). This witness signed his name as Giovanni Suda.

170. Ibid., fos. 243v–244r ('Io fui in Paesi de Turchi, e so che quando Turchi che in Paesi cristiani si saranno fatti Cristiani tornando fugiti al loro paese, e massime coll'attestato del cadì d'essere stati fatti cristiani, o a forza, o p[er] fugire, non saranno in conto alcuno maltrattati in quei lor Paesi'), 251r (sentence).

Chapter 6

Introductory note: This essay originated as a lecture given to the Kosovan Academy of Sciences and Arts; it was dedicated to the memory of Dr Ibrahim Rugova. It concerns the most influential Catholic churchman in Kosovo in the 17th century. Pjetër Bogdani was born in 1625, and studied in Italy, being ordained as a priest in 1650. In 1656 he became Bishop of Shkodër, and in 1679/80 he succeeded his uncle, Ndre Bogdani, as Archbishop of

Skopje. (That archdiocese contained the whole modern territory of Kosovo.) Pjetër's letters and reports to Rome, describing the conditions of the Catholic Church in Kosovo, are rich sources of information; but his most important written work, the subject of this essay, was the book he published in 1685. Four years later he would welcome the Austrian forces that invaded Kosovo (as described above, pp. 133–4). While tending the Austrian commander, Piccolomini, when he was dying of the plague, Bogdani also became infected; he died in Prishtina in Dec. 1689.

1. P. Bogdani, *Cuneus prophetarum de Christo salvatore mundi, et eius evangelica veritate, italice et epirotice contexta* (Padua, 1685) (reprinted, ed. E. Sedaj and I. Rugova, 2 vols. (Prishtina, 1989)). References will be given to the original edn., by volume- and page-number; the modern Albanian version of the text will be taken from the facing page in the Sedaj-Rugova edn.

2. Robert Elsie has written: 'It is Bogdani's use of the Albanian language which sets him apart from all other early Albanian writers. He had a conscious interest in old and forgotten words and a much richer vocabulary which he skilfully employed to form new abstract concepts' (*History of Albanian Literature*, 2 vols. (Boulder, CO, 1995), i, p. 77). See M. Sciambra, *Bogdanica: studio su Pietro Bogdani e l'opera sua*, ii (Bologna, 1965) (I am very grateful to Prof. Francesco Altimari for a copy of this work); and the essays by A. Kostallari, 'Pjetër Bogdani dhe gjuha letrare shqipe', and S. Mansaku, 'Vepra e Pjetër Bogdanit si burim për historinë e gjuhës shqipe', in A. Kostallari, ed., *Pjetër Bogdani dhe vepra e tij* (Tirana, 1991), pp. 17–52 and 145–57.

3. See, for example, K. Frashëri, 'Pjetër Bogdani dhe lëvizja çlirimtare në shekullin e 17-të', in A. Kostallari, ed., *Pjetër Bogdani dhe vepra e tij* (Tirana, 1991), pp. 53–83. I have discussed the events of 1689 (N. Malcolm, *Kosovo: A Short History* (London, 1998), pp. 144–56), and have demonstrated that the so-called 'Patriarch of the Kelmendi' who organized volunteer fighters in Prizren in November 1689 was Bogdani, not the Serbian Patriarch Arsenije.

4. For a fine example of this approach, see the monograph by Ibrahim Rugova, *Vepra e Bogdanit (1675–1685): Cuneus prophetarum* (Prishtina, 1982; I cite the 2nd edition, Prishtina, 1990).

5. Cf. the thoughtful comments on this point in Z. Mirdita, 'Aspekte teologjike në veprën "Cuneus prophetarum" të Pjetër Bogdanit (1630–1689)', *Urtia* (1994), pp. 38–48.

6. Bogdani, *Cuneus*, i, pp. 27–8 ('nassip'); 30–1 (cosmology); 35 (quotation).

7. G. Hering, *Ökumenisches Patriarchat und europäische Politik, 1620–1638* (Wiesbaden, 1968), p. 171.

8. P. Bogdani, *Letra dhe dokumente nga Arkivi i Kongregatës 'de Propaganda Fide' si dhe nga Arkivat Sekrete të Vatikanit*, ed. O. Marquet (Shkodër, 1997), p. 484: 'perché ingiuriava il Muhametto'.

9. On d'Aviano see M. Heyret, *P. Marcus von Aviano O.M.Cap., Apostolischer Missionar und päpstlicher Legat beim christlichen Heere* (Munich, 1931).

10. Bogdani, *Letra*, pp. 216 (3 Jan. 1669, giving information about an expected Ottoman campaign against Kotor), 267 (25 July 1672, sending a map of his diocese, as 'secretly observed by me' ('da me occultamente osservato')).

11. Ibid., p. 51.

12. L. Marlekaj, *Pietro Bogdani e l'Albania del suo tempo* (Palo del Colle, 1989), pp. 68–9, 325 ('vincere in parte le tenebre dell' ignoranza'; 'L'Evangeli in Albanese, Il specchio spirituale in Albanese, Il Rituale Romano in Albanese, La Dottrina Piccola in Albanese'). (I am very grateful to Dr Robert Elsie for the loan of a copy of Marlekaj's important work.) Marlekaj identifies the 'Gospels' here as Buzuku's Missal; but the possibility should not be excluded that Bogdani was actually referring to an Albanian translation of the Gospels which has not survived. For details of Budi's translations see D. S. Shuteriqi, *Shkrimet shqipe në vitet 1332–1850* (Tirana, 1976), pp. 62–5; Elsie, *History*, i, pp. 60–1. Bellarmine's text was known in two versions: a shorter one, first published in 1597 (translated by Bernardo da Verona), and a longer one, first published in 1602 (translated by Budi).

13. Bogdani, *Letra*, p. 307 (29 Dec. 1675). Unfortunately no copy of this book has yet been found; Mario Roques searched for it in vain in Venice and other Western cities (see his *Recherches sur les anciens textes albanais* (Paris, 1932), pp. 33–4), but Bogdani's statement that he took all copies to Shkodër suggests that if any copies survive, they will be somewhere in the Balkans—apart from the one copy which he later sent to the Propaganda Fide in Rome (see Bogdani, *Letra*, p. 315).

14. Bogdani, *Letra*, p. 297 (undated; shortly before 25 June 1675): 'l'Albania ha grandissima scarzezza, e quasi affatto priva di Libri in propria lingua'; 'non solo perciò acciecati gli Popoli dall'ignoranza vivono fra infiniti errori et abusi...Ma anche trovandosi la Natione tra Turchi, Greci e Serviani, di continuo la Lingua va perdendosi'; 'nella Lingua Albanese sua naturale la venuta del Messia, diffendendosi principalmente contro quelli errori che egli ha scoperto serpegiando tra quella gente'.

15. Ibid., p. 297.

16. See the entries in C. T. Lewis and C. Short, *A Latin Dictionary* (Oxford, 1879).

17. Bogdani, *Cuneus*, i, pp. 33–4 (Purgatory); ii, pp. 71–2 (Peter).

18. Ibid., i, pp. 36 (water), 37 (falling stars), 59 (crucifixion).

19. Bogdani, *Letra*, p. 223 (1 Apr. 1669): 'le tenebre delle menzogne nelle quali è constituito per la continua prattica che hanno in una Babilonia di sette, massime de Turchi et scismatici'.

20. Bogdani, *Letra*, pp. 143–4, 427.

21. Ibid., p. 150.

22. Ibid., p. 181.

23. Ibid., p. 298: 'rimediare alli sudetti bisogni con una soda confermatione de Cristiani nella Santa Fede e conversione innumerabile de Turchi montagnoli'. I translate 'montagnoli' here as 'malësore', because Bogdani was referring to the inhabitants of the Malësi, the highlands of northern Albania; 'highlanders' is an approximate English equivalent.

24. Ibid., p. 112.

25. Ibid., pp. 319 ('Turchi frescamente venuti alla fede di Christo'), 385 ('gran copia de Infideli').

26. Ibid., pp. 279–80. By Sept. 1674 Bogdani estimated that 300 Muslims had been converted in his diocese in the previous three years. A *sancakbeyi* was the governor of a *sancak*, a military-administrative district.

27. Bogdani, *Cuneus*, ii, p. 98.

28. On this standard four-part structure see Z. Remiro ['Remiro Andollu'], 'La Sagrada Congregación frente al Islám: apostolado de la prensa en lengua árabe', in J. Metzler, ed., *Sacrae congregationis de propaganda fide memoria rerum*, vol. i, part 1 (Rome, 1971), pp. 707–31, esp. pp. 722–3.

29. Bogdani, *Letra*, p. 307.

30. Bogdani, *Cuneus*, i, sig. §1r (vol. i, p. 76 in the Sedaj-Rugova edition).

31. Bogdani, *Letra*, pp. 307 ('la Vita di Christo Salvatore'), 315 ('la Vita di Christo Salvatore con le sue profetie').

32. Bogdani, *Cuneus*, ii, pp. 7, 114.

33. Bogdani, *Letra*, p. 301: 'nelle sue fattighe per fare più chiaramente constare alli Infedeli la veracità e fundamenti della Santa fede in proprio linguaggio e carattere'.

34. Ibid., p. 307: 'vado tutta via affatigandomi. E perché sono necessarijssimi li testi arabici circa le profetie per maggior confusione delli infideli, supplico humilmente la Sacra Congregatione si degni farmi la carità d'una Biblia Arabica; servirà ancora in più e più congressi pacifichi che loro Turchi soliono havere meco circa la matteria di fede.'

35. On the lengthy history of this project see N. Kowalsky, 'Zur Vorgeschichte der arabischen Bibelübersetzung der Propaganda von 1671', *Neue Zeitschrift für Missionswissenschaft*, 16 (1960), pp. 268–74, and M. P. Pedani Fabris, 'Ludovico Marracci: la vita e l'opera', in M. Borrmans et al., *Il Corano: traduzioni, traduttori e lettori in Italia* (Milan, 2000), pp. 9–29, esp. p. 23.

36. Bogdani, *Letra*, p. 279: 'in lingua turchesca et illirica, havendo lo cognitione anche leggere e scrivere il carattere del ultima oltre il parlar perfettamente la prima'.

37. In 1651 he had asked the Propaganda Fide to send him a Turkish dictionary and a Turkish or Arabic 'alphabet' (ibid., p. 51); but his comment of 1674, quoted above, suggests that he had made little or no progress with written Turkish. (The Arabic 'alphabet' was probably the single large sheet setting out the alphabet with its Latin equivalents, prepared by the Maronite scholar V. Scialac and printed by the Propaganda Fide in 1624, 1631 and 1633: see R. Smitskamp, *Philologia orientalis* (Leiden, 1992), p. 173.)

38. Bogdani, *Cuneus*, ii, p. 154.

39. Ibid., i, p. 70. The Italian word is 'Heresiarchi'; the Albanian text has 'krenatè gidhè t'kechiavet' ['krerë të të gjitha të këqijave'], 'creators of all ills', which seems like an attempt to explain the meaning of 'heresiarch' in a language that lacked any direct equivalent term. This is one of several cases in the first part of the *Cuneus* where the internal linguistic evidence suggests that the Italian may have been written first; the rarity of such cases in the second part tends to confirm, I think, the supposition that it was the original text. But these comments are merely impressionistic; a systematic study of this issue is needed.

40. Ibid., ii, p. 154.

41. I am very grateful to Professor Harry Norris for this suggestion, and for the information that this phrase, or variants of it, can be found in Bektashi or Hurufi poetry in Albanian.

42. Bogdani, *Letra*, p. 52. On Guadagnoli see Z. Remiro, 'Un saggio bilingue, latino e arabo, di controversia islamo-cristiana nella Roma del sec. XVII', *Euntes docete: commentaria urbaniana*, 22 (1969), pp. 453–80, esp. pp. 460–2.

43. Bogdani, *Letra*, p. 279. Little is known of Malvasia, except that he was from Bologna, had worked as a missionary in Arabic-speaking territory, and taught in Rome for the Propaganda Fide in the 1620s; the *Dilucidatio* appears to have been his only publication (see Remiro, 'Un saggio bilingue', p. 464, and M. Forlivesi, *Scotistarum princeps Bartolomeo Mastri (1602–1673) e il suo tempo* (Padua, 2002), pp. 88, 345).

44. See Remiro, 'Un saggio bilingue'. For a Latin version of Ahmed ben-Abdallah's treatise, see 'Ahmet Ben-Abdala', *Epistola theologica de articulis quibusdam fidei*, ed. Z. Grapius (Rostock, 1705).

45. F. Guadagnoli, *Apologia pro Christiana religione* (Rome, 1631), p. 208: 'Si enim super cornu Tauri sita est terra, in quonam loco Taurus ipse sitos pedes habet?...Praeterea Taurus indiget pabulo, quo nutriatur, cum sit animal: Quod nam pabulum habet? Debet etiam mori cum sit animal...corruptionis defectum patiens: quando ergo moritur terra cadit.'

46. Bogdani, *Cuneus*, i, p. 34. The Italian text here, which includes the phrase 'mentre erano soggetti alla corruzione' (translated here), is closer to Guadagnoli's phrasing (cf. my comment in n. 39, above). Cf. also Bogdani, *Letra*, p. 217.

47. Respectively: the medieval Latin translation, printed by Theodore Bibliander (*Machumetis Saracenorum principis...Alcoran* (Basel, 1543), p. 97: 'in fonte luteo'); the French translation by André du Ryer (*L'Alcoran de Mahomet* (Paris, 1651), p. 366: 'une fontaine'); the translation by Lodovico Marracci, published by the Seminary press at Padua nine years after Bogdani's death (*Alcorani textus universus* (Padua, 1698), p. 424: 'in fonte luti nigri'); M. Asad, *The Meaning of the Qur'an* (Bristol, 2003), p. 503 (adding also that the phrase could mean 'an abundance of water', and hence a spring). I refer to the 'apparent statement' in the Koran because, as Asad points out, the verb can be understood as 'he found it setting', i.e. 'it appeared to him that it was setting'.

48. Guadagnoli, *Apologia*, p. 209: 'in fontem feruentis aquae'.

49. Bogdani, *Cuneus*, i, pp. 29–30 (diagrams), 31 (quotation).

50. B. Malvasia, *Dilucidatio speculi verum monstrantis, in qua instruitur in fide christiana Hamet filius Zin Elabedin in regno Persarum princeps* (Rome, 1628), pp. 11–13, 16; Guadagnoli, *Apologia*, pp. 376–8; Bogdani, *Cuneus*, i, pp. 9–10.

51. Malvasia, *Dilucidatio*, p. 11 ('non ex carnali coniugio'); Bogdani, *Cuneus*, i, p. 9.

52. Malvasia, *Dilucidatio*, pp. 29–33; Bogdani, *Cuneus*, i, pp. 12–15. There is a briefer treatment of this theme in Guadagnoli, *Apologia*, pp. 379–81.

53. Bogdani, *Cuneus*, i, pp. 17 (reproducing material from Ciantes, *De sanctissima trinitate*, pp. 5–6, 9), 18 (summarizing Ciantes, pp. 11–17, 18–37).

54. See the entry 'Joseph-Marie Ciantes' in A. Vacant et al., eds., *Dictionnaire de théologie catholique*, 15 vols. (Paris, 1903–46), ii, col. 2,472.

55. Bogdani, *Cuneus*, i, p. 33. Bogdani's explicit reference to Macedo's account of Limbo (p. 33, paragraphs 5–6) corresponds to pp. 484–5 of Macedo's book; the account Bogdani goes on to give of Purgatory (pp. 33–4, paragraph 7) summarizes material on p. 468 of Macedo's book.

56. For a full account of Macedo's life, which included a prominent role as a defender of Portuguese independence, see I. de Sousa Ribeiro, *Fr. Francisco de Santo Agostinho de Macedo: um filósofo escotista português e um paladino da Restauração* (Coimbra, 1951), pp. 7–54.

57. Bogdani, *Letra*, p. 440.

58. G. Morosini, *Via della fede mostrata a'gli ebrei* (Rome, 1683), sig. §§1r.

59. See I. Golub, *Ivan Paštrić* (Split, 1988); T. Mrkonjić, *Il teologo Ivan Paštrić (Giovanni Pastrizio) (1636–1708): vita, opere, concezione della teologia, cristologia* (Rome, 1989).

60. Bogdani, *Letra*, p. 440 ('carissimo mio Padrone'); cf. also pp. 360, 365, 462, 500. Cf. also Marlekaj, *Pietro Bogdani*, p. 100. On Jeronim see J. Radonić, 'Jeronim Paštrić, istorik XVII veka', *Glas Srpske Akademije Nauka*, 190 (= ser. 2, 95) (1946), pp. 45–195; as Radonić shows, Jeronim was also close to the Propaganda Fide, and was given access to its archives when composing his historical works (p. 165). On the 'Illyrian' church and its wider role see J. Burić, *Iz prošlosti hrvatske kolonije u Rimu* (Rome, 1966).

61. These were the two aims specified in the Papal Encyclical of 15 Jan. 1622 which created the Propaganda Fide: see A. Reuter, 'De iuribus et officiis Sacrae Congregationis "de Propaganda Fide" noviter constitutae seu de indole eiusdam propria', in J. Metzler, ed., *Sacrae congregationis de propaganda fide memoria rerum*, vol. i, part 1 (Rome, 1971), pp. 112–45, esp. p. 119.

62. Bogdani, *Cuneus*, i, Preface ('Te primite perpara letterarit'), sig. a2v (i, p. 90 in the Sedaj-Rugova edn.).

63. T. Mrkonjić, 'Gregorio Barbarigo e Giovanni Pastrizio', in L. Billanovich and P. Gios, eds., *Gregorio Barbarigo, patrizio veneto, vescovo e cardinale nella tarda Controriforma (1625–1697)*, 2 vols. (Padua, 1999), ii, pp. 1,169–78, esp. pp. 1,171 (elected Protector), 1,172 (family connections with Split); S. Serena, *S. Gregorio Barbarigo e la vita spirituale e culturale nel suo seminario di Padova*, 2 vols. (Padua, 1963), ii, pp. 361–431 (correspondence with Paštrić).

64. See G. Barzon, 'Per lo studio del Seminario di Padova: economia, amministrazione, alunni e professori', in Billanovich and Gios, eds., *Gregorio Barbarigo*, i, pp. 637–701.

65. G. Fedalto, 'Il Cardinale Gregorio Barbarigo e l'Oriente', in Billanovich and Gios, eds., *Gregorio Barbarigo*, ii, pp. 977–1,001, here p. 1,000 ('dove occorresse che fossero stati deputati dalla Sede Apostolica e dalla Congregazione della Propaganda').

66. M. Cassese, 'Gregorio Barbarigo e il rapporto con ebrei e non cattolici', in Billanovich and Gios, eds., *Gregorio Barbarigo*, ii, pp. 1,023–56, here p. 1,038.

67. See G. Bellini, *Storia della tipografia del Seminario di Padova, 1684–1938* (Padua, 1938).

68. Ibid., p. 35. On Barbarigo's relations with the Propaganda Fide, see also G. Poletti, *Scritti vari* (Siena, 1910), pp. 344–64.

69. I. Zamputi, 'Shënime mbi kohën dhe jetën e Pjetër Bogdanit', *Buletin për shkencat shoqërore* (1954), no. 3, pp. 34–54; Shuteriqi, *Shkrimet shqipe*, p. 79. Note also that the book was published with a formal 'imprimatur' from the ecclesiastical authorities in Padua: Bogdani, *Cuneus*, i, sig. b2v (Sedaj-Rugova edn., i, p. 98).

70. P. Gios, ed., *Lettere di Gregorio Barbarigo a Cosimo III de' Medici (1680–1697)* (Padua, 2003), pp. 81, 83.

71. Bogdani, *Cuneus*, ii, pp. 145–50 (unfortunately the Sedaj-Rugova edn. omits pp. 146–7; the Armenian and Syriac texts are on p. 146).

72. These four pages, the last in the book, are also unfortunately omitted in the Sedaj-Rugova edn. (which also omits the Albanian index that follows the Italian index).

73. Bellini, *Storia della tipografia*, p. 312.

74. Bogdani, *Cuneus*, i, p. 70; ii, p. 22. For comments on the etymologies see the Sedaj-Rugova edn., i, pp. 35–6.

75. Bogdani, *Letra*, p. 461: 'Le Profetie sono poste anche in arabo, et hebreo come per doj nationi incredule'. Cf. the comment in the prefatory statement by Barbarigo's Auditor-General, Joannes Clericatus, that the book was for the instruction of the faithful under the Turk and 'for dragging other infidels away from the errors of Judaism and Islam' (Bogdani, *Cuneus*, i, sig. §1v (Sedaj-Rugova edn., p. 78): 'pro aliis infidelibus ex erroribus Iudaismi, & Mahumethanismi eruendis').

76. Ibid., p. 462: 'vestite alla Albanese e Serviana per dare in humore quella povera gente e consolarla al meglio che ho potuto'. The term 'Serbian' here may be primarily geographical.

77. Ibid., p. 469: 'Il maggiore e più ardente desiderio…è di portarlo in persona nella mia Chiesa, acciò che sparga per quanto può i documenti della Santa fede in quei Popoli'.

78. Ibid., p. 461.

79. M. Callegari, 'La tipografia del Seminario di Padova fondata dal Barbarigo', in Billanovich and Gios, eds., *Gregorio Barbarigo*, i, pp. 231–51, esp. pp. 246–50 (noting that by late 1686, after two years of operation, the press had accumulated a debt of 41,000 lire).

80. Bogdani, *Letra*, p. 461 ('Miracolo').

81. Callegari, 'La tipografia', pp. 247, 248 (n.).

82. Cf. G. Gjini, *Ipeshkvia Shkup Prizren nëpër shekuj* (Zagreb, 1992), p. 181; Bogdani, *Cuneus*, Sedaj-Rugova edn., i, pp. 25–6.

83. The only prefatory item retained in this issue of the book was Bogdani's 'Te Primite Perpara Letterarit'; but the last page of that five-page text was omitted.

84. See Serena, *S. Gregorio Barbarigo*, i, pp. 141–52; Cassese, 'Gregorio Barbarigo', p. 1,045.

85. Gios, ed., *Lettere*, pp. 70, 75 ('Io ho creduto sempre l'impresa di Constantinopoli la più facile e la più riuscibile').

86. Serena, *S. Gregorio Barbarigo*, i, p. 149.

87. N. Arnu, *Presagio dell'imminente rovina, e caduta dell'imperio ottomano, delle future vittorie, e prosperi successi della christianità* (Padua, 1684), esp. pp. 42–7. On the printing of this book, for which Arnu paid the costs, see Callegari, 'La tipografia', p. 233.

88. M. a Pobladura, 'De amicitia S. Gregorii Barbadici cum servo Dei Marco ab Aviano, O.F.M.CAP', *Collectanea franciscana*, 31 (1961), pp. 61–79.

89. Ibid., pp. 63, 75.

90. Bogdani, *Cuneus*, i, sigs. +1r-+2r (Sedaj-Rugova edition, pp. 108–12). On Ričardi see V. Klaić, *Život i djela Pavla Rittera Vitezovića (1652–1713)* (Zagreb, 1914), p. 49.

91. Klaić, *Život i djela*, pp. 56, 58. Klaić mentions this poem, but speculates that Bogdani himself had visited Vienna in order to lobby the Emperor (pp. 63–4)—a claim for which there is no evidence. The poem is signed 'Paulus Ritter'; Shuteriqi misidentified him as 'an Austrian poet' (*Shkrimet shqipe*, p. 83 (n.)); the error was corrected in Rugova, *Vepra e Bogdanit*, p. 59 (n.). The connection with Ritter Vitezović may have come through Ričardi: the latter was probably related to a priest in Dubrovnik, Father Franjo Ričardi, who was a friend of Bogdani's (see Klaić, p. 49 (n.), and Bogdani, *Letra*, p. 500).

92. Bogdani, *Cuneus*, sigs. (+4)2v-(+5)2v (Sedaj-Rugova edn., pp. 138–46); here sig. (+5)2r (Sedaj-Rugova edn., p. 144) ('Si cangieranno al fine/Nella Croce la Luna; in sacri Tempi/L'Empie Meschite, & i Serragli in Chiostri').

93. See above, n. 22.
94. Bogdani, *Cuneus*, i, p. 42; ii, p. 40.
95. Ibid., ii, p. 59.
96. Ibid., i, p. 5.
97. Ibid., ii, p. 82.

Chapter 7

1. D. T. Bataković, *Kosovo i Metohija u srpsko-arbanaškim odnosima* (Prishtina, 1991), pp. 22–4: 'Posle spaljivanja Skoplja...Pikolomini povukao se u Prizren gde ga je dočekalo oko 20.000 srpskih ustanika, s kojima je, izgleda, sklopio ugovor o zajedničkoj borbi protiv Turaka. Nedugo zatim, Pikolomini je umro od kuge, a njegovi naslednici nisu uspeli da spreče svoje vojnike da pljačkaju i zlostavljaju stanovništvo. Razočarani ponašanjem hrišćanske vojske...srpski ustanici počeli su odustajati od dogovorenog savezništva. Patrijarh Arsenije III Crnojević bezuspešno je pokušavao da sa carskim oficirima utvrdi novi sporazum...Arbanasi katoličke vere, uprkos obećanjima da će joj pomoći, napustili su austrijsku vojsku uoči odsudnog obračuna kod Kačanika, početkom 1690. Srpska milicija, odupirući se premoćnoj sultanovoj ordiji, povlačila se prema zapadu i severu zemlje. Turska odmazda praćena pljačkom i besomučnim pokoljima nad nevernom rajom trajala je puna tri meseca...U strahu od surove odmazde, sa Arsenijem III, prema severu stalo da beži i stanovništvo Kosova i susednih krajeva...Na poziv Leopolda I, patrijarh Arsenije III preveo je, zajedno sa delom visokog sveštenstva i znatan deo ozbeglog naroda (više desetina hiljada ljudi) u Rimsko-nemačko Carstvo, na tle južne Ugarske, pošto je dobio obećanja da će njegovom narodu tamo biti priznat poseban politički i verski status...Velika seoba 1690. bila je krupna prekretnica u istoriji srpskog naroda. Samo na Kosovu i u Metohiji zapusteli su gradovi a pojedina sela ostala su bez ijednog stanovnika...Najteža poslednica Velike seobe je veliki demografski poremećaj, jer je posle povlačenja Srba s Kosova i Metohije počelo obimnije, uglavnom nasilno, naseljavanje arbanaških plemena sa malisorskih visoravni. U decenijama posle Velike seobe, Arbanasi, mahom islamizovani, kao pustonosna reka preplavili su zapustela središta srpskih zemalja. Pljačkaška narav arbanaških plemena zahvaljujući njihovoj fantastičnoj moći reprodukcije, razvila se u opasnu pretnju biološkom opstanku srpskog naroda na Kosovu i u Metohiji.' (The version of this passage in D. T. Bataković, *The Kosovo Chronicles*, tr. D. Vulićević (Belgrade, 1992), pp. 47–9, adds a sentence not present in the Serbian text: 'The period following the Great Migration of the Serbs marked the commencement of three centuries of ethnic Albanian genocide against the Serbs in their native land.') Note that Bataković uses 'Austrian' here as a synonym (or metonym) of 'Imperial'; this usage is very widespread in the historical literature, and I shall also follow it in this essay.

2. K. Prifti et al., eds., *Historia e popullit shqiptar*, 4 vols. (Tirana, 2000), i, pp. 580–3: 'e dyta me gjeneral Pikkolominin në krye u nis për në Kosovë, ku u prit nga shqiptarët. Shqiptarët ishin gati të pranonin mbrojtjen e perandorit austriak. Të njëjtin veprim bënë edhe shqiptarët e Kelmendit. Kur Pikolomini hyri në Prishtinë, shqiptarët e Kosovës deklaruan se ishin me perandorin. 6000 shqiptarë ortodoksë (Albanensen) u

bashkuan me austriakët. Pikolomini të njëjten situatë ndeshi edhe në Prizren. Banorët e qytetit i dolën përpara dhe e pritën me nderime. Rreth 5000 shqiptarë me kryepeshkopin e tyre, Pjetër Bogdanin, e përshëndetën me breshëri të shtënash...Burimet austriake, angleze e papale pohojnë se pranë Pikolominit ishin mbi 20000 shqiptarë...Pas vdekjes së gjeneral Pikolominit (nëntor 1689) qëndrimi i shqiptarëve ndryshoi për disa arsye. Në radhë të parë ndikoi këtu qëndrimi i pasardhësve të Pikolominit dhe të oficerëve të tjerë austriakë. Ata filluan t'i trajtojnë keq shqiptarët...Duka i Holshtajnit...u përpoq në Prizren të çarmatoste shqiptarët, kurse në Lumë urdhëroi djegien e disa fshatrave...Forcat austriake dhe kryengritësit shqiptarë u tërhoqën në Kaçanik. Duka i Holshtajnit u detyrua të organizonte një këshill ushtarak, i cili vendosi t'u bëjë thirrje shqiptarëve që kishin qenë pranë Pikolominit, por ishte tepër vonë. Megjithatë, shqiptarët, besnikë të austriakëve, morën pjesë në luftën me tartarët e hanit të Krimesë...Me ushtrinë austriake u larguan nga Serbia e Kosova shumë kryengritës, besnikë të Austrisë. Mbi këtë fakt u ngrit teza e historiografisë serbe mbi të ashtuquajturën "shpërngulje të madhë të serbëve nga Kosova dhe mbi popullimin e saj nga shqiptarët". Është e vërtetë se midis atyre që u tërhoqën së bashku me ushtrinë austriake ishte patriarku i Pejës, Arsen III Cërnojeviçi...Por serbët që u larguan me të nuk ishin aq të shumtë në numër sa të bëhet fjalë për një shpërngulje të madhe të tyre nga Kosova në ato vitë...nga forcat që u vunë përkrah forcave austriake, dy grupe ishin më kryesorët: shqiptarët dhe "serbët". Nga një përllogaritje e përafërt del se numri i shqiptarëve ishte dy herë i madh se ai i "serbëve". Përveç dokumenteve të komandës ushtarake...shumë shqiptarë qëndruan deri në fund me austriakët. Edhe ndër të shpërngulurit që nuk i kalonin të 10,000 vetat shqiptarët ishin më të shumtë. Sipas një interpretimi që meriton të përmendet, edhe termi "serb", i cili përdorej në dokumente, nënkuptonte shqiptarët ortodokë që bënin pjesë në jurisdiksionin e kishës së Pejës. Në këtë rast duhet pranuar se kryengritësit e Kosovës, që u bashkuan me austriakët, ishin thuajse të gjithë shqiptarë.'

3. S. J. Shaw and E. K. Shaw, *History of the Ottoman Empire and Modern Turkey*, 2 vols. (Cambridge, 1976), i, pp. 220–1. (The first volume is credited to S. J. Shaw alone.)

4. S. Clissold, ed., *A Short History of Yugoslavia* (Cambridge, 1968), p. 109.

5. P. F. Sugar, *Southeastern Europe under Ottoman Rule, 1354–1804* (Seattle, 1977), p. 222.

6. B. Jelavich, *History of the Balkans*, 2 vols. (Cambridge, 1983), i, pp. 92–3.

7. In the account that follows of the events of 1689–90, the sources for all unreferenced factual statements can be found in N. Malcolm, *Kosovo: A Short History* (London, 1998), pp. 139–62.

8. Archives du Ministère des Affaires Étrangères, Paris, Correspondance politique, Autriche, vol. 51, fo. 174r: 'In Pristina 5000m Arnaut rebuttati à Turchi, e molti principali de circonuicini lochi...giurarono fedeltà all Imperatore'. [On this manuscript account see below, n. 81.]

9. Details of the ethnic composition of the population of Prishtina in this period are not available. My comment here is based on the general consideration that the proportion of Orthodox Slavs converting to Islam in this area was low, and on the analogous case of Vushtrri (Vuçitërn, Vučitrn), a town to the north of Prishtina: when Evlija Çelebi visited it in 1660 he found that 'most' of its inhabitants 'do not speak Bosnian but do speak Albanian and Turkish' (R. Dankoff and R. Elsie, eds., *Evliya Çelebi in Albania and Adjacent Regions (Kosovo, Montenegro, Ohrid)* (Leiden, 2000), p. 17).

10. The authors of the Albanian textbook appear to have relied at this point on the account given in S. Rizaj, *Kosova gjatë shekujve XV, XVI dhe XVII: administrimi, ekonomia, shoqëria dhe lëvizja popullore* (Prishtina, 1982), pp. 511–19, at p. 512, which cites the figure of 6,000 Albanians from R. Knolles and P. Rycaut, *The Turkish History*, ed. J. Savage, 2 vols. (London, 1701), ii, pp. 352–3. That text states (p. 352) that the Austrians marched 'towards *Pristina* and *Clina*, where they were joined by 6000 *Arnauts*...which People never being in obedience to the *Turks*, now came to yeild themselves Subjects and Slaves to his Imperial Majesty'. The original text by Rycaut does not describe these 'Arnauts' as 'never being in obedience to the *Turks*' (that phrase was wrongly transferred from another sentence by the editor, Savage); it states that Piccolomini's men marched 'towards *Pristina* and *Clina*, where they had understood from the advanced Guards, that 6000 *Arnauts*...remained in expectation to join with the *Germans*, and to oppose the *Turks* with all the People of the Country...Being arrived at *Pristina*, they concluded a Treaty with those People' (P. Rycaut, *The History of the Turks, beginning with the Year 1679* (London, 1700), p. 351).

11. See Malcolm, *Kosovo*, pp. 111–14.

12. M. Jačov, ed., *Spisi tajnog vatikanskog arhiva XVI–XVIII veka* (Belgrade, 1983), p. 141. In this report Bogdani also stated that the Serbs could supply another 7,000 fighters; this figure presumably related not to the total Serb population, but to those elements with which he had sufficiently close connections to be able to call on them for support—though the basis of his calculation is not known.

13. F. Veterani, *Memorie...dall'anno 1683, sino all'anno 1694* (Vienna, 1771), p. 108 ('20 mille Arnauti ridotti dal Picolomini alla fedel' ubbidienza di Cesare').

14. Archives du Ministère des Affaires Étrangères, Paris, Correspondance politique, Autriche, vol. 51, fo. 177r.

15. F. Wagner, *Historia Leopoldi Magni Caesaris Augusti*, 2 vols. (Vienna, 1719–31), ii, p. 124.

16. Kriegsarchiv, Vienna, Alte Feldakten, Türkenkrieg, 1689-11-18.

17. L. Soranzo, *L'Ottomanno* (Milan, 1599), pp. 167, 175 ('Albanesi, che uiuono alla Romana'; 'più d'Albanesi, che Seruiani'). [On Soranzo's main source of information about the Albanian lands, see above, pp. 42–4.]

18. Generallandesarchiv, Karlsruhe, MS 46/3714, item 3 (Augsburg, 6 Feb. 1690).

19. R. Veselinović, 'Die "Albaner" und "Klimenten" in den österreichischen Quellen zu Ende des 17. Jahrhunderts: historisch-geographische und ethnographische Abhandlung', *Mitteilungen des Österreichischen Staatsarchivs*, 13 (1960), pp. 195–230; cf. Malcolm, *Kosovo*, p. 155.

20. On the use of Catholic Albanian fighters by the Ottomans see Malcolm, *Kosovo*, p. 151.

21. Generallandesarchiv, Karlsruhe, MS 46/3714, item 1 ('ils sont [*sic*] pris com[m]unication avec 20m Albanois, qui ont tourné leurs armes contre les Turcs'). (The '2' here might possibly be read as a zig-zag '1'; I take it as a '2' both on visual grounds and because of the corroboration of the other early reports.)

22. See for example Dankoff and Elsie, eds., *Evliya Çelebi in Albania*, pp. 41, 65 and *passim*.

23. Anon, *Der neu-eröffneten Ottomanischen Pforten Fortsetzung* (Augsburg, 1701), p. 517b.

24. Archives du Ministère des Affaires Étrangères, Paris, Correspondance politique, Autriche, vol. 51, fo. 177r ('Stauano fuori di Priseren 6000 e più Albanesi, e di quelli med.^{mi} altre uolte assoldati da Turchi nominati Arnaut').

25. Contarini, *Istoria*, p. 168 ('i Capi delle vicine Nazioni, che vennero a tributare à Cesare giuramento di fedeltà').

26. S. Pulaha, *Qëndresa e popullit shqiptar kundër sundimit osman nga shek. XVI deri në fillim të shek. XVIII: dokumente osmane* (Tirana, 1978), pp. 184–5. Cf. also the letter written by Toma Raspasani on 22 July 1690, stating that the clans of Surroi, Gashi and Krasniqi had remained constantly loyal to the Emperor: I. Zamputi and S. Pulaha, eds., *Dokumente të shekujve XVI–XVII për historinë e Shqipërisë*, iv (Tirana, 1990), p. 342. These clans lived not in 'Serbia' as that term was used by Bogdani (he took the river Drin as marking the border of it), but in 'Albania'.

27. I. Zamputi, *Relacione mbi gjendjen e Shqipërisë veriore e të mesme në shekullin XVII*, 2 vols. (Tirana, 1963–5), i, p. 434. The question of how large the remaining Christian (both Catholic and Orthodox) population was in the Prizren region by the late 17th century is difficult to answer. An Ottoman register for the *cizye* tax (payable by non-Muslims) for 1668 specifies 995½ *cizye hanes* (literally, '*cizye* households') in the sancak of Prizren; more than half of these were in the kazas (administrative districts) of Bihor and Trgovište (Rožaj), with the figures for the remaining areas being 161 in the kaza of Prizren, 156½ in the kaza of Suhareke, 86 in the kaza of Gjakovë, and 92 in the Has district (P. Thëngjilli, *Shqiptarët midis lindjes dhe perëndimit (1506–1839): fusha fetare*, i (Tirana, 2002), p. 69). But the *cizye hane* was a taxation unit, and there is much uncertainty as to how it should be interpreted in this period. Petrika Thëngjilli assumes (pp. 67, 81) that each unit was equivalent to 3.8 actual households; applying the standard multiplier of 5, this means that each *cizye hane* represented 19 people (thus: 3,059 in the kaza of Prizren, 2,974 in the kaza of Suhareke, 1,634 in the kaza of Gjakovë, and 1,748 in the Has district). The fullest discussion of the *cizye hane* problem is in Nenad Moačanin's study of Slavonia, *Town and Country on the Middle Danube, 1526–1690* (Leiden, 2006), pp. 35–44, 183–232; Moačanin notes some special cases where one *cizye hane* could stand for 10–20 households (pp. 208, 217), finds that 30–40 per cent of non-Muslim households were not paying the *cizye* at all (p. 205), and suggests that in war-time the summary *cizye* registers may have recorded only the new settlers in the region (pp. 41, 206). Nevertheless, even with all these uncertainties, it seems highly unlikely that the Prizren region could have provided 20,000 men of fighting age from the Christian population.

28. E. Fermendžin, 'Izprave god. 1579–1671 tičuće se Crne Gore i stare Srbije', *Starine Jugoslovenskog Akademije Znanosti i Umjetnosti*, 25 (1892), pp. 164–200, at p. 199 ('In questa terra di Nassi, da 28 anni fa, vi era gran numero de christiani, adesso vi sono rimasto del sesso feminile da 300 anime e di huomini pochissimi, havendo il resto abiurato la fede per sfugire le gravezze e tributi'). (I take 'Nassi' here to be a mistranscription of 'Hassi'; the area is described as 15 miles from Gjakovë.) Cf. Andrea Bogdani's report of 1670, which specified 20 Catholic households in the 'Hassi' district, and added that there were very many Catholic women living in Muslim households, which brought the total to 500 Catholic souls (Archivio storico 'de Propaganda Fide', Rome, SOCG 431, fo. 161v).

29. On the crypto-Christians see above, pp. 60–3.

30. Archives du Ministère des Affaires Étrangères, Paris, Correspondance politique, Autriche, vol. 51, fo. 175r ('Rassiani').

31. A report from Prishtina of 19 Dec. 1689 stated that Raspasani, the 'Vicar of Albania', was engaged in obtaining the acceptance of Austrian rule by various places ('zu unterwerffung unterschiedenen orthen'); Kriegsarchiv, Vienna, Exp. Prot. 1690 (vol. 383), fo. 41r.

32. The claim that Arsenije was pursuing a positively pro-Ottoman policy has been made by Stanislao Kahnè: 'L'azione politica del patriarca di Peć Arsenio Črnojević dal 1682 al 1690', *Orientalia christiana periodica*, 23 (1957), pp. 267–312. But Kahnè's argument seems speculative on some key points.

33. A. Ivić, *Istorija Srba u Vojvodini* (Novi Sad, 1929), p. 315 (1693 figures). A larger figure for those who entered Hungary with Arsenije, 60,000, was given by Cardinal Kollonich (Kolonić) in a letter written in Vienna in Dec. 1703. The letter was to the Pope, and at this point in it Kollonich was boasting that he was preparing Arsenije and his people to accept union with Rome, so he may have been inclined to exaggerate the scale of the impending achievement; he also appears to have been referring to all the Serbs who had moved to Habsburg territory during the war, not merely to the ones who had moved in the 'Great Exodus' (see N. Nilles, *Symbolae ad illustrandam historiam ecclesiae orientalis in terris coronae S. Stephani*, 2 vols. (Innsbruck, 1885), i, p. 28). The two estimates by Arsenije remain the most authoritative we have.

34. Lj. Stanojević, ed., *Stari srpski zapisi i natpisi*, 6 vols. (Belgrade and Sremski Karlovci, 1902–26), iii, p. 94, no. 5283 ('37000 familija').

35. P. Julinac, *Kratkoie vredeniie v istoriiu proikhozhdeniia slaveno-serbskago naroda* (Venice, 1765); photo-reproduction ed. M. Pantić (Belgrade, 1981); p. 156. Julinac added the mystifying (and perhaps deliberately misleading) statement that this information was derived from an official Imperial report to Vienna.

36. J. Rajić ['Raić'], *Istoriia raznikh slavenskikh narodov, naipache Bolgar, Khorvatov, i Serbov*, 4 vols. (Vienna, 1794–5), iv, p. 135 ('37000 familii *Serbskikh* s Patriarkhom').

37. J. C. von Engel, *Geschichte des Ungrischen Reichs und seiner Nebenländer*, 4 vols. (Halle, 1797–1804), iii, p. 485 ('37,000 Serwische Familien, mit ihrem Patriarchen').

38. M. von Schwartner, *Statistik des Königreichs Ungern*, 3 parts in 2 vols. (Buda, 1809–11), ii, p. 113(n.) ('Ich habe ein eigenhändigen Memorial dieses merkwürdigen Mannes gelesen'...'40000 seiner Glaubensgenossen').

39. J. von Csaplovics, *Slavonien und zum Theil Croatien: ein Beitrag zur Völker- und Ländekunde*, 2 vols. (Pest, 1819), ii, p. 29 ('mit etwa 36,000 (einige geben diese Zahl auf 30, andere wieder auf 35,000 an) grössten Theil, servianischen, weniger albanisch-climentinischen Familien (vielleicht *rectius* Köpfen) herüber'). The claim about 'Albanian-Kelmendi' families perhaps arises from a confusion with the events of 1737, when a significant number of Serb and Kelmendi families did retreat northwards to Habsburg territory.

40. A. Stojačković ['Stojacskovics'], *Über die staatsrechtlichen Verhältnisse der Serben in der Wojwodina und überhaput in den Ländern der ungarischen Krone* (Timişoara, 1860), p. 14. Modestly, he summarized his conclusions as 'at least 500,000 souls' ('mindestens 500 000 Seelen').

41. Cited in I. Ruvarac, *Odlomci o Grofu Djordju Brankoviću i Arseniju Crnojeviću patriarhu* (Belgrade, 1896), p. 97. Ruvarac notes that this was drawn from Vasilije Petrović's

history of Montenegro, published in Moscow in 1754; that book thus pre-dated Julinac's work, and the basis of its claim is completely unknown.

42. K. von Czoernig, *Ethnographie der Oesterreichischen Monarchie*, 3 vols. (Vienna, 1855–7), ii, p. 157 and n. ('with 40,000 families, mostly Serbian and Rascian'; 'A[rsenije] Crnojević says this expressly in a Court petition of 1706' ('mit vierzig tausend, grössentheils *serbischen und rascischen Familien*'; 'A. Chernovich sagt diess ausdrücklich in einem Hofgesuche vom Jahre 1706')).

43. L. Szalay, *A Magyarországi szerb telepek jogviszonya az állomhoz* (Pest, 1861), p. 26 ('harminczhét ezer családdal'); J. Jireček, 'Die serbischen Privilegien, Verhandlungs-Congresse und Synoden. I: Die Zeit von 1690 bis 1740', *Oesterreichische Revue*, ser. 2, vol. 7 (1864), pp. 1–12, at p. 6 ('Ueber 30,000 Familien'); F. Vaníček, *Specialgeschichte der Militärgrenze, aus Originalquellen und Quellenwerken geschöpft*, 4 vols. (Vienna, 1875), i, p. 119 ('36.000 Familien'); J. H. Schwicker, *Politische Geschichte der Serben in Ungarn* (Budapest, 1880), p. 15.

44. A. E. Picot, *Les Serbes de Hongrie: leur histoire, leurs privilèges, leur église, leur état politique et social* (Prague, 1873), p. 75 ('c'est une tradition constante que cette population avait été recensée par famille et non par tête').

45. S. Gopčević, *Makedonien und Alt-Serbien* (Vienna, 1889), p. 223 (giving the figure of 37,000 families and adding: 'given the size of Serb families, we may estimate that the total quantity of people was at least half a million, if not more' ('Bei der Grösse der serbischen Familien kann man die Volksmenge auf wenigstens eine halbe Million schätzen, wenn nicht mehr')). On the story of this book see M. Heim, *Spiridion Gopčević: Leben und Werk* (Wiesbaden, 1966), pp. 92–114.

46. Ruvarac, *Odlomci*, p. 102.

47. D. Popović, *Velika seoba Srba 1690: Srbi seljaci i plemići* (Belgrade, 1954), p. 27.

48. J. Cvijić, *La Péninsule balkanique: géographie humaine* (Paris, 1918), p. 131 ('35 à 40.000 familles'). For a valuable study of Cvijić, which also pays special attention to his attitude towards the Albanians, see K. Clewing and E. Pezo, 'Jovan Cvijić als Historiker und Nationsbildner: zu Ertrag und Grenzen seines anthropogeographischen Ansatzes zur Migrationsgeschichte', in M. Krzoska and H.-C. Maner, eds., *Beruf und Berufung: Geschichtswissenschaft und Nationsbildung in Ostmittel- und Südosteuropa im 19. und 20. Jahrhundert* (Münster, 2005), pp. 265–97.

49. http://budapest.mfa.gov.yu under 'Dijaspora-Szórvány' (accessed 15/12/2006) ('više desetina hiljada porodica'); A. N. Dragnich and S. Todorovich, *The Saga of Kosovo: Focus on Serbian-Albanian Relations* (Boulder, CO, 1984), p. 66; M. Marković, 'La Signification de Kosovo dans l'histoire serbe', in A. Jevtić ['Jevtitch'], *Dossier Kosovo* (Lausanne, 1991), pp. 179–92, at p. 181 ('environ 150 000 Serbes'); K. Kučerová, *Chorváti a srbi v strednej európe (k etnickým, hospodárskym a sociálnym otázkam v 16–17. storočí)* (Bratislava, 1976), p. 100; I. Kušniráková, 'Pravoslávna komunita v Komárne v 17.–18. storočí v kontexte privilégií uhorských panovníkov', *Slovenská archivistika*, 37 (2002), no. 2, pp. 43–54, at p. 44: '36000 srbských rodin'... 'približne 370 až 400 tisíc ľudí'.

50. D. Popović, *Srbi u Budimu od 1690 do 1740* (Belgrade, 1952), p. 23. I exclude from this total 14 people from central Hungary, the Banat, and Bačka, whom Popović assumes to have come before 1690. Of course many of the Serbs who came to central Hungary in 1690 later moved elsewhere; but since this is merely a random sample, confined to

those whose place of origin is stated in the records, and since there is no reason to think that people from certain areas moved disproportionately thereafter, the validity of the evidence is not affected. It should also be noted that the Serb community in Buda had been very small before 1690 (ibid., p. 12).

51. Ibid., p. 24 ('"Arnauta"... što znači Cincara'—and noting that they set up their own 'arnautski esnaf' or Albanian guild in Buda). Cf. also the list of heads of household of the Buda Serbs for 1706, which includes a 'Vučo Despot Arnaut': G. Vitković, 'Spomenici iz budimskog e peštanskog arhiva', Glasnik Srpskog Učenog Društva, odeljak 2, vol. 3 (1873), pp. 1–303, and vol. 6 (1875), pp. v–lxx, 1–486; here vol. 3, p. 71. In February 1693 an official in Esztergom noted the presence of Muslims among the Serb refugees at Szentendre: 'die grosse anzahl Rätzen, worunter auch Türkhen sein sollen, die sich in der Insul St: Andre befindten' (Kriegsarchiv, Vienna, Exp. Prot. 1693 (vol. 391), fo. 82r). For evidence of 'Arnauts' in the Austrian military see M. Kostić, Završni bilans polemike o srpsko-arbanaskom ustanku protiv Turaka uz austrijsku vojsku 1689/90 (Belgrade, 1962), pp. 5–6; Malcolm, Kosovo, p. 162. Not all of the Arnauts in Austrian service had necessarily been recruited in Kosovo: a report by Luigi Marsigli on the defence of Niš noted that a besieging enemy would have to extend his lines to the nearby 'Albaneser berg', which furnished '60. combattenti': Generallandesarchiv, Karlsruhe, MS 46/3714, item 25, fo. 3r (4 July 1690).

52. See A. Ivić, Migracije Srba u Slavoniju tokom 16., 17. i 18. stoleća, Srpski etnografski zbornik, 36 (Subotica, 1926), pp. 126–7, and his Istorija Srba u Vojvodini, p. 289.

53. See Ivić, Migracije, p. 132, and Malcolm, Kosovo, p. 164.

54. Malcolm, Kosovo, p. 163.

55. This argument is developed in T. Djordjević, 'Stanovništvo u Srbiji posle velike seobe 1690 godine', Naš narodni život, 4 (1931), pp. 114–38, at pp. 131–2. Djordjević also notes that the majority of villages retained their Serb names, which would presumably not have happened if they had been permanently abandoned by their Serb inhabitants.

56. See Malcolm, Kosovo, p. 159. Konrad Clewing has disagreed with this interpretation, commenting that I have fallen victim here to the linguistic complexity of the German text (J. Reuter and K. Clewing, Der Kosovo Konflikt: Ursachen, Verlauf, Perspektiven (Klagenfurt, 2000), p. 30). But I have used not the German translation but the original Italian, which I believe I have interpreted correctly: see Veterani, Memorie, p. 130.

57. J. Radonić, Rimska kurija i južnoslovenske zemlje od XVI do XIX veka (Belgrade, 1950), p. 422. I assume that the standard multiplier of 5 for each household is too low in this case, since Bogdani also claimed that this population could supply 3,000 fighters.

58. Cvijić, La Péninsule balkanique, p. 131 ('la grande migration... était constituée surtout par la population urbaine').

59. J. Müller, Albanien, Rumelien und die österreichisch-montenegrinische Gränze (Prague, 1844), p. 74; Archivio storico 'de Propaganda Fide', Rome, SOCG 482, fo. 290v.

60. See Malcolm, Kosovo, pp. 194–6; Reuter and Clewing, Der Kosovo Konflikt, pp. 34–8.

61. Malcolm, Kosovo, p. 332.

62. For this phrase (from Bataković, Kosovo Chronicles, p. 49) see above, n. 1.

63. For the texts see J. Radonić ('Radonitch'), Histoire des Serbes de Hongrie (Paris, 1919), pp. 203–16.

64. For a still valuable survey of this history, see Picot, Les Serbes de Hongrie.

65. J. C. von Bartenstein, *Kurzer Bericht von der Beschaffenheit der zerstreuten zahlreichen Illyrischen Nation in kaiserl. königl. Erblanden* (Frankfurt and Leipzig, 1802), pp. 15, 35. This work was later issued in a Serbian translation: *Kratak izveštaj o stanju raseja-noga mnogobrojnoga ilirskoga naroda po car. i kralj. naslednčkim zemaljama,* tr. A. Sandić (Vienna, 1866).

66. In 1861 László Szalay cited the correct text, but then emended it to 'deserite' (*A Magyarországi szerb telepek,* p. 24); he was perhaps influenced by Aleksandar Stojačković, who had translated it as 'verlasset Eure Heimath' in the previous year (*Über die staatsrechtichen Verhältnisse,* p. 14). See also the comments on this in L. Hadrovics, *L'Église serbe sous la domination turque* (Paris, 1947), p. 139, and S. Čakić, *Velika seoba Srba 1689/90 i Patrijarh Arsenije III Crnojević* (Novi Sad, 1982), pp. 174-6.

67. Cited in Ruvarac, *Odlomci,* p. 129.

68. K. Subotić, 'O ideji srpske Vojvodine i narodno-crkvene autonomije na koncu XVIII. veka', *Letopis Matice Srpske,* 183 (1895), pp. 16-48, at pp. 38 ('da je pri ugovaranju izmedju Pikolominija i Crnojevića bilo reči o vojvodini'), 48 ('Srpski narod...je po prirodi svoje crkve bio jedno organizirano društvo, istina društvo bez teritorija, ali *jedna politička celina*'...'Ta autonomija je bila plod ugovora izmedju naroda i suver-ena'). A strong echo of this tradition can be found in an influential modern history of the Balkans: 'the patriarchate...assumed the functions of the former [*sc.* pre-Ottoman] Serbian government...When occasion arose, it conducted foreign policy and even provided military leadership. This was the case at the end of the seventeenth century when the Hapsburg armies had penetrated deeply into the Balkans...Until the beginning of the eighteenth century the Serbian church was in fact the Serbian state' (L. S. Stavrianos, *The Balkans since 1453* (1st publ. 1958), 2nd edn. (London, 2000), p. 240).

69. [A. T. Brlić] *Die freiwillige Theilname der Serben und Kroaten an den vier letzten österreichisch-türkischen Kriegen* (Vienna, 1854), p. iv ('unter das Panier Oesterreichs'...'sie sind treu und redlich bis in die jüngste Zeit dabei verharret, so dass man es als Grundsatz serbisch-nationaler Politik nennen kann: mit Oesterreich in den innigst-freundschaftlichen Beziehungen zu stehen. Dieses Gebot der nationalen Interessen ist in den Herzen der Serben tief gewurzelt').

70. See R. Veselinović, *Arsenije III Crnojević u istoriji i književnosti,* Srpska Akademija Nauka, posebna izdanja, 151 (Belgrade, 1949), pp. 74-7.

71. S. Novaković, 'Iz hronike Despota Djurdja Brankovića, s dodatkom nekojih dokume-nata koji se njega tiču', *Glasnik Srpskog Učenog Društva,* 33 (1872), pp. 135-90, at p. 140 ('Savez s Austrijancima protiv Turaka bio je jedino djelo, koje se može u nekoliko pravdati. Sve ostalo je teško razumjeti. Najnesrećnije je djelo seoba').

72. S. Niketić, 'Istorijski razvitak srpske crkve', *Glasnik Srpskog Učenog Društva,* 31 (1871), pp. 45-88, at p. 65 ('samo varljiva obećanja Austrije i glupost Arsenije III, mogli su tako što izmisliti i učiniti').

73. 'Prince Lazarovich-Hrebelianovich' and 'Princess Lazarovich-Hrebelianovich' (Eleanor Calhoun), *The Servian People: Their Past Glory and their Destiny,* 2 vols. (London, n.d. [1911]), ii, p. 587.

74. H. W. V. Temperley, *History of Serbia* (London, 1919), p. 128. Note the use of the term 'Kaiser', which for all but the most historically aware of Temperley's readers would

have had a set of connotations quite different from those relating to a 17th-century Holy Roman Emperor.

75. *The Servian People*, i, p. 328.

76. Cited in Ruvarac, *Odlomci*, p. 109 ('otačastvo ... u kom danas Arnaut, ljuti Arnaut žari i pali').

77. J. N. Tomić ['Tomitch'], *Les Albanais en Vieille-Serbie et dans le Sandjak de Novi-Bazar* (Paris, 1913), p. 37 ('la population serbe ... n'évacua pas les territoires limitrophes de la véritable Albanie, mais, subjuguée, elle fut contrainte à une islamisation et albanisation accélérées'). This widely circulated text was a translation of his *O arnautima u Staroj Srbiji i Sandžaku* (Belgrade, 1913).

78. Tomić, *Les Albanais*, p. 33 ('Par contre, les Albanais musulmans en masse s'étaient unis au pacha d'Ipek, Mahmoud Begovitch et s'étaient avec lui retirés vers le sud').

79. Veselinović, *Arsenije III Crnojević*, p. 23 ('Jedino su Srbi i Arbanasi ustajali dobrovoljno protiv Turaka').

80. S. Rizaj, 'Mbi të ashtuquajturën dyndje e madhe serbe nga Kosova në krye me Patrikun Arsenije Çarnojeviq (1690)', *Gjurmime albanologjike*, seria e shkencave historike, 12, for 1982 (1983), pp. 81–103.

81. *Additional note*: Since this essay was written, a very valuable account of the Imperial campaign in Kosovo has been published by Nuri Bexheti: *Der 'Grosse Türkenkrieg' und die Albaner: die militärische Präsenz der Balkanvölker am 'Grossen Türkenkrieg' (1683–1699)* (Saarbrücken, 2009), pp. 74–162. Bexheti's researches confirm on several points the account of these events presented in my history of Kosovo and elaborated in this essay. He also identifies the author of the Paris manuscript account as Alessandro Belleardi, an Italian count and military man in Imperial service (pp. 86–7); however, Belleardi was not himself present in Kosovo, so my general characterization of this work as compiled at second hand from a variety of source-materials (Malcolm, *Kosovo*, p. 147) remains valid.

One other work, unknown to me when I wrote this essay in 2006, added a few relevant details from the Ottoman *mühimme defter*s (registers of the executive orders, with related materials, of the government in Istanbul): F. F. Anscombe, 'The Ottoman Empire in Recent International Politics—II: The Case of Kosovo', *The International History Review*, 28 (2006), pp. 758–93, at pp. 767–91. Some of the documents relate to the Ottoman authorities' attempts during 1690 to persuade those peasants who had fled from parts of eastern Kosovo to return (p. 778); the most important of these, a decree of Mar. 1690, was discussed in Malcolm, *Kosovo*, p. 163 (cf. above, n. 54). However, the majority of the Ottoman documents either precede the Austrian campaign in Kosovo or date from more than a year after it ended; they shed no light on the numbers or the ethnic identities of those who fled in 1690; and they do not say anything directly about the identities either of the 5–6,000 people who welcomed the Austrians outside Prizren, or of the larger local force that was then recruited. (From other, later, documents Anscombe deduces that some of them may have previously served in the Ottoman army; but this detail was already known, from the Paris manuscript: see above, n. 24. One of his documents, of Feb. 1690, does state that Albanian Catholic clans from the nearby Malësi, such as the Gashi and Fandi, had risen in support of the Ottomans at some point; but I had noted the evidence of that document on p. 151 of my book (cf. above, n. 26).) Overall, Anscombe's findings are fully consistent with the account I have given of those matters. The only thing that puzzles slightly is his insistence that these Ottoman documents, which he calls 'the most valuable indigenous evidence', are of such decisive importance that all previous historians' accounts are vitiated by their alleged failure to refer to them. It is not clear why documents written in Istanbul, more than 400 miles away, should be seen as 'indigenous' to Kosovo, nor why we should grant them more value than documents generated inside Kosovo at the time by people—Albanian Catholic priests and Austrian military men—who were actively involved in these events (or even to summaries of such eye-witness documents, made soon thereafter). Every piece of evidence may have something to contribute, of course; yet no account of what happened in Kosovo during the Austrian campaign could possibly be assembled from the very patchy details of the *mühimme defter*s. To give such an account, we must still rely overwhelmingly on 'Western' sources of the kind that I have mostly used.

Chapter 8

This essay is dedicated to Dr Uran Ferizi, with deep gratitude for his friendship and advice, and for his company (and the hospitality of his family) on several visits to the Albanian lands—including some to the territories of Ali Pasha.

1. J. W. Baggally, *Ali Pasha and Great Britain* (Oxford, 1938).
2. K. E. Fleming, *The Muslim Bonaparte: Diplomacy and Orientalism in Ali Pasha's Greece* (Princeton, NJ, 1999). Fleming refers to the British Library manuscripts as being in the British Museum, and mistakenly locates the Leake papers there. A misprinted pressmark for one manuscript in Baggally (*Ali Pasha*, p. 55, n. 1) also appears in Fleming when the same passage is quoted (*Muslim Bonaparte*, p. 115, n. 72).
3. I. Koçollari, *Ali Pasha dhe Shqipëria në arkivat britanike* (Tirana, 2013).
4. The date of birth is uncertain; 1740 is also given by some sources, but the evidence points mostly to *c.*1750 (see D. N. Skiotis, 'From Bandit to Pasha: First Steps in the Rise to Power of Ali of Tepelen, 1750–1784', *International Journal of Middle East Studies*, 2 (1971), pp. 219–44, at pp. 228–9). On the principle of intra-*bey* marriage see Eqrem Bey Vlora, *Lebenserinnerungen*, 2 vols. (Munich, 1968–73), i, pp. 58–9; N. Clayer, *Aux origines du nationalisme albanais: la naissance d'une nation majoritairement musulmane en Europe* (Paris, 2007), pp. 34–5. The scathing remarks of Ismail Qemal Bey Vlora, 'Ali Pasha...coming from an obscure family of Tepeleni, had no title at all to play any rôle in Albania' (*The Memoirs of Ismail Kemal Bey*, ed. S. Story (London, 1920), pp. 4–5), can be discounted on grounds of deep and historic familial enmity.
5. For valuable accounts see Skiotis, 'From Bandit to Pasha'; F. F. Anscombe, 'Albanians and "Mountain Bandits"', in F. F. Anscombe, ed., *The Ottoman Balkans, 1750–1830* (Princeton, NJ, 2006), pp. 87–113. Anscombe emphasizes (p. 88) the complete irrelevance in this context of Eric Hobsbawm's theory of banditry.
6. See Skiotis, 'From Bandit to Pasha', pp. 230–44; for a useful summary account see N. Clayer, 'Ali Paşa Tepedelenli', *Encyclopaedia of Islam*, 3rd edn., http://reference-works.brillonline.com/entries/encyclopaedia-of-islam-3/ali-pasa-tepedelenli-

COM_23950. Among general biographies, the best is still G. Remérand, *Ali de Tébélen, Pacha de Janina (1744-1822)* (Paris, 1928).

7. G. L. Arsh, ed., *Ē Rōsia kai ta pasalikia Alvanias kai Ēpeirou, 1759-1831: engrapha rōsikōn archeiōn*, tr. I. Smusliaeva (Athens, 2007), pp. 211–18 (L. Benaki, report of 23 Sept./5 Oct. 1810), at p. 211.

8. A. Andréadès, 'Ali Pacha de Tébelin, économiste et financier', *Revue des études grecques*, 25 (1912), pp. 427–60, at pp. 437–40 (*çiftlik* statistics); H. Holland, *Travels in the Ionian Isles, Albania, Thessaly, Macedonia &c. during the Years 1812 and 1813* (London, 1815), p. 117 (income in piastres and pounds; figures given on p. 115 suggest a slightly different rate, which would make this roughly £216,000; the Bank of England inflation calculator puts that at £14.6 m in 2017). In 1810 the British agent George Foresti gave the higher estimate of 5 m piastres: British Library, London (hereafter: 'BL'), MS Add. 20,183, fos. 43r–50v (Foresti to Canning, from Ioannina, 6 Nov. 1810), at fo. 50r. Thanks to the survival of archival evidence, Ali's wealth is one of the few aspects of his life to have received detailed treatment by modern scholars: see e.g. A. Uzun, 'Tepedelenli Ali Paşa ve mal varlığı', *Belleten*, vol. 45, no. 244, for 2001 (2002), pp. 1,035–77, and E. Muço, *Yanya valisi Ali Paşa ve emlakı* (Istanbul, 2010). However, it cannot be explored in this essay, which has a very different focus.

9. G. L. Arsh, *Ē Alvania kai ē Ēpeiros sta telē tou IĒ' kai stis arches tou ITH' aiōna*, tr. A. Dialla, ed. V. Panagiōtopoulos (Athens, 1994), p. 373. For the last year of his life (1821–2), Uzun estimates the total income of Ali and his sons, taken together, at just over 15 m piastres: 'Tepedelenli Ali Paşa', p. 1,060. On the importance of tax-farming see H. Sezer, 'Tepedelenli Ali Paşa ve oğullarının çiftlik ilişkin yeni bilgi-bulgular', *Ankara Üniversitesi Osmanlı Tarihi Araştırma ve Uygulama Merkezi dergisi*, 18 (2005), pp. 333–57, at pp. 336–40, and D. Dimitropoulos, 'Aspects of the Working of the Fiscal Machinery in the Areas Ruled by Ali Paşa', in A. Anastasopoulos and E. Kolovos, eds., *Ottoman Rule in the Balkans, 1760-1850: Conflict, Transformation, Adaptation* (Rethymno, 2007), pp. 61–7.

10. See Ph. Mavroeidē, *Aspetti della società veneziana nel '500: la Confraternità di S. Nicolò dei Greci* (Ravenna, 1989), *passim* (Venice); C. Kafadar, 'A Death in Venice (1575): Anatolian Muslim Merchants Trading in the Serenissima', *Journal of Turkish Studies*, 10 (1986), pp. 191–218, at p. 196 (Ancona).

11. BL, MS Add. 56,527 (Hobhouse, journal), fo. 41v (hostage system); Holland, *Travels*, p. 149 (hostage system); T. S. Hughes, *Travels in Sicily Greece and Albania*, 2 vols. (London, 1820), i, p. 440 (imposition as heir); J. Bessières, *Mémoire sur la vie et la puissance d'Ali-Pacha, visir de Janina* (Paris, 1820), p. 8 (confiscation).

12. G. L. Arsh, *Albaniia i Epir v kontse XVIII–nachale XIX v.* (Moscow, 1963), pp. 270–2 (cultivating Church); idem, *Ē Alvania kai ē Ēpeiros*, p. 370 (favoured Greeks; churches, bells); Andréadès, 'Ali Pacha', p. 428(n.) (subsidy).

13. [J.] Hawkins, 'On the Site of Dodona', in R. Walpole, ed., *Travels in Various Countries of the East, being a Continuation of Memoirs relating to European and Asiatic Turkey* (London, 1820), 473–82, at p. 473. On Hawkins see H. S. Torrens, 'Hawkins, John (1761–1841)', *Oxford Dictionary of National Biography*.

14. BL, MS Add. 34,919, fos. 79r–81v (Hamilton to Lord Hawkesbury, from Ioannina, 6 May 1803), at fo. 80v.

15. Holland, *Travels*, pp. 137, 195; Hughes, *Travels*, ii, p. 214; F. S. N. Douglas, *An Essay on Certain Points of Resemblance between the Ancient and Modern Greeks* (London, 1813), p. 50 (referring to Montesquieu, *De l'esprit des lois*, V.13).

16. G. de Vaudoncourt, *Memoirs of the Ionian Islands, considered in a Commercial, Political, and Military Point of View... including the Life and Character of Ali Pacha*, tr. W. Walton (London, 1816), p. 267.

17. G. A. Makrēs and S. P. Papageōrgiou, *To chersaio diktuo epikoinōnias sto kratos tou Alē Pasa Tepelenlē: enischusē tēs kentrikēs exousias kai apopeira dēmiourgias eniaias agoras* (Athens, 1990), p. 65 (Souli, Delvinë, Himarë); M. Gjoni, *Bregdeti dhe Ali Pashë Tepelena* (Sarandë, 2006), pp. 24-6 (Delvinë, Himarë).

18. S. N. Naçi, *Pashallëku i Shkodrës nën sundimin e Bushatllive në gjysmën e dytë të shekullit të XVIII (1757–1796)* (Tirana, 1964), pp. 229–30 (Ohrid). However, Ali's eldest son, Muhtar, would be made governor of the Ohrid *sancak* in the year 1796-7: see H. Sezer, 'Tepedelenli Ali Paşa'nın oğulları', *Tarih araştırmaları dergisi*, vol. 17, no. 28, for 1995 (1996), pp. 155–64, at p. 156.

19. Makrēs and Papageōrgiou, *To chersaio diktuo*, p. 65 (Arta); Gjoni, *Bregdeti dhe Ali Pashë*, pp. 32-50 (Delvinë, Himarë).

20. Holland, *Travels*, p. 449; Arsh, ed., *Ē Rōsia kai ta pasalikia*, pp. 211-18 (L. Benaki report, 23 Sept./5 Oct. 1810), at p. 212.

21. Holland, *Travels*, p. 85 (exports); Archives du Ministère des Affaires Étrangères, Paris (hereafter: 'AMAE'), Correspondance politique, Îles Ioniennes, 18 (microfilm P 14343) (July 1811–March 1812), fos. 4r–15r (Lesseps report, 6 July 1812), fo. 6r (customs).

22. For the routes see the map in Makrēs and Papageōrgiou, *To chersaio diktuo*, p. 134. After his suppression of Himarë Ali was able to use the small ports of Porto Palermo and Sarandë, but these were ill-served by land routes into the interior.

23. A. Boppe, *L'Albanie et Napoléon (1797–1814)* (Paris, 1914), pp. 6-8; I. Ushtelenca, *Diplomacia e Ali Pashë Tepelenës (1786–1822)* (Tirana, 1996), pp. 44-5.

24. N. Bonaparte, *Correspondance générale*, ed. T. Lantz et al., 15 vols. (Paris, 2004–18), i, p. 1,275 (10 Nov.) ('Vous avez très bien fait, citoyen général, de vous refuser aux prétentions d'Ali-Pacha. Tout en l'empêchant d'empiéter sur ce qui nous appartient, vous devez cependant le favoriser autant qu'il sera en vous. Il est de l'intérêt de la République que ce pacha acquière un grand accroissement, batte tous ses rivaux, afin qu'il puisse devenir un prince assez conséquent pour pouvoir rendre des services à la République. Les établissements que nous avons sont si près de lui, qu'il n'est jamais possible qu'il puisse cesser d'avoir intérêt d'être notre ami. Envoyez des officiers du génie et d'état-major auprès de lui, afin de vous rendre en état de la situation, de la population et des coutumes de toute l'Albanie; faites faire des descriptions géographiques, topographiques de toute cette partie si intéressante aujourd'hui pour nous, depuis l'Albanie jusqu'à la Morée; et faites en sorte d'être bien instruit de toutes les intrigues qui divisent ces peuples').

25. Ibid., i, p. 1,119 (16 Aug.) ('C'est en vain que nous voudrions soutenir l'Empire de Turquie; nous verrons sa chute de nos jours...Le fanatisme de la liberté, qui déjà commence à aborder en Grèce, y sera plus puissant que le fanatisme religieux').

26. See S. J. Shaw, *Between Old and New: The Ottoman Empire under Sultan Selim III, 1789-1807* (Cambridge, MA, 1971), pp. 245-6.

27. A. de Beauchamp, *The Life of Ali Pacha, of Jannina, Late Vizier of Epirus, Surnamed Aslan, or the Lion, Including a Compendious History of Modern Greece*, 2nd edn. (London, 1823), pp. 94–101; Boppe, *L'Albanie et Napoléon*, pp. 9–19; Ushtelenca, *Diplomacia e Ali Pashës*, pp. 46–55. In the epic poem about Ali's life written by his secretary and counsellor Haxhi Shehret, it is claimed that Roze had been trying to organize a revolt in Çamëri in Ali's absence: I. Koçollari, ed. and tr., *Alipashaida e Haxhi Shehretit* (Tirana, 1997), pp. 208–20.

28. de Beauchamp, *Life of Ali Pacha*, p. 100 (French prisoners); Cambridge University, Classics Faculty Archive, Leake papers, Notebook 22 (unpaginated), after entry for 20 July 1809 ('the heads…'). The *kaymakam* was the vizier who deputized for the Grand Vizier in his absence.

29. It arrived at Cythera on 9 Oct. and conquered Zakynthos on 24 Oct.; on this fleet's Ionian campaign see R. C. Anderson, *Naval Wars in the Levant, 1559–1853* (Liverpool, 1952), pp. 367–71.

30. On the Potemkin episode see K. Prifti et al., eds., *Historia e popullit shqiptar*, 4 vols. (Tirana, 2000), i, p. 641; Arsh, ed., *Ē Rōsia kai ta pasalikia*, pp. 211–18 (L. Benaki, report of 23 Sept./5 Oct. 1810), at p. 213.

31. Remérand, *Ali de Tébélen*, pp. 62–3; Ushtelenca, *Diplomacia e Ali Pashës*, pp. 57–9.

32. For the text of the convention see C. P. de Bosset, *Proceedings in Parga and the Ionian Islands* (London, 1819), pp. 84–8; for the juggling see K. Şakul, 'Ottoman Attempts to Control the Adriatic Frontier in the Napoleonic War', in A. C. S. Peacock, ed., *The Frontiers of the Ottoman World* (Oxford, 2009), pp. 253–70. Of Butrint William Leake would write in 1805 that it was 'now held by Ali Pasha, who maintains a Garrison of twenty Albanians, and refuses to resign the place till he is repaid the expences of the garrison, since the time he expelled the French. He enjoys in the mean time the profits of the fisheries, pasture land and Woods which he farms of the Porte for about Fifteen Purses a year': The National Archives, Kew (hereafter: 'TNA'), FO 78/57, fos. 98r–112v (Leake, report to Lord Mulgrave, 22 Aug. 1805), at fo. 104r. One purse was 500 piastres (cf. above, n. 8).

33. Ushtelenca, *Diplomacia e Ali Pashës*, pp. 65–6 (recruitment plan, Russian hostility); G. Glover, *Fighting Napoleon: The Recollections of Lieutenant John Hildebrand, 35th Foot, in the Mediterranean and Waterloo Campaigns* (Barnsley, 2016), p. 86(n.) (Villette); İ. Demir, 'Tepedelenli Ali Pasha and the West: A History of his Relations with France and Great Britain, 1798–1820', MA thesis, Bilkent University, Ankara (2007), p. 78(n.) (Sultan's order, dated Ş 1214 [= Feb. 1800 in the Ottoman Malî calendar]).

34. C. I. Chessell, 'Britain's Ionian Consul: Spiridion Foresti and Intelligence Collection (1793–1805)', *Journal of Mediterranean Studies*, 16 (2006), pp. 45–61, at pp. 47–8. I use here the form of his name that was commonly used in the English documents.

35. BL, MS Add. 34,946, fo. 193r ('Jam aliis ad te litteris meis amorem meum erga celeberrimam nationem tuam exhibui; nihilominus etiam omnia mandata consulum vestr[or]um accuratissime citissimeque adimplevi non minus legatique vestri', 'maneo amicus tu[u]s perpetuus, fidelis sincerusque').

36. Cf. de Beauchamp, *Life of Ali Pacha*, pp. 101–2: 'Lord Nelson, when in the Aegean Sea, despatched one of his officers to compliment him upon his victory at Preveza'. Years later the French representative at Ali's court, François de Pouqueville, would write that after Preveza Nelson sent Ali a letter of congratulations, and a cannon, followed

by several emissaries: AMAE, Correspondance consulaire et commerciale (hereafter: CCC), Janina 5, no. 166 (29 Oct. 1812), at p. [2]. On Strane see D. Wilson, 'List of British Consular Officials in the Ottoman Empire and its Former Territories, from the Sixteenth Century to about 1860', http://www.levantineheritage.com/pdf/List_of_British_Consular_Officials_Turkey(1581–1860)-D_Wilson.pdf, p. 28.

37. BL, MS Add. 34,916, fos. 114r–115r (translation of letter from Ioannina, 4/16 Jan. 1800; the original is in BL, MS Add. 34,947, fo. 240r ('de laudatissimis tuis factis contra communem inimicum', 'post initam societatem inter meum imperatorem et regem tuum', 'vix quidem possum me retinere, quin iterum excellentiae tuae zelum reverentiamque meam erga illustrissimam tuam nationem omnimodo manifestem; utut eadem ostendi illustrissimo milord Hoken, qui in meis regionibus…peregrinator…cum quo locutus sum de diversis et quidem de hodiernis circumstantiis', 'promptitudinem meam pollicituros, qua ut bonus vicinus possim ipsi utilis esse', 'e parte autem mea quidquid in mea potestate sit et vobis utile, illud denegaturum nunquam invenio' 'gladius inauratus laboris [hujatis?] slopetum ejusdem laboris, et amphoreum argenteum pro aqua, quae omnia sunt producta nostrae regionis, quaeque etsi simplicia, tamen quia a sincero amico mittuntur, acceptanda sunt')). For Foresti's contacts with Nelson, from early 1799 onwards, see N. H. Nicolas, ed., *The Dispatches and Letters of Vice Admiral Lord Viscount Nelson*, 7 vols. (London, 1845–6), vols. iii–vi, *passim*.

38. BL, MS 34,919, fos. 79r–81r. The full text is printed in Baggally, *Ali Pasha and Great Britain*, pp. 85–9.

39. See (for the case of Lefkada), P. G. Rontogiannēs, *Istoria tēs nēsou Leukados*, 2 vols. (Athens, 1982), ii, pp. 108–29.

40. Arsh, *Albaniia i Epir*, pp. 206–10.

41. A. M. Stanislavskaia, *Russko-Angliiskie otnosheniia i problemi Sredizemnomoria, 1798–1807* (Moscow, 1962), pp. 292 (petitions), 310–11 (corps); Ushtelenca, *Diplomacia e Ali Pashës*, p. 81 (alliance). Lord Aberdeen noted that 'upwards of 1200' Souliots (more than a third of their entire population) had come to Corfu by early Jan. 1804: British Museum, London, Department of Greek and Roman Antiquities, Aberdeen diary, vol. 1, fo. 137r.

42. Ibid., p. 293. Lt.-Gen. Laurent de Gouvion Saint-Cyr was sent to Naples in May 1803 to command part of the army there under Murat. Despite Ali's anti-French actions in 1798, Napoleon had ordered Murat in Feb. 1801 to write to Ali assuring him 'that I have maintained my friendly feelings for him', and three months later had told Talleyrand to send an officer on a mission to Ioannina 'to find out what position this prince is taking and whether he is inclined to favour an uprising in Greece' (Bonaparte, *Correspondance générale*, iii, pp. 577 ('que j'ai conservé de l'amitié pour lui'), 695–6 ('pour connaître les dispositions de ce prince et s'il est disposé à favoriser un mouvement en Grèce')). There is no evidence that this mission was carried out.

43. TNA, FO 78/57, fos. 20r–23v, Leake to G. Hammond (16 Nov. 1803); T. Arsov, *Marbles and Politics: William Martin Leake's Missions in the Ottoman Balkans, 1799–1810* (Istanbul, 2010), pp. 44–5.

44. See H. McKenzie Johnston, *Ottoman and Persian Odysseys: James Morier, Creator of Hajji Baba of Ispahan, and His Brothers* (London, 1998), pp. 1–6, 13–19, 27–50.

45. TNA, FO 78/44, fos. 3r–8v (instructions to Morier), at fos. 4v–5r, 6r.

46. Balliol College Archives, Oxford, MS Morier E1, file 1, no. 27 (D. Morier to I. Morier, from Ioannina, 26 June 1804), fo. [1r].

47. TNA, FO 78/44, fos. 79r–82v (J. P. Morier to Hawkesbury, from Ioannina, 30 June 1804), at fos. 79r–v, 80v–81r.

48. TNA, FO 78/57, fos. 50r–53r (Leake to Harrowby, from HMS *Victory*, off Cape St Sebastian, 5 Oct. 1804), at fos. 51v–52r. Ali also requested a small ship. Nelson reacted favourably, writing on 16 Apr. to Lord Hobart that 'Of this we can be sure, that if we do not give him the two Artillery-men and the Vessel, the French will': Nicolas, ed., *Dispatches and Letters of Nelson*, v, p. 499.

49. TNA, FO 78/44, fos. 79v–80v.

50. TNA, FO 78/44, fos. 81v–82r.

51. Ibid., fos. 84r–92v (J. P. Morier to Hawkesbury, from Ioannina, 30 June 1804), at fo. 91r–v.

52. Ibid., fo. 86r.

53. Ibid., fos. 94r–103r (J. P. Morier to Harrowby, from Athens, 31 July 1804), at fos. 96v–97r (Çams), 101r–102v (retraction, most likely place).

54. TNA, FO 78/57, fos. 39r–44r (instructions to Leake, July 1804), at fos. 40v–41r. On Leake see J. H. Marsden, *A Brief Memoir of the Life and Writings of the late Lieutenant-Colonel William Martin Leake* (London, 1864); Sh. Hoxha, *Kontributi i Uilljëm Martin Likut në fushën e studimeve albanologjike* (Prishtinë, 2007); Arsov, *Marbles and Politics*.

55. TNA, FO 78/57, fos. 50r–53r (Leake to Harrowby, from the Victory, off Cape St Sebastian, 5 Oct. 1804), at fos. 51v–52v. On Nelson's relations with Foresti see Chessell, 'Britain's Ionian Consul', pp. 56–7. That Foresti was supportive of Ali was a fact known to the Russians, who accused him of informing Ali about everything they did on the islands: Arsh, *Albaniia i Epir*, p. 212.

56. W. M. Leake, *Travels in Northern Greece*, 4 vols. (London, 1835), i, pp. 8–36.

57. TNA, FO 78/57, fos. 58–60r (Leake to Harrowby, from Corfu, 21 Jan. 1805), at fo. 59r; Nicolas, ed., *Dispatches and Letters of Nelson*, v, p. 270 (Nelson to S. Foresti, 22 Oct. 1803).

58. TNA, FO 78/47, fos. 28r–31v (Leake to J. P. Morier, for the British Government, from Corfu, 19 Jan. 1805), at fos. 28r–29r.

59. TNA, FO 78/47, fos. 29r–31v.

60. TNA, FO 78/44, fos. 122r–127r (instructions, 19 Oct. 1804), at fos. 123v–126v.

61. TNA, FO 78/47, fos. 39r–44r (Morier to Harrowby, from Corfu, 28 Jan. 1805), at fos. 39v–43r.

62. Stanislavskaia, *Russko-Angliiskie otnosheniia*, pp. 327–8.

63. TNA, FO 78/57, fos. 72r–74v (Leake to Harrowby, from Tripolitsa, 8 Mar. 1805), at fo. 72r (Leake); Balliol College Archives, Oxford, MS Morier E1, file 2, no. 6 (D. Morier to C. Morier, from Ioannina, 18 Feb. 1805), fo. [1r] (Morier).

64. TNA, FO 78/47, fos. 60r–78r (Morier to Harrowby, from Ioannina, 26 Feb. 05), at fos. 60r–62r, 65v–69v. The request to transport the Souliots was anti-Russian insofar as it involved removing the fighters recruited by Russia on Corfu; but the idea had actually been suggested by the Russian Consul at Arta, a Greek in long-standing Russian service called Geōrgios Phlōrēs (generally referred to as George Flory) in a meeting with Ali in Jan. 1805. Flory said that the Souliots had been allowed to go to the Ionian

Islands by the Ottoman government, so Ali must take up the issue at Istanbul, but that he (Flory) would be happy if they could be permanently transported to a distant Russian colony. He told Mocenigo that Greeks generally would warm to the idea of Russia giving sanctuary to Greek refugees. See Arsh, ed., *Ē Rōsia kai ta pasalikia*, pp. 24–5 (on Flory), 142–3 (his proposal).

65. TNA, FO 78/47, fos. 70r–72r. The advice clearly made some impression, as Ali Pasha told George Flory about it in April. Ali complained that Russia was now dictating British policy; but Flory reported to the Russian government that Morier was undermining Russian policy, by trying to reduce the chances of a Greek uprising against Ali. See Arsh, *Ē Alvania kai ē Ēpeiros*, pp. 377, 380. The bishop was the Metropolitan of Arta, who had become Ali's close adviser.

66. TNA, FO 78/47, fos. 72v–75v. (For the value of a 'purse' see above, n. 32.)

67. Ibid., fos. 93r–101v (J. P. Morier to Lord Harrowby, from Corfu, 8 Apr. 1805), at fos. 93v–101r; fo. 105r (enclosure, list of ammunition).

68. Ibid., fos. 121r–122r (J. P. Morier to Lord Nelson, from Corfu, 8 Apr. 1805).

69. Ibid., fos. 181r–184v (J. P. Morier to Arbuthnot, from Ioannina, 20 June 1805), at fos. 181v–183r.

70. Ibid., fos. 203–204r (J. P. Morier to Mulgrave, from Ioannina, 31 July 1805), at fo. 203r. He added (fo. 203r–v) that 'The family of Botchari, one of the Sulliote chiefs, still remains in his hands, and will probably be kept to answer for the good behavior of that Chief, who is at Sta Maura [*sc.* Lefkada].'

71. TNA FO 78/53, fos. 3r–4v (J. P. Morier to Ali, from Salonica, 25 Oct. 1805), at fos. 3v–4r.

72. TNA, FO 78/57, fos. 98r–112v (Leake to Mulgrave, from Ioannina, 22 Aug. 1805), fos. 98r–v (travels, map), 101v (Preveza), 107v–110r (passes), 111r–112r (Greek peasants, 12,000 men, larger force). For his arrival on 28 June see Balliol College Archives, Oxford, MS Morier E1, file 2, no. 23 (D. Morier to C. Morier, from Ioannina, 27 and 29 June 1805), fo. [1v].

73. TNA, FO 78/47, fos. 93r–101v (J. P. Morier to Harrowby, from Corfu, 8 Apr. 1805), at fo. 100r; ibid., fos. 209r–211r, (J. P. Morier to Lord Mulgrave, from Ioannina, 18 Sept. 1805), at fo. 209r.

74. S. N. Naçi, *Pashallëku i Shkodrës ne vitet e para të shek. XIX (1796–1831)* (Tirana, 1986), pp. 38–41.

75. Leake, *Travels in Northern Greece*, i, p. 1.

76. TNA, FO 78/47, fos. 212r–219r (J. P. Morier to Mulgrave, from Salonica, 17 Oct. 1805), fo. 215r–v (inheritance of Berat, erosion). On his relationship with Ali see S. P. Papageorgiou, 'The Attitude of the Beys of the Albanian Southern Provinces (Toskaria) towards Ali Pasha Tepedelenli and the Sublime Porte (mid-18th–mid-19th centuries): The Case of "der'e madhe" of the Beys of Valona', *Cahiers balkaniques*, 42 (2014), pp. 1–34, at pp. 11–14. On the two sons see Sezer, 'Tepedelenli Ali Paşa'nın oğulları', pp. 155–8.

77. TNA, FO 78/47, fos. 177r–178v (J. P. Morier to Mulgrave, from Corfu, 21 May 1805), at 177r (report of taking of Elbasan); Arsh, *Albaniia i Epir*, pp. 224–5.

78. TNA, FO 78/47, fos. 209r–211r (J. P. Morier to Mulgrave, from Ioannina, 18 Sept. 1805), at fos. 209v–210r; Naçi, *Pashallëku i Shkodrës (1796–1831)*, pp. 45–6.

79. TNA, FO 78/57, fos. 128r–131r (Leake to Mulgrave, from Ioannina, 7 Nov. 1805), at fos. 129v, 130r.

80. See Arsov, *Marbles and Politics*, pp. 57–63.

81. TNA, FO 78/57, fos. 138r–143v (W. Leake to Mulgrave, from Tripolitsa, 11 Mar. 1806), at fos. 140v–141v.

82. On the negotiations see Shaw, *Between Old and New*, pp. 333–4; on the contacts with the Serbs, see L. Demény, 'Relaţiile ruso-sîrbe în anii 1806–1812', in E. Stănescu, ed., *Studii istorice sud-est europene*, vol. 1 (Bucharest, 1974), pp. 127–57, at pp. 133–7.

83. Shaw, *Between Old and New*, pp. 334–5 (diplomatic offensive), 344–5 (Sébastiani, agents), 349 (Sébastiani).

84. Boppe, *L'Albanie et Napoléon*, pp. 28–31 (Bessières 1798); AMAE, CCC, Janina 1 (microfilm 15536), unfoliated, Bessières, 'Note sur l'Albanie & sur Ali-Pacha', p. [2], 'se faire declarer souverain de l'Albanie, et obtenir la Cession de l'Egypte [à] la France, qui, pour reconnaître ce service, [aurait] garanti son independence'; H. Dehérain, 'Une correspondance inédite de François Pouqueville, consul de France à Janina et à Patras', *Revue de l'histoire des colonies françaises*, 9 (1921), no. 2, pp. 61–100, at pp. 62–5 (Pouqueville up to 1805); D. Iliadou, 'Le cas Pouqueville (1770–1838)', in I. A. Papigkē et al., *Meletēmata stē mnēmē Vasileiou Laourda: Essays in Memory of Basil Laourdas* (Salonica, 1975), pp. 425–48, at pp. 425–7 (Pouqueville up to 1805).

85. AMAE, CCC, Janina 1 (microfilm 15536), unfoliated, note to Bessières, 13 Sept. 1805, pp. [2–3] ('Mais ce qui importe à la France, c'est qu'[il] y ait une Puissance Musulmane en Europe, et que les sujets de la Porte ne vendent pas leur pays à des Etrangers').

86. Ibid., Bessières report to Talleyrand, undated, pp. [5] ('J'espere à Present que l'Empereur des français me protegera, comme le Reste de ses sujets, et alors je ne craindrais plus les intrigues des Russes, et je regarderai mon Existance politique comme parfaitement assurée'), [13] ('Mon souverain et Mon Maitre'), [14] (Corfu offer, 'mon independance sera assurée, et j'espere qu'il me placera au Rang des souverains de l'Europe').

87. Ibid., Bessières report to Talleyrand, undated, pp. [12, 14] (60,000); Pouqueville report no. 13, to Talleyrand, from Ioannina, 21 Apr. 1806, p. [3] (plan).

88. TNA, FO 78/53, fos. 21r–27r (J. P. Morier to Fox, from Ioannina, 25 Apr. 1806), at fo. 21r (change of plans); Balliol College Archives, Oxford, MS Morier E1, file 3, no. 18 (D. Morier to C. Morier, 20 Apr. 1806) (heatwave).

89. Bonaparte, *Correspondance générale*, vi, p. 527 (Napoleon to Talleyrand, 19 June 1806); AMAE, CCC, Janina 1 (microfilm 15536), unfoliated, Talleyrand to Pouqueville, 21 June 1806.

90. TNA, FO 78/53, fos. 21r–27v (1st conversation), at fos. 22r–23v (Pouqueville), 25r ('for the…'); 28r–36v (J. P. Morier to Fox, from Ioannina, 27 Apr. 1806) (2nd conversation), at fos. 28v (complaint), 28r–v (Corfu), 33v (three demands).

91. On Flory see above, n. 64.

92. Arsh, ed., *Ē Rōsia kai ta pasalikia*, pp. 155–68 (Flory report, from Corfu, 16 May 1806), at pp. 159–65 ('je tâchais les amuser en attendant quelque amélioration, et le dénoûment [sic] des circonstances politiques', 'Je suis Musulman, mais je ne suis point fanatique; j'abhorre mon Divan et son administration; je sens sa décadence, et je prévois sa chute. Je désire vivre avec honneur dans ce petit district où je commande, et mourir homme en place', 'J'en serai fâché et obligé de tourner ailleurs mes

dispositions. Tout le monde est en guerre, je me formerai sans doute un parti, je ne vous dis pas d'avantage'); pp. 168–70 (Flory, accompanying letter), at p. 169.

93. TNA, FO 78/53, fos. 46r–56r (J. P. Morier to Fox, from Ioannina, 4 June 1806), at fo. 48v ('source of…'); fos. 75r–85r (D. Morier to J. P. Morier, from Corfu, 22 May 1806), at fo. 80v (liar). 'Rayah' (*reaya*) was an Ottoman term for peasant subjects of the Sultan, especially Christian ones.

94. TNA, FO 78/53, fo. 122r–v (J. P. Morier to Fox, from Ioannina, 10 June 1806), at fo. 122r.

95. TNA, FO 78/57, fos. 151r–153v (Leake to Fox, from Corfu, 16 June 1806), at fo. 151v (Kotor visit); fos. 155r–158v (Leake to C. J. Fox, from Corfu, 18 June 1806), at fo. 157v ('invade Turkey…').

96. Arsov, *Marbles and Politics*, pp. 61–2; TNA, FO 78/53, fos. 124r–125v, 132r–v, 134r (J. P. Morier reports to Fox, from Patras, 14 July, Trikala, 27 Sept., and Patras, 17 Oct. 1806 respectively).

97. Baggally, *Ali Pasha*, pp. 23–7; Shaw, *Between Old and New*, pp. 349–53.

98. A. Aspinall, ed., *The Correspondence of Charles Arbuthnot*, Camden ser. 3, vol. 65 (London, 1941), pp. 1–5 (Arbuthnot to unidentified correspondent, from Cholmondeley Castle, 11 Oct. 1808), at p. 4.

99. Shaw, *Between Old and New*, pp. 357–9; Haus-, Hof- und Staatsarchiv, Vienna (hereafter: 'HHStA'), Türkei VI, 1, 1st foliation, fos. 52r–53r (von Stürmer report, from Istanbul, 27 Feb. 1807) at fo. 53r (demands, 'D'après mes notions la Porte Ottomanne seroit assez disposée à souscrire à ces conditions, mais elle ne sait comment s'y prendre pour calmer l'enthousiasme du peuple, qui est en masse sous les armes'); fos. 56r–61v (von Stürmer report, from Istanbul, 10 Mar. 1807), at fo. 57r ('quelques Bombes jettées au hazard'). On Sébastiani organizing the defence, see E. Driault, *La Politique orientale de Napoléon: Sébastiani et Gardane, 1806-1808* (Paris, 1904), pp. 89–110.

100. Aspinall, ed., *Correspondence of Arbuthnot*, p. 2.

101. Shaw, *Between Old and New*, pp. 345–8; A. F. Miller, *Mustapha Pacha Baïraktar* (Bucharest, 1975), pp. 124–31; A. Yaycioglu, *Partners of the Empire: The Crisis of the Ottoman Order in the Age of Revolutions* (Stanford, CA, 2016), pp. 163–5, 168–9.

102. AMAE, CCC, Janina 1 (microfilm 15536), unfoliated, Bessières report to Talleyrand, p. [7] ('une parfaite intelligence'); Miller, *Mustapha Pacha*, p. 126 (agreement).

103. AMAE, CCC, Janina 1 (microfilm 15536), unfoliated, Pouqueville reports from Ioannina, nos. 32 (18 Sept. 1806) (Paramythia), 38 (5 Oct. 1806) (pashas).

104. Ibid., Pouqueville reports from Ioannina, nos. 43 (25 Nov. 1806) (Russian ambassador, 10,000 men, three targets), 44 (11 Dec. 1806) (Sultan's blessing); Ushtelenca, *Diplomacia e Ali Pashës*, p. 103.

105. Ushtelenca, *Diplomacia e Ali Pashës*, pp. 105–7; on the French help see Boppe, *L'Albanie et Napoléon*, pp. 64–70.

106. S. J. Shaw and E. K. Shaw, *History of the Ottoman Empire and Modern Turkey*, 2 vols. (Cambridge, 1976), i, pp. 273–4.

107. Ushtelenca, *Diplomacia e Ali Pashës*, p. 106.

108. Bonaparte, *Correspondance générale*, vii, p. 837 (Napoleon to J. Bonaparte, from Finkenstein, 27 May 1807) ('Le pacha de Janina est ennemi des Russes, mais cet homme est faux. Il n'y a pas d'inconvénient que vous lui ayez envoyé quelques

secours; mais il ne faut pas pousser cela trop loin, il suffit de belles paroles'). The particular reason for Napoleon's judgement is not clear; most probably, French intelligence had obtained copies of some English despatches reporting Ali's pledges of Anglophilia.

109. See G. de Vaudoncourt, *Memoirs of the Ionian Islands, considered in a Commercial, Political, and Military Point of View... including the Life and Character of Ali Pacha*, tr. W. Walton (London, 1816), pp. 253–4; Arsh, *Ē Alvania kai ē Ēpeiros*, p. 413(n.).

110. Boppe, *L'Albanie et Napoléon*, pp. 74–6, 82–3.

111. Shaw, *Between Old and New*, pp. 388–9.

112. Ushtelenca, *Diplomacia e Ali Pashës*, pp. 111–12 (message from Tilsit); J.-J. Tromelin, 'Itinéraire d'un voyage fait dans la Turquie d'Europe... dans l'automne de 1807', *Revue des études napoléoniennes*, year 6, vol. 12 (July–Dec. 1917), pp. 344–81; year 7, vol. 13 (Jan.–June 1918), pp. 96–124 (report).

113. Ushtelenca, *Diplomacia e Ali Pashës*, pp. 112–13; I. Ushtelenca, *Rregjimenti shqiptar i Napoleon Bonapartit në Korfuz* (Tirana, 2007), p. 21 (regiment); Bonaparte, *Correspondance générale*, vii, p. 1,183 (Napoleon to Clarke, from Fontainebleau, 12 Oct. 1807) ('qu'il doit beaucoup ménager Ali-Pacha; qu'il est absurde de mettre en doute si je dois lui céder ou non Parga; que ce n'est pas à mes généraux à rien céder... Recommandez-lui de ne pas être dupe de la finesse d'Ali-Pacha et de ne se permettre aucune négociation diplomatique').

114. V. Panagiōtopoulos, D. Dēmētropoulos and P. Michaēlarēs, eds., *Archeio Alē Pasa Sullogēs I. Chōtzē Gennadeiou Vivliothēkēs tēs Amerikanēs Scholēs Athēnōn*, 4 vols. (Athens, 2007), i, pp. 622–3 (Berthier to Ali, from Corfu, 3 Dec. 1807).

115. HHStA, Türkei VI, 1, 4th foliation, fos. 1r–7v (Stürmer report from Istanbul, 6 Nov. 1807), at fo. 2r.

116. Ibid., 3rd foliation, fos. 1r–9r (Stürmer report, from Istanbul, 10 Aug. 1807) (shock); 38r–47v (Testa report, from Istanbul, 8 Sept. 1807), at fos. 40v–41r (Ionian Islands); 85r–88r (Stürmer report, from Istanbul, 25 Oct. 1807), at fo. 85r (territorial fears).

117. Sir Augustus Paget, ed., *The Paget Papers: Diplomatic and Other Correspondence of the Right Hon. Sir Arthur Paget*, 2 vols. (London, 1896), ii, pp. 291–375.

118. Ibid., ii, pp. 322–3 (G. Canning to Paget, from London, 14 Aug. 1807) ('to ascertain...'), 370 (Paget report, from the Dardanelles, 8 Oct. 1807) (intercession); Arsov, *Marbles and Politics*, pp. 65–7 (detention, release).

119. Hertfordshire Archives and Local Studies, Hertford (hereafter: HALS), MS Leake 85499 (Paget to Leake, from the Dardanelles, 19 Oct. 1807), fos. [1v–2r].

120. Cambridge University, Classics Faculty Archive, Leake papers, Notebook 18 (unpaginated), entries for 6 Nov. 1807 ('in a...'), 12 Nov. 1807 ('to my...'; Leake also noted that Ali described the French as 'atheists and not Christians' ('apistoi & ochi christianoi')); TNA, FO 78/57, fos. 191r–202r (Leake to G. Canning, from HMS *Delight*, 18 Nov. 1807), at fos. 192r–194r; fo. 205r–v is a copy of Leake's letter to Ali (in Greek) from Sarandë.

121. TNA, FO 78/57, fos. 194v–199r.

122. Ibid., fos. 214r–217r (Leake to Collingwood, from Messina, 20 Nov. 1807), at fos. 214r–215v.

123. Ibid., fos. 211r–212v (Leake to G. Canning, from Siracusa, 10 Dec. 1807), at fos. 211r–212r.

124. G. L. Newnham Collingwood, ed., *A Selection from the Public and Private Correspondence of Vice-Admiral Lord Collingwood: Interspersed with Memoirs of his Life*, 4th edn. (London, 1829), pp. 320–1 (Collingwood to Lord Castlereagh, from HMS *Ocean*, at Siracusa, 9 Dec. 1807), at p. 321; pp. 322–3 (Collingwood to Ali, from HMS *Ocean*, at Siracusa, 9 Dec. 1807), at p. 323.

125. Centre des Archives Diplomatiques, Nantes (hereafter: 'CAD'), Janina, consulat, 290PO/1/3, p. 1 (Pouqueville to de Champagny, from Ioannina, 11 Jan. 1808); pp. 17–19 (Pouqueville to de Champagny, from Ioannina, 6 Feb. 1808), at p. 18; p. 119 (Pouqueville to de Champagny, from Preveza, 8 May 1808).

126. G. Siorokas, 'O Alē Pasas kai oi autokratorikoi Galloi tēs Eptanēsou (nea stoicheia apo to anekdoto archeio tou C. Berthier)', *Dōdōnē: epistēmonikē epetēris tēs Philosophikēs Scholēs tou Panepistēmiou Iōanninōn*, 3 (1974), pp. 273–334, at pp. 322–4 (Ali to Berthier, from Ioannina, 23 Jan. 1808), pp. 322 ('to empodion tōn trophōn apo touta ta merē eis ta nēsia') 323 ('einai adunaton na paraitēsō tēn proskolēsin mou eis tous Frantzezous kai na zētō tēn philian ekeinōn, opou einai echthroi tou vasileiou mou'). A month later Berthier would again complain to Ali about his failure to respond to a request for food, including 600 head of cattle: Panagiōtopoulos, Dēmētropoulos, and Michaēlarēs, eds., *Archeio Alē Pasa*, i, pp. 679–80 (Berthier to Ali, from Corfu, 24 Feb. 1808).

127. Boppe, *L'Albanie et Napoléon*, p. 94.

128. Bonaparte, *Correspondance générale*, viii, pp. 40–1 (Napoleon to de Champagny, from Paris, 12 Jan. 1808), at p. 41; pp. 139–40 (Napoleon to J. Bonaparte, from Paris, 8 Feb. 1808), at p. 140 ('Vous devez considérer Corfou comme plus important que la Sicile…Souvenez-vous bien de ce mot: dans la situation actuelle de l'Europe, le plus grand malheur qui puisse m'arriver est la perte de Corfou').

129. Miller, *Mustapha pacha*, pp. 255–6 (Sébastiani, *divan*); Panagiōtopoulos, Dēmētropoulos, and Michaēlarēs, eds., *Archeio Alē Pasa*, i, pp. 624–5 (Razēs to Kōstas the grammatikos, for Ali, from Istanbul, 8 Dec. 1807), at p. 624 (payments to Halet).

130. HHStA, Türkei VI, 1, 5th foliation, fos. 77r–84v (Stürmer report, 11 Mar. 1808), at fos. 78v–79r ('Il m'a été assuré en confiance, que la Porte ne cherche qu'à amuser Sebastiani, et qu'elle est très décidée à n'acquiescer à aucune de ses demandes'); Miller, *Mustapha pacha*, p. 256 (instruction to official).

131. HHStA, Türkei VI, 4th foliation, fos. 93r–103v (Stürmer report, 24 Dec. 1808), at fo. 104v (Napoleon); G. Siorokas, 'Scheseis tōn Gallōn me to pasaliki tou Mperatiou (1807–1808)', *Dōdōnē: epistēmonikē epetēris tēs Philosophikēs Scholēs tou Panepistēmiou Iōanninōn*, 4 (1975), pp. 349–76, at pp. 371–2 (G. Liperakēs to C. Berthier, from Berat, 22 Feb. 1808) (p. 371: couriers).

132. Boppe, *L'Albanie et Napoléon*, p. 95; I. Ushtelenca, *Shteti dhe qeverisja e Ali Pashë Tepelenës* (Tirana, 2009), p. 109(n.).

133. Panagiōtopoulos, Dēmētropoulos, and Michaēlarēs, eds., *Archeio Alē Pasa*, i, pp. 622–3 (Berthier to Ali, from Corfu, 3 Dec. 1807), at p. 622; Bonaparte, *Correspondance générale*, viii, pp. 104–5 (Napoleon to Berthier, from Paris, 29 Jan. 1808), at p. 105 ('mon intention est que vous en prenez sur-le-champ possession pour fortifier le cap et y établir une bonne batterie').

134. Panagiōtopoulos, Dēmētropoulos, and Michaēlarēs, eds., *Archeio Alē Pasa*, i, pp. 675–7 (Bessières to Ali, from Corfu, 3 Mar. 1808), at p. 676; 690–2 (Berthier to Ali, 18 Mar. 1808), at p. 690; 699–700 (Bessières to Ali, from Corfu, 18 Mar. 1808), at p. 699.

135. Ibid., pp. 692–7 (Ali to Bessières, from Ioannina, 10 Mar. 1808), at p. 696 ('to Vothrōnton, tēn Pargan tēn Prevezan kai tēn Vonitzan, dia tēn diaphulaxin tōn opoiōn, kai olē ē Arvanētia einai etēmē na chusē to aima tēs').

136. CAD, Janina, consulat, 290PO/1/3, pp. 62–4 (Pouqueville to de Champagny, from Ioannina, 29 Mar. 1808), at p. 63; Pouqueville suspected (p. 64) that the letter might be fictitious.

137. Ibid., pp. 17–19 (Pouqueville to de Champagny, from Ioannina, 6 Feb. 1808), at p. 18 (arms deliveries); 29 (Pouqueville to de Gallo, for J. Bonaparte, from Ioannina, 18 Feb. 1808) (people forbidden); 73–87 (Pouqueville to Sébastiani, from Ioannina, 14 Apr. 1808), at p. 73 (house arrest). Ali also received 50 artillery pieces from Istanbul in April: Ushtelenca, *Diplomacia e Ali Pashës*, p. 138.

138. Bonaparte, *Correspondance générale*, viii, pp. 368 (Napoleon to de Champagny, from Bordeaux, 11 Apr. 1808), 660 (Napoleon to de Champagny, from Bayonne, 29 May 1808), 762 (Napoleon to de Champagny, from Bayonne, 16 June 1808) ('exciter contre Ali-Pacha les petits pachas ses voisins, qui sont mécontents de lui, et l'affaiblir de toutes les manières, en donnant des secours d'armes et d'argent, secrètement cependant, à tous ses ennemis').

139. CAD, Janina, consulat, 290PO/1/3, pp. 6 (Pouqueville to Berthier, from Ioannina, 23 Jan. 1808) (Elbasan); 30–1 (Pouqueville to de Champagny, from Ioannina, 13 Feb. 1808), at p. 30 (losing); 41–3 (Pouqueville to Berthier, from Ioannina, 19–21 Feb. 1808), at p. 42 (peace).

140. TNA, FO 78/57, fos. 191r–202r (Leake to G. Canning, from HMS *Delight*, 18 Nov. 1807), at fo. 195v ('tha polemēsomen mazu sas, tha pesomen mazu sas').

141. HHStA, Türkei VI, 1, 6th foliation, fos. 41r–42v (Stürmer report, 11 May 1808), at fo. 41r–v (referring to the pashas of Shkodër, Ioannina and Delvinë—the last being probably a slip for Vlorë/Berat).

142. Siorokas, 'Scheseis tōn Gallōn' pp. 371–2 (Liperakēs to Berthier, from Berat, 22 Feb. 1808), at pp. 369–70; 372–3 (Ibrahim to Berthier, from Berat, 21 Mar. 1808), pp. 372–3, at p. 372 ('C'est la crainte de [*sic*] peuple, qui m'empéche de vous obeir. Il est vrai qu'auparavant je fis vous croire facile le passage des troupes françoises en ce côté; mais or, en voyant toute l'Albanie allarmé par la même raison, je ne puis pas convenir contre l'opinion des [*sic*] ses barbares et des autres Vesirs').

143. TNA, FO 78/61, fo. 65r (Leake to G. Canning, from London, 1 Feb. 1808).

144. Ibid., fos. 28r–29v (D. Morier to Hammond, from Malta, 29 Jan. 1808), 30r–31r (D. Morier to G. Canning, from Malta, 12 Apr. 1808), 32r–35v (D. Morier to G. Canning, from Malta, 22 Apr. 1808).

145. Newnham Collingwood, ed., *Selection from the Correspondence of Collingwood*, pp. 370–1 (Ali to Collingwood, from Ioannina, 2 June 1808), 383–4 (Collingwood to Ali, from HMS *Ocean*, off Cadiz, 20 June 1808), 424–5 (Ali to Collingwood, from Ioannina, 2 Aug. 1808).

146. Ibid., pp. 320–1 (Collingwood to Lord Castlereagh, from HMS *Ocean*, at Siracusa, 9 Dec. 1807); cf. also Sir Robert Adair, *The Negotiations for the Peace of the Dardanelles,*

in 1808–9, 2 vols. (London, 1845), i, pp. 2–3 (Halet Pasha to Capt. Stewart, from Istanbul, 13 Feb. 1808), at p. 3.

147. TNA, FO 78/61, fos. 36r–v (D. Morier to G. Canning, from Malta, 14 May 1808), 75r–79r (Leake to G. Canning, from Malta, 26 Dec. 1808), at fo. 75v (referring to Apr. departure).

148. Adair, *Negotiations*, i, pp. 21–4 (Adair to Capt. Hervey, from Malta, 9 Sept. 1808), at pp. 21–2.

149. HALS, MS Leake 85505, endorsed 'Ali Pacha to the King', fos. [1r–2r]; printed in Marsden, *Brief Memoir*, pp. 27–8. A slightly different translation is in TNA, FO 78/61, fos. 52r–53v.

150. See Miller, *Mustapha pacha*, pp. 259–75; Yaycioglu, *Partners of the Empire*, pp. 182–7.

151. Miller, *Mustapha pacha*, pp. 259–60 (Ismail, Ali), 278 (Muhtar).

152. See ibid., pp. 278–361; Yaycioglu, *Partners of the Empire*, pp. 187–200.

153. Adair, *Negotiations*, i, pp. 13–17 (Adair to G. Canning, from Palermo, 17 Aug. 1808), at p. 14; pp. 19–21 (Adair to G. Canning, from Malta, 9 Sept. 1808), at p. 20.

154. Newnham Collingwood, ed., *Selection from the Correspondence of Collingwood*, pp. 424–5 (Ali to Collingwood, from Ioannina, 2 Aug. 1808), at p. 424; TNA, FO 78/61, fos. 75r–79r (Leake to G. Canning, from Malta, 26 Dec. 1808), at fo. 76r.

155. TNA, FO 352/1, fo. 223r (summary by S. Canning of G. Canning, message to Adair, from London, 20 Aug. 1808).

156. The quantity of artillery was reported by Pouqueville after its eventual arrival: CAD, MS Janina, consulat, 290PO/1/4, p. 119 (Pouqueville to the Foreign Minister of the Kingdom of Italy, from Ioannina, 2 Apr. 1809).

157. HALS, MS Leake 85506 (G. Canning to Leake, from London, 21 Oct. 1808), fos. [1r–3v]; printed in Marsden, *Brief Memoir*, pp. 28–31. On the shipment of arms see Arsov, *Marbles and Politics*, p. 73.

158. HALS, MS Leake 85508 (Baker to Adair, from HMS *Success*, 10 Nov. 1808), fo. [2r–v].

159. TNA, FO 78/61, fos. 55r–57r (Canning to Ali, from London, 19 Aug. 1808), at fo. 56r.

160. A. Cunningham, *Anglo-Ottoman Encounters in the Age of Revolution*, ed. E. Ingram (London, 1993), p. 158.

161. Newnham Collingwood, ed., *Selection*, pp. 482–5 (Collingwood to Mulgrave, from HMS *Ocean*, at Malta, 21 Jan. 1809), at p. 483.

162. For evidence of Ali's consistently hostile policy towards the French during 1808, see the summaries of Pouqueville's letters to the governor of Corfu in A. Mézin, *Français et ottomans en Illyrie et dans l'Adriatique au temps de Napoléon: inventaire des papiers du général Donzelot (1764–1843)* (Istanbul, 2009), pp. 88–107.

163. Newnham Collingwood, ed., *Selection*, p. 484.

164. See Adair, *Negotiations*; Cunningham, *Anglo-Ottoman Encounters*, pp. 103–43, esp. pp. 111–14; S. Richmond, *The Voice of England in the East: Stratford Canning and Diplomacy with the Ottoman Empire* (London, 2014), pp. 36–43. The negotiations remained difficult to the end. Adair finally extorted an agreement from the Ottoman representative by actually hoisting the sails of his ship on 1 Jan., in readiness to leave: FO 78/63, fos. 87r–88r (Adair to G. Canning, from the Dardanelles, 5 Jan. 1809), at fo. 87r.

165. Newnham Collingwood, ed., *Selection*, pp. 490–2 (Collingwood to Adair, from Malta, 2 Feb. 1809), at p. 490.

166. Adair, *Negotiations*, ii, pp. 129 (Adair to Ali, from the Dardanelles, 6 Jan. 1809), 131-3 (Adair to Ali, from Pera, 1 Mar 1809), at p. 133 (jumped gun—referring to a letter of 2/14 Dec. to Foresti, of which the text and translation are in TNA, FO 78/65, fos. 76r-v and 78r-79v).

167. CAD, MS Janina, consulat, 290PO/1/4, p. 64 (Pouqueville to La Tour-Maubourg, from Ioannina, 16 Feb. 1809). The official, Selim Aga, was an Englishman, a former artillery officer who had converted to Islam.

168. TNA, FO 78/61, fos. 75r-79r (Leake to Canning, from Malta, 26 Dec. 1808), at fos. 76v-78r.

169. TNA, FO 78/65, fos. 11r-14v (Leake to Canning, from Malta, 12 Feb. 1809), at fos. 13v, 14v.

170. Ibid., fos. 17r-20v (Leake to Canning, from Preveza, 6 Mar. 1809).

171. Ushtelenca, *Shteti dhe qeverisja*, p. 85. This was an improvement on his previous methods: in 1807 he had murdered three French couriers (I. Koçollari, *Policia sekrete e Ali Pashës* (Tirana, 2009), pp. 363-4).

172. Panagiōtopoulos, Dēmētropoulos and Michaēlarēs, eds., *Archeio Alē Pasa*, ii, pp. 23-4 (Bessières to Ali, from Corfu, 27 Feb. 1809), at p. 24 ('ē Ēpsiloti sou sinphoros me tous Inglezous etimazeste dia na kamnete katadromin eis tēn Parga').

173. TNA, FO 78/65, fos. 31r-34v (Leake to Adair, from Missolonghi, 23 Mar. 1809), at fo. 32v.

174. Panagiōtopoulos, Dēmētropoulos and Michaēlarēs, eds., *Archeio Alē Pasa*, ii, pp. 25-8 (Bessières to Ali, from Corfu, 13 Mar. 1809), at p. 26 ('Oi suchnes antapokrises opou ē Upsiloti sou echēs me tous Inglezous, ta dora tōn topiōn kai mparoutē kai alles paromiais polemikais etimasies opou ē Ēpsiloti sou elavetan'). This is the original retained by Ali; Leake's copy is TNA, FO 78/65, fos. 36r-37v.

175. TNA, FO 78/65, fo. 33r-v.

176. Ibid., fos. 42r-45v (Leake to Canning, from Preveza, 9 Apr. 1809), at fos. 43r-44v.

177. Newnham Collingwood, *Selection*, pp. 520-2 (Collingwood to Mulgrave, from HMS *Ville de Paris*, off Minorca, 5 May 1809), at pp. 520-1.

178. CAD, Janina, consulat, 290PO/1/4, p. 147 (Pouqueville to Donzelot and Bessières, from Arta, 22 Apr. 1809).

179. Pouqueville heard this news on the previous day: ibid., p. 146 (Pouqueville to Donzelot and Bessières, from Arta, 21 Apr. 1809). On 9 Apr. Leake had learned from Ali that the Russians were threatening to break off their peace talks on these grounds: TNA, FO 78/65, fos. 42r-45v (Leake to Canning, from Preveza, 9 Apr. 1809), at fo. 42r.

180. HALS, MSS Leake 85511 (Eyre to Leake, from HMS *Magnificent*, off Fano, 2 May 1809), at fo. [1v]; Leake 85515 (Ball to Leake, from Malta, 20 July 1809), at fo. [1v].

181. Cambridge University, Classics Faculty Archive, Leake papers, Notebook 21 (unpaginated), entry for 10 May 1809 (referring also to Ali's 'late conversations with Mr Turner upon the state of his health in which I have been the Interpreter').

182. HALS, MS Leake 85529 (Adair to Leake, from Pera, 10 Aug. 1809), at fo. [1v]; for the request see TNA, FO 78/65, fos. 98r-99v (Leake to Adair, from Ioannina, 4 July 1809), at fo. 98r.

183. See H. McKenzie Johnston, *Ottoman and Persian Odysseys*, pp. 88–105, 120–4; I. Amini, *Napoleon and Persia: Franco-Persian Relations under the First Empire* (Washington, DC, 1999), pp. 90–197.

184. HALS, MS Leake 85530 (Adair to Leake, from Pera, 16 Aug. 1809), fos. [2v–4r]. Both the claim that Jones had prevented a Russian–Persian agreement and the claim that Adair could order him to institute one were fictitious.

185. TNA, FO 78/65, fos. 53r–61v (Leake to Adair, from Preveza, 25 Apr. 1809), at fo. 54r.

186. Ibid., fos. 72r–75r (Leake to Canning, from Ioannina, 31 May 1809), at fos. 72v–73r; HALS, MSS Leake 85527 (Adair to Leake, from Pera, 24 June 1809, printed in Adair, *Negotiations*, ii, p. 175) (urged); Leake 85529 (Adair to Leake, from Pera, 10 Aug. 1809), fo. [1r] (frustrated).

187. HALS, MSS Leake 85531 (Adair to Leake, from Pera, 11 Oct. 1809), at fo. [1v]; Leake 85532 (Adair to Leake, 13 Oct. 1809), at fo. [1r].

188. Mézin, *Français et ottomans*, pp. 118 (Pouqueville to Donzelot, from Ioannina, 7 Apr. 1809), 302 (Ibrahim to Donzelot, from Berat, 31 Jan. 1809).

189. TNA, FO 78/65, fos. 63r–66v (Leake to Canning, from Ioannina, 16 May 1809), at fos. 64v–65r.

190. Ibid., fos. 68r–70v (Leake to Canning, 20 May 1809), at fos. 68v–69r.

191. See Naçi, *Pashallëku i Shkodrës (1796–1831)*, pp. 74, 78. In July Pouqueville reported that Ali was in fact trying to get his son Muhtar installed as Pasha of Shkodër: Mézin, *Français et ottomans*, p. 127 (Pouqueville to Donzelot, from Ioannina, 27 July 1809).

192. TNA, FO 78/65, fos. 113r–116r (Leake to Adair, from Ioannina, 4 Sept. 1809), at fo. 115v (peace, Çams); fos. 126r–128v (Leake to Adair, from Preveza, 30 Oct. 1809), at fo. 128r ('reprimanded him…'); CAD, Janina, consulat, 290PO/1/4, unpaginated section (Pouqueville to La Tour-Maubourg, from Ioannina, 2 Oct. 1809) (conflict resumed, grandson); Mézin, *Français et ottomans*, pp. 141 (Pouqueville to Donzelot, from Ioannina, 21 Oct. 1809) (only citadel of Berat), 313 (news report, 15 Jan. 1810, move to Vlorë).

193. Cambridge University, Classics Faculty Archive, Leake papers, Notebook 22 (unpaginated), after entry for 20 July 1809.

194. TNA, FO 78/65, fos. 68r–70v (Leake to Canning, from Ioannina, 20 May 1809), at fos. 69r–70r.

195. Ibid., fos. 117r–119v (Leake to Canning, from Ioannina, 5 Oct. 1809), at fos. 117v–118v.

196. Glover, *Fighting Napoleon*, pp. 37–9 (troops); D. Gregory, *Napoleon's Jailer: Lt. Gen. Sir Hudson Lowe: A Life* (Madison, WI, 1996), p. 64 (secrecy).

197. Newnham Collingwood, ed., *Selection*, pp. 535–9 (Collingwood to Stuart, from HMS *Ville de Paris*, off Toulon, 15 July 1809), at p. 537 (proposal); pp. 550–3 (Collingwood to Lady Collingwood, from HMS *Ville de Paris*, 30 Oct. 1809), at p. 552 (reluctant); Anderson, *Naval Wars*, p. 472 (dates); cf. BL, MS Add. 36,543, fos. 87r–88v, exemplum of *London Gazette*, no. 16,322 (pp. 1,945–8), 5–9 Dec. 1809 (despatches of 3–16 Oct., reporting conquests).

198. Holland, *Travels*, pp. 14, 35.

199. FO 78/68, fos. 235r–240v (Adair to Marquess (Richard) Wellesley, from Pera, 1 June 1810), at fo. 240v.

200. HALS, MS Leake 85518 (Lowe to Leake, from Cephalonia, 15 Oct. 1809). F. H. Marshall has suggested that a letter from Ali to Leake, dated 24 Sept. and sent from Delvinaki,

referred to the British expedition when it mentioned 'the coming of those Englishmen': 'Four Letters of Ali Pasha to William Martin Leake', *Byzantinisch-neugriechische Jahrbücher*, 9 (1932), pp. 158–68, at pp. 158, 160 ('ton erchomon autōn tōn egklezōn'). But the letter was dated by the Julian calendar, i.e. written on 6 Oct.; the reference was evidently to the coming of Byron and Hobhouse, whose arrival at Arta must have been reported by Leake.

201. Mézin, *Français et ottomans*, p. 137 (departure 30 Sept.). Leake had planned to take advantage of Ali's absence to leave Ioannina for one of his topographical tours of the Greek countryside: TNA, FO 78/65, fos. 117r–119v (Leake to Canning, from Ioannina, 5 Oct. 1809), at fo. 119r. His first reference to a possible occupation of the Ionian Islands was in his despatch of 12 Oct.: ibid., fos. 121r–122r (Leake to Canning, from Ioannina, 12 Oct. 1809), at fo. 121v.

202. CAD, Janina, consulat, 290PO/1/4, unpaginated section (Pouqueville to Donzelot and Bessières, from Ioannina, 9 Oct. 1810), at p. [1].

203. BL, Add. 56,527, fos. 36v (29 Sept.), 45r (5 Oct.), 58v (19 Oct.).

204. For the claim see for example V. Vallucci, *Lord Byron e Ali Pascià Tepelene: Childe Harold II e le strategie della Gran Bretagna nel Mare Ionio* (Rome, 2005), pp. 34, 65; and, with a far-fetched sexual speculation about Byron's role, P. Cochran, *Byron and Hobby-O: Lord Byron's Relationship with John Cam Hobhouse* (Newcastle, 2010), pp. 79–93.

205. TNA, FO 78/65, fos. 130r–132r (Leake to Adair, from Ioannina, 5 Sept. 1809), at fo. 130r–v; cf. also fos. 123r–125r (Leake to Canning, from Preveza, 1 Nov. 1809), at fo. 123r–v.

206. Ibid., fos. 143r–144r (Leake to Canning, from Ioannina, 19 Nov. 1809), at fo. 143r; fos. 145r–147r (Leake to Stuart, from Ioannina, 19 Nov. 1809), at fo. 146r–v.

207. BL, MS Add. 20,190, fo. 260r–v (Oswald to Leake, from Zakynthos, 7 Nov. 1809).

208. Marshall, 'Four Letters', pp. 162–4 (Ali to Leake, '27 Nov.' [9 Dec.] 1809), at p. 162 ('me arketous Arvanitas upo tēn exousian tou eis tēn douleusin tōn Phrantzezōn'). Pharmakēs, who commanded a significant number of men, had previously been fighting against Ali's son Veli in the Peloponnese.

209. HALS, MSS Leake 85513 (Navy Office to Leake, 25 May 1809); Leake 85516 (Percy Fraser to Leake, from the Arsenal, Malta, 15 Sept. 1809); Leake 85536 (report on forests, endorsed 27 Dec. 1809). For the 1803 offer see above, p. 159.

210. TNA, ADM 49/168, pp. 146–8 (Leard to Fraser, from Durrës, 9 Feb. 1810), at p. 147 (3 Jan., 'a considerable...', 'the exportation...'); pp. 154–6 (Fraser to Admiralty Board, from Malta, 11 June 1810), at p. 154 ('of a...'); pp. 156–7 (Leard and Fraser letters, 17 June–31 July) (3 shipments, 1 Aug.). The Admiralty Board reacted by contesting Leard's terms and repudiating his service, but was eventually forced to admit that he had performed well. On this episode see P. K. Crimmin, '"A Great Object with us to Procure this Timber": The Royal Navy's Search for Ship Timber in the Eastern Mediterranean and Southern Russia, 1803–1815', *International Journal of Maritime History*, 4 (1992), no. 2, pp 83–115, and idem, 'Hunting for Naval Timber in the Adriatic, 1802–1815', in J. Tulard et al., *Français et anglais en Méditerranée, 1789–1830* (n.p., 1992), pp. 149–57.

211. Leake, *Travels*, iv, pp. 224 ('tired', expense, displeasure), 547 (early Jan., northerners ('Ghege')).

212. Marshall, 'Four Letters', pp. 162–4 (Ali to Leake, '27 Nov.' [9 Dec.] 1809), at p. 162 ('tēn prothumian mou eis ola ekeina opou apovlepoun tēn douleusin kai eucharistēsin tou genou sas').

213. HHStA, Türkei VI, 3, 2nd foliation, fos. 49r–55v (Stürmer report, 10 Feb. 1810), at fos. 50v–51r ('pour éviter de plus grands maux').

214. Ibid., fos. 49v–50r.

215. Remérand, *Ali de Tébélen*, p. 143; Baggally, *Ali Pasha and Great Britain*, pp. 47–50; Rontogiannēs, *Istoria tēs nēsou Leukados*, ii, pp. 231–3 (giving the Julian date for the start of the campaign). The Greek troops were the newly recruited regiment of 'Greek Light Infantry'; one British soldier who participated in the attack described them as 'a fine looking body of men but, as it turned out, *utterly useless* as soldiers', noting that when they were engaged in the attack on the fortress of Lefkada they 'behaved so ill and caused such confusion and disappointment that they were never tried again' (Glover, ed., *Fighting Napoleon*, p. 40).

216. Mézin, *Français et ottomans*, pp. 158–60 (Pouqueville reports to Donzelot, 31 Mar. 5 Apr., 6 Apr., 14 Apr. 1810). Cf. AMAE, CCC, Janina 3, no. 32 (Pouqueville to de Champagny [now the duc de Cadore], from Preveza, 14 Apr. 1810): 'after much prevarication, Ali Pasha now openly declares himself our enemy' ('après bien de tergiversations, Ali-Pacha se déclare ouvertement contre nous').

217. AMAE, CCC, Janina 3, no. 39 (Pouqueville to Cadore, from Preveza, 19 Apr. 1810), at p. [5] (800 soldiers); Mézin, *Français et ottomans*, p. 160 (Pouqueville to Donzelot, from Preveza, 17 Apr. 1810) (Parga).

218. Marshall, 'Four Letters', pp. 165–8 (Ali to Leake, '27 Mar.' [8 Apr.] 1810), at pp. 165 (scenario), 167 ('to kuriōteron meson [o]pou stereōnei tēn asphaleian tēs exousias mou eis toutous tous topous, tēn ēsuchian mou kai tēn eleutherian apo kathe endechomena upopta', 'tēn sumphōnian mas kai uposchesin sou').

219. BL, MS Add. 20,171, fo. 93r–v (Lowe to Leake, from Lefkada, 18 May 1810), at fo. 93r.

220. On 19/31 Mar. Ali had written to Hudson Lowe from Preveza, asking him to forward a letter to Leake on Malta; the letter of 8 Apr. was similarly sent to Lowe on 28 Mar./9 Apr.: BL, MS Add. 20,177, fos. 10r, 12r. On Leake's later life see Arsov, *Marbles and Politics*, p. 95.

221. BL, MS 43,229, fos. 157r–158v (G. Foresti to Aberdeen, from Corfu, 10 Oct. 1806), at fo. 157v.

222. The indirect evidence is strong. On 2[/14] Dec. 1803 Ali's secretary Mehmet sent to Aberdeen from Ioannina a letter beginning, 'My Lord, Since I am Certain that your Grace is my General's and Master's friend, and loves him; it is with utmost satisfaction, that have the honour to give your Grace the notice of Sully's [*sc.* Souli's] Conquest' (BL, MS 43,229, fo. 14r); from this it seems very likely that Aberdeen had met Ali. Aberdeen's incomplete travel diary shows that after a journey across Greece he reached Patras on 6 Nov. 1803 and was there until the 12th; it also shows that he was on Corfu by 9 Jan. Although it lacks details of the weeks in between, it does contain six pages of jottings of Albanian vocabulary (British Museum, London, Department of Greek and Roman Antiquities, Aberdeen diary, vol. 1 (unfoliated) (vocabulary, Patras); vol. 2, fo. 136r (Corfu)). George Foresti was presumably working for his father on Corfu, and would have made a suitable guide for the 19-year-old Earl

on a brief trip to Ioannina. Aberdeen would become Prime Minister in 1852, 30 years after Ali's death.

223. BL, MSS Add. 43,229, fos. 335r–337v (G. Foresti to Aberdeen, from Malta, 29 Sept. and 6 Oct. 1808); Add. 43,230, fo. 6r–v (G. Foresti to Aberdeen, from Malta, 16 June 1809).

224. BL, MS Add. 20,183, fos. 3r–4v (G. Foresti to Lowe, from Përmet, 5 Jan. 1810). The nature of the threat is obscure; it may have involved forcible detention. Ali's emissary had been prevented from passing beyond Zakynthos, and Foresti had had the task of telling Ali that he had failed to use the correct channels for dealing with the British authorities (fo. 3r–v). Foresti's journey to Përmet may have been made in an attempt to catch up with Ali, who was on his way to make a triumphal entry into Berat three days later: see Leake, *Travels*, iv, p. 547.

225. AMAE, CCC, Janina 3, no. 21 (Pouqueville to Cadore, from Preveza, 19 Mar. 1810) (reporting arrival on 9 Mar.); TNA, FO 78/85, fo. 141r–v (Foreign Office to Treasury, Sept. 1815) (Oswald initiative, employed 14 Mar. 1810–14 Sept. 1815); fos. 147r–148v (Foresti to J. P. Morier, from London, 5 Oct. 1815), at fo. 147r–v (£3 per day to Leake, £500 per year to Foresti); fo. 149r–v (copy of Adair to Foresti, from Pera, 12 June 1810).

226. Hughes, *Travels*, ii, p. 190.

227. BL, MS Add. 20,184, fos. 63r–65v (Oswald to Lowe, from Zakynthos, between 21 and 29 Feb. 1810), at fos. 64v–65r.

228. BL, MS Add. 20,117, fos. 21r (Ali to Lowe, from Preveza, 15/27 Apr. 1810), 22r (Ali to Lowe, from Preveza, 18/30 Apr. 1810) ('Per la buona vicinanza & amicizia, che regna fra Noi, non si dovrebbe dare ricetto e prottezione alle persone che abandonono la loro Patria, e Natural Sudditanza, e la prego di rimediare al passato, e di non permettere in avenire, che succedino altre emigrazioni').

229. BL, MSS Add. 20,168, fos. 38r–39v (Lowe to Oswald, from Lefkada, 17 May 1810), at fo. 38r (alarm, 2,000 men); fos. 63v–64r (Lowe to Oswald, from Lefkada, 21 May 1810) (different place, could bombard fortress); Add. 20,169, fos. 130r–129r, retrograde (Lowe to Süleiman, from Lefkada, 27 May 1810), at fo. 129v ('la perfetta Amicizia, ed Armonia che regna tra i nostri Governi').

230. BL, MS Add. 20,183, fos. 13r–16v (G. Foresti, minute of discussion with Ali on 2 July; enclosed with letter to Oswald, from Ioannina, 5 July 1810), at fo. 15r.

231. BL, MS Add. 20,169, fos. 74v–76r (Lowe to Oswald, from Lefkada, 15 July 1810), at fos. 75r–76r.

232. TNA, FO 352/1, fos. 462r–463v (Oswald to Adair, from Zakynthos, 18 June 1810), at fos. 462v–463r (on falsity); fo. 464r–v (copy in translation of La Tour-Maubourg's complaints); fo. 466r–v (Ali to Oswald and S. Foresti, from Ioannina, 1/13 June 1810), at fo. 466r ('Il mio Governo è molto irritato contro di me'); fo. 470r–471v (copy of La Tour-Maubourg's complaints, in Italian, with Ali's refutatory comments).

233. Ibid., fos. 341r–357r (S. Canning, 'Memoranda', 10 July–24 Oct. 1810), at fos. 341v–342r (18, 19 July); TNA, FO 78/70, fos. 102r–104v (S. Canning to Wellesley, from Pera, 20 July 1810), at fo. 104r (promised).

234. Ushtelenca, *Diplomacia e Ali Pashës*, pp. 182–4 (official); TNA, FO 352/1, fos. 341r–357r (S. Canning, 'Memoranda', 10 July–24 Oct. 1810), at fo. 348r (1 Sept.).

235. CAD, Janina, consulat, 290PO/1/4, unpaginated section (Pouqueville to Cadore, from Ioannina, 25 July 1810) (*firman*); (Pouqueville to La Tour-Maubourg, from Ioannina,

30 July 1810) (English help); Mézin, *Français et ottomans*, p. 319 (Pouqueville to Donzelot, from Ioannina, 11 Aug. 1810) (forgery). BL, MS Add. 20,183, fos. 29r–30v (G. Foresti to Lowe, from Ioannina, 25 July 1810), at fo. 29r (arrival of *firman*); fos. 43r–50v (G. Foresti to S. Canning, from Ioannina, 6 Nov. 1810), at fos. 44v–45r ('the final..', 'Aly Pacha..').

236. Bonaparte, *Correspondance générale*, ix, p. 285 (Napoleon to Cadore, from Saint-Cloud, 23 June 1810).

237. BL, MS Add. 20,183, fos. 34r–35v (G. Foresti to Lowe, from Ioannina, 22 Sept. 1810), at fo. 34r; TNA, FO 78/70, fos. 27r–34r (G. Foresti to S. Canning, from Ioannina, 29 Sept. 1810), at fo. 28v ('Among the..').

238. BL, MS Add. 20,183, fos. 36r–39v (G. Foresti to S. Canning, from Ioannina, 29 Sept. 1810), at fo. 37v.

239. Ushtelenca, *Diplomacia e Ali Pashës*, pp. 184–9 (blockade); BL, MS Add. 20,183, fos. 52r–53v (G. Foresti to Canning, from Ioannina, 11 Nov. 1810), at fo. 53v (peace agreement); fos. 61r–64v (G. Foresti to Canning, from Ioannina, 24 Dec. 1810), at fo. 62r (shortages). Despite the agreement, Ali continued with a gradual conquest of the territory of Vlorë: see fos. 67r–69v (G. Foresti to Canning, from Berat, 13 Jan. 1811), at fo. 69r. For a description of the generally miserable state of Vlorë earlier in 1810 see J. Galt, *Letters from the Levant; containing Views of the State of Society, Manners, Opinions, and Commerce, in Greece, and Several of the Principal Islands of the Archipelago* (London, 1813), pp. 4–24.

240. BL, MS Add. 20,183, fos. 52r–53v, 55r–56v, 58r–v (G. Foresti to S. Canning, from Ioannina, 11 Nov., 23 Nov., 5 Dec., respectively).

241. Ibid., fos. 67r–69v (G. Foresti to S. Canning, from Berat, 13 Jan. 1811), at fos. 67r (offended), 67v (proposal, answer). For La Tour-Maubourg's continued denunciations in this period, see Mézin, *Français et ottomans*, pp. 60–1.

242. TNA, FO 78/70, fos. 27r–34r (G. Foresti to S. Canning, from Ioannina, 29 Sept. 1810), at fo. 31v.

243. BL, MS Add. 20,183, fos. 43r–50v (G. Foresti to S. Canning, from Ioannina, 6 Nov. 1810), at fos. 46r (fighters, Spain), 47r–v (greatest fear), 49r (ordinance, £5 m).

244. Ibid., at fos. 43v–44r ('animated the..', 'remained behind..'), 44v ('my Residence..').

245. V. H. Aksan, *Ottoman Wars, 1700–1870: An Empire Besieged* (Harlow, 2007), pp. 272–8.

246. CAD, Janina, consulat, 290PO/1/6, pp. 72–4 (Pouqueville to Cadore, 28 Jan. 1811), at p. 73.

247. TNA, FO 78/74, fos. 127r–130r (G. Foresti to S. Canning, from Preveza, 1 Aug. 1811), at fo. 127v.

248. BL, MS Add. 20,110, fos. 35r–36r (Lowe to G. Foresti, from Zakynthos, 7 Mar. 1811), at fo. 35v.

249. BL, MS Add. 20,183, fos. 79r–80v (G. Foresti to Col. Smith, from Ioannina, 14 Mar. 1811), at fos. 79v–80r.

250. Ibid., fos. 87r–88r (G. Foresti to Lowe, from Ioannina, 15 Mar. 1811), at fo. 87v.

251. BL, MS Add. 20,110, fos. 37r–40r (Lowe to Oswald, from Zakynthos, 17 Mar. 1811), at fos. 38r (France), 39r (possession).

252. BL, MS Add. 20,171, fos. 132r–135r (Lowe to Oswald, from Lefkada, 8 Apr. 1811), at fo. 134v.

253. BL, MS Add. 20,183, fo. 96r–v (S. Canning to G. Foresti, from Pera, 4 May 1811), at fo. 96r.

254. Ibid., fos. 90r–91r (G. Foresti to Lowe, from Ioannina, 15 Apr. 1811), at fo. 90r.

255. BL, MS Add. 20,171, fos. 136r–138v (Lowe to Rowley, from Lefkada, 18 May 1811), at fo. 136v.

256. BL, MSS Add. 20,183, fos. 67r–69v (G. Foresti to Lowe, from Berat, 13 Jan. 1811), at fo. 69r; Add. 20,110, fos. 28r–31v (Lowe to Campbell, from Lefkada, 16 Feb. 1811), at fo. 31r; Arsh, *Albaniia i Epir*, p. 250 (forts, garrisons).

257. CAD, Janina, consulat, 290PO/1/9, pp. 481–3 (Pouqueville to Bassano, 1 June 1811), at p. 481; BL, MS Add. 20,183, fo. 115r–v (G. Foresti to Lowe, from Ioannina, 15 June 1811), at fo. 115r.

258. CAD, Janina, consulat, 290PO/1/6, pp. 4–6 (Pouqueville to Lesseps, from Ioannina, 2 Jan. 1811), at pp. 4–5; pp. 40–3 (Pouqueville to Cadore, from Ioannina, 14 Jan. 1811).

259. Mézin, *Français et ottomans*, p. 62 (La Tour-Maubourg to Donzelot, from Istanbul, 23 Feb. 1811) (exception); CAD, Janina, consulat, 290PO/1/6, pp. 166–76 (Pouqueville to Cadore, from Ioannina, 1 Mar. 1811), at p. 175 (general prohibition); Janina, consulat, 290PO/1/7, pp. 194–5 (Pouqueville to Cadore, from Ioannina, 6 Mar. 1811) (assurance); pp. 225–30 (Pouqueville to Lesseps, from Ioannina, 14 Mar. 1811), at p. 226 (secret); pp. 314–5 (Pouqueville to Cadore, from Ioannina, 7 Apr. 1811), at p. 315 (high price); Janina, consulat, 290PO/1/8, p. 384 (Pouqueville to La Tour-Maubourg, from Ioannina, 4 May 1811).

260. Mézin, *Francais et ottomans*, p. 60 (La Tour-Maubourg to Donzelot, from Pera, 14 Dec. 1810) CAD, Janina, consulat, 290PO/1/6, pp. 83–4 (Pouqueville to Donzelot and Lesseps, from Ioannina, 2 Feb. 1811), at p. 83.

261. CAD, Janina, consulat, 290PO/1/7, pp. 199–203 (Pouqueville to Cadore, from Ioannina, 7 Mar. 1811), at p. 202; BL, MS Add. 20,171, fos. 136r–138v (Lowe to Rowley, from Lefkada, 18 May 1811), at fo. 137v. Eventually, in Aug., Pouqueville would write to Paris that the claim to deprive Ali of these positions had been an illusory promise to the French, merely to gain time: CAD, Janina, consulat, 290PO/1/10, pp. 629–35 (Pouqueville to Bassano, from Ioannina, 3 Aug. 1811), at p. 632.

262. BL, MS Add. 20,183, fos. 101r–102v (translation of: *kaymakam paşa* to Ali, from Istanbul, 25 May 1811), at fos. 101r–v ('gl'infiniti oltraggi che Vostra Altezza ha fato e fa al Governo di Francia in tempo che la Porta vi scrisse tante volte di non far simile cose', 'fare secretamente tutte quelle Preparazioni che saranno sufficienti ad espellere via i Francesi nel caso facessero qualche Movimento'), 102r (300,000).

263. CAD, Janina, consulat, 290PO/1/9, pp. 502–4 (Pouqueville to La Tour-Maubourg, 12 June 1811), at p. 503 ('fatigué des attentats d'ali pacha, et de sa constante opposition aux approvisionnements de corfou est determiné a ne pas souffrir la continuation de ses insultes. son intention est de declarer la guerre a Ali pacha, si la porte ne peut reussir a le retenir dans le devoir').

264. AMAE, Correspondance politique, Îles Ioniennes, vol. 18, fo. 32r–v (La Tour-Maubourg, from Büyükdere, to Lesseps, 7 July 1811), at fo. 32r (threat in Apr.); CAD, Janina, consulat, 290PO/1/9, pp. 564–9 (Pouqueville to Donzelot and Lesseps, 30 June 1811), at p. 566 ('mais je vous assure que mon Gouvernement ne m'abandonnera pas et que je ne me separerai pas de lui. Si Bonaparte veut la Guerre, il peut la déclarer, qu'il agisse franchement en brave, sans chercher de détours').

265. AMAE, Correspondance politique, Turquie, vol. 222, fos. 51r–56v (La Tour-Maubourg to Bassano, from Büyükdere, 24 July 1811), at fo. 51r ('de changer de Vues en lui montrant dans un rebelle, qu'il haït et qu'il veut détruire, un homme désormais précieux à conserver pour la défense des frontières de l'Empire'), 51v (react to pressure).

266. Ibid., fos. 58r–60v (text of note).

267. Ibid., fos. 51r–56v (La Tour-Maubourg to Bassano, from Büyükdere, 24 July 1811), at fos. 52r–53r (initial reaction), 53r–54r (threat to leave, change of tune).

268. Remérand, *Ali de Tébélen*, p. 166 (departure 2 Sept.); AMAE, CCC, Janina 4, no. 152 (Pouqueville to Bassano, from Ioannina, 10 Oct. 1811) (*firmans*); Correspondance politique, Turquie, vol. 222, fos. 119r–120v (La Tour-Maubourg to Bassano, from Büyükdere, 4 Sept. 1811), at fo. 119r ('austère et indépendant', 'toutes les séductions des Anglais et d'Ali-Pacha'); TNA, FO 352/1, fo. 600v (G. Foresti to S. Canning, from Ioannina, 7 Oct. 1811) ('meant only...')

269. CAD, Janina, consulat, 290PO/1/14, pp. 317–18 (Pouqueville to Bassano, from Ioannina, 17 Nov. 1811), at p. 317 (no authority, only responses); TNA, FO 352/2A, fo. 128r–v (rough translation of: Ali to his agent, from Ioannina, 9/21 Nov. 1811); fo. 129r–v (original letter, in Greek, fragment); AMAE, CCC, Janina 4, no. 173 (Pouqueville to Bassano, from Ioannina, 16 Nov. 1811) (40 purses). For the value of the piastre in 1812 see Holland, *Travels*, pp. 115, 117, and W. Turner, *Journal of a Tour in the Levant*, 3 vols. (London, 1820), i. p. xvii.

270. Mézin, *Français et ottomans*, p. 63 (La Tour-Maubourg to Donzelot, from Istanbul, 24 June 1811).

271. CAD, Janina, consulat, 290PO/1/10, pp. 604–9 (Pouqueville to La Tour-Maubourg, from Ioannina, 23 July 1811), at p. 607 (Dukat); pp. 638–40 (Pouqueville to Bassano, from Ioannina, 9 Aug. 1811), at p. 639 (bribed, suborned); AMAE, Correspondance politique, Îles Ioniennes, vol. 18, fo. 72r–v (Lesseps to 'Monseigneur', from Corfu, 15 Aug. 1811), at fo. 72r (Vlorë seized 1 Aug.).

272. CAD, Janina, consulat, 290PO/1/10, pp. 642–7 (Pouqueville to Bassano, from Corfu, 14 Aug. 1811), at p. 644 (presents, promises); AMAE, CCC, Janina 4, no. 143 (Pouqueville to Bassano, from Ioannina, 24 Sept. 1811), at p. [1] (handed over). Recognizing the hopelessness of his position, Ibrahim had already begun negotiating with Ali, sending his only son to Ioannina as a hostage: TNA, FO 78/74, fos. 131r–132v (G. Foresti to S. Canning, from Ioannina, 8 Sept. 1811), at fo. 132v. Ali would keep Ibrahim under guard at Konica for a year, before transferring him to Ioannina: AMAE, CCC, Janina 6, no. 153 (Pouqueville report, from Ioannina, 3 Oct. 1812), at p. [2].

273. AMAE, CCC, Janina 4, no. 143 (Pouqueville to Bassano, from Ioannina, 24 Sept. 1811), at p. [2]; Naçi, *Pashallëku i Shkodrës, 1796–1831*, p. 96 (Mustafa Pasha).

274. TNA, FO 78/74, fos. 131r–132v (G. Foresti to S. Canning, from Ioannina, 8 Sept. 1811), at fo. 131r (French officer).

275. Boppe, *L'Albanie et Napoléon*, pp. 133–5 (alliance); Remérand, *Ali de Tébélen*, pp. 172–4 (alliance, campaign); AMAE, CCC, Janina 4, no. 161 (Pouqueville to Bassano, from Ioannina, 24 Oct. 1811), at p. [1] (heavy defeat); Nottingham University Library, Nottingham [henceforth: NUL], MS Pw Jd 96 (G. Foresti to S. Foresti, from Ioannina, 26 Nov. 1811), fo. [1r].

276. BL, MS Add. 20,177, fos. 231r–232r (Ali to Lowe, from Ioannina, 20 Aug. 1811), at fo. 231v ('non vedo niente eseguito, e giustamente devo dolermi, e sorprendermi', 'quanti Sagrifizi feci, e farò per amor vostro lo fò con tutta la mia Soddisfazione come si trattasse di cose che me medesimo riguardassero').

277. Ibid., fos. 234r, 245r, 250r (Ali to Lowe, from Ioannina, 14/26 Aug., 23 Sept., 18/30 Sept. 1811).

278. BL, MS Add. 20,170, fos. 296r–301v (Lowe to Smith, from Lefkada, 12 Oct. 1811), at fo. 297v.

279. BL, MS Add. 20,183, fos. 134r–137r (G. Foresti to Lowe, from Ioannina, 30 Sept. 1811), at fos. 134v–135r.

280. BL, MS Add. 20,170, fos. 271r–275v (Lowe to Smith, from Lefkada, 7 Oct. 1811), at fos. 272r–273r; for the earlier view see above, p. 209.

281. BL, MS Add. 20,170, fos. 302r–306r (Lowe to Smith, from Lefkada, 14 Oct. 1811), at fos. 304v–305r.

282. Ibid., fos. 331v–337r (Lowe to Smith, from Lefkada, 23 Oct. 1811), at fos. 332r–333v.

283. Ibid., fos. 342v–346r (Lowe to Smith, from Lefkada, 30 Oct. 1811), at fo. 344v; fos. 346r–348r (Lowe to Rowley, from Lefkada, 1 Nov. 1811), at fo. 347r.

284. BL, MS Add. 20,183, fos. 149r–152v (S. Foresti to Smith, from Zakynthos, 3 Nov. 1811, copied in one column, with Lowe's remarks in another), at fos. 149r–151r.

285. BL, MS Add. 20,171, fos. 351r–357r (Lowe to Smith, from Lefkada, 5 Nov. 1811), at fos. 353v–354r.

286. Gregory, *Napoleon's Jailer*, pp. 77–8; NUL, MS Pw Jd 105 (Airey to Maitland, from Zakynthos, 10 Feb. 1812) (departure).

287. NUL, MS Pw Jd 98 (Airey to Maitland, from Zakynthos, 22 Dec. 1811), at fos. [1r–2r].

288. NUL, MS Pw Jd 105 (Airey to Maitland, from Zakynthos, 10 Feb. 1812), at fo. [2r].

289. NUL, MS Pw Jd 122 (Airey, proclamation, 13 Apr. 1812); Panagiōtopoulos, Dēmētropoulos and Michaēlarēs, eds., *Archeio Alē Pasa*, ii, pp. 248–9 (S. Foresti to Ali, from Zakynthos, 14 Apr. 1812), at p. 248 ('la buona armonia, e sincera amicizia').

290. NUL, MS Pw Jd 121 (Airey to Bentinck, from Zakynthos, 17 Apr. 1812), at fos. [1r–2r].

291. NUL, MSS Pw Jd 217/2 (Arata to McCombe, from Lefkada, 20 Mar. 1812) (report of assassination); Pw Jd 217/3 (Ali to Airey, from Tepelenë, 19/31 Mar. 1812) (denial); Pw Jd 217/4 (Airey to Ali, from Zakynthos, 2 Apr. 1812), at fos. [1v–2r] ('una Calunnia cosí falsa, nera ed abbominevole contro l'Altezza Sua'); Pw Jd 217/9 (Ali to S. Foresti, from Tepelenë, 1 Apr. 1812) (offer to punish); Pw Jd 217/14 (Ali to S. Foresti, from Ioannina, 16/28 Apr. 1812) (pleading).

292. Sir Robert Wilson, *Private Diary of Travel, Personal Services, and Public Events, during Mission and Employment with the European Armies in the Campaigns of 1812, 1813, 1814*, ed. H. Randolph, 2 vols. (London, 1861), i, p. 1 (8 Apr.); D. Manley, 'Liston, Sir Robert (1742–1836), Tutor and Diplomat', *ODNB* (career); Richmond, *Voice of England*, pp. 89–90, 110 (appointment, delay).

293. TNA, FO 78/79, fos. 79r–82v (Mar. 1812), at fos. 79r–82r.

294. NUL, MS Pw Jd 218/1 (Ali to Bentinck, from Ioannina, 16/28 Apr 1812) ('il Zelo e l'attacamento'). The gunpowder was presumably given in accordance with Airey's suggestion, made in Feb.: see above, at n. 288.

295. NUL, MS Pw Jd 2343 (Castlereagh to Ali (extract), from London, 23 May 1812).

296. CAD, Janina, consulat, 290PO/1/15, pp. 1–2 (Pouqueville to Bassano, from Ioannina, 1 Jan. 1812) (offer refused); pp. 32–4 (Pouqueville to Bassano, from Ioannina, 23 Feb. 1812) (fall, 300).

297. Ibid., pp. 80–6 (Pouqueville to Bassano, from Ioannina, 7 Apr. 1812), at p. 81; this report includes a long account of the destruction of Kardhiq.

298. Holland, *Travels*, pp. 491–5.

299. CAD, Janina, consulat, 290PO/1/15, pp. 37–43 (Pouqueville to Bassano, from Ioannina, 29 Feb. 1812), at p. 41.

300. Ibid., at p. 43 (Çamëri); AMAE, CCC, Janina 4, no. 176 (Pouqueville to Bassano, from Ioannina, 20 Nov. 1811), at pp. [2–3] (Vlorë); CCC, Janina 5, no. 89 (Pouqueville to Bassano, from Ioannina, 31 May 1812), at p. [6] (franc = piastre).

301. Mézin, *Français et ottomans*, p. 338 (Guès to Donzelot, from Corfu, undated); Boppe, *L'Albanie et Napoléon*, pp. 191–2.

302. Mézin, *Français et ottomans*, pp. 258 (Guès to Donzelot, from Ioannina, 23 Feb. and 8 Mar. 1812), 333 (report to duc de Feltre, from Corfu, undated), 338 (Guès to Donzelot, before 20 Mar. 1812). Mustafa was imprisoned and starved to death by Ali: Holland, *Travels*, p. 196.

303. Mézin, *Français et ottomans*, p. 338 (Franck to Donzelot, from Corfu, 25 June 1812) (reporting journey to Ioannina, 20 May).

304. TNA, FO 78/77, fos. 12r–13r (S. Canning to Wellesley, from Pera, 17 Jan. 1812), at fo. 12r–v.

305. Richmond, *Voice of England*, pp. 104–16.

306. TNA, FO 78/77, fos. 154r–158r (G. Foresti to S. Canning, from Istanbul, 20 Apr. 1812).

307. Ibid., fos. 211r–212r (S. Canning to Wellesley, from Pera, 13 May 1812), at fos. 211v–212r.

308. Ibid., at fo. 211v (oral assurance); fos. 213r–215r (S. Canning to G. Foresti, from Pera, 10 May 1812), at fos. 213r–214v.

309. Ibid., fos. 211r–212r (S. Canning to Wellesley, from Pera, 13 May 1812), at fo. 211r (dep. 13 May); fos. 233r–242r (text of treaty, 16 May); fo. 253r–v (S. Canning to G. Foresti, from Pera, 22 May 1812).

310. AMAE, CCC, Janina 5, no. 80 (Pouqueville report, from Ioannina, 18 May 1812), at pp. [1] ('Oui et très content, puisque la France nous aidera par une puissante diversion'), [2] ('Jamais sans le concours de la France', 'je leur ai dit tout ce qu'ils voulaient, mais j'ai prevenu le grand visir, de ne pas les écouter. je [vais] tromper les Anglais, jusqu'a la fin & les faire croire, que je sois leur ami'), [3] ('du premier coup de canon tiré en Pologne', 'afin de defendre nostre pays & la Morée de quelque invasion des Anglais, afin, consul, que nous combattions ensemble, pour les chasser des isles joniennes').

311. Ibid., nos. 91 (Pouqueville report, from Ioannina, 3 June 1812), 103 (Pouqueville report, from Ioannina, 22 June 1812), at p. [2] ('les difficultés & les obstacles que je rencontre dans mes negociations'). The Bentinck papers do not record any such visit.

312. For Adair's refusal see above, at n. 187.

313. AMAE, CCC, Janina 5, after no. 105, no. 6 in Preveza sequence (Pouqueville report, from Ioannina, 8 July 1812), at p. [1] ('cette paix…va consommer la ruine de notre patrie; votre Empereur, avec raison, sera indigné avec nous; dieu m'est temoin que j'ai tout fait pour en empècher la conclusion').

314. Ibid., before no. 113 (Lesseps to Bassano, from Corfu, 11 July 1812), at p. [1] ('secrète-ment et verbalement, qu'il reveroit, craignoit et aimoit Sa Majesté l'Empereur Napoleon; qu'il se soumettroit aveuglement à ses ordres').

315. Ibid., no. 127 (Pouqueville report, from Ioannina, 30 July 1812, quoting a letter from La Tour-Maubourg which had arrived on 21 July), at p. [4].

316. Wilson, *Private Diary*, pp. 394–5 (Liston to Tyrconnell, from Istanbul, 25 Dec. 1812).

317. NUL, MSS Pw Jd 145 (Ali to S. Foresti, from Ioannina, 15/27 July 1812); Pw Jd 2344 (Ali to Bentinck, from Ioannina, 18/30 Sept. 1812); Pw Jd 173 (Liston to G. Foresti, from Istanbul, 29 Oct. 1812), at fo. [1r–v].

318. AMAE, CCC, Janina 6, e.g. nos. 130, 131, 149, 157 (Pouqueville reports, from Ioannina, 20 Aug., 24 Aug., 27 Sept., 9 Oct. 1812).

319. Ibid., no. 166 (Pouqueville report, from Ioannina, 29 Oct. 1812), at p. [13] ('je refusai le subside et depuis ce moment les Anglais m'abhorrent').

320. Ibid., no. 163 (Pouqueville report, from Ioannina, 25 Oct. 1812), at p. [1] ('division', 'il faut oublier, ou au moins dissimuler le passé...enfin il faut se servir d'Ali-Pacha tel qu'il est'); no. 166 (29 Oct.), at pp. [15–19] (advantages). At almost the same time, the Foreign Minister was instructing Pouqueville to cultivate Ali, in the hope of persuad-ing him that a pro-French policy was in his interests: NUL, MS Pw Jd 2371 (Bassano to Pouqueville, from Vilnius, 18 Oct. 1812).

321. AMAE, CCC, Janina 6, after no. 166, 'Bulletin no. 48' (compilation of news, dated Ioannina, 1 Nov. 1812); Holland, *Travels*, p. 185.

322. AMAE, CCC, Janina 6, no. 176 (Pouqueville report, from Ioannina, 17 Nov. 1812), at p. [2] ('les plus ferventes protestations de vouloir servir Sa Majesté').

323. Ibid., before no. 186, 'Bulletin no. 53' (compilation of news, dated Ioannina, 28 Nov. 1812); no. 186 (Pouqueville report, from Ioannina, 1 Dec. 1812), at p. [1] ('fort chancelante et incertaine'); no. 190 (7 Dec. 1812), at pp. [2–3] ('nouvelle coalition', 'une fausse nouvelle qu'il reçoit, un caprice suffisent pour détruire les projets les mieux calculés et les plus sages').

324. Boppe, *L'Albanie et Napoléon*, pp. 202–4 (noting that by the time Guès reached Paris in May, the situation had irrevocably changed); Mézin, *Français et ottomans*, p. 259.

325. NUL, MS Pw Jd 2367 (Italinsky report), enclosed in MS Pw Jd 2365 (G. Foresti to Bentinck, from Preveza, 16 Feb. 1813). The figure for those who returned was quite accurate, but the total at the start had been much higher; modern estimates are 650,000 and 27,000.

326. NUL, MSS Pw Jd 2356 (G. Foresti to Bentinck, from Preveza, 8 Feb. 1813), at fo. [1r]; Pw Jd 2374 (S. Foresti to Bentinck, from Zakynthos, 9 Mar. 1813), at fo. [1v]; Pw Jd 2377 (Russian agent, report, from Corfu, 2 Mar. 1813), at fo. [1v] ('due mila albanesi più disposti a servire la causa dell'umanità in caso d'attacco della Piazza, che a difen-dere i Francesi'). 'Albanians' here meant people from the Albanian territories.

327. NUL, MS Pw Jd 2361 (anon., report on Corfu, 24 Jan. 1813), at fo. [1r].

328. NUL, MS Pw Jd 2360, fo. [1r–v] (Andréossy to Donzelot, from Tarabya, 22 Oct. 1812), at fo. [1v] ('Il y a long temt [*sic*] qu le G.S. a l'Intention d'aneanter Ali Pacha, il avoit abandoné plusieurs fois ce projet, il y reveille aujourdhui'); this was enclosed in MS Pw Jd 2356 (G. Foresti to Bentinck, from Preveza, 8 Feb. 1813).

329. TNA, FO 78/85, fos. 119r–126v (G. Foresti, accounts), at fo. 121v.

330. Ushtelenca, *Diplomacia e Ali Pashës*, pp. 222–3; Mézin, *Français et ottomans*, p. 217 (Pouqueville to Donzelot, from Ioannina, 15 Mar. 1813) (Gjirokastër). In Aug. Pouqueville reported that Ali had Ibrahim killed (*ibid.*, p. 227: Pouqueville to Donzelot, from Ioannina, 11 and 16 Aug. 1813); but this may have been a rumour put out by Ali. Thomas Hughes, who was in Ioannina in Feb. 1814, would write that 'this venerable old man, the father-in-law of Ali's two sons, may be seen like a wild beast through the iron bars of his dungeon' (*Travels*, ii, p. 191).

331. TNA, CO 136/1, enclosure to no. 11 (Campbell to Bathurst, from Zakynthos, 15 July 1813), at fo. [9r].

332. CAD, Janina, consulat, 290PO/1/4, pp. 151–2 (Pouqueville to Donzelot and Bessières, from Preveza, 26 Apr. 1809), at p. 152 (300 houses); AMAE, CCC, Janina 5, after no. 127, Preveza series, no. 10 (Pouqueville report, from Preveza, 31 July 1812), at p. [1]; Holland, *Travels*, p. 67. On the fortifying see above, at n. 255.

333. NUL, MS Pw Jd 2362 (S. Foresti to Bentinck, from Zakynthos, 13 Feb. 1813), at fo. [3r].

334. Holland, *Travels*, p. 120; NUL, MSS Pw Jd 2369 (G. Foresti to Bentinck, from Preveza, 2 Mar. 1813) (Colovo's journey); Pw Jd 2373 (G. Foresti, paper on Parga, 1 Mar. 1813), at fos. [2r–3r].

335. TNA, FO 78/82, fos. 205r–207v (Ali, 'Relazione Istorica' on Parga, 11/23 Sept. 1814), at fos. 206v–207r.

336. Boppe, *L'Albanie et Napoléon*, pp. 204–7; and see the map in de Bosset, *Proceedings in Parga*. On Papasoglou, a Smyrniot Greek who had been admiral of the Mamluk navy at the time of Napoleon's invasion of Egypt (and then recruited by Napoleon, becoming commander of the 'Chasseurs d'Orient'), see A. Boppe, 'Le Colonel Nicole Papas Oglou et le bataillon des Chasseurs d'Orient, 1798–1815', *Carnet de la Sabretache: revue d'histoire militaire retrospective*, 8 (1900), pp. 13–30, 112–27 (giving also an explanation of the peculiar status of Agia: pp. 118–20).

337. Ushtelenca, *Diplomacia e Ali Pashës*, pp. 229–30.

338. Hughes, *Travels*, ii, p. 59; TNA, CO 136/2, fos. 37r–38r (Ali to Campbell, from Preveza, 16/28 Feb. 1814), at fo. 37r–v ('infiniti ladroncinj ed altri malanni'); fos. 39r–40v (Campbell to Ali, from Zakynthos, 10 Mar. 1814).

339. TNA, CO 136/2, fos. 43r–44v (Campbell to Ali, from Zakynthos, 11 Mar. 1814), at fo. 43r (visit by Foresti 10–11 Mar. 1814); CO 136/3, fos. 58r–59v (Campbell, letter of introduction for Said Ahmed, 8 May 1815), at fo. 58v (visit of 14 Mar. 1814).

340. TNA, CO 136/2, fos. 33r–36v (Campbell to Bathurst, from Zakynthos, 14 Mar. 1814), at fos. 35v–36v.

341. de Bosset, *Proceedings in Parga*, pp. 57–9. Papasoglu had enjoyed friendly relations with Ali in 1807: see Boppe, *L'Albanie et Napoléon*, pp. 69–72.

342. TNA, CO 136/2, fos. 45r–47v (Campbell to Bathurst, from Zakynthos, 30 Mar. 1814), at fos. 46r–47r.

343. Ibid., fos. 57r–58v (Campbell to Bathurst, from Zakynthos, 31 Mar. 1814), at fo. 57r–v.

344. Ibid., fo. 57v (pretended); TNA, FO 78/82, fos. 37r–40v (Liston to Castlereagh, from Istanbul, 25 Apr. 1814), at fos. 37r–40r.

345. TNA, FO 78/82, fo. 43r (Liston to Castlereagh, 11 May 1814).

346. G. Pauthier, *Les Îles Ioniennes pendant l'occupation française et le protectorat anglais* (Paris, 1863), pp. 81–155 (Apr., May); Rémérand, *Ali de Tébélen*, p. 211 (June).

347. TNA, FO 78/82, fos. 112r–114r (Liston to Castlereagh, from Istanbul, 10 Oct. 1814), at fos. 112v–113v (agent, letter, quotations); fos. 115r–116r (Ali to Castlereagh, from Ioannina, 11/23 Sept. 1814), at fo. 115r ('per il Trattato del 1802, passò in assoluto dominio e Sovranità del mio Governo … e da esso inseguito cessami in Feudo').

348. TNA, FO 78/85, fo. 62r–v (Castlereagh to Ali, from Vienna, 19 Jan. 1815) (replying to letter of 15/27 Oct. 1814).

349. Ibid., fos. 64r–65v (Ali to Castlereagh, 14/26 Apr., from Preveza); TNA, CO 136/3, fos. 56r–57r (Ali to Campbell, from Preveza, 15/27 Apr. 1815) (requesting letter of introduction for Said Ahmed); fos. 90r–93r (report by Zervo on conversation with Ali, Corfu 21 June 1815), at fo. 92v ('some favourable …').

350. E. Prevlakēs and K. Kalliatakē Mertikopoulou, eds., Ē Ēpeiros, o Alē Pasas kai ē ellēnikē epanastasē: proxenikes ektheseis tou William Meyer apo tēn Preveza, 2 vols. (Athens, 1996), i, pp. 17–24 (Meyer to Planta, from London, 29 May 1819), at p. 21.

351. TNA, CO 136/3, fos. 49r–53v (Campbell to Bathurst, from Corfu, 12 May 1815), at fos. 50v–51r; fos. 203r–206r (Campbell to Commandant of Parga, 11 May 1815), at fo. 206r.

352. TNA, FO 78/85, fos. 72r–73r (Bathurst to Ali (draft), from London, 14 Oct. 1815), at fo. 72r ('now under …'); fo. 143r (Said Ahmed to Bathurst, from London, 29 Sept. 1815); fo. 145r–v (Bathurst to Said Ahmed (draft), from London, 30 Sept. 1815) (practice of government).

353. See de Bosset, Proceedings in Parga; Baggally, Ali Pasha and Great Britain, pp. 64–75.

354. See above, at nn. 60 (Morier), 121 (Leake).

355. See above, at nn. 90 (Morier), 163 (Collingwood), 168 (Leake), 280–1 (Lowe).

356. See above, at n. 149.

357. See above, at nn. 165 (Collingwood), 166 (Adair), 184 ('Let his …'), 187 (Adair, unverifiable).

358. See above, at nn. 308 (Canning), 347 ('that His …').

359. See above, at nn. 59 (Arbuthnot), 64 (Morier).

360. See above, at nn. 182 (troops), 232–3 (countering French Ambassador).

361. CAD, Janina, consulat, 290PO/1/14, pp. 367–370 (Pouqueville to Bassano, from Ioannina, 3 Dec. 1811), at p. 370 ('il s'informe minutieusement de l'état de l'europe'); Holland, Travels, p. 127. On his appetite for news see also V. Veliu, Relacione diplomatike ndërmjet Ali Pashës dhe Napoleonit (1797–1814) (Skopje, 2010), pp. 215–16.

362. Holland, Travels, p. 149 (Germany etc.); NUL, MS Pw Jd 2356 (G. Foresti to Bentinck, from Preveza, 8 Feb. 1813), at fo. [1v] (news from Vienna); AMAE, CCC Janina 6, no. 152 (Pouqueville report, from Ioannina, 1 Oct. 1812), at p. [1] ('scandaleuses'). On this issue see also S. P. Aravantinos, Istoria Alē Pasa tou Tepelenlē, 2 vols. (Athens, 1895), i, pp. 342–3.

363. Newnham Collingwood, ed., Selections, pp. 370–1 (Ali to Collingwood, from Ioannina, 2 June 1808), at p. 371.

364. HHStA, MS Türkei VI, 2, 1st foliation, fos. 65r–66r (von Stürmer report, from Istanbul, 26 Sept. 1808), at fo. 66r; Spiridion's letter, evidently seen also by von Stürmer, was dated 4 Aug.

365. TNA, FO 78/61, fos. 46r–47r (D. Morier to Ali, from Malta 14 July 1808); CAD, Janina, consulat, 290PO/1/3, unpaginated section, Pouqueville to de Champigny, 12 Oct. 1808 (every two weeks, extracts to Istanbul), and Pouqueville to de Champigny, 26 Oct. 1808 (Mefoud Effendi).

366. TNA, FO 78/65, fos. 113r–116r (Leake to Adair, from Ioannina, 4 Sept. 1809), at fo. 115r; NUL, MS Pw Jd 217/3 (Ali to Airey, from Tepelenë, 19/31 Mar. 1812).

367. See above, at nn. 156, 170 (artillery etc.), 243 (vital protection), 294 (gunpowder), 317 ('if his...').

368. Fleming, *Muslim Bonaparte*, pp. 8 ('In the...'), 115 ('By 1811...'), 116 ('British concern...'). The only clear example of a 'threat' was not to British power in the region, but to William Leake personally, when Ali threatened to hold him at Ioannina in 1809. But as Leake explained, this was caused by 'his fear of being abandoned by Great Britain and left to contend single-handed against France...in the event of such a Crisis, as he apprehends, he will not allow me to quit Ioannina, as my departure will deprive him of all farther hope of assistance from Great Britain' (TNA, FO 78/65, fos. 130r–132r (Leake to Adair, from Ioannina, 5 Sept. 1809), at fo. 130r–v). This could hardly be seen as evidence of 'Ali's obvious strength and superior position'.

369. Fleming, *Muslim Bonaparte*, p. 116 (printed also in Baggally, *Ali Pasha and Great Britain*, pp. 87–9).

370. Fleming, *Muslim Bonaparte*, p. 116.

371. Ibid., p. 117.

372. Ibid., p. 155.

373. Ibid., p. 119 ('Ali came...'), 157 ('it was...', 'realization that...').

374. Ibid., p. 182. In some ways, Fleming's own account of Ali reinforces the stereotype of capricious malice. Discussing his conflict with Souli, she makes no mention of the security issue, writing that 'There seems...to be no indication that the war between Ali and the Souliotes marked anything more than a personal vendetta' (p. 148). And on the killing of the men of Kardhiq, she passes over the fact that they had just fought a war against him, writing that 600 men unsuspectingly accepted an invitation to a 'feast' at the *han* (p. 171).

375. Ibid., p. 164 ('adjusted his...'); Holland, *Travels*, pp. 182–4 (telescopes etc., freedom from prejudice, seeking information), 527 (plan for Salih); Hughes, *Travels*, ii, p. 54 (plan for Salih, abandoned).

376. Fleming, *Muslim Bonaparte*, p. 164 (Leake, *Travels in Northern Greece*, iv, p. 221). Later on the same page, in a passage not quoted by Fleming, Leake writes: 'he even entertains lively fears for his own safety, as he often inquires whether, in case of being driven out of his native country, he should find security for his person and property in the British dominions.'

377. CAD, Janina, consulat, 290PO/1/15, pp. 80–6 (Pouqueville report, from Ioannina, 7 Apr. 1812), at p. 80 ('j'ai versé tant de sang, que je n'ose regarder en arrière!'); pp. 117–19 (Pouqueville report, from Ioannina, 6 Mar. 1812), at p. 118 (assassinations, serving-boys).

378. [J.] Sibthorp, 'Extract from the Journal of the Late Dr. Sibthorp, relating to Parts of the Ancient Elis, Arcadia, Argolis, Laconia, Messenia, and the Islands on the Western Shores of Greece', in R. Walpole, ed., *Travels in Various Countries of the East, being a Continuation of Memoirs relating to European and Asiatic Turkey* (London, 1820), pp. 75–106, at p. 98.

379. de Vaudoncourt, *Memoirs*, pp. 82 (Parga), 88 (Vonitsa).

380. Above, at n. 92 (Flory, 1806); Arsh, ed., *Ē Rōsia kai ta pasalikia*, pp. 205–6 (Benaki to Roumiantsev, from Corfu, 2/14 Aug 1809), at p. 205 ('un fidèle vassal'), pp. 242–4

(Benaki to Nesselrod, from Venice, 20 Sept./2 Oct. 1814), at p. 244 (request by Ali); pp. 247–51 (Nesselrod(?) to Benaki, from Paris, 1/13 Aug. 1815), at pp. 249–50 (Ali's messages, Parga).

381. See above, n. 120.

382. The standard modern history of the Albanian lands portrays Ali as seeking separation from the Ottoman state from the 1790s onwards: Prifti et al., eds., *Historia e popullit shqiptar*, i, p. 640. For a more romantic nationalist view of him, as the creator of a specifically Albanian state, see G. Meksi and V. Meksi, *Ali Pashë Tepelena* (n.p. [Tirana], 2004), esp. pp. 293–4.

383. See above, at n. 100.

384. See above, at n. 64.

385. Yaycioglu, *Partners of the Empire*, pp. 67 ('administrative, fiscal...'), 76 ('the dynasticization...'), 240 (competing models—the third involving collectively elected community leaders).

386. Different considerations apply, however, to Ali's sons Muhtar and Veli, whose careers conformed more closely to the 'order of notables' model: Muhtar, for instance, supplied large forces to the Ottoman army on several occasions, and was appointed at different times to the governorships of the *sancak*s of Ohrid, Euboea, Karlıeli, Trikala, Delvinë, Lepanto and Vlorë, being given the rank of *beylerbeyi* in 1810 as a reward for fighting the Russians (Sezer, 'Tepedelenli Ali Paşa'nın oğulları', p. 156). Overall they were awkwardly situated somewhere between this model and the practice of their father, who presumed on their loyalty to him. (One recent study claims that 'Ali and his sons could be counted upon to contribute forces to the Ottoman military effort' (F. Anscombe, 'Continuities in Ottoman Centre–Periphery Relations, 1787–1915', in A. C. S. Peacock, ed., *The Frontiers of the Ottoman World* (Oxford, 2009), pp. 235–51, at p. 244); but this ignores Ali's repeated refusals to supply forces himself, eliding the distinction that needs to be made between him and his sons.)

387. AMAE, CCC, Janina 1, no. 13 (Pouqueville to Talleyrand, from Ioannina, 21 Apr. 1806), at p. [3]; CCC, Janina 4, no. 165 (Pouqueville to Bassano, from Ioannina, 31 Oct. 1811), at p. [1] ('balancer l'autorité du grand seigneur').

388. See above, at n. 50.

389. See above, at nn. 61 (Morier), 119 (Leake instructions), 121 (Leake report).

390. Arsh, ed., *Ē Alvania kai ē Ēpeiros*, pp. 388–414 (Kapodistrias, 'Notions sur Aly Visir de Gianina', 1812), at p. 408 ('r[o]yauté de l'Epyre et de l'Albanie').

Chapter 9

Introductory note: This essay was first presented at a conference in Prizren in 2003, marking the 125th anniversary of the League of Prizren. Some knowledge of the general history of the League was therefore presumed; this note is for the benefit of readers who are less familiar with the subject. Following anti-Ottoman revolts in Hercegovina and Bosnia in 1875, the Ottoman Empire became embroiled in wars first against Serbia and Montenegro, and then against their sponsor-power Russia, during the period 1876–8. Russia imposed a peace settlement, the Treaty of San Stefano, in March 1878, which would have involved large territorial changes; the other Great Powers rejected this, and called the Congress of Berlin. The resulting Treaty of Berlin (July 1878) granted territorial gains to Serbia and Montenegro, including the transfer to the latter of the district of Gusinje (Guci) and Plav (Plavë), at the northern tip of the Ottoman province of Kosovo. This caused huge resentment in Kosovo itself. In June 1878, before the Congress of Berlin had finished its work, a meeting of Albanian notables at Prizren proclaimed the formation of a 'League', a military-defensive organization with the simple aim (to begin with) of resisting any attempt to cede land to neighbouring states. Three months later a senior Ottoman official, sent to Kosovo both to supervise the new border changes and to persuade the local population to accept them, was killed by an angry crowd in Gjakovë. The strength of local opposition to the ceding of Gusinje and Plav would lead the Great Powers to agree an alternative plan, under which the Ottoman Empire would give Montenegro the small coastal city of Ulcinj. During 1879 the aims of the League developed in a more 'autonomist' direction, as it began to demand self-government for the Albanian lands within the Ottoman Empire. In late 1880 it took over the administration of Kosovo, becoming the *de facto* government there; but in the spring of 1881 an Ottoman army violently reconquered the area. Although the League of Prizren was then disbanded, it retained a lasting significance as the first modern 'autonomist' movement, and would subsequently be regarded by many Albanians as a forerunner of the movement for full independence.

1. A. Roberts, *Salisbury: Victorian Titan* (London, 1999), pp. 187, 193.
2. See especially W. N. Medlicott, *Bismarck, Gladstone, and the Concert of Europe* (London, 1956), pp. 79–98.
3. For a thorough study of British public opinion and political debate on these issues, see W. G. Wirthwein, *Britain and the Balkan Crisis, 1875–1878* (New York, 1935); on Gladstone's role see also R. T. Shannon, *Gladstone and the Bulgarian Agitation, 1876* (London, 1963).
4. For a valuable study of the occasional references to Albania in the *Times* newspaper during this period, see R. J. Crampton ['Kramton'], 'Anglia dhe Shqiptarët më 1878–1881', in A. Buda et al., eds., *Konferenca kombëtare e studimeve për lidhjen shqiptare të Prizrenit, 1878–1881*, 2 vols. (Tirana, 1979), pp. 398–408, esp. pp. 399–402.
5. The National Archives, Kew (hereafter: 'TNA'), FO 424/88/101D, St. John to Salisbury, 22 Sept. 1879. I am very grateful to Bejtullah Destani for supplying copies of this and several of the other TNA documents cited in this essay.
6. S. Rizaj, ed., *Dokumente angleze mbi lidhjen shqiptare të Prizrenit dhe fillimin e copëtimit të Ballkanit (1877–1885)*, 2 vols. (Prishtina, 1996), ii, pp. 266–70.
7. British Government, *Accounts and Papers, 1880*, vol. 42, Turkey, no. 15, part 2, nos. 67 (St. John to Granville, 5 June 1880), 73 (St. John to Fitzmaurice, in Fitzmaurice's despatch of 22 July 1880).
8. Ibid., no. 75 (Fitzmaurice to Granville, 22 July 1880); and cf. no. 64, summarizing Kristoforidhi's account. (Kristoforidhi (1827–95), born in Elbasan, had converted to Protestantism and worked for the British and Foreign Bible Society, for which he translated parts of the Bible into Albanian.) St. John reacted angrily to being thus contradicted (see TNA, FO 30/29/344, no. 163 (St. John to Granville, 24 Jan. 1881)); he also responded in a somewhat surreptitious way, writing an anonymous article for the

Times (15 Sept. 1880) in which his own views were set out at length (see Crampton, 'Anglia dhe Shqiptarët', pp. 401–2).

9. See B. Hrabak, 'Prvi izveštaji diplomata velikih sila o Prizrenskoj Ligi', *Balcanica*, 9 (1978), pp. 235–89, at p. 250; F. Baxhaku and K. Kaser, eds., *Die Stammesgesellschaften Nordalbaniens: Berichte und Forschungen österreichischer Konsuln und Gelehrter (1861–1917)* (Vienna, 1996), pp. 38, 49, 55.

10. On Austrian policy see H. D. Schanderl, *Die Albanienpolitik Österreich-Ungarns und Italiens, 1877–1908* (Wiesbaden, 1971), pp. 22, 48–56.

11. TNA, FO 424/74/324 (Kirby Green to Salisbury, 8 Sept. 1878).

12. Ibid.

13. Rizaj, ed., *Dokumente angleze*, i, pp. 254–5 (Kirby Green to Salisbury, 30 Sept. 1878), 256–7 (Blunt to Layard, 30 Sept. 1878).

14. TNA, FO 424/76/485 (Kirby Green to Salisbury, 11 Nov. 1878).

15. TNA, FO 881/4268/70 (Kirby Green to Salisbury, 18 Apr. 1880) (printed in B. Destani, ed., *Albania & Kosovo: Political and Ethnic Boundaries, 1867–1946* (London, 1999), p. 122).

16. TNA, FO 881/4268/99 (Kirby Green to Salisbury, 25 Apr. 1880) (printed in Destani, ed., *Albania & Kosovo*, p. 128).

17. See TNA, FO 881/4268/237 (memorandum by Sale, dated 4 June 1880) (printed in Destani, ed., *Albania & Kosovo*, pp. 149–50).

18. Rizaj, ed., *Dokumente angleze*, ii, pp. 299–306 (Kirby Green to Granville, 29 May 1880), here pp. 299–300.

19. TNA, FO 881/4327/31 (Kirby Green to Granville, 25 June 1880) (printed in B. Destani, ed., *Montenegro: Political and Ethnic Boundaries, 1840–1920*, 2 vols. (London, 2001), p. 31).

20. Rizaj, ed., *Dokumente angleze*, ii, p. 304.

21. TNA, FO 881/4268/293 (Goschen to Granville, 22 June 1880) (printed in Destani, ed., *Albania & Kosovo*, pp. 151–2).

22. See S. Gwynn and G. M. Tuckwell, *The Life of the Rt. Hon. Sir Charles Dilke Bart., M.P.*, 2nd edn., 2 vols. (London, 1918), i, pp. 328–9. The proposal seems impractical to the point of absurdity; but I am grateful to Professor Ian Harris for pointing out that it may have been modelled on the constitutional situation that prevailed when the Elector of Hanover became George I of England in 1714. Hanover was theoretically an autonomous sub-unit of the Holy Roman Empire, and it was united only in a personal union with the British crown.

23. British Library, London, MS Add. 43,911, fo. 64r (Goschen to Dilke, 8 June 1880).

24. Ibid., fo. 128r (Greek chargé to Dilke, 5 Dec. 1880, enclosing text of a telegram sent by him to Athens: 'Among friends of Greece here, there seems to be a liking for the idea of a personal union of Albania with us, in order to strengthen our resources. If you approve, this would be a propitious time' ('Parmi amis Grèce ici parait en faveur projet union personelle Albanie avec nous pour renforcer nos moyens. En cas approbation moment serait favorable')).

25. Gwynn and Tuckwell, *Life of Dilke*, ii, p. 250.

26. TNA, FO 424/74/353 (Layard to Salisbury, 10 Sept. 1878). On the murder see N. Malcolm, *Kosovo: A Short History* (London, 1998), pp. 222–3.

27. See T. J. Spinner, *George Joachim Goschen: The Transformation of a Victorian Liberal* (Cambridge, 1973), esp. pp. 68–78; A. D. Elliot, *The Life of George Joachim Goschen, First Viscount Goschen, 1831–1907*, 2 vols. (London, 1911), i, pp. 198–240.

28. Wirthwein, *Britain and the Balkan Crisis*, p. 58. As a son of the Marquess of Lansdowne, Lord Edmond Fitzmaurice had a courtesy title, and was able to sit in the House of Commons.

29. TNA, FO 424/100/31–4 (Goschen to Granville, 26 July 1880) (printed in Rizaj, ed., *Dokumente angleze*, ii, pp. 324–33).

30. K. Prifti, ed., *Lidhja shqiptare e Prizrenit në dokumentet osmane, 1878–1881* (Tirana, 1978), pp. 76–9; Spinner, *George Joachim Goschen*, p. 70.

31. A. Ramm, ed., *The Political Correspondence of Mr Gladstone and Lord Granville, 1876–1886*, 2 vols. (Oxford, 1962), i, p. 187 (Gladstone to Granville, 27 Sept. 1880: 'In the last resort, to offer Albania to the Kalamas [*sc.* Albanian territory up to the Kalamas valley] (where the country inhabited by Greeks begins) its formal or practical independence').

Chapter 10

1. *The Memoirs of Ismail Kemal Bey*, ed. S. Story (London, 1920); Myfit Bey Libohova, *Politika ime ndë Shqipëri, 1916–1920* (Gjirokastër, 1921 [reprinted Tirana, 2004]); Hasan Bey Prishtina, *Nji shkurtim kujtimesh mbi kryengritjen shqyptare të vjetit 1912* (Shkodër, 1921 [reprinted n.p., 1995]).

2. S. Vlora, *Kujtime nga fundi i sundimit osman në Luftën e Vlorës*, tr. A. Asllani, ed. M. Verli and L. Dushku (Tirana, 2013); I. Strazimiri, *Lufta kundër pavarësimit të Shqipërisë* (Tirana, 2010).

3. I. Temo, *İttihad ve Terakki anıları* (Istanbul, 1987 [1st publ. Medgidia, 1939]); S. Vllamasi, *Ballafaqime politike në Shqipëri (1899–1942)*, ed. M. Verli (Tirana, 1995); T. Boletini, *Kujtime: Pranë Isa Boletinit* and *Përballë sfidave të kohës*, ed. M. Verli, 2 vols. (Tetovë, 1996 [reprinted Tirana, 2003]); S. Kosova, *Shqipëria e viteve 1912–1964 në kujtimet e Spiro Kosovës*, ed. M. Verli, 2 vols. (Tirana, 2008–9); Eqrem Bey Vlora, *Lebenserinnerungen*, 2 vols. (Munich, 1968–73).

4. N. Zaimi, *Daughter of the Eagle: The Autobiography of an Albanian Girl* (New York, 1937). On her birth and upbringing see the obituary, 'Nexhmie Zaimi, Author of "Daughter of the Eagle", Passes Away', *Dielli*, Apr.-June 2003, p. 9.

5. I. Kadare, *Kronikë në Gur* (Tirana, 1971).

6. The National Library of Albania (Biblioteka Kombëtare e Shqipërisë), Tirana, press-mark dr. l.b.13.

7. M. Kruja, *Kujtime vogjlije e rinije* (Tirana, 2007).

8. Biblioteca provinciale dei padri Cappuccini, Trento (hereafter: BPPC), MS AR 4 28/1. I am very grateful to the Capuchin library for permission to consult and quote from this manuscript.

9. Ibid., fasc. 1, fo. 40r ('mi fu posto nome Lazzaro conforme l'uso di alcuni Albanesi, di porre due o tre nomi…Mio Padre, Antonio, figlio di Lazzaro Tuscia, della stirpe Giolalla, era persona civile, e agiata, e godeva fame di uomo dabbene. La mia Madre

Cristina (Ziu) era della famiglia Duoda ricca e conosciuta in città. Essendo primogenito ebbi il privilegio di esser chiamato col nome del nonno').

10. Ibid., fasc. 1, fos. 37r–38r ('L'Albania antica'). The reason why the foliation begins on fo. 37 is not clear; the chapter-numbering leaves no room for doubt that this is the start of the work. Some of the authors and/or works mentioned by Tusha here are hard to identify with certainty. His 'Panajati' may perhaps be Panagiōtis Aravantinos, author of *Chronographia tēs Ēpeirou* (Athens, 1856) (in which case his knowledge of the work was presumably second-hand). His 'P. Jungh Gesuita' presumably refers to Giacomo Jungg, who taught at the Xaverian school in Shkodër; but the only work known to have been published by this writer at the time of composition of Tusha's text was his *Elementi grammaticali della lingua albanese* (Shkodër, 1881), which contains no historical observations whatsoever. The others he mentions are Giuseppe Juhani, P. Francesco Bossi M.Or., and P. Leonardo M.O. (these two abbreviations being presumably for the Order of Minims; on Father Leonardo see above, at n. 49).

11. BPPC, MS AR 4 28/1, fasc. 1, fos. 38r–39r, 'L'albania nel suo stato attuale' (fo. 39r: 'l'Albania giace ancora nel barbarismo, nella inciviltà, nell'estrema miseria. Li vive ancora come nel medio evo;…e la vita che si mena in campagna è come quella vita pastorale, che menavano gli antichi del vecchio testamento').

12. Ibid., fasc. 1, fo. 39r–v ('Descrizione di Scutari', 'deliziosa città…è capoluogo dell'Albania, il centro del commercio, e la prima per ricchezza, bellezza naturale, e buon clima', 'un poco separato dai Cristiani'). The total population of Shkodër fell during the second half of the century, from *c*.38,000 in the late 1850s (H. Hecquard, *Histoire et description de la Haute Albanie ou Guégarie* (Paris, n.d. [1858]), p. 13) to *c*.35,000 in the first decade of the 20th century, when Theodor Ippen estimated that there were 22,000 Muslims, 12,000 Catholics and 1,000 Orthodox, plus a number of Gypsies (*Skutari und die nordalbanische Küstenebene* (Sarajevo, 1907), p. 38, noting also the division of the city into 9 Muslim and 3 Catholic districts).

13. BPPC, MS AR 4 28/1, fasc. 1, fo. 39v ('più belle, e specialmente una via detta Paruzza ha cominciato a sentire un poco l'influenza del moderno progresso', 'un bellissimo convento…un grande seminario'). The Parruca family was one of the richest Catholic merchant families in the city (with a smaller Muslim branch), specializing in the silk trade; Filip Parruca contributed substantially to the cost of building the Catholic cathedral in 1858–67, and the family house he built later became the Italian Consulate (see F. Leo and L. Davico, *Il Consolato d'Italia a Scutari fra storia, testimonianze, architettura*, ed. R. Orlando (Catanzaro, 2008), pp. 31–2). A 'Parruca Square' (Sheshi Parruca) remains in Shkodër today; the street described by Tusha was a continuation of the road that runs north-eastwards from that square (now Rruga Qemal Draçini). The building of the seminary, friary, cathedral, archbishop's residence and other institutions gave a much more visibly Catholic character to Shkodër; until the early-to-mid-19th century there had been no Catholic church inside the city, and the bishop had resided outside it (Ippen, *Skutari*, pp. 39–40).

14. BPPC, MS AR 4 28/1, fasc. 1, fo. 40r ('Questo dolce si chiama [y]semerii ed è composta di farina, burro, e zucchero; la donna ne mangia *circa* un chilogramma in quel punto. Dato il felice annunzio della mia nascita, si raccolsero circa 15, o venti donne, parenti della famiglia della madre, e vennero in massa a visitarla. Ognuna portava un

dato numero di ova (che secondo i recenti ordini dovrebbero essere o quattro, o al più sei), e con quelle ova guardando il bambino, gli fregava la faccia. Quindi mettevano ognuna alcune piastre sotto il guanciale di mia madre, e quel denaro doveva darsi al nunzio, o [th]irzs. Stantechè io fui il primo bambino, il volto di mia madre era coperto da un sottile e largo fazzoletto orientale (sciamii ciubuke), ed alle cortesie usite delle donne, essa non dava risposta, nè diceva parola alcuna, ma solamente dava la mano; e questo in segno di pudore, essendo io il primo nato. Giaceva la mia madre in un ampio materasso disteso sul parimento, era coperta da imbottita bella e lussureggiante, e pesava il suo capo sopra lungo guanciale di fodera rossa; ed essendo parimente bianco-vermiglio il lenzuolo, e l'imbottita di setta o d'oro, facevano una bella mostra'). The piastre (or kuruş) was a silver coin, worth 40 paras and containing roughly one gram of pure silver; the Ottoman lira was worth 100 piastres. The primary meaning of 'çubuk' in Turkish is a rod, wand or bar; in relation to textiles it means a stripe or rib.

15. Ibid., fasc. 1, fo. 40v.

16. Ibid., fasc. 1, fo. 41r ('Dopo la madre, ebbe cura speciale di me la nonna paterna, la quale mi allevò in sua stanza i primi due o tre anni', 'Quantunque sia natura dei fanciulli albanesi di non star mai quieti nè a casa, nè dovunque, pure io divenni mansueto', 'Io fui buon fanciullo, grazie alle molte sollecitudini dei miei genitori, e dalla nonna. Essi rare volte mi lasciavano uscir di casa, e per lo più stava a chiuso, al contrario dei nostri fanciulli, che stanno tutto il giorno per le strade, a giocare ed infangarsi. Ebbi sempre amore alla quiete, alla pace, ed al ritiramento', 'Spesso giuocaua cogli asciiki, o ossetti, e articoli delle giunture e dei ginocchi degli animali: questi ossetti vengono alcune volte colorite in rosso, ed è il giuoco prediletto dei ragazzi').

17. Ibid., fasc. 1, fos. 41r (confirmation), 41v ('Come allora io era felice! Quando penso alla contentezza di quell'età, mi sento venire le lagrime al confronto col tempo presente', 'Signor Marco, di Venezia, persona istruita e galantuomo; ora però defunto', 'un certo Nicoletta', 'Filippo Cioba Albanese', 'un italiano Garibaldino, di sopranome Battaglia'). Shkodër was raised to the rank of an archdiocese in 1867; the German Karl Pooten served as Archbishop until his death in 1886. On this Jesuit school see I. A. Murzaku, *Catholicism, Culture, Conversion: The History of the Jesuits in Albania (1841–1946)* (Rome, 2006), p. 176.

18. BPPC, MS AR 4 28/1, fasc. 1, fo. 41r ('crescono come animali senza istruzione, ed appena cresciute si chiudono in casa', 'vi fù sempre qualche maestra privata o monaca; ed adesso vi sono le Stimatine, che insegnano gratis, ed hanno quasi 300 scolare', 'ed i fanciulli dei ricchi per lo più sono accompagnati alla scuola dai loro servi'). On the Franciscan and Stigmatine schools see M. Prenushi, 'Vështrim historik mbi gjendjen dhe zhvillimin e arsimit në gjuhën shqipe dhe të huaj në Shkodrën e shekullit XIX', *Studime historike*, 28 (1974), no. 3, pp. 65–83, at pp. 71, 74.

19. BPPC, MS AR 4 28/1, fasc. 1, fos. 42r–46r, chs. 6–8 ('La casa paterna', 'I mobili albanesi').

20. Ibid., fasc. 1, fo. 46r–v ('ostinazione al divin volere', 'e vestito per l'ultima volta le vesti albanesi, mi inviai al Collegio, corteggiato da una moltitudine grande di parenti ed amici benevoli', 'il più contento uomo del mondo').

21. On the early history of the seminary see Murzaku, *Catholicism*, pp. 128–33. Murzaku cites the official instructions of the Propaganda Fide, specifying five years of

secondary schooling, but Lazër Tusha notes that by his time this had become six. The other Pontifical Serminaries are those of Columbus, Ohio (1892) and Bangalore (1962).

22. BPPC, MS AR 4 28/1, fasc. 1, fos. 46v–47v ('un vero servo di Dio; uomo contemplativo, perfetto in tutte le virtù', 'belle lettere', 'eloquenza e poesia').

23. P. Bartl, ed., *Albania sacra: geistliche Visitationsberichte aus Albanien*, i: *Diözese Alessio* (Wiesbaden, 2007), p. 393 (friary).

24. BPPC, MS AR 4 28/1, fasc. 1, fo. 48r ('Villeggiatura a Trosciani – Morte del Padre – Descrizione dei funerali').

25. Ibid., fasc. 1, fos. 48v–49r ('segno di estremo lutto', 'Tutti i membri di queste Compagnie, avvisati dai vecchiardi, dovettero venire a seppelirlo, pagando per l'anima sua 2 piastre. Vennero pure a seppelirlo tutti i parenti ed amici; e si fece una comitiva di circa 300 Scutarini. Vennero pure tutti i sacerdoti che si trovavano a Scutari (giacchè noi chierici eravamo in villeggiatura.[)] Vennero i 6.Gesuiti, ed i 6. Francescani; e circa in 20 vennero nella stanza del morto, e cantarono un De profundis, e poi si misero in fila a due a due, cantando salmi'), 49v ('si sgrafiano e si fanno sangue, e battono fortemente il petto', 'In alcuni luoghi sogliano rompere un gran pignata quando esce di casa il morto; dicendo che in quella pignata sono racchiusi tutti i mali, e rompendola i mali svaporano'). Lazër notes, with an evident touch of pride in his family's socio-economic status, that the funeral banquet for his father cost 2,000 piastres.

26. Ibid., fasc. 1, fo. 50r–v.

27. Ibid., fasc. 2, fos. 3r–v ('tutta Turca', 'è paese sanissimo, ed i signori di Scutari e di altri paesi vanno ogni anno a villeggiare, e a fare i bagni (cioè a lavarsi nel mare...)'), 4r ('e abbondaran le tartarughe, che furon nostro cibo prediletto a Salci; ma gli Albanesi non se ne curano, e neppur sanno ben condirle', 'se non li avesse sacceggiati il Montenegro più barbaro del Turco'). Pal Shantoja would later (1888–92) serve as parish priest of Barbullush: see http://www.kishakatolikeshkoder.com/Institutetper cent20rregulltare/oblatet/te-dhena-te-pjesshme-per-famullite-e-barbullushit.htm.

28. BPPC, MS AR 4 28/1, fasc. 2, fos. 4v–5r ('Le Conseguenze della guerra', 'una guerra accanita col Turco, e cogli stessi paesani, che benchè stufi del Turco pure resistevano al Montenegro', 'gente robusta, e lavoratori instancabili').

29. Ibid., fasc. 2, fo. 5r ('ripieni di fanatismo Turco preferirono lasciar in pace le loro case e i loro terreni e i loro beni stabili in regolo al Montenegro...e per la loro falsa religione si ridussero ad estrema miseria', 'si mischiarono in tutte nostre arti e mestieri...ve[n]dendo essi le cose a vil prezzo per poco guadagno', 'Da quasi cinque anni il commercio di Scutari è morto, come qui si dice').

30. Ibid., fasc. 2, fo. 6r ('Ritorno nel secolo').

31. Ibid., fasc. 2, fo. 6r ('non mi riconobbe più e negò la parola data e non mi volle'), 6v ('doveva con penitenza nuova espiare a peccati vecchi', 'nel Bazar, nella mia bottega lasciatami dal Padre, e presi ad attendere agli affari di famiglia,; dove anche ora mi trovo').

32. Ibid., fasc. 2, fo. 6v ('perchè non era stato kysmet (come dicevano essi)').

33. Ibid., fasc. 2, fos. 6v ('feci di tutto per non lasciarla (anche contra la volontà dei superiori); ma Dio non volle, perchè io era indegno per le mie colpe...Feci qualche tentativo anche più tardi, e nulla ottenni, ed anche ora mi trovo come allora. Diversi sono i

desideri dalla vita che meno. Faccio il commerciante contro mia voglia. L'avvenire poi è in mano di Dio; però spero che mi sarà ora favorevole in una santa impresa a cui mi accingo'), 7r ('pretesto', 'mancanza di vocazione').

34. Ibid., fasc. 2, fos. 8r–v ('I miei vestiti', 'Il sistema è orientale, il lusso asiatico moderato dala povertà del paese', 'i Turchi cittadini vestono come i Cristiani con qualche piccola differenza; perchè nel vestito Turco, che è assai più maestoso, spicca il color bianco, e nel Cristiano il nero e il rosso. I Turchi invece di larghe braghe vestono una specie di breve sottola bianca fino ai ginocchi, che chiamano fistan, ma larghissima e candida come la neve, e accresce maestà e gravità alla persona colle sue numerosissime pieghe'), 9r–10r (priests, *hoxhas*, women's clothes).

35. Ibid., fasc. 2, fos. 10r–11v ('La piazza Albanese', 'spesso si sente in bocca quel Jahudi-pazaar, doppio sistema giudaica di vendere, e rare volte si adopera il cosidetto Elbassan-pazaar, o Selaniki-pazaar, metodo di vendere a prezzo fisso…a Scutari quasi nulla ha il prezzo fisso, eccettuato il pane dei fornai, che per lo più sono Schismatici, fuori di pochi Turchi'). Theodor Ippen noted that the bakers were mostly 'Bulgarians' (*sc.* Macedonians) from Struga, which lies just to the north of Ohrid (*Skutari*, p. 30).

36. Ibid., fasc. 2, fos. 12r–14r ('Un invito alle nozze').

37. Ibid., fasc. 2, fos. 14v–15r ('Le superstizioni', 'molti errori, molti pregiudizi, molti timori e precauzioni, che dominano dapertutto in Albania sia tra i Turchi che tra i Cristiani', 'Il Signore, al dir di loro, alla nascita di ognuno scrive nel cranio tutti gli avvenimenti, che devongli accadere durante la vita; e perciò nelle disgrazie dicono, questo esser già al eterno da Dio destinato e scritto', 'questo fanatismo li rende forti in guerra', 'Guardano nel dorso di quell'osso, e predicono guerre, eserciti, pace, morti in famiglia, morti nel vicinato o tra parenti o molte cose. Se quell'osso ha un buco in cima, morirà di certo presto presto il padrone di casa. Se l'osso nella sua prospettiva ha dei segnali rossi, il sangue scorrerà a rivi nel nostro paese, se vi ha dei segnali bianchi, quelli significano sepolchri, e morirà uno di casa', 'altre superstizioni pessime', 'quello che è più meraviglioso si è la certezza e la precisione, con quale predicono queste cose, e che poi per lo più veramente avvengono. Quindi io sono persuaso che realmente il demonio non habbia ancor levato il dominio, che ha avuto sempre nei nostri paesi, perchè realmente ha parte in queste cose').

38. Ibid., fasc. 2, fo. 15r–v ('in paragone a quelle maggiori superstizioni, che sono in pieno vigore tra i nostri Cristiani', 'Scitim', 'tormentare i tentare gli uomini', 'scitue', 'Il mio giudizio è, che il demonio veramente opera tali cose nei nostri paesi').

39. Ibid., fasc. 2, fo. 16r ('usitatissima', 'Quando un mio fratellino, di nome Nicolò, fù trovato morto una mattina colla bocca piena di sangue, attribuirono tale morte improvvisa ad operazioni magiche di strega, perchè anche il lume si trovò da sè smorzato. Era facile trovare poi la stregha. Quel primo povero o povera che venisse a chiedere limosina quella mattina, quello sarebbe il mezzano di tali stregonerie; quallora però non ubidisse a sputare in terra, perchè sputando ella non sarebbe colpevole. Veramente venne la mattina una povera vecchia a questuare. Le chiedemmo uno sputto, e le promettemmo abbondante limosina in denaro. Quella sospettando qualche scherzo non volle giammai sputare, e se ne andò via; e fu tenuta come cagionevole della morte di mio fratello').

40. Ibid., fasc. 2, fo. 16r–v ('Certo però che si crede esistenti le culscedre, le sfingi, e certi esseri inesprimabili nelle solitudine, che incantano i viatori').

41. Ibid., fasc. 2, fo. 16v ('Certi sacerdoti hanno il dono da Dio (o altrimenti) di fare simili favori con brevetti, come di sanar malattie, scacciar demoni, perfezionare i sensi o le membra...Si usano brevetti anche per gli animali, e qui è in voga la superstizione del *mal occhio*. Ed in questa pure ha parte il demonio, non essendo cose naturali').

42. Ibid., fasc. 2, fo. 16v ('la forza e prepotenza, quasi il despotismo, dei bravi d'allora, le uccisioni e le vanità, gli incontri, e la memoria trasmessa da padre in figlio di vendette da prendersi per antiche offese e quasi dimenticate uccisioni').

43. Ibid., fasc. 2, fo. 17r ('Quindi è una catena di uccisioni in Albania, specialmente nelle montagne', 'in mezzo alla piazza', 'mezz'ora dopo').

44. Ibid., fasc. 2, fo. 17v ('per nature o per fede', 'a questo vile tra i montagnuoli nelle loro radunanze si dà il bicchierino d'acquavita per traverso sotto il ginnocchio, seduti come sono alla Turca colle gambe incrocicchiate. E così disonorandolo, lo spingono alla vendetta, che quanto più tarda, tanto arriva più crudele').

45. Ibid., fasc. 3, fo. 2r–v ('Le amicizie in Albania', 'Per l'amico un albanese si annegher-ebbe, si slanciarebbe nel fuoco, cascherebbe da alto precipizio, si condannerebbe a perenne prigione, a fame, a stenti, a privarsi di ogni proprio avere, anche della propria vita. E se gli Albanesi mancano ad altri precetti del Signore, io stimo che puntual-mente osservano quello che dice: Ama il prossimo tuo come te stesso; imperochè spesso lo amano più di sè stessi').

46. Ibid., fasc. 3, fo. 2v ('specialmente se [sono] Italiani', 'Però adesso ho tralasciato quell'intima confidenza che aveva con ognuno senza distinzione di persone, perchè l'esperienza mi insegnò che mi ingannava, ed ho cominciato a provare alquanta dif-fidenza con alcuni, dopo chè caddi nelle insidie altrui').

47. Ibid., fasc. 3, fo. 3r ('Fra gli Albanesi ho molta amicizia e famigliarità cogli avventori della mia bottega, e coi buoni contadini, come pure coi sinceri Scutarini e con quelli che amano la virtù, lo studio delle lettere, e che pensano e giudicano delle cose netta-mente e senza pregiudizii', 'Vi sono anche amicizie impure, purtroppo frequenti spe-cialmente tra la gioventù...gli albanesi si amano (ed anche si odiano) intimamente senza motivi carnali, o per egoismo, ma per sincerità cordiale').

48. Ibid., fasc. 3, fos. 3v ('Falsa vocazione', 'una interna voce, un interno desiderio, una vocazione interna sempre ad altra Religione', 'una falsa vocazione, una illusione'), 4r–v (Lezhë-Shkodër-Lezhë), 5r ('la mal contentezza assieme agli stente, ai cattivi tratta-menti, ed alle celie, diedero l'ultimo crollo alla mia finta vocazione'), 5v (Mariano of Palmanuova).

49. Ibid., fasc. 3, fos. 6r–10r.

50. Ibid., fasc. 3, fos. 10v ('Il mio Commercio', 'Tutto il nostro commercio si riduce in comprar roba dai signori, e, formandone abiti, venderli poi ai contadini. A quest'arte ab antico rimase il nome di boimalii', 'tela, panno, setta, e oro', 'contadini Turchi, gente sincera, buona, e nostri amicissimi'), 11r ('la maggior nostra ricchezza consiste in crediti', 'Noi negoziamo coi più ricchi villani, e tutti mi vogliono bene; e quando andai per il Bairam a passeggiare ad essi, mi trattarono come un gran signore, perchè quasi tutti i villaggi circonvicini mi devono denaro, e non poco, perchè chi mi deve due mila piastre, chi tre mila, e fino a quattro mila una famiglia sola'), 11v (villagers, smaller items). 'Boimalii' does not appear in modern dictionaries; possibly it derives from 'boj' (a Gheg form of 'bëj', to 'make') and 'mall', meaning 'goods'. (I am very grateful to Dr Uran Ferizi for this suggestion.)

51. Ibid., fasc. 3, fo. 12r ('puro guadagno, dopo aver pagati tutti gli agenti, i garzoni, i sarti, e l'affitto della bottega', 'abbiamo varie terre, abbiamo due case, tre vigne, un prato vigna e capanna a Barbullusci, un fertile terreno a Gurizii, alcuni crediti privati, e denaro ad interesse; come pure la madre e la nonna hanno denaro, da cui ricavano ogni anno l'interesse di dieci per cento, come si suole tra i Cristiani qui in Albania, mentre i Turchi danno e prendono il 15 per cento'); Barbullush is a village roughly 9 miles south of Shkodër; Gur i Zi is a village 3 miles south-east of Shkodër.

52. Ibid., fasc. 3, fo. 12r ('o, come direbbero qui maestro di bottega', 'a riscuotere i nostri crediti, ed è molto amico e pratico coi villani').

53. Ibid., fasc. 3, fos. 12v–14v ('Un viaggio alle Montagne'), 14v–15r ('Le Feste in Albania', 'la Madonna del Buon Consiglio', 'alla venuta dei barbari Turchi fù trasportata sopra l'aere dagli Angeli, e depositata a Gennazano, dove si venera tuttora miracolosamente in aria sospesa, nulla poggiandola sopra la nicchia del ricco altare. Ed i Scutarini conservano speranza nel cuore, che quella benedetta immagine della loro Prottetrice ritornerà presto alle terre albaniche', 'che fà assai del bene (ed in questa Congregazione sono anch'io, e tengo una medaglia)').

54. Ibid., fasc. 3, fo. 15r ('poche e assai meschine', 'girano per la città, gridando e urlando', 'una specie di chitarra', 'ciapare', 'cantori pagati, e grandi bevute d'acquavita, e salti e canti indescrivibili', 'perchè dicono che allora il dragone si divora la luna e lo spaventano, e lo uccidono').

55. Ibid., fasc. 3, fos. 16v–18r (Bushat), 18v–19v (Madonna di Scutari); fasc. 4, fos. 2r–3v (food), 4r–v (Lake Shkodër), 4v–7r (Skanderbeg).

56. Ibid., fasc. 4, fos. 7v ('Vera Vocazione Divina', 'Questo Capitolo descriverà, quando avremo con seguito quello, a cui il Signore ci ispira'), 8v ('Cap. 33.°, ed ultimo. Entrata, e Perseveranza').

57. Ibid., fasc. 2, cover ('Questa narrazione interessante, per la ingenua verità , se sia abreuiata, corretta in quanto a lingua e ortografia ed i vocaboli [?] scritti chiaramente, e segnati in nota se sieno albanesi o turche, e moderata la stizza contro ai Maomettani, e venga messa alla stampa'), fasc. 4, fo. 12r ('Questo non mi appartiene'). On De Rada see R. Elsie, *History of Albanian Literature*, 2 vols. (Boulder, CO, 1995), i, pp. 158–70. The later history of Lazër's manuscript is unknown, apart from the fact that it was bequeathed to the Capuchin library by Luigi Menapace, a writer and journalist who lived in Trento and died in 1986 (see the catalogue entry by Adriana Paolini in http://manus.iccu.sbn.it//opac_SchedaScheda.php?ID=193929).

Chapter 11

1. For a valuable overview of those contributions, see Zef Mirdita, *Krishtenizmi ndër Shqiptarë* (Prizren, 1998), pp. 243–347. This essay is dedicated to Professor Mirdita, in gratitude for his acts of personal kindness, and in admiration of his major contributions to scholarship. I am also grateful to Robert Elsie for his comments on this essay.

2. The only study known to me is the excellent but very brief article by Kahreman Ulqini, 'Dy fjalë për albanologun Ernesto Cozzi (1870-1926)', *Kultura popullore*, 20 (1999), nos. 1-2, pp. 189–93.

3. These details are from the anonymous obituary in *Zâni i Shna Ndout*, 14, no. 3 (Mar. 1926), pp. 33–6, at 33–4. I am very grateful to Giovalin Çuni and Magi Laca, of the 'Marin Barleti' Library, Shkodër, for kindly sending me a copy of this article.

4. *Lajmtari i zemres së Jezu Krishtit*, 36, n. 3 (Mar. 1926), pp. 33–5, at p. 33: 'per të cillat Perendija e kishte stolisë me aftsí të veçantë e me fuqí mendjet e shndedjet'. Again, I am very grateful to Giovalin Çuni and Magi Laca for a copy of this article.

5. Edith Durham wrote that Cozzi had had 'several years' medical training' (*High Albania* (London, 1909), p. 107), and that he was 'medically trained and very skilful with wounds' (*The Struggle for Scutari (Turk, Slav, and Albanian)* (London, 1914), p. 210). On the service as a military chaplain see below, n. 25.

6. *Lajmtari* (as in n. 4, above), p. 34.

7. On Marconi see E. Deusch, *Das k.(u.)k. Kultusprotektorat im albanischen Siedlungsgebiet in seinem kulturellen, politischen und wirtschaftlichen Umfeld* (Vienna, 2009), pp. 110 (n.), 458–9.

8. *Lajmtari* (as in n. 4, above), p. 34 ('Gjân'). Sumë is in the Postribë district, just to the north-east of Shkodër; Xhan lies further to the north-east, near Kir.

9. E. Cozzi, 'La donna albanese, con speciale riguardo al diritto consuetudinario delle Montagne di Scutari', *Anthropos*, 7 (1912), no. 3, pp. 309–35, and nos. 4–5, pp. 617–26, at p. 317 (n.): 'Suma, dove fui parroco dal 1901–1903'.

10. See F. Cordignano, ed., *L'Albania a traverso l'opera e gli scritti di un grande Missionario italiano il P. Domenico Pasi S. I. (1847–1914)*, 3 vols. (Rome, 1933–4), ii, p. 344(n.). One of the obituaries states that Cozzi remained at Sumë until 1904 (see *Zâni i Shna Ndout* (as in n. 3, above), p. 34); but the report edited by Cordignano (ii, p. 344) shows that his successor was already in place in Sumë before the end of 1903. [*Additional note*: In 1884 Sumë had been served by the parish priest of Xhan, and in 1863 there had been no priest in either parish: see P. Bartl, ed., *Albania sacra: geistliche Visitationsberichte aus Albanien*, iv: *Diözese Pulati* (Wiesbaden, 2017), pp. 319, 332.]

11. E. Cozzi, 'La vendetta del sangue nelle Montagne dell'Alta Albania', *Anthropos*, 5 (1910), no. 1, pp. 654–87, at p. 676: 'per una sola parola di dileggio vidi cadere cinque montagnoli sulla porta della mia chiesa (Suma).' ('Montagnolo', which I translate as 'highlander', is Cozzi's term for 'malësor'.)

12. Ibid., p. 674: 'curata da chi scrive, guariva in breve, ed al presente si trova maritata in Montenegro.' Puzzlingly, Cozzi dates this episode to 1905.

13. Archivio storico della Sacra Congregazione di Propaganda Fide, Rome, nuova serie, 1920, vol. 656, Rub. 109 (protocollo 2886), part 3, fo. 239v. On this document (which will be referred to hereafter as Cozzi, 'Atti'), see above, p. 303.

14. *Zâni i Shna Ndout* (as in n. 3, above), p. 34. Kodhel is in the Zadrimë district, close to Dajç, half-way between Shkodër and Lezhë.

15. *Lajmtari* (as in n. 4, above), p. 34. Lazër Mjeda was just one year older than Cozzi, and had served as secretary to Marconi; he became Bishop of Sapë in 1901 by special papal dispensation (as he was below the canonical age of 35). At the end of 1904 Mjeda became Coadjutor to the Archbishop of Shkodër, and received a titular archbishopric, moving to Shkodër in 1905. See M. W. E. Peters, *Geschichte der Katholischen Kirche in Albanien, 1919–1993* (Wiesbaden, 2003), p. 284; Deusch, *Das Kultusprotektorat*, p. 436; and the studies in N. Ballabani, ed., *Imzot Lazër Mjeda: mbrojtës dhe lëvrues i identitetit shqiptar* (Prishtina and Sankt Gallen, 2011).

16. *Zâni i Shna Ndout* (as in n. 3, above), p. 34; G. Valentini, introduction to E. Cozzi, 'La donna albanese', *Shêjzat*, 17 (1973), nos. 1–4, pp. 94–126, 232–41 (a reprinting of Cozzi's article, with a brief introduction), at p. 94.

17. In his letter to Carl Patsch of 5 Mar. 1909 (see n. 34, below) Cozzi wrote that since January of that year he had moved to the new parish of 'Rjoli'. The obituary in *Zâni i Shna Ndout* (as in n. 3, above) mistakenly dates the move to Rrjoll to 1914 (p. 34). Rrjoll, Reç and Lohje were all clans (*fises*) of Malësia e Madhe. Edith Durham described Rrjoll as 'a small tribe of one bariak [*sic*]', and noted that it was 'but a two and a half hours' walk' from Reç (*High Albania*, p. 108).

18. Cozzi, 'Atti' (see n. 13, above), part 3, fo. 236v.

19. *Lajmtari* (as in n. 4, above), p. 34, naming the Archbishop as Jak Serreqi, who was installed there in June 1910; Cozzi was certainly acting for him when he travelled to Vienna in 1912 (see below, at n. 119).

20. On 'Malësia e Madhe' see n. 31, below.

21. Durham, *High Albania*, p. 107.

22. *Lettere edificanti dei padri della Compagnia di Gesù della Provincia Veneta*, xx (Venice, 1910), p. 51, quoted in Ulqini, 'Dy fjalë', p. 189.

23. Deusch, *Das Kultusprotektorat*, pp. 460–2. On Serreqi see Peters, *Geschichte der Katholischen Kirche*, p. 289.

24. Ibid., p. 730. Deusch's book is by far the most thorough study of the functioning of the 'Kultusprotektorat'.

25. Ibid., p. 461: 'wegen seiner überragenden Bildung und seiner unleugbaren Tüchtigkeit sowie mit Rücksicht auf seine Beliebtheit...Don Ernesto Cozzi ist Triestiner [*sic*: an error for "Trientiner"], ehemaliger Militärkaplan, seit 1901 im Lande, spricht Deutsch und hat das Albanische vollkommen erlernt. Der einzige dunkle Punkt betreffs seiner wäre, dass er in politischer Beziehung vor zwei Jahren eine Unvorsichtigkeit insoferne begangen hat, dass er sich zu weit mit Don Nicolò Ashta eingelassen hatte und durch diesen in eine indirekte Berührung zu Aladro und Schiaparelli gekommen ist.' The reference to being a military chaplain is puzzling, as this is not mentioned (for the period before the First World War) in any other account of Cozzi's life; possibly he had spent some time in this capacity between 1895 and 1901.

26. N. Ashta, 'Kanuni i malcís', *Albania*, 1897, pp. 149–52, 178–81; 1898, pp. 86, 106–7, 156; 1899, pp. 67–70; these articles were translated as 'Das Gewohnheitsrecht der Stämme Mi-Schodrak (Über-Scutariner Stämme) in den Gebirgen nördlich von Scutari', *Zeitschrift für Ethnologie*, 33 (1901), pp. 358–63. The latter work was accompanied by a similar text by Lazër Mjeda (pp. 353–8: 'Das recht der Stämme von Dukadschin').

27. On Aladro see S. Skendi, *The Albanian National Awakening, 1878–1912* (Princeton, NJ, 1967), pp. 318–24, and E. Deusch, 'Albanische Thronbewerber: ein Beitrag zur Geschichte der albanischen Staatsgründung', *Münchner Zeitschrift für Balkankunde*, 4 (1981–2), pp. 89–150; 5 (1983–4), pp. 121–64; 6 (1990), pp. 93–151 (at 4, pp. 96–101). Nathalie Clayer notes that, through intermediaries, Aladro did gather some support among the Catholic clergy of the Shkodër region: *Aux origines du nationalisme albanais: la naissance d'une nation majoritairement musulmane en Europe* (Paris, 2007), p. 422.

28. On Ghika, who was from a prominent Romanian family (of Albanian origin), see Skendi, *Albanian National Awakening*, pp. 324–31, and Deusch, 'Albanische

Thronbewerber', 4, pp. 148–50 (commenting that he was not taken seriously by the Albanians).

29. Deusch, *Das Kultusprotektorat*, pp. 434–5. Aladro's secretary was Viskë Babatasi, from Korçë, who served him from 1902 to 1908 (Skendi, *Albanian National Awakening*, p. 320; Clayer, *Aux origines*, p. 424; Deusch, 'Albanische Thronbewerber', 4, pp. 97, 100). However, the catalogue of Arkivi Qëndror i Shtetit, Tirana (hereafter: 'AQSh'), records a letter written by the priest Pjetër Tusha on 14 Oct. 1907 stating that Luigj Gurakuqi was taking on the secretarial role at that time (Fondi 132, Arqipeshkvia e Shkodrës, 1907, dosja 22). I am very grateful to Dr Nevila Nika for facilitating my visits to the AQSh.

30. Valentini, introduction to Cozzi, 'La donna albanese' (as in n. 16, above), p. 94: 'Dalla stesura, calligraficamente perfetta e senza pentimenti del suo grande e massiccio manoscritto, si può dedurre che egli pensasse d'aver fatto con ciò opera definitiva.'

31. Ibid., p. 95. As Cozzi explained, the two main divisions of the northern Albanian mountains were Malësia e Madhe ['the Great Highlands'], containing the *fises* of Hot, Grudë, Kelmend, Kastrat, Shkrel, Reç, Lohje and Rrjoll, and Malësia e Vogël ['the Little Highlands'], containing those of Shalë, Shosh, Kir, Plan, Toplanë and Xhan ('La donna albanese', p. 309 (n.)). Roughly speaking, the former is a broad arc of territory stretching from north of Shkodër north-eastwards below the present Montenegrin border; the latter is a smaller area nestling beneath that arc, to the north-east of Shkodër.

32. On Patsch see H. D. Szemethy, 'Patsch, Carl Ludwig', in *Neue Deutsche Biographie*, xx (Berlin, 2001), pp. 101–2 (http://www.deutsche-biographie.de/pnd11605882X.html).

33. C. Patsch, *Das Sandschak Berat in Albanien* (Vienna, 1904).

34. Bayerisches Hauptstaatsarchiv, Munich, Südostinstitut MS 271, Cozzi to Patsch, 9 Mar. 1909: 'Ich habe schon seit einigen Jahren, nach meinen Kräften, viel Material über die Sitten u. Gebräuche der Bergbewohner Ober-Albaniens (besonders der Bergstämme des Vilajets von Scutari) gesammelt; aber leider habe ich noch nicht diese Notizien in Ordnung gebracht; und überdies möchte ich die Sitten u. Gebräuche der Kleinen Malzia mit den der grossen Malzia, wo ich gegenwärtig thätig bin, ver-gleichen, und so meine kleine Arbeit ergänzen: leider aber als Missionär habe ich zu wenig Zeit dafür. Ich müss auch erwähnen, dass ich meine Aufsätze in meiner Muttersprache (italienisch) geschrieben habe. Sie werden mir in Rücksicht auf diese Umstände gewiss ihre gütige Verzeihung eingedeihen [*sic*] lassen, dass ich Ihr Anerbieten nicht annehmen kann.' I am very grateful to Bärbel Köhler of the Bayerisches Hauptstaatsarchiv and to Konrad Clewing of the Südostinstitut for their help in providing copies of Cozzi's letters to Patsch.

35. E. Cozzi, 'Malattie, morte, funerali nelle montagne d'Albania', *Anthropos*, 4 (1909), nos. 5–6, pp. 903–18, at p. 909: 'Proprio mentre scrivevo quest'articolo (29. Marzo 1909), veniva chiamato a visitare una donna cinquantenne….'

36. Valentini, introduction to Cozzi, 'La donna albanese' (as in n. 16, above), p. 96. I am very grateful to Father Diego Brunello SJ for confirming that this MS is not among the Cordignano papers preserved at the Archive of the Venetian Province of the Society of Jesus at Gallarate.

37. For the first three of these, see above, nn. 35, 11 and 9, respectively. The fourth was 'Credenze e superstizioni nelle montagne dell'Albania', *Anthropos*, 9 (1914), nos. 3–4, pp. 449–76.

38. I am very grateful to Dr Andrzej Miotk SVD, who has searched the surviving correspondence of Wilhelm Schmidt in the archive of the Societas Verbi Divini, Rome, without finding any references to Cozzi. I am also grateful to Prof. Dr Joachim Piepke, of the Anthropos Institut, Sankt Augustin, who confirms that the Institut does not retain any archival materials from this period.

39. On his early life and work see E. Brandewie, *When Giants Walked the Earth: The Life and Times of Wilhelm Schmidt SVD* (Fribourg, 1990), pp. 11–48.

40. K. J. Rivinius, *Im Dienst der Mission und der Wissenschaft: zur Entstehungsgeschichte der Zeitschrift Anthropos* (Fribourg, 2005), pp. 268–308, gives a photo-reproduction of the full text of the prospectus. Here p. 272 (= p. 4 of the original): 'die meist nur kurze Dauer derselben, die mangelhafte oder vollständig fehlende Bekanntschaft mit den Sprachen der betreffenden Völker'.

41. Ibid., p. 272: '*Hier erscheint nun die Stellung des Missionars als eine einzigartig günstige.* Er ist schon durch seinen Missionsberuf genötigt, die *Sprache des Volkes*, bei dem er wirkt, gründlich zu erlernen... Er verweilt nicht nur ein par Tage oder Wochen bei dem Volke, *sondern ganze Jahre und Jahrzehnte*; er sieht also nicht bloss einzelne Stücke aus dem Leben dieses Volkes, sondern in seiner vollen Ausdehnung, in seiner regelmässigen Folge wie in seinen wechselnden Einzelheiten spielt es sich vor seinen Augen ab....'

42. Ibid., p. 280 (= p. 12 of the original). In 1911 one Mark was equivalent to one English shilling or 25 US cents (K. Baedeker, *Austria-Hungary* (Leipzig, 1911), 'Money Table').

43. On this point see Brandewie, *When Giants Walked the Earth*, p. 55.

44. W. Schmidt, *Die Ursprung der Gottesidee*, 12 vols. (Münster, 1912–55). See the comments in W. Petermann, *Die Geschichte der Ethnologie* (Wuppertal, 2004), pp. 600–3.

45. Rivinius, *Im Dienst der Mission*, pp. 284–5 (= pp. 16–17 of the original).

46. Ibid., pp. 289–305 (= pp. 21–37 of the original).

47. 'Lo stato agricolo in Albania, con speciale riguardo alle montagne di Scutari', *Revue d'ethnographie et de sociologie*, 1 (1910), pp. 33–49.

48. See Brandewie, *When Giants Walked the Earth*, p. 58. On Van Gennep more generally see N. Belmont, *Arnold Van Gennep, créateur de l'ethnographie française* (Paris, 1974). The journal was at first called *Revue des études ethnographiques et sociologiques*; it was renamed in 1910.

49. E. Cozzi, 'Le tribù dell'Alta Albania: appunti sulla loro organizzazione sociale e politica con dati statistici', ed. G. Valentini, in *Studime e tekste, dega 1: juridike, n. 1* (Rome, 1944), pp. 229–69.

50. Bayerisches Hauptstaatsarchiv, Munich, Südostinstitut MS 271, Cozzi to Patsch, 4 Mar. 1912: 'Da es voraussichtlich ein allgemeiner Aufstand in Albanien ausbrechen wird, habe ich in kurzer Zeit eine Arbeit in italienischer Sprache verfasst, um die sociale u. politische Organization der Bergstämme Ober-Albaniens zu schildern, u. ich möchte dieselbe sofort drücken lassen.'

51. Ibid. In 1911 one Austrian Krone was equivalent to 10½ English pence, or 21 US cents (Baedeker, *Austria-Hungary*, 'Money Table').

52. See G. Valentini, 'Prefazione', in Cozzi, 'Le tribù', pp. 231–2, and his preface to Cozzi, 'La donna albanese', in *Shtêjzat* (see above, n. 16), pp. 94–6. Valentini incorrectly gave the date of the *Il Trentino* article as '29' Dec.; I am very grateful to Marina Chemelli, of the Biblioteca Comunale di Trento, for supplying a copy of the original article. Cozzi's letter to Patsch of Mar. 1912 (see above, n. 50) included a complete list of contents of the planned work, concluding with an 'Appendice—Dati statistici'.

53. Cozzi, 'Le tribù', p. 233: 'In questo schizzo che non ha la pretenzione di essere uno studio scientifico, al quale occorrerebbe una assai vasta cultura delle scienze giuridiche che a me manca affatto'.

54. Cozzi, 'Malattie, morte', p. 903: 'mi proposi per passatempo di descrivere con esattezza ed insieme con semplicità quanto erami sembrato più interessante nella vita di queste tribù montagnole'; 'La donna', p. 309: 'questi appunti, scritti alla buona nei rari momenti di ozio'.

55. Cozzi, 'Malattie, morte', pp. 905, 906; 'La vendetta', pp. 658, 662; 'La donna', p. 326 (also 'Credenze e superstizioni', p. 462).

56. Cozzi, 'Malattie, morte', p. 914; 'La vendetta', pp. 654, 660, 666; 'La donna', pp. 320, 331; 'Credenze e superstizioni', p. 453; 'Lo stato agricolo', p. 36.

57. Cozzi, 'La vendetta', pp. 656, 682.

58. See above, pp. 314–18.

59. Cozzi, 'Le tribù', p. 267; 'La vendetta', p. 666; 'Lo stato agricolo', p. 39.

60. Cozzi, 'Malattie, morte', p. 914: 'vi ha in questi pianti funebri montagnoli una brutalità di dolore, che noi comprendiamo male, ed il cui spettacolo ci è forse insopportabile. La scena è affatto antica, mentre la ritroviamo presso i primi poeti greci; i monumenti figurati la rappresentano di sovente, ma sopra tutto nelle prime epoche dell'arte. Noi abbiamo nei nostri musei dei vasi con dipinture nere, e delle tavole di terra cotta che sono l'illustrazione fedele delle cerimonie albanesi. Gli uomini del V. secolo e quelli dell'età anteriore si avvicinavano in ciò del tutto agli Albanesi'.

61. Ibid., p. 912: '*per me sgidh shpirtin* vale a dire "per liberare lo spirito del defunto"'; p. 918: 'una parte della famiglia indo-europea'.

62. Cozzi, 'Credenze e superstizioni', p. 458.

63. Cozzi, 'La donna', pp. 321, 326.

64. Cozzi, 'La vendetta', p. 661.

65. Cozzi, 'Malattie, morte', p. 910: 'l'ammalato albanese non teme affatto la morte, ma teme invece assai il dolore. Nella mia pratica di medico per questi montagnoli ebbi largo campo di convincermi di questo fatto. Non si può credere quale emozione, quale ansia mal celata provi il montanaro prima d'una operazione anche la più semplice; e pur tuttavia nei momenti del massimo dolore la può sopportare eroicamente. Nè ciò è una contradizione; l'albanese è più vicino allo stato primitivo di natura che non noi, e per esso non è vergogna il mostrar apertamente, che il dolore gli è ingrato e pesante; come non rifuggivano dal mostrar ciò neppure gli eroi d'Omero'.

66. Cozzi, 'La donna', pp. 310: 'come meteora'; 310–11: 'tutti gli Albanesi, in pubblico, affettano una grande indifferenza verso il sesso femminile, e specialmente verso le proprie moglie; ma ciò è cosa più di apparenza, di prammatica'; 311: 'in realtà trattano il debil sesso amorevolmente e con rispetto, e nulla v'ha di più toccante che i rapporti tra fratello e sorella e dei figli verso la madre'; 'Questi fieri abitatori dell'Alpi albanesi non

disdegnano viaggiando la compagnia del debil sesso; s'intrattengono con esso giovial-
mente, ma sempre con correttezza nelle parole e negli atti.'

67. Ibid., p. 312: 'Tutt'altro invece si presenta la vita congiugale nell'intimo della famiglia:
ma bisogna entrare e vivere a lungo con essi nelle lor case per conoscere i rapporti
d'affetto che corrono fra marito e moglie. Ricordo sempre le parole che mi dicea un
montanaro, mio amico: "*Nuk kee bes, zotnii, saa dashtnii kena per graat t'ona, e saa
fort rúhena, qi mos t'a diin kushi*" vale a dire, "Non puoi credere, signore, quanto
affetto portiamo alle donne nostre, e quanto procuriamo che non lo sappia nessuno."'

68. Ibid., p. 331 (n.): 'assolutamente falsa'. Cozzi was referring to the work by Steinmetz
(issued in Patsch's series), *Eine Reise durch die Hochländergaue Oberalbaniens* (Vienna,
1904), p. 17. He was perhaps especially irked by Steinmetz's confident assertion that
while previous travellers in the region had thought that a strict moral code prevailed
in such matters, 'this is based on a merely superficial acquaintance with the actual
reality' ('so beruht dies auf einer nur oberflächlichen Bekanntschaft mit dem
Tatsächlichen'). Towards the end of his journey, in the late summer of 1903, Steinmetz
had been given hospitality by Cozzi in Sumë (*Eine Reise*, p. 65).

69. Ibid., p. 332 (n.), referring to Siebertz, *Albanien*, p. 144 ('überaus laxer Natur'): 'non
basta fare un viaggio da Scutari a Prizrend per lanciare simili giudizi...ogni onesto, il
quale conosca un pò la vita intima di questo popolo, deve convenire che tale asserzi-
one è semplicemente una calunnia.'

70. Cozzi, 'La donna', p. 329: 'gravi maltrattamenti personali'.

71. Ibid.: 'ammalato di qualche malattia secreta'; 'Malattie, morte', p. 904. Cozzi attributed
the spread of syphilis here to the practice some men had of going to beg in the cities,
where they temporarily abandoned their own customs. He noted that it was less widespread in Malësia e Madhe, despite the fact that the sexual morality of men there
'leaves rather more to be desired than that of Malësia e Vogël' ('lasci assai più a desid-
erare che non nella Piccola').

72. Cozzi, 'La vendetta', p. 658: 'non si deve giudicare così sfavorevolmente la vendetta del
sangue, come fanno vari autori; nè credere che le frequenti uccisioni che avvengono in
Albania, sia perchè gli Albanesi di odiano a vicenda, e non vi possa esistere fra loro
amore e concordia.'

73. Ibid.: 'quasi naturalmente'. He notes here a similar observation on blood-feuds among
the Ethiopians by the eminent missionary Cardinal Massaja.

74. Ibid.: 'un efficace ritegno'; 'ai quali tante volte piace di chiamare col nome di barbari e
crudeli questi albanesi'; 'no: per il Albanese la vendetta è un sentimento di sdegno,
idealizzato quasi a dovere religioso e civile.' (This last phrase occurs also in Cozzi, 'Le
tribù', p. 248, where he comments that many of the crimes that occur in 'civilized'
countries are unknown in these mountains.)

75. Ibid., p. 676. The feud was still in progress as he wrote.

76. Ibid., pp. 659–60.

77. Cozzi, 'Malattie, morte', pp. 908–10.

78. Cozzi, 'La donna', pp. 618–20.

79. Ibid., pp. 318–20. On the sworn virgins, women who renounce the prospect of marriage and motherhood, and take on some aspects of the male role, see A. Young,
Women who Become Men: Albanian Sworn Virgins (Oxford, 2000).

80. Cozzi, 'Credenze e superstizioni', pp. 450–66. (I reproduce Cozzi's spellings, with standard modern spellings in square brackets. A kulshedër was a many-headed dragon; an orë and a zanë were female sprites or fairies.) Cozzi gives several examples of such divinations that proved remarkably accurate.

81. Cozzi, 'Lo stato agricolo', pp. 37–9.

82. Cozzi, 'Le tribù', esp. p. 242.

83. Cozzi, 'La vendetta', p. 657; 'Malattie, morte', p. 913; 'La donna', pp. 325–6 (second and third wives), 328 (widows' children—noting also that this is allowed in Islamic law), 333 (on the efforts of the clergy to end these 'abusi').

84. Cozzi, 'La vendetta', p. 679 and (n.). On this mission (the 'Missione volante', known locally as 'Misioni shëtitës shqiptar') see Cordignano, ed., L'Albania (see above, n. 10), and I. A. Murzaku, Catholicism, Culture, Conversion: The History of the Jesuits in Albania (1841–1946) (Rome, 2006), pp. 209–40.

85. Cozzi, 'Malattie, morte', pp. 911, 916.

86. Cozzi, 'La donna', p. 310.

87. Cozzi, 'Credenze e superstizioni', p. 476: 'parole cabalistiche'; 'in quanto che rifiutand-ovisi, i Cristiani si rivolgerebbero di certo ai ministri della religione turca'.

88. Cozzi, 'Malattie, morte', p. 905 (n.); 'La vendetta', p. 658; 'La donna', p. 325 (n.); 'Lo stato agricolo', p. 37; 'Credenze e superstizioni', p. 453 (hoxha).

89. Cozzi, 'La vendetta', p. 655.

90. Cozzi, 'Lo stato agricolo', p. 49: 'ma...siamo in Turchia, la cui trascuratezza e non-curanza sono diventate proverbiali. La Turchia pei suoi sudditi non solo non ha mai fatto nulla, ma ha lasciato andare a male anche quello che esisteva.'

91. Cozzi, 'La donna', p. 311 (n.): 'Mi dà occasione di vergare questa nota anche la guerra ad oltranza che in oggi (Aprile 1911) si combatte tra questi monti fra le truppe del governo ed i nostri alpigiani stanchi già del tirannico regime giovane-turco. L'energia, l'audacia, il coraggio, di cui danno prova le donne della grande Malcija, sono superiori a qualunque elogio.'

92. See C. Libardi, I primi moti patriotici albanesi nel 1910-1911-1912, specie nei Dukagini, 2 parts (Trento, 1935), part 1, pp. 55–69; Eqrem Bey Vlora ['E.b.V.'], Die Wahrheit über das Vorgehen der Jungtürken in Albanien (Vienna, 1911), p. 36.

93. See Durham, Struggle for Scutari, pp. 68–80; P. Bartl, Die albanesischen Muslime zur Zeit der nationalen Unabhängigkeitsbewegung (1878–1912) (Wiesbaden, 1968), pp. 177–8.

94. Durham, High Albania, pp. 103 (quotation), 103–7.

95. Ibid., pp. 227–8. The origins of this display of Catholic power and prestige are explained by Camillo Libardi (who helped to organize it): I primi moti patriottici albanesi, part 1, pp. 15–16.

96. Royal Anthropological Institute, London (hereafter: 'RAI'), Durham MS 47 (1). I am very grateful to Sarah Walpole and David Shankland for their help and hospitality at the RAI.

97. RAI, Durham MS 42 (1).

98. RAI, Durham MS 42 (6), entries for 16, 17, 19 and 28 Oct. 1911. Rrjoll had evidently suffered some heavy reprisals; but Camillo Libardi noted that it was unusual in having taken sides neither with the rebels nor with the Ottoman authorities (I primi moti, part 2, p. 20).

99. RAI, Durham MS 42 (6), entry for that date.

100. Ibid., entry for that date.

101. AQSh, Fondi 132, Arqipeshkvia e Shkodrës, 1912, dosja 29 (8 Jan. 1912), fos. 2r ('Atto fatto nella bandiera di Reçi'), 4r ('stragrande miseria ed indigenza'), 4v (total).

102. Ibid., fo. 5r ('due tribù di Reci e Rjolli').

103. See above, at n. 50.

104. RAI, Durham MS 42 (7), p. 3. A 'jemadan' (xhamadan) was an embroidered jacket or waistcoat.

105. Ibid., p. 4; Durham, *Struggle for Scutari*, p. 128: 'It was only, however, some foolish men of the Temali-Dushmani tribe, who, angry because they received no maize from the Government, fired fifty shots or so in the air, as defiance, childishly.'

106. RAI, Durham MS 42 (7), p. 25.

107. Ibid., p. 51.

108. RAI, Durham MS 42 (8), entries for those dates. On Balesium see M. von Šufflay ['Shuflaj'], *Qytetet dhe keshtjellat e Shqipërisë, kryesisht në mesjetë*, tr. L. Malltezi (Tirana, 2009), p. 52.

109. RAI, Durham MS 47 (5), p. 17; this follows a note on a blood feud dated 7 Mar. 1912. The account of Cozzi's remarks includes his comments on Balesium (p. 19).

110. Durham, *High Albania*, p. 107. Another version of this statement, attributed to Cozzi at Reç, is given in E. Durham, *Some Tribal Origins, Laws, and Customs of the Balkans* (London, 1928), p. 123: 'they believe in two powers, Light and Darkness, which are in conflict—Good and Evil. These tattoos are in some way connected with it. So is the Serpent, which they sometimes tattoo and also draw on walls.'

111. RAI, Durham MS 42 (10), first section (unpaginated).

112. See Durham, *Some Tribal Origins*, pp. 116–31. The 'Bogomil' theory about the medieval Bosnian Church has, however, been thoroughly dismantled by modern scholarship: see especially J. V. A. Fine, *The Bosnian Church: A New Interpretation* (Boulder, CO, 1975), and M. Wenzel, 'Bosnian Tombstones—Who Made them, and Why?', *Südost-Forschungen*, 21 (1962), pp. 102–43.

113. E.g. Durham, *Some Tribal Origins*, p. 225. Confirmation came also from other sources: in another notebook she added the comment on this topic: 'Bishop Bumci, Father Fishta & Dom Ernesto, all corroborate this belief' (RAI Durham MS 47 (8), section 'F', unpaginated).

114. Durham, *Some Tribal Origins*, pp. 243–84; a reference here to Cozzi in relation to shoulder-blade divination recounts a conversation with him.

115. Ibid., p. 123.

116. There is a notable contrast here with the case of Franz Nopcsa, whose lengthy manuscript work on northern Albanian customary law makes numerous references to Cozzi's articles on the blood feud and on Albanian women: see F. Baxhaku and K. Kaser, eds., *Die Stammesgesellschaften Nordalbaniens: Berichte und Forschungen österreichischer Konsuln und Gelehrter (1861-1917)* (Vienna, 1996), pp. 317–428, *passim*.

117. RAI, Durham MS 42 (11), entry for that date.

118. Archive of the Venetian Province of the Society of Jesus, Gallarate, MS 182: 'Ernesto Cozzi, Diario III parte' [hereafter: Cozzi, Diary], p. 1. It is very unfortunate that the

other two 'parts' of this diary are no longer extant. I am extremely grateful to Padre Diego Brunello SJ for his help and hospitality during my visit to Gallarate.

119. This was the 23rd Eucharistic Congress; the 1st had been held in Lille in 1881. Originally developed as a lay initiative, but then given papal authorization, eucharistic congresses were international gatherings combining worship and prayer (with a special emphasis on veneration of the eucharist) with seminars and discussions, the larger aim being to combat secularism in modern society.

120. Cozzi, Diary, p. 1: 'perorare la causa albanese'; 'tutte le montagne sopra Scutari'.

121. Ibid., pp. 1-5 (p. 5: 'S. M. con un inchino si allontanò senza dare alcuna risposta in merito'). On Bianchi, an Italian who was born in Albania and trained there as a priest, see Peters, *Geschichte der Katholischen Kirche*, pp. 260-1.

122. Cozzi, Diary, pp. 5-6.

123. RAI, Durham MS 42 (10), entry for 25 Oct.

124. AQSh, Fondi 132, Arqipeshkvia e Shkodrës, 1912, dosja 9, fos. 1-2 (Shkodër, 18 Sept. 1912): 'chefs religieux'; 'chefs et bajraktars'; 'conservera sa individualité etnique [*sic*] albanaise et aura un [*sic*] autonomie administrative en tout semblable a celle qui [*sic*] jouissent les nationalités les plus privilègés [*sic*] dans la Monarchie Aust. Hongroise'.

125. Ibid., fos. 1-2 (French), 3 (Italian). The Italian draft is unsigned and undated; but the fact that both documents survive in the archive of the Archdiocese of Shkodër, together with the information about Serreqi's position supplied here by Cozzi and Durham, makes it seem very likely that the Archbishop was involved.

126. Cozzi, Diary, pp. 6-8.

127. Ibid., pp. 9-12.

128. Ibid, pp. 12 (Lombardo), 14: 'Ero solo in casa e dormivo placidamente. Allo scoppio che ridusse tutto il locale in un mucchio di rovine, sfondando tutte le porte ed infrangendo tutti i vetri, balzo da letto e col mannlicher in mano mi precipito nel cortile per tema di qualche nuovo scoppio'; 'un colpo di Essad Pashà in riposta al messaggio di Vito Lombardo'.

129. Ibid., p. 21: 'nota spia del governo ottomano'. A *mahallë* was a small sub-division of an inhabited area.

130. Ibid., pp. 23-4.

131. Ibid., pp. 15, 18-19: 'una nuova êra di pace, di tranquillità, di progresso e di civiltà'; 'non farà alcuna distinzione di religione essendo questa cosa affatto privata'.

132. Ibid., pp. 26 ('sia come sacerdote, sia come medico'), 27.

133. Durham, *Struggle for Scutari*, pp. 204-5.

134. RAI, Durham MS 42 (10), entry for 24 Oct.; Cozzi, Diary, p. 29.

135. RAI, Durham MS 42 (10), entry for that date.

136. Cozzi, Diary, p. 31: 'che si erano dichiarati solidali coi cristiani e che pertanto erano rimasti nelle loro case'. Edith Durham noted this as follows: 'D. Ernesto's man from Rioli reports that the Xtians there have disarmed all the Moslems & robbed them of everything. Everyone except P. Lorenzo takes for granted every Moslem will have to leave land. Extraordinary wild joy of all over at last turning tables on Moslems' (RAI, Durham MS 42 (10), entry for 28 Oct.).

137. Cf. the comments on this in Durham, *Struggle for Scutari*, p. 204: 'The Montenegrins had, however, summoned them as "cat's-paws", meaning to use them as fighting men, and then throw all the blame on them. The Montenegrin soldiers, under the direction

of their officers, seized all loot worth having, loaded it upon the gangs of women who had come for the purpose, and sent it under escort to Podgoritza.'

138. Cozzi, Diary, pp. 39–40: 'Esorto segretamente i capi montagnoli a non prestare aiuto ai montenegrini, i quali altro non bramano che essi vengano esposti, dove più grave è il pericolo di lasciar la vita.'

139. Ibid., p. 45: 'stanchi del Montenegro che cercano solo di sfruttare il meglio che possono e di menarlo a naso colle loro finte promesse'.

140. Ibid., p. 52: 'il governo montenegrino vuole avere fra le sue truppe almeno questi capi devoti alla sua causa per poter influire sull' opinione pubblica europea a mezzo di false informazioni, che cioè le montagne albanesi fanno causa comune con lui, e desiderano il suo dominio: ma se dapprincipio gli Albanesi s'erano gettati nelle sue braccia spinti dalla disperazione, ora si sono già accorti, "quanto sa di sale il pane offerto da Re Nicola", e nuovamente fanno voti che il turco vinca...e sperano.'

141. Ibid., p. 54.

142. Ibid., p. 57: 'delle crudeltà e dei sacchi'. Austria-Hungary and Italy had agreed in late October to seek the creation of an autonomous Albania, though autonomy would amount to independence only if Ottoman sovereignty were abolished. On 12 and 13 November both powers told King Nikola to withdraw from the Albanian port of Shëngjin, and the Italian message emphasized Italy's commitment to the integrity and autonomy of Albania: see J. D. Treadway, *The Falcon and the Eagle: Montenegro and Austria-Hungary, 1908–1914* (West Lafayette, IN, 1983), pp. 118–20.

143. Cozzi, Diary, p. 59: 'La pellicola venne poi rappresentata all'estero colla dicitura: "omaggio a Re Nicola dei missionari cattolici albanesi." Poveri omaggi!? E povero pubblico turlupianto dai reclames di Re Nicola.'

144. Ibid., pp. 61–4.

145. Ibid., p. 66: 'qui a Grizhe è una continua orgia, in tutta la estensione della parola.'

146. Ibid., p. 75: 'Ai nostri montagnoli invece, per ingannarli, fu detto loro che il governo montenegrino li avrebbe lasciati far bottino a Scutari per tre giorni, e ciò per deferenza verso di loro!!! Oh! civiltà barbina di Re Nicola!' Six months later, Edith Durham heard an account of this from two other Catholic priests: 'Both Padres said it is true that the King tried to bribe all the tribes to help take Scutari at the end by a promise of 3 days plunder. The tribes were by then disgusted with Monte: & far from going to help discussed attacking the Montes: & would almost certainly have done so had the siege lasted a few days longer' (RAI, Durham MS 42 (13), unpaginated, entry after 19 Aug. 1913).

147. Cozzi, Diary, pp. 87 ('freddezza'), 88.

148. Ibid., p. 95.

149. Ibid., p. 98: 'pretesto'; 'gli abborriti albanesi che si difendono eroicamente'.

150. Ibid., p. 100: 'ora però cambia, sia subentrato un cambiamento; mentre tutta l'ira e l'odio dei dirigenti montenegrini è contro i cattolici; e si impreca contro il fedifrago Arcivescovo di Scutari, contro il clero albanese, le montagne....'

151. Ibid., p. 103: 'si era recato da Miss Edith Durham, benefattrice degli Albanesi, per chiederle la carità.' This episode was described by Durham herself: 'the little priest of Summa came with two Summa men, all in great misery, to beg some clothes...I gave the poor man a blanket as well as clothing. Outside the hotel he was arrested by the police, and taken before Stanko Markovitch, who threatened him that if he was ever

caught asking help of the Englishwoman again, he should be hanged' (*Struggle for Scutari*, p. 261).

152. Cozzi, Diary, pp. 104 ('tutti i maomettani e cattolici dell'Alta Albania ad abiurare la lor fede e farsi ortodossi'), 105 ('un mio amico Hysen Shyti di Vonthai venne barbaramente fucilato sol perchè si rifiutò a farsi ortodosso').

153. Ibid., pp. 115–19. On Dobrečić see Treadway, *The Falcon and the Eagle*, p. 249, n. 44.

154. Cozzi, Diary, p. 20.

155. Ibid., pp. 121–4. On Brigadier (later Brigadier General) Jovan Bećir, who was Prince Danilo's commanding officer, see S. Pavlović, *Balkan Anschluss: The Annexation of Montenegro and the Creation of the Common South Slavic State* (West Lafayette, IN, 2008), p. 84, n. 17. Edith Durham noted that Prince Danilo gained an unpleasant reputation for executing prisoners, and that 'Brigadier Bechir, who was with him, was nicknamed the Montenegrin Nero' (*Struggle for Scutari*, p. 248).

156. Cozzi, Diary, pp. 126–7, 128 ('tutti armati fino ai denti'), 129, 130 ('non senza paura di venir arrestato').

157. Ibid., p. 131. Cozzi's comment about the conditions evidently expresses a relative judgement; in absolute terms, conditions were very bad. Edith Durham, who had entered Shkodër on 25 April, recorded that 'The people were half dazed with terror and starvation...The schools, churches, hospitals and Consulates had all been aimed at, rather than the citadel or barracks. All had been struck, and some wrecked...The cathedral was a wreck...the Montenegrin troops had poured in, and when I arrived were looting hard' (*Struggle for Scutari*, pp. 280, 282).

158. Cozzi, Diary, pp. 134–5.

159. Ibid., p. 136: 'La schiavitù politica e religiosa musulmana tramontò per sempre; l'incubo montenegrino scomparve; e sull'orizzonte spunta l'alba di giorni migliori. Fiat!'

160. Archive of the Venetian Province of the Society of Jesus, Gallarate, MS Albania 3, contains a photograph of Cozzi in military uniform dated Vienna, 25 Nov. 1914, and stamped on the reverse: 'Militärseelsorge der K. u. K. 7. Infanterietruppendivision'.

161. *Zâni i Shna Ndout* (as in n. 3, above), p. 35: 'u gjetë shpesh fill e per ball me anmik, nder llogoret mâ të parat'.

162. Ibid.

163. See above, n. 115. While he may have lost his notes, he did (as we have seen) retain the manuscript of his projected work.

164. *Zâni i Shna Ndout* (as in n. 3, above), p. 35.

165. Archivum Romanum Societatis Iesu, Rome (hereafter: 'ARSI'), MS 1002, 'Missio albanensis provinciae venetae', vol. 3, fasc. 1, to Monsignor Laurenti, from Shkodër, 17 Dec. 1918: 'assai decaduta'; 'Altre e altre cose di simile o analoga materia avrei a dire, e tutte necessarie pel bene morale dell'Albania, ma ciò può farsi solo a voce'. I am very grateful to Father Brian Mac Cuarta SJ for his welcome and his advice at the ARSI. On Genovizzi see Murzaku, *Catholicism, Culture, Conversion*, pp. 145–6, 149, 187, 189, 224.

166. ARSI, MS 1002, vol. 3, fasc. 1, 'Stato religioso in Albania e nel Montenegro', 15 June 1919. Murzaku describes this text, which is unsigned, as a report by a 'special envoy' (*Catholicism, Culture, Conversion*, p. 152); but it is in Genovizzi's handwriting, and

shows a degree of local knowledge that a temporary envoy would be unlikely to have attained.

167. ARSI, MS 1002, vol. 3, fasc. 1, 'Stato religioso in Albania e nel Montenegro', p. 1: 'quasi un nulla quanto all'attività apostolica'; 'perdono abitualmente la giornata in chiacchere prolungate.'

168. Ibid., fasc. 1, pp. 2 ('1° Si direbbe che una metà del Clero albanese sono Preti per motivo di interessi materiali; 2° Domina in essi l'inerzia e l'avarizia; 3° Passano abitualmente le giornate fumando tabacco, chiaccherando e oziando'), 3.

169. Ibid., fasc. 1, p. 6: 'Mandare in Albania quanto prima un Visitatore Apostolico che sia esperto e uomo di carattere ecc., e che percorre adagio adagio le singole diocesi; sia anche non troppo vecchio, se no non reggerebbe ai difficili viaggi che si devone fare. Suggerirei poi che esso sia uno straniero e non un albanese perchè gli albanesi, avvezzi come sono sin dall' infanzia a vedere i loro abusi ecclesiastici, non ne fanno tanto caso…Atto a questo grave ufficio sarebbe p. es. il Rdo Don Ernesto Cozzi, nato ed ordinato prete nella diocesi di Trento, e che da *circa* 15 anni vive in Albania come missionario volontario.'

170. Ibid., fasc. 1, p. 6. Gjura (1875–1939) had taught in the Jesuit College in Shkodër, and had studied theology in Innsbruck; he would become Archbishop of Durrës in 1929 (see Peters, *Geschichte der Katholischen Kirche*, p. 272).

171. ARSI, MS 1002, vol. 3, fasc. 1, 'Stato religioso in Albania e nel Montenegro', p. 7: 'Come episcopabili suggerirei ancora Don Ernesto Cozzi e Don Pietro Giura sopranominati, che sono amendue di circa 40 anni e che hanno sempre mostrato uno zelo e un' attività ecclesiastica singolare; sono dotati di scienza più che mediocre e conoscono pure diverse lingue. Sebbene D. Ernesto Cozzi non sia albanese, pure gode la simpatia e la fiducia di tutti gli albanesi, parla bene la loro lingua, conosce a fondo i costumi di questa nazione, ed è capace non meno di D. Pietro Giura di por mano alla riforma bramata qui in Albania.' Cozzi was in fact within three weeks of his 49th birthday; this underestimate may be taken as evidence of his physical vigour.

172. Cozzi, 'Atti' (see n. 13, above), fos. 515r–526v: 'Giornale-spese della visita apostolica.'

173. Cozzi, 'Atti'; Archivio Segreto Vaticano, Archivio della Delegazione Apostolica di Albania (hereafter: ASVat, ADA), vol. 1, fasc. 3, fos. 242–326. An Albanian translation of most of the report is given in Gjergj Gashi, *Vatikani dhe Arbëria, 1700–1922* (Tirana, 1998), pp. 205–484; key points are summarized (from Gashi's version) in Peters, *Geschichte der Katholischen Kirche*, pp. 21–6.

174. On Shllaku see Peters, *Geschichte der Katholischen Kirche*, pp. 291–2; Deusch, *Das Kultusprotektorat*, pp. 552(n.), 588.

175. Cozzi, 'Atti', fo. 3r: '1° di fare della politica talvolta disastrosa; 2° di eccessivo attaccamento al denaro; e di manomissione dei beni ecclesiastici; 3° di nepotismo o di protezionismo irragionevole; 4° di eccessiva trascuratezza delle cose del culto, della disciplina ecclesiastica, della direzione e correzione del clero, della visita pastorale.'

176. Ibid., fo. 3r: 'condennato alla inerzia per la sua eccessiva pinguedine e per i suoi disturbi…gravi disordini e numerose uccisioni.'

177. On Bumçi see Peters, *Geschichte der Katholischen Kirche*, pp. 261–2; Deusch, *Das Kultusprotektorat*, pp. 463–4. On Bianchi see above, n. 121.

178. Cozzi, 'Atti', fo. 3r: 'L'attuale amministratore Don Giuseppe Gionli è l'*unico* prete in Albania che tutti dicono esemplare e capace di reggere una Diocesi.'

179. Ibid., fo. 7r: 'Eccessivo attaccamento all'interesse ed estrema avarizia specialmente nelle spese di culto; sfruttamento del popolo ... Eccessiva dimestichezza coi secolari e con le donne: da che spesso nascono gravissimi scandali; Tendenze politiche, spesso disordinate e causa di gravi danni.'

180. Ibid., fo. 8r: 'In genere il popolo conserva ancora uno spirito di fede e di attaccamento alla religione; ma va crescendo ogni giorno l'indifferentismo. La religione del popolo è però superficiale ed apparente, e assume quasi una forma di superstizione.'

181. Ibid., fo. 67r-v ('concubinato').

182. Ibid., fos. 68v, 69v.

183. Ibid., fos. 60v, 69v.

184. Ibid., fos. 64v-65v: 'come vere monache'; 'una vita veramente edificante'.

185. Ibid., fo. 71r.

186. Ibid., fo. 67v.

187. Ibid., fo. 72r-v: 'il grande attaccamento che hanno alle tradizioni, alle superstizioni, ai costumi dei loro antenati, mentre il loro diritto consuetudinario forma l'unica norma della loro vita pubblica e privata, e con ciò stesso l'unico ostacolo allo sviluppo morale e sociale di questo popolo'; 'la mancanza di governo, mentre ogni tribù si regge tutt'ora quasi indipendente secondo le proprie leggi e tradizioni'; 'lo spirito di indipendenza morale e politica che anima queste popolazioni'.

188. Ibid., fos. 63v-64r: 'essendo l'albanese conservativo per eccellenza'; 'un governo militare inesorabile che sapesse amministrare la giustizia, imporre ed applicare efficacemente le leggi'; 'sviluppare la cultura intellettuale e religiosa a mezzo di scuole'.

189. Ibid., fo. 9r.

190. M. W. E. Peters, *Der älteste Verlag Albaniens und sein Beitrag zu Nationalbewegung, Bildung und Kultur: die 'Buchdruckerei der Unbefleckten Empfängnis' zu Shkodra (1870-1945)* (Hamburg, 2007), pp. 221-2 (citing *Lajmtari i Zemres së Krishtit*, 31 (1921), no. 36: 'Die Ernennung einer Gesandtschaft ist ein konkreter Erweis der Liebe und Sorge, welche der Heilige Stuhl und insbesondere Papst Benedikt XV. immer schon für die vollständige Freiheit und den wahren Fortschritt Albaniens gehabt haben ... Ich werde mein Leben geben für die Blüte dieses Albaniens, welches für mich gleichzeitig auch die zweite Heimat ist').

191. The date is given in *Zâni i Shna Ndout*, 9, no. 2 (Feb. 1921), pp. 18-19; again, I am grateful to Giovalin Çuni and Magi Laca for a copy of this article.

192. AQSh (see above, n. 29), Fondi 132, Arqipeshkvia e Shkodrës, 1921, dosja 38, fo. 2r: 'sentimenti di paterno affetto e di singolare benevolenza ... verso l'Episcopato, il Clero ed il popolo albanese'.

193. Ibid., dosja 24 (24 Apr. 1921; 1 July 1921: 'stato deplorevole').

194. Ibid., dosja 38, fo. 7r: 'Amministratore Apostolico'.

195. Ibid., dosja 38, fo. 7r ('la rinunzia non lo esonera dal grave dovere di dare un completo e dettagliato resoconto della sua amministrazione'); ASVat, ADA (see above, n. 173), vol. 1, fasc. 2, fos. 208-10, 214-215.

196. Peters, *Geschichte der Katholischen Kirche*, p. 285.

197. Ibid., pp. 36, 271.

198. Ibid., pp. 36-7, 260-1, 282.

199. Ibid., pp. 41-2.

200. Ibid., pp. 56-7.

201. ASVat, ADA, vol. 1, fasc. 6, fos. 599–600.

202. Cozzi, 'Atti', fos. 73v–74r. The Archbishop, he noted, had ordered the clergy to excommunicate publicly all parents that sent their sons to this school.

203. All the details given here are from the valuable account in I. A. Murzaku, *Returning Home to Rome: The Basilian Monks of Grottaferrata in Albania* (Grottaferrata, 2009), pp. 125–9, summarizing Cozzi's report to Van Rossum, 'Attività scolastica protestantica-americana e Chiesa Ortodossa in Albania' (20 June 1921), in Archivio della Sacra Congregazione per le Chiese Orientali, Rome, Prot. 119, fasc. II.

204. Ibid., pp. 132–6.

205. ASVat, ADA, vol. 1, fasc. 1, fos. 2v–3r: 'è doloroso che questa piccola nazione la quale avrebbe così estremo bisogno di pace tranquillità e lavoro concorde di tutte le forze per il suo sviluppo constituzionale, economico e sociale, venga gettata così di frequente in preda a lotte intestine con enorme spese di sangue e di danaro'; 'sebbene l'Albania individualmente sia stata riconosciuta come stato indipendente, tuttora prendendo in considerazione i confini fissati senza alcun principio d'equità e di giustizia dalle potenze d' Europa e che non corrispondono certo alle esigenze etnografiche e topografiche ed agli interessi economici e strategici del paese, troppi motivi di odio e d'invidia vennero accumulati fra gl' albanesi ed i vicini jugoslavi e greci, si che mai cesseranno gli intrighi.'

206. Ibid., fasc. 1, fo. 36v (23 May 1924): 'nelle cose albanesi è ben difficile il poter fare delle previsioni a motivo del carattere impulsivo e volubile del popolo, e delle influenze estere che in nessun paese si fan sentire come in Albania.'

207. Ibid., fasc. 6, fo. 547 (18 July 1921).

208. Peters, *Geschichte der Katholischen Kirche*, p. 43: 'qui et bonorum christianorum fama gaudeant'.

209. ASVat, ADA, fasc. 6, fos. 563r (16 Nov. 1923), 570r (5 Apr. 1924: 'ha preso ad esse [elezioni] una parte troppo attiva, adoperandosi pubblicamente per il trionfo di uno dei partiti'), 574 (7 June 1924: 'ha preso attiva parte a recenti manifestazioni politiche, particolarmente in occasione delle cerimonie funebri per la uccisione del giovane mussulmano omicidia di Essad Pascià').

210. Ibid., fasc. 1, fos. 65r–66v: 'corifei del partito suo e già profughi a Belgrado'.

211. Ibid., fasc. 1, fo. 66v: 'Ormai cattolici, ortodossi e musulmani sono sfiduciati e avviliti nel veder il loro paese percorso da bande straniere (russe e montenegrine); ed invocano una mano liberatrice. Che l'Albania colla sua deplorevolissima situazione economica e col consequente oscillare della politica interna ed il vario succedersi a breve scadenza dei governi; colle profonde insanabili gelosie e antagonismi dei partiti che impediscono ogni collaborazione; col parassitismo e favoritismo che qui predominano, possa consolidarsi, organizarsi & prosperare senza l'aiuto straniero, nessuno più lo crede.' On the acts of violence see Peters, *Geschichte der Katholischen Kirche*, p. 51.

212. See above, n. 159.

213. Perhaps the last significant document is his 'Protocollo no. 1950' of 5 Apr. 1925, in which he instructed the Albanian bishops that 'the action of the clergy cannot become subservient to the particular actions of politics and of political parties; it must be inspired solely by the religious and moral formation and renovation of individuals, and by the Christian restoration of society' (ASVat, ADA, vol. 1, fasc. 6, fos.

599–600: 'l'azione del clero non può asservirsi alle particolari azioni della politica e dei partiti, ma deve ispirarsi unicamente alla formazione e rinnovazione religiosa e morale degli individui e alla restaurazione cristiana della società').

214. These details are drawn from two documents in the Archive of the Venetian Province of the Society of Jesus, Gallarate, MS Albania 3, 'Necrologia di Mons. Ernesto Cozzi': a letter from his sister Carolina (quotation: 'io non mi alzerò più dal letto') to an unnamed Church dignitary, and a letter from Suor Feliciana, a niece of Archbishop Marconi who was with Carolina at the time, printed in *Il nuovo Trentino* in early Mar. 1926.

215. Ibid., 'Necrologia di Mons. Ernesto Cozzi', envelope of newspaper cuttings, undated cutting (perhaps from *Il nuovo Trentino*): 'L'Albania ne ha accolta la salma come quella di un figlio di adozione.'

216. *Lajmtari* (as in n. 4, above), p. 34: 'Ishte fort i pershpirtshem, zelltár, i durueshem, fjalëamel, i butë, i dashtun, zêmerbardhë e i shkueshem me gjithkend, (sa deri fmít e vogjel flitshin me tê si me folë me prindin e vet). Ishte fort i drejtë, besnik, i palodh-shëm e qindrak në të kryeme të detyrve të veta.'

217. Archive of the Venetian Province of the Society of Jesus, Gallarate, MS Albania 3, 'Necrologia di Mons. Ernesto Cozzi', envelope of newspaper cuttings, *Corriere della sera*, 8 Apr. 1926: 'in poco più d'un quinquennio, seppe superare ostacoli e difficoltà innumeri placando gli animi, stroncando abusi, negando privilegi, ed esigendo dal clero un sano e sacro spirito apostolico.'

Chapter 12

1. *The Adriatic Review*, vol. 1, no. 1 (Sept. 1918), pp. 11–14. I am very grateful to the staff of the Widener Library, Harvard University, where I consulted this and the other Albanian-American journals referred to in this essay.

2. See R. Elsie, *History of Albanian Literature*, 2 vols. (Boulder, CO, 1995), i, pp. 365–86; B. Fevziu, *Histori e shtypit shqiptar 1848–1996* (Tirana, 1996), pp. 46–9, 133.

3. Noli remained for nearly a decade a bitter opponent of Zog after being driven from power in 1924, but underwent a quiet rapprochement with him in the 1930s. Konica, although well known to be critical of Zog, gave him his official support and was appointed Minister Plenipotentiary in Washington. Dako became a leading apologist for Zog, as his 1937 publication shows. Kostandin Çekrezi supported Zog in the 1920s but was imprisoned by him in 1932, later fleeing to America, where he led an anti-Zogist movement; his relations with Noli deteriorated to the point where the latter described him as 'an irresponsible, unprincipled, unscrupulous juggler' (letter of 18 Dec. 1942, quoted in B. J. Fischer, *Albania at War, 1939–1945* (London, 1999), p. 243). For further details of Çekrezi's career see W. Bland and I. Price, *A Tangled Web: A History of Anglo-American Relations with Albania* (London, 1986), pp. 72–7, 133, 139.

4. Çekrezi, *Albania Past and Present*, pp. 4–5.

5. K. Dako, 'The Albanians', *Ylli i mengjezit*, vol. 1, no. 3 (15 Feb. 1917), pp. 67–73, at pp. 67–8.

6. For a summary of the key arguments see N. Malcolm, *Kosovo: A Short History* (London, 1998), pp. 28–40.

7. E. S. Piccolomini (Pope Pius II), *Cosmographia Pii Papae in Asiae & Europae eleganti descriptione* (Paris, 1509), fo. 13r; F. C. H. L. Pouqueville, *Voyage dans la Grèce, comprenant la description ancienne et moderne de l'Épire, de l'Illyrie grecque, de la Macédoine cisaxienne…et du Péloponèse*, 5 vols. (Paris, 1820–1), ii, pp. 510–25; N. Nikoklēs, *De albanensium sive Schkipitar origine et prosapia* (Göttingen, 1855). On Nikoklēs see N. R. Çabej, *Autoktonia e shqiptarëve në studimet gjermane* (Prishtina, 1990), pp. 31–2. This Caucasian hypothesis was not the only rival to the Illyrian theory; some Renaissance writers supposed that the Albanians had migrated from Italy.

8. The key breakthrough here was made by Joseph Ritter von Xylander, who, arguing against an even stranger hypothesis (that the Albanians were 'Tatars'), demonstrated that Albanian was an 'Indo-Germanic' language: Xylander, *Die Sprache der Albanesen oder Schkipetaren* (Frankfurt-am-Main, 1835), esp. pp. 292–320.

9. F. Tajani, *Le istorie albanesi* (Salerno, 1886), part 1, pp. xxi–xxii.

10. Johann Thunmann's work was published as *Untersuchungen über die Geschichte der östlichen europäischen Völker* (Leipzig, 1774). One section of this work has been reprinted under the title *Über die Geschichte der Albaner und der Wlachen* (Hamburg, 1976). Herodotus describes the Pelasgians as non-Greek and autochthonous (unlike the Dorian Greeks, who had migrated to their present location in the Peloponnese): *The Histories*, tr. G. Rawlinson (London, 1997), I.56–7, pp. 30–1.

11. A. Masci, 'Essai sur l'origine, les moeurs et l'état actuel de la nation albanaise', tr. C. Malte-Brun, in C. Malte-Brun, ed., *Annales des voyages, de la géographie et de l'histoire*, 24 vols. (Paris, 1808–14), iii, pp. 145–234.

12. C. Malte-Brun, *Précis de la géographie universelle, ou description de toutes les parties du monde*, 2nd edn., 8 vols. (Paris, 1812–29), vi, pp. 200–15 (p. 204: 'la langue albanaise est un chaînon distinct, ancien et important de la grande chaîne des langues pélasgo-helléniques').

13. G. Crispi, *Memoria sulla lingua albanese* (Palermo, 1831), esp. pp. 4–6, 33–4 (portraying Albanian as essentially a pre-Homeric version of Greek).

14. J. G. von Hahn, *Albanesiche Studien*, 3 vols. (Jena, 1854), i, pp. 214–19.

15. Fevziu, *Histori e shtypit*, p. 127; P. Vasa ('Wassa Effendi'), *The Truth on Albania and the Albanians: Historical and Critical Issues*, tr. E. St. J. Fairman [1st published 1879], ed. B. Destani (London, 1999), pp. 4–8. For details of some other expressions of the 'Pelasgian' theory see Xh. Gosturani, *Historia e albanologjisë* (Tirana, 1999), pp. 105, 128–9, 132.

16. K. Dako, *Zogu the First, King of the Albanians (A Sketch of his Life and Times)* (Tirana, 1937), p. 13.

17. F. Noli, 'Mehmet Bey Konitza', *Illyria*, vol. 1, no. 8 (1 Aug. 1916), pp. 4–6, at p. 6.

18. K. Dako, 'The Independence of Albania a Necessity for International Peace', *Ylli i mengjezit*, vol. 1, no. 6 (2 Apr. 1917), pp. 161–9, at p. 163.

19. Dako, 'The Albanians', p. 68.

20. K. Çekrezi, 'Past and Present Conditions of Albania', *Illyria*, vol. 1, no. 7 (1 July 1916), pp. 1–3, at p. 1.

21. Herodotus, *Histories*, II.50–3, pp. 149–51.

22. Malte-Brun, *Précis de la géographie*, vi, p. 205; Crispi, *Memoria sulla lingua albanese*, pp. 25, 33–4. (Most of Crispi's examples are taken from Malte-Brun.)

23. von Hahn, *Albanesische Studien*, i, pp. 249, 251; Vasa, *The Truth on Albania*, pp. 11–13.

24. Çekrezi, *Albania Past and Present*, p. 4; K. Dako, 'The Religious Beliefs of the Albanians', *Ylli i mengjezit*, vol. 1, no. 5 (15 Mar. 1917), pp. 129–31.

25. K. Dako, 'The Albanian Language', *Ylli i mengjezit*, vol. 1, no. 4 (28 Feb. 1917), pp. 97–9, at p. 99.

26. K. Çekrezi, 'Southern Albania or Northern Epirus?' (editorial), *Illyria*, vol. 1, no. 2 (1 Apr. 1916), pp. 5–6, at p. 6.

27. Mehmet bey Konica, 'The Albanian Question', *The Adriatic Review*, vol. 1, no. 4 (Dec. 1918), pp. 145–64, at p. 148. While modern scholars reject these derivations, they do accept similar claims in relation to the place-names Dalmatia and Dardania.

28. The most extreme example of this tendency was a work by Bernardo Bilotta, *Gli enti sacri della Bibbia ne' numi mitologici venerati da' Pelasgi Albanesi del gentilesimo* (Castrovillari, 1897), which treated not only classical names but biblical ones too as riddles to be solved in Albanian: thus Semiramis was 's'e e mirë ëmë?' ('isn't she a good mother?'), and the Hebrew Noemi (Naomi) was 'njoh ema', 'I know how to weave'. (This rare work, listed in E. Legrand, *Bibliographie albanaise* (Paris, 1912), p. 183, is known to me only from the review of it by Faik Konica in *Albania: La Revue albanaise*, vol. 'A' (1897), pp. 100–1; even Konica, who was not lacking in a taste for whimsy, found Bilotta's theory hard to swallow.)

29. Dako, 'The Albanian Language', p. 97.

30. Dako, 'The Albanians', p. 68.

31. Çekrezi, *Albania Past and Present*, p. 10.

32. Ibid., p. 36.

33. F. Konica, *Albania: The Rock Garden of Southeastern Europe*, ed. G. M. Panarity (Boston, 1957), p. 30.

34. Ibid., p. 33.

35. K. Dako, 'The Strength of the National Consciousness of the Albanian People', *Ylli i mengjezit*, vol. 3, no. 5 (Aug. 1918), pp. 129–32, at p. 130.

36. Çekrezi, 'Past and Present Conditions', p. 1; Çekrezi, *Albania Past and Present*, p. 39.

37. F. Noli et al., 'Memorandum on Albania', *The Adriatic Review*, vol. 1, no. 3 (Nov. 1918), pp. 97–104, at p. 98. Later in the same text they referred to 'the unspeakable Turk' (p. 103); cf. Çekrezi's remark about 'the despised Turk': Çekrezi, *Albania Past and Present*, p. 36.

38. Ismail Qemal Vlora, 'Albania and the Albanians', first published in *The Quarterly Review*, reprinted in *Ylli i mengjezit*, vol. 2, no. 5 (29 Sept. 1917), pp. 129–34, at p. 134.

39. Eqrem Bey Vlora, *Die Wahrheit über das Vorgehen der Jungtürken in Albanien* (Vienna, 1911); A. Herbert, *Ben Kendim: A Record of Eastern Travel*, ed. D. MacCarthy (London, 1924), pp. 200, 205.

40. Quoted in Konica, *Albania: The Rock Garden*, p. xxix.

41. I am very grateful to Ihsan bey Toptani (born into one of the great landowning families of central Albania in 1908, and brought up with virtually no religious instruction) for a fascinating discussion of this point.

42. For a valuable survey of Albanian Muslim writers and scholars, see H. Kaleshi, *Kontributi i shqiptarëve në diturite islame* (Prizren, 1991); for an important overview of Albanian Catholicism, see Z. Mirdita, *Krishtenizmi ndër shqiptarë* (Zagreb, 1998). Unfortunately there is no comparable study of the Orthodox Albanians.

43. Lady Mary Wortley Montagu, *Letters and Works*, ed. Lord Wharncliffe and W. Moy Thomas, 2 vols. (London, 1893), i, p. 291.

44. Konica, *Albania: The Rock Garden*, pp. 135–6.

45. Ibid., p. 50.

46. Çekrezi, *Albania Past and Present*, pp. 201, 204. For an earlier version of these comments see Çekrezi, 'The Religious and Educational Question in Albania' (editorial), *The Adriatic Review*, vol. 1, nos. 5–6 (Jan.–Feb. 1919), pp. 187–91.

47. Çekrezi, *Albania Past and Present*, p. 202.

48. Dako, 'Religious Beliefs of the Albanians', p. 129.

49. Çekrezi, *Albania Past and Present*, p. 202.

50. T. Zavalani, *Historia e Shqipnis*, 2 vols. (London, 1957–66), i, p. 218 ('Pa dashtë me paksue randësin e faktorve historik që shkaktuen përhapjen e Muhamedanizmit në Shqipni, duhet të theksojmë se kanë luejtë rol edhe vetijat e tyne si racë. Sepse bjen në sy fakti se Shqipnija u zhvillue ndën sundimin ottoman në nji drejtim krejt të përkundërt nga ai i popujve te tjerë të Balkanit. Shkaku mund të jet se Shqiptarët ishin gatue shpirtnisht ndën influencën e paganizmit të Romës që i-u shtue traditave pagane të Iliris. Pranimi i fes kristiane nuk u ba për Iliret kanali për të ngjallë ndërgjegjen kombtare. Kështu që, prej koheve të lashta, nji dallim i qartë në mes të fes dhe kombësis ka karakterizue mendësin dhe aktivitetin shoqnuer të Shiptarve').

List of Manuscripts

Avignon

Archives départementales de Vaucluse

D 36: University of Avignon, 'Livre concernant les noms...des primiciers, docteurs...et gradués'.

Cambridge

Cambridge University, Classics Faculty Archive

Leake papers, Notebook 18: Oct.–Dec. 1807.
Leake papers, Notebook 21: Apr.–May 1809.
Leake papers, Notebook 22: June–Nov. 1809.

Gallarate

Archive of the Venetian Province of the Society of Jesus

Albania 3: photograph of E. Cozzi, 1914; 'Necrologia di Mons. Ernesto Cozzi'; C. Cozzi, letter; newspaper cuttings concerning E. Cozzi.
182: E. Cozzi, 'Diario III parte'.

Hertford

Hertfordshire Archives and Local Studies ('HALS')

Leake 85499: Sir Arthur Paget to W. Leake, 19 Oct. 1807.
Leake 85505: 'Ali Pacha to the King' [Apr. 1808], draft translation, Aug.–Sept. 1808.
Leake 85506: G. Canning to W. Leake, from London, 21 Oct. 1808.
Leake 85508: A. St J. Baker to Sir Robert Adair, from HMS *Success*, 10 Nov. 1808.
Leake 85511: G. Eyre to Leake, from HMS *Magnificent*, off Fano, 2 May 1809.
Leake 85513: Navy Office to Leake, 25 May 1809.

Leake 85515: Sir Alexander Ball to Leake, from Malta, 20 July 1809.

Leake 85516: P. Fraser to Leake, from the Arsenal, Malta, 15 Sept. 1809.

Leake 85518: H. Lowe to Leake, from Cephalonia, 15 Oct. 1809.

Leake 85527: Sir Robert Adair to Leake, from Pera, 24 June 1809.

Leake 85529: Sir Robert Adair to Leake, from Pera, 10 Aug. 1809.

Leake 85530: Sir Robert Adair to Leake, from Pera, 16 Aug. 1809.

Leake 85531: Sir Robert Adair to Leake, from Pera, 11 Oct. 1809.

Leake 85532: Sir Robert Adair to Leake, from Pera, 13 Oct. 1809.

Leake 85536: Report on forests, endorsed 27 Dec. 1809.

Innsbruck

Tiroler Landesarchiv

O. Ö. Geheimer Rat, Selekt Ferdinandea, Pos. 86: Petru Şchiopul to Archduke Ferdinand, Sept. 1592; B. Rossi to Ferdinand, Aug.–Nov. 1594; A. Bruni to Rossi, Oct. 1594.

Karlsruhe

Generallandesarchiv

46/3714: Letter from a secretary of the English Embassy in Istanbul, 19 Jan. 1690; von Baden, plan of operations, Augsburg, 6 Feb. 1690; L. Marsigli report, 4 July 1690.

Kew

The National Archives ('TNA')

ADM 49/168: summaries of Navy Board correspondence, 1807–21.

CO 136/1: papers on administration of Ionian Islands, 1813.

CO 136/2: papers on administration of Ionian Islands, 1814.

CO 136/3: papers on administration of Ionian Islands, 1815.

FO 30/29/344: C. St. John to Granville, Jan. 1881.

FO 78/44: J. Morier, papers, 1804.

FO 78/47: J. Morier, papers, Jan.–Oct. 1805.

FO 78/53: J. Morier, papers, Jan.–Oct. 1806.

FO 78/57: W. Leake, papers, 1803–7.

FO 78/61: papers of D. Morier, W. Leake et al., 1808.

FO 78/63: Sir Robert Adair papers, Nov. 1808–June 1809.

FO 78/65: papers of W. Leake, J. Morier, et al., Feb. 1809–Nov. 1809.

FO 78/68: Sir Robert Adair, reports, Jan.–July 1810.

FO 78/70: S. Canning, letters, May–Dec. 1810.

FO 78/74: S. Canning, reports, June–Dec. 1811.

FO 78/77: S. Canning, reports, Jan.–July 1812.

FO 78/79: Sir Robert Liston, papers, 1812.

FO 78/82: Sir Robert Liston, reports, 1814.

FO 78/85: correspondence relating to Ottoman Empire, 1815.

FO 352/1: S. Canning, papers, 1809–11.

FO 352/2A: S. Canning, papers, 1810–11.

FO 424/74: W. Kirby Green, report, Sept. 1878; Sir Henry Layard report, Sept. 1878.

FO 424/76: W. Kirby Green, report, Nov. 1878.

FO 424/88: C. St. John, report, Sept. 1879.

FO 424/100: G. Goschen to Granville, July 1880.

FO 881/4268: W. Kirby Green, reports, Apr. 1880; M. Sale, memorandum, June 1880; G. Goschen to Granville, June 1880.

FO 881/4327: W. Kirby Green to Granville, June 1880.

Lisbon

Instituto dos Arquivos Nacionais

Tribunal do Santo Ofício, Inquisição de Lisboa, proc. 8488: Gino case, 1579.

London

British Library ('BL')

Add. 20,110: H. Lowe, correspondence, 1811–12.

Add. 20,168: H. Lowe, letters, June 1809–Sept. 1811.

Add. 20,169: H. Lowe, letters, May–Dec. 1810.

Add. 20,171: H. Lowe, letters, 1808–9, Feb. 1810–Sept. 1812.

Add. 20,177: letters to H. Lowe, 1805–11.

Add. 20,183: G. Foresti, letters to H. Lowe.

Add. 20,184: J. Oswald, letters to H. Lowe, 1809–12.

Add. 20,190: letters to H. Lowe, 1808–10.

Add. 34,916: letters to Nelson, Jan.–Mar. 1800.

Add. 34,919: letters to Nelson, Feb.–Aug. 1803; W. Hamilton to Lord Hawkesbury.

Add. 34,946: letters to Nelson, 1799.

Add. 34,947: letters to Nelson, 1800.

Add. 36,543: R. Church, papers relating to Ionian Islands, 1810–13.

Add. 43,229: letters to Lord Aberdeen.

Add. 43,230: letters to Lord Aberdeen.

Add. 43,911: letters to C. Dilke, 1880.

Add. 56,527: J. Hobhouse, journal, July–Dec. 1809.

British Museum, Department of Greek and Roman Antiquities

Lord Aberdeen, travel diary, vol. 1: Mar.–Sept. 1803, Jan.–Feb. 1804.

Lord Aberdeen, travel diary, vol. 2: Sept.–Nov. 1803.

Royal Anthropological Institute ('RAI')

Durham MS 42 (1): E. Durham, diary, 1910–11.

Durham MS 42 (6): E. Durham, diary, 1911–12.

Durham MS 42 (7): E. Durham, diary, Feb.–Apr. 1912.

Durham MS 42 (10): E. Durham, notebook and diary, Oct. 1912.

Durham MS 42 (11): E. Durham, diary, July–Oct. 1912.

Durham MS 42 (13): E. Durham, diary, Aug.–Oct. 1913.

Durham MS 47 (5): E. Durham, notebook, 1911–12.

Durham MS 47 (8): E. Durham, notebook, undated.

Madrid

Archivo Histórico Nacional (AHN)

Libro 898 (microfilm 2540): Sicilian Inquisition reports.

Libro 899: Sicilian Inquisition reports.

Libro 901 (microfilm 2543): Sicilian Inquisition reports.

Mantua

Archivio di Stato

Archivio Gonzaga, busta 968: reports from Rome, 1597.

Mdina, Malta

Archive of the Inquisition, Cathedral Museum

Processi, 47B: case 268, Tole, 1629.
Processi, 130: case 33, Giovanni Pietro Christodulo, 1771–2.

Milan

Biblioteca Ambrosiana

S 102 sup.: Lazaro Soranzo, 'Relatione' [a version of *L'Ottomanno*].

Munich

Bayerisches Hauptstaatsarchiv

Südostinstitut MS 271: E. Cozzi, letters to C. Patsch, 9 Mar. 1909 and 4 Mar. 1912.

Nantes

Centre des Archives Diplomatiques ('CAD')

Janina, consulat, 290PO/1/3: F. Pouqueville, minutier, Jan.–Dec.1808.
Janina, consulat, 290PO/1/4: F. Pouqueville, minutier, Dec. 1808–Dec. 1809.
Janina, consulat, 290PO/1/6: F. Pouqueville, minutier, Jan.–Mar. 1811.
Janina, consulat, 290PO/1/7: F. Pouqueville, minutier, Mar.–Apr. 1811.
Janina, consulat, 290PO/1/8: F. Pouqueville, minutier, May 1811.
Janina, consulat, 290PO/1/9: F. Pouqueville, minutier, May–July 1811.
Janina, consulat, 290PO/1/10: F. Pouqueville, minutier, July–Aug. 1811.
Janina, consulat, 290PO/1/14: F. Pouqueville, minutier, Nov.–Dec. 1811.
Janina, consulat, 290PO/1/15: F. Pouqueville, minutier, Jan.–June 1812.

Naples

Archivio Storico Diocesano di Napoli ('ASDN')

Sant'Ufficio ('SU'), filza 56.659: Strayl case, 1586.

SU, filza 89.1075: Anastasia of Paramythia case, 1598.

SU, filza 119.1529: Theodora Tedea case, 1606–7.

SU, filza 189.2476: Pietro d'Alba case, 1634.

Nottingham

Nottingham University Library ('NUL')

Pw Jd 96: G. Foresti to S. Foresti, from Ioannina, 26 Nov. 1811.

Pw Jd 98: G. Airey to Maitland, from Zakynthos, 22 Dec. 1811.

Pw Jd 105: G. Airey to Maitland, from Zakynthos, 10 Feb. 1812.

Pw Jd 121: G. Airey to Bentinck, from Zakynthos, 17 Apr. 1812.

Pw Jd 122: G. Airey, proclamation, 13 Apr. 1812.

Pw Jd 217/2: Major Arata to Lt Col. McCombe, from Lefkada, 20 Mar. 1812.

Pw Jd 217/3: Ali to Airey, from Tepelenë, 19/31 Mar. 1812.

Pw Jd 217/4: G. Airey to Ali, from Zakynthos, 2 Apr. 1812.

Pw Jd 217/9: Ali to S. Foresti, from Tepelenë, 1 Apr. 1812.

Pw Jd 217/14: Ali to S. Foresti, from Ioannina, 16/28 Apr. 1812.

Pw Jd 218/1: Ali to Bentinck, from Ioannina, 16/28 Apr. 1812.

Pw Jd 2343: Lord Castlereagh to Ali (extract), from London, 23 May 1812.

Pw Jd 2356: G. Foresti to Bentinck, from Preveza, 8 Feb. 1813.

Pw Jd 2360: A. Andréossy – F. Donzelot correspondence, Oct.–Dec. 1812.

Pw Jd 2361: anon., report on Corfu, 24 Jan. 1813.

Pw Jd 2362: S. Foresti to Bentinck, from Zakynthos, 13 Feb. 1813.

Pw Jd 2365: G. Foresti to Bentinck, from Preveza, 16 Feb. 1813.

Pw Jd 2367: A. Italinsky report, from Istanbul, giving bulletin from Vilnius, 26 Dec. 1812.

Pw Jd 2369: G. Foresti to Bentinck, from Preveza, 2 Mar. 1813.

Pw Jd 2371: Bassano to Pouqueville, from Vilnius, 18 Oct. 1812,

Pw Jd 2373: G. Foresti, memoir on Parga, 1 Mar. 1813.

Pw Jd 2374: S. Foresti to Bentinck, from Zakynthos, 9 Mar. 1813.

Pw Jd 2377: Russian agent, report, from Corfu, 2 Mar. 1813.

Oxford

Balliol College Archives

Morier E1: D. Morier letters, file 1.

Paris

Archives du Ministère des Affaires Étrangères ('AMAE')

Correspondance consulaire et commerciale ('CCC'), Janina 1 (microfilm 15,536) (1800–7).

CCC, Janina 3 (microfilm P 11,395) (Jan. 1810–Mar. 1811).

CCC, Janina 4 (Apr.–Dec. 1811).

CCC, Janina 5 (Jan.–July 1812).

CCC, Janina 6 (Aug.–Dec. 1812).

Correspondance politique, Autriche, vol. 51: report on Piccolomini's campaign of 1689–90.

Correspondance politique, Îles Ioniennes, vol. 18 (microfilm P 14,343) (July 1811–Mar. 1812).

Correspondance politique, Turquie, vol. 222 (microfilm P 629): F. La Tour-Maubourg, reports, July–Dec. 1811.

Bibliothèque nationale de France

lat. 8994: Roman Inquisition to Archbishop of Cosenza, 1592.

Rome

Archivio del Collegium Germanicum et Hungaricum

Hist. 145: G. Nappi, 'Annali del Seminario Romano'.

Archivio della Sacra Congregazione de Propaganda Fide ('ASCPF')

SC Servia 1: Gj. Nikollë, report, 1743.

SC Servia 4: D. d'Afragola, report, 1845, G. Krasniqi, report, 1845, Bogdanović, letter and report, 1846, Bogdanović, reports, 1849, 1850.

SC Servia 5: Bucciarelli, report, 1872.

SOCG 431: A. Bogdani, report, 1670.

SOCG 482: P. Bogdani, report, 1681.

SOCG 792: M. Mazarek, report, 1760.

SOCG 872: M. Mazarek, report, 1785.

SOCG 895: M. Mazarek, report, 1791.

SOCG 922: G. Krasniqi, report, 1820.

nuova serie, 1920, vol. 656, Rub. 109 (protocollo 2886): E. Cozzi, 'Atti' (report on Apostolic Visitation of Albania).

Archivum Romanum Societatis Iesu ('ARSI')

1002, 'Missio albanensis provinciae venetae', vol. 3, fasc. 1: F. Genovizzi, letter to Msgr Laurenti, 17 Dec. 1918; F. Genovizzi, 'Stato religioso in Albania e nel Montenegro', 15 June 1919.

Tirana

Arkivi Qëndror i Shtetit ('AQSh')

Fondi 132, Arqipeshkvia e Shkodrës, 1907, dosja 22: P. Tusha, letter, 14 Oct. 1907.

Fondi 132, Arqipeshkvia e Shkodrës, 1912, dosja 9: draft treaty between leaders of *vilayet* of Shkodër and Montenegro, 18 Sept. 1912.

Fondi 132, Arqipeshkvia e Shkodrës, 1912, dosja 29: E. Cozzi, statement and letter, 8 Jan. 1912.

Fondi 132, Arqipeshkvia e Shkodrës, 1921, dosja 24: E. Cozzi, letters to J. Serreqi, 24 Apr. 1921; 1 July 1921.

Fondi 132, Arqipeshkvia e Shkodrës, 1921, dosja 38: E. Cozzi, letters to J. Serreqi, 29 Jan. 1921; Nov. 1921.

Biblioteka Kombëtare e Shqipërisë

dr. 1.b.13: Sevasti Qiriazi-Dako, 'Jetëshkrimi i Sevasti Qiriazit'.

Trento

Biblioteca provinciale dei padri Cappuccini ('BPPC')

AR 4 28/1: L. Tusha ('Tuscia'), 'La mia vita in Albania'.

Trieste

Archivio di Stato, Trieste

Microfilm of Archivio municipale di Capodistria, MS 550: Libro del Consiglio S (1591).

Udine

Archivio storico dell'Arcidiocesi di Udine ('ASAU')

Sant'Officio ('SO'), busta ('b.') 1302: fasc. 884, 886, 893, 907, 908, 914 (cases of 1639, 1640, 1641).

SO, b. 1304: fasc. 937 (cases of 1643).

SO, b. 1348: sewn vol. of summary reports (cases of 1638, 1641, 1643).

Vatican City

Archivio Segreto Vaticano ('ASVat')

Archivio della Delegazione Apostolica di Albania ('ADA'), vol. 1, fasc. 1: E. Cozzi, letters to Propaganda Fide, 1921, 23 May 1924, Jan. 1925.

ADA, vol. 1, fasc. 3: copy of E. Cozzi, 'Relazione' (first part of 'Atti').

ADA, vol. 1, fasc. 6: Propaganda Fide, letters to E. Cozzi, 16 Nov. 1923, 5 Apr. 1924, 7 June 1924; E. Cozzi, 'Protocollo no. 1950', 5 Apr. 1925.

Fondo Borghese, ser. III, MS 128: F. Patrizi, notes on Albania, 1590s.

Fondo Borghese, ser. IV, MS 229: A. Bruni to A. Ingegneri, 17 Oct. 1596.

Processus consistoriales, 114: report, 1728.

Segr. Stato, Legaz. Avignone, 12: G. Bruni to Cardinal Como, Jan. 1581.

Segr. Stato, Legaz. Avignone, 15: G. Bruni to Cardinal Como, Apr. 1584.

Visitationes ad limina, 728: Karadžić, reports, 12 Dec. 1713 and 12 June 1716.

Biblioteca Apostolica Vaticana

Barb. Lat. 5361: A. Bruni, treatise.

Venice

Archivio di Stato ('ASVen')

Provveditori da terra e da mar, filza 529: report of interview with 'Nicon', 7 Oct. 1689; Zmajević to Molin, 22 Nov. 1689.

Provveditori da terra e da mar, filza 530: Molin, report, 5 Mar. 1690.

Savi all'eresia (Santo Ufficio) ('SU'), busta ('b.') 86 (1628), fasc. 1: Peter of Shkodër case, Alexander of Kurbin case, B. Matagushë case.

SU, b. 87 (1630): Nicolaus of Fan case.

SU, b. 101 (1644–5): Gj. Bastar case, N. Bassan case, Gj. Isin case.

SU, b. 124 (1687): Bardi case.

Biblioteca del Museo Correr

Wcovich Lazzari 25, busta 9: A. Bruni, treatise.

Biblioteca Nazionale Marciana

IT VII 1068: report from Vienna, Dec. 1689.

Istituto per la storia della società e dello stato veneziano, Fondazione Cini, Venice

Microfilm 136 of Archivio Segreto Vaticano, nunziatura di Venezia: report of 22 Apr. 1690.

Vienna

Haus-, Hof- und Staatsarchiv ('HHStA')

Türkei VI, 1: reports from Ottoman Empire, 1807–8.

Türkei VI, 2: reports from Ottoman Empire, 1808–9.

Türkei VI, 3: reports from Ottoman Empire, 1809–10.

Kriegsarchiv

Alte Feldakten, Türkenkrieg, 1689-11-18: von Strasser, report to von Baden.

Exp. Prot. 1690 (vol. 383): report from Prishtina, 19 Dec. 1689.

Exp. Prot. 1693 (vol. 391): report from Esztergom, Feb. 1693.

Bibliography

Adair, Sir Robert, *The Negotiations for the Peace of the Dardanelles, in 1808–9*, 2 vols. (London, 1845).

Ahmed ben-Abdallah ['Ahmet Ben-Abdala'], *Epistola theologica de articulis quibusdam fidei*, ed. Z. Grapius (Rostock, 1705).

Aksan, V. H., *Ottoman Wars, 1700–1870: An Empire Besieged* (Harlow, 2007).

Albèri, E., ed., *Relazioni degli ambasciatori veneti al senato*, 15 vols. (Florence, 1839–63).

Alkan, M., 'The End of the *Akıncı* Corps in the Ottoman Empire', in *IBAC 2012: 2nd International Balkan Annual Conference: The Balkans at a Crossroads*, ed. B. Çınar, 2 vols. (Istanbul, 2013), ii, pp. 492–501.

Amabile, L., *Il Santo Officio della Inquisizione in Napoli* (Castello, 1892).

Amantos, K., *Scheseis Ellēnōn kai Tourkōn apo tou endekatou aiōnos mechri tou 1821* (Athens, 1955).

Amini, I., *Napoleon and Persia: Franco-Persian Relations under the First Empire* (Washington, DC, 1999).

Anderson, R. C., *Naval Wars in the Levant, 1559–1853* (Liverpool, 1952).

Andréadès, A., 'Ali Pacha de Tébelin, économiste et financier', *Revue des études grecques*, 25 (1912), pp. 427–60.

Andreadis, G., *The Crypto-Christians: Klostoi: Those who Returned; Tenesur: Those who have Changed* (Salonica, 1995).

Anna Comnena, *The Alexiad*, tr. E. A. S. Dawes (Cambridge, Ontario, 2000).

Anon., ed., *Turcici imperii status* (Leiden, 1630).

Anon., *Der neu-eröffneten Ottomanischen Pforten Fortsetzung* (Augsburg, 1701).

Anon., ed., 'Reise des Ritters Hans Bernard von Eptingen nach Palästina, im Jahr 1460', *Der Schweizerische Geschichtsforscher*, vii (Bern, 1828), pp. 313–402.

Anon., ed., 'Journal de voyage à Jérusalem de Louis de Rochechouart, évêque de Saintes (1461)', *Revue d'Orient latin*, 1 (1893), pp. 168–274.

Anon., 'Ancient Illyrians in Entente', *The Adriatic Review*, vol. 1, no. 1 (Sept. 1918), pp. 11–14.

Anon., Obituary of Ernesto Cozzi, *Lajmtari i zemres së Jezu Krishtit*, 36, n. 3 (Mar. 1926), pp. 33–5.

Anon., Obituary of Ernesto Cozzi, *Zâni i Shna Ndout*, 14, no. 3 (Mar. 1926), pp. 33–6.

Anon., 'Nexhmie Zaimi, Author of "Daughter of the Eagle", Passes Away', *Dielli*, Apr.–June 2003, p. 9.

Anon., 'Dijaspora-Szórvány', http://budapest.mfa.gov.yu (accessed 15/12/2006).

Anscombe, F. F., 'Albanians and "Mountain Bandits"', in F. F. Anscombe, ed., *The Ottoman Balkans, 1750–1830* (Princeton, NJ, 2006), pp. 87–113.

Anscombe, F. F., 'The Ottoman Empire in Recent International Politics—II: The Case of Kosovo', *The International History Review*, 28 (2006), pp. 758–93.

Anscombe, F. F., 'Continuities in Ottoman Centre-Periphery Relations, 1787–1915', in A. C. S. Peacock, ed., *The Frontiers of the Ottoman World* (Oxford, 2009), pp. 235–51.

Aravantinos, P., *Chronographia tēs Ēpeirou* (Athens, 1856).

Aravantinos, S. P., *Istoria Alē Pasa tou Tepelenlē*, 2 vols. (Athens, 1895).

Ariosto, A., *Itinerarium (1476–1479)*, ed. F. Uliana (Alessandria, 2007).

Arnold, T. W., *The Preaching of Islam: a History of the Propagation of the Muslim Faith*, 3rd edn. (London, 1935).

Arnu [Arnoux, Harnoux], N., *Presagio dell'imminente rovina, e caduta dell'imperio ottomano, delle future vittorie, e prosperi successi della christianità* (Padua, 1684).

Arsh, G. L., *Albaniia i Epir v kontse XVIII–nachale XIX v.* (Moscow, 1963).

Arsh, G. L., *Ē Alvania kai ē Ēpeiros sta telē tou IĒ' kai stis arches tou ITH' aiōna*, tr. A. Dialla, ed. V. Panagiōtopoulos (Athens, 1994) [with an appendix of documents not in the original edn.].

Arsh, G. L., ed., *Ē Rōsia kai ta pasalikia Alvanias kai Ēpeirou, 1759–1831: engrapha rōsikōn archeiōn*, tr. I. Smusliaeva (Athens, 2007).

Arsov, T., *Marbles and Politics: William Martin Leake's Missions in the Ottoman Balkans, 1799–1810* (Istanbul, 2010).

Asad, M., tr., *The Meaning of the Qur'an* (Bristol, 2003).

Ashta, N., 'Kanuni i malcís', *Albania*, 1897, pp. 149–52, 178–81; 1898, pp. 86, 106–7, 156; 1899, pp. 67–70.

Ashta, N., 'Das Gewohnheitsrecht der Stämme Mi-Schodrak (Über-Scutariner Stämme) in den Gebirgen nördlich von Scutari', *Zeitschrift für Ethnologie*, 33 (1901), pp. 358–63.

Aspinall, A., ed., *The Correspondence of Charles Arbuthnot*, Camden ser. 3, vol. 65 (London, 1941).

Babinger, F., *Mehmed the Conqueror and His Time*, tr. R. Manheim, ed. W. C. Hickman (Princeton, NJ, 1978).

Baçe, A., 'Qyteti i fortifikuar i Kaninës', *Monumentet*, 7–8 (1974), pp. 25–54.

Badia Elias, J., *La Inquisició a Catalunya (segles XIII–XIX)* (Barcelona, 1992).

Baedeker, K., *Austria-Hungary* (Leipzig, 1911).

Baggally, J. W., *Ali Pasha and Great Britain* (Oxford, 1938).

Baião, A., 'A Inquisição em Portugal e no Brazil', *Archivo historicao portuguez*, 7 (1909), pp. 227–40.

Baldacci, A., *Nel paese del Cem: viaggi di esplorazione nel Montenegro orientale e sulle Alpi albanesi* (Rome, 1903).

Baldini, U., 'Capodilista, Gabriele', *Dizionario biografico degli italiani* (Rome, 1960–), xviii, pp. 635–8.

Ballabani, M., ed., *Imzot Lazër Mjeda: mbrojtës dhe lëvrues i identitetit shqiptar* (Prishtina and Sankt Gallen, 2011).

Balsamo, J., 'Il Turco vincibile. Un "corpus turc" à la fin du XVIᵉ siècle: La Noue, Naselli, Soranzo, Esprinchard', in Gruppo di studio sul cinquecento francese, *Scritture dell'impegno dal rinascimento all'età barocca* (Fasano, 1997), pp. 205–16.

Barjaktarović, M., 'Dvovjerske šiptarske zadruge u Metohiji', Srpska Akademija Nauka, *Zbornik radova*, vol. 4 (Etnografski Institut, vol. 1) (1950), pp. 197–209.

Barleti, M., *The Siege of Shkodra*, tr. D. Hosaflook (Tirana, 2012).

von Bartenstein, J. C., *Kurzer Bericht von der Beschaffenheit der zerstreuten zahlreichen Illyrischen Nation in kaiserl. königl. Erblanden* (Frankfurt-am-Main and Leipzig, 1802).

von Bartenstein, J. C., *Kratak izveštaj o stanju rasejanoga mnogobrojnoga ilirskoga naroda po car. i kralj. nasledničkim zemaljama*, tr. A. Sandić (Vienna, 1866).

Bartl, P., *Die albanesischen Muslime zur Zeit der nationalen Unabhängigkeitsbewegung (1878–1912)* (Wiesbaden, 1968).

Bartl, P., *Der Westbalkan zwischen spanischer Monarchie und Osmanischem Reich: zur Türkenkriegsproblematik an der Wende vom 16. zum 17. Jahrhundert* (Wiesbaden, 1974).

Bartl, P., ed., *Quellen und Materialien zur albanischen Geschichte im 17. und 18. Jahrhundert*, 2 vols. (Munich, 1975–9).

Bartl, P., 'Die Kelmendi: zur Geschichte eines nordalbanischen Bergstammes', *Shêjzat (Le Pleiadi)* (1977), pp. 123–38.

Bartl, P., ed., *Albania sacra: geistliche Visitationsberichte aus Albanien*, i: *Diözese Alessio* (Wiesbaden, 2007).

Bartl, P., ed., *Albania sacra: geistliche Visitationsberichte aus Albanien*, ii: *Erzdiözese Durazzo* (Wiesbaden, 2011).

Bartl, P., ed., *Albania sacra: geistliche Visitationsberichte aus Albanien*, iii: *Diözese Sappa* (Wiesbaden, 2014).

Bartl, P., ed., *Albania sacra: geistliche Visitationsberichte aus Albanien*, iv: *Diözese Pulati* (Wiesbaden, 2017).

Barzon, G., 'Per lo studio del Seminario di Padova: economia, amministrazione, alunni e professori', in L. Billanovich and P. Gios, eds., *Gregorio Barbarigo, patrizio veneto, vescovo e cardinale nella tarda Controriforma (1625–1697)*, 2 vols. (Padua, 1999), i, pp. 637–701.

Başar, F., 'Osmanlı devletinin kuruluş döneminde hizmeti görülen akıncı aileleri: I: Mihaloğulları', *Türk dünyası tarih dergisi*, no. 63 (Mar. 1992), pp. 20–6.

Başar, F., 'Osmanlı devletinin kuruluş döneminde hizmeti görülen akıncı aileleri: III: Turahanoğulları', *Türk dünyası tarih dergisi*, no. 65 (May 1992), pp. 47–50.

Bataković, D. T., *Kosovo i Metohija u srpsko-arbanaškim odnosima* (Prishtina, 1991).

Bataković, D. T., *The Kosovo Chronicles*, tr. D. Vulićević (Belgrade, 1992).

Baxhaku, F., and K. Kaser, eds., *Die Stammesgesellschaften Nordalbaniens: Berichte und Forschungen österreichischer Konsuln und Gelehrter (1861–1917)* (Vienna, 1996).

Bayerle, G., *Pashas, Begs and Effendis: A Historical Dictionary of Titles and Terms in the Ottoman Empire* (Istanbul, 1997).

[de Beauchamp, A.,] *The Life of Ali Pacha, of Jannina, Late Vizier of Epirus, Surnamed Aslan, or the Lion, Including a Compendious History of Modern Greece*, 2nd edn. (London, 1823).

Beebe, K., *Pilgrim and Preacher: The Audiences and Observant Spirituality of Friar Felix Fabri (1437/8–1502)* (Oxford, 2014).

Bellini, G., *Storia della tipografia del Seminario di Padova, 1684–1938* (Padua, 1938).

Belmont, N., *Arnold Van Gennep, créateur de l'ethnographie française* (Paris, 1974).

Bennassar, B., and L. Bennassar, *Les Chrétiens d'Allah: l'histoire extraordinaire des renégats, XVIᵉ–XVIIᵉ siècles* (Paris, 1989).

[Bessières, J.,] *Mémoire sur la vie et la puissance d'Ali-Pacha, visir de Janina* (Paris, 1820).

Bethencourt, F., *The Inquisition: A Global History, 1478–1834* (Cambridge, 2009).

Bexheti, N., *Der 'Grosse Türkenkrieg' und die Albaner: die militärische Präsenz der Balkanvölker am 'Grossen Türkenkrieg' (1683–1699)* (Saarbrücken, 2009).

Bibliander, T., ed., *Machumetis Saracenorum principis... Alcoran* (Basel, 1543).

Bilotta, B., *Gli enti sacri della Bibbia ne' numi mitologici venerati da' Pelasgi Albanesi del gentilesimo* (Castrovillari, 1897).

Binark, İ., ed., *6 Numaralı mühimme defteri*, 3 vols. (Ankara, 1995).

Binark, İ., et al., eds., *12 Numaralı mühimme defteri*, 3 vols. (Ankara, 1996).

Birken, A., *Die Provinzen des Osmanischen Reiches* (Wiesbaden, 1976).

Black, C., *The Italian Inquisition* (New Haven, CT, 2009).

Bland, W., and I. Price, *A Tangled Web: A History of Anglo-American Relations with Albania* (London, 1986).

Boccadamo, G., *Napoli e l'Islam: storie di musulmani, schiavi e rinnegati in età moderna* (Naples, 2010).

Bogdani, P., *Cuneus prophetarum de Christo salvatore mundi, et eius evangelica veritate, italice et epirotice contexta* (Padua, 1685).

Bogdani, P., ed. E. Sedaj and I. Rugova [reprint of the 1685 edn., with facing translation in modern Albanian], 2 vols. (Prishtina, 1989).

Bogdani, P., *Letra dhe dokumente nga Arkivi i Kongregatës 'de Propaganda Fide' si dhe nga Arkivat Sekrete të Vatikanit*, ed. O. Marquet (Shkodër, 1997).

Boletini, T., *Kujtime: Pranë Isa Boletinit* and *Përballë sfidave të kohës*, ed. M. Verli, 2 vols. (Tetovë, 1996 [reprinted Tirana, 2003]).

Bonaparte, N., *Correspondance générale*, ed. T. Lantz et al., 15 vols. (Paris, 2004–18).

Bonnici, A., *Medieval and Roman Inquisition in Malta* (Rabat, 1998).

Bono, S., *Schiavi musulmani nell'Italia moderna: galeotti, vu' cumprà, domestici* (Naples, 1999).

Boppe, A., 'Le Colonel Nicole Papas Oglou et le bataillon des Chasseurs d'Orient, 1798–1815', *Carnet de la Sabretache: revue d'histoire militaire retrospective*, 8 (1900), pp. 13–30, 112–27.

Boppe, A., *L'Albanie et Napoléon (1797–1814)* (Paris, 1914).

Borgia, N., *I monaci basiliani d'Italia in Albania*, 2 vols. (Rome, 1935–42).

de Bosset, C. P., *Proceedings in Parga and the Ionian Islands* (London, 1819).

Bostan, İ., 'The Establishment of the Province of *Cezayir-i Bahr-i Sefid*', in E. Zachariadou, ed., *The Kapudan Pasha: His Office and His Domain* (Rethymno, 2002), pp. 241–51.

Botero, G., *Relationi universali*, 2 vols. (Vicenza, 1595).

Brandewie, E., *When Giants Walked the Earth: The Life and Times of Wilhelm Schmidt SVD* (Fribourg, 1990).

Brasca, S., *Viaggio in Terrasanta 1480*, ed. A.-L. Momigliano Lepschy (Milan, 1966).

Braudel, F., *The Mediterranean and the Mediterranean World in the Age of Philip II*, tr. S. Reynolds, 2 vols. (London, 1972).

von Breydenbach, B., *Sanctarum peregrinationum in montem Syon…opusculum* (Mainz, 1486).

British Government, *Accounts and Papers, 1880*, vol. 42, Turkey (London, 1880).

[Brlić, A. T.,] *Die freiwillige Theilname der Serben und Kroaten an den vier letzten österreichisch-türkischen Kriegen* (Vienna, 1854).

Bryer, A., 'The Crypto-Christians of the Pontos and Consul William Palgrave of Trebizond', in A. Bryer, *Peoples and Settlements in Anatolia and the Caucasus, 800–1900* (London, 1988), item XVII.

Burić, J., *Iz prošlosti hrvatske kolonije u Rimu* (Rome, 1966).

Çabej, N. R., *Autoktonia e shqiptarëve në studimet gjermane* (Prishtina, 1990).

Cahen, C., P. Hardy and H. İnalcık, 'Djizya', in *The Encyclopaedia of Islam*, 2nd edn., ed. H. A. R. Gibb et al. (Leiden, 1960), ii, pp. 559–66.

Čakić, S., *Velika seoba Srba 1689/90 i Patrijarh Arsenije III Crnojević* (Novi Sad, 1982).

Callegari, M., 'La tipografia del Seminario di Padova fondata dal Barbarigo', in L. Billanovich and P. Gios, eds., *Gregorio Barbarigo, patrizio veneto, vescovo e cardinale nella tarda Controriforma (1625–1697)*, 2 vols. (Padua, 1999), i, pp. 231–51.

Cantelli, G., *Albania propria overo superiore detta anche Macedonia occidentale* [engraved map, single sheet] (Rome, 1689).

Cassese, M., 'Gregorio Barbarigo e il rapporto con ebrei e non cattolici', in L. Billanovich and P. Gios, eds., *Gregorio Barbarigo, patrizio veneto, vescovo e cardinale nella tarda Controriforma (1625–1697)*, 2 vols. (Padua, 1999), ii, pp. 1,023–56.

Çekrezi, K. ['Chekrezi, C.'], 'Southern Albania or Northern Epirus?', *Illyria*, vol. 1, no. 2 (1 Apr. 1916), pp. 5–6.

Çekrezi, K. ['Chekrezi, C.'], 'Past and Present Conditions of Albania', *Illyria*, vol. 1, no. 7 (1 July 1916), pp. 1–3.

Çekrezi, K. ['Chekrezi, C.'], *Albania Past and Present* (New York, 1919).

Çekrezi, K. ['Chekrezi, C.'], 'The Religious and Educational Question in Albania', *The Adriatic Review*, vol. 1, nos. 5–6 (Jan.–Feb. 1919), pp. 187–91.

Chareyron, N., *Pilgrims to Jerusalem in the Middle Ages*, tr. W. D. Wilson (New York, 2005).

Chessell, C. I., 'Britain's Ionian Consul: Spiridion Foresti and Intelligence Collection (1793–1805)', *Journal of Mediterranean Studies*, 16 (2006), pp. 45–61.

Chivu, G., et al., eds., *Documente și însemnări românești din secolul al XVI-lea* (Bucharest, 1979).

Ciantes, G., *De sanctissima trinitate ex antiquorum hebraeorum testimoniis evidenter comprobata discursus* (Rome, 1667).

Ciriaco of Ancona, *Epigrammata reperta per Illyricum a Cyriaco Anconitano apud Liburniam* (n.p., n.d).

Clayer, N., *L'Albanie, pays des derviches: les ordres mystiques musulmans en Albanie à l'époque post-ottomane (1912–1967)* (Berlin, 1990).

Clayer, N., *Aux origines du nationalisme albanais: la naissance d'une nation majoritairement musulmane en Europe* (Paris, 2007).

Clayer, N., 'Ali Paşa Tepedelenli', *Enclyclopaedia of Islam*, 3rd edn., http://referenceworks.brillonline.com/entries/encyclopaedia-of-islam-3/ali-pasa-tepedelenli-COM_23950

Clewing, K., and E. Pezo, 'Jovan Cvijić als Historiker und Nationsbildner: zu Ertrag und Grenzen seines anthropogeographischen Ansatzes zur Migrationsgeschichte', in M. Krzoska and H.-C. Maner, eds., *Beruf und Berufung: Geschichtswissenschaft und Nationsbildung in Ostmittel- und Südosteuropa im 19. und 20. Jahrhundert* (Münster, 2005), pp. 265–97.

Clissold, S., ed., *A Short History of Yugoslavia* (Cambridge, 1968).

Cochran, P., *Byron and Hobby-O: Lord Byron's Relationship with John Cam Hobhouse* (Newcastle, 2010).

Comnena, Anna: *see* Anna Comnena.

Conrady, L., *Vier rheinische Palaestina-Pilgerschriften des XIV. XV. und XVI. Jahrhunderts* (Wiesbaden, 1882).

Conring, H., ed., *De bello contra Turcos prudenter gerendo* (Helmstadt, 1664).

Coon, C. S., *The Mountains of Giants: a Racial and Cultural Study of the North Albanian Mountain Ghegs* (Cambridge, MA, 1950).

Cordignano, F., ed., *L'Albania a traverso l'opera e gli scritti di un grande Missionario italiano il P. Domenico Pasi S. I. (1847–1914)*, 3 vols. (Rome, 1933–4).

Cozzi, E., 'Malattie, morte, funerali nelle montagne d'Albania', *Anthropos*, 4 (1909), nos. 5–6, pp. 903–18.

Cozzi, E., 'La vendetta del sangue nelle Montagne dell'Alta Albania', *Anthropos*, 5 (1910), no. 1, pp. 654–87.

Cozzi, E., 'Lo stato agricolo in Albania, con speciale riguardo alle montagne di Scutari', *Revue d'ethnographie et de sociologie*, 1 (1910), pp. 33–49.

Cozzi, E., 'La donna albanese, con speciale riguardo al diritto consuetudinario delle Montagne di Scutari', *Anthropos*, 7 (1912), no. 3, pp. 309–35, nos. 4–5, pp. 617–26.

Cozzi, E., 'Le tribù dell'Alta Albania: appunti sulla loro organizzazione sociale e politica con dati statistici', *Il Trentino*, 24 Dec. 1913.

Cozzi, E., 'Credenze e superstizioni nelle montagne dell'Albania', *Anthropos*, 9 (1914), nos. 3–4, pp. 449–76.

Cozzi, E., 'Le tribù dell'Alta Albania: appunti sulla loro organizzazione sociale e politica con dati statistici', ed. G. Valentini, in *Studime e tekste, dega 1: juridike, n. 1* (Rome, 1944), pp. 229–69.

Cozzi, E., 'La donna albanese', *Shêjzat*, 17 (1973), nos. 1–4, pp. 94–126, 232–41.

Crampton ['Kramton'], R. J., 'Anglia dhe Shqiptarët më 1878–1881', in A. Buda et al., eds., *Konferenca kombëtare e studimeve për lidhjen shqiptare të Prizrenit, 1878–1881*, 2 vols. (Tirana, 1979), pp. 398–408.

da Crema, A., *Itinerario al Santo Sepolcro, 1486*, ed. G. Nori (Pisa, 1996).

Crimmin, P. K., '"A Great Object with us to Procure this Timber": The Royal Navy's Search for Ship Timber in the Eastern Mediterranean and Southern Russia, 1803–1815', *International Journal of Maritime History*, 4 (1992), no. 2, pp. 83–115.

Crimmin, P. K., 'Hunting for Naval Timber in the Adriatic, 1802–1815', in J. Tulard et al., *Français et anglais en Méditerranée, 1789–1830* (n.p., 1992), pp. 149–57.

Crispi, G. [Z. Krispi], *Memoria sulla lingua albanese* (Palermo, 1831).

della Croce, I., *Historia antica, e moderna, sacra, e profana, della città di Trieste* (Venice, 1698).

Crowson, A., *Butrinti venecian: Venetian Butrint* (London, 2007).

von Csaplovics, J., *Slavonien und zum Theil Croatien: ein Beitrag zur Völker- und Ländekunde*, 2 vols. (Pest, 1819).

Cunningham, A., *Anglo-Ottoman Encounters in the Age of Revolution*, ed. E. Ingram, (London, 1993).

Cvijić, J., *La Péninsule balkanique: géographie humaine* (Paris, 1918).

von Czoernig, K., *Ethnographie der Oesterreichischen Monarchie*, 3 vols. (Vienna, 1855–7).

Dako, K. ['C.'], 'The Albanians', *Ylli i mengjezit*, vol. 1, no. 3 (15 Feb. 1917), pp. 67–73.

Dako, K. ['C.'], 'The Albanian Language', *Ylli i mengjezit*, vol. 1, no. 4 (28 Feb. 1917), pp. 97–9.

Dako, K. ['C.'], 'The Religious Beliefs of the Albanians', *Ylli i mengjezit*, vol. 1, no. 5 (15 Mar. 1917), pp. 129–31.

Dako, K. ['C.'], 'The Independence of Albania a Necessity for International Peace', *Ylli i mengjezit*, vol. 1, no. 6 (2 Apr. 1917), pp. 161–9.

Dako, K. ['C.'], 'The Strength of the National Consciousness of the Albanian People', *Ylli i mengjezit*, vol. 3, no. 5 (Aug. 1918), pp. 129–32.

Dako, K. ['C.'], *Zogu the First, King of the Albanians (A Sketch of his Life and Times)* (Tirana, 1937).

Dankoff, R., and R. Elsie, eds., *Evliya Çelebi in Albania and Adjacent Regions (Kosovo, Montenegro, Ohrid)* (Leiden, 2000).

Dansette, B., 'Les Pèlerinages occidentaux en Terre Sainte: une pratique de la "Dévotion Moderne" à la fin du Moyen Age? Relation inédite d'un pèlerinage effectué en 1486', *Archivum franciscanum historicum*, 72 (1979), pp. 106–33, 330–428.

Darovec, D., *Breve storia dell'Istria*, tr. M. Rebeschini (Udine, 2010).

Davidson, N. S., 'The Inquisition of Venice and its Documents: Some Problems of Method and Analysis', in A. Del Col and G. Paolin, eds., *L'Inquisizione romana in Italia nell'età moderna: archivi, problemi di metodo e nuove ricerche* (Rome, 1991), pp. 117–31.

Davison, R. H., *Reform in the Ottoman Empire, 1856–1876* (Princeton, NJ, 1963).

Dawkins, R. M., 'The Crypto-Christians of Turkey', *Byzantium*, 8 (1933), pp. 247–75.

Dehérain, H., 'Une correspondance inédite de François Pouqueville, consul de France à Janina et à Patras', *Revue de l'histoire des colonies françaises*, 9 (1921), no. 2, pp. 61–100.

Del Col, A., 'I criteri dello storico nell'uso delle fonti inquisitoriali moderne', in A. Del Col and G. Paolin, eds., *L'Inquisizione Romana: metodologia delle fonti e storia istituzionale* (Trieste, 2000), pp. 51–72.

Del Col, A., *L'Inquisizione in Italia, dal XII al XX secolo* (Milan, 2006).

Demény, L., 'Relațiile ruso-sîrbe în anii 1806–1812', in E. Stănescu, ed., *Studii istorice sud-est europene*, vol. 1 (Bucharest, 1974), pp. 127–57.

Demir, İ., 'Tepedelenli Ali Pasha and the West: A History of his Relations with France and Great Britain, 1798–1820', MA thesis, Bilkent University, Ankara (2007).

Denke, A., ed., *Konrad Grunembergs Pilgerreise ins Heilige Land, 1486: Untersuchung, Edition und Kommentar* (Cologne, 2011).

Destani, B., ed., *Albania & Kosovo: Political and Ethnic Boundaries, 1867–1946* (London, 1999).

Destani, B., ed., *Montenegro: Political and Ethnic Boundaries, 1840–1920*, 2 vols. (London, 2001).

Deusch, E., 'Albanische Thronbewerber: ein Beitrag zur Geschichte der albanischen Staatsgründung', *Münchner Zeitschrift für Balkankunde*, 4 (1981–2), pp. 89–150; 5 (1983–4), pp. 121–64; 6 (1990), pp. 93–151.

Deusch, E., *Das k.(u.)k. Kultusprotektorat im albanischen Siedlungsgebiet in seinem kulturellen, politischen und wirtschaftlichen Umfeld* (Vienna, 2009).

Di-Blasi, G. E., *Storia del regno di Sicilia dall'epoca oscura e favolosa sino al 1774*, 20 vols. (Palermo, 1847).

Dimitropoulos, D., 'Aspects of the Working of the Fiscal Machinery in the Areas Ruled by Ali Paşa', in A. Anastasopoulos and E. Kolovos, eds., *Ottoman Rule in the Balkans, 1760–1850: Conflict, Transformation, Adaptation* (Rethymno, 2007), pp. 61–72.

Djordjević, T., 'Stanovništvo u Srbiji posle velike seobe 1690 godine', *Naš narodni život*, 4 (1931), pp. 114–38.

Djurdjev, B., *Iz istorije Cme Gore, brdskih i malisorskih plemena* (Sarajevo, 1954).

Douglas, F. S. N., *An Essay on Certain Points of Resemblance between the Ancient and Modern Greeks* (London, 1813).

Dragnich, A. N., and S. Todorovich, *The Saga of Kosovo: Focus on Serbian–Albanian Relations* (Boulder, CO, 1984).

Driault, E., *La Politique orientale de Napoléon: Sébastiani et Gardane, 1806–1808* (Paris, 1904).

Duijzings, G., *Religion and the Politics of Identity in Kosovo* (London, 2000).

Duka, F., 'Aspekte social-ekonomike dhe demografike të Himarës gjatë sundimit osman (shek. XV–XVI)', in L. Nasi et al., eds., *Himara në shekuj* (Tirana, 2004), pp. 62–95.

Duka, F., 'Shoqëria dhe ekonomia në Çamërinë osmane: kazatë e Ajdonatit dhe Mazrakut (gjysma e dytë e shek. XVI)', *Studime historike*, (2007), pp. 25–38.

Dumont, A., *Le Balkan et l'Adriatique: les bulgares et les albanais; l'administration en Turquie; la vie des campagnes; le panslavisme et l'hellenisme*, 2nd edn. (Paris, 1874).

Durham, M. E., *High Albania* (London, 1909).

Durham, M. E., *The Struggle for Scutari (Turk, Slav, and Albanian)* (London, 1914).

Durham, M. E., *Some Tribal Origins, Laws, and Customs of the Balkans* (London, 1928).

Durrieu, P., 'Valona, base d'une expédition française contre les Turcs projetée par le roi Charles VIII (1494–1495)', *Comptes rendus des séances de l'Académie des Inscriptions et Belles-Lettres*, 59 (1915), no. 2, pp. 181–90.

Elliot, A. D., *The Life of George Joachim Goschen, First Viscount Goschen, 1831–1907*, 2 vols. (London, 1911).

Elsie, R., *History of Albanian Literature*, 2 vols. (Boulder, CO, 1995).

Elsie, R., 'The Christian Saints of Albania', *Balkanistica*, 13 (2000), pp. 35–57.

Elsie, R., *Early Albania: A Reader of Historical Texts, 11th – 17th Centuries*, Balkanologische Veröffentlichungen, xxxix (Wiesbaden, 2003).

Elsie, R., *The Tribes of Albania: History, Society and Culture* (London, 2015).

von Engel, J. C., *Geschichte des Ungrischen Reichs und seiner Nebenländer*, 4 vols. (Halle, 1797–1804).

Esch, A., 'Gemeinsames Erlebnis—individueller Bericht: vier Parallelberichte aus einer Reisegruppe von Jerusalempilgern 1480', *Zeitschrift für historische Forschung*, 11 (1984), no. 4, pp. 385–416.

Esprinchard, J., *Histoire des Ottomans, ou empereurs des Turcs, iusques à Mahomet III*, 2nd edn. (Paris, 1609).

Eubel, C., *Hierarchia catholica medii aevi*, iii (Munich, 1910).

Evliya Çelebi, *Evliya Çelebi in Albania and Adjacent Regions (Kosovo, Montenegro, Ohrid)*, ed. and tr. R. Dankoff and R. Elsie (Leiden, 2000).

Fabri, F., *Evagatorium in Terrae Sanctae Arabiae et Aegypti peregrinationem*, ed. K. ['C.'] D. Hassler, 3 vols. (Stuttgart, 1843–9).

Farlati, D., *Illyrici sacri*, 8 vols. (Venice, 1751–1819).

Fedalto, G., 'Il Cardinale Gregorio Barbarigo e l'Oriente', in L. Billanovich and P. Gios, eds., *Gregorio Barbarigo, patrizio veneto, vescovo e cardinale nella tarda Controriforma (1625–1697)*, 2 vols. (Padua, 1999), ii, pp. 977–1,001.

Fermendžin, E., 'Izprave god. 1579–1671 tičuće se Crne Gore i stare Srbije', *Starine Jugoslovenskog Akademije Znanosti i Umjetnosti*, 25 (1892), pp. 164–200.

Fevziu, B., *Histori e shtypit shqiptar 1848–1996* (Tirana, 1996).

[Feyerabend, S., ed.,] *Reyssbuch dess heyligen Lands, das ist ein grundtliche Beschreibung aller und jeder Meer und Bilgerfahrten zum heyligen Lande* (Frankfurt-am-Main, 1584).

Fine, J. V. A., *The Bosnian Church: A New Interpretation* (Boulder, CO, 1975).

Finkel, C. B., 'The Provisioning of the Ottoman Army during the Campaigns of 1593–1606', in A. Tietze, ed., *Habsburgisch-osmanische Beziehungen*, Beihefte zur Wiener Zeitschrift für die Kunde des Morgenlandes, xiii (Vienna, 1985), 107–23.

Finkel, C. B., *The Administration of Warfare: The Ottoman Military Campaigns in Hungary, 1593–1606* (Vienna, 1988).

Fischer, B. J., *Albania at War, 1939–1945* (London, 1999).

Fiume, G., 'Marineo, Vincenzo Beccadelli di Bologna, marchese di', in *Dizionario biografico degli italiani* (Rome, 1960–), lxx, p. 415.

Fiume, G., *Schiavitù mediterranee: corsari, rinnegati e santi di età moderna* (Milan, 2009).

Fleming, K. E., *The Muslim Bonaparte: Diplomacy and Orientalism in Ali Pasha's Greece* (Princeton, NJ, 1999).

Floristán Imízcoz, J. M., ed., *Fuentes para la política oriental de los Austrias: la documentación griega del Archivo de Simancas (1571–1621)*, 2 vols. (Leon, 1988).

Floristán Imízcoz, J. M., 'Los contactos de la Chimarra con el reino de Nápoles durante el siglo XVI y comienzos del XVII', *Erytheia: revista de estudios bizantinos y neogriegos*, 11–12 (1990–1), 105–39; 13 (1992), 53–87.

Forlivesi, M., *Scotistarum princeps Bartolomeo Mastri (1602–1673) e il suo tempo* (Padua, 2002).

Frashëri, K., 'Pjetër Bogdani dhe lëvizja çlirimtare në shekullin e 17-të', in A. Kostallari, ed., *Pjetër Bogdani dhe vepra e tij* (Tirana, 1991), pp. 53–83.

Freundlich, L., *Albaniens Golgotha: Anklageakten gegen die Vernichter des Albanervolkes* (Vienna, 1913).

Galt, J., *Letters from the Levant; containing Views of the State of Society, Manners, Opinions, and Commerce, in Greece, and Several of the Principal Islands of the Archipelago* (London, 1813).

Ganz-Blättler, U., *Andacht und Abenteuer: Berichte europäischer Jerusalem- und Santiago-Pilger (1320–1520)* (Tübingen, 1990).

Gashi, Gj., *Vatikani dhe Arbëria, 1700–1922* (Tirana, 1998).

Gaspari, Sh., 'Nji dorshkrim i vjetës 1671 mbi Shqypni', *Hylli i Dritës* 6 (1930), pp. 377–88, 492–8, 605–13; 7 (1931), pp. 154–61, 223–7, 349–55, 434–47, 640–4, 699–703; 8 (1932), pp. 48–50, 98–104, 208–10, 265–7, 310–14.

Geisheim, F., ed., *Die Hohenzollern am heiligen Grabe zu Jerusalem, insbesondere die Pilgerfahrt der Markgrafen Johann und Albrecht von Brandenburg im Jahre 1435* (Berlin, 1858).

Gerlach, S., *Stephan Gerlachs dess Aeltern Tage-Buch*, ed. S. Gerlach (Frankfurt-am-Main, 1674).

Ghinassi, G., ed., 'Viaggio a Gerusalemme di Nicolò da Este, descritto da Luchino dal Campo, ed ora per la prima volta messo in luce', in *Miscellanea di opuscoli inediti o rari dei secoli XIV e XV* (Turin, 1861), pp. 99–160.

Ginzburg, C., 'L'inquisitore come antropologo', in R. Pozzi and A. Prosperi, eds., *Studi in onore di Armando Saitta dei suoi allievi pisani* (Pisa, 1989), pp. 23–33.

Gios, P., ed., *Lettere di Gregorio Barbarigo a Cosimo III de' Medici (1680–1697)* (Padua, 2003).

Giovio, P., *Historiarum sui temporis tomus primus* (Venice, 1566).

Gjergj-Gashi, Gj., *Martirët shqiptarë gjatë viteve 1846–1848* (Zagreb, 1994).

Gjini, G., *Ipeshkvia Shkup Prizren nëpër shekuj* (Zagreb, 1992).

Gjoni, M., *Bregdeti dhe Ali Pashë Tepelena* (Sarandë, 2006).

Glover, G., *Fighting Napoleon: The Recollections of Lieutenant John Hildebrand, 35th Foot, in the Mediterranean and Waterloo Campaigns* (Barnsley, 2016).

Godefroy Ménilglaise, [D.-C.,] marquis de, ed., *Voyage de Georges Lengherand, mayeur de Mons en Haynaut, à Venise, Rome, Jérusalem, Mont Sinaï & Le Kayre, 1485–1486* (Mons, 1861).

Gökbilgin, M. T., *Rumeli'de Yürükler, Tatarlar ve Evlâd-ı Fâtihân* (Istanbul, 1957).

Golub, I., *Ivan Paštrić* (Split, 1988).

Gomez-Géraud, M.-C., *Le Crépuscule du Grand Voyage: les récits des pèlerins à Jérusalem (1458–1612)* (Paris, 1999).

Gonzalez-Raymond, A., *La Croix et le croissant: les inquisiteurs des îles face à l'Islam, 1550–1700* (Paris, 1992).

Gopčević, S., *Makedonien und Alt-Serbien* (Vienna, 1889).

Gosturani, Xh., *Historia e albanologjisë* (Tirana, 1999).

Graciotti, S., *La Dalmazia e l'Adriatico dei pellegrini 'veneziani' in Terrasanta (secoli XIV–XVI): studio e testi* (Venice, 2014).

Gregory, D., *Napoleon's Jailer: Lt. Gen. Sir Hudson Lowe: A Life* (Madison, WI, 1996).

Grinevetsky, S. R., et al., eds., *The Black Sea Encyclopedia* (Heidelberg, 2015).

Grisar, J., *Maria Wards Institut vor römischen Kongregationen (1616–1630)* (Rome, 1966).

von Groote, E., ed., *Die Pilgerfahrt des Ritters Arnold von Harff* (Cologne, 1860).

Guadagnoli, F., *Apologia pro christiana religione* (Rome, 1631).

de Gubernatis, D., and A. M. de Turre, *Orbis seraphicus: historia de tribus ordinibus a seraphico patriarcha S. Francisco institutis […] tomus secundus*, ed. M. A. Civetia and T. Domenichelli (Quaracchi, 1886).

Gutteridge, A., 'Cultural Geographies and "the Ambition of Latin Europe": The City of Durres and its Fortifications, c.400 – c.1501', *Archeologia medievale*, 30 (2003), pp. 19–65.

Gwynn, S., and G. M. Tuckwell, *The Life of the Rt. Hon. Sir Charles Dilke Bart., M.P.*, 2nd edn., 2 vols. (London, 1918).

Hadrovics, L., *L'Église serbe sous la domination turque* (Paris, 1947).

'de Haedo, D.' [A. de Sosa], *Topographia e historia general de Argel, repartida en cinco tratados* (Valladolid, 1612).

von Hahn, J. G., *Albanesische Studien*, 3 vols. (Jena, 1854).

von Hahn, J. G., *Reise von Begrad nach Salonik* (Vienna, 1861).

Hanson, W. S., and I. A. Oltean, 'The "Valu lui Traian": A Roman Frontier Rehabilitated', *Journal of Roman Archaeology*, 25 (2012), pp. 297–318.

Hasluck, F. W., *Christianity and Islam under the Sultans*, ed. M. M. Hasluck, 2 vols. (Oxford, 1929).

Hawkins, [J.,] 'On the Site of Dodona', in R. Walpole, ed., *Travels in Various Countries of the East, being a Continuation of Memoirs relating to European and Asiatic Turkey* (London, 1820), 473–82.

Hecquard, H., *Histoire et description de la Haute Albanie ou Guégarie* (Paris, n.d. [1858]).

Heers, J., and G. de Heyer, eds., *Itinéraire d'Anselme Adorno en Terre Sainte (1470–1471)* (Paris, 1978).

Heim, M., *Spiridion Gopčević: Leben und Werk* (Wiesbaden, 1966).

Herbert, A., *Ben Kendim: A Record of Eastern Travel*, ed. D. MacCarthy (London, 1924).

Hering, G., *Ökumenisches Patriarchat und europäische Politik, 1620–1638* (Wiesbaden, 1968).

Herz, R., ed., *Die 'Reise ins Gelobte Land' Hans Tüchers des Älteren (1479–1480): Untersuchungen zur Überlieferung und kritische Edition eines spätmittelalterlichen Reiseberichtes* (Wiesbaden, 2002).

Heyret, M., *P. Marcus von Aviano O.M.Cap., Apostolischer Missionar und päpstlicher Legat beim christlichen Heere* (Munich, 1931).

Hippler, C., *Die Reise nach Jerusalem: Untersuchungen zu den Quellen, zum Inhalt und zur literarischen Struktur der Pilgerberichte des Spätmittelalters* (Frankfurt-am-Main, 1987).

Holland, H., *Travels in the Ionian Isles, Albania, Thessaly, Macedonia &c. during the Years 1812 and 1813* (London, 1815).

Horstmann, C., 'Ratschläge für eine Orientreise (aus MS. Cotton Append. VIII, f. 108ff.)', *Englische Studien*, 8 (1885), pp. 277–83.

Howard, D. R., *Writers and Pilgrims; Medieval Pilgrimage Narratives and their Posterity* (Berkeley, CA, 1980).

Hoxha, Sh., *Kontributi i Uilljëm Martin Likut në fushën e studimeve albanologjike* (Prishtina, 2007).

Hrabak, B., 'Prvi izveštaji diplomata velikih sila o Prizrenskoj Ligi', *Balcanica*, 9 (1978), pp. 235–89.

Hughes, T. S., *Travels in Sicily Greece and Albania*, 2 vols. (London, 1820).

Hupchick, D. P., *The Bulgarians in the Seventeenth Century: Slavic Orthodox Society and Culture under Ottoman Rule* (Jefferson, NC, 1993).

de Hurmuzaki, E., et al., eds., *Documente privitóre la istoria Românilor*, 19 vols. (Bucharest, 1887–1938).

Iliadou, D., 'Le cas Pouqueville (1770–1838)', in I. A. Papigkē et al., *Meletēmata stē mnēmē Vasileiou Laourda: Essays in Memory of Basil Laourdas* (Salonica, 1975), 425–48.

İnalcık, H., 'Timariotes chrétiens en Albanie au XVᵉ siècle d'après un registre de timars ottoman', *Mitteilungen des Österreichischen Staatsarchivs*, 4 (1951), pp. 118–38.

İnalcık, H., *The Middle East and the Balkans under the Ottoman Empire: Essays on Economy and Society* (Bloomington, IN, 1993).

Ioly Zorattini, P., *I nomi degli altri: conversioni a Venezia e nel Friuli Veneto in età moderna* (Florence, 2008).

Ippen, T. A., *Skutari und die nordalbanische Küstenebene* (Sarajevo, 1907).

Ivić, A., *Migracije Srba u Slavoniju tokom 16., 17. i 18. stoleća*, Srpski etnografski zbornik, 36 (Subotica, 1926).

Ivić, A., *Istorija Srba u Vojvodini* (Novi Sad, 1929).

Jačov, M., ed., *Spisi tajnog vatikanskog arhiva XVI–XVIII veka* (Belgrade, 1983).

Jelavich, B., *History of the Balkans*, 2 vols. (Cambridge, 1983).

Jireček, J., 'Die serbischen Privilegien, Verhandlungs-Congresse und Synoden. I: Die Zeit von 1690 bis 1740', *Oesterreichische Revue*, ser. 2, vol. 7 (1864), pp. 1–12.

Jochalas, T., 'Über die Einwanderung der Albaner in Griechenland (eine zusammenfassende Betrachtung)', in P. Bartl, M. Camaj and G. Grimm, eds., *Dissertationes albanicae in honorem Josephi Valentini et Ernesti Koliqi septuagenariorum* (Munich, 1971), pp. 89–106.

Johannes von Frankfurt, *Opuscula: itinerarius, arenga, collatio*, ed. M. L. Bulst-Thiele (Heidelberg, 1986).

de Jong, F. F., 'The Kızılbaş Sects in Bulgaria: Remnants of Safavi Islam?', *The Turkish Studies Association Bulletin*, 9, no. 1 (Mar. 1985), 30–2.

Julinac, P., *Kratkoie vredeniie v istoriiu proikhozhdeniia slaveno-serbskago naroda* (Venice, 1765); photo-reproduction ed. M. Pantić (Belgrade, 1981).

Jungg, G., *Elementi grammaticali della lingua albanese* (Shkodër, 1881).

Kadare, I., *Kronikë në gur* (Tirana, 1971).

Kafadar, C., 'A Death in Venice (1575): Anatolian Muslim Merchants Trading in the Serenissima', *Journal of Turkish Studies*, 10 (1986), pp. 191–218.

Kahnè, S., 'L'azione politica del patriarca di Peć Arsenio Črnojević dal 1682 al 1690', *Orientalia christiana periodica*, 23 (1957), pp. 267–312.

Kaleshi, H., *Kontributi i shqiptarëve në diturite islame* (Prizren, 1991).

Kaleshi, H., and H.-J. Kornrumpf, 'Das Wilajet Prizren: Beitrag zur Geschichte der türkischen Staatsreform auf dem Balkan im 19. Jahrhundert', *Südost-Forschungen*, 26 (1967), pp. 176–238.

Kamen, H., *The Spanish Inquisition* (London, 1976).

Karaiskaj, Gj., *Pesë mijë vjet fortifikime në Shqipëri* (Tirana, 1981).

Karaiskaj, Gj., *Die spätantiken und mittelalterlichen Wehranlagen in Albanien: Städte, Burgen, Festungen und Kastelle*, ed. M. W. E. Peters (Hamburg, 2010).

Karpat, K. H., *Studies on Ottoman Social and Political History: Selected Articles and Essays* (Leiden, 2002).

Kaser, K., *Hirten, Kämpfer, Stammeshelden: Ursprünge und Gegenwart des balkanischen Patriarchats* (Vienna, 1992).

Kayapınar, A., 'Dobruca yöresinde XVI. yüzyılda gayr-i Sünni İslam'ın izleri', *Alevilik-Bektaşilik araştırmaları dergisi*, 1 (2009), 85–102.

Kiel, M., *Ottoman Architecture in Albania, 1385–1912* (Istanbul, 1990).

Kiel, M., 'Das türkische Thessalien: Etabliertes Geschichtsbild versus Osmanische Quellen. Ein Beitrag zur Entmythologisierung der Geschichte Griechenlands', in R. Lauer and P. Schreiner, eds., *Die Kultur Griechenlands in Mittelalter und Neuzeit: Bericht über das Kolloquium der Südosteuropa-Kommission 28.–31. Oktober 1992* (Göttingen, 1996), pp. 109–96.

Kiprovska, M., 'The Mihaloğlu Family: *Gazi* Warriors and Patrons of Dervish Hospices', *Osmanlı araştırmaları*, 32 (2008), pp. 193–222.

Kiszling, R., 'Glaubenskampfe in Albanien um die Jahrhundertswende', *Mitteilungen des Österreichischen Staatsarchivs*, 12 (1959), pp. 426–32.

Klaić, V., *Život i djela Pavla Rittera Vitezovića (1652–1713)* (Zagreb, 1914).

Knolles, R., and P. Rycaut, *The Turkish History*, ed. J. Savage, 2 vols. (London, 1701).

Koçollari, I., ed. and tr., *Alipashaida e Haxhi Shehretit* (Tirana, 1997).

Koçollari, I., *Policia sekrete e Ali Pashës* (Tirana, 2009).

Koçollari, I., *Ali Pasha dhe Shqipëria në arkivat britanike* (Tirana, 2013).

Kohl, J. G., ed., *Pilgerfahrt des Landgrafen Wilhelm des Tapferen von Thüringen zum Heiligen Lande im Jahre 1461* (Bremen, 1868).

Konica, F., Review of B. Bilotta, *Gli enti sacri della Bibbia*, in *Albania: La Revue albanaise*, vol. 'A' (1897), pp. 100–1.

Konica ['Konitza'], F., *Albania: The Rock Garden of Southeastern Europe*, ed. G. M. Panarity (Boston, 1957).

Konica, Mehmet bey, 'The Albanian Question', *The Adriatic Review*, vol. 1, no. 4 (Dec. 1918), pp. 145–64.

Kosova, S., *Shqipëria e viteve 1912–1964 në kujtimet e Spiro Kosovës*, ed. M. Verli, 2 vols. (Tirana, 2008–9).

Kostallari, A., 'Pjetër Bogdani dhe gjuha letrare shqipe', in A. Kostallari, ed., *Pjetër Bogdani dhe vepra e tij* (Tirana, 1991), pp. 17–52.

Kostić, M., 'Ustanak Srba i Arbanasa u Staroj Srbiji protiv Turaka 1737–1739 i seoba u Ugarsku', *Glasnik Skopskog Naučnog Društva*, 7–8 (1930), pp. 203–35.

Kostić, M., *Završni bilans polemike o srpsko-arbanaskom ustanku protiv Turaka uz austrijsku vojsku 1689/90* (Belgrade, 1962).

Kovačev ['Kowačev'], R., 'Register aus dem osmanischen Archiv in Konstantinopel für die Stadt Varna und ihre Umgebung (zweite Hälfte des 16. Jh.)', *Bulgarian Historical Review*, 31 (2003), pp. 29–68.

Kowalsky, N., 'Zur Vorgeschichte der arabischen Bibelübersetzung der Propaganda von 1671', *Neue Zeitschrift für Missionswissenschaft*, 16 (1960), pp. 268–74.

Krasniqi, M., *Lugu i Baranit: monografi etnogjeografike* (Prishtina, 1984).

Kreuer, W., ed., *Tagebuch der Heilig Land-Reise des Grafen Gaudenz von Kirchberg, Vogt von Marsch/Südtirol im Jahre 1470: Bearbeitung und Kommentierung des von seinem Diener Friderich Steigerwalder verfassten Reiseberichts* (Paderborn, 1990).

Kruja, M., *Kujtime vogjlije e rinije* (Tirana, 2007).

Kučerová, K., *Chorváti a srbi v strednej európe (k etnickým, hospodárskym a sociálnym otázkam v 16.–17. storočí)* (Bratislava, 1976).

Kunt, İ. M., *Sancaktan eyalete: 1550–1650 arasında Osmanlı ümerası ve il idaresi* (Istanbul, 1978).

Kušniráková, I., 'Pravoslávna komunita v Komárne v 17.-18. storočí v kontexte privilégií uhorských panovníkov', *Slovenská archivistika*, 37 (2002), no. 2, pp. 43–54.

Langer, J., 'Nord-Albaniens und der Herzegowina Unterwerfungs-Anerbieten an Österreich, 1737–1739', *Archiv für österreichische Geschichte*, 62 (1881), pp. 239–304.

Lappa, D., 'Religious Conversions within the Venetian Military Milieu (17th and 18th Centuries)', *Studi veneziani*, 67 (2013), pp. 183–200.

Laugier de Tassy, J. P., *Histoire du royaume d'Alger, avec l'état présent de son gouvernement, de ses forces de terre & de mer, de ses revenus, police, justice politique & commerce* (Amsterdam, 1725).

Lavenia, V., *Un'eresia indicibile: Inquisizione e crimini contro natura in età moderna* (Bologna, 2015).

'Lazarovich-Hrebelianovich, Prince' and 'Princess Lazarovich-Hrebelianovich' (Eleanor Calhoun), *The Servian People: Their Past Glory and their Destiny*, 2 vols. (London, n.d. [1911]).

Leake, W. M., *Travels in Northern Greece*, 4 vols. (London, 1835).

Legrand, E., *Bibliographie albanaise* (Paris, 1912).

Le Huen, N., *Le Grant Voyage de Jherusalem* (Paris, 1517).

Lenormant, F., *Turcs et monténégrins* (Paris, 1866).

Leo, F., and L. Davico, *Il Consolato d'Italia a Scutari fra storia, testimonianze, architettura*, ed. R. Orlando (Catanzaro, 2008).

Lewis, C. T., and C. Short, *A Latin Dictionary* (Oxford, 1879).

Libardi, C., *I primi moti pattriotici albanesi nel 1910-1911-1912, specie nei Dukagini*, 2 parts (Trento, 1935).

Libohova, Myfit Bey, *Politika ime ndë Shqipëri, 1916–1920* (Gjirokastër, 1921 [reprinted: Tirana, 2004]).

Limanoski, N., *Islamizacijata i etničkite promeni vo Makedonija* (Skopje, 1993).

Luetić ['Luetiq'], J., 'Lundruesit detarë, marina tregtare dhe veprimtaria e porteve të Vlorës, Durrësit e Lezhës dhe lidhjet nautike-komerciale të shqiptarëve me dubrovnikasit në vitet 1566–1584', *Gjurmime albanologjike*, ser. shk. hist., 14, for 1984 (1985), pp. 111–36.

Luka, K., 'Pamje mbi ekonominë dhe topografinë e viseve të Hotit, të Kuçit, të Piprit dhe të Kelmendit në fund të shek. XV', *Studime historike* (1980), no. 4, pp. 219–52.

Lybyer, A. H., *The Government of the Ottoman Empire in the Time of Suleiman the Magnificent* (Cambridge, MA, 1913).

Macedo, F., *Scholae theologiae positivae ad doctrinam catholicorum, & confutationem haereticorum apertae* (Rome, 1664).

McKenzie Johnston, H., *Ottoman and Persian Odysseys: James Morier, Creator of Hajji Baba of Ispahan, and His Brothers* (London, 1998).

Magini, G. A., *Geografia, cioè descrittione universale della terra*, tr. L. Cernoti (Venice, 1598).

Makrēs, G. A., and S. P. Papageōrgiou, *To chersaio diktuo epikoinōnias sto kratos tou Alē Pasa Tepelenlē: enischusē tēs kentrikēs exousias kai apopeira dēmiourgias eniaias agoras* (Athens, 1990).

Malcolm, N., *Kosovo: A Short History* (London, 1998).

Malcolm, N., 'Response to Thomas Emmert', *Journal of Southern Europe and the Balkans*, 2 (2000), pp. 121–4.

Malcolm, N., 'Crypto-Christianity and Religious Amphibianism in the Ottoman Balkans: The Case of Kosovo', in C. Hawkesworth, M. Heppell and H. Norris, eds., *Religious Quest and National Identity in the Balkans* (Basingstoke, 2001), pp. 91–109.

Malcolm, N., 'The Kelmendi: Notes on the Early History of a Catholic Albanian Clan', *Südost-Forschungen*, vols. 59–60 (2001), pp. 149–63.

Malcolm, N., 'Myths of Albanian National Identity: Some Key Elements, as Expressed in the Works of Albanian Writers in America in the Early Twentieth Century', in S. Schwander-Sievers and B. J. Fischer, eds., *Albanian Identities: Myth and History* (London, 2002), pp. 70–87.

Malcolm, N., 'Pjetër Bogdani's *Cuneus prophetarum* (1685): The Work and its Religious Context', *Studime*, 13 (2006), pp. 5–32.

Malcolm, N., 'Diplomacia britanike dhe Lidhja e Prizrenit, 1878–1880', in J. Bajraktari, ed., *Lidhja shqiptare e Prizrenit dhe vendi i saj në histori* (Prishtina, 2008), pp. 41–56.

Malcolm, N., 'The "Great Migration" of the Serbs from Kosovo: History, Myth and Ideology', in O. J. Schmitt and A. Frantz, eds., *Albanische Geschichte: Stand und Perspektiven der Forschung* (Munich, 2009), pp. 225–51.

Malcolm, N., 'Ernesto Cozzi (1870–1926): A Neglected Figure in Albanian Studies and in the History of Albania', in A. Ramaj, ed., *Poeta nascitur, historicus fit—ad honorem Zef Mirdita* (Sankt Gallen, 2013), pp. 455–504.

Malcolm, N., *Agents of Empire: Knights, Corsairs, Jesuits and Spies in the Sixteenth-Century Mediterranean World* (London, 2015).

Malcolm, N., 'An Unknown Description of Ottoman Albania: Antonio Bruni's Treatise on the *beylerbeylik* of Rumeli (1596)', *Revue des études sud-est européennes*, 53 (2015), pp. 71–94.

Malipiero, D., *Annali veneti dall'anno 1457 al 1500*, ed. A. Sagredo, Archivio storico italiano, ossia raccolta di opere e documenti finora inediti o divenuti rarissimi risguardanti la storia d'Italia, vii (Florence, 1843).

Malte-Brun, C., *Précis de la géographie universelle, ou description de toutes les parties du monde*, 2nd edn., 8 vols. (Paris, 1812–29).

Malvasia, B., *Dilucidatio speculi verum monstrantis, in qua instruitur in fide christiana Hamet filius Zin Elabedin in regno Persarum princeps* (Rome, 1628).

Manley, D., 'Liston, Sir Robert (1742–1836), Tutor and Diplomat', *Oxford Dictionary of National Biography* (https://www.oxforddnb.com/).

Mansaku, S., 'Vepra e Pjetër Bogdanit si burim për historinë e gjuhës shqipe', in A. Kostallari, ed., *Pjetër Bogdani dhe vepra e tij* (Tirana, 1991), pp. 145–57.

Marković, M., 'La Signification de Kosovo dans l'histoire serbe', in A. Jevtić ['Jevtitch'], *Dossier Kosovo* (Lausanne, 1991), pp. 179–92.

Marlekaj, L., *Pietro Bogdani e l'Albania del suo tempo* (Palo del Colle, 1989).

Marracci, L., ed. and tr., *Alcorani textus universus* (Padua, 1698).

Marsden, J. H., *A Brief Memoir of the Life and Writings of the late Lieutenant-Colonel William Martin Leake* (London, 1864).

Marshall, F. H., 'Four Letters of Ali Pasha to William Martin Leake', *Byzantinisch-neugriechische Jahrbücher*, 9 (1932), pp. 158–68.

Masci, A. [Mashi, E.], *Discorso sull'origine, costumi e stato attuale della nazione albanese* (Naples, 1807).

Masci, A. [Mashi, E.], 'Essai sur l'origine, les moeurs et l'état actuel de la nation albanaise', tr. C. Malte-Brun, in C. Malte-Brun, ed., *Annales des voyages, de la géographie et de l'histoire*, 24 vols. (Paris, 1808–14), iii, pp. 145–234.

Masini, E. *Sacro arsenale ò vero prattica dell'officio della S. Inquisitione ampliata* (Rome, 1639).

Mavroeidē, Ph. ['F. Mavroidi'], *Aspetti della società veneziana nel '500: la Confraternità di S. Nicolò dei Greci* (Ravenna, 1989).

Medlicott, W. N., *Bismarck, Gladstone, and the Concert of Europe* (London, 1956).

Meksi, G., and V. Meksi, *Ali Pashë Tepelena* (n.p. [Tirana], 2004).

Mendes Drumond Braga, I. M. R., *Entre a Cristandade e o Islão (séculos XV–XVII): cativos e renegados nas franjas de duas sociedades em confronto* (Ceuta, 1998).

Merxhushi, N., and M. Minga, *Paramithia, qytetërimi mes tragjedive* (Tirana, 2011).

Mézin, A., *Français et ottomans en Illyrie et dans l'Adriatique au temps de Napoléon: inventaire des papiers du général Donzelot (1764–1843)* (Istanbul, 2009).

Mihačević, L., *Po Albaniji: dojmovi s puta* (Zagreb, 1911).

Mikov, L., *Izkustvoto na heterodoksnite miusiulmani v Bŭlgariia (XVI–XX vek): Bektaši i Kŭzŭlbaši/Alevii* (Sofia, 2005).

Miller, A. F., *Mustapha Pacha Baïraktar* (Bucharest, 1975).

Minchella, G., 'Porre un soldato alla inquisitione': i processi del Sant'Ufficio nella fortezza di Palmanova, 1595–1669* (Trieste, 2009).

Miović, V., *Dubrovačka republika u spisima Osmanskih sultana* (Dubrovnik, 2005).

Mirdita, Z., 'Aspekte teologjike në veprën "Cuneus prophetarum" të Pjetër Bogdanit (1630–1689)', *Urtia* (1994), pp. 38–48.

Mirdita, Z., *Krishtenizmi ndër Shqiptarë* (Prizren, 1998).

Mitchell, R. L. N., 'A Muslim-Christian Sect in Cyprus', *The Nineteenth Century and After*, 63 (Jan.–June 1908), pp. 751–62.

Mjeda, L., 'Das Recht der Stämme von Dukadschin', *Zeitschrift für Ethnologie*, 33 (1901), pp. 353–8.

Moačanin, N., *Town and Country on the Middle Danube, 1526–1690* (Leiden, 2006).

Monter, W., *The Frontiers of Heresy: The Spanish Inquisition from the Basque Lands to Sicily* (Cambridge, 1990).

Moosa, M., *Extremist Shiites: The Ghulat Sects* (Syracuse, NY, 1988).

Moretti, S., 'Une communauté étrangère dans la Venise des XVe et XVIe siècles: le cas des Albanais', in J. Bottin and D. Calabi, eds., *Les Étrangers dans la ville: minorités et espace urbain du bas Moyen Âge à l'époque moderne* (Paris, 1999), pp. 183–94.

Morosini, G., *Via della fede mostrata a'gli ebrei* (Rome, 1683).

Mrkonjić, T., *Il teologo Ivan Paštrić (Giovanni Pastrizio) (1636–1708): vita, opere, concezione della teologia, cristologia* (Rome, 1989).

Mrkonjić, T., 'Gregorio Barbarigo e Giovanni Pastrizio', in L. Billanovich and P. Gios, eds., *Gregorio Barbarigo, patrizio veneto, vescovo e cardinale nella tarda Controriforma (1625–1697)*, 2 vols. (Padua, 1999), ii, pp. 1,169–78.

Muço, E., *Yanya valisi Ali Paşa ve emlakı* (Istanbul, 2010).

Muir Mackenzie, G., and A. P. Irby, *Travels in the Slavonic Provinces of Turkey-in-Europe*, 3rd edn., 2 vols. (London, 1877).

Müller, J., *Albanien, Rumelien und die österreichisch-montenegrinische Gränze* (Prague, 1844).

Murphey, R., *Ottoman Warfare, 1500–1700* (London, 1999).

Murzaku, I. A., *Catholicism, Culture, Conversion: The History of the Jesuits in Albania (1841–1946)* (Rome, 2006).

Murzaku, I. A., *Returning Home to Rome: The Basilian Monks of Grottaferrata in Albania* (Grottaferrata, 2009).

Mutafčieva, V. P., and S. A. Dimitrov, *Sur l'état du système des timars des XVIIe–XVIIIe siècles* (Sofia, 1968).

Myfit Bey Libohova: *see* Libohova, Myfit Bey.

Naçi, S. N., *Pashallëku i Shkodrës nën sundimin e Bushatllive në gjysmën e dytë të shekullit të XVIII (1757–1796)* (Tirana, 1964).

Naçi, S. N., *Pashallëku i Shkodrës ne vitet e para të shek. XIX (1796–1831)* (Tirana, 1986).

Napoleon: *see* Bonaparte.

Neeffs, E., 'Un Voyage au XVe siècle', *Revue catholique*, 9 (1873), pp. 268–91, 321–36, 425–51, 553–81.

Németh, S. K., 'Die Disputation von Fünfkirchen', in R. Dán and A. Pirnát, eds., *Antitrinitarianism in the Second Half of the 16th Century* (Budapest, 1982), pp. 147–55.

Newett, M. M., ed., *Canon Pietro Casola's Pilgrimage to Jerusalem in the Year 1494* (Manchester, 1907).

Newnham Collingwood, G. L., ed., *A Selection from the Public and Private Correspondence of Vice-Admiral Lord Collingwood: Interspersed with Memoirs of his Life*, 4th edn. (London, 1829).

Nicolas, N. H., ed., *The Dispatches and Letters of Vice Admiral Lord Viscount Nelson*, 7 vols. (London, 1845–6).

Niketić, S., 'Istorijski razvitak srpske crkve', *Glasnik Srpskog Učenog Društva*, 31 (1871), pp. 45–88.

Nikoklēs, N., *De albanensium sive Schkipitar origine et prosapia* (Göttingen, 1855).

Nilles, N., *Symbolae ad illustrandam historiam ecclesiae orientalis in terris coronae S. Stephani*, 2 vols. (Innsbruck, 1885).

Noli, F., 'Mehmet Bey Konitza', *Illyria*, vol. 1, no. 8 (1 Aug. 1916), pp. 4–6.

Noli, F., et al., 'Memorandum on Albania', *The Adriatic Review*, vol. 1, no. 3 (Nov. 1918), pp. 97–104.

Nopcsa, F., *Die Stammesgesellschaften Nordalbaniens: Berichte und Forschungen österreichischer Konsuln und Gelehrter (1861–1917)*, ed. F. Baxhaku and K. Kaser (Vienna, 1996).

Norris, H. T., *Islam in the Balkans: Religion and Society between Europe and the Arab World* (London, 1993).

Novaković, S., 'Iz hronike Despota Djurdja Brankovića, s dodatkom nekojih dokumenata koji se njega tiču', *Glasnik Srpskog Učenog Društva*, 33 (1872), pp. 135–90.

Nušić, B., *S Kosova na sinje mora: beleške s puta kroz Arbanase 1894. godine* (Belgrade, 1902).

Ongania, F., ed., *Il Montenegro da relazioni dei provveditori veneti (1687–1735)* (Rome, 1896).

Orbini, M., *Il regno de gli Slavi hoggi corrottamente detti Schiavoni* (Pesaro, 1601).

Paget, Sir Augustus, ed., *The Paget Papers: Diplomatic and Other Correspondence of the Right Hon. Sir Arthur Paget*, 2 vols. (London, 1896).

Panagiōtopoulos, V., *Plēthusmos kai oikismoi tēs Peloponnēsou, 13os–18os aiōnas* (Athens, 1985).

Panagiōtopoulos, V., D. Dēmētropoulos and P. Michaēlarēs, eds., *Archeio Alē Pasa Sullogēs I. Chōtzē Gennadeiou Vivliothēkēs tēs Amerikanēs Scholēs Athēnōn*, 4 vols. (Athens, 2007).

Papageorgiou, S. P., 'The Attitude of the Beys of the Albanian Southern Provinces (Toskaria) towards Ali Pasha Tepedelenli and the Sublime Porte (mid-18th‒mid-19th centuries): The Case of "der'e madhe" of the Beys of Valona', *Cahiers balkaniques*, 42 (2014), pp. 1–34.

Patrizi, F., *Paralleli militari*, 2 vols. (Rome, 1594–5).

Patsch, C., *Das Sandschak Berat in Albanien* (Vienna, 1904).

Pauthier, G., *Les Îles Ioniennes pendant l'occupation française et le protectorat anglais* (Paris, 1863).

Pavlović, S., *Balkan Anschluss: The Annexation of Montenegro and the Creation of the Common South Slavic State* (West Lafayette, IN, 2008).

Pedani ['Pedani-Fabris'], M. P., ed., *Relazioni di ambasciatori veneti al Senato*, xiv: *Costantinopoli: relazioni inedite (1512–1789)* (Padua, 1996).

Pedani ['Pedani Fabris'], M. P., 'Ludovico Marracci: la vita e l'opera', in M. Borrmans et al., *Il Corano: traduzioni, traduttori e lettori in Italia* (Milan, 2000), pp. 9–29.

Pedani, M. P., *Dalla frontiera al confine*, Quaderni di Studi Arabi, Studi e testi, 5 (Venice, 2002).

Peirce, L., *Morality Tales: Law and Gender in the Ottoman Court of Aintab* (Berkeley, CA, 2003)

Pertusi, A., *Martino Segono di Novo Brdo, vescovo di Dulcigno: un umanista serbo-dalmata del tardo Quattrocento* (Rome, 1981).

Petančić ['Petantius'], F., *De itineribus in Turciam libellus* (Vienna, 1522).

Petermann, W., *Die Geschichte der Ethnologie* (Wuppertal, 2004).

Peters, M. W. E., *Geschichte der Katholischen Kirche in Albanien, 1919–1993* (Wiesbaden, 2003).

Peters, M. W. E., *Der älteste Verlag Albaniens und sein Beitrag zu Nationalbewegung, Bildung und Kultur: die 'Buchdruckerei der Unbefleckten Empfängnis' zu Shkodra (1870–1945)* (Hamburg, 2007).

Photiadēs, K., *Oi exislamismoi tēs Mikras Asias kai oi kruptochristianoi tou Pontou* (Salonica, 1993).

Piccolomini, E. S., *Cosmographia Pii Papae in Asiae & Europae eleganti descriptione* (Paris, 1509).

Picot, A. E., *Les Serbes de Hongrie: leur histoire, leurs privilèges, leur église, leur état politique et social* (Prague, 1873).

Pinto, G., 'I costi del pellegrinaggio in Terrasanta nei secoli XIV e XV (dai resoconti dei viaggiatori italiani)', in F. Cardini, ed., *Toscana e Terrasanta nel medioevo* (Florence, 1982), pp. 257–84.

Pippidi, A., *Byzantins, Ottomans, Roumains: le Sud-Est européen entre l'héritage impérial et les influences occidentales* (Paris, 2006).

a Pobladura, M., 'De amicitia S. Gregorii Barbadici cum servo Dei Marco ab Aviano, O.F.M.CAP', *Collectanea franciscana*, 31 (1961), pp. 61–79.

Poletti, G., *Scritti vari* (Siena, 1910).

Popović, D., *Srbi u Budimu od 1690 do 1740* (Belgrade, 1952).

Popović, D., *Velika seoba Srba 1690: Srbi seljaci i plemići* (Belgrade, 1954).

Pouqueville, F. C. H. L., *Voyage en Morée, à Constantinople, en Albanie, et dans plusieurs autres parties de l'Empire Ottoman pendant les années 1798, 1799, 1800 et 1801*, 3 vols. (Paris, 1805).

Pouqueville, F. C. H. L., *Voyage dans la Grèce, comprenant la description ancienne et moderne de l'Épire, de l'Illyrie grecque, de la Macédoine cisaxienne... et du Péloponèse*, 5 vols. (Paris, 1820–1).

Pozzi, M., *Filippo Pigafetta consigliere del principe*, 2 vols. (Vicenza, 2004).

Pratesi, R., 'Ariosto, Alessandro', *Dizionario biografico degli italiani* (Rome, 1960–), iv, pp. 166–8.

Prenushi, M., 'Vështrim historik mbi gjendjen dhe zhvillimin e arsimit në gjuhën shqipe dhe të huaj në Shkodrën e shekullit XIX', *Studime historike*, 28 (1974), no. 3, pp. 65–83.

Prescott, H. F. M., *Friar Felix at Large: A 15th-Century Pilgrimage to the Holy Land* (New Haven, CT, 1950).

Preto, P., *I servizi segreti di Venezia* (Milan, 1994).

Prevlakēs, E., and K. Kalliatakē Mertikopoulou, eds., *Ē Ēpeiros, o Alē Pasas kai ē ellēnikē epanastasē: proxenikes ektheseis tou William Meyer apo tēn Preveza*, 2 vols. (Athens, 1996).

Prifti, K., ed., *Lidhja shqiptare e Prizrenit në dokumentet osmane, 1878–1881* (Tirana, 1978).

Prifti, K., et al., eds., *Historia e popullit shqiptar*, 4 vols. (Tirana, 2000).

Prishtina, Hasan Bey, *Nji shkurtim kujtimesh mbi kryengritjen shqyptare të vjetit 1912* (Shkodër, 1921 [reprinted: n.p., 1995]).

Pulaha, S., 'Krahinat e sanxhakut të Dukagjinit gjatë shekullit XVI', *Studime historike*, 27 (1973), no. 3, pp. 3–51.

Pulaha, S., ed., *Defteri i regjistrimit të sanxhakut të Shkodrës i vitit 1485*, 2 vols. (Tirana, 1974).

Pulaha, S., 'Formation des régions de selfgouvernment [*sic*] dans les Malessies du sandjak de Shkodër aux XVᵉ–XVIIᵉ siècles', *Studia Albanica*, 13 (1976), no. 2, pp. 173–9.

Pulaha, S., *Qëndresa e popullit shqiptar kundër sundimit osman nga shek. XVI deri në fillim të shek. XVIII: dokumente osmane* (Tirana, 1978).

Pulaha, S., *Popullsia shqiptare e Kosovës gjatë shekujve XV–XVI (studime dhe dokumente)* (Tirana, 1983).

Pușcariu, S., *Studii istroromâne*, 3 vols. (Bucharest, 1906–29).

Raça, Sh., *Shtegtimet dhe ngulimet e shqiptarëve në Greqi shek. XIII–XVI* (Prishtina, 2004).

Raça, Sh., 'Disa aspekte studimore mbi Sulin dhe Suliotët', *Studime historike*, (2012), pp. 201–22.

Radonić ['Radonitch'], J., *Histoire des Serbes de Hongrie* (Paris, 1919).

Radonić, J., 'Jeronim Paštrić, istorik XVII veka', *Glas Srpske Akademije Nauka*, 190 (= ser. 2, vol. 95) (1946), pp. 45–195.

Radonić, J., *Rimska kurija i južnoslovenske zemlje od XVI do XIX veka* (Belgrade, 1950).

Rajić ['Raić'], J., *Istoriia raznikh slavenskikh narodov, naipache Bolgar, Khorvatov, i Serbov*, 4 vols. (Vienna, 1794–5).

Rakić, M., *Konzulska pisma 1905–11*, ed. A. Mitrović (Belgrade, 1985).

Ramm, A., ed., *The Political Correspondence of Mr Gladstone and Lord Granville, 1876–1886*, 2 vols. (Oxford, 1962).

Reeves, E., 'Occult Sympathies and Antipathies: The Case of Early Modern Magnetism', in W. Detel and C. Zittel, eds., *Wissensideale und Wissenskulturen in der frühen Neuzeit* (Berlin, 2002), pp. 97–114.

Remérand, G., *Ali de Tébélen, Pacha de Janina (1744–1822)* (Paris, 1928).

Remiro, Z., 'Un saggio bilingue, latino e arabo, di controversia islamo-cristiana nella Roma del sec. XVII', *Euntes docete: commentaria urbaniana*, 22 (1969), pp. 453–80.

Remiro ['Remiro Andollu'], Z., 'La Sagrada Congregación frente al Islám: apostolado de la prensa en lengua árabe', in J. Metzler, ed., *Sacrae congregationis de propaganda fide memoria rerum*, vol. i, part 1 (Rome, 1971), pp. 707–31.

Renda, F., *L'Inquisizione in Sicilia* (Palermo, 1997).

Reuter, A., 'De iuribus et officiis Sacrae Congregationis "de Propaganda Fide" noviter constitutae seu de indole eiusdam propria', in J. Metzler, ed., *Sacrae congregationis de propaganda fide memoria rerum*, vol. i, part 1 (Rome, 1971), pp. 112–45.

Reuter, J., and K. Clewing, *Der Kosovo Konflikt: Ursachen, Verlauf, Perspektiven* (Klagenfurt, 2000).

Richmond, S., *The Voice of England in the East: Stratford Canning and Diplomacy with the Ottoman Empire* (London, 2014).

Riera i Sans, J., *Sodomites catalans: història i vida (segles XIII–XVIII)* (Barcelona, 2014).

Ritig, S., 'Primacijalni naslov splitske i barske metropolije', *Bogoslovska smotra*, 11 (1923), pp. 89–95.

Rivinius, K. J., *Im Dienst der Mission und der Wissenschaft: zur Entstehungsgeschichte der Zeitschrift Anthropos* (Fribourg, 2005).

Rizaj, S., *Kosova gjatë shekujve XV, XVI dhe XVII: administrimi, ekonomia, shoqëria dhe lëvizja popullore* (Prishtina, 1982).

Rizaj, S., 'Mbi të ashtuquajturën dyndje e madhe serbe nga Kosova në krye me Patrikun Arsenije Çarnojeviq (1690)', *Gjurmime albanologjike*, seria e shkencave historike, 12, for 1982 (1983), pp. 81–103.

Rizaj, S., ed., *Dokumente angleze mbi lidhjen shqiptare të Prizrenit dhe fillimin e copëtimit të Ballkanit (1877–1885)*, 2 vols. (Prishtina, 1996).

Roberts, A., *Salisbury: Victorian Titan* (London, 1999).

Röhricht, R., 'Die Jerusalemfahrt des Heinrich von Zedlitz (1493)', *Zeitschrift des Deutschen Palästina-Vereins*, 17 (1894), 98–114, 185–200, 277–301.

Röhricht, R., *Deutsche Pilgerreisen nach dem Heiligen Lande*, 2nd edn. (Innsbruck, 1900).

Röhricht, R., and H. Meisner, eds., *Das Reisebuch der Familie Rieter*, Bibliothek des Litterarischen Vereins in Stuttgart, clxvii (Tübingen, 1884).

Romeo, G. *L'Inquisizione nell'Italia moderna*, 2nd edn. (Bari, 2004).

Rontogiannēs, P. G., *Istoria tēs nēsou Leukados*, 2 vols. (Athens, 1982).

Roques, M., *Recherches sur les anciens textes albanais* (Paris, 1932).

Ross, E., *Picturing Experience in the Early Printed Book: Breydenbach's Peregrinatio from Venice to Jerusalem* (University Park, PA, 2014).

Rostagno, L., 'Note sulla simulazione di fede nell'Albania ottomana', in G. Calasso et al., *La bisaccia dello sheikh: omaggio ad Alessandro Bausani islamista nel sessantesimo compleanno* (Venice, 1981), pp. 153–63.

Rostagno, L., *Mi faccio turco* (Rome, 1983).

Rudt de Collenberg, W., 'Le Baptême des musulmans esclaves à Rome au XVIIe et XVIIIe siècles', *Mélanges de l'École Française de Rome*, 101 (1989), pp. 1–181, 519–670.

Rugova, I., *Vepra e Bogdanit (1675–1685): Cuneus prophetarum* (Prishtina, 1982; 2nd edn., Prishtina, 1990).

Ruvarac, I., *Odlomci o Grofu Djordju Brankoviću i Arseniju Crnojeviću patriarhu* (Belgrade, 1896).

Rycaut, P., *The History of the Turks, beginning with the Year 1679* (London, 1700).

du Ryer, A., tr., *L'Alcoran de Mahomet* (Paris, 1651).

Şakul, K., 'Ottoman Attempts to Control the Adriatic Frontier in the Napoleonic War', in A. C. S. Peacock, ed., *The Frontiers of the Ottoman World* (Oxford, 2009), pp. 253–70.

da Sanseverino, R., *Viaggio in Terra Santa*, ed. G. Maruffi (Bologna, 1888).

Santoro, S., 'Lo stato degli studi sull'urbanistica di *Epidamnos-Dyrrachium*', in M. Buora and S. Santoro, eds., *Progetto Durrës: l'indagine sui beni culturali albanesi dell'antichità e del medioevo: tradizioni di studio a confronto* (Trieste, 2003), pp. 149–208.

Schanderl, H. D., *Die Albanienpolitik Österreich-Ungarns und Italiens, 1877-1908* (Wiesbaden, 1971).

Schefer, C., ed., *Le Voyage de la Saincte Cyté de Hierusalem fait l'an mil quatre cens quatre vingts* (Paris, 1882).

Schmid, J., ed., *Luzerner und Innerschweizer Pilgerreisen zum Heiligen Grab in Jerusalem vom 15. bis 17. Jahrhundert* (Lucerne, 1957).

Schmidt, W., *Die Ursprung der Gottesidee*, 12 vols. (Münster, 1912–55).

Schmitt, O. J., *Das venezianische Albanien (1392-1479)* (Munich, 2001).

Schmitt, O. J., *Südosteuropa und die Adria im späten Mittelalter* (Bucharest, 2012).

Schön, T., 'Ein Pilgerfahrt in das heilige Land im Jahre 1494', *Mitteilungen des Österreichischen Instituts für Geschichtsforschung*, 13 (1892), pp. 435–69.

von Schwartner, M., *Statistik des Königreichs Ungern*, 3 parts in 2 vols. (Buda, 1809–11).

Schwicker, J. H., *Politische Geschichte der Serben in Ungarn* (Budapest, 1880).

Sciambra, M., *Bogdanica: studio su Pietro Bogdani e l'opera sua*, ii (Bologna, 1965).

Seitz, J., *Witchcraft and Inquisition in Early Modern Venice* (Cambridge, 2011).

Selaniki Mustafa Efendi, *Tarih-i Selaniki*, ed. M. İpşirli, 2 vols. (Istanbul, 1989).

Serena, S., *S. Gregorio Barbarigo e la vita spirituale e culturale nel suo seminario di Padova*, 2 vols. (Padua, 1963).

Setton, K. M., *The Papacy and the Levant (1204-1571)*, ii, *The Fifteenth Century* (Philadelphia, 1978).

Sezer, H., 'Tepedelenli Ali Paşa'nın oğulları', *Tarih araştırmaları dergisi*, vol. 17, no. 28, for 1995 (1996), pp. 155–64.

Sezer, H., 'Tepedelenli Ali Paşa ve oğullarının çiftlik ilişkin yeni bilgi-bulgular', *Ankara Üniversitesi Osmanlı Tarihi Araştırma ve Uygulama Merkezi dergisi*, 18 (2005), pp. 333–57.

Sferra, D., et al., *L'Albania veneta: la Serenissima e le sue popolazioni nel cuore dei Balcani* (Milan, 2012).

Sforza, G., 'Un libro sfortunato contro i Turchi (documenti inediti)', in C. Cipolla et al., *Scritti storici in memoria di Giovanni Monticolo* (Venice, 1922), pp. 207–19.

Shannon, R. T., *Gladstone and the Bulgarian Agitation, 1876* (London, 1963).

Shaw, S. J., *Between Old and New: The Ottoman Empire under Sultan Selim III, 1789-1807* (Cambridge, MA, 1971).

Shaw, S. J., and E. K. Shaw, *History of the Ottoman Empire and Modern Turkey*, 2 vols. (Cambridge, 1976).

Shkurti, S., *Der Mythos vom Wandervolk der Albaner: Landwirtschaft in den albanischen Gebieten (13.-17. Jahrhundert)*, ed. K. Kaser (Vienna, 1997).

Shuteriqi, D. S., *Shkrimet shqipe në vitet 1332-1850* (Tirana, 1976).

Sibthorp, [J.,] 'Extract from the Journal of the Late Dr Sibthorp, relating to Parts of the Ancient Elis, Arcadia, Argolis, Laconia, Messenia, and the Islands on the Western Shores of Greece', in R. Walpole, ed., *Travels in Various Countries of the East, being a Continuation of Memoirs relating to European and Asiatic Turkey* (London, 1820), pp. 75–106.

Siebertz, P., *Albanien und die Albanesen: Landschafts- und Charakterbilden* (Vienna, 1910).

Siorokas, G., 'O Alē Pasas kai oi autokratorikoi Galloi tēs Eptanēsou (nea stoicheia apo to anekdoto archeio tou C. Berthier)', *Dōdōnē: epistēmonikē epetēris tēs Philosophikēs Scholēs tou Panepistēmiou Iōanninōn*, 3 (1974), pp. 273–334.

Siorokas, G., 'Scheseis tōn Gallōn me to pasaliki tou Mperatiou (1807–1808)', *Dōdōnē: epistēmonikē epetēris tēs Philosophikēs Scholēs tou Panepistēmiou Iōanninōn*, 4 (1975), pp. 349–76.

Skendi, S., *The Albanian National Awakening, 1878–1912* (Princeton, NJ, 1967).

Skendi, S., 'Crypto-Christianity in the Balkan Area under the Ottomans', *Slavic Review*, 26 (1967), pp. 227–46.

Skiotis, D. N., 'From Bandit to Pasha: First Steps in the Rise to Power of Ali of Tepelen, 1750–1784', *International Journal of Middle East Studies*, 2 (1971), pp. 219–44.

Smitskamp, R., *Philologia orientalis* (Leiden, 1992).

Sohrweide, H., 'Der Sieg der Safaviden in Persien und seine Rückwirkungen auf die Schiiten Anatoliens im 16. Jahrhundert', *Der Islam: Zeitschrift für Geschichte und Kultur des islamischen Orients*, 41 (1965), pp. 95–223.

Sommerville, J. P., 'The New Art of Lying: Equivocation, Mental Reservation, and Casuistry', in E. Leites, ed., *Conscience and Casuistry in Early Modern Europe* (Cambridge, 1988), pp. 159–84.

Šopov ['Schopoff'], A., *Les Réformes et la protection des chrétiens en Turquie, 1673–1904* (Paris, 1904).

Soranzo, L., *L'Ottomanno* (Ferrara, 1598).

Soranzo, L., *L'Ottomanno* (Milan, 1599).

Soranzo, L., *Ottomannus... sive de rebus Turcicis liber unus*, tr. J. Geuder von Heroltzberg (Hanau, 1600).

Soranzo, L., et al., *Turca nikētos, hoc est, de Imperio Ottomannico evertendo, et bello contra Turcas prospere gerendo consilia tria* (Frankfurt-am-Main, 1601).

Soranzo, L., *The Ottoman of Lazaro Soranzo*, tr. A. Hartwell (London, 1603).

Soranzo, L., *Ottomannus: von Zustand, Macht und Gewalt, auch anderen verborgenen heimlichen Sachen des Ottomanischen Türkischen Reiches*, tr. C. Cresse, ed. H. Hattenhauer and U. Bake (Frankfurt-am-Main, 2009).

de Sousa Ribeiro, I., *Fr. Francisco de Santo Agostinho de Macedo: um filósofo escotista português e um paladino da Restauração* (Coimbra, 1951).

Spinner, T. J., *George Joachim Goschen: The Transformation of a Victorian Liberal* (Cambridge, 1973).

Stadtmüller, G., 'Das albanische Nationalkonzil vom Jahre 1703', *Orientalia christiana periodica*, 22 (1956), pp. 68–91.

Stanislavskaia, A. M., *Russko-Angliiskie otnosheniia i problemi Sredizemnomoria, 1798–1807* (Moscow, 1962).

Stanojević, Lj., ed., *Stari srpski zapisi i natpisi*, 6 vols. (Belgrade and Sremski Karlovci, 1902–26).

Stavrianos, L. S., *The Balkans since 1453*, 2nd edn. (London, 2000).

Steinmetz, K., *Eine Reise durch die Hochländergaue Oberalbaniens* (Vienna, 1904).

Stojačković ['Stojacskovics'], A., *Über die staatsrechtlichen Verhältnisse der Serben in der Wojwodina und überhaupt in den Ländern der ungarischen Krone* (Timişoara, 1860).

Stojanovski, A., *Dervendžistvoto vo Makedonija* (Skopje, 1974).

Strazimiri, I., *Lufta kundër pavarësimit të Shqipërisë* (Tirana, 2010).

Strejček, F., ed., *Jana Hasišteinského z Lobkovic putování k Svatému Hrobu* (Prague, 1902).

Subotić, K., 'O ideji srpske Vojvodine i narodno-crkvene autonomije na koncu XVIII. veka', *Letopis Matice Srpske*, 183 (1895), pp. 16–48.

von Šufflay, M., *Srbi i Arbanasi (njihova simbioza u srednjem vijeku)* (Belgrade, 1925).

von Šufflay, M., *Qytetet dhe kështjellat e Shqipërisë, kryesisht në mesjetë*, tr. L. Malltezi (Tirana, 2009).

Sugar, P. F., *Southeastern Europe under Ottoman Rule, 1354–1804* (Seattle, 1977).

Szalay, L., *A Magyarországi szerb telepek jogviszonya az állomhoz* (Pest, 1861).

Szemethy, H. D., 'Patsch, Carl Ludwig', in *Neue Deutsche Biographie*, xx (Berlin, 2001), pp. 101–2.

Tajani, F., *Le istorie albanesi* (Salerno, 1886).

Tedeschi, J., *The Prosecution of Heresy: Collected Studies on the Inquisition in Early Modern Italy* (Binghamton, NY, 1991).

Temo, I., *İttihad ve Terakki anıları* (Istanbul, 1987).

Temperley, H. W. V., *History of Serbia* (London, 1919).

Theiner, A., ed., *Vetera monumenta Poloniae et Lithuaniae gentiumque finitimarum historiam illustrantia*, 4 vols. (Rome, 1860–4).

Theiner, A., ed., *Vetera monumenta slavorum meridionalium historiam illustrantia*, 2 vols. (Rome and Zagreb, 1863–75).

Thëngjilli, P., *Renta feudale dhe evoluimi i saj në vise shqiptare (shek. XVII–mesi i shek. XVIII)* (Tirana, 1990).

Thëngjilli, P., *Shqiptarët midis lindjes dhe perëndimit (1506–1839): fusha fetare*, i (Tirana, 2002).

Thëngjilli, P., *Shqiptarët midis lindjes dhe perëndimit (1506–1750): fusha politike*, ii (Tirana, 2006).

Thunmann, J., *Untersuchungen über die Geschichte der östlichen europäischen Völker* (Leipzig, 1774).

Thunmann, J., *Über die Geschichte der Albaner und der Wlachen* (Hamburg, 1976).

Tomić, J., 'Gradja za istoriju gornje Arbanije', *Spomenik Srpske Kraljevske Akademije*, 42 (= ser. 2, vol. 37) (1905), pp. 51–77.

Tomić, J., 'Patrijarh Arsenije ill Crnojević prema Mlečićima i ćesaru 1685–1695', *Glas Srpske Kraljevske Akademije*, 70 (= ser. 2, vol. 43) (1906), pp. 66–161.

Tomić, J., *O arnautima u Staroj Srbiji i Sandžaku* (Belgrade, 1913).

Tomić, J. ['I. Tomitch'], *Les Albanais en Vieille-Serbie et dans le Sandjak de Novi-Bazar* (Paris, 1913).

Topping, P., 'Albanian Settlements in Medieval Greece: Some Venetian Testimonies', in A. E. Laiou-Thomadakis, ed., *Charanis Studies: Essays in Honor of Peter Charanis* (New Brunswick, NJ, 1980), pp. 261–71.

Torrens, H. S., 'Hawkins, John (1761–1841)', *Oxford Dictionary of National Biography* (https://www.oxforddnb.com/).

Treadway, J. D., *The Falcon and the Eagle: Montenegro and Austria-Hungary, 1908–1914* (West Lafayette, IN, 1983).

Tričković, R., 'U susret najtežim iskušenjima: XVII vek', in R. Samardžić et al., eds., *Kosovo i Metohija u srpskoj istoriji* (Belgrade, 1989), pp. 115–26.

Tromelin, J.-J., 'Itinéraire d'un voyage fait dans la Turquie d'Europe…dans l'automne de 1807', *Revue des études napoléoniennes*, year 6, vol. 12 (July–Dec. 1917), pp. 344–81; year 7, vol. 13 (Jan.–June 1918), pp. 96–124.

Truhelka, Ć., 'Über die Balkan-Yürüken', *Revue internationale des études balkaniques*, 1–2 (1934–5), pp. 89–99.

Tucoo-Chala, P., and N. Pinzuti, eds., 'Le Voyage de Pierre Barbatre à Jérusalem en 1480', *Annuaire-Bulletin de la Société de l'Histoire de France*, for 1972–3 (1974), pp. 74–172.

Tülüveli, G., 'Honorific Titles in Ottoman Parlance: A Reevaluation', *International Journal of Turkish Studies*, 11 (2005), pp. 17–27.

Turner, W., *Journal of a Tour in the Levant*, 3 vols. (London, 1820).

Ugolini, L., 'Pagine di storia veneta ai tempi di Scanderbeg e dei suoi successori (con due documenti inediti)', off-printed from *Studi albanesi*, 3–4 (1933–4).

Ulqini, K., 'Dy fjalë për albanologun Ernesto Cozzi (1870–1926)', *Kultura popullore*, 20 (1999), nos. 1–2, pp. 189–93.

Uluçay, Ç., 'Yavuz Sultan Selim nasıl padişah oldu?', *Tarih dergisi*, 6 (1954), no. 9, pp. 53–90.

Urošević, A., *Gornja Morava i Izmornik*, Srpski etnografski zbornik, vol. 51 (Naselja i poreklo stanovništva, vol. 28) (Belgrade, 1935).

Ushtelenca, I., *Diplomacia e Ali Pashë Tepelenës (1786–1822)* (Tirana, 1996).

Ushtelenca, I., *Rregjimenti shqiptar i Napoleon Bonapartit në Korfuz* (Tirana, 2007).

Ushtelenca, I., *Shteti dhe qeverisja e Ali Pashë Tepelenës* (Tirana, 2009).

Uzun, A., 'Tepedelenli Ali Paşa ve mal varlığı', *Belleten*, vol. 45, no. 244, for 2001 (2002), pp. 1,035–77.

Vacant, A., et al., eds., *Dictionnaire de théologie catholique*, 15 vols. (Paris, 1903–46).

Valentini, G., 'Prefazione' to E. Cozzi, 'Le tribù dell'Alta Albania: appunti sulla loro organizzazione sociale e politica con dati statistici', in *Studime e tekste, dega 1: juridike, n. 1* (Rome, 1944), pp. 231–2.

Valentini, G., ed., *La legge delle montagne albanesi nelle relazioni della missione volante 1880–1932* (Florence, 1969).

Valentini, G., Preface to E. Cozzi, 'La donna albanese', *Shêjzat*, 17 (1973), nos. 1–4, pp. 94–6.

Vallucci, V., *Lord Byron e Ali Pascià Tepelene: Childe Harold II e le strategie della Gran Bretagna nel Mare Ionio* (Rome, 2005).

Vaníček, F., *Specialgeschichte der Militärgrenze, aus Originalquellen und Quellenwerken geschöpft*, 4 vols. (Vienna, 1875).

Vanzan, A., 'La Pia Casa dei Catecumeni in Venezia. Un tentativo di *devshirme* cristiana?', in A. Destro, ed., *Donne e microcosmi culturali* (Bologna, 1997), pp. 221–55.

Vaquer Bennasar, O., *Captius i renegats al segle XVII: mallorquins captius entre musulmans renegats davant la Inquisició de Mallorca* (Palma, 2014).

Vasa, P. ['Wassa Effendi'], *The Truth on Albania and the Albanians: Historical and Critical Issues*, tr. E. St. J. Fairman, ed. B. Destani (London, 1999).

Vassilich, G., 'Sull'origine dei Cici: contributo all'etnografia dell'Istria', *Archeografo triestino*, ser. 3, 1 (1905), pp. 53–80; 2 (1906), pp. 209–47.

de Vaudoncourt, G., *Memoirs of the Ionian Islands, considered in a Commercial, Political, and Military Point of View...including the Life and Character of Ali Pacha*, tr. W. Walton (London, 1816).

Veinstein, G., 'Une source ottomane de l'histoire albanaise: le registre des *kadi* d'Avlonya (Vlorë), 1567–1568', in Ch. Gasparès, ed., *Oi Alvanoi sto mesaiōna* (Athens, 1998), pp. 371–84.

Veliu, V., *Relacione diplomatike ndërmjet Ali Pashës dhe Napoleonit (1797–1814)* (Skopje, 2010).

Veselinović, R., *Arsenije III Crnojević u istoriji i književnosti*, Srpska Akademija Nauka, posebna izdanja, cli (Belgrade, 1949).

Veselinović, R., 'Die "Albaner" und "Klimenten" in den österreichischen Quellen zu Ende des 17. Jahrhunderts: historisch-geographische und ethnographische Abhandlung', *Mitteilungen des Österreichischen Staatsarchivs*, 13 (1960), pp. 195–230.

Veterani, F., *Memorie...dall'anno 1683, sino all'anno 1694* (Vienna, 1771).

Vida, G., *De' cento dubbi amorosi di Hieronimo Vida iustinopolitano*, ed. A. Vida (Padua, 1621).

Vinaver, V., 'Toma Peleš, jedan od radnika na dizanju ustanka protiv Turaka krajem XVI veka', *Istoriski glasnik*, 3–4 (1950), pp. 134–8.

Vinaver, V., 'Dubrovačko-albanski ekonomski odnosi krajem XVI veka', *Anali Historijskog Instituta u Dubrovniku*, 1 (1952), pp. 207–31.

Vitković, G., 'Spomenici iz budimskog e peštanskog arhiva', *Glasnik Srpskog Učenog Društva*, odeljak 2, vol. 3 (1873), pp. 1–303, and vol. 6 (1875), pp. v–lxx, 1–486.

de Vivo, F., *Information and Communication in Venice: Rethinking Early Modern Politics* (Oxford, 2007).

Vllamasi, S., *Ballafaqime politike në Shqipëri (1899–1942)*, ed. M. Verli (Tirana, 1995).

Vlora, Eqrem Bey ['E.b.V.'], *Die Wahrheit über das Vorgehen der Jungtürken in Albanien* (Vienna, 1911).

Vlora, Eqrem Bey, *Lebenserinnerungen*, 2 vols. (Munich, 1968–73).

Vlora, Ismail Qemal Bey, 'Albania and the Albanians', *Ylli i mengjezit*, vol. 2, no. 5 (29 Sept. 1917), pp. 129–34.

Vlora, Ismail Qemal Bey, *The Memoirs of Ismail Kemal Bey*, ed. S. Story (London, 1920).

Vlora, Syrja Bey, *Kujtime nga fundi i sundimit osman në Luftën e Vlorës*, tr. A. Asllani, ed. M. Verli and L. Dushku (Tirana, 2013).

Vratislav, V. ['Baron Wenceslas Wratislaw'], *The Adventures of Baron Wenceslas Wratislaw of Mitrowitz*, tr. A. H. Wratislaw (London, 1862).

Vryonis, S., 'Religious Changes and Patterns in the Balkans, 14th–16th Centuries', in H. Birnbaum and S. Vryonis, eds., *Aspects of the Balkans: Continuity and Change* (The Hague, 1972), pp. 151–76.

Wagner, F., *Historia Leopoldi Magni Caesari Augusti*, 2 vols. (Vienna, 1719–31).

Walther, P., *Fratris Pauli Waltheri guglingensis itinerarium in Terram Sanctam et ad Sanctam Catherinam*, ed. M. Sollweck (Tübingen, 1892).

Webb, D., *Medieval European Pilgrimage, c.700 – c.1500* (Basingstoke, 2002).

Wenzel, M., 'Bosnian Tombstones—Who Made them, and Why?', *Südost-Forschungen*, 21 (1962), pp. 102–43.

Wettinger, G., *Slavery in the Islands of Malta and Gozo, ca. 1000–1812* (San Gwann, 2002).

Wiet, E., 'Mémoire sur le pachalik de Prisrend', *Bulletin de la Société de Géographie*, ser. 5, vol. 12 (1866), pp. 273–89.

Williams, G., ed., *The Itineraries of William Wey, Fellow of Eton College, to Jerusalem, AD 1458 and AD 1462; and to Saint James of Compostella, AD 1456* (London, 1857).

Wilson, D., 'List of British Consular Officials in the Ottoman Empire and its Former Territories, from the Sixteenth Century to about 1860', http://www.levantineheritage.com/pdf/List_of_British_Consular_Officials_Turkey(1581–1860)-D_Wilson.pdf.

Wilson, Sir Robert, *Private Diary of Travel, Personal Services, and Public Events, during Mission and Employment with the European Armies in the Campaigns of 1812, 1813, 1814*, ed. H. Randolph, 2 vols. (London, 1861).

Wirthwein, W. G., *Britain and the Balkan Crisis, 1875–1878* (New York, 1935).

Wortley Montagu, Lady Mary, *Letters and Works*, ed. Lord Wharncliffe and W. Moy Thomas, 2 vols. (London, 1893).

Xylander, J. Ritter von, *Die Sprache der Albanesen oder Schkipetaren* (Frankfurt-am-Main, 1835).

Yaycioglu, A., *Partners of the Empire: The Crisis of the Ottoman Order in the Age of Revolutions* (Stanford, CA, 2016).

Yerasimos, S., *Les Voyageurs dans l'Empire Ottoman (XIVᵉ–XVIᵉ siècles): bibliographie, itinéraires et inventaire des lieux habités* (Ankara, 1991).

Young, A., *Women who Become Men: Albanian Sworn Virgins* (Oxford, 2000).

Zagorin, P., *Ways of Lying: Dissimulation, Persecution and Conformity in Early Modern Europe* (Cambridge, MA, 1990).

Zaimi, N., *Daughter of the Eagle: The Autobiography of an Albanian Girl* (New York, 1937).

Zamputi, I., 'Shënime mbi kohën dhe jetën e Pjetër Bogdanit', *Buletin për shkencat shoqërore* (1954), no. 3, pp. 34–54.

Zamputi, I., 'Bashkimi i maleve shqiptare në fillim të shekullit të XVII-të: ekspedita e Vuco Pashës mbi Kelmend me 1638', *Buletin për shkencat shoqërore* (1957), no. 3, pp. 63–95.

Zamputi, I., *Relacione mbi gjendjen e Shqipërisë veriore e të mesme në shekullin XVII*, 2 vols. (Tirana, 1963–5).

Zamputi, I., ed., *Dokumente të shekujve XVI–XVII për historinë e Shqipërisë*, ii (Tirana, 1990).

Zamputi, I., ed., *Dokumente të shekujve XVI–XVII për historinë e Shqipërisë*, iii (Tirana, 1990).

Zamputi, I., and S. Pulaha, eds., *Dokumente të shekujve XVI–XVII për historinë e Shqipërisë*, iv (Tirana, 1990).

Zavalani, T., *Historia e Shqipnis*, 2 vols. (London, 1957–66).

Zeebout, A., *Tvoyage van Mher Joos van Ghistele*, ed. R. J. G. A. A. Gaspar (Hilversum, 1998).

Zefiq, F., *Shqiptarët Kelmendas në Hrtkovc e Nikinc (1737–1997)* (Zagreb, 1997).

Zuallart, J. ['G. Zuallardo'], *Il devotissimo viaggio di Gierusalemme* (Rome, 1587).

Index